Books by Jonathan Kwitny

The Crimes of Patriots: A True Story of Dope, Dirty Money, and the C.I.A.

Endless Enemies: The Making of an Unfriendly World

Vicious Circles: The Mafia in the Marketplace

Shakedown (a novel)

The Mullendore Murder Case

The Fountain Pen Conspiracy

Acceptable Risks

JONATHAN KWITNY

POSEIDON PRESS

NEW YORK   LONDON

TORONTO   SYDNEY

TOKYO   SINGAPORE

POSEIDON PRESS
SIMON & SCHUSTER BUILDING
ROCKEFELLER CENTER
1230 AVENUE OF THE AMERICAS
NEW YORK, NEW YORK 10020

DESIGNED BY KAROLINA HARRIS
MANUFACTURED IN THE UNITED STATES OF AMERICA

1   2   3   4   5   6   7   8   9   10

LIBRARY OF CONGRESS CATALOGING-IN-PUBLICATION DATA
KWITNY, JONATHAN.
ACCEPTABLE RISKS / JONATHAN KWITNY.
P.   CM.
1. AIDS (DISEASE)—CHEMOTHERAPY—MORAL AND ETHICAL ASPECTS.
2. AIDS (DISEASE)—PATIENTS—LEGAL STATUS, LAWS, ETC.—UNITED STATES.
3. PHARMACEUTICAL POLICY—UNITED STATES.
4. DRUG LEGALIZATION—UNITED STATES.   I. TITLE.
RA644.A25K95   1992
174'.2—DC20   92-17548
CIP
ISBN 0-671-73244-7

AUTHOR'S NOTE

This book is not a history of any disease, or social period, or scientific activity. It is not an exposé of any person or institution. If it were, additional people and events would be included. Their omission is not a slight, or an error.

This is the story of two American citizens exposed by accident to problems they had no particular prior interest in, or responsibility to solve. It is the story of how they took it upon themselves to lead and help, and how this required them, at considerable risk and sacrifice, to defy outmoded laws and conventions of society that they saw doing harm rather than good. With determination, and care for other people, and without violence, they set their own good sense against established power.

And they won—not completely, because except in ball games and comic books no one ever does. But they made America change in order to correct an injustice, and by doing so they prolonged countless lives. And they proved that the United States is still that rare breed among countries—a true democracy where entrenched power can be made to bend to the will and good sense of citizens, and where no citizen need consider himself ordinary.

This is the story of a couple of real-life heroes. It tells how any of us, at the right place, at the right time, with enough courage, can become heroes.

For those curious about the methodology of its telling, an explanation follows the story. But two points need emphasis up front.

Because this is a narrative rather than a news story, I have put into notes, rather than into the text, irreconcilable comments from some of the persons talked about. In accord with the publisher's style, the notes have been placed at the end of the text. But where I think there is important rebuttal, I have said so in the text, and I urge readers to read the accompanying notes to understand why I chose the version I used in the text.

Every author has many people to thank, and I will thank many at the end of the story. But one person—my friend Ellen Sackstein— was so vital to the necessary cutting and editing of this book that every reader who enjoys it ought to know of her contribution.

For Bert and Phyllis Baker

and for Judy Jackson

By what legal or moral right do we abide a system that tells huge numbers of gravely ill Americans they can't try these therapies until a bunch of people in a federal building in Rockville, Maryland, say so? . . .

Is the system used in the U.S. to regulate and review developments in medical science unnecessarily slowing the delivery of new, potentially lifesaving advances to the American people?

DANIEL HENNINGER, *The Wall Street Journal*

It's not good for people to be put in a situation where they're begging for their lives from a central government authority.

SAMUEL BRODER, Director, National Cancer Institute

It is always easier to get forgiveness than it is to get permission.

U. UTAH PHILLIPS

ONE

*T*he early-morning sunlight drifted over the San Gabriel Mountains and fell upon Los Angeles. It fell gently on the beachfront patios of Malibu, and the moist, flowering lawns of Beverly Hills and Brentwood. It fell more harshly on the tangled miles of concrete freeways, where cars, already queued at entry ramps, hooked onto other cars in endless trains that tied the luxury enclaves of the north to the ugly architectural Babel of central Los Angeles.

There, beneath the intersection of two elevated freeways, the Santa Ana and the Harbor, the sunlight pushed down an alley and past locked wire gates into a courtyard mostly filled by two parked cars, a weathered sedan and a yellow-and-white Volkswagen microbus. In this neighborhood, there were more broken bottles and spent shell casings than tended lawns.

Past the sedan and the microbus, the light poked through the slits of ceiling-level security windows into the ground-floor apartment in one of those flat, characterless two- or three-story stucco buildings that make up much of Los Angeles.

Inside was a long, narrow artist's studio: at one end a jumble of canvases, tables laden with paints and brushes, a ladder leaning against a wall, shelves crowded with boxes, tools, and artifacts. In the studio center, a living area had been cleared out—the furniture one grade above Salvation Army, except for a large-screen late-model Sony television receiver and carefully assembled stereo components. Overlooking all this, at the opposite end of the studio from the canvases, was an elevated platform bed, at the edge of which a heavy figure stirred.

A man's hairy leg swung over the edge of the platform, the foot finding the rung of a ladder. Then another foot, to the rung below. Behind, a smaller figure was still sleeping in the bed, revealing only a flash of naked back.

Beneath the bed, the ladder rungs stretched into storage shelves: Half-empty bottles of whiskeys and liquors on the top shelf (though a connoisseur's collection of wines was neatly racked in another corner of the room). Next shelf, jars of spices and spaghetti sauce, cans of tuna and gourmet cat food. Then a shelf of exotic cookbooks tending, but not doctrinairely, toward the Asian and vegetarian. A row of old magazines. Housecleaning paraphernalia. And on the bottom shelf, record albums, hundreds of them, jackets worn. At places, the row fell open to reveal the album covers: Toscanini, Schubert, the B-52's, *The Best of Joan Baez.*

Corti took three steps from the foot of the bed and was in the bathroom. In the mirror, he faced a man who had fundamentally changed his life in the past few years, and was satisfied with the result.

He picked slacks and a shirt from the closet wedged between the bathroom and the refrigerator. His body was solid: six-two, two hundred pounds. He walked past the bright red $2,500 Pinarello Record racing bike, with full Campagnola racing components, parked against the wall, and stroked it.

He stopped by the coffee table and eyed the photographs he had pulled out last night: His old place in Beverly Hills. The electrical-equipment business he'd founded. The two pictures of blond women, in their early twenties and looking California-healthy—like photos at the front of a Playmate-of-the-Month pictorial, lovely women still in their street clothes but with body shapes that made you want to turn the page to see more. And these women had been his wives.

He put the pictures away. The business, the fancy house, the marriages, the trappings of success, had only trapped him. Now, at forty-three, he had found someone just as young and good-looking as the women in the pictures. His father had kidded him last year about being a cradle robber—and admitted to having been something of a cradle robber himself.

Corti looked up and saw another picture, on canvas, perched on an easel, incomplete. It was a painting, a dizzying repetition of patterned marks, like gull wings, thrown up Jasper Johns style. The colors were red, yellow, white, green, and brown—but all muted, autumnal shades, colors not usually seen in southern California.

Maybe this week he'd finish it.

Corti slipped on his shoes, said a few words to the cats that had been watching him, and poured food into their bowl. Then he walked into the sunlit courtyard and waved to Victor, his landlord and neighbor, who was looking down from the second-floor window. He unlocked the gate and drove the yellow VW microbus past Victor's sedan and out onto the street.

He stopped at a doughnut shop and emerged with coffee and a

muffin. Munching, he proceeded south on the Harbor Freeway: Past the Los Angeles Memorial Coliseum, where the 1984 Olympics had just been held. Past the University of Southern California, where Corti had studied art history. (Practicality had pushed him to Long Beach State and a degree in economics, but the art had stayed with him, and he still rooted for the Trojans in football season.)

At Imperial Boulevard he turned west toward the ocean. After a few more turns, he was in the parking lot of a four-story stucco-and-glass building: the Robert F. Kennedy Medical Center. Corti had idolized Robert Kennedy long before going to work in the building that bore his name. Kennedy had championed ordinary people struggling to make headway against the system. Corti admired that. And Kennedy was a doer. Corti had always been short on patience for people who talked about problems and didn't act. Kennedy acted.

The clocks in Kennedy Hospital said five minutes after seven o'clock when Corti pushed past the emergency-room doors and into the intensive care unit. Late. He caught a scolding eye from the charge nurse at the nurses' station, who glanced up from her video monitors to give it to him. Then she turned back to watching heartbeats, as Corti circled behind her and into the nurses' lounge. The shift's five other nurses were already assembled, the coffee poured, the report from the nightshift underway. Corti took a seat. He was the only man in the room.

The intensive care unit drew the cream of the hospital's nurses. Just twelve beds, two to a nurse, and each patient's life hung in the balance each minute. Corti, barely out of nursing school, had got the job. He liked helping people. Medicine intrigued him. But he also liked the intensive care unit's hours. Three twelve-hour shifts on successive days, then three days off, provided consistent care for critically ill patients, and also provided long blocks of time unbounded by the ordinary workday for his painting and biking.

After a scowl noting Corti's lateness, the head nurse proceeded down the list of cases. Intensive care nurses had to know the condition of each other's patients. Periodic "Code Blue" emergencies demanded team care. A nurse's decision on what drug and how much of it to administer could save or cost a life in the minutes before a doctor arrived.

For Corti, there was a man named Roberts. Fifty. Heart attack two days ago. The doctor had ordered administration of lidocaine, tapered off in the standard way. And the doctor had said Roberts could get out of bed today for the first time. Given normal luck, the patient would be promoted soon to the definitive observation unit, or DOU

—a kind of a halfway house after intensive care for patients who still needed close monitoring but were on the road to recovery. Probably, Roberts would walk out of the hospital in a couple of weeks. If he gave up smoking and his love for deep-fried foods, he'd lead a relatively normal life.

That was a better prospect than was faced by Corti's other patient, a sixty-two-year-old woman named Katherine Pewters, who was suffering from severe chronic obstructive pulmonary disease. Without the respirator hooked to her mouth she would be dead. She had been in intensive care a week, with no sign of improvement. The one factor in her favor was that she was under the care of a doctor named Kenneth Landis, who Corti had repeatedly been told was one of the leading lung-disease experts in the Southwest.

Out among the beds now, Corti adjusted Mrs. Pewters's respirator settings and intravenous feeding and medication levels as Landis had ordered. He had grown fond of Mrs. Pewters, though there was little he could do for her, and though she was a lot of work. Her veins had deteriorated to where it was hard to insert an IV needle into one without collapsing it. In desperation, he had finally turned to a type of needle designed for infants, and placed it in an unusual spot, her ankle. His creativity succeeded.

As with most intensive care patients, Corti found the presence of family a big help. At least one of Mrs. Pewters's children was there most of the time, to help Corti turn her, examine her for bedsores, hold her hand, and try to ease the fear she must have felt. Her son had even written a poem praising Corti, entitled "God Sent Jim."

Roberts, too, had a daughter who was at the hospital through the day. This morning Corti needed her. As soon as Roberts found out he was allowed out of bed, he wanted—to Corti's astonishment—to walk out of the unit to a smoking area to light up. Corti forbade it, but without the daughter's help might have lost the argument.

The cigarette debate was still going on in late morning, when Dr. Landis, the lung specialist, made his rounds. He stopped to see Mrs. Pewters and another patient, then spotted Corti and headed for him. Youthfully graying and mustachioed, Landis *looked* like a doctor, the kind of man who could persuasively endorse headache remedies on television. Corti saw him coming and assumed there was news about Mrs. Pewters.

"Jim, can I talk to you?" Landis said.

They headed for a corner.

"We've got something new," Landis said. "There's a patient in the DOU with pneumocystis carinii pneumonia."

Well, Corti thought. It was bound to happen. RFK Hospital had its first AIDS case.

Until 1981, pneumocystis carinii pneumonia, or PCP, had been an extremely rare disease. Then people started showing up with it in various hospitals. And then the disease was found to be part of the AIDS syndrome.

"He's thirty-three years old," Landis continued. "We've got him on Bactrim."

"Is he doing well?"

"I think we'll get him out of the pneumonia. Obviously with AIDS there's more to it than that. He could be on a normal floor, but they've got him in the DOU just because everybody's so afraid of this disease. He's all alone over there. Why don't you go see him?"

The two men locked eyes, and Corti understood. Landis knew Corti was gay. Corti hadn't been making any secret of that, or that he was living with another man.

"He's not getting the care he should," Landis went on. "Some nurses over there are afraid to even go in the room. They talk to him from the hall. I've watched them. They don't even fluff up his pillow."

"Shit," Corti muttered.

"His name's Pritchett, Allan Pritchett," Landis said. "He's in one-twenty-six."

"I've got a lunch break in a few minutes," Corti said. "I'll go then."

Corti did what he could for Roberts and Mrs. Pewters. Then he pushed through the swinging doors of the intensive care unit and headed down the beige corridor of the DOU.

TWO

*A*round most of the doorways in the DOU were clusters of visitors, joking with patients and nurses. At the open door of room 126 there was no one. Corti looked in. Every other room along the corridor housed two patients. In room 126, only one bed was occupied.

The man in it looked okay to Corti—except that he was thirty-three years old and had just learned he was dying.

"Can I come in?" Corti asked.

The man just stared at him.

"Look, I'm well acquainted with what you've got. I'd like to try to help."

Nothing.

"I work with AIDS Project Los Angeles," Corti said. "I care about this disease."

Pritchett continued staring, but now Corti could see tears welling in his eyes.

Finally, the patient spoke. "Are you gay?" he asked.

"Yes."

Now tears began to flow down Pritchett's cheeks. Corti went to the bed and held his hand while Pritchett continued to sob. At least, Corti thought, he knows there's somebody who's not afraid to touch him.

"My lover died," Pritchett said at last.

"Was it AIDS?"

"They don't even know. I guess so. Oh, I'm so damned happy to have somebody I can talk to."

"Well," Corti said, holding Pritchett's shoulders, "it's good to have somebody *I* can talk to. Try not to mind the other nurses. It's the first time they've run into this disease and they don't understand it. How long have you been here?"

"Four days."

"Is the medicine doing any good?"

"The doctor thinks so. I feel a lot better."

"You sweating much?"

"Soaking the sheets. Not as bad now. I think the drug's helping."

"You're still a little short of breath," Corti observed. "But your temperature's coming down. I've talked to Ken, and he thinks you'll be out of here okay. He's a good doctor. You're in good hands with him. Do you have friends who can support you?"

"I have friends," Pritchett said. "I had a lover. He died six months ago. My neighbor has AIDS. I've been helping him." Pritchett lay back on the bed. "Hell, now he can start helping me."

Corti began the routine questions he had learned to ask patients. Pritchett was a sales representative for a large corporation, which had insured him through a health maintenance organization. The HMO clinic hadn't known what to do with an AIDS case, and had sent him to this hospital. The hospital had put him in Landis's care.

When Corti fished for details, Pritchett's story about friends who could help him fight the disease proved empty. Nobody, really, could even visit him in the hospital. His father was dead. His mother lived in the Midwest; she had learned a while back that he was gay, but she hadn't wanted to hear more about it, and Pritchett certainly

hadn't told her he had AIDS. There was a sister he talked to sometimes on the telephone, but she too lived far away.

Another bad edge to the AIDS problem, Corti thought. The people
who needed help the most had the least of it. The real and perceived
embarrassments of homosexuality had cut gay men off from their
normal family support systems before they even came down with the
disease. Then, when they desperately needed help, as Roberts and
Mrs. Pewters needed help, gay men were often alone.

Corti thought about his own family—how thrilled he had been that
his father accepted young John Upchurch after Upchurch became
his live-in lover. His father had made the joke about cradle robbing.
It was a joke not about Upchurch's maleness, but about his youth.
"Yeah, I used to like the young ones myself," he had said, and Corti
felt good. But when Corti began bringing Upchurch to his family's
Thanksgiving dinner, many in the family began to boycott the dinner, and let him know why. That was a familiar story in the gay
ghettos.

Corti wound up his questions, and Pritchett sat forward, composed
and earnest. "I know that everybody dies from this," he said. "But I
know I'm going to be able to beat it. Is that funny?"

"No."

"You know I said I had this neighbor. His name's Reuben. He has
AIDS. He was sick a long time ago. But he looks okay now. He's
been well for months."

"Yeah, that can happen," Corti said. "That's the strange history of
this disease."

"No, Reuben takes something," Pritchett insisted. "He takes something somebody found for him. It's called ribavirin. You can buy it in
Mexico."

"Ribavirin," Corti repeated. "I've heard of it. I don't know much
about it."

"I have to get it."

"I'll talk to Ken about it. As long as you're in the hospital, he's your
doctor, and he's in charge of what medication you take."

"Reuben says his doctor won't give it to him here. He has to get it
in Mexico."

"You know," Corti said, "I've heard a lot of remedies bandied
about at the AIDS meetings. There's some other medicine people
are getting in Mexico, too. But nobody's proven that any of it works.
Guys are still dying of this disease."

Corti didn't know how much to say. He didn't want to add to

Pritchett's depression. But he also didn't want to encourage a patient to abandon the care of Ken Landis to chase a mirage.

"Just because your friend Reuben seems well doesn't mean he's cured," Corti added. "That's the nature of the disease, illness comes and goes."

"The medicine doesn't have to cure you," Pritchett said. "It just has to keep you well until the cure comes along. They'll find a cure. I know one of these days when I turn the television on the announcement will be there, there's been a new break in AIDS. Until then I'm going to take care of myself."

"I'll talk to Ken about it."

Corti spent his thirty-minute lunch break and fifteen-minute coffee break with Pritchett that day—and most days following. He began to feel not just sympathy but comradeship with the patient. Corti told him about his own life—selling the house and business, banking the money for a cushion, moving to central L.A., and painting. Maybe the paintings would sell someday, maybe not. But the business had bored him and grayed his hair. So he had gone to nursing school a few years ago. Now he could support his real needs in a salaried, three-day-a-week nursing job he really liked.

Pritchett seemed cheerful, more optimistic in the face of his predicament. He improved and was allowed to walk the corridors wearing a surgical mask. People still backed off, but they didn't scatter. He continued to talk about ribavirin, the drug from Mexico. Finally Corti went to Landis about it.

"Yeah, I've heard of it," Landis said. "It's a broad-spectrum antiviral agent. It's available over the counter in some countries. Mexico, for one. Until now, it's just been one more thing people take trying to get rid of colds. It's never been tested or approved for use here."

"This guy Pritchett's determined to take it. He's convinced it's keeping his next-door neighbor well till they find a cure for AIDS."

"I couldn't prescribe it for him in this hospital even if I wanted to. It isn't legally available in the U.S."

"He'll be out in a few days. He wants to get it in Mexico."

"How's he going to do that? He's in no shape for that kind of trip."

"I could help him," Corti said.

"It's illegal to bring nonapproved drugs across the border. It's smuggling. If you were caught you might both end up charged with a felony."

"You mean I could go to jail for it," Corti said.

"You bet."

"Would the drug hurt him?"

"Probably not. People in other countries have been taking it for years." Landis fished in his desk for some notes. "They talked about it at an AIDS symposium a few months ago. No reported ill effects," he said. He put the notes away. "I don't know that it's ever cured anything, either," he smiled.

"But who cares at this point," Corti said. "I mean, what's he got to lose? You can get Pritchett over the PCP. But he's only going to get PCP again, or Kaposi's sarcoma, or some other AIDS-related disease. And he'll get gradually weaker, and one day he won't respond to treatment and he'll die."

"That's the outlook, sadly enough."

"And there's some stuff in Mexico with some science behind it that they haven't even bothered to test here, and he wants to take it. But you can't give it to him and the pharmacies here can't sell it. Why, because it might be dangerous? Hell, dying is dangerous."

Landis smiled. "It's the way the system works," he said. "It was designed to protect the public."

He thought a minute. He was, after all, on the medical-ethics committee of the county bar association. Corti wanted advice, and deserved the best advice available. It did sound a little bit cavalier, going down to Mexico and bringing back some unapproved drug. On the other hand, Landis could appreciate the frustration of someone who was dying from a disease like AIDS with no officially recognized treatment—and the frustration of someone like Corti who wanted to help.

"You know," Landis said, "there's a drug called Atrovent, a very good bronchodilator we use for asthma. And I remember it was available in Europe and Canada for at least five years before the Food and Drug Administration approved it here. I used to go to conference after conference and hear Atrovent praised to the skies. And the FDA was always there promising imminent approval. And years would pass, and nothing would happen. And I was prohibited by law from giving it to patients who would have been a lot more comfortable if they could have had it. I remember how frustrated I felt. And that was really minor compared to this. People like our friend Pritchett are dying every day, and there's no known effective treatment. Ribavirin's been swallowed by thousands of Mexicans and Europeans. Nobody seems to have keeled over from taking it."

And, he thought, if it worked . . .

"What the hell," Landis said to Corti. "The patient's got AIDS. If he's going to be happier taking this stuff, why shouldn't he? Maybe there's something to it, who knows? Beyond getting him over this pneumonia, I sure don't have anything else to offer him. Just be careful crossing the border."

"Congratulations," Corti told Pritchett at lunch that day. Corti had taken to eating his sandwich in Pritchett's room each noon. "You're getting out Thursday."

"I guess that's good news."

"And I've got a day off Saturday. Why don't I drive you down to Tijuana and we look into this ribavirin business?"

THREE

Driving south in sunshine on Interstate 5 in the yellow-and-white microbus, Corti and Pritchett talked about their lovers, their lives, and the disease that had sent them on their mission. The curve of incidence was rising alarmingly and it seemed nothing was being done.

They whipped up a mutual outrage. No one even knew where the disease came from. Trees? Monkeys? It was all rumor. The government wasn't addressing the problem. Research was scant. The doctors had few answers.

"They can treat the PCP, but they don't know anything about AIDS," Pritchett said. "My lover died virtually untreated. Reuben, my neighbor, he went to this doctor in Hollywood who was supposed to specialize in AIDS. He didn't get any treatment at all. He found out about ribavirin reading a gay newspaper. He asked friends, and somebody found him some. Now he feels like he's better. Who's going to say he isn't, you know? All I know is I want some, too."

The road wound through a gauntlet of just-built housing projects and golf courses. Here and there, construction crews were at work building more houses. Aircraft took off and landed at a string of military airfields. Activity everywhere, but nobody was working on AIDS, Corti thought.

Ever southward they drove, past San Diego. Crossing the border, Corti and Pritchett encountered no guards or customs men. No questions, no searches. All that told them they had entered Mexico was the cacophony of Spanish signs along Tijuana's Third Street as they drove in: MARRIAGES, DIVORCES, STERLING SILVER JEWELRY, CUBAN CIGARS. And probably the most common sign of all: FARMACIA.

Around the corner on the main drag, the Avenida de la Revolución, a pulsing disco beat emanated from Tijuana Tilly's Fifth Avenue Restaurant and Disco Bar. The gaudy sign promised ninety-nine-cent beer and no cover charge. The sidewalks were lined with trinkets for sale: plastic horses, pig banks, sombreros, dolls, and leather goods.

From storefronts, kids cried, *"Amigos,* spend your money here!" Margaritas Village offered margaritas in fourteen flavors. Caesar's Hotel declared it had invented the Caesar salad, original recipe still being served.

And among all this, one large, gleaming, glass and polished-steel modern-looking department store: Maxim's. It was the first place Corti and Pritchett entered.

The pharmacy department had exactly one box of ribavirin on hand, containing twelve foil-wrapped tablets of 200 milligrams each. That was a two-day supply, according to the dosage levels Pritchett had heard about.

Pritchett bought the box at the marked peso price, equivalent to $18 in U.S. currency. Then they went to a smaller pharmacy down the street. There they found two boxes, and learned that the Mexican Government had fixed the price of ribavirin at the U.S. equivalent of $17.50 a box. Corti spotted some black-market exchange dealers on the street who would dole out pesos at slightly above the official rate, which meant that ribavirin would be even cheaper using Mexican currency. He and Pritchett went from drugstore to drugstore, finding a box or two here and there at prices of $17 to $20. Pritchett bought wherever they found a low-end price.

Then they wandered into the Regis Farmacia, a kind of small, rundown Walgreen's, with aisles of health and beauty aids and a pharmacy counter at one end. Behind the pharmacy counter were long metal shelves crowded with boxed medications. Two brothers named Castro introduced themselves as the owners; one was also chief pharmacist. In good English, after introductions all around, the Castros and an assistant told them the store had eighteen boxes of ribavirin on hand, $17.20 a box, or the equivalent in pesos.

"Is there a quantity break?" Corti asked.

Roberto Castro smiled. "Every ten boxes you buy, we give one free," he said.

Pritchett bought ten boxes.

"I hope it helps you," Castro said.

Corti looked up quizzically.

"For SIDA, no? I hope it makes you well."

SIDA was AIDS in Spanish. These people knew very well why

two gringos had driven down from Los Angeles to buy ribavirin, Corti thought. He smiled and nodded. "I hope so, too," he said.

These are nice people, Corti thought. And they are in the ribavirin business.

Around the corner on the Avenida de Niños, they found an almost identical situation at the Olympia Farmacia. There was a friendly dialogue, but they made no purchase. Pritchett decided the eighteen boxes they had already bought would do until the next trip. They had visited fifteen pharmacies in all, and Corti thought he had sized up the Tijuana ribavirin market.

"This is the first time I've seen this," he told Pritchett when they went out on the street again. "People are gearing up for the AIDS business. They're getting ready to make money."

"Maybe they've got local customers, too," Pritchett said.

"There's no AIDS in Tijuana," Corti corrected him. "At least not that anybody's reported yet. It's something white guys from Los Angeles get. And these people can sell the treatment for what to them is big bucks. They're happy to make the money."

Corti had visited Tijuana often with his family when he was growing up. He knew the routine they could expect at the border on the way back. He bought two bottles of tequila, bagged separately, at a liquor store; he and Pritchett each were allowed one bottle tax-free on reentry to the United States. Inside the microbus, he put both bottles of tequila into one bag, and into the other dumped the eighteen little blue-and-white cardboard boxes of ribavirin Pritchett had bought. Then he put both bags between the front seats.

Crossing back into the Land of the Free wasn't at all like the unimpeded crossing into Mexico. Returning, you had to stop at what looked like a big toll plaza. Dozens of booths were ranged in a sweeping curve, like the closed end of a horseshoe. Cars lined up in lanes. Inside each booth was a federal agent. High above, overlooking this scene, was a building, its top floor mostly windows, where other federal agents peered with binoculars, scanning for suspicious behavior inside the waiting cars. If something caught their eye, it would trigger a computer message to an agent in a booth below: something special to ask or look for.

After a twenty-minute wait, Corti's reentry conversation went exactly as he planned it.

"How long you been in Mexico?" asked the man in the booth, peering into the car through the window.

"Just the day," Corti said.

"Bringin' anything back?"

"Bottle each of tequila."

Pritchett sat silent in the passenger seat and stared straight ahead. The man waved them through.

FOUR

*P*ritchett shared the pills with his neighbor, Reuben. He phoned Corti regularly. He said he continued to feel better, though he was no longer taking anything prescribed by the hospital that could have improved him. Reuben swore by the pills.

"I'm going to have to find a way to get a steady supply," Pritchett said.

"Saturday's free. Let's go down again," Corti replied.

They went straight to the Castro brothers at Regis Farmacia and bought 20 boxes, then to the Olympia and bought 20 more. It cost about $670 for 44 boxes, including the 4 free ones. That provided about 44 days of medication for both Pritchett and Reuben. Ribavirin was a costly affair. No health-insurance plan would reimburse the money. Legally, ribavirin didn't exist in the United States.

The border crossing went exactly as before.

Two evenings later Corti and his lover John Upchurch were sprawled on the sofa at home watching a rented movie when the phone rang.

"Hi," said a male voice. "I'm a friend of Allan Pritchett. I'm calling for Jim Corti."

"I'm Jim Corti."

"I understand you might be going to Tijuana soon."

Startled, Corti said nothing.

"If you're going, could you pick up some ribavirin for me? I'm sick. I can't get down there myself."

"Well—I might be going down. How much are you looking for?" But as soon as the man started to answer, Corti thought better of it, and interrupted him. "Who's your doctor?"

"My doctor isn't involved in this."

"Maybe your doctor ought to be involved. I'd prefer it that way," Corti said.

"He says he doesn't know anything about ribavirin. He just says it's not available here. And that there's nothing else to give me. Listen, people are saying this could work. It was in the paper. I want to try it. I want a month's worth. Fifteen boxes."

"Suppose I do it," Corti said, still thinking about the idea. "I need the money up front."

"Sure."

"Fifteen boxes is going to be around $255."

"Fine."

Whoever the caller was, he was obviously not going to be discouraged easily. "All right. Can you bring it over to"—and he gave his address.

"When should I come?"

"Tomorrow evening, around eight?"

"Okay."

He called Pritchett immediately and told him what had happened. "What's going on?" he asked.

"I may have mentioned it to somebody," Pritchett said. "I think the stuff's working. Anyway, it's the only medicine there is."

"So you told somebody I was making regular runs to Tijuana?"

"I told a few people you took me."

"A few people? How many?"

"A few people."

Shit, Corti thought. What was he getting himself into? He pondered it through the evening, discussing it with Upchurch. Okay, these were dying men. They had no way out, except maybe this last hope. But should Corti turn himself into a hired drug smuggler to solve their problem? And by supplying this untested drug, could he be risking harm to the very people he wanted to help?

He went to Landis's office. After expressing regrets about the death of Mrs. Pewters, he laid the ribavirin situation on the line.

Landis thought it over. "This AIDS business is really getting to me," he confessed to Corti. "I run into it in my committee meetings, I run into it in my practice. The patients just have all kinds of special problems I've never encountered before. We're obviously dealing with more than just bugs and drugs. The psychological and sociological ramifications of this disease are so overwhelming!"

Corti nodded.

"You know," Landis went on, "PCP is sometimes the first sign a man is gay. That's how the family finds out. I've seen cases where a family sometimes wants the kid to die. Wants the kid to die!"

Corti remembered Thanksgiving.

Landis was thinking it over. It wasn't just that Corti was gay and these were AIDS patients. Landis had seen Corti empathize with all kinds of critically ill patients. Corti was just generally a good man. And there had been substantial scientific studies of ribavirin, too.

"It's a drug that's considered potent against viruses," he told Corti. "The FDA in its typical conservative fashion hasn't approved it. But this isn't like Steve McQueen going to the Caribbean for some crazy coffee enema to cure a malignancy. This does make sense. I have no objection to your getting them ribavirin. I think it's meritorious behavior."

Landis made clear he couldn't be in the business of prescribing illegal drugs for other doctors' patients. But with all that said, he left no doubt in Corti's mind that he wasn't discouraging a supply of ribavirin for these men, who were diagnosed as having an incurable illness with a six-month life expectancy.

Corti drove home, his mind now set.

That night a man Corti had never seen before knocked on his door and handed him $255 cash. There was barely any conversation. Corti took the man's phone number and first name, and said he'd call when he was back from the next trip.

Corti got twenty calls the first week. Most were not patients themselves, but parents and friends of patients—all people who said that because of age or distance or some other reason they couldn't go themselves. Corti, still nervous about wholesale smuggling, told the callers he was only making a few trips to Tijuana to feel the place out, that he might not go back for several weeks. But they would persist.

"My friend's really sick. Please do this," a voice would say. And he would cave in.

The next trip, he brought back sixty boxes—two weeks' supply for eight patients.

Callers would ask what he wanted for making the trips, something he hadn't really considered. "I'd take a couple of tanks of gas," he began to tell them. "And," he would disclose, "I get a free box for every ten I buy. I'll keep that."

"What are you going to do with it?" somebody asked him.

"Give it to somebody who doesn't have any money," he said.

Strangers were now coming to his door every day or so, delivering hundreds of dollars in cash. Somehow there seemed to be money left over, and he began buying for people who couldn't pay in advance.

A mother had come to Los Angeles from Houston to care for her AIDS-stricken son, an out-of-work dancer. She herself had been an actress. Now she was making ends meet as a secretary.

"My son is hurting so bad," she told Corti over the telephone, her Houstonian drawl audible through the sobs. "Nothing's working for him. He's in fever sweats. We can't get rid of the fever. He's losing weight. Please get him some pills and I'll pay you when I get paid."

"Sure," Corti said. And he fronted the money.

She came by the studio as soon as he had returned from Tijuana, at six o'clock on a Saturday. She stopped just inside his doorway, not coming in.

"I'm Marilyn," she said. Leaning against a work table, she carefully counted $120 in $5, $10, and $1 bills. The money was so obviously dear to her that Corti grew embarrassed at the idea of taking it. As she counted, she talked on about how her son had studied music at Juilliard, then finally won a role in an off-Broadway hit, *Best Little Whorehouse in Texas*. Her life seemed to have become consumed by pride in her son. And now fear for him.

Corti handed her seven boxes of ribavirin, and she began to cry. She kissed him. She was gone in twenty minutes, but she stayed on Corti's mind.

Four days later, she called again. She was crying so much she could hardly talk. At first Corti feared the worst. But then he heard the words. "His fever's gone," she was sobbing. "He's stopped sweating. He feels so good. We've got to get him more of these pills."

Corti hardly knew what to say. Was it possible the ribavirin had made such a decisive difference so fast? Was it more likely that something left of the son's immune system had been poised to relieve the fever anyway, and had swung into action by coincidence four days after the regimen of ribavirin began? Could it also be that the psychological boost of taking any hopeful new drug, the so-called placebo effect, was really responsible for the turn-around? Could these factors all have worked together?

And at this moment, for purposes of this case, did it really matter?

"We'll get him more of it," Corti assured her.

And he always did. Sometimes she would come by with home-made cookies for him. Sometimes she was shy of cash. He let her run up the bill when she wasn't working.

And there were more calls. Other people said the ribavirin was having an effect, sometimes a dramatic one. And they cited the same four symptoms it relieved: weight loss, fevers, sweats, and energy loss. These phone calls would not have proven ribavirin's efficacy to *The New England Journal of Medicine*, and they didn't prove it to Corti, either. But the calls were having a profound effect on him.

Two Long Beach men came by whose health he would follow over the years: Randy Wendelin, who had tested positive for the AIDS virus in a newly developed blood test, but who was still symptom-free, and Wendelin's lover Neil Cahoj, who was already very sick. Almost as soon as he started taking ribavirin, Cahoj began getting better, and he credited the new drug. He said it relieved weight and energy loss, fevers, and sweats.[1]

Corti didn't know whether the ribavirin was working. But he was contributing positively to people's lives. Of that he had no doubt. The trips to Tijuana on his days off were no longer something he felt hesitant about. They had become an obligation to him. He knew that one man's trips to the border to bring back a shopping bag of pills was small reply to this epidemic. But he felt good about what he was doing.

Each time he made the run to Tijuana, before he even left the southern fringes of Los Angeles a hundred miles from the Mexican border, he passed a large glass-and-concrete building fronting onto Interstate 5. If you asked him what it was, he could not have told you. The sign on the building said INTERNATIONAL CHEMICAL AND NUCLEAR CORPORATION.

FIVE

Martin Delaney had been involved in the politics of the gay community even less than Jim Corti had. He had been brought up in Chicago, in a large Irish Catholic family. His father was an industrial machinist, who had tried a midcareer switch to real estate, failed at it, and gone back to the factory. His mother also worked, as a bookkeeper for a group of doctors.

As a boy, Delaney was encouraged to study science, and he had contemplated a career as a nuclear physicist. But by high school he had set his sights on the priesthood instead, an interest he later attributed to what he called his "save-the-world complex." His mother's brother was a priest. And not just any priest, either, but Mayor Daley's pastor. The family was close to the Democratic political machine that ruled the city.

Delaney followed the traditional track to the priesthood in Chicago, progressing through a series of Jesuit-run institutions: Quigley Prep, Loyola University, and finally St. Mary of the Lake, a seminary that had produced so many prominent members of the Catholic hierarchy it was known among the clergy as the West Point of the church. During his postgraduate work, however, Delaney began chafing at the reclusive life, and at the notion that he should accept church precepts on faith alone. With each year, his questions about dogma became more troubling. The priests had always told him, "Don't ask those questions now, you'll understand later." But "later" had arrived, and the questions weren't answered.

In a crisis of faith, he left the seminary and took a job teaching in a primary school. Before long, he had become lead negotiator for the local teachers' union, and attended classes on how to conduct successful meetings and how to bargain. He discovered he was good at meetings. He was blessed with a perpetually young-looking choirboy face, attractive without being intimidating. He had a knack for sensing what other people in the room were thinking, knowing the right moment to press a point or change the subject or keep his mouth shut.

But after seven years, the job grew tiresome. He was trying to please parents, kids, teachers, and the school board at the same time, and it was thankless. At a party, he met a Xerox executive, who eventually offered him a job presenting executive seminars for a Xerox consulting subsidiary. He took it. Soon Delaney was designing the seminars. He seemed to be a rising star at Xerox until his failure to marry and observe other social norms, such as bringing female companions to dinners, became an issue in his career path. By the late 1970s, some coworkers began suspecting the truth—that he was a homosexual—and reacted derisively.

Delaney quit Xerox and joined a small private consulting firm run by two women. He thought female leadership would take care of his problem. But the women took on another male associate, Mark Bradley (last name changed here on request), who needed a day job while he pursued an acting career. Delaney and Bradley became lovers. Then he heard one of the owners complaining about "all those homosexuals around." And she fired Bradley. Delaney was convinced it was because of their relationship. So this arrangement, too, had fallen apart.

Delaney quit, and he and Bradley moved to the San Francisco area, the cultural capital of male homosexuality in the United States. There they figured they could at last pursue their lives and careers free from discrimination. Even though Delaney had moved across the country because of his sexual orientation, however, he did not choose to define his life, as many did, with the San Francisco gay community.

He rented a townhouse in Sausalito, one of the swanky suburbs of Marin County. Set on a hillside, the house had a deck in back with a gorgeous vista of the bay. Delaney was good at writing corporate training programs and running them, and had no trouble finding work doing that. He rarely traveled to the Castro area in downtown San Francisco, the focal point of gay culture. He didn't, as a matter of routine, even read the gay press.

The next few years was the brief, golden era of gay culture in the United States. Despite the kind of problems Delaney had encountered in Chicago, there was a growing tolerance of sexual diversity in much of the country, and gay men were openly declaring their orientation. In San Francisco and New York they were even flaunting it, holding parades and public parties, and electing candidates to office. In the late 1970s and early 1980s, before the AIDS epidemic, it was possible for gay men to bask in liberation from what had, for centuries, been an embarrassing secret.

In the midst of all this, Delaney had chosen a relatively conventional existence: an executive career and a quiet, monogamous suburban life. Still, fate continued to stymie him. This time, it was his health. Beginning in 1978, Delaney suffered recurrent attacks of hepatitis. He felt a wreck. Eventually, he had to turn down some sales and marketing seminars he was asked to run, and to confine himself to writing the programs at home. He checked into and out of hospitals.

In late 1980, doctors biopsied his liver and found cirrhosis. He was not a drinker. The hepatitis was killing him, and doctors had no cure. Some advised treatment with steroids; others advised against that. Nearly disabled now, Delaney began to lose hope.

Then a friend saw an item in *The San Francisco Chronicle* about a chronic hepatitis research project underway at nearby Stanford University. What was there to lose? Delaney enrolled in a double-blind clinical study of two drugs. By the time the study began, the supervising doctors told him he probably had only two years to live.

The two drugs being tried together were interferon and ARA-A— an immune booster combined with an antiviral agent. In accord with standard scientific procedure and FDA regulations, half the injections given out were placebos—inactive duds designed to look like the real drugs but with no pharmaceutical properties. The doctors running the experiment wanted to be sure that if the patients who got the drugs improved, the improvement came from the drugs and not from the placebo effect. The only way to know was to deprive an identical patient population of the drugs and see what happened to those patients. Since two drugs were being tested, a participant had only a one-in-three chance of getting both interferon and ARA-A, which was the treatment course the doctors sponsoring the test thought was best. One patient in three got no effective drug treatment at all, just placebos.

Delaney felt impatient with those odds. He cajoled a nurse into giving him secret information about known side effects of the drugs. This would allow him to determine whether the injections he was getting contained one drug, two drugs, or placebo. By dispensing this knowledge, the nurse broke the fundamental bond of objectivity that scientists consider necessary to ensure the integrity of an experiment. To Delaney, the integrity of the experiment seemed less important than extending his own life beyond the two years he had been given, and he was able to find a nurse who thought so, too. As it turned out, Delaney was one of those getting the combination of real drugs after all.

At first, the drugs sapped his strength still further. But after six months, the chronic hepatitis had disappeared and he felt his former energy returning. The cure had worked. For a while, he was overjoyed. But the day after Thanksgiving 1981, he awoke with a severe burning sensation in his right foot, which quickly spread to both feet. It turned out that the drugs had an unanticipated side effect: nerve damage, called neuropathy.

Ever afterward, he would suffer foot pain. He looked for loose-fitting shoes for those occasions when he had to wear shoes at all. He would suffer silently through meetings and other business occasions; when they finished, he would look immediately for a place to take his shoes off. He often dosed heavily on prescription painkillers.

Discovering such side effects was an important purpose of the first phase of carefully controlled experiments that are required to get a drug approved for market by the U.S. Government. The object is to protect patients. But the Stanford study was second phase. The bad side effects supposedly had been assessed in earlier trials on a smaller number of patients, and Delaney had been assured there were no bad side effects. He was angry, and disillusioned with the way government-approved clinical trials were run.

But there was never any question in Delaney's mind that he was better off walking around on sore feet than he would have been not walking around at all. During his long treatment, Delaney had become good friends with five other chronic hepatitis sufferers. Among the six friends, Delaney had been the only one in the experiment—the only one able to obtain interferon and ARA-A. Delaney was back to a full work routine in 1982. All five others died.

Yet, despite the apparent lifesaving benefit of the experimental drug regimen, the Stanford researchers and their U.S. Government overseers at the Food and Drug Administration had decided to end the interferon and ARA-A tests. They had decided that the drugs were too risky and the benefits too uncertain to be used on people. Delaney was alive because of his fluke exposure to experimental drugs that other patients would never get the chance to try.

Delaney never again felt like his old self. The disease had killed 90 percent of his liver cells before the drugs had reversed it. The normal liver contains a great overabundance of cells as protection against the inevitable destruction of some by infections that visit the body during a normal life. In Delaney, liver function had fallen below that line of overabundance, to where it left him sometimes sluggish and ill. But his disabilities were not what concerned him. He felt lucky to be alive. Tests showed that his blood was free of the virus that two years earlier had threatened to kill him.

By the time Jim Corti was encountering his first AIDS case in Los Angeles in the fall of 1984, Martin Delaney was riding high on the Reagan boom years. He had been discovered by the Bank of America's private banking division, which paid him to develop its training and marketing programs.

Commuting as a private consultant from home to the Bank of America's headquarters building in San Francisco, he showed executives how to find rich potential clients—how to obtain lists of people who had recently bought Mercedes-Benzes or other expensive cars, who carried American Express gold cards, or who figured in newspaper stories suggesting high finance. From his home, he wrote manuals and scripts for videotapes. He ventured out to conduct seminars for branch executives.

In October 1984, he and Bradley went to Hawaii on vacation. Bradley seemed badly in need of it. His acting career launched, Bradley had just completed his two biggest parts. He had played the male lead in the San Francisco production of a drama Al Pacino had starred in in New York. The reviews were good. Then came a starring role in a Grade B horror-comedy film. All the while, Bradley managed to hold down his day job helping produce coin sets for collectors at the U.S. Mint in San Francisco.

Though the acting opportunities had been exhilarating at first, they had become draining by the end. The surf and sun of Hawaii were supposed to reinvigorate Bradley. For a while, they seemed to work. But in the weeks after their return, his energy faded again.

One day in late October, Delaney came home from a day at the bank and began grilling steaks on the wooden deck as he often did. Business was good, the air was bracing, the sky was blue and the view of a freighter sailing out of San Francisco harbor was magnificent. But Bradley seemed strangely indolent and gloomy on the sofa.

It was their custom to eat on the sofa, while they watched Tom Brokaw deliver the day's news. The big Sony color monitor was backed up alongside the sliding doors to the deck, so the harbor scene was still visible over Brokaw's shoulder. But Bradley was strangely quiet, without his usual commentary.

Finally, he pulled back from his food and rolled up the hem of his shorts, revealing a small rash on his leg. Delaney looked up, puzzled.

"Look at this," Bradley insisted.

"Yeah, so what?" Delaney said. "You've got a little sore on your leg."

"You remember when I had the swollen lymph nodes?"

"Swollen lymph nodes. You mean the lump in your groin."

"Yeah."

"That was three or four years ago. You thought you had cancer."

"Yeah."

"They did a biopsy and everything was normal and it went away."

Bradley just looked at him, a kind of horror on his face that Delaney honestly didn't understand.

"Right?" Delaney asked.

Bradley didn't speak. The whole thing was strange. Bradley was normally a tough guy. If he had a sore on his leg he would try to cover it up, not display it.

"So go see Bolan." Delaney shrugged. Bob Bolan was an internist, the doctor who had told Bradley he didn't have cancer.

"I've got an appointment with him tomorrow," Bradley said. He seemed angry that Delaney wasn't equally upset.

The next day Delaney was at home at the computer, writing, when Bradley came in from the doctor.

"What happened?" Delaney asked.

"Just give me some time, and we'll get to it," Bradley said.

Through dinner he started talking about trivial things, items on the news. Only after the dishes were cleared away did he suddenly explode into tears. He shook, he sobbed, but Delaney couldn't get words out of him. Finally, he spoke.

"I've been having swollen lymph nodes for a long time. Not just in my groin. In my armpits. All over the place. Can't you see what's been going on with me? I've been losing weight. You know how tired I've been. Now this sore."

"Well, did you go see Bolan?"

"I saw him yesterday."

"Why didn't you tell me?"

"Because Bolan wouldn't say what it was. Even though I knew. He just kept pointing to the *Physicians' Desk Reference* and saying, 'There are no answers in this book. There are no answers in this book.' Then he set me up for today with a guy at San Francisco General."

"And?" It was like pulling teeth.

"They say it's all part of a broader syndrome."

It was the word "syndrome" that finally delivered the shock to Delaney. His mind went reeling. They were speaking about the unspeakable. In recent months, the papers had been reporting about a new virus that had been isolated by Robert Gallo, the heralded scientist from the National Institutes of Health in Bethesda, and a French scientist named Luc Montagnier. The virus was responsible for a fatal disease that was attacking gay men and threatening humanity at large. Wrapped up in his own life, Delaney hadn't paid it that much attention. Now he realized that doctors had diagnosed his lover Mark as having acquired that syndrome—a sexually transmitted disease that was universally fatal.

"How sure are they?" Delaney asked.

"Sure. They've got a new blood test."

"But how—how could it have happened? We haven't gone to the bathhouses. That's where it's spread."

"I know."

"We've been sitting up here on this goddamned hill talking about how the bathhouses ought to be closed."

"I know."

"Then how?"

"Probably years ago. When you were sick. Or when we broke up. Or something. What does it matter?"

"What?"

"Years ago. I went out a few times."

"To the bathhouses?"

"No. Just out."

"How often?" Delaney said in disbelief.

"A few times."

"We've got to start taking care of you," Delaney said. New fears were rushing at him. People were supposed to do better with this disease if they were basically strong and healthy. Bradley had already been sick. Maybe he lacked the strength now to fight it.

"You better go see somebody, too," Bradley said.

Delaney nodded perfunctorily. He thought Bradley meant that a doctor might be able to advise him on how to care for a sick companion.

Bradley started sobbing again, exasperated by Delaney's slowness to understand. "Martin, if I've got it I probably gave it to you."

Delaney laughed nervously. "Don't be silly. I'm finally healthy. I haven't had any of these symptoms. I feel fine."

"Martin, that doesn't matter. If I've got it, how could you not have it?"

It seemed there was no end to the avalanche of horrors. Delaney had never thought for one second that he could have AIDS. He had always been something of a prude sexually. He disapproved of the bathhouses. And anyway, he had been sexually inactive most of the past few years because of his hepatitis. When the virus was spreading, he hadn't even *thought* about sex. AIDS was something other people got.

"You've got to go to a doctor," Bradley was insisting. "With your hepatitis problems, this could be even worse for you than for me. We need to do something now."

"But from everything I've read, there's no action to take. There's nothing you can do anyway."

And then Delaney knew that had been the wrong thing to say.

Bradley slumped back. "I know," he said. "I know. It's all over already. Life is over. I just can't believe this. I can't believe it. And this is all my fault."

Hours seemed to pass in moments. "I can't believe it," Bradley was repeating.

Watching his lover lapse into hopelessness, Delaney felt his own attitude stiffen. Hopelessness was the wrong approach. "We don't *have* to believe it," he suddenly heard himself declare. "You know I've already been through all this. They told me four years ago I had two years to live and I'm still here."

"This is different," Bradley said.

"No, it's not. It's the same goddamned bullshit. We'll fight this thing the same way I fought the hepatitis. Whatever it takes, we're going to do it."

"Martin, you can't fight it. They've got nothing for it."

"Hey, I saw five people die from chronic hepatitis because the doctors told them they had nothing for it. And they *did* have something for it. They gave the drugs to me and I lived."

Bradley just kept shaking his head, tears streaming down his cheeks. Delaney was past the moment when he might have wanted to cry. He didn't feel defeated. "We'll fight this thing and we'll start in the morning. We'll find out everything we can."

He put his arms around Bradley, who collapsed into them.

"I want you to make this resolution with me, that we're going to do whatever we can to fight this, and we're going to start in the morning," Delaney told him.

Bradley just lay there.

"I want you to promise me."

"Okay," Bradley said lamely.

SIX

"**I** think you ought to stop work," Delaney told him the next morning. "We need to put all our energy into this fight. Call the mint and tell them you're leaving. I'm going to go out and start researching this thing."

Bradley nodded. He had already come to the same conclusion. "I've got to go back to the hospital for more tests anyway."

Delaney went to newsstands and rounded up copies of gay-targeted publications, including the *Bay Area Reporter,* the *San Francisco Sentinel* and *Coming Up.* They were weekly newspapers he had seldom paid attention to. Now he looked at them, and the news they contained was scary rather than hopeful. AIDS was ravaging the community. There was talk of terror and grief, not treatment.

Back home, he called Gabe Garcia, the Stanford doctor who had helped run the hepatitis program he had been through. But Garcia offered no hope.

"It's a tough problem," Garcia told him. "We just don't have any tools to work with."

Delaney began phoning friends, culling their recollections and their own back copies of articles from the gay press. There were drugs the government was looking at that showed promise in test tubes. But they were all many years away from being in drugstores.

Then a gay friend from Chicago told him there was a drug already available in Mexico. Not much was known about it, but it seemed to bolster the immune system. According to the *Bay Area Reporter* a few months back, it might prolong the interlude of health enjoyed by an infected person before the diseases of the AIDS syndrome began. It might work for a matter of years. The drug was called isoprinosine.

"Why Mexico?" Delaney asked. "Why can't we just get it here?"

His friend laughed. "Because it's not approved by the government."

"Maybe it doesn't work then," Delaney offered.

His friend laughed again. "Maybe it doesn't. You know something else that does? From what the paper said, I don't think they've even tested isoprinosine in the United States."

"Well, we might as well at least try it. What do we have to lose?"

"You'll have to go to Mexico, then."

"So there's something that might have some value, it's not proven, but it might, and the government won't let you buy it here."

"You're shocked?"

"Yeah, I am. Why can't you just go to the drugstore and get this drug? What does the government want to protect us from if we're dying?"

"It's a stupid system," the friend explained.

"Do you know anybody who's taking this stuff?" Delaney asked.

"As a matter of fact, yes." And he reeled off a few names. Two were of people Delaney knew, and he called them. They said they thought the drug was helping; at least they had felt good and suffered no illness since they had begun taking it. It seemed Delaney had found a good place to start the fight for Bradley's life.

When Bradley came in, Delaney tried to cheer him with the news about isoprinosine. But Bradley seemed downcast.

"What happened?" Delaney asked him.

"Just more tests. Endless tests. And they had me meet with some guy from a counseling service."

"It sure doesn't seem to have improved your spirits," Delaney said.

"Marty, there's just no hope. The guy is a professional counselor. He says to me, 'If I were you, I would go out there on the streets and live my life right now, and the less time you spend here worrying, the better.' He says to forget about a cure and just have the best life I can. And I say, 'Oh, in other words I'm going to die, right?' And he keeps saying, 'Well, no, I didn't say that. It's just there is no cure for this.' This was a gay man, Marty. Some of the doctors are gay men, too."

"Well, maybe they're wrong," Delaney said angrily. He had found the article about isoprinosine from the newspaper, and tossed it at Bradley. "Ask the doctor about this," he said.

Bradley looked it over, and agreed to ask about isoprinosine at San

Francisco General Hospital, part of the University of California Medical School.

"I've heard about it," said the hospital AIDS specialist. "It's an immune modulator. It could offer some hope, but we really don't know much about it yet. I guess you just have to wait and see if it gets tested."

Bradley was incredulous. "What do you mean 'wait and see.' You've already told me I've got this virus. How long before I get AIDS and die? What's my life expectancy now, a year?"

"Well, you've got a point," the doctor said. "You might as well go get what's in Mexico. I guess that's reasonable, because you don't really have any other choices." Bradley was all the more alienated by the dispassionate tone of the answer. This was his *life*, for Christ's sake!

He told Delaney. Delaney phoned a friend whose sister lived in Mexico City. The friend arranged for him to wire the sister several hundred dollars to buy isoprinosine and ship it north. He sent the money, but after a week of phone calls there was no drug. Finally, Delaney found out the family was feuding, and the sister had just pocketed his money.

Delaney turned to Bradley after hanging up the phone. "I think I should just hop in my car and drive down to the border. Tijuana. At least see what's available."

"Okay. Let's try it," Bradley said.

"I don't think you ought to go. Not the first time, anyway."

"I feel okay."

Delaney thought it over. "No. It's a foreign country. We won't know what'll happen. I assume it's illegal. I'm going to have to smuggle whatever I get back into the country. You don't need that kind of stress right now."

He left on a Saturday in his new Mazda. Traffic was bad, and by the time he reached Tijuana it was 5 P.M. Fifteen years had passed since his last visit. He remembered it as a small, dirty town. Now he was confounded by the traffic and bustle. He worried it might take all weekend to locate what he was looking for.

He drove around, eying the *farmacias,* surprised there were so many. He found a large one with an empty parking space in front and stopped. The sign overhead said "Regis."

He walked in and asked a clerk for isoprinosine. The clerk brought out a man named Castro, who spoke English. What Castro brought to the counter amazed Delaney. They had loads of isoprinosine, stacked up in white boxes. They seemed glad to see another gringo coming in with cash asking for isoprinosine.

The price was $2.50 for a box of twenty pills. The dosage he had heard talked about was six pills a day. He had enough money for a hundred boxes, which would be more than enough for now. If the drug seemed to do any good, he would give some to other friends as well.

"This is a snap," he thought, as Castro loaded a bag with pills and handed it to him.

Only outside the store did he stop to think. Getting into Mexico had been no problem. The problem was going to be getting out. Would he get arrested? Would they seize the pills? Of the two, arrest was no worse, he decided. He would risk lying to the government to try to protect his cargo. He bought two clay pots and a souvenir blanket from a tourist stand. He put some of the pills in the pots, and stored them on the front seat with the new blanket, so he'd have something to declare. He stuck most of the pills in the trunk under some old blankets.

As he pulled into the line of cars nearly a mile from the border, he realized he was crossing probably the most carefully guarded border point the U.S. had. The government's "war on drugs" had started, and security seemed intense. It was also Saturday evening. Half of teenage California had gone to Tijuana to party. The wait was an hour. Delaney was glad Bradley wasn't sharing the ordeal.

"How long you been in Mexico?"

"Just the day."

"What were you doin' there?"

"A tourist."

"What are you bringin' back?"

"Tourist stuff." Delaney glanced over at the pots and the blanket. So did the agent. The agent waved him on.

He hit Interstate 5 with a burst of exhilaration. He pushed the accelerator, grinning as the Mazda cut north through the warm night. He had gotten away with it. After all the tears, all the phone calls, and the disappointment with the friend's sister, he was across the border and headed home with a hundred boxes of what he hoped was healing power.

Then, a few miles up the road, he saw red lights flashing in the night ahead. His foot instinctively pulled off the accelerator. It was another roadblock. His heart sank. Another line. What did these people want?

"Any agricultural products? Oranges?"

The agent peered into the car behind a bright flashlight that blinded Delaney.

"No," Delaney replied after some hesitation. This time he felt as if he were lying even though he was telling the truth.

"Are you bringing in any immigrants?"

"No."

The agent at the border had quickly waved him through. This man flashed his light around, seemed to be debating whether to search the Mazda. What would happen if he found the pills? Maybe that wasn't this man's department. Maybe he'd just let him go. Delaney had no idea.

"Okay." The agent backed away and headed for the next car. Delaney drove on, sweating. All he wanted was to get back home. After half an hour, he felt safe enough to pull over and call Bradley. Mission accomplished; he was headed for Sausalito. He made it at 5 A.M.

SEVEN

Almost as soon as Bradley started taking the pills, he and Delaney noticed improvement.

Each morning would begin with an agonizing search of the skin rashes to see if a spot had turned into a reddish lump, signaling the onset of Kaposi's sarcoma. K.S., as it was called, was a form of skin cancer previously rare and now associated with AIDS. Unlike other skin cancers, K.S.'s purple lesions spread, sometimes fast, always ugly. Even the dying retained enough of their self-esteem to worry about the disfigurement of Kaposi's.

But instead of worsening, Bradley's skin infection cleared up altogether. To be sure, the chronology of Delaney's return with the isoprinosine and the clearing up of Bradley's skin infection did not constitute scientific proof that the drug had cured, or relieved, anything. But the psychological lift afforded by this noticeable improvement after taking a new drug was certain.

Delaney was fascinated. Within days of his successful trip, he went to a gay community meeting in San Francisco to hear the AIDS situation discussed. He phoned friends to make sure they knew there was a possibly helpful drug, and that he had a supply. Bradley avoided the meetings and public discussion. He was an actor, and he was terrified that word would get out he was infected. Even a rumor could cost him work. What producer would want to begin shooting a film, or rehearsing a play, with an actor who might at any moment erupt with a disfiguring skin disease, or have to go to the hospital with pneumocystis carinii pneumonia? Or die?

For Delaney, there was a return of the sense of community service that had once impelled him toward the priesthood. Word began to spread. The phone rang.

"I'm really interested in isoprinosine," a strange voice would say. "Do you have some you can spare?"

Pretty soon he had given away what he thought he and Bradley could spare. And he began turning callers down.

"Well," they would say, "it's for a friend. I don't have a car. Can I give you his phone number, and you can decide what to do after you talk to him?" He was spending more and more time on the phone, taking numbers.

One night he was having dinner with an old friend from Chicago, now working as a marketing specialist for another bank in San Francisco. And the friend had a friend who was really sick, who needed the drug. The man already had come down with pneumocystis carinii pneumonia, and was near death.

Two weeks had passed since Delaney's trip to Tijuana, and he was going back. He invited the sick man to go with him.

His passenger was visibly ill—limp, breathing poorly. He seemed scared about traveling to Mexico, and absolutely terrified of what was happening to his health. He said little on the way down, clutching a bottle of water he had brought because he didn't trust the drinking water in Mexico. Delaney asked him if he had tried isoprinosine yet.

"No. I've been trying to get it."

"Wasn't there anybody else who could drive you down?"

"Somebody went for me last week, and was supposed to bring it back."

"What happened?"

"He was stopped at the border. They confiscated everything. Five hundred dollars' worth. They talked about arresting him. Said if he tried it again, they would."

Delaney took a deep breath and gunned the Mazda into Mexico. He was carrying more than $600, and his passenger nearly $500. They went first to the Regis Farmacia. When they had bought its shelves bare of isoprinosine, they went to other pharmacies as well. They found that some smaller pharmacies weren't as well stocked but charged less—as little as $2 a box.

Approaching the border checkpoint, cargo once again hidden in the trunk under tourist trinkets, Delaney was nervous. He was thinking about the man who only last week was stopped at the border, threatened with arrest, his precious and costly cargo lost to the feds. They reached the booth.

Suddenly, Delaney thought he detected something strange in the demeanor of the agent. The questions began as usual. But when the agent saw Delaney's passenger—wheezing, coughing, gaunt, and glassy-eyed—his head jerked back from the Mazda window. There was fear on his face. In half the time, and with half the number of questions of the previous week, the agent waved Delaney through. In the side mirror, Delaney could still see him, pulling back, holding his breath, stepping aside from an imagined airborne viral attack.

As they headed up Interstate 5, Delaney turned to his passenger. "So you're going with me now. Why didn't you go last week with the guy who went down?" he asked.

"People thought I was too sick."

"You're sick now."

"I wanted to go this time so I could plead my case if it came down to it. I just can't afford to have another load confiscated."

Delaney began to wonder whether carrying a visibly sick passenger might be a key to safe passage. It might not work all the time, but it might work when he needed it to. "Maybe you're the reason we got through," he said.

A few days later, at another public meeting about AIDS, he picked up a brochure from a stack by the door. It was a four-page medical paper written by a lawyer in Texas. He took a copy home to Bradley.

"There's something interesting here," he said. "This guy claims that two drugs available in Mexico actually cure AIDS. One of them is isoprinosine."

"God, I hope so," Bradley said.

"Well, *cures* may be extravagant. I doubt the guy I drove down last weekend has been cured. But this is the interesting part. The other drug is called ribavirin. Ribavirin is an antiviral that's been used in a lot of countries against flu and so forth. This paper says to use it in combination with the isoprinosine, which is an immune modulator. You know what that reminds me of?"

"Tell me."

"That's exactly what they gave me to cure the hepatitis. An antiviral and an immune modulator—ARA-A and interferon. Together. It makes sense. And it worked!"

Bradley took the idea to San Francisco General for his checkup the next day. But the hospital doctors were no more excited about ribavirin than they had been about isoprinosine. Ribavirin was being looked at by a laboratory run by the Centers for Disease Control in Atlanta, they said. Early reports were that it retarded or killed the AIDS virus in test tubes. But that was a long way from trials on live patients, which hadn't been attempted yet. If Bradley wanted to take it, okay, but the doctors advised he'd be better off enjoying life and leaving experiments to medical science.

Delaney took off for Tijuana again. But he returned empty-handed. There had been, it turned out, a recent rush of demand for ribavirin from Los Angeles patients. The shelves were bare. Delaney would have to come back next week. Delaney was also stunned to find ribavirin being quoted at $18 a box, many times the price of isoprinosine.

Bradley was disconsolate at the news. "God, this costs a lot. I don't know what I'm going to do. I can't afford it. But I have to have it."

"Yes," Delaney said. "And you will have it, regardless of the cost. It's a necessity, and we'll get it."

"I don't know what I'm going to do," Bradley went on, once more unreceptive to the optimism. "If my health is going to fail me . . ."

"Don't worry. You live here, and I'll take care of you as long as this is going on."

Bradley's voice continued to rise. "I can't even give you my share of the rent this month. I've got nothing coming in."

"I knew that when I asked you to quit work," Delaney said. "These banks are paying me plenty. Stop worrying. We'll take care of your health first, then see what happens."

"Thanks," Bradley said. But there was as much anger as gratitude in his voice.

"Remember when I was sick?" Delaney said. "People came in and cleaned my house for me, paid my rent, brought me food. When a crisis comes, you pitch in whatever you can. Our community is in a war. Every meeting I go to, they take up collections to care for this person and that person. Every meeting, more people ask me to get them drugs in Mexico. Some can pay, some can't. There are people who give a hundred dollars a month to care for total strangers. There are people who give more. It's outrageous these drugs are illegal so you can't get medical insurance for them. But that's how it is."

"I guess that's how it is," Bradley repeated.

Delaney drove the eighteen-hour round trip to Tijuana again a few days later, this time with several thousand dollars in his pockets. About half was from people who had asked him to make a buying run for them. About half was from his own bank account. He began making the trip every week or so.

EIGHT

*B*ack in Los Angeles, Jim Corti was fussing with his wine collection between trips to Tijuana, when he was seized by an idea that seemed inspired. He went to the phone and dialed Larry Wardzala.

In college, he and Wardzala had been the closest of friends, and fraternity brothers. Both had served terms as president of the fraternity. Both had become engaged to women who, in successive years, were chosen sweetheart of the fraternity. Corti had married his sweetheart, which became the source of much kidding and serious discussion between him and Wardzala in later years, after they had identified themselves as gay.

Each understood something about the other that no new friend could ever understand or be part of. They stayed neighbors in Long Beach, and shared a devotion to wine collecting. They had bought some vintages that quickly appreciated in value. By the time they were thirty, they had spent evenings together consuming $300 bottles of wine with apples and a few pieces of cheese.

But they had drifted apart in the 1970s, after Corti started a business and moved to Beverly Hills. Years passed and they rarely saw each other. A year or two ago, Corti had learned from mutual friends that Wardzala had switched from wine to gin, become an alcoholic, and joined Alcoholics Anonymous. Corti meant to call, but never did.

Suddenly now, dusting off some wine bottles in late 1984, Corti thought about Wardzala. If his friend was still on the wagon, maybe he'd want to dispose of his wine collection.

After some small talk, Corti broached the subject. "I hear you got into A.A.," he said.

"Two years now," Wardzala told him.

"So what are you going to do with your wine collection?"

"Well, Gomez, it's like this," Wardzala said. Back in college, Wardzala had begun calling Corti "Gomez," in reply to which Wardzala had become known between them as "Gonzalez." "I don't drink anymore," Wardzala went on. "So I wondered if you'd be interested in my wine collection. That's why I had you call me."

Why he had me call him. Corti just smiled. Wardzala hadn't changed.

"Well, I'd sure like to take a look at it," Corti said.

"Then come over. It hasn't gone anywhere."

"Maybe next week," Corti said.

"Sounds swell," Wardzala said. "Pick a day. By the way—I have AIDS."

"Yeah, me too," Corti joked.

There was no reply from the other end of the line.

"You're joking, aren't you," Corti said.

"No." The voice was subdued, not bantering now. "I had pneumonia three months ago."

It was a while before Corti could find his voice. "Can I come down now?"

"Sure."

Corti began to explain to Upchurch, his lover, who had come into the room. But Upchurch understood.

"It's getting close, isn't it?" Upchurch said.

They piled into the VW microbus and headed for Long Beach. The old friends talked and cried, but Wardzala's continuing good spirits kept the occasion from becoming somber. In the end, Wardzala helped load twenty-five cases of fine French and California wine into Corti's van. When Corti pulled out his checkbook, Wardzala waved him off.

"Don't worry about it," he said.

Corti pulled something else out of his pocket. "There's something I want you to try, Larry. No promises it'll do anything, but it won't hurt."

"What is it?"

"It's called ribavirin. It fights viruses. You can only get it in Mexico. Some people with the virus have said it's helped them."

"Ah, I've read about that crap. It's not going to do anything."

"Probably not. But maybe it will. Just try it."

Wardzala took the shrink-wrapped packets of pills.

Over the next few weeks, Corti and Wardzala had dinner twice weekly, sometimes with others, mostly alone. They went to the beach and to the mountains, retracing trips they had made when they were younger. They talked about wine experiences, and mutual girl friends and mutual boy friends. They laughed the kind of laughter that borders on tears.

They talked about the Phone Booth Quartet, a college singing group half of whose membership they had constituted. Among other popular 1960s songs they had performed was "Seasons in the Sun," about a young man, dying, and his feelings toward the friend who cuckolded him:

> Adieu, Françoise, it's hard to die
> When all the birds are singing in the sky
> Now that the spring is in the air
> With your lovers everywhere
> Just be careful, I'll be there
>
> We had joy, we had fun, we had seasons in the sun
> But the wine and the song like the seasons are all gone.

They tried to sing it, but could get only halfway through. Corti thought tears had interrupted them. Then he realized Wardzala's lungs had become too congested to hold the breath to sing. Within days, Wardzala became ill, too weak to care for himself. There was no treatment.

The rest was a nightmare. To make matters worse, two of Wardzala's friends, a young woman and a male former lover, came to help care for him and started feuding with Wardzala's family over the daily routine. The young people saw the family as part of the life they thought Wardzala had rejected, and the family saw the young people as intruders and perhaps seducers. Corti, disgusted by the discord to start with, felt both sides trying to use him and his knowledge of the disease to fuel their feud.

Then the contest fell to who was entitled to Wardzala's possessions and insurance money on his death. In his last days, Corti's old friend was being pressured by competing sides to structure a will and give powers of attorney.

"I imagine you could do with less bickering from those ninnies in the next room," Corti said on one visit.

"They all mean well," Wardzala replied. "Everybody's under pressure."

"Yeah, but you're the one they're supposed to be concerned with."

Wardzala managed a slight smile. "By the way, they're also down on me for giving the wine away to you. They said you ought to pay for it."

"I offered to pay for it in the first place."

"I know, I know. Give me a check for $500."

"Larry, there are some bottles in that collection that are probably worth $500 by themselves."

"But they don't know that. It will keep the vultures happy if I just get some money for it."

Corti gave him a check. Wardzala was almost too weak to take it.

It was worse a few nights later, when Corti and Upchurch arrived at Wardzala's bungalow for a visit, and found him slipped into dementia, crawling about on his hands and knees, drooling onto the floor. Corti and the others struggled to get him back to bed.

When they left the room, Upchurch said, "If I ever got like that, I'd want somebody to get me out of it."

"There is no mercy at all," Corti sobbed. "You ask yourself, 'Where is God?' "

A few nights later Corti found Wardzala in bed, lucid, but even weaker. The sick man could barely reach out to him.

"I can die now," he rasped. "My friends and my mother have agreed on the legal conditions. I guess I shouldn't disappoint them."

Corti just nodded. They both rolled their eyes.

Wardzala went on talking hoarsely about their college days, sometimes lapsing into non sequiturs.

"Sing for me," Wardzala said.

"Sing?" Corti said. "You mean like Zorba, dancing through whatever went wrong?"

"Yeah."

"Sing what?"

"You know, the songs. Sing the sweetheart song."

Corti sang "The Sweetheart of Sigma Chi." Wardzala smiled. Corti began "The Lady in Red," a comic drinking song about a woman debauched by college men and thrown out of a bar into the winter night before finally being rescued. Halfway through, Corti saw Wardzala was asleep.

He kissed Wardzala on the forehead, and left.

The next day he phoned the house and got an answering-machine message Wardzala had taped long before. Corti understood very well why Wardzala couldn't come to the phone right now. He was dead. That fast.

Corti responded by dedicating time to AIDS Project Los Angeles, a local support group, driving to suburban communities to tell in plain language how the disease was transmitted, and how to care for those who had it. He talked about the potential benefits of ribavirin.

He also increased the frequency of his trips to Tijuana in the yellow-and-white microbus, which had become known among AIDS patients and their relatives as the "Virus Van." And twice a week, on days off, he would rise at 5 A.M., hop on the shiny red Pinarello

Record bicycle with the Campagnola accessories, and head north along the coast.

It would take him about five hours to reach Santa Barbara, 115 miles away. From Hendrickson's Bicycle Shop there, he would call Upchurch, and say he was headed home. Sometimes Upchurch would meet Corti in the microbus halfway, and they would drive back together. Other times—and Corti prided himself on this—he would ride back with a local racing team, sometimes beating them.

On those trips, once again AIDS seemed far away.

NINE

*I*n the early spring of 1985, Delaney answered his phone and heard the name Paul Boneberg.

"I'm running an organization called Mobilization Against AIDS," Boneberg said. "We've got a community forum coming up, and I'd like you to speak."

"How'd you get my name?" Delaney asked.

"You're bringing in drugs, right? That's what we want you to talk about. The Mexican connection."

"Yeah? I think I've seen some of your literature at meetings," Delaney said.

"So what do you say?"

Delaney felt pushed. "Tell me a little more about yourself."

"Mainly I'm interested in raising hell," Boneberg said. "I used to own a bookstore in the Castro. Got into gay politics. I was president of the Stonewall Gay Democratic Club. I organized the National March for Lesbian and Gay Rights during the Democratic convention last summer."

This guy's a real promoter, Delaney thought.

"And because it was so successful," Boneberg went on, "various activists asked me to start something permanent, and Mobilization is what we came up with."

"You know, I've never really had direct contact with gay lib," Delaney said. He was still feeling his way, and Boneberg seemed to be pressing him front and center.

"So come on out to this thing. There'll be an FDA enforcement guy there. We need to hear you."

"I don't know how much I'll feel like saying with an FDA enforcement guy around, either," Delaney said.

"Don't worry. If they want to know what you do, they already know. The important thing is to pin them down on their policy. Find out what they'll allow and what they won't, what they tell the border guards, and why they're blocking these drugs at all."

"So why do you need me? You seem pretty forceful."

"You've been there. Besides, the audience needs to know what's available. You can tell them."

"Okay," Delaney sighed. "I'll do what I can."

He showed up at the appointed place, the Swedish-American Hall on Market Street, and was surprised to find a small room crowded with maybe fifty to seventy people. Five of them, including Delaney, were panelists.

Delaney immediately picked out Mark Roh, the FDA man—tall, thin, in his mid-thirties, with dark-rimmed glasses and a business suit. From Roh's style and way of presenting himself, Delaney decided right off that Roh was also a gay man. A pierced ear he saw when he shook Roh's hand confirmed the impression. Asking Boneberg about it, Delaney learned that Roh and his brother had been openly active in gay events for years; Delaney just hadn't been present.

Delaney's understanding of Roh's sexual orientation rendered him all the more amazed at what transpired. Roh was the first speaker.

"AIDS really isn't my specialty," he began. He said he specialized in medical devices, like artificial body parts. "I don't really know much about AIDS," he added. Brows furrowed around the room. Why was he there, then? Caustic remarks were audible.

Roh continued with a brief survey of potential AIDS drugs that left the crowd obviously dissatisfied. He looked helpless. (Roh's own account follows in a note.) Given the confines of FDA policy, the picture he painted of AIDS treatments was necessarily bleak. He didn't know of any promising available products. By the FDA's standards, there were none. The only substances Roh mentioned being studied at all were being looked at in laboratory test tubes. One, suramin, would undergo its first tightly controlled human trial later that year. The others were all years away even from clinical testing, let alone consumer use. Roh didn't mention ribavirin and isoprinosine, which most audience members knew Delaney was bringing in from Mexico.

Boneberg quickly turned the platform over to Delaney.

"I don't know what I can and can't say with a public official present," Delaney began, and he found himself being about as vague as Roh had been. The audience rebelled against him, too.

"How do you get the stuff in?" one man called out.

"What are the rules?" another asked.

"I want to hear from Mr. Roh what he thinks about ribavirin and isoprinosine," someone else said, eliciting a chorus of supportive monosyllables.

Delaney felt relief as eyes, and pressure, fell on Roh.

"What about ribavirin and isoprinosine, Mr. Roh?" Boneberg said.

Roh looked uncomfortably from side to side, as if longing for assistance. Finally, he said, "I don't know what you're talking about. I never heard of these drugs."

The ensuing silence was broken by Delaney's statement, which seemed to sum up the general feeling in the room: "I'm *horrified*," Delaney began. "Mr. Roh, you're not even reading the gay press. I know the FDA was very late in recognizing this syndrome in the first place. But it's obvious now. And if you're in enforcement in California, this is going to land in your lap."

"We've had our experience over the years with many magical cures coming from Mexico," Roh said. "They were always fraudulent. We have a research and approval system in this country that has proven itself. I am not going to become a party to making quackery available, so that some fly-by-night drug company can make garbage, so they can earn $200, so that some gay person can inject it into his arm."

"Are you saying that about ribavirin and isoprinosine?" someone asked.

"I'm not up on every single compound that somebody thinks is the new miracle drug," Roh replied.

Delaney hit full stride then. Without mentioning Bradley's name, he told the story of Bradley's recovery from AIDS-induced skin infections after beginning a course of isoprinosine. He had heard a dozen similar stories, he said.

"And as for ribavirin, it's a very well known antiviral compound, one of very few effective antivirals in history. It's being studied right now by Richard Roberts of Cornell University in New York, with FDA approval, and based on that, your own agency, Mr. Roh, is at this moment considering approving it for use in some viral infections, where its effectiveness has been demonstrated in clinical tests. Well, if it works on other viruses, why not on AIDS? Your people may not have done all the tests they want, but our people are dying."

Roh appeared tongue-tied, in full retreat.[2] (See note for Roh's account.)

"We don't know for sure how these drugs will work," Delaney

added, "but it makes more sense than the next best thing, which is dying without trying anything."

Suddenly the audience was alive again with questions. "Where do you buy it?" "How do you get it into the country?"

Delaney again protested that he didn't want to risk giving specifics with an FDA representative present.

Boneberg produced the solution. "If you're interested in more information, I'm going to put a piece of paper in the back of the room. Just leave your name and address and phone number on that paper, and I don't know what Martin Delaney can tell you exactly, but maybe the tooth fairy will come around to your mail box and answer these questions."

It got a good laugh. And the list at the end of the night contained more than thirty names and addresses. More than half the audience had signed up.

When the meeting was over, Delaney and Boneberg exchanged a few words. Both men knew what was needed. And Delaney headed home to his computer.

He turned out a manual attempting to answer the rush of questions the audience had. He described what the pills and their packaging looked like. He identified the trade names sometimes used in Mexico for the ingredients in ribavirin and isoprinosine (Vilona and Pranosine). He named the pharmacies where the drugs could be bought, and gave directions. He listed the prices usually charged, and warned against overcharges by profiteers. He urged comparative shopping. He discussed the consensus dosage, and recounted both the success stories and the limits on the successes. He advised how to get through customs by looking calm and conventional, maybe carrying a camera, or bringing a woman friend or relative along.

And he especially urged that persons taking the drugs be under the care of a doctor who was fully advised of the drug regimen.

The letters went out to everyone who had signed up for information. They bore no return address, and were signed "The Tooth Fairy." The recipients easily made the connection to the joke at the meeting. Again, Delaney's phone began to ring.

"I appreciated the letter," callers would say. "I'd like to drive down there, but I'm just too sick. I need your help. When are you making your next trip?"

A man showed up at Delaney's door, a young man leaning on a cane, and looking like only one thing Delaney had ever seen before —pictures of prisoners freed at Auschwitz. He invited the man in, but the stranger clutched at the railing by the door and said he did not feel up to even descending the stairs into Delaney's living room. "I'm Joe," he said. Feebly, he offered Delaney an envelope containing $300 for a one-month supply of pills. His phone number was scrawled on the envelope.

Delaney hesitated to accept. It was one thing to say that ribavirin and isoprinosine would empower an infected but relatively healthy body like Bradley's to ward off the usual AIDS-related diseases. But did these drugs really stand a chance of helping this wasted man, whose sunken, hollow eyes now looked out at Delaney beseechingly?

On the other hand, did this man have any alternative? Did Delaney have the right to play God and deny him his last hope?

Delaney took the envelope but continued to hold it in front of him, half hoping the sick man would take it back. "How did you ever make it here in your condition?" Delaney asked.

"I drove."

"You look too sick to drive."

"I just got over my second case of PCP. I need to get back to work now."

"You look too sick to work, too."

"I'm a computer programmer," the man said with a hint of indignation. "I can make good money when I'm well enough to work."

The man was clutching onto his identity with the same feeble determination as he was clutching onto the railing. Whoever he used to be is gone now, Delaney thought to himself.

"You know," Delaney said, "the people who seem to have been helped by these drugs have really been in an earlier stage of the disease. This might not do you any good."

"What difference does it make?" the man asked.

"You might just be wasting your money."

"What else would I have to do with it?"

Delaney nodded, embarrassed. He put the envelope in his pocket.

T E N

All along, Delaney and his lover, Mark Bradley, had assumed that if one of them was infected, so was the other. Delaney just hadn't shown symptoms yet. Bradley's diagnosis had been confirmed by a blood test, then in an experimental run at San Francisco General Hospital, part of the University of California Medical School. When the test became commercially available at an anonymous gay-run testing service in the spring of 1985, Delaney took it.

The result amazed them. Negative. Maybe, ironically, the hepatitis and Delaney's resulting lack of sexual energy over several critical years had saved him from this even more terrible scourge.

In May 1985, Bradley heard an item on a local news show about an experiment being run on a possible AIDS drug: suramin, a chemical that had been used in Africa for half a century to treat sleeping sickness. The test was being run at San Francisco General, where Bradley was being monitored anyway. He mentioned it to Delaney.

"Suramin," Delaney repeated. "That's what that FDA man, Mark Roh, talked about at the panel discussion a few months ago."

Inquiring at the hospital, Bradley was quickly scheduled to meet Dr. Paul Volberding, director of all San Francisco General's AIDS activities. He was running the study under the auspices of the National Cancer Institute, part of the government's huge health complex in Bethesda, Maryland. The NCI had sponsored test-tube research on suramin, then given it to a handful of AIDS patients.

Delaney was impressed on hearing Volberding's name at dinner that evening. "If you were to list the handful of guys with the biggest international reputations as AIDS experts, Volberding would be in there," he said. "You're at the top of the medical establishment now."

"Isn't that the same medical establishment that's keeping ribavirin and isoprinosine out of the country?" Bradley asked sarcastically.

"Well, maybe they're finally doing something useful. Hell, this is what we've wanted all along, for them to start testing a promising drug. You have to have *some* faith that the medical authorities are going to cure this disease if they get to work."

Next morning, Bradley sat in Volberding's office, not very comfortably, answering the standard questions.

"Are you currently taking any other medication?"

"Ribavirin and isoprinosine."

Volberding set down his pad and leaned forward, obviously unhappy at the news. "I'm going to advise you to stop taking those drugs," he said. (Volberding's account follows in a note.)

"Why?"

"Drugs can be very dangerous," Volberding said. "You'll have to discontinue them to go on suramin anyway."

"Well, I really don't want to stop these drugs," Bradley said. "I think they've made me better. Kept me well."

"It is absolutely necessary if you are to get suramin," he was told.

"We don't know the nature of the interactions these other drugs might have with suramin. Besides, I really don't think the isoprinosine and ribavirin are helping anyway, or will ever help."

The doctor moved around the desk and pulled up a chair alongside Bradley. He drew a diagram with a pencil.

"This is the virus," he said. "This is what it looks like. It's inside you everywhere. It's in the tissue." And he drew what that looked like. "You'll never get rid of this virus," Volberding said. "If I were you, I would get out on the street and just live your life."

"That's—that's the most despondent thing I've ever heard," Bradley said. "I'm not going to just accept that. I'm not going to just wither away."

"Then the suramin test is the best option you have. Like the virus, suramin also gets in everywhere. And it's been proven in the laboratory to kill the virus, or at least block it from replicating. The hope we have is that it might stop the virus from replicating within you, and maybe kill it."

"If I get off these other drugs, will the suramin prevent me from getting sick the way they have?"

"Suramin is the only drug even under study. We don't know much about ribavirin, and we certainly don't know that ribavirin has anything to do with your not being sick. But we know that in the laboratory studies on suramin it killed the virus. We want to give it six months and see what it does in people."

Bradley sat back and closed his eyes. He looked at Volberding. He nodded.[3] (See notes for Volberding's account.)

But when he got home, he found that now Delaney was wavering, especially after they had gone over the fine print of the test protocol Bradley had brought home. "I've done a little investigating," Delaney began. "Some patients were treated at NCI, and word is the testers got negative viral cultures out of them."

"That's just what Volberding said," Bradley told him.

"But there's lots of potential danger, too." Delaney picked up the test protocol and glanced at it again. "Fevers, nausea, constipation, fatigue, general malaise. This is a very serious drug."

"They said those things *might* happen. *Might.*"

"And on the other hand, your health now with the ribavirin and isoprinosine seems pretty good. The skin infections have gone away. Your nagging flu's gone away. You've been okay for almost six months."

"But I'm not working, you're paying all my fucking bills and I've still got this virus."

"Yeah, I know, and the best medical minds in the country have come up with suramin as a solution. But it's still a test. There are inherent risks in doing it. Don't worry about the bills. I can take care of that. The question is your health. It's your choice. Think about it."

"I have thought about it," Bradley said. "It looks really promising and I want to do it."

"Probably right," Delaney said. "If it doesn't go well, you can always go back to what you're doing now. Or start the ribavirin and isoprinosine again in addition to the suramin."

"Volberding said that's a no-no. The interaction of the drugs might be dangerous, and it might interfere with the results of the study."

"The question is your health, not the study. Are you going into this because you want to help science, or because you want to save your life?"

Bradley turned away in silence.

"I know," Delaney said. "He's your doctor. When you're sick, you want to trust your doctor."

The next day Bradley went into the hospital for his first dose. His intravenous needle was hooked to a syringe bigger than he had ever seen before. Every minute or so a bit of liquid containing the drug was released into his body. The process took nearly an hour, and he had to hang around the rest of the day for blood tests. Then he had to traipse back to the hospital with a urine specimen every three days and a semen specimen once a week. And, he was informed, he might feel a little sick. This was strong medicine; that's why it stood a chance against the virus. He might even run a fever.

That evening his temperature was 104 degrees. He was more exhausted than he had ever been before. He couldn't drag himself from bed the rest of the evening. Delaney felt a well of doubt and fear in his stomach.

"It's okay," Bradley said. "Maybe it means it's working."

ELEVEN

*I*n May 1985, Jim Corti and his lover, John Upchurch, spent a weekend at a hotel on the beach at San Simeon, playing in the ocean and working on tans, from which they took no small amount of narcissistic pleasure. That Saturday night Upchurch complained of an earache. Feeling flushed, he took his temperature and it was over 100.

They each remarked that it was the first time they could recall his being sick.

By coincidence, Upchurch was due for a physical the week after they returned. He was quitting a job Corti had got him at RFK Medical Center and taking one with better hours at Hollywood Presbyterian Hospital.

After the physical, Hollywood Presbyterian called and said something unusual had turned up in Upchurch's chest X-ray. He needed to see a doctor, and have more X-rays of his lung.

For about two weeks Upchurch had been suffering fever, and he had started to cough. He wasn't a smoker. At night, he sweated and felt warm. In the day, he complained of aches and muscle pains.

On weekend afternoons, he and Corti sometimes took picnic baskets to Griffith Park, where they would hike a mile and a half uphill to Dante's Roost on the side of Mount Hollywood. There, in a garden overlooking the city, they would enjoy gourmet sandwiches and champagne. The first weekend of June, Upchurch begged off making the trip. He said his joints and muscles were sore. He must have the flu.

Both men had medical backgrounds. Both knew it wasn't the flu.

The doctor called and said the new chest X-rays were marginal. They would need another look later. Corti and Upchurch were both scared to death.

Upchurch had a third chest X-ray, taken near the office of an internist Corti knew in Long Beach. The internist, Tom McCloy, had agreed to analyze it. They chose McCloy, an old friend, because they desperately wanted a clean medical letter so Upchurch could start the new job at Hollywood Presbyterian Hospital.

All the way to Long Beach they talked optimistically.

"At least it's finally going to be over," Corti said. "I know when we talk to Tom we'll know what's what."

"And if my fever's gone, the way I think it is, he can write the letter and I can start work."

McCloy worked in a ten-story high-rise off Atlantic Avenue. The setting sun was in their eyes as they took the newly obtained X-ray to his office. He studied it and examined Upchurch. Upchurch asked Corti into the room.

"There are shady patches in the upper lobes of both lungs," McCloy said. "There's an infiltration of something. It could be a lot of things. Nothing we can nail down with this."

Corti looked at the X-ray. He had seen it before. It looked like pneumocystis carinii pneumonia, PCP, the principal cause of death in AIDS patients. The survival rate of the pneumonia itself was 50 percent. The overall life expectancy from the time of diagnosis, including those who did survive the pneumonia, was six to eight months. He thought from Upchurch's face that Upchurch didn't recognize PCP in the X-ray. He hoped not.

"Is this serious enough to keep me from going to work on my new job?" Upchurch asked.

"You've also got a 101.8 fever, and you're coughing," McCloy said.

Corti was scared to death. Should Upchurch be hospitalized? McCloy was the doctor, and Corti trusted him.

"Is there any way we can get around this so I can work?" Upchurch was saying, almost pleading by this time. He had quit his job at RFK to take a little break, but he needed this new job now.

"The X-ray will probably need further interpretation," McCloy said. "I'm not going to hold you back because of the X-ray. But I can't clear you for work until the fever clears up. I'll have the X-ray analyzed further and get back to you."

Corti knew the news was worse than that, but sensed that McCloy was trying to soft-pedal it until he was positive, out of concern for Upchurch's feelings.

Corti and Upchurch drove back up the freeway in silence. They entered the studio and sat on the couch with the three cats. Upchurch's favorite was a big Siamese named Ajax. For a long time, he stroked the cat, refusing to look up at Corti. Then, when he did, Corti saw tears in his eyes, and then down his cheeks.

"Look, John, there's something crummy going on here and we've got to talk about it," Corti said. "We need to make an appointment with the people in the Valley."

Upchurch knew who he meant. The word "AIDS" didn't have to be said. Drs. Joel Weisman and Gene Rogalski, in the San Fernando Valley, had the biggest AIDS practice on the West Coast. Weisman was one of the doctors credited with identifying the AIDS syndrome in the first place.

"You think that's it?" Upchurch asked.

"We have to rule it out," Corti said. "They're the best there is."

Corti had met Upchurch on a trip to Laguna Beach six years earlier. Upchurch was living the beach life, having completed a degree at a local junior college. Corti was attending a business conference. At the end of the day's meetings, Corti stopped off at a popular bar, The Boom-Boom Room. He saw a cute kid in a Greek fisherman's hat playing video games. Their eyes met, and they smiled at each other. Corti had a couple of drinks and the kid was still there.

"Do you smile at everybody like that?" Corti asked.

"That's one way to get to know you," the kid said.

"You want to get to know me? I'm pretty easy," Corti said. "Can I buy you some drinks?"

"A drink maybe."

"How about some drinks?"

"You can try if you want."

They left the video machine and went back into the bar, where they talked for several hours, at first about Upchurch's hat and Corti's cowboy boots, later about Laguna Beach, Fire Island, and the French Riviera, all of which they had both enjoyed. They both liked the song on the jukebox.

They moved on to a nearby hotel and, later, agreed to meet the next weekend. After a few more meetings, Corti decided that Upchurch, then twenty, was too young, and decided to stop seeing him. He left Upchurch waiting without a phone call when Upchurch had been expecting him at Laguna Beach that Friday night. Saturday morning, there was a beating on the door of Corti's house in Beverly Hills. It was Upchurch.

"Nobody stands me up," Upchurch said. "Certainly not somebody I care about. If you ever want to see me again, you owe me an apology."

Corti had reached out and pulled him in. Upchurch didn't leave except to go back and get his things. He moved in one month after their first meeting.

In explaining the move, Upchurch decided to confront his family for the first time with the news that he was gay. The added news that he was living with an older man didn't help. Corti supported him emotionally through the trouble.

The family's inevitable wrath fell upon Corti, who made himself useful as a lightning rod. "What have you done to my little brother?" Upchurch's brother barked. "What is an older man doing living with our young son?" his mother pleaded. Upchurch talked to them often, explaining that he had been the one who chased down Corti. Finally, the family came to town for a weekend and after a few nervous exchanges they seemed accepting.

Then came Corti's change in careers, and the move to the downtown studio. That had taken some adjusting for them both, but they grew content that it was right. In fact, their whole world had finally come to seem healthy and peaceful.

Now this.

They called Weisman's office immediately, and brought the Mc-Cloy X-ray to Steve Knight, a specialist on Weisman's team. It was Tuesday, June 18, 1985. A day later, when they returned for an exam and diagnosis, Knight was out and they saw his colleague, Gene Rogalski. Rogalski stunned them both. He said Knight had left word that the X-rays were negative. Rogalski examined Upchurch's chest and found it clear. He ran a blood-gas test and said Upchurch's oxygen levels were perfectly normal. Upchurch, he said, just had bronchitis.

Corti was baffled, but wanted to believe. "Fine, maybe he knows. Maybe I'm reading the X-ray wrong," he told himself.

Rogalski gave Upchurch a prescription for the antibiotic erythromycin, and they headed home ecstatic. If the hotshots of the trade had looked at it and said it was bronchitis, maybe it was bronchitis.

"It's like the governor just came down with a stay of execution!" Upchurch exclaimed.

Upchurch took the erythromycin for a week, but only got worse. His fever was higher, his pulse quicker. The doctor said to keep taking the antibiotic. Upchurch took cool showers and Tylenol. He had no appetite. He lost weight. He sweated. He lost energy. Days became nights became days. After every shift, Corti came home from the hospital hoping to find Upchurch better; he never was. After another week, they knew it wasn't bronchitis.

They scheduled another visit to the Valley. This time they saw Knight, who ordered a new X-ray. It showed every lobe in the lung covered with a ground-glass pattern.

"We're going to have to admit you to the hospital," Knight said. "Presumptively, it looks like PCP."[4] (See note for sourcing.)

Upchurch and Corti were frozen in terror as Knight made arrangements. Both assumed they were facing imminent death.

At the time, Sherman Oaks Hospital was among the best AIDS hospitals in the country. Upchurch was brought to its AIDS unit at 145 pounds, down from 152. Corti weighed himself at 185 pounds, down, he thought, from his usual 200. He didn't look or feel sick, but if Upchurch was dying, so, by all reason, was he.

Now he faced another crisis. The woman at the admissions desk was asking him the routine questions while Upchurch was being wheeled around for tests.

"Insurance?" she asked.

Corti had known it was coming, but had been too busy worrying about death to deal with it. Upchurch had quit RFK Hospital, and never got the expected job at Hollywood Community. Technically, he had no medical insurance. But if Sherman Oaks denied admission, Upchurch might have to go to a lesser facility and forfeit treatment by the doctors of choice, both now and for the continuing care he was going to need if he survived the PCP. Often, the first thing a doctor asked of an AIDS patient was what kind of medical insurance the patient had. This was not necessarily a matter of greed. The insurance determined what kind of care the doctor could offer. Without insurance, it might be impossible to admit the patient to a decent hospital. Few doctors would take on an uninsured patient.

"Insurance?" the woman repeated.

"Prudential," Corti said, and gave the woman Upchurch's old Prudential health card from RFK. Corti sweated through the rest of the interview with a fright worse than when he crossed the border back into the U.S. with a load of illegal pills.

Upchurch was given a room and put on Bactrim, the same drug Corti had helped administer to Allan Pritchett the previous fall at RFK. Pritchett had made it out of the hospital, and the last Corti had heard, he was still alive. Surely Upchurch would come home, too.

That thought in mind, Corti dashed to RFK and made a beeline for administration. He pleaded with the employee-benefits director, thankful he had taken the time to chat her up in a friendly way whenever he had seen her in the cafeteria over the past year. He needed this favor. If Upchurch couldn't be continued on the Prudential rolls an extra month, it could cost him his life. Upchurch's original written resignation had been effective as of June 1. In fact, he had left in time for the long Memorial Day weekend in late May. The written resignation still said June 1. Couldn't the hospital just give him June? Then everything would be all right.

The woman smiled, tapped her pencil a few times, and agreed.

TWELVE

*W*hen Corti told the story to Upchurch back at Sherman Oaks, it was about the only piece of good news Upchurch had received. After four days, nothing had improved. The X-rays looked worse. Upchurch couldn't eat and could barely breathe. The ratio of oxygen to carbon dioxide in his blood fell to dangerous levels, and he was put on a ventilator life-support system. They both knew the chilling implications of a ventilator. The doctors started him on another drug, pentamidine.

Corti rarely left the hospital except to go to work. Upchurch's family drove in from La Verne fifty miles east. Corti's patched-up relations with them were strained again as he was thrown together with them night and day. The tension eventually burst to the surface, with the question that had been smoldering in their minds the whole time.

"Why is John sick and you're not?" one of Upchurch's sisters finally asked him.

It was the kind of question he normally could have handled with aplomb. Now, as she eyed him squarely, he only stammered and cried. No one could make out what he said.

"Are you a carrier? Could we get it from you?"

"I don't think that's possible," he said. He had thought they had become friends. He had worked hard to make that happen. Obviously it wasn't so. There was a gulf between them, and Corti knew, as many men knew, that a gulf lay between the whole gay community and the bulk of mainstream America.

The tension continued—even when *Time, Newsweek,* and the other periodicals one inevitably encounters in hospital waiting rooms all suddenly bore cover stories about AIDS. Rock Hudson, the all-American film star who had charmed the nation bantering on screen with the all-American girl, Doris Day, was dying of the disease. Hudson had gone to France to try a purported cure, HPA-23, though there was no real evidence that HPA-23 worked.

Because of Hudson, President Reagan, for the first time, was confronting AIDS. Maybe, Corti thought, the rest of the world would wake up. Meanwhile, though, the magazine stories all had lots of questions, but no answers for deathly ill people like John Upchurch.

For weeks, Upchurch fought his struggle on the respirator while Corti kept vigil. Corti quit riding his bicycle. His only recreation was running out of the hospital for deep-fried fast food, on which he gorged compulsively. He gained thirty pounds while Upchurch lay bedridden. In its own, harmful way, larding on weight reassured him that he wasn't suffering the telltale AIDS symptom of weight loss. He was eating himself sick to affirm that he was healthy.

As for Upchurch, the doctors said that each passing day he stayed in his near-coma reduced his ultimate chance of survival by half. Now the days had turned to weeks. He was unconscious, emaciated, fed through a nose tube. Sometimes he barely responded to stimuli.

At other times he tried to pull the irritating tube and ventilator out of his nose and mouth and had to be restrained and even sedated.

Under the stress, Corti kept complaining to the hospital staff about Upchurch's care, in a manner he would later recognize as excessive. The feeding bags weren't the right size, he would argue. The tubes hadn't been changed often enough. He complained about anything he could think of. When he was at work he called in to the hospital asking fussy questions. The staff put up with him.

Upchurch's X-rays went from bad to disastrous. Every lobe of his lungs was overwhelmed with PCP organisms. The doctors said they no longer believed he would make it.

"The best thing we can do now is just make no further changes in the ventilator," they said. And they stopped even ordering the arterial blood-gas tests that would tell if Upchurch's lungs were improving.

They continued him on the pentamidine, but otherwise the doctors seemed to lose interest in Upchurch. From his own experiences at Kennedy Hospital, Corti recognized the way doctors react to hopeless cases, shaking their heads, saying, "There's nothing more we can do." They were giving the patient up for dead.

Corti and the family agreed that if Upchurch appeared to die—if his heart stopped—no heroic measures would be taken to try to revive him. Still, Upchurch's constitution was so hardy his body held on. The ventilator was going full blast, twenty-four cycles a minute of pure oxygen. Corti would sit at Upchurch's side for hours, crying, resigned to the notion that Upchurch was as good as dead.

Then one night, at his vigil, Corti thought he noticed a change. Upchurch's toes were warm. Blood had begun circulating again to the peripheral parts of his body. He alerted a doctor, who ordered an arterial blood-gas count. Anxiously, Corti awaited the results, feeling the still-warm toes, and a new flicker of hope. And then the results: Upchurch's lungs were working. The oxygen levels in the blood were up. The infection must be clearing. It was the middle of the night. The doctor ordered the ventilator turned down a notch. And Corti knew at that moment that Upchurch would make it out of the hospital.

Two weeks later the tubes were removed. They hugged. They talked. They wished blessings on the woman at RFK who had extended Upchurch's medical benefits. The bill was now over $200,000, and Prudential would pay it. Soon, Upchurch was told he could go home in a week. It was September. The PCP was licked.

But in their joy, as Corti was rubbing skin cream on Upchurch's legs, still dry and scaly from the hospital stay, he noticed a small raised purple spot. He recognized it at once as Kaposi's sarcoma. Almost before he could react emotionally, he scanned Upchurch's body. There, on the back of an elbow, was another small raised purple spot.

Kaposi's can linger for years with little effect on the body—just one or two small purple spots. It can also spread like brushfire over the skin, disfiguring the patient. And it can strike internally, ravaging the brain, stomach, and other vital organs. When that happens, it kills. It is so terrifying to people with the AIDS virus that they often cannot talk about it without glancing instinctively at their exposed skin to reassure themselves that it isn't there.

Corti excused himself, went out in the hall and started crying. When he felt able to talk, he went to Steve Knight, the immunologist. Knight examined Upchurch, taking punch biopsies of the two small raised purple spots. The next day, he returned with the diagnosis Corti knew was coming. Upchurch had not known. He was devastated. He prided himself on his handsome, boyish looks. Now, all he could imagine was being spotted all over with K.S. More than that, it was a reminder, all too soon, that while he had won the battle against PCP he was in a war that no one had ever won. Corti knew it, too. They cried for two days.

And Corti began to think again of his own mortality. How much time did he really have?

Two days before Upchurch was to go home, Dr. Joel Weisman stopped by the room. Weisman, head of the Valley medical group, was perhaps the most prominent doctor specializing in gay men's diseases in the western United States. Corti resented him because he thought Upchurch's doctors had given up on Upchurch during the crisis, and had reduced their level of attention. Of course, Corti was worried exclusively about one patient, and Weisman and his group had many patients. And the bottom line was, whatever Weisman did, Upchurch had been brought safely past the pneumonia.

"How's our miracle boy doing?" Weisman asked. It was no secret that Upchurch had been all but given up for dead before his amazing recovery.

"Fine," Upchurch said. "I want to go home. I'm grateful for what you've done."

Corti cringed at the compliment to Weisman.

"Well, don't you worry about a thing," Weisman said. "Chances are we'll have you on suramin before the month is up. It's a new drug the government's studying, the first antiviral they think may work against this virus."

"I've heard of it," Corti said. "It's the one used in Africa against sleeping sickness."

"That's right," Weisman said. "We think it may work against AIDS, too. It's worth trying."

But the treatment never materialized.

On each of two subsequent checkups at Weisman's office—where Upchurch was examined by Knight, the immunologist—he and Corti asked about suramin. Finally, Knight told them, "A lot of people want it, but there are problems with it. I can't say exactly when you'll get it."

Corti fished for more specifics, but Knight wouldn't provide them. "A lot of people want it," he repeated.

Corti got the idea there must have been some bad results in the clinical tests of suramin being run that summer in San Francisco.

"You know, even if there was a ten percent chance, people would be willing to take that chance," Corti told Knight.

Knight just smiled. Neither he nor Weisman offered any treatment. Under federal drug laws, there was no treatment to offer.[5]

It had been months now since Corti had made a Mexican run. He had lost touch with the community he had been serving. His telephone-answering machine had become a black hole. Messages were neither heard nor returned. Now Upchurch seemed in stable health, his energy and appetite restored. Starting him on ribavirin and isoprinosine seemed a good idea.

So, once more, Corti headed south. He discovered that several other men were now making buying trips for large groups, both in Los Angeles and San Diego. They would sometimes socialize in Tijuana eateries. One, a muscular former Navy pilot, was already suffering from early AIDS symptoms himself. He stuck in the memory because his name was Thomas Jefferson. He even claimed to have backing from the office of Republican Senator Pete Wilson, who until recently had been mayor of San Diego.

Corti also got back in touch with the local AIDS speaking bureau. Once again, he began going to suburban high schools, nurses' and doctors' conferences, Lions Club and PTA meetings. After the Rock Hudson publicity, demand had increased. He spoke in lay language. He omitted nothing—about sexual conduct, or that his own lover had come down with the disease. Or that he probably had it, too.

And he began looking around for an M.D. who would treat the

disease more aggressively than the bigshots had. Surely there was a doctor who would supervise the use of drugs like ribavirin and isoprinosine, even if the medical establishment in Washington hadn't blessed them yet.

THIRTEEN

*F*riday was treatment day for Mark Bradley at the San Francisco General Hospital/University of California suramin study. As usual, he came home looking half dead, and Delaney felt scared. Also, as usual, Delaney had assembled the makings of a hearty dinner, having been told that Bradley should eat well to promote his strength. But Bradley's strength seemed nonexistent as he staggered to the bed and collapsed.

Delaney tried to engage him in talk. "The guy from the *Tribune* called, and they're going to run that article," he said. An *Oakland Tribune* reporter had heard about the Mexican smuggling runs Delaney and various patients were making, and wanted to write about them. Delaney and Bradley had debated at length whether Delaney should cooperate. The reporter sounded sympathetic, but Bradley was nervous that publicity could get Delaney in trouble.

"I think you're wrong about the FDA," Delaney began again, still trying to animate Bradley. "They need public pressure before they'll let ribavirin and isoprinosine into the country. The reporter guaranteed I'd be anonymous, just identified as 'a quiet, pleasant-faced business consultant' named Wayne."

"Yeah," Bradley said, eyes still closed.

"So I think it's safe."

"Yeah," Bradley said again.

Delaney then described the prospective dinner menu as appetizingly as he could, and pleaded with Bradley to eat.

"Uh-huh . . . yeah . . . I'll eat. . . . Just let me rest for an hour."

Delaney went to the kitchen, seasoned and roasted a chicken, cleaned and cut up a salad, boiled water for corn, and shouted occasional questions at the bedroom to make sure his customer was still conscious. A grunt would come back, never much of an answer.

Finally the table was set, the chicken decked for carving, the salad tossed, and the corn removed from the water at the perfect moment between raw and soggy, and Delaney's call to dinner went unanswered. And a second, and a third. He raced downstairs to where Bradley lay motionless. Was he breathing? Yes. Delaney shook him, and Bradley came out of his fog and raised to one elbow.

"I'll be up, I'll be up," he said. "Just give me a second."

Delaney grimaced and paced outside the room. A few minutes later he went in and found Bradley asleep again. They repeated the ritual. "You ought to eat," he said. "Yeah, I will, just give me a second," Bradley said.

Delaney tried a couple of more times during the course of the evening, but to no avail. It was the next morning before Bradley could really talk.

"I'm sorry about the food," he sighed.

"The point isn't the food," Delaney said. "The point is that you still feel so rotten."

Bradley nodded. "It doesn't go away, you know? Like, at first I'd be this way for a few days, but at least I'd know how it felt to be okay again before I went in for another injection. Now, it's like I'm never okay."

"So quit."

"I can't quit."

"Mark, it's September. You've been on this stuff nearly four months. It's supposed to be making you better, not worse."

"It is making me better. Every lymph node has shrunk. I've got no swelling anywhere."

"But you're a walking zombie."

"Jesus, don't you do this, too. Every person I meet gives me this routine about how can you put anything like that into your body."

"But look at you."

"Yeah, look at me. I'm still alive. Have you seen what happens when you reach a full-blown diagnosis of AIDS and you're dying? I saw these patients in wheelchairs, going blind. I'm going to do any drug that doesn't kill me to avoid that. The risks I'll accept. If it kills me, maybe it's better to go quickly."

"You don't know this is going to do anything more for you than the ribavirin did, and you felt fine when you were taking that."

"Suramin kills the virus. The NCI studies showed negative cultures after a few weeks."

"That's the very kind of bullshit I'm talking about," Delaney exploded. "I've seen three journal articles out now that say those negative cultures don't mean anything. They just mean the virus is hard to culture. They're getting negative cultures with all sorts of stuff, but the patients still go on to the next stage of the disease. All we know about suramin is that it's destroying what's left of your health. And the study! They doubled the dose without even telling you."

"That was a mistake."

"But it's the kind of mistake that's not supposed to happen in federally supervised studies. You signed up to take five hundred milligrams of this drug a week, and that was dangerous enough, and they doubled you to a goddamned gram without even telling you."

"They told me, eventually."

"But you're supposed to sign a consent to what they do. They're not supposed to double the dose and then tell you later."

"They say there are three or four other hospitals in the study and they were all giving a gram. I have to trust them."

"Mark, if you're going to get Kaposi's, one of us will see it."

"What do you mean?"

"The way you keep examining yourself. You think I don't notice?"

Bradley sighed again. "I can't help it," he said.

FOURTEEN

A few days later they were sitting together in the anteroom of the AIDS unit at San Francisco General. "I'm sure it's going to be okay," Delaney was saying.

"The throat's really bothering me," Bradley complained.

"Read this," Delaney said, trying to distract him by brandishing the *Oakland Tribune* article:

AIDS Victims Pin Hopes on Drug Smugglers
By Peter Aleshire, Copyright 1985, The Tribune.

"Yeah, it's a great story," Bradley said. "Dying patients detained at border, expensive pills confiscated."

Delaney pulled it back and began reading in a mocking voice: "The FDA has to be careful about allowing the indiscriminate use of drugs we don't know much about." He looked up. "What do they mean? They know more about ribavirin and isoprinosine than they do about suramin, and they're giving *that* out." He began reading again. "We still have to proceed with caution. Many of these AIDS patients are in a very, very delicate balance, which is currently keeping them alive. If we charge ahead like a bull in a china shop, we may upset that delicate balance and shorten many people's lives."

He threw down the paper. "How can they on the one hand tell you the disease is fatal, and then on the other tell you not to take anything for it because you could upset the 'delicate balance' that's keeping you alive?" Delaney asked.

A nurse approached and ushered Bradley into one of the examining rooms. A member of the AIDS team Bradley had gotten to know started looking him over. "So you've got a sore throat," the doctor said, almost to himself. Tongue depressor and light in hand, he peered into Bradley's mouth.

"Probably Kaposi's," the doctor said, withdrawing the light. "I've seen it start this way. Sooner or later, it was likely to come. But people have stayed alive for years with it. Why don't you take a seat outside and I'm going to have one of the senior staff examine you further and we'll decide what to do."

Bradley felt as if he were free-falling down a tunnel. When he emerged from the examining room, he was shaking. Already fatigued from the suramin treatment, he looked uncertain to make it to his chair. Delaney rushed to him to keep him from collapsing.

"My god," Bradley was saying. "This drug is supposed to help and now I've got Kaposi's."

The word hit Delaney like a physical blow. "Wh-Where?" he stammered.

"My throat," Bradley said. "That's where it hurt, isn't it?"

"Kaposi's in your throat? Are they sure? What are they going to do?"

"They're going to have one of the senior doctors examine me. My god, Martin, why is this happening? We didn't go to the bathhouses. We've lived like saints. And all the people who were living the life we said they shouldn't are walking around fine. And I've got Kaposi's."

"C'mon," Delaney said. He didn't know what else to say. Inside, he felt as devastated as Bradley.

They sat there a full hour, Bradley a sobbing, emotional wreck, Delaney white, nearly dumb.

Finally, the other physician called Bradley in. Delaney tried to marshal some comforting thoughts, something to say after Bradley got the bad news. People had survived Kaposi's for years. They would tough it out together.

Then he saw Bradley emerge, shaking and walking rudderlessly as before. Delaney rushed to him again.

"C'mon," he said. "We will tough this out. We know people who've had Kaposi's a long time."

"It's not Kaposi's. This doctor says it's not, it's just a sore throat. He gave me these." Bradley held up a bottle of antibiotic capsules.

"Well—well, then, that's wonderful," Delaney said.

Bradley shook his head and Delaney saw tears in his eyes again. "How can they do that to you? How can they say things like that? Kaposi's is everybody's worst fear. It's the beginning of the end. Who am I supposed to believe?"

"I don't know," Delaney said, his arm around Bradley, supporting him as they left. "Let's hope the guy who gave you the pills is right."

They returned to the apartment and sat through the late afternoon, watching the sun set, feeling depressed.

Delaney finally broke the silence. "Do you ever ask them why you feel like this? Something must be terribly wrong."

"You always ask me that," Bradley said. "I feel helpless in there. If I ask them, they say everything's all right."

"I told you before you ought to ask to see Volberding. He's supposed to be the big national hotshot running the program, and he's never around."

"He's got the whole department to run, I guess," Bradley said. "He told me he's got a good staff running the test."

"Well, did you ask this afternoon how one doctor could diagnose you as having Kaposi's sarcoma and the next doctor an hour later tells you it was a mistake and gives you antibiotics?"

"No, I had other things on my mind," Bradley said.

For a moment, the gloom settled over them once more. Then the phone rang. Delaney got it.

"Hi, Martin," the voice said. "This is Peter Aleshire of the *Oakland Tribune* again. I've had some interesting news from the FDA and the Customs Service. They're caving in a bit."

"No shit."

"They say now they'll allow isoprinosine and ribavirin to come in so long as it's a quantity 'for personal use,' not for distribution."

"How much is that?" Delaney asked.

"That's the catch," Aleshire said. "You don't know. Customs says the FDA won't allow them to say what a 'personal-use quantity' is. And the FDA won't comment. So it's all a guessing game."

"You know why, don't you?" Delaney smiled. "If they announce a quantity, it sounds as if they've determined the correct dosage. In their eyes, it would be tantamount to approving the drug."

"Well, I can tell you the people at customs sure don't like it," the reporter said. "Enforcing it's going to be a real headache when they can't say how many pills are allowable and how many aren't."

"Well, I'm sure it won't cover the loads I bring in," Delaney said. Then he thanked Aleshire for probably relieving some border hassles for patients who were physically able to drive nine hours down and nine hours back to buy their own supplies. And he wondered why the hell patients should have to do that.

FIFTEEN

*T*he drive had become almost second nature to Delaney. So had the company of strangers who volunteered to come along, to help carry pills and dupe customs inspectors.

But on this particular warm, clear day, he was glad fate had arranged for him to travel alone. Mark was over his throat infection. After the Kaposi's scare, life had begun to seem normal even during the persistent craziness of the suramin testing. Delaney had his favorite Pink Floyd tape playing as he wheeled the Mazda through the sunshine and over the border. He had even grown to like walking around Tijuana, shopping for cheap clothes. It was fun, bargaining the price down a few dollars on an already underpriced leather jacket, counting from the sparse roll of bills in one pocket, knowing all the while that he had $10,000 cash—albeit other people's money—in his other pockets.

A new leather jacket under one arm, he turned the corner at Tijuana Tillie's and found the counter at the Regis Farmacia again. This week's order was the biggest yet. When the two Castros heard it, their eyes bulged. They carted up box after box to the counter. After filling eight large shopping bags, they were out of pills.

"You are carrying out more merchandise than my entire pharmacy is worth," said Roberto Castro, laughing. "For this much merchandise you could buy my pharmacy."

The jacket still under one arm, handles of six shopping bags wound around his fingers, Delaney exited the pharmacy. A young clerk chased down the Tijuana street after him with two more bags. They reached the Mazda, dumped the bags in the backseat and locked it.

Then Delaney headed for the Olympia, and then for yet another pharmacy. Each time, he emerged with three more shopping bags. He could barely cram them into the backseat. Perplexed, he pulled out of the parking space on a main thoroughfare and found a secluded side street.

There he sat, in the sun, the tape player blaring, pulling the strips of shrink-wrapped tablets out of their blue-and-white cartons. He was piling the strips of pills in the car, and chucking the empty cartons into a large trash bin on the street. Higher grew the mounds of shrink-wrapped pills in their twelve-pill strips; so too grew the collection of boxes in the trash bin. Eventually, the bin filled, and Delaney began stuffing the boxes into the rapidly emptying shopping bags. Even with the boxes discarded, the size of the pill cargo was getting worrisome.

He took a shopping bag loaded with just the shrink-wrapped pills around behind the car, and opened the trunk. He pulled out the spare tire, and began stuffing the pills into its cavity. When the tire was so full he could barely squeeze it back onto its moorings, he replaced it and began stuffing pills in the spaces around the tire in the well of the trunk.

When the well was full, he covered it, closed the trunk, and opened the rear street-side door of the Mazda. Tugging at the side panel by the door, he pried it loose, first under the window, then along the sides of the door. Holding it still in place at the bottom, he began cramming pills between the side panel and the metal door.

When that space was full, he snapped the panel back into place, went around to the other side of the car, and did the same thing there. He filled all four doors. Still, there remained five bags containing thousands more pills. He reached into the crevice behind the rear seat, and tugged, remembering scenes he had seen in movies. But the Mazda wasn't built for smugglers. The seat wouldn't pull cleanly away from the backrest. There was no easy cavity to exploit.

When he finally managed to move the seat slightly, his hand came back scraped and bloodied from the springs underneath. Still, there was some space, and Delaney began wedging the pills into it, continuing to scratch his hands as he did so.

But even with the back crevice filled and some pills left on the front seat where they could easily be explained away as a personal supply, there were too many pills. Delaney locked the car and took four mostly filled shopping bags of pills back to the Regis. He asked if he could leave the bags behind the counter and pick them up later.

Castro looked at Delaney's sweaty clothes and bloody hands, and laughed heartily. "Sure. Whenever you want them, *amigo.*"

Delaney used a sink in the pharmacy to clean up, then drove for the border. He gripped the steering wheel palms up, to hide the scraped backs of his hands, and bluffed the customs man.

"Just this one sack of pills for personal use," he told the man at the border, showing a paper bag with a dozen boxes of ribavirin. He held up the bag, still careful to show only his relatively clean palms. The guard nodded.

Delaney sped out of sight of the customs area, then left the main highway for the border town of Chula Vista. He began looking for a motel room, where he could unload the pills he had brought with him and go back for the rest. But he couldn't find a vacant room in town. It was after 5 P.M., and daylight was running out.

He spotted what looked like a dump, behind some small industrial buildings not far from the main road. He drove onto the service road behind the buildings. They were shut tight for the weekend. He approached the dump. On the edge of the piles of refuse were some large rusting factory parts, broken beams, and wooden crates.

He opened the trunk of the Mazda, took out the spare tire, and began unloading pills into one of the shopping bags. He stored it under a rusting factory wheel propped up on one end by some wooden beams. The wheel looked as if it had been there awhile, and wasn't likely to be hauled away soon. He followed the same course with bag after bag, emptying each crevice in the car, replacing the side panels, the seat and the tire, and putting the bags full of pills under the factory wheel. Then he drove back to Tijuana.

Returning to the Regis, he collected the shopping bags from behind the counter. Parked again on the side street, he began laboriously, once more, stuffing the strips of shrink-wrapped pills in and around the spare tire, into the door frames of the car and into the cavity behind and under the rear seat.

He headed back to the border, wishing now that one of his customers had come with him, someone who could scout ahead on foot and make sure he did not encounter the same customs agent he had earlier. There was nothing to do now but sweat it out in the dark and hope.

From seven or eight cars back, he could see the attendants in the booths in his row and the rows around him. He didn't spot the man he had dealt with a couple of hours ago. He hoped as he waited that there would be no sudden shift changes before he got through.

His luck continued. The encounter was as simple as it ever had been—a few perfunctory questions and he was back on the road. Around a bend, he wheeled off the freeway, and followed the service road around behind the small industrial park, to where the discarded machine parts lay in the dirt and gravel. Crawling around in near-total darkness now, he couldn't find the bags he had left. He turned the car around again, and aimed its headlights at the area where he knew the bags had to be. On his knees now, in the dirt, he groped about with his hands. From under the rusting factory wheel, he retrieved his bags of pills, and tossed them into the backseat of the Mazda.

Dirty, tired, a bit scared, his hands still sore, he raced back to Interstate 5 and hurtled north into the night. He didn't even reach for the radio.

"What am I doing?" he kept asking himself. "I'm a consultant to half a dozen major banks, advising executives. This is my weekend, and I'm carrying huge wads of bills around Tijuana, scraping my hands, lying to customs agents, crawling around dumps, driving through the night. If I'm lucky I'll be home before dawn. What then? And what for?"

It was the job of the government and the medical establishment to fight this epidemic. Yet from everything he saw, they were either in the way, or, in Mark's case, making matters worse.

It was 4 A.M. by the time he reached Sausalito, and crawled into bed.

He awoke at 9 to the sound of his doorbell. He fished for his pants, slipped them on, and stumbled down the hall toward the front door. There, he was surprised to confront a familiar-looking but not exactly recognizable young man.

"I'm Joe," the man said. "I brought you some money a few days ago. You said you'd be going to Tijuana Saturday. Today's Sunday."

It was the Auschwitz man, Delaney realized. But there was more color to him now. He seemed less emaciated somehow. There was life to this man; a few days ago he had seemed already dead. And Delaney hadn't even delivered the ribavirin to him yet.

"You look a lot better than you did the other day," Delaney said.

"I had a blood transfusion yesterday," the man replied. "And now I've got ribavirin to look forward to. You don't know how great it makes me feel to think there's something that might work, that I can try. I am just so indebted to you, I can't thank you enough for what you're doing."

"Yeah," Delaney said. "Let me get you your pills."

"Who was that?" Bradley asked when the man was gone.

"Somebody who says I made him feel a whole lot better before I even gave him the ribavirin. I can't get over the way he looked. He was at the house a few days ago and I thought he was going to die on the front stoop. He said he'd had PCP twice already. I didn't even want to take his money. Now he looks like he might survive the drive home at least."

"What do you suppose did it?"

"He said it was the hope that maybe the drug will work. And he had a transfusion yesterday."

"Transfusions can make that kind of difference," Bradley said. "But it peters out. He'll be back the way he was in a few days. You don't look so great yourself."

Delaney told him about the trip and they both laughed.

Then they stopped. "I thought a lot about this whole business on the drive back," Delaney said. "Sometimes it seems just plain crazy. Then I see someone like this guy—and I kind of think it's not crazy. That this is really worth doing."

Bradley nodded.

"Anyway," Delaney said, "we've got ten thousand dollars' worth of pills sitting there in the living room. I better go deliver some of them."

S I X T E E N

*T*he caller had said: "My lover's dying. We don't have much money. No car." Delaney had taken the address.

As he drove over the Golden Gate Bridge and looked out on what he had long regarded as one of the most beautiful views in the world, he knew he was headed for a seedy district of drug addicts and prostitution, where burned-out people lived in cheap tenements. But he still wasn't prepared for quite how bad things were when he turned off Van Ness and onto Eddy Street.

Littered sidewalks led past boarded-up storefronts under two- and three-story hotels. He found a parking place in front of the address he'd been given. But he didn't feel particularly safe getting out of the car.

It was an unusually hot afternoon. He walked up three flights of stairs, repelled by the urine stench and the graffiti on the walls. When he knocked, the door opened to a tiny, acrid apartment.

He stood looking at a poorly and effeminately dressed man, who greeted him frantically and asked him in. The man looked maybe fifty, delicate, and nearing the limits of his sanity. He was what Delaney called "an auntie type." His hands shook palsy-like as he spoke.

Delaney knew at once it was the man who had called him. But all

Delaney could think about was that it stank in this room. He looked around. Why were all the windows closed? Were they afraid of noise? Or of fresh air? He wondered.

How far this was from any life he had known himself!

"This is the only person I've ever loved," the man was saying, beginning a stream of babble, never making eye contact. "We don't know anybody in this town. We came here just a year ago from Iowa. I want to go back there to visit my mother, but I just can't. He's been so sick, for six months. It all happened so fast. This was such a beautiful and handsome person."

Delaney scanned the knickknacks and photographs that had been scattered to try to make the place livable. There were pictures of the couple in better health. The man babbling at him wasn't fifty, but probably more like thirty-five. His younger lover, the one with AIDS, looked Hispanic—and was dressed in women's clothing.

The babbler was talking about his job as a bookkeeper. He revealed that his lover had been one of those lucky drag queens who attained employment as a transvestite in bar shows. There were a lot of drugs in that scene, Delaney thought. And the closer he looked at the photographs in this dingy apartment, the more he began to see the lover as a hard drug user.

"These pills you have from Mexico," the first man was saying. "Do you really think they'll help? Can they save him?" He talked so fast he left almost no time for Delaney to answer. Delaney turned again to face him, but the man still wouldn't look him in the eye. "Aren't you going to ask me about money?" he was saying. "We don't have any insurance. I want to know about these pills before I pay you."

"I don't need to take your money if you can't afford it," Delaney said. "Do you have a doctor?"

"Not a regular doctor, no. I was treated for V.D. by a doctor once, but that was a clinic. When will he get better? How long will it take? We don't have much money. I've tried to help him with things I've got from the health-food store. . . ." He gestured, and Delaney's eyes fell upon a shelf of herb teas and vitamins. Delaney began to shake his own head. This sorry array was obviously collected by someone who either didn't know enough to go to his doctor about sickness, or had given up on medical science altogether. The man continued, in his whiny, helpless tone. "He's taken the teas. Nothing seems to change anything. Do you think what you've got will really help?"

"I don't know whether it will help anyone," Delaney said.

"His weight's dropped terribly the past two months," the man went on.

"Let me see him," Delaney said.

They went into the only other room in the apartment, and it was worse than Delaney had imagined. The figure he saw shriveled up in a fetal position on a bed looked near death—emaciated, in a pool of sweat, bed clothes filthy. There were used Kleenexes all over the room. A glass of water sat on a lone dresser by the bed. The man had barely enough voice to tell Delaney, after several queries, that he had not seen a doctor since becoming ill. He spoke in a thick Spanish accent.

"Will the pills help?" the sick man added hoarsely.

Delaney gave his stock answer: "Some people say it's helped them, some people say it hasn't. I can't tell you whether it will do you any good. But what alternatives do you have?" Then, looking at the man, he added, "You ought to be in a hospital."

"No, no, I can't do that," the man replied, not moving in bed.

"San Francisco General will take anyone, and they have some of the most experienced AIDS specialists in the country," Delaney said.

"I was there once. I can't do that."

Delaney didn't want to press him further. These men are out of touch with the world, he thought. They are terrified. It was pathetic. An air of death hovered about the apartment.

The sick man's eyelids were barely open, the eyes rolled back. Delaney began to explain how to take the ribavirin and isoprinosine, if that is what he chose to do. The sick man interrupted him to say, "I'm very tired."

The first man asked what to do. Delaney wanted to say there was nothing to do at this late stage of the disease, but he had determined never to deny people hope. He left two boxes of pills, said again that he didn't know if they would help, and told both men that the patient ought to be in a hospital.

"We can't do that," the older man repeated, shaking his head more vigorously, still staring at the floor. "We can't do that."

He and Delaney left the room. "Are you ill yourself?" Delaney asked.

"Probably. I don't know," the man said.

"Have you been tested?"

"No, no."

Delaney encouraged him again to see a doctor. If there was anyone the ribavirin and isoprinosine might help, it would more likely be this man than his lover. But this was not a rational encounter.

Delaney could not get the scene out of his head as he drove around to make other deliveries. These weren't the kind of people who inhabited his comfortable existence. These were a couple of scared animals in a hole. If San Francisco had been so unkind to them, God only knew how they must have been treated in Iowa.

He began to think about gays. There were like people everywhere who shared a fundamental drive of life with Delaney that most other people could never fully understand. And they had been punished miserably for this shared trait, which they had not created but merely recognized. What had been done to these two men to put them in the spot they were in? He thought of gays he knew from places that were probably a lot more tolerant than Iowa—gays who had told him of being pushed out of the family house, cut out of wills, even forced to undergo electroshock therapy because they were the way they were. And if they were not supposed to be that way, why *were* they that way?

And after life had been thus unfair to them, AIDS had doubled the blow. The family found out not just that the son was gay but that he was dying, all at the same time. And the family tended to blame the entire gay community. The two men he had just seen had probably been ridden out of Iowa on a rail, only to find refuge in that little hole in the tenderloin of San Francisco. They were afraid of doctors, afraid of the outside world. But they had called Martin Delaney.

Suddenly it came to him that the city must be filled with men like them, dying, caged, alone. The AIDS statistics that showed up in the medical records counted the people who went to doctors, who sought some kind of medical care. This guy would be carried out of his tenement in a body bag. There would be no autopsy. Cause of death: cardiac arrest. And except for his pathetically helpless lover, did anyone in the whole world know or care?

As soon as Delaney got home, he called Joe Brewer.

S E V E N T E E N

Brewer was a psychologist whose group-therapy sessions had helped Delaney and other patients deal with their anguish during the hepatitis drug experiments at Stanford. Delaney had always respected him for creating an anchor of stability amidst the panic as so many patients suffered and died.

Recently he had run into Brewer at AIDS meetings. With a therapy practice centered in the gay community, Brewer counseled lots of

AIDS patients, some of whom took ribavirin and isoprinosine that Delaney smuggled from Mexico. Brewer had been interested in Delaney's smuggling. Now Delaney asked Brewer to meet him at a small Japanese restaurant near Brewer's office in the Castro area, where they had dined before.

"Joe, I never expected it to balloon like this. I just did a ten-thousand-dollar deal. The next trip'll be just as big. And I've still got my work. Before I go to Tijuana again, I fly to Honolulu to give a seminar for First Hawaiian Bank. Then I go back to smuggling."

"It must be tough," Brewer commiserated. "But people all over San Francisco are depending on you. I know some of them."

"San Francisco, hell," Delaney aid. "Word spreads. I'm getting orders from Chicago, St. Louis. . . . I met a doctor from New York who tested positive, and I gave him some, and now his patients are ordering. And his friends' patients. All my spare time is tied up in this. So's my money."

"It's kind of ridiculous when you get down to it," Brewer said. One guy can't be expected to fight this disease by supplying the whole country with illegal drugs. For one thing, we don't even know for sure they work. Somebody needs to come up with a system."

"That's why I wanted to talk," Delaney said. "Right now, we've got four drugs that show signs of working against the virus. The government is involved in two. There's suramin, which has been around for years for sleeping sickness. It's being tested on the AIDS virus, though I think it's doing Mark more harm than good."

"Agreed," Brewer said. "I've got patients suffering through the same test."

"Then there's something called Compound S, which some people call AZT. The government developed it, then licensed it to a big drug company, Burroughs Wellcome. They're going to start nation-wide hospital trials next year, so maybe in a few years we'll have a clue to whether it works or not. Meantime, people are dying and can't get any.

"Then we come to the last two drugs," Delaney said. "Ribavirin and isoprinosine, which are made by two little companies, ICN and Newport Pharmaceuticals. They're approved overseas, but not here. There's an FDA-sanctioned test for ribavirin wrapping up now, but only in connection with some lung disease that kids get, and the manufacturer had to work for years to get *that* started. They say they won't start testing it against AIDS till at least next year."

"Though thousands of patients are taking the stuff anyway," Brewer said.

"We know these drugs make a lot of people feel better. Maybe the drugs are working against the virus. Maybe it's just the placebo effect. Maybe the drugs are even harmful, though there's no evidence of it."

"This ought to be resolved," Brewer said. "If the drugs work, they ought to be publicized and approved. If the government is going to take forever, there's no reason we couldn't organize our own study in the community and get it done."

"Exactly!" Delaney exclaimed. "We know the doctors who are monitoring patients on these drugs. Some of them are in your neighborhood. All we need is for them to supply the data on dosages and T-cell counts and occurrence of new infections and so forth, and we collate it. All we've got to do is get them to cooperate. There's nothing magic about these studies. The jerks up at San Francisco General are killing Mark and a bunch of other people with suramin right now. I was lucky to get out of the Stanford hepatitis study alive. We can do at least as well as that."

As dinner progressed, a conspiracy took shape. Neither Delaney nor Brewer had heard of any previous drug study that relied on local doctors, bypassing the FDA. It would probably violate some federal laws. But Delaney was already violating federal laws.

"I've supervised statistical research in psychology," Brewer said. "Why not with AIDS? Most of the research that's done in psychology is pretty sloppy, and yet it's accepted as fact all the time. I'm certain we can do better than most stuff I see."

"There are a hundred people a day dying from this disease, Joe, and it's only going to get worse. We've got a chance to do something about it. The goddamned government never will."

When the dishes were cleared, Delaney pulled out a pile of Xeroxed documents. "Look what's already been done," he said. "Just for ribavirin, talking about safety and potential effectiveness, here's several dozen published articles from scientific journals, going back to 1972. *Science* magazine, *Lancet*, the most respected journals in medicine. The drug works against some influenza viruses, Lassa fever virus, herpes viruses, you name it. Only minor side effects. Available all over the world for viruses—except here. And now even the FDA is close to approving it for a kids' lung disease."

Delaney began summing up some of the papers. Ribavirin seemed to reduce production of an enzyme called reverse transcriptase that the AIDS virus needs in order to reproduce itself. Brewer was impressed by Delaney's quick self-education in medicine.

Suddenly interrupting his own jargon, Delaney looked up from the papers and caught Brewer's eyes. "Why shouldn't our guys be allowed to take this stuff, Joe? Especially if medical science hasn't got anything else to offer them, and says they're going to die soon if they do nothing?"

"And this other pile," Brewer said. "I assume it's about isoprinosine."

"The drug's been studied at least since 1971 under a bunch of different names," Delaney said. "And in all these studies the reports say virtually no side effects. Now, here's an Italian university study on cancer patients last year.[6] Isoprinosine significantly boosts immune responses in human subjects. Why not use this drug against a disease that kills you by lowering your immune responses?"

Delaney documented his point with study after study. One study, with U.S. Government participation, showed a restoration of immune cells in all three AIDS patients tested.[7]

"Jesus, Joe, I know it's only three patients, but it worked against AIDS in people." The words were pouring out of Delaney. Brewer took them in, fascinated, nodding, trying to follow in the mass of documents.

"And let me tell you something else," Delaney went on. "Ribavirin is an antiviral agent. Isoprinosine is an immune-system modulator. It only makes sense that the two of them will work best together. That's exactly what cured me of the hepatitis when people taking just one drug without the other died. And yet nobody is interested in testing these two drugs in combination. Under FDA rules, each company has to test and prove its own drug alone first. A joint test doesn't help anybody but the patient. The FDA and the big university research institutions won't do anything until the companies propose it and pay for it."

"But we can cut through that," Brewer said, still shuffling through the photocopies. "Okay. You know what I'm going to do? I work with a dozen doctors who deal with AIDS all the time. We treat each other's patients. I'm going to send copies of some of these papers to them and see what their reaction is."

"Those are the very doctors we'll need for a study," Delaney said. "They can monitor the patients we supply drugs to, and feed us the lab data. We get data on patients who take ribavirin and isoprinosine, and data on their other patients who don't."

"You're talking about a control group now," Brewer said.

"That's what the FDA wants."

"That's tough. Look, there are two kinds of studies you can do. One is a retrospective study. That looks at what's already happened to patients who have been taking the drugs. It could be done fast. The trouble is, medical science doesn't pay much attention to retrospective studies because they can be biased. People tend to submit the data that proves their case, and ignore the other data that doesn't. What you're talking about now is a *prospective* study, which means treating new patients under a protocol, a set of rules, designed in advance to compare the progress of patients who get the treatment with the progress of patients who don't. That's the more respected kind of study, but it takes a lot more time."

"Let's do both," Delaney said. "Let's get some scientific basis for saying whether this stuff works or not so we can tell our people whether to take it. Let's move as fast as we can. If the results are positive, we publicly demand the FDA do whatever it has to do to get these drugs out."

"It's worth a shot," Brewer said. "I'll send these studies to some doctors. We also ought to meet with a guy named Don Gorman who's started a research library for Boneberg and his Mobilization group."

"Talking to Mobilization's a good idea," Delaney agreed. "They're probably tax exempt. We're going to need some kind of nonprofit tax cover for this. We're going to need a computer and statisticians. This is going to cost money."

EIGHTEEN

Accompanying Brewer to Mobilization's new research library—which was just a small room for storing documents—Delaney was disappointed that the director, Gorman, wasn't more enthusiastic.

"I think it's a good idea, Don," Delaney said.

"I think it's a *great* idea. But Boneberg'll have fits."

"Why?"

"Don't you see where this is leading?"

Delaney and Brewer looked at him blankly.

"Hell," Gorman said. "It means people have to get tested for the virus. If you don't test, you don't know whom to give the drugs to, the doctors can't monitor them, and you can't do your study."

"So?" Delaney said. "Of course, people ought to get tested. How else are they going to get treated?"

"You think so and I think so. But the board of Mobilization doesn't think so. It's Boneberg's big issue. Most other gay political groups, too. They're scared to death we're all going to be rounded up and thrown in concentration camps. This guy Lyndon LaRouche is campaigning for a constitutional amendment to have us all quarantined. William F. Buckley, Jr., wants us tattooed with some kind of scarlet letter."

"But surely a guy like Boneberg can see that the most important thing is still to find out whether you're sick and try to keep yourself alive."

"No," Gorman said. "At least once at every directors' meeting he makes his little speech about how the most important thing is to keep ourselves out of jail until they find the cure. The majority of the board feels that way. Try talking to Tim Wolfred, the executive director of the AIDS Foundation. These guys are dead set against even the slightest suggestion that people ought to be tested. And the Civil Liberties Union is behind them."

"So why can't people just get tested anonymously?" Delaney asked. "Use a number instead of a name. Deal with doctors we can trust, and only the guy taking the test gets the result."

"They don't trust anybody that much. Some guy like LaRouche could come along and unblind the number system."

"Shit," Delaney said.

"And what else is behind it, of course, is that they think testing's pointless, because they don't really believe anything helps. That's where they and I differ. It may be that the people who most need to see a successful study are the board at Mobilization."

"I can't believe this," Delaney said. "We're going to have a tough enough time with the medical establishment. How can our own community fight us!"

"Well, maybe we can still work it out," Gorman said. "I want you to talk to Ken McPherson. He's another member of the board at Mobilization. I think he'll agree with me on this. You know what may have to happen?"

"I'm afraid to ask," Delaney said.

"This could split us off from Mobilization, make it two different groups."

"This is crazy."

"Yeah. Well, maybe that's what has to happen. Let's both talk to McPherson. You sure the doctors will cooperate?"

"Why wouldn't they?" Delaney said. "Until now all the data they assemble's just gone to waste. They talk about it with each other, but nobody ever totals it up. This'll benefit everybody."

"Optimist," Gorman said.

Within a week, Gorman had set up a meeting for Delaney with McPherson. Delaney decided to hang it all out.

"The FDA is a bunch of bums," he asserted. "Do you really think they care about dying queers? If we can get doctors whose patients use these illegal drugs to start recording the results, we'll be able to prove what effect it's having. We've got to. You've read the projections in the papers. Incidence of AIDS is doubling every year. If we don't do this now, ourselves, then by 1992 we'll all be dead."

McPherson turned to Gorman, and some other allies from the Mobilization board who were sitting in. "We've been bitching all along that the government is moving too slowly," he said. "This is put up or shut up. You and I know that ribavirin and isoprinosine seem to be helping people. We have to record the results and start getting that information out."

Several of them agreed to confront Boneberg and the rest of the Mobilization board with an ultimatum.

"Are you crazy?" Boneberg responded. "There are politicians trying to put our people in concentration camps. The only way you can run these experiments is by encouraging people to test themselves for the virus. We can't encourage testing."

"Who cares if you're in a concentration camp if you're dead?" Gorman replied. After a few more rounds of argument, Gorman and another director resigned from Mobilization on the spot, taking the tax-exempt research organization with them. McPherson said he intended to stay with both groups.

The San Francisco gay leadership was now roiled in controversy. Delaney remained focused on one goal: find and promote a treatment for AIDS. "We've got to launch this study with as much fanfare as possible," he told his new colleagues. "Every newspaper, every television station in town has to promote this. We need to reach potential funders, potential cooperating doctors, and every patient we can."

Brewer said he knew the owner of the Valencia Rose, a popular club in the Castro, and they could hold a press conference there.

"We also need a name," Delaney said. "Something to differentiate this study from whatever else Gorman is doing."

Brewer looked down on the desk in front of him and saw an unrelated paper bearing the word "inform."

"How about Project Inform?" he said.

On October 22, 1985, the press turned out at the Valencia Rose for the inauguration of Project Inform. Surprised reporters, who expected the usual ragtag community protest group, were greeted by men in business suits handing out fancy press kits. The mainstream *San Francisco Chronicle* and *Examiner* were still skeptical. Could you get scientifically acceptable data in this fashion, without government approval? Where was the study design?

The design was still being drawn, Delaney said. And it would be drawn to produce scientifically acceptable data. The prospective part of the study would involve maybe four hundred volunteers who had tested positive for the virus; two hundred would take ribavirin and isoprinosine in combination, and another two hundred, the control group, wouldn't take either drug.

Had a community-based drug study been done before? No, nor apparently even attempted, Delaney said. But there was no choice. "The federal Food and Drug Administration has been treating AIDS as business-as-usual. Given the nature of this disease, that's just not adequate. Years go by, and we're told to wait for results, even when the diagnosis says we've got six months to live."

Delaney talked about the preliminary studies that suggested ribavirin and isoprinosine might work against AIDS. "No matter what the medical authorities say, people are using these drugs," he told the reporters. "What we want to do is provide a safe, monitored environment to learn what effects they are having."

The papers and television and radio stations were quick to find establishment research doctors to disparage the experiment. "It seems to be a very well-intentioned effort, and I wish them well," Dr. Volberding of San Francisco General told the *Chronicle*. But, he added, "to be honest I don't think the chances are very good they can find anything that is very convincing."

In all, Delaney was happy with the coverage. The project had been treated with respect. Peter Aleshire's continuing sympathetic treatment in the *Oakland Tribune* helped the rest of the mainstream press accept Delaney's underground approach.

What puzzled Delaney was that the gay press seemed less enthusiastic about what he was proposing than the mainstream press. He was constantly surprised by the way many gay leaders feared publicity about AIDS. They had finally achieved public tolerance of homosexuality, and now they saw it jeopardized by anyone who tended to link sexual preference in people's minds with a fatal disease.

To Delaney, though, saving lives was more important. Somehow, he would have to overcome the fears of his own community's leaders.

He thought about the Iowa men who had been living in the San

Francisco tenement. He had gotten a call a month ago that the sick man was dead. The surviving lover actually wanted to give back the remaining pills so someone else who was sick could use them.

Delaney wondered how many other dramas like that were being played out in San Francisco and around the country. Who was the dead man? Was he a citizen? Did he have a green card? Is that why they were afraid to take him to a hospital or to deal with the medical system? How did the Centers for Disease Control incorporate such men into their statistics?

Driven by a painful anxiety, Delaney refused to let his feeling of helplessness interfere with his mission. He had called Joe, the Auschwitz man, who had rallied after a blood transfusion, and had ordered more pills. But a woman answered the phone. Experience told Delaney that was a bad sign.

"Is Joe there?"

"Who is this calling?"

Another bad sign. "My name's Martin Delaney."

"You're the man who helped Joe get the pills. I'm his sister. Joe's passed on. But I want to thank you. It meant a lot to him."

People cling to life, Delaney thought. Some people die with the expectation that this is what happens to you when you are eighty-six years old. But he was tired of seeing people like these, in their thirties or younger, hounded by the question, How can this happen to me?

NINETEEN

*F*or a while, at least, Project Inform's study was in Brewer's hands. Several statisticians and community doctors, intrigued by news reports after the press conference, agreed to help him devise a protocol. Delaney had to tend to his consulting work, to his smuggling runs—and to his ever more severely sick lover, who refused to remove himself from the federally sponsored University of California–run suramin study.

As Bradley grew weaker, the information available about the study grew more ominous. Volberding, the big expert, seemed to have almost vanished from the project. It appeared to be directed instead by an underling two years past his residency.

Bradley had also been solicited for a separate study of swollen lymph nodes, run by another Volberding staffer, Dr. Donald Abrams. The shrinkage of Bradley's lymph nodes had been one of the few encouraging results from the suramin injections. Now, Bradley and Delaney discovered, Abrams didn't find that encouraging at all. It was Abrams's disconcerting theory that swollen lymph nodes were a positive sign that the body's natural immune system was fighting the disease; when lymph nodes shrunk back to normal, he theorized it meant that the body had given up.

Then came a call from Brewer, confirming ugly rumors about what was happening to other patients in the suramin study. One of Brewer's psychotherapy patients who had been in the study had just died of liver failure, and another was dying of it. Still more ominous, Brewer noted that both men had been in relatively good health going into the study a few months before. Brewer was angry.

Yet Bradley had been told at the hospital that nothing serious was happening.

Then he was invited to a meeting with the researchers on November 13, 1985, at the hospital. A patient he met told him the meeting had been demanded by a group of patients who were alarmed over the deterioration they had suffered.

When the meeting came, Volberding wasn't there. The young researcher who had taken over the study showed up late, then sounded upbeat about prospects for the drug, though he couldn't give numbers yet. But he said he wanted to correct the word going around that people were becoming seriously ill from suramin. Some were sick, but not many, and not seriously.

"Except two people died," Delaney exclaimed when Bradley told him about it that night.

But it wasn't due to the suramin, Bradley said. "And they passed out new consent forms covering the risks of the increased dosage."

"Which they increased two months ago without the consent forms, and without telling you first."

"I signed mine."

Delaney shook his head helplessly. It was uncharacteristic of Bradley to accept things so passively, he thought. He wondered if passivity was one more side effect of the suramin.

"Look, how do you think I feel?" Bradley said. "I feel impotent and self-conscious, just being in this situation. Not working. Having you pay for my drugs, my rent, my car." Delaney had just bought him a secondhand Honda to make the hospital commute easier.

"I'm in a position to help," Delaney said.

"I don't want this to be the cornerstone of our relationship."

"Well, it's not. It won't always be this way, but right now you're sick and our first concern is getting you well. The suramin sure doesn't seem to be doing it."

Bradley was quiet a moment. "One of the new side effects they mentioned is possible kidney failure," he said.

Delaney looked at him. "Do you really want to continue this?"

"Yes, I really want to continue this. It could make me well."

"But you're sick all the time now."

"I don't care. I'll be sick for the duration if it's going to cure me."

But over the next two weeks his resolve faded. He became bloated, feverish. He was bedridden half the time. He asked for an appointment at San Francisco General, but was told the doctors were too busy. Three times he visited the hospital to see a doctor and was turned away. His concentration began to lapse. He would reach for words in conversations and couldn't find them. He came to a red light and couldn't react. He wrecked the secondhand Honda.

Then came Thanksgiving at Delaney's sister's house. Bradley's hair was falling out—something he was sure the doctors hadn't warned him of. He felt paranoid, and began to wonder if his mind was going, too. He could scarcely walk. His weight had dropped precipitously.

"I want you to stop taking this drug," Delaney told him on the way home. "You're sick as hell. You haven't had PCP, you haven't had Kaposi's, or any other serious AIDS infection. All you've had is this damned suramin."

"Yeah, maybe I should stop," Bradley finally agreed. "Let me go see somebody." The concession, after so many months of insistence, startled Delaney. They decided Bradley would see a doctor the following Monday even if he had to force his way in.

That Sunday night was the worst of Bradley's life. He thought he was dying. He found himself chanting, "Let me make it till morning," as if it were a mantra.

Finally in the waiting room of San Francisco General, Bradley began raising his voice to an elderly gentleman receptionist.

"I've got to see a doctor now."

"All the doctors are busy. Do you have an appointment?"

"I've got to see a doctor now. I'm sick. I'm on this goddamned drug and something is wrong."

Bradley's suramin injection had been postponed from Friday because of the Thanksgiving holiday, but he had already made up his mind he wasn't taking it.

The receptionist continued to stall him. Bradley collapsed into a chair.

He looked up once and saw the nurse for the project preparing the large syringe for an injection—obviously his.

He went after the receptionist again. Suddenly, Lillian appeared, a short, dark-haired former radiology technician who had become the project paperwork administrator. She was the one person at the hospital who Bradley thought really cared.

"I want to see a doctor," he was shouting. "I won't take any more of the drug."

"No, I know, you're not taking it," Lillian said. He was thrown back by her easy agreement. She had been running the experiment on doctors' orders for months. She told the nurse preparing the syringe to go get a doctor.

"Should I continue when I feel like this?" he asked.

"No. Absolutely not." Lillian kept her professional manner, but was obviously angered by how sick Bradley was. "Everybody else has stopped due to the complications of this drug. People are experiencing all sorts of problems."

Bradley was stunned. Had he heard her correctly? After all he had been through, was she suddenly telling him that he was the only fool still taking this toxic drug? He collapsed back into a chair to wait. The nurse who had been preparing the syringe appeared. He asked again if it was true.

"Everybody else has stopped," Lillian repeated. "People are dying of liver failure."

A staff physician who sometimes supervised Bradley's injections ushered Bradley into an examining room.

"Lillian said everybody has stopped but me," Bradley said, his voice a mix of panic and anger.

The doctor said nothing, but busily took out equipment for drawing blood.

"You mean to tell me that I'm the last patient on this drug?"

"Well, I asked you, and you chose to continue," the doctor said, strapping the tubing around Bradley's arm and probing for a vein.

"But I didn't know everybody was getting sick."

"Well, most stopped very recently," the doctor said, as Bradley's blood flowed into the tube. "There. We'll have the results tomorrow," he said.

"The other doctor took my blood back when I said I started getting like this. I was never told what the results were."

"Let me go look," the doctor said.

He came back a few minutes later looking concerned, holding a small piece of paper with numbers on it.

"Your adrenal levels are way down," he said. "I'm going to give you a shot of hydrocortisone. And a prescription for hydrocortisone by mouth." He withdrew a hypodermic from a drawer.

"You mean the test result has been sitting here for almost a month?" Bradley said.

The doctor was silent as he gave Bradley the shot and began writing the prescription. Then he said, "I'm also going to give you an appointment to see an endocrinologist next month, and we'll have you admitted to the hospital for tests."

"What do you mean 'next month'!" Bradley said, suddenly enraged again. "If there's something wrong, shouldn't I be admitted now? I've been complaining for four months that there's something wrong. Why wasn't this done sooner?"

"Well," the doctor began. And then he didn't say anything.

"Now you're telling me I can't get in the hospital for a month. What if something goes wrong over the holidays?"

"No, no, you'll be fine," the doctor assured him. "Just take these hydrocortisone tablets and come back in a few days. We'll also give you an intravenous of liquid before you leave now. You're dehydrated."

While Bradley lay on the table taking in the liquid, the young doctor whom Volberding had designated as principal researcher of the suramin project came in. The two men eyed each other nervously.

"You'll feel better in a while," the doctor said matter-of-factly.

Bradley glared back at the doctor. "I'm looking forward to it," he said.[8] (See note for the doctors' recollections.)

That night Bradley began to bloat again, but worse this time than before. He was checked again at the hospital. Over the next week, he gained nearly twenty pounds, obviously water. His face became round. His knees and ankles swelled. He felt better; his energy level was up. But they were frightened of what the bloating meant.

He phoned the hospital. "Don't worry, it's only a little water," the doctor said. "Come in and see me next week."

At least, Bradley thought, he could finally get a doctor on the phone.

"This is bullshit," Delaney said. "I want to go with you when you go back there. There's obviously something terribly wrong."

"No. I'll handle it myself."

"You better," Delaney said. "If you come back without some kind of satisfactory explanation I'm going in there and raise hell."

Arriving for his appointment, Bradley recognized a man in the elevator as another patient who had spoken at the meeting a few weeks earlier.

"Have you had an adrenal problem?" Bradley asked.

With his glassy, dilated eyes, the man looked like a drug addict. "Yeah," he said. "They're giving me steroids. Lots of them. Makes you feel good."

Off the elevator and into the waiting room, Bradley saw yet another patient, sitting wan and expressionless.

"Have you had problems on the suramin?" Bradley asked. His voice was forceful and demanding now, not casual. The man just mumbled. He seemed unable to communicate, the way Bradley had been on Thanksgiving. He was yellow, drawn. Finally Bradley understood what the man was trying to say.

"They won't let me in to see the doctor," the man was saying.

"Who are you?" Bradley said. "Give me your name and telephone number."

The man seemed unable to respond. Bradley took out a pocket notebook and ballpoint pen and placed it in the man's hands. With obvious difficulty, the man wrote his name, Paul Davis, and a phone number.

"Don't worry," Bradley said, taking the paper. "I had the same problems. We're going to get to the bottom of it."

The man nodded.

"My ankles are swollen," Bradley told the doctor. "I'm bloated."

"I've made an appointment for you to be admitted for endocrine tests here in the hospital in January."

"I don't want to wait until January. You've done this to me with this drug. You've got to help me out of it."

"The adrenal problem is not from the suramin. It's from the virus. Believe me, this isn't a big enough thing to hassle people with over the holidays. If you taper the steroids down, the water problem will be okay. It's already getting better from what you told me on the phone."

Bradley had to admit that it was. In a few days, on the new dosage, he lost the twenty pounds of water he had gained.

Delaney still wanted to intervene. Bradley insisted that he not, and even forbade Delaney and others to see him in the hospital. "I don't want you or anybody to see me sick," he said.

Right after New Year's 1986, just before being admitted to the hospital, Bradley was allowed another brief talk with the young principal researcher of the suramin study. "It's the disease that's causing this. It's not the suramin," the doctor insisted.

"That I don't believe," Bradley said. "I never had this problem before I took this drug."

But after he was admitted, the hospital's chief endocrinologist told him the same thing—the suramin hadn't caused the problem. And the doctor put him on a new steroid. "You're dehydrated, you're losing salt," he said. In a few days the problems seemed to be adjusted. But the doctor warned, "You've lost ninety percent of your adrenal function and you're never going to recover it." The doctor gave him a tag to wear around his neck at all times, warning that he had adrenal insufficiency.

"You're going to need to wear this as long as you live," he said.

Back home, Bradley felt in some ways better than he had in months. In other ways, the steroids were imposing new afflictions. He was bloating again. And his hair was falling out rapidly. In his despair, he accepted an offer from Delaney to buy him a wig. All they could find was a woman's wig, for $300, which they then took to a barber for a haircut. Bradley wore it one day, but felt so awkward in it he put it away.

He called Paul Davis, the desperately sick patient whose phone number he had obtained in the waiting room of the suramin study. Davis, too, felt much better, but had suffered serious body damage, and was on steroids. They met for coffee. Once more, Delaney wanted to come, but Bradley insisted on keeping the remaining parts of his life in his own control. He met Davis alone.

"I've got a friend who's a lawyer," Davis said. "I want you to see him."

"How many of us are there who are angry over this?"

"You're the only other one I know who's still alive. There are at least five people dead, out of twenty-three who started. None of them died of any of the normal AIDS infections. They seem to have died from the effects of the suramin." (See note 9 for information about a dispute over the number and cause of deaths.)

Bradley blanched.

"The National Cancer Institute warned last year that this stuff had 'significant toxicity,'" Davis added. "It was worse than they told us. They knew. Look at this." And he put a multipage Xeroxed document on the table.

Bradley thumbed through it, looking bewildered.

"It's the original protocol for the study, written by the National

Cancer Institute," Davis said. He took the document back from Bradley, turned to a particular page and began reading: " 'In the literature of the 1930s and 1940s there are references to a toxic effect of suramin on the adrenal glands. . . . Generally this complication was noted in patients receiving high doses.' " He thrust the document at Bradley. "See? They knew. And didn't tell us. And let it happen."

Bradley took it from him and read over the passage. "Well, it also says, 'Further analysis cast doubt on these reports, and most authorities who have used this drug . . . have not reported adrenal gland toxicity.' "

"Yeah, but don't you see, they never even tested us for it," Davis said. "They never checked for adrenal damage until we got so sick we almost died. It was almost too late. Look at this."

Davis thrust another paper into Bradley's hands, a chart showing symptoms associated with the various stages of adrenal failure. "This was part of the protocol, too," Davis said. "See? When you show up with any of these symptoms"—and he pointed—"you're supposed to be taken off the drug. And they never even checked us for these."

"How did you get all this stuff?" Bradley asked.

"I can't tell you. But there's something else you ought to know. Lillian's job's in jeopardy."

Bradley looked up, stunned. "Why?"

"I guess because she told the patients too much."

"Too much? She told me I was the last person in the experiment still taking the drug. If she hadn't told me that, they were going to give me another shot," Bradley said. "She may have saved my life."

"Will you go see this lawyer?"

"Okay."

"He'll be expecting you."

The lawyer propped his feet up on the desk of his small office in the Castro. "It's a case, all right," he said. "But are you sure you want to bring it? That's the question I've been asking Paul Davis."

"These bastards have really screwed us up," Bradley said. "And lied to us."

"Right now, we don't have solid proof of that. With work, maybe we could get it. But suppose we do. Do you know what will happen if we bring this suit?"

Bradley looked at him.

"It will be a huge media event," the lawyer said. "The newspapers will be after you. Television. These doctors will fight back with everything they've got, and they've got a lot. The hospital is insured. The insurance company will hire the best lawyers in the country to prove that you've got a fatal disease. They'll say AIDS caused any damage that was done to your body. And how could the hospital harm you further? That's the question the jury would confront, over and over. And what happens to your career when it's in all the newspapers and on TV that you've got AIDS?"

Bradley was angered. "I don't have AIDS. I've got a virus. I've never had any serious AIDS-related infections."

"I know," the lawyer said. "You've got ARC. AIDS-related conditions. And to you and me it's a big difference. But do the producers you want jobs from understand? Do they all know the difference between ARC and AIDS? Look, I'm not trying to talk you out of it. If you really want to go ahead, maybe I make a bundle of money, too. But are you ready for the stress this will impose, and the possibility it will weaken you against the disease and maybe take years off your life? You've got to ask yourself how badly you want to do this."

Bradley nodded soberly, and said he'd think about it. When he got home, he called Volberding, the doctor supervising all AIDS work at San Francisco General. To Bradley's surprise, he got through.

"Why didn't you find this sooner?" he demanded. "I saw the original study protocol. It very specifically said there was a risk of adrenal damage."

Volberding seemed prepared for a confrontation. "You knew that there were risks. You signed the consent form."

"But the consent form didn't say anything about adrenal damage. I've lost my adrenal function, I've got to take steroids the rest of my life, and steroids lower my immune response. I'm fighting a virus that lowers my immune response, and now I have to take steroids that make it worse."

"Everybody knew it was an experimental drug, and there are things that can go wrong. You decided to take that chance."

"I decided to take that chance based on the idea that I would be monitored properly."

"Well, you were monitored properly."

"If I was monitored properly this wouldn't have happened. I've been coming in for months with the exact symptoms of adrenal failure. And nobody checked me. I saw a chart that said we were supposed to be taken off the drug if our cortisol count fell. You never took my cortisol count."

"You were being monitored according to all the guidelines in our protocol."

"Your original protocol said there was a risk of adrenal damage. I saw it."

Volberding argued that AIDS infections could have caused the adrenal damage. "As far as we know, that's where it came from. Not the suramin."

Bradley shook his head, exasperated. "I've seen a lawyer," he said. There was no reaction.

"If I agree not to sue, what guarantees do I have I will get medical care with this thing the rest of my life?"

"You have care. Just come in here when you need to."[9] (See note for details on the suramin study, including several disputed points.)

TWENTY

*I*n Los Angeles, Jim Corti was still looking for a doctor who believed in treating AIDS patients with the most aggressive therapies available. A friend told him about Michael Scolaro, a psychiatrist who had converted his practice to internal medicine in order to treat AIDS patients.

"He's committed his whole life to fighting this epidemic," the friend said. "Kind of like you."

On a drug-buying run to Tijuana in January 1986, Corti talked to a patient of Scolaro's. Corti had been bringing AIDS patients on his trips for months, training them how to buy and smuggle drugs for themselves, so he could reduce his own time on the road.

The patient, David Peterson, was driving, and two others were with them. They were talking about the FDA's new rules, adopted after a newspaper ran articles about smugglers in San Francisco. Now, each person was free to bring in his own three-month supply, and the trips might be easier.

But after the pills were bought, and Peterson's Chevy pulled up to the border station, they ran into an aggressive young guard. This is a redneck, Corti thought, looking into the frowning, acne-marked face of the guard, who was staring down at Peterson. He thinks we're queers and he hates us.

"Regular tourist things," Peterson declared, nervously. But under the guard's unrelenting questions and evil stare, he admitted they had "also bought some AIDS medicine."

"Don't you know it's illegal to bring drugs to this country?" The guard either hadn't heard about the FDA's new three-month policy or didn't care. Corti was about to explain it when the first-time traveler next to him in the back seat shouted, "We don't have drugs. We have medicine that you use to fight AIDS."

"Okay, we're gonna need to search the car," the guard said, reaching back for some papers. Corti's heart sank as the guard directed them military style to a secondary inspection area. Corti knew they had far more pills than could even liberally be construed as a three months' supply for just the four of them.

But as the guard handed Peterson some yellow papers—apparently a formal notice of being in deep trouble—an older inspector walked up and put a hand on the young guard's shoulder.

"Well, what do we have here?" the older guard said, eying the passengers. Corti thought he recognized the man from an earlier trip.

"All we're bringing across the border is some AIDS medicine, which we're entitled to, and this guy wants to search the car," Corti said.

"How much do you have?"

"We have three months' worth for each person."

"Well, you all look like decent people," the older man said. "Go on through. I can't blame you for wanting to take care of your own health."

As Peterson slowly pulled away, the faces of the two guards were frozen on Corti's memory. The older one winked at him.

After some black humor about the close call, Peterson began telling Corti about Scolaro—the only doctor he had found who would agree to monitor him on ribavirin and isoprinosine.

Scolaro had developed a nationwide reputation treating chronic pain. Then his gay lover, and some friends, came down with AIDS. Disappointed at the lack of response from other doctors, Scolaro decided to address the disease himself. Now, 95 percent of his patients were at various stages of AIDS virus infection.

Scolaro's office turned out to be a mere ten blocks or so from Corti's house—next door, by Los Angeles standards. So the next week Corti paid him a visit.

Next to Corti, Scolaro was barely noticeable—a wispy five feet four inches. He was gray-haired, conservatively dressed, and professorial. Corti was a foot taller, and only beginning to shed the pounds he had put on during Upchurch's illness. His shock of brown hair was unruly, and he had taken to wearing a Hawaiian shirt in colors as gaudy as the front page of *USA Today*.

Scolaro knew Corti was the source of the ribavirin his patients were taking. He told Corti he had studied the drug at the University of Southern California, watching for himself as ribavirin blocked creation of the enzyme, reverse transcriptase, that permitted the AIDS virus to reproduce. Corti immediately brought up a published study of such an experiment at Cornell, and at that point each man knew that in the other he had found someone who understood the language and literature of AIDS drugs.

"Are you afraid the FDA's going to come down on you for recommending unapproved drugs?" Corti asked.

"No," Scolaro said. He tossed Corti a letter to him on FDA letterhead. Scolaro was negotiating with the FDA to run the first formal study of ribavirin and isoprinosine in human AIDS patients—not at a university, but from his medical office.

"I've never heard of a study being done out of a doctor's office," Corti said.

"There's always a first time." Scolaro smiled. "I decided a year ago that when I know these drugs have shown activity against the virus, I have a moral obligation to give hope and comfort to a patient. I can't sit and squirm and say, 'What will the FDA say?' "

Scolaro figured that if he obtained FDA authority, he could get the drug directly from the manufacturer. Then if he produced positive data, he could push for bigger studies at major medical centers. So far, he said, the doctors at the FDA had been warm to his ideas. His only complaint was the mountain of paperwork required for an IND, or Investigational New Drug, permit, which would allow him to test ribavirin and isoprinosine on human subjects.

"Before you can even get an IND, you have to document the expected toxicity," Scolaro said. "You have to produce all the information that's available in the literature. You've got to make tables in advance showing the way you're going to collect data and record it. Then when you give the FDA something, they just send it back six weeks later with suggestions about changing it. And they give you a list of five more things you have to spell out for them that you didn't."

"Sounds like the bureaucratic equivalent of border guards," Corti commented.

Scolaro was doing the paperwork in his spare time. He had hired an assistant to try to raise grant money to pay salaries for her and additional staff.

"I think it's going to be many years before they come up with that magic-bullet cure for this disease," Scolaro said. "Meantime we've got to focus on combinations of any drugs we can find that will help patients live as long and as well as possible. Patients tell me other doctors won't go along with taking ribavirin. If these doctors had taken time to study the extensive literature on this drug—for me it would be unconscionable to oppose your patient taking something like that."

These were sentiments Corti had been waiting to hear from a doctor for a year and a half. He felt like applauding. "I talk to these doctors all the time," he said. "If you so much as mention drugs like ribavirin they sneer at you."

"And tell you it's not legal in this country." Scolaro smiled.

"Or they challenge you to provide clinical data on it, when they know damned well there isn't any clinical data yet."

"Because they haven't run the studies."

"What can I do to help?" Corti asked.

"There's plenty to do, if you have the time."

"I work three long shifts a week at RFK hospital. I'll make time for whatever has to be done."

"Do you have time to come over for dinner Saturday night?"

In the relaxed atmosphere of Scolaro's house, they toasted their prospective collaboration with red wine, consumed bowls of pasta prepared by Scolaro's housekeeper, and discussed the AIDS issues of the day, from prospective treatments to whether the virus could, as some people were then saying, be spread through saliva.

TWENTY-ONE

Corti brought Scolaro patients, including his lover, John Upchurch. Statistics now said Upchurch had about nine months to live after his semimiraculous recovery from PCP and the onset of Kaposi's sarcoma. He was taking ribavirin, isoprinosine, and several other drugs Scolaro had heard about. Despite bouts of tiredness, he also volunteered many days in Scolaro's office, filing and collecting data from patients' charts.

One day Corti burst in with news that a doctor he'd learned of had been experimenting with a compound called DNCB (dinitro-chlorobenzene) that he thought might work as a dermatological immune booster against Kaposi's sarcoma. Corti wanted to get it for Upchurch and others who were suffering from the disease. But Corti couldn't find a source. Did Scolaro know how to get it?

Scolaro pulled out a reference book, opened it, and declared that DNCB was a chemical sometimes used in photo processing. "Let's find a chemical-supply house," he said. Corti marveled at the idea of a doctor willing to try something that wasn't in the medical texts—a probably harmless long shot—on the chance that it would extend the lives of doomed strangers. The compound was located. But Corti called Scolaro later in the day: the chemical supply house had a problem selling to a private party. Scolaro told Corti to have the chemical shipped and billed to Scolaro at St. Vincent's Medical Center, where Scolaro was on the staff. Corti could pay him the money later.

As it turned out, the DNCB provided a good indicator of a subject's immune function. Placed in a solution and put on the skin of a relatively healthy person, it produced red welts; on the skin of a person like Upchurch, whose immune system had been ravaged, it produced little or no reaction. But the DNCB had no discernible curative effect on Kaposi's. Still, the episode drew Corti further into Scolaro's camp.

"I can't tell you how overjoyed I am to find a doctor who would do this," he said.

"What?" Scolaro smiled. "A doctor who would try something from the far corner to try to save a dying man? A few weeks ago I had a patient with the kind of chronic total diarrhea that has proved fatal for a lot of AIDS patients. Nothing else worked, so I tried a chelating agent I read about in a veterinary manual, something they use on horses. I figured there was nothing to lose. And it stopped the guy up. If veterinary medicine is what it takes to save a patient, I'm willing to try that, too."

There were regular late-night dinners at Scolaro's house, catered by the housekeeper and featuring jugs of wine. Sometimes they were joined by Upchurch, or Scolaro's dying lover, Gene, or Scolaro's small gray dog, who occasionally flew through the room knocking over wine glasses. Always present, however, was Nikki Gramatikos, the assistant who was looking for money to run the ribavirin-isoprinosine study.

Corti and Gramatikos struck up a quick friendship. She had several grant applications in the works. The most important potential funder was AmFAR—the American Foundation for AIDS Research, probably the most-publicized AIDS-related group in the country. AmFAR had been cofounded by Mathilde Krim of the Memorial Sloan-Ket-

tering Cancer Center in New York, and Michael Gottlieb, a noted
AIDS expert affiliated with UCLA. The other important grant application was to the Ledler Foundation, a Los Angeles institution that
sometimes supported medical research.

If either came through, they could proceed with the study—they
hoped with FDA approval, but if necessary, without it. If the grants
didn't materialize, the cost of research staff and laboratory work
would be prohibitive.

Evenings at Scolaro's house began with stacks of literature. Each
participant arrived with some, ranging from prominent medical journals to underground newspapers. Each journal or newspaper had a
tag or paper clip indicating the item considered significant; most had
yellow highlighting in various places. The stacks of reading materials
were passed around until everyone had looked through everything.
Scolaro would often scout new publications while the others read
articles he had located previously.

Corti discovered it was almost impossible to find something Scolaro *hadn't* read. He came in once with an article he had photocopied
from a medical journal that had arrived at the hospital that day.
"Here's a brand-new study that shows the virus *does* live in saliva,"
he told Scolaro.

"Yes," Scolaro shot back, "but they could find very little, even in
men with full-blown AIDS diagnosis. It doesn't mean saliva is an
effective means of spreading the disease."

Scolaro had already read the article and absorbed it. Corti began
switching from wine to soft drinks to try to keep as alert as the doctor.

They talked about how the study would be organized. How much
should doctors be paid? Should they hire an AIDS expert, or try to
find a good doctor who was a novice in the field and could be trained
by Scolaro?

When the food was dished out, the stories would start.

"I got another 'you-don't-know-what-you're-doing' call today,"
Scolaro said one evening. He had put a patient on acyclovir, a drug
for herpes that Scolaro reasoned might inhibit AIDS progression
since the two viruses seemed to activate each other. The patient had
told his internist, who called Scolaro in a rage.

"He says, 'What basis in the literature do you have to support
this?'" Scolaro recounted. "So I tell him, 'Basically, there is no literature, other than what's come out of the National Cancer Institute
on bone-marrow transplants. They found that acyclovir at three or
four times the recommended dosage for herpes, over a long time,
inhibited the development of other infections.'

"And this internist starts getting contentious, trying to put me down. He says, 'If you don't have a study you can point to, you are wrong to recommend to my patient that he take this.' Then he started asking about my background, where I had done my training. And I told him I was a psychiatrist."

Scolaro stopped. Corti and Gramatikos understood immediately what had happened. The word "psychiatrist" told other doctors Scolaro wasn't to be taken seriously on medical matters.

"I got this patient through a nun at St. Vincent's," Scolaro continued after a few bites of food. "She sent him to me for a second opinion. Here was a kid who had been through PCP, who was on no treatment of any kind. There was a recent paper on acyclovir, showing it might inhibit some infections. So I gave it to him."

He told of another case where doctors criticized him for using steroids on patients with severe pneumocystis carinii pneumonia, or PCP, who were near death from lung inflammation. "I used a cortisone derivative on them, and they healed," Scolaro said. "So other doctors called, and said, 'You're using steroids in patients who have no immune system.' And I said, 'Yeah, but they were going to die.' They don't seem to want to understand.[10] I've talked to doctors about taking part in the ribavirin-isoprinosine study. They're reluctant to do it. They feel it's breaking the law. Or they're afraid the FDA will come down on them. They're afraid of being accused of quackery. They say they want to wait and see what the government does."

"A lot of people are going to die before the government does anything," Corti said.

TWENTY-TWO

*W*hen the study proposal was ready, Gramatikos drove to Laguna Hills to deliver it at the office of Newport Pharmaceuticals, the company that makes isoprinosine. At first she was delighted to be received warmly by Newport's top research scientist and an assistant. Although the proposal could as well have been handed over to a secretary, these senior officials took time to sit Gramatikos down for coffee and small talk. But then the small talk got to her.

She noticed a decoration on the wall, a mockup of a white-black-and-gold California license plate with the designation HTLV-3.

"A license plate with the name of the AIDS virus?" she asked in disbelief. "Don't you think it would upset a lot of people who have this in their blood?"

"Well, I never thought of that," he said. But he was still smiling. "I thought it was very clever." [11]

She told Corti about it when she got back to work. "This is business for them," she said. "Not saving lives, but making bucks."

Just then Scolaro walked past, escorting a man out of his office and looking despondent.

"That was a patient," he said after the man had left, "who may be walking around today because I gave him steroids when he had PCP. It checked an inflammation until the PCP cleared up. Then he got lymphoma, so I sent him over to the clinic at UCLA. And the doctor there took a look at his medical history and said he absolutely could not condone the use of steroids in an AIDS patient. You know what the doctor said? He said, 'Yes, I know Scolaro. He's one step above a voodoo priest.' A voodoo priest! I'm the one who recommended that this patient go over to UCLA in the first place."

"Because of the steroids?" Corti asked.

"Not just that. He heard I was encouraging the use of an unapproved drug. This patient was on ribavirin."

"Well, you've heard it all before," Gramatikos said. "You just have to keep your chin up."

"Except this doctor is different. The guy who thinks I'm a witch doctor is a highly regarded AIDS specialist. I sent this patient to him because of his reputation."

"What difference should his reputation make if he's wrong?"

"The difference is he's Michael Gottlieb. And Gottlieb heads AmFAR, which is the outfit our grant proposal is before. He's got our study in his hands." [12] (See note for Gottlieb's denial.)

A few weeks later the letter came, announcing that AmFAR had rejected the grant proposal. It was signed by someone other than Gottlieb. It said simply that the study did not fit the AmFAR guidelines for support. AmFAR was more interested in funding public education about AIDS than in funding the study of new drugs. But in Scolaro's mind, despite Gottlieb's insistence to the contrary, Gottlieb remained responsible for the rejection. Then, a little later, came the next rejection, from the Ledler Foundation.

Gramatikos talked to the executive director of the foundation, Lloyd Rigler.

"Guess why it was turned down," she told Scolaro afterward. "You know who they go to for advice on medical grants?"

He guessed before she told him.

"Michael Gottlieb," she said. "He's a friend of Rigler's."

"Small world." [13]

But the worst blow was yet to come.

Newport Pharmaceuticals wrote that Dr. Alvin J. Glasky, its founder and chief executive, had decided not to allow isoprinosine to be used in the joint study. Gramatikos called Glasky, but it did no good.

"They say they want isoprinosine studied to see what it does on its own against AIDS before they allow it to be studied with some other drug," she told Scolaro.

He was bitterly discouraged, but understood the problem. "Whether our test was successful or unsuccessful, it would confuse the issue of the benefit of their own particular drug, which is before the FDA for testing on its own. They're afraid if ribavirin has some problem it will be associated with isoprinosine. And that they might wind up with legal liability for it."

"But the whole idea was that these drugs would be more effective in combination than each would be individually," Gramatikos said. "It will be the patients who lose."

"I know," he said. That was the system.

A few days later, Scolaro called Gramatikos aside to say he would not have money to pay her much longer. She had better look for a regular job.

With the study apparently dead, Corti left RFK Medical Center to take a more time-consuming job in the AIDS unit at Hollywood Community Hospital. He wanted to spend more time with AIDS patients, and RFK didn't have many.

It provided no solace when the newspapers said that Dr. Alvin J. Glasky had been fired by the board at Newport while he was in the hospital being treated for a heart problem.

Corti studied Newport's history. Glasky had invented isoprinosine thinking it was an antiviral drug. Only by accident was it discovered that the drug's most promising qualities were as an immune booster. In the late 1970s, Glasky had arranged studies that to him demonstrated the drug's efficacy against a form of encephalitis. When the FDA refused to allow his company, Newport, to distribute isoprinosine free to victims of the disease, Glasky grew furious. He was convinced that studies showed the drug effective on 180 of 200 test subjects with the encephalitis; the FDA faulted the sample of subjects. [14]

In quite a departure from normal drug-company procedure, Glasky sued the FDA. He lost. The courts said it was the FDA's call.

Then came the AIDS epidemic, and isoprinosine again appeared promising, according to some of the government's own studies. In the December 21/28, 1985, issue of the leading British medical journal, *The Lancet*, six doctors from prominent institutions, including the National Cancer Institute's famous Robert C. Gallo, reported that in test tubes isoprinosine and another drug impeded the AIDS virus when it tried to invade healthy T-cells.

"At a clinical level," the doctors concluded, "this means that [isoprinosine] may prove helpful in the early stages of AIDS." Another published study came to the same conclusion.

In December 1985, New Zealand approved the drug for use against ARC, the symptoms brought on by the AIDS virus before the eruption of full-blown AIDS. Isoprinosine was now approved for use against one thing or another in eighty-nine countries. No one had found any serious side effects to the drug.

Buoyed by all that, Glasky paid for another study. Under a protocol approved by the FDA, he compiled data showing the drug improved the immune system of ARC patients, as measured by their T-cell counts. But when the data was turned in, the FDA stunned him by rejecting the drug anyway. Now the FDA said that even though it had approved the T-cell study, the study was irrelevant. In order to get a drug approved you had to kill the virus in the body—cure AIDS —or at least prove over many years that patients who took your drug outlived patients who didn't. The FDA, demanding a cure for AIDS, had decided to discount the benefits of merely slowing the virus's spread from T-cell to T-cell.

Glasky went to FDA headquarters in Rockville, Maryland, outside Washington, to protest. He met a phalanx of FDA brass led by Dr. Ellen Cooper, head of the agency's antiviral program—and thus its AIDS fight. She wouldn't budge. She told Glasky that his original study had been approved to advance the state of knowledge, not to qualify isoprinosine for distribution.

So Glasky, who had already tried suing, did something else unusual for a drug-company chief executive. Claiming he found Cooper's action "rather incredible," he held a press conference denouncing the FDA.

"I feel isoprinosine is one of the drugs of choice for AIDS," he told reporters. "It's a crime that politics is going to keep it from ever being used in the U.S. In order to get a drug approved, you have to have the NIH [National Institutes of Health] Mafia behind it. To run a study that didn't have the establishment behind it was foolhardy." [15]

Glasky got some favorable coverage. But he also got a quick hook from his financial backers. As far as they were concerned, if the FDA rejected you when you came courting with a dozen roses, you sent three dozen next time. You did not send a vial of acid.

In the spring of 1986, when Glasky had heart trouble, the backers simply changed the locks on the doors at the company he had founded and installed new leadership. Newport and Glasky began a round of lawsuits against each other, but none of that helped Scolaro, or AIDS patients.

Corti headed for Mexico.

TWENTY-THREE

*I*t was turning out to be a bad day. Corti was making a $20,000 buy for New York City clients, and hadn't been able to round up anyone to go with him. He left Los Angeles around noon. On the way down his muffler blew out, and the yellow Virus Van was making an unseemly noise. When he got to the store just on the U.S. side of the border where he normally bought black-market pesos, the dealer wasn't in; that meant Corti would be losing about two cents on the dollar in Tijuana. Then, when he got there, he had a flat tire, and dirtied himself changing it.

Corti had been getting used to sailing through border inspections under the FDA's new, looser rules. He put the pills—five large cardboard boxes of them, his biggest load ever—under a blanket in the back of the van and headed home. The broken muffler still announced his presence ahead of him.

The line at the border was half a mile long. It was an hour before he neared the inspection booths. When he was seven or eight car lengths away, he recognized the officer for his lane. Months ago he had identified her, by grooming and dress, as one of an unusual number of lesbians who had been drawn to the uniformed immigration and customs services as a career.

She was about forty, a bit stocky, with short-cropped hair and no jewelry. Like the others, she would always wave him through.

"More ribavirin?" she'd say.

"Yeah."

"Is that stuff really doing any good?"

"Seems to be."

"God bless ya."

And he'd go on. Once she'd even told him, "We have a common interest."

He followed the cars to her booth, passing up his last chance to change lanes. Then, when he was three cars from the booth, trapped by traffic, a man came to relieve her. Corti froze. It was the young redneck with the acne, the guard Corti had determined never to see again. There was no way out. He watched his favorite woman border guard disappear. He longed to call out to her, but couldn't.

The new guard recognized him instantly. He punched Corti's license plate into his computer. Slowly, in a charade of magisterialness, he went through the formal routine.

"How long were you in Mexico?"

"Just today."

"What did you buy?"

"I bought some ribavirin and isoprinosine for my own personal use."

"How much?"

"Three months' worth."

"May I see it?"

"Sure." And Corti offered the small bag next to him in the seat.

The guard didn't take it. He smiled. "What's back there?"

"You can look at it if you want."

The guard opened the van and started overturning the boxes. "What's this?"

"Ribavirin."

"Three months' worth?"

"It's for my friends who are too sick to get it themselves."

"You'll need to go to secondary inspection."

Well, Corti thought, he had been through secondary inspection before. Maybe there would be a more understanding guard there.

"Follow me," the redneck said. He signaled to two other officers nearby, who joined the escort. Corti could scarcely believe it, but they had their hands on their guns. And they weren't headed for the usual secondary-inspection area. They went the other way, to someplace new. Corti saw cars being torn apart by crews with tools, looking for drugs. The van was directed into a stall with tables on either side. The lights were bright enough for a movie set.

A deep voice said, "Will you take the boxes out and set them on the table, please?"

Corti did.

The officers dumped all the medicine out of the blue-and-white boxes. Corti noticed other officers walking or driving by, staring at them. The redneck came up close, with the hint of a smile.

"We're going to have to detain you for this," he said.

Corti felt his heart sink. "Am I under arrest?" he asked.

"No. We need to clarify what this is, and what you intend to do with it." The armed escort led him to an office and took turns questioning him.

What is this? Why do you have it? What exactly do you intend to do with it? What is this drug? Who is it for? Is this a black-market operation?

Corti had with him a list of clients all over the country, from New York to Los Angeles. He even considered turning it over. Nobody gave a damn at that point if they got in trouble. They wanted the drugs. And it was their $20,000 investment he was protecting.

He said, "These drugs are for sick people who are not able to get here. These drugs are for people who are dying from AIDS."

Corti was led into an adjoining room, closed in only by glass and a few metal frames that held the glass. The door closed. He saw several of the officers conversing, occasionally pointing at him. By now, they all began to look like young rednecks with acne. Finally one of them came in.

"We're going to confiscate the goods, and we're going to detain you," the officer said.

"Am I under arrest?"

"No. Not yet."

Another officer entered the room and began staring at him. Corti pondered his best move.

"Maybe this could all be cleared up with a phone call," he said.

The last man to come into the room spoke, avoiding Corti's suggestion. "It's not a question of what you're bringing in. It's a question of how much you're bringing in, and you tried to obscure it from us." The man paced from one end of the small room to the other, then turned his glare toward Corti again. "That," he said very slowly, "is smuggling."

Corti forgot his fear. He looked the officer right back in the eye. "If your friends were dying, you'd do the same thing."

"If the queen had balls, she'd be the king," the man replied. He laughed and walked away.

Corti asked to speak to the agent in charge.

No one answered, but another man eventually came into the room.

"Why do you have so much?" he asked. "Are you black-marketing this?"

There was something different, maybe more sincere, about this man's demeanor. Corti decided to gamble.

"I'll give you names, phone numbers, and prescriptions from M.D.'s," he offered. "Call and ask these people whether I'm black-marketing or not."

"We're not here to make phone calls. We're here to stop drug smuggling," the man said. "These are drugs."

"Let me make one call," Corti said.

"Who do you want to call?"

"Senator Wilson's office."

"Why Wilson? You know him?"

"No. But I think his people might help."

"Help you?" Both men knew Wilson was a Republican, and considered conservative.

"I think so," Corti said.

"Go ahead. Make your call." The officer led Corti into another office.

Nervously, Corti drew out of his wallet a paper he had been given months ago by Thomas Jefferson, a fellow ribavirin smuggler from San Diego, Senator Wilson's hometown. Corti dialed the number. A man answered.

"Is Robert there?" Corti asked, reading the name written on the paper.

"No."

His heart sank again.

"But maybe I can help you," the man said.

New hope. Corti identified himself and tried to explain briefly what had happened.

"Good god," the man said, sympathetically.

"I'm not sure if I'm under arrest," Corti said. "But they're threatening to confiscate twenty thousand dollars of AIDS medicine."

"What telephone number are you at?"

Corti told him.

"Let me talk to someone there."

The newest officer on the scene, who had led Corti into the office where he now sat, took the phone. He listened, for what seemed forever. Then he set the phone down without hanging it up, and waved through the glass for the redneck, who had been watching. The redneck took Corti back to the first room.

"Am I under arrest, or what?" Corti asked.

"It's beginning to look that way."

Half an hour passed. Corti sat in the glass-windowed room alone. Finally an older officer came in. He looked Corti up and down.

"We're going to give you the opportunity to return these goods to Mexico and get your money back," he said. "Do you think you can do that?"

"Yes."

He escorted Corti to the van.

"Load your car back up," he said. Corti did.

The officer walked in front of the van as Corti drove it. They arrived at a lane headed back to Tijuana, though the van was still facing Los Angeles.

"If you make a U-turn here, it takes you back to Tijuana," the officer told him. "If you drive straight, you go to Los Angeles. Good luck."

"I think I understand," Corti said.

"Good," the man said. Then, as Corti watched, the man took the paperwork he had been given, wadded it in his hand, and turned and walked away.

Corti eased away, trying to limit the broken-muffler noise, picked up speed, and pushed toward L.A., never looking back. He left the freeway on the first off-ramp and took side roads, racing past gas stations, fast-food joints, and motels. He pulled into the lot of the Valli Hi motel and parked so the car wasn't visible from the road. Shaking, he checked in, went to the room, and fumbled for the numbers of smugglers he had trained and trusted. He reached one, who drove immediately to the motel. In the night, hidden from the road, they transferred all the drugs from the van to the car, which then headed back for Los Angeles. Still shaking, Corti returned to his room to sleep the night.

Before he left in the morning, he called Senator Wilson's office and asked for the man he had spoken to the night before. A woman said the man was away. Corti dictated a message. "I'm a Democrat, and I'm pretty liberal," it said. "But I can't thank you enough."

"I'll pass the message on," the woman told him.

Corti headed home to relay the story to Upchurch. But Upchurch was asleep. He had never regained his full stamina after his bout with PCP. The story waited a day.

Corti determined to get to know Thomas Jefferson better. When he called with his thanks, Jefferson began telling him about a friend, Chuck, and his lover in Los Angeles who were in desperate straits.

"One of them's sick, the other's infected," Jefferson said. "When I phoned them a few days ago, they actually had a suicide pact. They've been going to Chuck's family doctor, who doesn't understand this disease. He's given them nothing but doom and gloom. I told them there was hope, and about ribavirin and isoprinosine. They said they'd try it, but I haven't been able to get to L.A. yet. Can you go see them, and give them some pills and steer them to a doctor up there who understands this stuff?"

"I will, and I know just the doctor," Corti said.

He found Chuck and his lover, cooped up in a house, still depressed, but ready to buy pills and listen to advice. When Corti started to deliver his usual lecture about the need for a regimen of decent diet, rest, and stress reduction, he discovered that Jefferson had been over the same ground on the phone. They agreed to start the pills immediately, and to book an appointment with Michael Scolaro.

Corti left feeling good—and feeling still more impressed with Jefferson.

A week later, Chuck called to thank him. They had been to see Scolaro. They were excited to hear from a doctor confirmation of what Jefferson and Corti had told them about the hope of fighting the disease. "It's like our lives have started again after months of living under a death sentence. The doctor I grew up with said there was no way to fight back. Now—we may die, you know? But at least we're among allies. There's something we can do. I'm going to try to go back to work."

Corti told Upchurch about the experience, and about Jefferson. And he had still more news of his own.

"I had a blood test," Corti said.

"What for?" Upchurch asked him.

"I wanted to do it."

And he handed Upchurch the envelope from the gay men's health center in Long Beach. Upchurch pulled out the paper and read. He seemed overcome by emotion, hugged Corti, said nothing.

"At first I felt absolute elation," Corti said. "Like the governor had just made the phone call—death sentence lifted. Then I began feeling guilty. Like, how was I going to tell you I'm negative?"

"I'm glad you did," Upchurch said. "I don't know what's going to happen to me. But I used to worry about what's going to happen to the cats, and the house. Now I don't have to worry. Nothing that we've done so far is wasted. You're healthy."

"I still feel guilty," Corti said. "I don't want it to be any kind of separation, any borders."

"It isn't."

But the next morning Corti awoke to find Upchurch already up, seated on the sofa and crying.

"What's wrong?" Corti asked.

"Nothing," Upchurch said.

"You don't cry if nothing's wrong."

Upchurch raised the coffee mug he was holding and threw it across the room, smashing it against the wall and spraying the coffee. It was the first time Corti had seen him do anything violent.

"Why do I have this?" Upchurch screamed at him. "I never hurt anybody." He began repeating, over and over, "I never hurt anybody."

Corti waited till Upchurch was quiet. "Let's go get some breakfast up in the mountains," he said.

Later, Corti stopped by Scolaro's office to tell him the good news about his test. Nikki Gramatikos had left to take a job handling public relations for a chain of rehabilitation centers. Corti found Scolaro already in good spirits over some news of his own.

"A woman at the FDA wrote me wondering whatever happened to our study," Scolaro said. "They think there may be some underlying merit to testing an antiviral in combination with an immune booster, and they'd like to see it get underway. Think about it. After all these months, now *they* are writing *me* to do something."

"That's great," Corti said.

"When Newport pulled isoprinosine out of the study a few months ago, I just gave up. Now maybe it's worth another try."

"How are you going to get around Newport? Without isoprinosine you don't have a combination."

"The woman at the FDA suggests using another immune booster, an agent called thymopentin, or TP-5. It's made by Ortho Pharmaceuticals, and Ortho has already approved a study in combination with another drug. For our purposes, the TP-5 shouldn't be too much different from isoprinosine."

"So you're going to be busy writing more protocols again now."

"It looks that way."

"Well, now that you've got the immune booster taken care of, I'm afraid there may be a problem with the antiviral—the ribavirin. The price of the damned stuff has shot up unbelievably. Last week they were asking three times what I was buying it for in January."

"Why's the price going up?"

"I don't know. But I've got a lot of unhappy buyers. I've been trying to get to ICN to find out what's going on. They make the stuff. But they don't seem to want to talk about it."

"Keep after them."

TWENTY-FOUR

*I*n the spring of 1986, Martin Delaney grew increasingly impatient with Project Inform's proposed ribavirin-isoprinosine study. Unlike Scolaro, Delaney's team wasn't seeking approval from the FDA or the drug companies. He and Joe Brewer had intended the study to be underway by now. But nothing seemed to be happening.

Meanwhile, Delaney had been forced to step up his consulting work because of new financial demands, both from his subsidy of the drug imports and from Mark Bradley's illness. He had added Varian Associates, the big elecronics firm, to the list of mostly banking clients he ran seminars for.

Brewer, the one with the scientific expertise, was supposed to be getting the drug study started. When Project Inform had been announced in October 1985, the aim had been a quick survey of doctors' offices to tally the effect of ribavirin and isoprinosine on blood counts and general health. Meanwhile, they would start a prospective study of patients going on the drugs for the first time, under a specified protocol.

But when Delaney phoned Brewer, the news was usually discouraging. Brewer's initial mailings of scientific articles on ribavirin and isoprinosine had not stirred the anticipated excitement from local doctors.

"They were bemused," Brewer said of the doctors he had mailed the articles to. "Nobody much cared. Two or three said they used it as bathroom reading."

"Bathroom reading!" Delaney had long before been struck by the cynicism he felt from the doctors who showed up at community meetings, who wrote letters to the gay press, and who counseled his acquaintances. Most doctors seemed content to deny hope. Many even advised against having blood tests, on the ground that discovery of the AIDS virus could produce only anguish. If the test proved positive, there was nothing that could be done anyway, they said.

But hell, everyone in the gay community was afraid he had the virus. To Delaney, avoiding a blood test not only made despair a certainty, it promoted a sense of helplessness. And now these same doctors who advised against testing relegated scientific articles documenting the promise of ribavirin and isoprinosine to bathroom reading!

"We have no choice," Brewer said. "We have to go through the patients. The only way to get the data is to have the patients initiate the process."

"But how on earth do we find each individual patient?" Delaney asked. "Even if we could, it would take forever. The whole point was to use the doctors' offices as information centers."

"Doctors won't do it," Brewer replied. "It's a question of malpractice and confidentiality. We have to find out who the patients are on our own, and go to them to get them to sign release forms, and then get the doctors to give us the data."

"But they can give us the data anonymously. We don't need to identify the patients. No study does that."

"Every study starts with release forms."

"Maybe if they're done by hospitals, which already have patients. We don't have patients. Why can't these doctors go to their patients on their own and just ask whether they'd allow their blood results and T-cell counts to be released anonymously?"

"They say it's standard ethical procedure that a person's data is private, even without a name. I've talked to a lot of doctors. They won't do it."

"Is it standard ethical procedure to let patients die when there might be a treatment at hand?"

"Marty, even when they know their own friends and neighbors are infected, they say they're worried about being sued."

"It doesn't make any sense," Delaney said. "If a doctor goes to an AIDS patient and says, 'Hey, there's this study going on that might find out what the benefits are of the drugs you're taking, are you willing to have your blood data turned over,' the patient's not going to sue. Come on!"

"Not all of the doctors thought this was a good idea," Brewer said.

"Well, did *any* of them think it was a good idea?"

"What I'm getting from even friendly doctors is that they just can't take the hours to go through the charts. And they're not going to do something that isn't sanctioned."

"I just don't understand," Delaney said.

"We're not talking about a completely rational process," Brewer replied. "That's just not how doctors do things."

Delaney sighed, and thought. "Okay, we've got all these patients who have called the Project Inform phone number. Let's ask them to feel out their doctors about participating in the tests."

"I've been asking them," Brewer said. "They call back and say they asked their doctor to monitor them, and the doctor said, 'No. They're unapproved drugs. We don't know if they're safe. We don't know if they work.' That's what the doctors are saying."

"But the patients are already using the drug," Delaney said. "We're trying to find out whether it's hurting, helping, or doing nothing. Everybody agrees it needs to be done. What kind of twisted bureaucratic logic is this?"

"A few of the doctors offered the patient's blood work if the patient really insisted," Brewer said. "But the message to the patients was pretty consistently, 'Don't do it.' "

"Then we'll just have to hire our own staff to do the research and line up our own patients."

"But we're not going to be able to raise the money for that with the medical and scientific community against us. I've already talked to AmFAR. They won't help. They say they're not into this kind of thing; they want to do education."

"We can go to ICN," Delaney said. "*They've* got to want this done. This could be their ticket to getting FDA approval for ribavirin."

"We said at the beginning we weren't going to go to the manufacturers for money. People will think we're just a front for some drug company."

"From what you say, we don't have a choice."

Delaney called ICN's director of clinical research, Karl Johnson, and made an appointment. Then he drove to Costa Mesa.

As he followed the directions Johnson had given him, he suddenly realized: he had seen this building dozens of times. Every trip he had made to Tijuana to buy ribavirin had brought him right past the imposing steel-and-glass headquarters of the company that made the drug. It was barely out of Los Angeles. Yet he had to drive another hundred miles south to another country to buy the product. The irony overwhelmed him.

ICN's entrance, on the side of the building away from the road, was grander than its image as a small, struggling drug company had prepared him for. Delaney found himself striding across a majestic plaza with fountain and sculpture to reach the opulent-looking three-story headquarters. Inside, the entrance hall and wide corridors suggested more splendor than desperation.

But his business eye caught telltale signs of trouble. There weren't many people for all this space. The company had obviously over-bought, expecting to grow faster. Rooms were empty. And the furniture in Johnson's office looked worn; it lacked the grandeur of the building surrounding it. The office wasn't even well lit. And Johnson, the company's top clinical scientist, seemed to have no secretary. ICN must have expected that by now ribavirin would be for sale at drugstores throughout the U.S. The problems at this company were Washington's doing.

Delaney was surprised that Johnson, a former government scientist and medical professor at George Washington University, did not seem to be pushing his company's drug. "We don't know whether it works on AIDS," Johnson told him. "We haven't been able to do much research yet. What kind of evidence do *you* have?"

"Mostly anecdotal," Delaney began.

"That and fifty cents will get you a cup of coffee," Johnson replied between puffs of his cigarette.

Delaney tried to explain how powerful the anecdotal experience seemed, and how little AIDS patients had to lose. "The word on the street is that the drug is working well," he said. "Thousands of people are using it." And he outlined the two-part study Project Inform wanted to conduct.

"What experience do you have doing this kind of work?"

"None, really," Delaney said. "But we'll hire people. My role is really as a front man. I'm a business consultant. But we'll get the system and procedures in place."

"That ain't a lot to go on," Johnson said. "Do you have any idea how much money it takes to study a drug the way the FDA requires? We're already gearing up for two big studies. I can't convince management to put up the kind of money you'll need for another one."

"I guess I don't know what it will cost," Delaney admitted. "But this is a unique situation. We're burying forty or fifty men a month right within our own community in San Francisco. Nationwide, it's thousands a year and tripling every year. There are already estimates that half the gay community in San Francisco is infected. There's a lot I don't know about the science of all this, but our community is being wiped off the planet. This is the most rational approach available."

"I know, I know," Johnson said. "I read the papers, too. But your kind of people aren't viewed very positively down in *this* community —Orange County."

The remark gave Delaney an intended jolt. He wondered whether Johnson was spelling out a public-relations problem or telling him the way ICN management itself felt—that ICN was all for selling ribavirin to cure a child's lung virus, but that it didn't care if gays dropped dead.

Seeing his comment had sobered Delaney up, Johnson shifted to a softer tone. "How can I help you?" he asked. "What do you want me to do?"

"Fund the studies," Delaney told him.

"I can't do that. I don't have the money. Of course, it's obvious we should be funding it," Johnson said. "But that doesn't convince the powers that be around here. I can talk to management. What can you give me to use as a tool?"

"Lab data on some patients," Delaney said. "The names of a few physicians who think their patients are getting positive results. And our research protocol."

"I can't commit to anything," Johnson said. "But I appreciate what you're doing. It's what I'd be doing if I were in the same position."

Delaney got the idea Johnson considered himself an outsider at ICN, somehow distanced from the management team two floors above his office.

"Maybe I can toss you a nickel," Johnson said.

In the next few days, Delaney collected five impressive case histories, showing improved T-cell counts and the disappearance of infections with use of ribavirin. He shipped them to Johnson, who called back a few days later, sounding grim. He had taken the case histories to management to see if ICN would be willing to work with Project Inform.

"It's unclear the company can help collect data on patients who are not supposed to be taking this drug," Johnson said. "There's no history of how FDA regulations will apply to this. All I can give you is a thousand dollars, a couple of hundred dollars for each of these cases, to help pay your costs."

Delaney was badly disappointed.

"We do have some big studies about to get underway at Cornell and elsewhere," Johnson said. "I know that's going to take a lot longer than you'd like, but we're going to have to wait for that."

The tests will also be limited to ribavirin alone, Delaney thought, even though the combination with isoprinosine is what seems most promising. But he thanked Johnson for his effort and they hung up on good terms.

By February 1986, Brewer, and a few doctors willing to help him, had come up with a protocol. But it was for a much more difficult study than he and Delaney had originally envisioned.

TWENTY-FIVE

Delaney got a phone call from Marcus Conant, a respected veteran physician, who had first identified Kaposi's sarcoma in the Bay Area at the outbreak of the epidemic. Conant had brought together a group of doctors to meet regularly and discuss approaches to Kaposi's and other aspects of AIDS. Among them were top staff from the University Medical Center and San Francisco General Hospital. Conant had heard about Project Inform's intended study and wanted Delaney and Brewer to appear before his doctors' group to discuss their plan.

Delaney didn't think twice before accepting. These were the most prominent doctors in one of the two or three foremost AIDS study locations in the United States.

With great care, Delaney and Brewer edited the protocol for the proposed study, and Xeroxed it for distribution at the meeting. If some of these doctors would agree to cooperate, Project Inform would be back on track.

But Delaney's optimism vanished when he and Brewer arrived for the meeting at the University of California, San Francisco, Medical Center. It was right after lunch. Delaney and Brewer were dessert. They were ushered to a podium at the front of a long, narrow room, where about sixty doctors were already seated. Delaney, who gave seminars for a living, was a master at managing groups of this size. But he took one look at *this* group and wanted to leave.

Never in his life had he confronted such visible hostility. Around the room, his smiles were met by unfriendly glares. There was none of the usual welcoming or joking. He tried to break the ice with body language and light-hearted remarks, as he and Brewer handed out the protocols. But the ice would not break. Delaney looked at Brewer, but Brewer seemed unfazed by, or perhaps unaware of, the atmosphere. As Conant introduced him, Delaney felt his powers of group control draining from him. He began feeling short of breath.

"You've all heard of the plans for this unconventional research project," Conant was saying. "And I thought it would be useful to have Joe and Marty here to attempt to explain it to you."

Delaney's palms started sweating. Conant was talking about Delaney's background as a business consultant and Brewer's as a psychotherapist. Every other person in this room was a medical doctor.

They knew doctors might not have all the answers, but they believed that they alone had the tools to find the answers.

Conant's introduction was very neutral, and all too short.

As Delaney rose, he felt continued contempt from the audience. All he saw was looks of distrust and suspicion. These were the doctors whose criticisms of him he had read in the press and heard about at community meetings. These were the people who thought him a lunatic. Why hadn't he realized before the meeting what he would be getting into?

Delaney tried to explain who he and Brewer were, and why they were planning a study. He felt uncharacteristically tongue-tied. It was the single worst presentation he could recall giving.

"People in the community are using these drugs for better or worse," he said. "There is no alternative. It's irresponsible not to study them. We feel an obligation to find out if they are helpful or harmful. We feel the obligation to take on this study ourselves." He looked around the room, feeling like a comic who had lost his audience.

"In no way are we here to endorse the use of these drugs," he went on. "We are extremely careful to make clear in our literature that we are not recommending anybody use these drugs. We are giving information so people can make decisions. The use of these drugs has to be studied and it's in the best tradition of science to do so."

Then came Brewer's turn to describe the design for the study in scientific terms. He received the same icy stares. After he spoke, Conant returned to the podium. Delaney was sitting on the front edge of a table, feeling embarrassed about how poorly he had spoken. Conant asked for questions. The hostile barrage began.

Would there be a placebo control group? several people wanted to know.

"With what you know about AIDS," Delaney said, "I don't have to tell you that life expectancy is only nine months. So you don't need a placebo to find out what happens if you don't take the drug."

Could the study produce a believable result without a control group?

Brewer said he could create a control group by having doctors match patients who wanted to use the drugs with those who preferred not to. That set loose the first wave of derisive chuckles.

Then Donald Abrams, from the Volberding group at San Francisco General Hospital, took the floor. Didn't the mere presence of people doing a study like the one Project Inform had announced encourage people to take unproven drugs, he wanted to know.

For a moment, Conant himself came to their rescue. "Don, you could say that about any time you do a study," he told Abrams. "Any time a researcher studies a drug, it gives the impression the drug is worth getting, and some people will want to use it."

But Abrams was undeterred. Community doctors didn't know how to conduct research, he argued. The universities were barely qualified to do it. How could Delaney and Brewer, nonprofessionals, nonphysicians, do such research?

"Well, then, you do it," Delaney replied. "Nothing would please Joe and me more than for some of you to take this study over and kiss us goodbye. We have our businesses. But we firmly believe it has to be done and nobody else is willing to do it."

"There's no magic to the conduct of research," Brewer added. "It is a standardized process that exists in textbooks. It exists in journals."

Questions began hurtling from the audience, not even acknowledging what Delaney had said. Delaney's main argument, that people were taking the drugs anyway and it only made sense to study them, was ignored. Delaney found his answers were getting as belligerent as the questions.

"Thousands of people are already taking these drugs. . . . We didn't start this phenomenon, it exists separately from us. . . . The medical community can't just go on telling people not to take these drugs. . . . Safety! The whole point of what we're *doing* is about safety. . . . No one ever thought these drugs would cure the disease. The question is whether they make people live longer, make them more comfortable."

Brewer tried his calmer approach. "Wouldn't we all feel foolish if two years from now there are studies of these drugs that show they are useful, and we had bypassed this chance two years earlier to give them to people and help them?" he asked.

But the cold hostility of the questioning didn't abate. Arms waved. Every third question seemed to come from Abrams.[16] (See note for Abrams's recollection.) He castigated them for raising false hope among patients.

"I am less worried about false hope than I am about false hopelessness," Brewer said. But the replies fell on deaf ears.

Finally, amidst near chaos, Conant broke in to conclude the meeting. "It looks like you are going to continue to disagree," he said, in what seemed an almost comically deadpan understatement. And he thanked Delaney and Brewer for coming.

A third of the audience had spoken and not one had said anything favorable. As the crowd filed out, Delaney saw them grumbling among themselves. Instead of coming forward to thank Delaney for the presentation—as he was used to—this audience treated him as if he had a much more communicable disease than AIDS. Then he noticed with pleasant surprise that three doctors had come forward, almost sheepishly, to shake hands and thank him and Brewer.

"I think it's sort of a good idea, what you're doing," one said, and the others nodded.

"Why didn't you speak up?" Delaney asked.

The doctors backed off, smiling nervously. Somebody muttered something about "peer pressure." And they were gone without identifying themselves.

"What is it that bugs these guys so much?" Delaney repeated several times to Brewer as they left the meeting. Then he searched out loud for answers to his own question. "The factual points weren't that heated," he said. "What we were talking about in there were really philosophical questions, not medical questions. It was like being back in the seminary. What they were agitated about was that nonmedical people were invading their turf. If we succeed, it's like the collapse of the priesthood of medicine."

"People seemed geared to embarrass us," Brewer agreed. "Like it was set up. But a fourth of the doctors in there were gay. Abrams is. Conant is."

"I think they resent the fact that the gay community likes what we're doing," Delaney went on. "We're the little guy against the system. The community identifies with that. Abrams keeps getting heat in the gay press for being part of the system, and the system doesn't do anything. He's become a nay sayer. Always there with a negative comment. Whatever drug you're talking about, according to him it doesn't work. I think they're afraid they won't be taken seriously as researchers. Gay doctors are falling all over themselves to prove to everyone that they are conservative scientists and not gay flakes."

Brewer nodded.

"Well, this kind of puts in on record, the whole official medical hostility toward our concept," Delaney said. "It's going to make it more difficult for doctors inside or outside the gay community to work with us."

TWENTY-SIX

While the research idea stalled, Project Inform continued its monthly meetings at the Metropolitan Community Church, an ecumenical, nominally Christian institution catering to gays. Hundreds would show up, and Delaney and Brewer would spend hours patiently answering questions.

How much should I take? What should I take it with? My doctor says this will cause anemia. My doctor says this drug is unproven, that I should just wait and see. My T-cells are at 300; should I start taking it now or wait until I have symptoms?

Then the answers. Most doctors said, "Don't do anything until you're very sick," and then when you were, said, "There's nothing we can do for you." But ribavirin and isoprinosine seemed to delay the disease, they didn't cure it. The drugs worked best in healthier men. Doctors couldn't legally recommend the drug. The proper approach was to say, "I want to take this drug, will you help monitor me?" Then the answer might be different.

People in the audience invariably asked about other treatments. One doctor in Berkeley was telling her patients to drink eight gallons a day of distilled water. Some advocated enormous amounts of vitamin C—as much as 80 grams, which gave some AIDS patients stomach ulcers in addition to their other problems. Delaney simply said he saw no scientific basis for such remedies. Worst, Delaney believed, were the macrobiotic-diet advocates. "It's ridiculous to think that by starving yourself on a few grains of rice a day you're going to unleash the body's natural forces," he would argue. "If you have AIDS, you need all the protein and carbohydrates you can get."

After the meetings, some men would always linger to talk to him privately. Some reasked the same questions he had just answered, as if he had been concealing the truth publicly and would reveal it in private.

Others were very sick. They just wanted hope. "Tell me the story again about the guy whose T-cells went up by three hundred," they would say. They didn't want to hear about others, the ones who died.

One day in March 1986, Delaney got a call from a San Diego AIDS patient he had talked to before—Thomas Jefferson, a former Navy pilot, husband and father of two, who had recently declared his homosexuality after an AIDS diagnosis. He had even been smuggling AIDS drugs from Mexico. He was absolutely sold on the combination of ribavirin and isoprinosine and so was his doctor. Jefferson had progressed far enough into the AIDS syndrome to have been diagnosed with lymphoma, a lymph cancer. But after he went on the ribavirin-isoprinosine regimen, his flagging blood count almost miraculously normalized and the lymphoma abated.

Having heard about Delaney's work, Jefferson sent lab slips showing his amazing improvement. Delaney was so impressed he secretly wondered if Jefferson hadn't been misdiagnosed in the first place, though he never told that to Jefferson. Jefferson would call periodically to say that border guards had confiscated a load of pills, or that someone else had scored a dramatic health improvement.

Now Jefferson delivered some truly disturbing news. The price of ribavirin had suddenly skyrocketed. Throughout 1985, the price had been falling along with the falling value of the peso. Back when Delaney had started buying it, a box of twelve pills cost $18. But with Mexican currency on the skids, the same box, priced in pesos, had recently been obtainable for only about $7. A box lasted only two or three days.

"All of a sudden it's over twenty dollars a box," Jefferson said. "It's not clear who's raising the price—the pharmacies, the government, some middleman, or what."

"I ought to go down there next weekend anyway," Delaney said. "Let me check it out."

Every drugstore Delaney visited gave a price of $21 or $22 a box. "All I know is, the distributor is telling me this is what the cost will be from now on," one druggist explained. Others said pretty much the same thing. Delaney persuaded a few stores to drop the price on old stocks, but when they were gone the new price would prevail, he was told.

Back home, he found a raft of messages. By this time, Project Inform had sent instructions to thousands of people on how to make buys in Mexico. Now it seemed half of them were calling to complain about the price escalation. There were cries for a community meeting. Delaney agreed to call one.

At 9 A.M. Monday, he was on the phone to his contact, Karl Johnson, at ICN. "What the hell are you guys doing?" he demanded hotly. "You were making out all right, selling a drug that isn't licensed. I can see an increase, but you've tripled the price."

Johnson seemed surprised by Delaney's accusation. "I don't know anything about it," he kept saying.

Delaney repeated, more calmly, what the druggists had told him in Mexico, and what dozens of callers were telling him on the phone. "Who did this? Was it the pharmacies? Was it the company?"

Johnson again distanced himself from the rest of ICN. "Did those sons of bitches really do this?" he said. "Those sons of bitches in marketing must have done it. Let me call around and try to find out what's going on here."[17] (See note for Johnson's recollection.)

Already, however, flyers had started to appear around the Castro, charging that ICN was price-gouging to exploit desperately ill people. A public meeting was going to occur whether Project Inform sponsored it or not. Delaney scheduled a meeting for April 3.

Hundreds of patients and their friends showed up, enraged. Delaney denounced the price increase as unconscionable, and said he was negotiating with the company. Either the price would come down, or there would be action. People in the audience called for demonstrations in the streets. For two and a half hours, people rose to denounce ICN, and sometimes business in general. Delaney didn't say "no" to anything. He promised to relay the threats to the company.

In the usual milling crowd after the meeting Delaney recognized a figure he had seen hanging around quietly after previous meetings. This time the man seemed determined to assert himself.

He said he was David Winterhalter, and he frightened Delaney a bit at first. Strange people sometimes filtered in among the crowds at the community meetings. Some would linger afterward to argue various conspiracy theories, such as that the government had created the AIDS virus and loosed it on the world in order to wipe out the gay population. Delaney tried to avoid these people, and Winterhalter at first looked like one of them in his dirty blue jeans, T-shirt, long gray hair, and unkempt beard. But now he pushed forward.

"Can you give me a list of all the research that's been done on ribavirin and isoprinosine?" he began. Delaney said he would send a list if the man left an address. But the question persisted: Where were the studies being done? What were the qualifications of the researchers?

The intensity of Winterhalter's gaze and the relentlessness of his questions did nothing to dispel Delaney's unease. Delaney found himself going over ground he had already covered, but being pressed for new levels of detail. What did Delaney know about Compound S, the new substance the Centers for Disease Control had identified as working against the AIDS virus in a test tube?

"It's also known as AZT," Delaney said. "It was developed by the National Cancer Institute, which licensed it to Burroughs Wellcome, a big British-owned drug company. They've just started human testing."

"How did Burroughs Wellcome get it out of the government?" Winterhalter asked.

"A total fluke," Delaney said. And as Winterhalter plied him for details, Delaney found himself explaining the Orphan Drug Act Congress had passed to encourage drug companies to produce drugs for rare illnesses, for which the market might not be profitable. Government research centers that developed such drugs turned over exclusive manufacturing rights to drug companies. The gift of Compound S, or AZT, to Burroughs Wellcome seemed a boondoggle, because even though AIDS was technically a rare disease when the license was granted people knew the disease was mushrooming and the market would soon be abundant.

"The more I see of this business, the more I don't like it," Delaney said. "There are doctors on FDA advisory committees who earn their living consulting and running tests for the big drug companies. That's where they get their priorities. It's a built-in conflict of interest, but the FDA doesn't seem to see it."

"Have you tried to get this Compound S?"

"We can't get it—it isn't on the market anywhere."

"What are people saying about it?"

"That it works in test tubes, just like ribavirin. But ribavirin is on sale in Mexico and a lot of other places, and Compound S isn't. Otherwise, we'd be distributing it, too."

"Is there any kind of data on—"

Thinking this could go on forever, Delaney excused himself and said he had to leave.

"I'd like to help you in your work if I could," Winterhalter said. "Maybe office work. I have a computer."

"Oh? What kind is it?"

"I built it myself."

"Oh. From a kit?"

"No, I designed it. I do that."

"What kind of software does it run?"

"Stuff I wrote myself. It's a word processor. I can type letters, make posters and things."

"Whatever you want." This guy is either an untapped genius or a total nut, Delaney thought. A nut, he decided, and hurried away.

Before he could get out of the hall, however, he almost tripped over another familiar figure: Mark Roh, the FDA official who had spoken at an early meeting on AIDS drug policy. Delaney halted.

"Are you here for the FDA, or because you're interested?" he asked.

"I'm not here for the FDA," Roh told him. Suddenly Delaney noticed there were tears in Roh's eyes. "I just want you to know I support what you're doing," Roh said. "Everyone I've known in this town is dead or dying." Then Roh turned and walked away.

Delaney was moved. He guessed some personal tragedy had just befallen Roh, and he wondered what it was. He never found out.

TWENTY-SEVEN

The next morning ICN officials began phoning him. First, there was a call from a public-relations man, then calls from the regulatory-affairs director and the vice-president for operations.

"The company did engage in a price action," he was told. "But we didn't triple the price. It's unfair to look at it that way."

The Mexican Government set maximum prices for retail pharmaceuticals, based on negotiations with the manufacturer, ICN said. Three years earlier, ICN's subsidiary in Mexico had agreed with the government there on a fixed peso price for ribavirin. Since then, the peso had gone from about two hundred for a U.S. dollar to nearly six hundred for a U.S. dollar. Consequently, the dollar income ICN received from its Mexican unit for sales of ribavirin had shriveled. When the pricing agreement had come up for renewal, ICN had merely reinstated its original price in dollars against the devalued peso. What was wrong with that?

Delaney thought a minute. "I'll tell people what you've said," he told the executives. "But I don't think they'll buy it. The crowd was angry last night. They want demonstrations. There are flyers up all over town. Ribavirin now costs three times what it cost a couple of months ago. You've got to lower the price."

"But we can't lower it," he was told. "We've got a deal with the Mexican Government. We're not even supposed to be selling it to AIDS patients. We can't lower the price to accommodate them."

Delaney told Mark Bradley about the conversation. "You know," he concluded, "I've wondered all year how ICN got its profits out of Mexico, and how the pills could keep flowing for the same peso price when the peso was collapsing. Now I know what happened. The company was in serious trouble. When I visited the office, it seemed like a ghost town, operating at half speed. So in their eyes they came to a perfectly reasonable solution."

"But you're not going to let them get away with it."

"I hate to exploit this," Delaney said. "But our job is to worry about the community. I'll tell you where ICN's vulnerable. I just read in *The Wall Street Journal* that Kodak invested ten million dollars in ICN stock and options. That's what's paying for the study of ribavirin on AIDS patients at Cornell. Where we can really put the pressure on is through Kodak. There's got to be a way. A couple of hundred guys marching through the Castro with picket signs won't do it."

It was Thomas Jefferson who came up with the way. He drove to San Francisco to meet Delaney and attend the next community meeting.

Flyers were posted. Letters went out to the Project Inform mailing list, which now contained more than five thousand names:

In mid March the price of RIBAVIRIN, an anti-viral drug used by many AIDS and ARC patients, was TRIPLED by ICN PHARMACEUTI-CALS and their partner in testing it, EASTMAN KODAK COMPANY. . . .

CAN WE AFFORD TO LET THE PHARMACEUTICAL INDUSTRY GET AWAY WITH THIS? Is this what will happen with all promising AIDS treatments? . . .

The drug appears to be so inexpensive to manufacture that the company hopes to market it for agricultural purposes. Yet for AIDS patients, a year's supply—about a pound—now costs close to $4,000.

THURSDAY'S PUBLIC FORUM WILL DISCUSS STRATEGIES to bring pressure to force a price reduction.

Before the meeting even took place, Karl Johnson called again.

"Boy, you guys are really putting some heat on," he said. "ICN is following everything you do, every flyer printed."

"You think it's doing any good?" Delaney asked.

"You guys are right on target with Kodak, I'll tell you that. ICN is run by one man, Milan Panic. He founded it, and he controls it. Right now, Panic practically lives at Kodak. The studies at Cornell and Harvard are underway, and Kodak is paying most of the cost. It's a multiyear agreement, too."

Delaney told Jefferson about the conversation. "I think we've got somebody playing ball on our behalf over at ICN," he said.

At the packed meeting, Jefferson presented his plan: There would be a nationwide telephone and letter-writing campaign from hospital beds by AIDS patients. ICN was small fish. The calls and letters would go to Kodak, accusing it of profiteering from people with a deadly disease. Each call, each letter was to mention a planned boycott of Kodak film. Project Inform's own mailing list would be contacted. Jefferson's carefully kept phone logs would also yield thousands of interested people across the country. They would network with others.

Delaney asked if anyone knew people in Rochester, New York, where Kodak had its headquarters. Hands went up. Not only should Rochester patients write and call, Delaney said, they should spill the saddest stories possible to the local press.

Overall, audience response was strong. People rose, announcing some of the cities where they could deliver protests. There were also calls for a mass rally and demonstration. Someone suggested the weekend around Cinco de Mayo Day—May 5, a Mexican national holiday. The Mexican Government was in on the price rise, too. The groundswell of suggestions and enthusiasm in the audience was so strong Delaney began to feel like a bystander at his own party.

When the phone rang the next morning, he didn't know whether it was going to be ICN or a disgruntled ribavirin user with another protest idea. Instead, it was Winterhalter, wanting Delaney to go to Mexico with him, to start buying ribavirin, even at $22.

"I'll mail you our information package on how to do it," Delaney said. "Then you just drive down any time you want. You don't need me. Do you have a car?"

"Hell no. I have an airplane."

"An *air*plane?" Delaney had suspected from Winterhalter's dress and behavior that he might be homeless, living in a park somewhere.

"Sure, an airplane. It's something you ought to look into if you go down there very often."

You have an airplane. You don't even have any decent shoes, Delaney was thinking.

"Anyway, I don't want to wait for the mail," Winterhalter said. "Give me your address and I'll drive over there."

Jesus Christ, the last thing Delaney wanted was to give this nut his address.

"I can mail you a map of Tijuana, the whole works," Delaney said. "Show you just where to go."

"Naw, I'm going today. I've got a friend who's very sick who wants to try this. I found an airfield down there right by the border. By the way, that was a hell of a meeting you guys had last night. I'm gonna generate some letters and phone calls for this goddamn thing. I know people all over the country who will want to join on this one. Anyway, give me your address and I'll be by to pick up the map this morning and be on my way."

Delaney gave him the address, thinking even as he was doing so that it was a mistake.

"Sure you don't want to come with me?" Winterhalter said.

No sooner had Delaney hung up than the phone started ringing again, with people eager to help with the ribavirin protest. Delaney finally switched the phone over to the answering machine; he had to finish writing handouts for a training course he was due to give the following Monday at Seafirst Bank in Seattle. Just when he was finally absorbed in the bank work, Winterhalter drove up in a faded green Volkswagen bug.

"Sure you don't want to come?" he said when Delaney opened the door. "The plane's a four-seater, and there's only two other guys going down with me."

"No thanks." Delaney smiled, heading down the stairs. "Let me get you a map and a list of stores."

Winterhalter trailed behind him. "You know, I love coming to the meetings you hold and listening to the stories about how well people are doing on these drugs," he said. "It's not conclusive proof, but it's enough to go on. This is the only rational choice."

"We think so," Delaney said, pulling a packet of papers from his desk, Winterhalter right behind him.

"You know, I'm a chemical engineer, and sometimes—"

Delaney was looking at him, amazed.

"Well, I may not look it now. I left work after I got diagnosed six months ago. I've been living off disability and money I get from an apartment building I own. But I worked a long time for some companies in Silicon Valley. And sometimes in chemical engineering you set up experiments creating new compounds. During design and development, when you're working toward a new product, there's a time period where you don't have conclusive evidence, but you struggle with what you do have to determine the most rational approach, even though it isn't absolutely guaranteed. That's life. It might take decades to get compelling hard evidence on how something works, but you have to go forward or you never reach that conclusive evidence. And right now these drugs are the only rational choice—the only way to go forward."

Suddenly, Delaney decided he might really like this man. Then Winterhalter's questions started again, rapid-fire, about how many people had taken ribavirin and what Delaney knew about their blood results. Delaney started up the stairs, almost in flight, explaining that he had to get back to work.

"You said you didn't know much about Compound S."

"Except that Burroughs Wellcome owns it and we can't get it."

"Well, there's another one I've read about from the CDC. Suramin. What do you know about suramin?"

"Don't even think about that one," Delaney said. "Good luck on your trip."

Winterhalter was looking over the map in the doorway. Delaney finally nudged him out.

"Looks like a piece of cake," Winterhalter said as the door closed. "You're going to have to come down with me one of these days."

TWENTY-EIGHT

*T*he messages that had overflowed Delaney's answering machine while he was in Seattle told him that Jefferson's call-Kodak-from-the-hospital-bed plan must be working. AIDS patients and their friends reported getting calls back, not from Kodak but from the ICN public-relations staff, apologizing, explaining, appealing for understanding.

Then Delaney got his own call from the ICN P.R. chief. There were a couple of nervous jokes about how all the phone calls had sure kept the company hopping the past few days. Kodak had received hundreds of calls. Some had been referred directly to ICN chairman Panic. The P.R. man no longer seemed to be joking. Would Delaney please agree to talk the problem through with ICN's director of regulatory affairs? He was a former FDA man. Delaney said he'd take the call happily.

"We *can't* lower the price of the drug on the basis of protests of Americans AIDS patients because they're not supposed to be getting the drug in the first place," the regulatory-affairs man pleaded.

Delaney heard him out. Then a marketing man came on and explained that the company had been struggling with the Mexican Government for more than a year to win a "price correction" to make up for the money lost in the peso collapse. "If we go back now and say we don't want it, they'll never listen to us again," he said.

Then the P.R. man came back. "You've got to call off these demonstrations," he said. "It's in your interest as well as ours to get this drug approved by the FDA. You're putting us in a position where that's in real jeopardy. If Kodak gets so embarrassed by this that they back out, then the trials we need for FDA approval are going to be impossible. I hear you've got Tom Brokaw flying in to cover this thing. That's just too high an exposure."

Tom Brokaw? It was the first Delaney had heard of that.[18] He took it in stride. These people were clearly worried, and he sensed he had the upper hand. "We've got to get the price down," he said. "But there are a number of ways that could be done. I think it would be useful if we came down there and talked it out."

A meeting was set for the following Saturday. Panic, the founder and chairman, was out of town until then, and Delaney wanted him present for the meeting. Delaney had heard about Panic, a 1956 Yugoslavian immigrant (who pronounced his name PAN-ish). He was a big Democratic Party contributor. By reputation, he was an eccentric whose aggressive personality dominated the company.

In the days before the meeting, Delaney drilled Brewer in negotiating tactics, the same way he trained bankers. "Most people go into meetings and react," he told Brewer. "Those people tend to lose. You *plan* a meeting, you don't wing it."

They began role playing, pretending in turn to be each person who might be at the table for ICN, analyzing the opposition's motives and options, their personalities, and what Delaney called their "hot buttons." They did a similar analysis of themselves.

When Saturday came, Delaney and Brewer were led through the plaza, past the fountain and sculpture, through the grand entrance hall, and into a nicely paneled conference room at Panic's appointed hour, 7:30 A.M. On the other side of the table from them were Johnson (the medical chief), the regulatory-affairs man, the public-relations man, the marketing man, Panic, and Panic's personal assistant, a strikingly attractive and dark-complexioned woman of about thirty-five, with an exotic trace of a foreign accent.

Panic opened the meeting, then turned it over to his executives. "Mr. Panic has said that nothing could be changed," one said, and went on in that vein. The price rise was not exploitation. Because of the peso devaluation, the company had been losing money on every pill it sold. It could not, and would not, lower the price.

At that point, Panic stood, turned to his colleagues and said, "You guys work on it." Then, to Delaney's surprise, he abruptly whisked himself away to another appointment. It was only 8 A.M.

"But you've got to call off this demonstration," one of the executives then said, as if nothing unexpected had happened. "We've got to keep the Kodak board from being embarrassed with all this nonsense about price gouging and exploitation. It's only going to damage the patients if the tests can't go ahead as scheduled."

Delaney waited to speak until they were clearly through. Then he paused and began. "That is all flat-out unacceptable," he said. "I understand your pricing problems. But the community in San Francisco is enraged. We can't control them and don't want to. There'll be demonstrations next week." The ICN team grimaced.

"You do have some ways out," Delaney continued. As ICN knew, he said, Project Inform was looking for funding to pay for its own study of ribavirin, both alone and in combination with isoprinosine. That study was jeopardized by the price problem. Delaney suggested ICN could offer to pay for Project Inform's research staff and the cost of the lab testing.

And ICN could sell the pills to the study at cost, through bulk orders. He would pool individual American purchases. That way the retail price would stay high in Mexico, but Americans who wanted to use the drug could order it at what was, in effect, the old price.

"The proposals won't work," an ICN official said. And one by one, the executives explained why. The Kodak-financed studies at Cornell and Harvard were critical if ribavirin was ever to be marketed with FDA approval. The studies couldn't be endangered by having the company associate itself with this illegal neighborhood study of ribavirin with another drug.

Arguments were hurled back and forth across the table for hours. Both sides needed a solution. None appeared. Delaney and Brewer finally left, disappointed, to drive on to Tijuana for more drugs before they returned to San Francisco.

"Things have really broken down," Delaney said on the way out. "What do you want to do?"

Just then they noticed that Karl Johnson, the chief scientist, had followed them into the parking lot.

"It seems to be going nowhere," Delaney told him.

"No. You guys have got them by the balls," Johnson said. "Take everything you can get. This is the time to ask for the money. You don't understand what a corner you've got them in. They'll give you anything you ask for to get you to back off Kodak. You're on the right track if you hang tough. Keep up the pressure."

Then he walked away as discreetly as he had come. Delaney and Brewer looked at each other. On the way to Tijuana, bewildered, they pondered what had happened.

Monday morning they found out. All the executives from the meeting except Panic and Johnson placed a conference call. What, again,
did Delaney want?

"Here's our plan," Delaney began. "We want our research of ribavirin funded, along the lines of the plan we proposed to Karl Johnson
months ago. And we want a system to pool the orders of ribavirin
from the buyers, to get it at cost. You send the orders to Mexico. We
pick it up ourselves, and cut out the middleman."

"That's what we talked about Saturday," the regulatory-affairs man
replied. "And I've already checked it out with the FDA, pretty high
up. They said, 'If you start making deals at the border, we can't
accept that.' So I said, 'What if we did business in Mexico City,
where the factory is, fifteen hundred miles from the border?' They
said that was another matter. 'What you do in Mexico City is your
business.' "

"No good," Delaney said. "How are we going to get the stuff up to
the border from Mexico City?"

"You want this stuff badly enough, you'll figure it out. This is the
only way we can do it. We have to live with the FDA."

Delaney hesitated.

"Send us the research proposal," someone else said. "We have the
ICN Foundation that could fund it. You guys work with Karl Johnson
and draw something up."

Only the marketing man spoke up contrarily. "What if the Mexican
distributors object? We have to work with those people, too."

"Well," Delaney said, "who said they have to know?"

There was a pause.

"Okay," one of the ICN men said. "We'll sell it to you. How you
get it to the patients is for you to figure out. We'll work with our
Mexican subsidiary to find a bulk price."

"Seven dollars a box tops," Delaney said. "We'll come up with a
way to distribute it."

"And you'll call off the Cinco de Mayo demonstration and Tom
Brokaw."

That was easy to agree to. Both of Delaney's bargaining chips had
been imaginary.

Details were worked out in succeeding conference calls. In days,
Johnson flew to San Francisco to work on the study protocol.

"What do you suppose happened?" Delaney said. "Did Johnson
rebel against the company? Did all these guys rebel against Panic?
Did Panic set the whole thing up himself and bow out so he wouldn't
be connected with it?"

"Who cares?" Brewer said. "We won. The price will be lowered. And for the first time in the history of the epidemic, a community group is going to conduct research."

TWENTY-NINE

*I*CN gave Project Inform $75,000—more money than Delaney and Brewer had imagined getting. It allowed them to open an office and hire a staffer. And ICN indicated that if things went well, more money would become available for the prospective study.

First, though, somebody had to figure out a distribution system for the ribavirin.

After the community meeting to discuss the ICN settlement and call off the protests, Delaney saw David Winterhalter approaching excitedly. "Everything worked," Winterhalter said. The map had been correct. And the airfield he flew into—Brown Field, right at the border—was used mainly by U.S. Customs. Winterhalter had rented a junker of a car for $10 a day at the little airport. Then he had loaded his plane with smuggled ribavirin and isoprinosine just a few dozen yards from where customs planes and their crews sat idle.

Also, he said, he had devised a computer program that Project Inform might be interested in. He urged Delaney to come to his house to look at it. With a smile the equivalent of a white flag, Delaney agreed.

The house did not surprise him: a bungalow, old and rundown, on a poor block in Berkeley. The lawn was uncut, the bushes untrimmed. Except for a sparsely furnished bedroom and kitchen, the rooms contained nothing but boxes of books.

The scene outside the back door, however, could not have been imagined: a vegetable patch and barnyard, with chickens and ducks everywhere, plus half a dozen cats for rodent control. Delaney stepped into a cluster of overgrown grass, and out popped a chicken.

"I kill one or two a week. That's how I feed myself," Winterhalter explained.

Beyond the small barnyard was a garage that had been turned into a tool shed. Alongside it stood a big fuel tank on steel legs, and a green Volkswagen minibus with two smaller fuel tanks in the back.

"It's aviation fuel," Winterhalter said. "I stock up on it in bulk when it's cheap. You don't want to be at the mercy of the guys at the airport."

Delaney wondered if any smokers ever traveled the alley past the fuel tanks. He suppressed a joke about there goes the neighborhood. And this was an earthquake zone. On this property, he thought, must be a violation of every public-safety ordinance the city of Berkeley had. Somehow, though, he felt safe; Winterhalter exuded an air of confidence.

"Are the neighbors at all concerned?" Delaney finally asked.

"Oh, in this neighborhood nobody complains about what anybody does."

"Are you worried about people stealing things?"

"What have I got that anybody would want?" Winterhalter said. "Besides, there's usually other people around here. I let some runaway kids stay here, or homeless people. Just doesn't happen to be anybody right now."

Back inside, Winterhalter showed Delaney his computer—a row of circuit boards with no chassis, and an open keyboard with holes between the keys. But it worked.

"What can I do for you with it?" Winterhalter asked.

What the hell, Delaney thought. "Somebody's got to run the ribavirin operation," he said. "Pool the orders from around the country, collect the money, and feed it all to ICN. And then figure out how to distribute the drug. Project Inform can't be involved in selling the drug if we're going to be testing it. I don't want anyone to think we're some kind of a sales rep for ICN. The sales operation has to be independent."

"I can handle it," Winterhalter said. "First, I want you to fly down there with me."

In for a dime, in for a dollar. "Okay."

Bradley still thought the idea was ridiculous. "So even if the guy does have a plane, does that mean you trust him flying it?" he argued. But Delaney had bought into Winterhalter, a man who grew up on a small farm in Oklahoma, obtained a doctorate in chemical engineering, contracted AIDS, and was fighting back buoyantly. Winterhalter, self-possessed and driven, seemed able to make things happen on his own. Bradley was overruled.

Delaney showed up at the small airport in the wine country north of San Francisco. He pulled his new top-of-the-line Mazda sedan alongside the aging green minibus. Winterhalter's plane was a Cessna 180, single engine, ten years old.

Winterhalter unlocked the cyclone-fence gate, and they pulled the cars right up to the plane. He had brought two other men with him, both quiet and looking decidedly not well. They sat in Delaney's car, while Winterhalter fueled the plane from a hose connected to the tanks he carried in the back of the VW. He carried a generator and pump in the van, too.

"As you fill the gas tanks, you have to tip the wings, rock the plane like this, to make sure the fuel moves around," he announced over the noise of the generator. "That'll get rid of any air bubbles."

When the tanks were full, Winterhalter spent forty-five minutes checking the plane, describing every task to Delaney as he performed it. "Now pull this lever and see if the flap moves," he instructed. "That's right. Now look what happens when I push these pedals on the floor." Delaney saw the front wheel turn. The whole list was more than Delaney could absorb at one sitting, but he felt himself learning.

They went outside, opened the hood, and checked the oil, just as if it were a car. Winterhalter removed blocks from the air intakes. "They keep birds from nesting in there," he explained. He moved the propeller, then toured the plane, carefully inspecting it.

"See anything here?" he asked.

Delaney strained to see. "Nope."

"Well, you're wrong," Winterhalter said. And he pointed to a dent on the side of the plane. "It's essential that a pilot know the body of his plane intimately."

The inspection complete, they and the two sick men boarded the Cessna. Winterhalter took down everyone's weight. Then he instructed Delaney, "Go pull the blocks from under the wheels and bring them in the plane."

Winterhalter had Delaney riding up front behind a duplicate set of controls, wearing headphones, and listening to conversations with the flight-control center. After half an hour in the air, Winterhalter said, "Do you want to take the controls?"

"I don't know there's any reason to."

"I want you to." And Delaney did.

"Learn to fly," Winterhalter said, "You know, this is the easy part, when you're up in the air. A plane *wants* to fly. I don't want you to move the controls. Just keep it in stasis."

Delaney felt a rush of excitement. All the way south, Winterhalter pointed out ground objects he navigated by. A reservoir. A power plant. A highway intersection. Winterhalter told Delaney to try to make a straight line for the intersection. Delaney was surprised how quickly he was thrown off course.

"Wind," Winterhalter said. "Wind speed and wind direction." And he launched into a long discussion of air speed and altitude.

Suddenly Delaney's exhilaration was broken by the suspicion that Winterhalter was going through all this because he feared his own death, and needed someone to carry on. Delaney hadn't probed the exact state of Winterhalter's health, and Winterhalter hadn't volunteered it.

When it came time to descend, Winterhalter resumed the controls, but kept up the commentary, and, they landed at Brown Field, in the desert near the Mexican border. A couple of dozen other small planes were parked near the runway some of them clearly marked "U.S. Customs." A dozen cars and pickup trucks nearby were also marked "U.S. Customs." Once again, Delaney had the feeling that Winterhalter was a risk taker, but that he calculated his risks carefully; he seemed so self-assured and in control that Delaney followed him past a few groups of chatting customs men and into the airport, where Winterhalter filed flight papers and rented a car.

"So you need a way to get the pills from the ICN factory in Mexico City to customers around the U.S.," Winterhalter said as they drove to Tijuana. "Seems the best way to avoid the most problems with the government, and still make it as easy as possible for the customers to get the drugs, would be for me to form an independent sales organization to move the drugs from the factory to the border. Set up shop here in Tijuana. That would put the system back the way it was before the price increased. Plenty of people could drive down to pick it up as they always have. For the ones who can't, I'll drive it across and fly north with whatever's needed."

"I suppose you could have it shipped to Tijuana from Mexico City," Delaney said.

"There's a port just a few miles from here," Winterhalter agreed. "There are dozens of depots and warehouses where the stuff could be shipped to. I come down, pick it up, and take it to someplace in town we rent out—a storefront, a motel room, whatever. And people come pick it up the way they used to."

"The local pharmacists are going to lose a lot of business," Delaney said.

"Yeah, that's something to worry about. People sometimes get violent down here. We'll just have to be so discreet they don't find out who's short-circuiting them. And we'll need recruits to help move the goods and shepherd the buyers who come down."

"Tom Jefferson's people in San Diego could probably help," Delaney said. "I'm sure we'll find somebody."

They made the usual purchases at the Regis and the Olympia, noticing that the more expensive Maxim's now had a big sign in its window, "We have ribavirin." They stopped for tacos, rice, and beans and drove back to Brown Field without incident. Customs guards seemed to pay them no mind as they loaded the pills onto the Cessna.

Boarding the plane, however, Delaney noticed a tank of oxygen behind Winterhalter's seat. "Is that standard equipment?" he asked.

"Naw. It's just that my lungs are in such bad shape."

Delaney considered that the prospect of Winterhalter's becoming incapacitated might be real. He recounted in his mind the in-flight procedures, step by step, over and over.

Airborne, he was again given the controls. Just as he was getting used to it, Winterhalter reached back and in one swift move put a helmet backward over Delaney's head, blocking his view.

"What did you do that for?"

"You're flying blind. You need to be able to fly blind. Just look down at your instruments. Isn't this what we're all doing in this epidemic? We're trying to steer the ship as best we can, but in truth we're flying blind. We don't have answers. Still, we have to keep going."

Just like that, Delaney flew four hundred miles north to Napa Airport. Then, helmet off, he watched carefully as Winterhalter landed.

THIRTY

*W*eeks passed. Delaney's phone rang.

"Martin Delaney? This is Jim Corti in Los Angeles. I don't know how the hell you've done it, but you seem to have a lock on seven-dollar-a-box ribavirin. I buy for users all over the country—"

"I think I know who you are," Delaney said. "Tom Jefferson told me there was somebody doing this in L.A. He even mentioned your name."

"Yeah, I've met Jefferson. So if you know who I am, why did I just get grilled for an hour on the phone by your man Winterhalter? He wanted to hear everything I know about AIDS, what doctors I've worked with, what medicines—"

Delaney smiled. "Sorry. He was just making sure you're not a fed. That's what he's supposed to do."

"Well, what I want to know is what you've got going here. I've been at this two years, and then the price goes up, and for months now I've tried every fucking thing I can figure. I've arm-twisted the pharmacies, I've offered bribes, I went down to ICN and told them I bought more ribavirin than anybody else in the world, and I still can't get the price down. How the hell did you do it?"

Delaney told him the basic outline of the story.

"It was the calls to Kodak that did it," Delaney said.

"It's still hard to believe. I'll tell you what. I'm going to test you out with a modest order. Six hundred boxes. If you can deliver, I'll toss all my business into Winterhalter's operation. I have no vested interest keeping on doing this myself."

Now it was Delaney in disbelief, swallowing his words. "We can get as much or as little as you want," he said finally. "Seven dollars a box, plus twenty-five cents to defray costs." He paused. "Six hundred boxes is the biggest order we've ever had," he said. "Just remember to send a cashier's check."

Later, he laughed about it with Winterhalter. "Forty-five hundred dollars and he called it a test," Delaney said. "But what really impressed me was how ready he was to turn everything over to you. He's been at this two years, and yet he doesn't have an ego invested in it."

When the appointed afternoon came, Corti showed up in Tijuana as the letter from Winterhalter had instructed. He parked the Virus Van at a discreet distance, and walked to where he was told to wait, at the corner of Fifth and Revolución, wearing on his shirt a small green stick-on dot Winterhalter had sent him in the mail. As he waited, he noticed a few neatly dressed, middle-class-looking Americans emerge from the entrance to a multistory indoor parking garage down the street. Each of them was carrying an identical brown paper bag, and, as they walked past, he could see they also wore small green dots on their clothing. They smiled at him and nodded in recognition. He smiled and nodded back.

A few minutes later he saw more such people. Eight or ten groups left the garage. Some walked the other direction, some headed his way and passed him as he waited on the corner. They all carried brown bags and wore green dots. He guessed some to be grandparents of patients, some parents, some brothers or sisters, some friends.

Then Corti was approached by a man in T-shirt and jeans, sporting an unkempt gray beard. "David Winterhalter," the man said, and handed him two large bags of ribavirin. "I'll be back with more," Winterhalter said. "We decided to do it two bags at a time. That way if anybody stops me, they're only going to get what I'm carrying, not the whole carful." Corti examined the contents.

"Jesus, the stuff looks real," Corti said, taking them. "I don't know how you did this after I knocked myself out for the past two months and couldn't get to first base, but it's absolutely wonderful." He put them in the car.

Half a dozen bags later the shipment was complete. They shook hands. "Thank you. And I want you to thank Marty," Corti said.

A few days later Corti called Delaney and thanked him again. "I was half expecting to be dealing with some con man," he confided. "And then there was Winterhalter. No rings, no jewelry. Just straight talk."

"He's down-to-earth," Delaney agreed.

"So let me place an order for eighteen hundred boxes for your next trip. Just triple what we did this time."

Delaney tried to conceal his laugh. "That's a week from Saturday," he said. "Send the order to Winterhalter. He's handling it."

"Hey, I want to go down to Tijuana and run through the whole procedure with you. Get a sense of the size of the operation. I want to see if I can help. It's just mind-boggling to me that you could have arranged this. How long have you been at it?"

And suddenly Delaney felt himself being grilled—about the Castro brothers, the clerks at the Olympia Pharmacy, where the price used to be printed on a box of ribavirin before the package was redesigned. Most things, Delaney knew. Some, he didn't.

"I think you know Tijuana better than I do," he told Corti finally. "I'll concede that."

"Look, I've got a lot of people depending on me," Corti said. "I have to reassure myself."

"I know," Delaney said. "Somebody's going to counterfeit ribavirin someday, and you need to know it's not us. And that we're not feds. But remember, you could blow our operation, too. We just have to get to trust each other."

"It's amazing we haven't tripped over each other before," Corti said.

"I know. We've probably been bidding on the same lots without being aware of it."

They talked an hour, networking and cementing a friendship. Neither man could understand why doctors weren't recording the progress of patients on ribavirin and isoprinosine for scientific comparison. Delaney told Corti about the study Project Inform was organizing, and Corti told Delaney about Dr. Michael Scolaro's effort to run a similar study from his office. Both men cursed the perverse scheming of the FDA to keep AIDS patients from getting ribavirin. The drug had finally been approved for treating the babies' lung disease—but the FDA license provided that ribavirin could be sold in American drugstores only in aerosol form, specifically so that doctors couldn't prescribe it in dosages practical for AIDS patients.

The Friday afternoon of the next distribution weekend in Tijuana, Corti again met Winterhalter at a designated spot. Winterhalter showed Corti to the passenger's side of a rented car with U.S. plates, and climbed into the driver's side.

"I want to show you how it works," Winterhalter said. "But it's very important that everything you see stay secret. The local druggists have just lost a market that was bringing them tens of thousands of U.S. dollars a month. If they or any cops find out what's going on, it could be dangerous."

Corti nodded. Winterhalter drove around a few corners to Avenue Madero, and into the paved courtyard of La Villa de Zaragoza, a fairly modern motel laid out in Mexicali-style brown stucco. They drove past one courtyard, into another, more secluded from the street, and parked in front of a room.

"This is the first time we've let a buyer see the operation," Winterhalter said. And he pushed open the motel-room door. The beds had been turned on end and placed against the wall. On the floor, Corti saw Martin Delaney, surrounded by cardboard crates of ribavirin. It was more of the drug than he had ever seen.

"Holy shit," Corti said. "I'm in ribavirin heaven."

He joined in as Delaney, Winterhalter, and a couple of helpers prepared for the next day's pill transfers. Boxes of pills were removed from the shipping crates and placed in paper bags according to Winterhalter's computerized list of orders. A computer-prepared peel-off label was affixed to each bag.

As they worked, Delaney and Winterhalter filled in details of the operation for Corti. Winterhalter had organized himself as BARIG, short for the Bay Area Ribavirin Interest Group. But, despite the localized name, he was booking orders from around the country, paid for by money order or certified check through BARIG's post-office box.

Monthly, he sent a bulk order with certified check to the Mexico City ICN unit, which shipped the appropriate amount of ribavirin to a warehouse on the Tijuana docks. Delaney had worked out the arrangement by phone with ICN in Mexico City. The Mexican office prepared purchase vouchers for the parent ICN company in Costa Mesa, California, showing the official price of about $21 a box, with an advance payment received of $7. The parent company made good the rest of the money through bookkeeping entries. The price fixed with the Mexican Government stayed $21 a box on the books of the subsidiary, while BARIG paid $7.

Meanwhile, Winterhalter, doing everything by computer, mailed out purchase instructions to the buyers, including a green stick-on dot to identify them. Groups of from one to two dozen buyers were scheduled to assemble each hour at a given street corner in Tijuana. Corners would be rotated through the day for security. The groups would be met by Winterhalter or a representative and escorted to the chosen point of transfer, usually an upper floor of the parking garage.

The operation had taken on grand proportions. So far, it seemed charmed. Winterhalter, Delaney, and a vanload of volunteers would arrive in Tijuana on a Friday and rent out rooms for all of them at the motel, plus a room for operations. Then they would pick up the crates of ribavirin at the docks. Through the afternoon and evening they would attack the crates with razor blades and begin packaging the drugs in brown-paper bags that Winterhalter bought by the boxful.

"Don't you think the motel staff might give you away?" Corti asked.

"No," said Winterhalter. "I leave an extra hundred dollars for them when I pay the bill."

When the packaging was completed, Delaney made his usual suggestion that they call it a day, and return to their rooms for an early sleep. Corti proposed that as long as they were in Tijuana they might as well party. When others welcomed the idea, it became clear that Corti's live-wire personality was going to recharge the atmosphere of the operation. In the muggy weekend night, the group joined the thousands of other Californians jamming the streets.

Delaney agreed to the taco-and-tequila sessions at Corti's favorite alfresco restaurants, though Delaney couldn't drink. But he drew the line at going into a drag-show bar Corti liked to visit for fun. What amazed Delaney was that everywhere they went in Tijuana people would approach with hands extended, and a warm "Señor Jim," or "Señor Corti, good to see you." Corti was obviously one of the most gregarious people he had ever met.

Corti carefully observed the next day's routine. Saturday morning, Delaney and Winterhalter visited the usual pharmacies to buy isoprinosine for clients who had ordered both drugs. The druggists complained about the lack of ribavirin orders, but accepted Winterhalter's claim that the price increase had wiped out demand for the drug. Then the isoprinosine was brought back to La Villa de Zaragoza and put into the bags with the ribavirin as the computerized labels indicated. Delaney and Winterhalter took turns driving the bags to the parking garage, while the other stayed behind in the rooms.

Then came the parade: grandmothers, children, friends, lovers, sisters, brothers, some patients themselves, representatives of buyers' groups from Hawaii, Florida, and New York—all coming to pick up pills, thanking the suppliers profusely.

"It's a credit to the gay community that you folks have done this," one elderly couple told Delaney.

"Billy's so sick," another woman said. "We hope this is going to help. But even if it doesn't, we thank you for trying."

A man speaking out from a small cluster of people said, "The doctors told us nothing would help. There wasn't any point in trying. The doctors just said, 'Wait and see.' I'm glad someone tried something rather than just waiting for the inevitable."

About 150 people showed up through the day. Some recognized Corti, having bought from him in the past. Many seemed delighted to see and talk to other people in circumstances like theirs.

On the way back to the motel, Delaney told Corti, "I thought it was going to be too complicated. That it would never work. But Winterhalter said, 'No, I can make it work.' And he has."

At the motel, they stuffed shrink-wrapped sheets of pills into Corti's Virus Van and the car Winterhalter had rented, and drove to Brown Field. There, they pushed the pills down into the tail of the Cessna. Corti marveled at what they were doing, in the moonlight, just a hundred feet from a customs post. Then they locked the plane and returned to the motel in the rented car for a final load, checking out as they left.

They were barely out of the parking lot when they noticed a Mexican police car tailing them. After several blocks, it pulled them over.

"Not again," Delaney said.

A cop peered in the window. "You didn't stop for the light, señor."

Winterhalter, who was driving, politely told the cop they had stopped.

"No, and you were weaving in your lane. You are in very much trouble. You must come with us to the police station."

Winterhalter sighed. "Is there some other way we can take care of this? We're in a hurry."

"Well, you can pay the fine of fifty dollars."

Winterhalter paid, and was waved off without a receipt.

"They skip the paperwork as a courtesy to us," Winterhalter joked to Corti.

"This would be funny," Delaney said, "except these bribes are expensive, and if anything really happened and they looked in the trunk and saw all those pills, we might actually end up in jail. Or worse, if they tell any of the drugstores."

"You know the one time they didn't stop us?" Winterhalter said. "Two weeks ago. You know why?"

Delaney looked at him.

"Because the car we rented at Brown Field last time was one of those old Nashes that still say 'U.S. Navy' on the side," Winterhalter said. "Those are old Navy staff cars. From now on, we insist on renting those. They may not look like much, but they're protection."

That night they went to a San Diego restaurant for dinner with Tom Jefferson and some friends. Delaney had grown to like Jefferson, a former officer in the Vietnam War, who prided himself on his physique, even though AIDS had begun to erode it. The first time Delaney had visited Jefferson's house, he had spotted a prominently displayed picture of Jefferson appropriately unattired on a nude beach, posed like Adonis.

"Don't you be staring at that pecker," Jefferson barked.

Delaney had just laughed. Then what are you putting that picture up here for? he thought, but didn't say anything.

Now Delaney announced to Corti, Winterhalter, and the others that Jefferson was the first new hire Project Inform would make with its $75,000 grant from the ICN Foundation. The announcement was toasted with margaritas.

Among those Jefferson brought to the dinner was a lesbian border guard he knew; she had a lot of advice. For one thing, she said, they didn't need to worry about carrying two loads across the border on the same day, or even on successive days. When license-plate numbers were punched into computers at the checkpoints, it took two days before the numbers registered in the mainframe computer; during that time, while the numbers were in temporary storage, cars wouldn't be recognized on repeat trips. This meant they could safely use a rented car to make as many trips as they liked from Tijuana to Brown Field on a weekend, as long as they didn't run into a single antagonistic border guard more than once.

"There are a lot of lesbians working the border," she said. "Any of us would pass you in a second. You have to watch out for the rednecks. But if you look okay, like a decent person, most officers will wave you by."

When dinner was over, Corti took off in the Virus Van, and Delaney and Winterhalter drove to Brown Field for the flight home. By now, Delaney was setting the flight path, taking off, and navigating —everything but landing.

THIRTY-ONE

*W*hile the smuggling seemed to be going more smoothly than most CIA operations Delaney had read about, the study Joe Brewer was supposed to be organizing was at a standstill. Delaney had less and less patience for the failure, but didn't know what to do about it.

Doctors didn't want to break new ground on an ethical issue, Brewer said. Some of the doctors he had trusted to help him had turned around and told other doctors to avoid the study for fear of losing their licenses. Plus, he said, "they think we're out of our field. We're not researchers. They want to let Volberding and the big boys at San Francisco General take care of it."

Delaney wanted to tell Brewer to find more cooperative doctors. In the end, he said, he just hoped ICN's formal study at Cornell and Harvard produced positive results.[19]

Meanwhile, word spread of another discouraging development: Dr. Donald Abrams, a pillar of the medical establishment, had undertaken a sixty-day study of isoprinosine among infected patients at San Francisco General Hospital. They had continued to die at the accustomed rate, and Abrams had proclaimed isoprinosine a proven failure and discontinued the study. Delaney was furious; he had heard from patients, though Abrams would later deny it, that most subjects in the test had already reached the late stage of the disease, at which isoprinosine was thought to do little.[20]

"He's telling the whole medical community it's a failure," Delaney complained to anyone who would listen. "Even with healthy patients you can't fairly evaluate this type of drug in sixty days. Without any peer review, without any publication, they're willing to accept his negative results."

Then, in late December 1986, Delaney got a call from Karl Johnson at ICN. The first formal academic study of ribavirin had been unblinded, with the researchers' announcement of who was taking the drug and who was taking the placebo.

"It looks like we have a big success," Johnson beamed. "It looks significant."

Delaney pressed him for numbers. "About a dozen people in the placebo group progressed to AIDS," Johnson said. "Nobody in the maximum-dose ribavirin group did. We're going to Washington, Panic and the whole executive team, right after New Year's. The company's going to push the FDA to hold a press conference, same as they did for the AZT test this fall."

Delaney was ecstatic. The winter holiday season of 1986–87 was surely a time for rejoicing. Drugs that might stall the epidemic appeared ready for FDA approval.

The AZT trial had been unblinded midway through. The drug was declared a roaring success by officials from the FDA as well as from Burroughs Wellcome. AZT seemed headed for quick licensing, as a life-extending medication for people with AIDS. Maybe within weeks ICN would be able to sell ribavirin legally in the United States. At least for a while, ribavirin kept virus-infected people from progressing to AIDS, so far more people would benefit from it than from AZT. Ten times as many people had the virus as had AIDS.

In January, Delaney got another call. FDA review of the ribavirin data was being delayed. FDA Commissioner Frank E. Young wanted to be personally involved. But Dr. Young's son had been critically injured in a train crash.[21] While Young raced between office and hospital to care for his son, ICN was going ahead with a limited press conference on its own. The company had registered with the Securities and Exchange Commission for a new securities offering, and the SEC was demanding disclosure of all relevant facts. The market implications of the ribavirin-AIDS study were tremendous.

THIRTY-TWO

On Saturday, January 10, 1987, Delaney, Corti, and more than a million other people saw an article under a two-column headline on the front page of *The New York Times*, written by the *Times*'s veteran medical writer Lawrence K. Altman, a physician himself. The story began: "WASHINGTON, Jan. 9—In a six-month study, the drug Ribavirin appeared to halt the progression of an early form of infection caused by the AIDS virus, a drug company announced today. It is the first time that a drug has seemed to prevent AIDS from developing in patients with early signs of infection with the virus."

ICN had stressed that the drug wasn't a cure for AIDS, the story cautioned. Test subjects still could expect to get the disease sometime. But the tone of the story was hopeful. Results were reported for 163 patients who tested positive for HIV, as the AIDS virus was now universally called. Of 52 patients with only the earliest symptoms, swollen lymph glands, who were given 800 milligrams a day of ribavirin, none developed AIDS during the course of the study. Of 55 patients who received a smaller dose, 600 milligrams a day of ribavirin, 6 developed AIDS. And of 56 patients who received a placebo, and no ribavirin, 10 developed AIDS.

Results were still awaited from a companion study testing ribavirin in patients at the next stage of the disease, who were already suffering from AIDS-related conditions, or ARC.

To be approved by the FDA, a new drug traditionally had to succeed in three phases of studies. In the first phase, a drug was studied in test tubes, in animals, and in a handful of people to determine toxicity and dosage. The ribavirin studies just completed were phase two, in which a drug was given to a few hundred people, to see if it promised effectiveness without severe toxicity. Ahead lay phase three, the costliest and most time-consuming, in which the drug would be used on a much larger patient group to see if it could be proven safe and effective.

Still, this was a fatal disease. Here was a drug without significant side effects at the dosages given. And those who took it did better than those who didn't, and those who took more of it did better than those who took less. AZT had been licensed for sale after a single phase two study of 280 people.

The *Times* said that while the larger studies were pursued, ICN had asked the FDA to let ribavirin be given immediately to HIV-infected patients. Immediate distribution seemed possible under a new plan that Dr. Young had announced soon after taking over as head of the FDA in 1984. Young, then dean of the University of Rochester Medical School, was appointed by President Reagan to help free the pharmaceutical industry of unnecessary regulation.

Under his plan, a so-called "Investigational New Drug," or IND, could be approved for patient treatment based on early study results if it was the only hope against a dire illness. The system was called, simply enough, "Treatment IND." But in the three years Young had been talking about it, not one drug had been distributed under Treatment IND. Now, ICN figured that if ever a drug would qualify, ribavirin ought to. And it requested such early use.

The *Times* article said the FDA was still evaluating the study data, but that "Dr. Young said that the FDA knew of ICN's plans for a news conference and that its actions were not unusual because many drug companies have released information at an early stage in the research of a potential drug." Like AZT, Delaney thought.

According to the test results, ribavirin not only worked in earlier-stage patients than AZT, it was relatively harmless. AZT caused severe anemia and bone-marrow damage in many patients, and threatened permanent damage to the body's chemistry. Ribavirin wasn't toxic at recommended dosages. For all these reasons, the initial news stories about the ribavirin test results warmed the hearts of Corti and Delaney. But it was the last purely good news about ribavirin that would appear for some time.

The following Monday's *Wall Street Journal* put quite a different spin on the story. The *Journal* reported that AIDS researchers were calling the ribavirin test results " 'sketchy,' 'inconclusive,' and 'premature.' " High up, the *Journal* quoted exactly one such researcher by name: " 'One needs to question the company's motivation for calling a press conference and then releasing such inconclusive results,' said Donald Abrams, assistant director of the AIDS clinic at San Francisco General Hospital," the *Journal* said. Later, the article quoted two other critics by name; one was Abrams's boss, Paul Volberding, who was also dismissive of any quick use of ribavirin.

Abrams and Volberding were quoted in local press accounts, too. Delaney was irate on the phone to Corti that night. "Nobody mentions," he complained, "that these guys earn their living in part from drug-company grants to do FDA-approved research. They've been down on ribavirin for years because we're importing it outside FDA channels. Now the press quotes them as if they were unbiased experts who have found flaws with ICN's research—which they haven't even seen yet." [22] (See note for doctors' reactions.)

Later in January, Delaney and Jefferson attended an antiviral conference ICN hosted at Newport Beach, scheduled long in advance of the controversy. Delaney found Karl Johnson not just optimistic but gloating.

"They've run into pancytopenia in the AZT trials," Johnson said.

"Sounds awful. What is it?" Delaney replied.

"It means it's killing off all forms of blood cells. I think it's going to knock AZT out of the box."

As sympathetic as he was to ICN's plight with ribavirin, Delaney was repelled by the spirit of competition between the drugs, and disusted that anyone would delight in bad news about something as promising as AZT. But he knew ICN's enemies were the same way.

"Well," Delaney said, "it's not completely surprising. My friend Jim Corti is a nurse in Los Angeles, and says they've had to cut back the dose by half on the AZT studies there because of anemia toxicity. Some people can tolerate it, some can't."

More weeks dragged by with no word from the FDA about making ribavirin available for use under the Treatment IND program.

Then, February 13, 1987, the *Journal* ran a page-one feature story with the bombshell news that the Securities and Exchange Commission had started "an investigation of possible stock manipulation and insider trading in ICN securities." The article spotlighted Panic's reputation as a promoter and the recent volatility of ICN's stock.

The *Journal* said ribavirin might turn out to be useful, but was "unproved." The article quoted the editor of the prestigious *New England Journal of Medicine* saying that releasing data at a press conference was "just plain outright wrong." No mention was made of the AZT press conference a few months earlier.

The *Journal* reported that back when ribavirin was approved for use against the babies' lung disease, the FDA required ICN to withdraw a press release it had issued. The FDA said that ICN had "grossly exaggerated" the effectiveness and safety of the drug beyond the specific disease the FDA had approved it for.

Also, the *Journal* reported, ICN had been giving "a 60 percent [price] discount [on ribavirin] to patients referred by a San Francisco AIDS-information group."

The head of that group, Martin Delaney, and his new confidant Jim Corti, weren't mentioned in the *Journal* story. But as controversy swirled around ribavirin, local television news programs paid them increasing attention. TV reporters had been assigned to videotape a smuggling trip, and both Delaney and Corti had cooperated.

Newsweek devoted a full page to "Uproar Over AIDS Drugs," and quoted Delaney on why AZT approval seemed close at hand, whereas ribavirin approval did not. AZT had been discovered in a government laboratory and awarded to a big drug company. "The government looks into a few narrowly defined products from the old-boy network and everything else gets the door slammed in its face," Delaney said. *Newsweek* described Project Inform flatteringly and published the new toll-free 800 number of its hotline.

Project Inform had also begun mass mailings of what would become a regular quarterly newsletter in an attractive desktop-publishing format. The mailing list started at six thousand and grew quickly. Readers were urged to support the quick provisional approval of ribavirin. Congress was urged to investigate the FDA, to appropriate money for trials of promising treatments, and to order customs to let people bring a year's supply of ribavirin or other promising pharmaceuticals into the country unchallenged.

But the government was moving in quite the opposite direction. On April 10, 1987, the FDA rejected ICN's request to have ribavirin released under Treatment IND and began a campaign attacking the ribavirin study data. What puzzled Delaney was that instead of the agency's making a public pronouncement, it went covert. FDA officials were quoted anonymously in the press saying that the study had been biased, and that the companion study of somewhat sicker ARC patients showed more deaths and medical problems among patients taking the drug than among those taking a placebo. ICN had not yet announced the results of that test.

These news stories stunned and saddened Delaney—and yet he didn't know what to make of them. The studies had been run by veteran scientists at Harvard, Cornell, Johns Hopkins, USC, and a couple of other top research facilities. For the studies to have been as badly flawed as was being suggested would have required deceit or gross incompetence. If there was evidence of either, why wouldn't the FDA make it public?

To the contrary, from what Delaney could learn, the researchers were standing behind their data, although refusing to talk publicly about it. One, Peter W. Mansell of the Center for Immunological Disorders of M. D. Anderson Hospital in Houston, was still planning to present a formal paper on the study at the Third International Conference on AIDS coming up in Washington.

A *Wall Street Journal* story quoted an anonymous congressional investigator who said that dangerous side effects to ribavirin had turned up in its use in the babies' lung disease, and were being covered up by ICN. The article said the FDA and a congressional committee headed by Representative John Dingell of Michigan were working on this. The article contained no denial from the company, only a statement that "top executives were out of the country and couldn't be reached for further comment."[23] (See note for resolution of these allegations, plus a note on journalism.)

The controversy grew so hot that Kodak announced it was selling its stake in ICN.

THIRTY-THREE

Not long after his newsletter went out, Delaney was surprised to receive a letter from Frank Young, the commissioner of the FDA. It was a form letter, but it was evidently aimed at a short list. It said the FDA was proposing codifying Young's Treatment IND policy as a formal regulation, in order to make it easier for the FDA to approve giving experimental drugs to desperately ill people. Young was requesting comments on the proposal.

Delaney was delighted. Maybe this meant Young had been trying to get Treatment IND working, and had been running into bureaucratic difficulty. Maybe that was why ribavirin hadn't been approved. He talked to Jefferson, Corti, and others, and began to plot a positive response. This could be nothing but good news for the whole AIDS community.

Then a friend in New York told him that the National Gay and Lesbian Task Force, the major gay lobbying group in the country, was opposing the new Treatment IND policy.

Delaney couldn't believe it. But a few more calls told him that the Gay Men's Health Crisis in New York, another big AIDS lobby, had sided with the Gay and Lesbian Task Force. So had many other local gay organizations.

In a fury, Delaney called Jeff Levi, executive director of the Gay and Lesbian Task Force. He had never met Levi, who was perhaps the nation's leading spokesman for gay causes. But once Delaney established that the task force really was opposing Treatment IND, he wasted no time lashing into Levi on the phone. "I don't think you're representing people with AIDS," he said. "Who are you representing? Who are you speaking for?"

"This is a scheme by the drug companies to get rid of government regulation," Levi replied.[24] "This is Ronald Reagan trying to deregulate the pharmaceutical industry."

"You're so caught up in liberal Democratic Party politics you can't see where your own interest lies," Delaney said. "Out here in the heartland, people want these drugs. They don't give a shit if it's coming from Reagan or anybody else."

"It's going to dump every kind of quack medicine on us and rob sick people blind. Don't just talk to me. Talk to Ralph Nader, Sidney Wolfe, all the public-interest groups. They're all against this. If they adopt this, it's going to undo twenty years of consumer-protection laws."

"You're just a goddamned gay bureaucrat," Delaney fumed. "People with AIDS are dying because of FDA bureaucrats. We don't need them to die because of gay bureaucrats. People have a right to get these drugs before they die, and you have no right to interfere."

The argument raged until Delaney almost slammed down the phone. More calls showed that AmFAR, People With AIDS, and every other big-name AIDS lobby had gone along with Levi. He was stunned.

He turned to Jefferson. "There's less danger from unproven drugs than from waiting years to get them approved," he said. "We don't have that kind of time. By God, we'll fight!"

The opening salvo came in the April 1987 issue of the Project Inform newsletter, reaching more than ten thousand subscribers.

> In what appears to be a major shift in policy, FDA commissioner Frank E. Young proposed a change in regulations which would allow greatly increased access to experimental treatments for patients with life-threatening illnesses. The new policy would permit drug companies to sell certain experimental medicines to two classes of patients. Slightly different regulations would address (1) patients with "immediately life-threatening diseases" (including advanced AIDS) and (2) "serious illnesses" (examples quoted in the proposal are Alzheimer's disease and multiple sclerosis; many assume that ARC would also qualify).

For six single-spaced pages, Delaney went on to analyze the proposal and the arguments for and against it. Not only should the AIDS community support the new Treatment IND rule as far as it went, Delaney wrote, but the proposed rule needed to go further. The drugs should be available to all HIV-infected people.

He wrote personal letters to board members of national gay organizations. The organizations had said Treatment IND would create profiteering; they wanted the drugs given out free. Unless the companies could charge for the drugs, Delaney argued, "only the richest pharmaceutical companies will be able to work on AIDS treatments. Allowing them to charge makes it possible for smaller companies to be involved. . . . It is often the small companies in any industry which produce the greatest breakthroughs."

There had been complaints that Treatment IND would hurt research because people who could get experimental drugs wouldn't volunteer for placebo-controlled studies. "Our objective is to stay alive, not to be test subjects," he said.

And he wrote a tempered version of all this to Commissioner Young, declaring that Young's proposal, "while perhaps less than ideal, is a striking and important step in the battle against AIDS."

The battle lines were being redrawn. The FDA was being courted as a potential ally. Gay partisans seemed to have become enemies.

Then Jefferson got a call from Larry Kramer, a New York playwright he had met. Kramer had devoted himself to organizing noisy political protests on behalf of those suffering from the disease. His demonstrations, full of his own flamboyance, attracted more attention than his plays had—particularly on television. He had gotten to know Phil Donahue, and appeared on Donahue's daytime talk show.

Kramer said Donahue was doing another show on AIDS, and asked Delaney to appear on it with him. Kramer had been intrigued by news of a "West Coast underground" in illegal drugs; no such organization existed in the East yet.

So Delaney found himself flown to New York, put up in a fancy hotel, picked up by a limo, and whisked into a TV studio ahead of hundreds of mostly gay men lined up outside hoping to sit in the audience. The confrontational and emotional appeals of Kramer and his supporters in the audience dominated the program. They accused various public-health officials of being bigots and murderers.

But Delaney got a chance to describe the many potential treatments that weren't on shelves because they were mired in the testing and approval process. And viewers were urged to call Project Inform's 800 number. Some three thousand did, that week alone. Twice AT&T called Project Inform to say it was shutting down the number because the avalanche of calls was clogging other customers' lines, and that if such calling continued Project Inform would have to upgrade its level of service.

Meanwhile, ABC's *20/20* program approached Delaney, wanting to do a segment on the drug issue. Tom Jefferson drove to Tijuana with the ABC cameras and correspondent for a tour of the drug shops.

It was spring 1987. David Winterhalter had grown sicker. A nerve disease infiltrated his AIDS-weakened immune system and attacked his legs. He went from a cane to crutches to a wheelchair and finally into the hospital.

With Winterhalter disabled, BARIG folded its tent. It was no longer much needed anyway. Desire for ribavirin waned as people heard about the government's devastating attacks on the drug. The rival drug AZT, which health authorities were praising, was approved under the Treatment IND rules and therefore was available. Although AZT, after it was licensed, was far more expensive than ribavirin, users could claim reimbursement from insurance companies because it was FDA-approved; ribavirin was paid for out of pocket. Besides, the peso had continued to fall, and those who still wanted ribavirin could get it for $13 a box in Mexico even without BARIG.

Delaney encouraged Winterhalter to take AZT. He did for a while, mainly to appease Delaney, but it didn't help. Winterhalter's T-cells —the core of his immune response system—were about gone. One day as Delaney visited him in the hospital in Berkeley, Winterhalter announced he had decided to end his life. He had lived by his own hand, growing his own food, flying his own plane, storing his own gasoline, making his own computer. He would not now be cared for.

"I feel good about BARIG," he said. "That was a fitting last act in life. I don't want to be a burden."

"You're no burden," Delaney said, reaching for Winterhalter's hand. "We're ready. We'll have no trouble taking care of you." He pleaded with Winterhalter to keep fighting.

"Shut up," Winterhalter said. "This is my decision, not yours. Don't try to change my mind."

He went home from the hospital in a wheelchair. His parents flew in from the Midwest.

One afternoon Delaney was called to the house. What few belongings there were had been packed away. Winterhalter told Delaney to take a small crate of drugs he had been using, and to distribute them to people who needed them. In the week he had been home from the hospital, he had sold the airplane and chickens by phone from his bed.

And he told Delaney he was going to take a bottle of Seconal. He pointed to a large plastic bag beside him, and said he had instructed his parents that if the pills didn't work within three hours, they were to put the bag over his head until he had stopped breathing.

"We do this on the farm with animals," he said. "There is a time when you put someone out of his misery, and this is the time."

The sun was streaming in through the window onto the bare walls and floor. There were only the bed, the television and VCR, and the nightstand with the bottle of pills, a glass of water, and the plastic bag. Winterhalter's parents came into the room. Winterhalter asked Delaney to hug him goodbye and then leave.

Tears in his eyes, Delaney did so. It was May 16, 1987.

Regrouping after the loss of a friend to AIDS was never easy. It seemed at times like a cruel relay race, one comrade competing and dying, but passing his torch on to the next. For Delaney, such sadness was mollified only by action.

In the week that followed Winterhalter's death, Delaney composed another letter to Commissioner Young at the FDA, tougher than the one he had sent before. This time, he asked for a personal meeting with Young. "We are deeply concerned with your agency's handling of ribavirin," it said. The FDA's reported interpretation of the recent test results seemed flawed and prejudiced. The experiences reported by large numbers of patients contradicted FDA suggestions of possible harm from use of the drug.

THIRTY-FOUR

*T*he Food and Drug Administration was accountable to two committees in the House of Representatives. One, chaired by Representative Ted Weiss of Manhattan, was in charge of checking to make sure that the FDA and other health and education agencies of government are doing their jobs right.

Weiss was a reliable, even doctrinaire supporter of consumer-protection groups and also of political minorities. When a political-minority organization like the National Gay and Lesbian Task Force complained about a consumer-protection matter, Weiss would be first to the barricades. So it was not surprising that in April 1987 Weiss's committee decided to look into FDA boss Frank Young's new Treatment IND proposal.[25]

Young suffered a long day before the committee. "I fear that the new regulations could permit another Thalidomide disaster," Weiss declared in his opening remarks. But because Weiss ran a relatively quiet ship, the hearing didn't attract much interest from reporters. Delaney was unaware of it. In mid-May, when Delaney heard that a Treatment IND regulation had been adopted, he assumed that Young's original proposal had sailed through as planned.

The other committee Frank Young had to worry about was headed by Representative John Dingell of Michigan. That committee was in charge of legislation governing the FDA. Like Weiss, Dingell was big on consumer protection and traditional Democratic Party support groups. But by temperament he was very different from Weiss—loud and idiosyncratic. He loved a juicy scandal. When some bean counter found that the Pentagon had paid $600 for a toilet seat, or $35 for a simple screw nut, it was Dingell who made sure the information reached page one and the network news. His staff was expert at managing leaks and working with reporters.

Dingell's committee also watched over the Securities and Exchange Commission's work policing the marketplace for stocks and bonds. The SEC was investigating the volatility of ICN stock. If a stock scandal could be combined with a drug scandal, Dingell had a double winner. He would lure the press away from any number of wars or celebrity divorce cases to cover it.

Frank Young was still smarting from accusations by Representative Weiss that his Treatment IND proposal meant he was going soft on drug companies. Now, Dingell offered Young the chance to have his armor polished before the public. How could he resist?

On May 28, Delaney was jolted by the televised fireworks before Dingell's subcommittee. No $600 toilet seat ever had a sterner finger pointed at it than Dingell pointed that day at his new national villain: ICN Pharmaceuticals of Costa Mesa, California. Delaney could scarcely believe his eyes and ears.

Dingell began the hearing by announcing that the AIDS crisis was attracting "a number of charlatans, rogues and knaves." He declared that the country was depending on the FDA—not to encourage development of a cure for the disease, but rather to "protect the public, both those who have the disease and those who may acquire it, from being taken advantage of at a time when they are most vulnerable." How well was the FDA combating charlatans, rogues and knaves? To find out, the committee would examine the FDA's handling of "the drug Ribavirin, marketed under the brand name of Virazole by ICN Pharmaceuticals Inc."

Others joined the bandwagon. Dingell's colleague, Representative Ronald L. Wyden of Oregon, spoke of "evidence of questionable conduct and activities by ICN." He said, "Congress must take steps to make sure that AIDS victims are not ripped off by those who look for a quick buck at their expense. . . . Let's make sure that the truth gets out about Ribavirin."

The search for truth that day did not include testimony from any representatives from the company, or any of the scientists from leading university hospitals who had signed highly promising test conclusions on ribavirin. The witnesses consisted only of a doctor from Brooklyn who had complained to the FDA about ICN, and then the phalanx of FDA officials who had worked on the ribavirin case, led by Frank Young himself.

The doctor was Bernard Bihari, head of the Kings County [Brooklyn] Addictive Disease Hospital, which had its share of AIDS patients. He testified that after ribavirin had been approved for the babies' lung disease early in 1986, an ICN salesman had approached him. Bihari didn't treat babies with lung disease. But he said the salesman had told him ICN "had decided that for humanitarian reasons . . . they were interested in making the drug available at cost to physicians who were treating AIDS."

Bihari said he considered this approach "sleazy and illegal." But what really led him to go to the FDA, he said, was the sudden price rise of ribavirin. The "at cost" figure the salesman had given him was triple the price being paid for the drug in Mexico.

"Shortly after that," Bihari testified, "I heard from people I know with AIDS who had been going to Mexico to get Ribavirin [that] the price in Mexican pharmacies had tripled. . . . And when they asked the pharmacies why they were raising the price, the pharmacy said that the ICN affiliate in Mexico had insisted that they raise the price to that level."

This was, of course, the same price rise Martin Delaney and Jim Corti had been shocked by the previous year. Even with the increase, ribavirin cost less than half what it cost to take AZT, which the FDA approved. Nevertheless, Delaney had investigated the cause of the ribavirin price increase—the peso collapse and renewal of ICN's three-year price agreement with the Mexican Government —and Delaney had found a way around it. Dr. Bihari, the only witness Congress and the press heard from, didn't investigate. He said he "assumed" what had happened:

"I assumed that . . . their purpose was to establish a network of physicians through whom they could distribute it . . . and that by getting their Mexican affiliate to raise the price, they would . . . increase the financial value of the network of physicians in the United States. . . . I was furious at what was clear to me was happening, and that ICN was planning to make profits illegally off the backs of people with AIDS. . . . So I called the FDA."[26] (See note for comments from Bihari, and from Dingell's office.)

Dr. Young was brought forward to testify about what the FDA had done. He was dressed all in white. Since coming to the FDA in 1984, Young had revived the custom of wearing white Public Health Service uniforms in public. He looked like a Coast Guard commander.

His testimony began with a boast that his agency was eager to fight AIDS, as evidenced by its approval of AZT for prescription use in record time. The fast action on AZT was achieved "because we were working very extensively with the sponsor [Burroughs Wellcome]," he said.

But when it came to "charlatans, rogues and knaves," Young showed he could be tough. He testified that the ribavirin studies had produced "safety concerns. . . . Major deficiencies have been identified by FDA reviewers." The danger was so great, Young testified, that the FDA was forbidding further studies of ribavirin on HIV patients pending review of new data.

Delaney couldn't believe it. Safety concerns? Major deficiencies? What was Young talking about? Delaney had just been on the phone with the researchers, and they were delighted with the results.

Young went on. The FDA had "concluded that the data did not demonstrate that Ribavirin provided sufficient evidence of therapeutic benefit to patients."

What kind of evidence did Young want? Delaney thought. None of the patients with a full dose of ribavirin had progressed to AIDS; six of those with a partial dose had progressed, and ten of those with no ribavirin had progressed.

Then Young said the FDA had rejected this data because of "the imbalance of the randomization of patients with low T-cell counts." Patients with low T-cell counts were clustered in the placebo group.

In other words, the FDA commissioner was telling Congress and the country, the test was rigged. The placebo group was sicker in the end because it had been sicker to begin with.

Delaney was dazed. All these scientists at Cornell, Harvard, Johns Hopkins, University of Southern California—if Young was right, they had been incompetent at best, corrupt at worst. Their tests were biased. Accidentally? Intentionally? Young didn't say.

Then Dr. Ellen Cooper, the FDA's chief reviewer of AIDS drugs, got more explicit. She had found that 43 patients entered the test with low T-cell counts; 10 had been assigned to the placebo group, 17 to the low-dosage ribavirin group and only 6 to the high-dosage ribavirin group. Of 7 patients with *very* low T-cell counts, 6 were assigned to the placebo group, and 5 progressed to AIDS. She testified that 16 patients who already had AIDS symptoms entered the test in violation of the protocol, and 12 were assigned to the placebo group.

"I concluded [from] the data presented from this study, you could not use it to evaluate efficacy," Dr. Cooper testified.

Then Dr. Lawrence Hauptman, who had also analyzed the data for the FDA, made the critical conclusion. "If you don't count these [sicker] patients, the treatment effect disappears," he testified. "If the randomization process had worked as it ought to have, it's very unlikely that the distribution of patients with T-4 counts less than 20 would have fallen out the way it did. . . . Extremely unlikely."

Congressman Wyden asked the FDA group, "Are you saying that there is the possibility of an intentional bias?"

"I guess you would have to say, whenever randomization fails that that possibility exists," Dr. Cooper said, noting that the data didn't necessarily prove criminality. But she testified that she had recommended an investigation of the M. D. Anderson Hospital in Houston, a study site whose sample was allegedly biased. Dr. Nasim Moledina, an FDA medical officer who reviewed the test data for Dr. Cooper, added that the USC site was also suspect. No one mentioned that doctors from Harvard, Cornell, and Johns Hopkins had also signed off on the studies.

Delaney immediately thought of Dr. Peter N. R. Heseltine of USC and Dr. Peter W. Mansell of M. D. Anderson Hospital. He had gotten to know both scientists over the phone. Neither was named in the testimony, but their colleagues knew very well who they were. They had just been accused before Congress and the country of scientific fraud. They were not there to defend themselves.

"From my view, it's kind of suspicious . . . the disproportionate number of sick people being placed in the placebo group," commented Congressman Dennis Eckart of Ohio.

"You're perfectly correct," replied Dr. Young.

Dr. Cooper also testified that back in December 1986 she had seen preliminary data from the ribavirin test on more seriously ill patients, those already suffering from AIDS-related conditions, or ARC. That study, which came later than the first, had just been completed in the spring of 1987. The researchers had told Delaney that the results were less dramatic than the results on the earlier-stage patients, but were also positive.

But Dr. Cooper testified that, according to the data she had seen, nine deaths had occurred—eight from the patient group taking the maximum dose of ribavirin, one from the group taking placebos. More recent figures showed fourteen deaths from the maximum-dose group, ten from the lesser-dose group, and only seven from the placebo group.

"When you have an imbalance like that," Dr. Cooper testified, "you have to leave open the possibility that the drug may have adversely influenced progression."

Suddenly, the FDA was not just saying that ribavirin was useless in preventing AIDS. The FDA was saying that ribavirin might actually *cause* AIDS! This almost backfired on Young when the congressmen began questioning him on how he could have released this deadly drug for the babies' lung disease. He assured them that tests had proven the drug safe in aerosol use, and that the FDA had made sure that ribavirin prescribed as an aerosol could not easily be converted to any form in which AIDS patients could use it. (So much for the news account of side effects suffered by babies.)

What happened to ICN and the researchers was of secondary importance as far as Delaney was concerned. What mattered most was the fate of ribavirin as a potential help for hundreds of thousands of people stricken with a fatal virus.

Congressman Norman F. Lent of Long island defined the hearing's position on that one. "Now, what does that—I'm a layman and not a physician—that would seem to indicate to the unskilled that the more of this stuff you took, the better your chances were of dying," he said.

"That's what it seems like," testified Dr. Moledina of the FDA.

The next morning, *The New York Times* headline said, "DATA ON AIDS DRUG CALLED MISLEADING / Lawmaker Accuses Company of Bias in Its Test Results After House Testimony." *The Wall Street Journal* headlined, "ICN May Have Pushed Virazole to Fight AIDS. House Panel Data Suggest Firm Tried to Sell Drug Without FDA Approval." And the *Journal* declared, without qualification, "FDA documents released by the subcommittee showed that [ribavirin] was ineffective, and possibly harmful, to AIDS patients." The story said that FDA officials testified that claims for ribavirin's effectiveness against AIDS "aren't true." The price of ICN's stock shares tumbled.

Delaney felt his world caving in. The next morning he and Jefferson met at the Project Inform office.

"What if we've been conned by these people?"

"I can't believe that."

"I've never had any reason to doubt Karl Johnson. He's a scientist."

"If we've been lied to, I'll be pissed as hell."

"It's hard to believe . . . all these doctors, at all these hospitals."

With such serious allegations, they wondered, why hadn't Congress invited the researchers to defend their studies? Or the company its drug?

THIRTY-FIVE

*T*he very next week, June 1 through 5, 1987, the Third International Conference on AIDS was held at the Washington Hilton Hotel. Delaney made it his business to be there. Almost every important AIDS scientist from around the world was on hand.

From the moment Delaney arrived, he sensed the conference was geared toward one thing above all others: the promotion of AZT. The AZT panels were given the largest meeting rooms. AZT was praised everywhere as the single hope for those with HIV.

Still, a meeting room was devoted to a presentation of the two ribavirin studies on June 2. Delaney found himself in a capacity audience as Peter Mansell of M. D. Anderson Hospital in Houston rose to present the first study. There, too, as Mansell stared down from the podium at them, were the FDA officials who had disgraced him the week before, questioning his ethics before Congress. Delaney had called Mansell after the congressional testimony, and knew how angry Mansell was.

Methodically, in scientific language and using slides to present his statistics, Mansell told the long history of ribavirin's study, decked out with all the dull dignity of science. Near the end, Mansell emphasized that he and his partners at the other study sites had analyzed the degree of illness in patients going into the study—including the "apparent discrepancies" the FDA had criticized them for. They had used the Cox Proportionate Hazard Model that had been adopted as a standard by the testing industry.

It was true, he said, that more patients with T-cells below 200—very low—had fallen into the placebo group. But if you isolated the low T-cell patients in each of the groups, the lowest mean T-cell point was in the lower-dose ribavirin group. They were sickest, but did much better than the placebo group.

Then Mansell presented calculations showing that under the standard Cox statistical system, the difference in T-cell counts going into the study did not account for all the difference in result. Nor did chance. The dosage of ribavirin was a "significant independent predictor" of whether the patient would progress to AIDS. In other words, the drug worked.

It was customary after such presentations for there to be a few questions from the audience, usually clarifying some detail about dosage or patient response. But no sooner had Mansell thanked the audience for listening than there was raucous rush of people to the podium. The audience was startled and roused by the unexpected activity.

"Dr. Mansell," a voice called out, "I would like to ask you if you or any of the other researchers have a financial interest in the approval of this drug or the company that makes it."

The room buzzed. Questions like that weren't usually asked at scientific conferences. Mansell, who had presented hundreds of papers over more than twenty years as a research scientist, stammered, obviously stunned. Apparently he didn't understand the implication that he or a relative might hold stock in ICN.

"I . . . think," he said, "that that is a question that should be asked. . . ."

While Mansell stammered, a man in a white uniform grabbed the podium.

"Frank Young, FDA," the man announced. "FDA has had the opportunity to examine these cases in detail, and as we testified at the Dingell hearing last week, we do not have evidence of effectiveness in this study." And he summed up the same points made before Congress, asserting that the patient groups had been biased. "The agency remains interested in receiving data on this drug," Young concluded. "Thank you."

Young was greeted by strong applause from a portion of the audience. It was like a political convention, not a scientific conference, Delaney thought. Mansell was probably the first scientist ever to have his research paper trashed by the head of the Food and Drug Administration from the same podium the scientist was still trying to speak from.

Mansell, having just suffered this denunciation, responded with what little humor he could muster. "I don't think that that's a question, exactly," he said of Young's explosion. Nobody laughed.

Then he said all the patient records were open for examination, and that the FDA so far hadn't come to look at them. He wasn't as forceful as Young, but seemed to be sticking to his guns.

Mansell's remarks brought a burst of applause from the pro-ribavirin section of the audience. But it was a minority. More "questioners" arose. The moderator himself jumped in to say that some patients in the placebo group had become ill suspiciously early. Even the moderator was accusing Mansell of bias.

Mansell's replies were stammering, and cut off by more attacks. His public humiliation became the gossip of the conference. Little was made of the other paper Delaney heard that day. Andrew Vernon of Johns Hopkins presented for the first time in public the results of the second ribavirin study, on the more seriously ill ARC patients. The overall number of deaths in that study had been so small that under the governing Cox Proportionate Hazard Model, you could not say the difference between the ribavirin groups and the placebo group had been statistically significant.

Still, the trend had been in favor of ribavirin. Patients had been only two-thirds as likely to advance to AIDS on ribavirin as on placebo. Delaney buttonholed everyone at the conference he could, arguing that even if the report was statistically inconclusive, it had directly contradicted the testimony of all the FDA doctors before Congress the week before.

Despite what the FDA said, the data showed that patients had *not* been worse off after taking ribavirin. There was *no* evidence suggesting the drug might increase the chance of getting AIDS. Quite the opposite. Patients had been a third *less* likely to develop AIDS and die after taking the drug. But no one seemed able to focus on that.

A few hours later, Delaney, spinning the TV dial in his hotel room, watched Frank Young shoot Peter Mansell's career down in flames on all three network evening news programs. Dan Rather reported that CBS's unnamed sources had disclosed that more people died of AIDS after taking ribavirin than died after taking a placebo.

The potential lifesaver had been saddled with a reputation as a death drug.

THIRTY-SIX

A few weeks after the conference in Washington, Young's office called. The commissioner wanted to meet with Delaney, if Delaney would come to Washington again. What provoked the call? Delaney didn't ask. Maybe it was his support of Young's Treatment IND proposal, or his request to meet with Young over what now seemed a terribly unjust treatment of ribavirin. Maybe it was the cumulative effect of his growing influence in the AIDS community. But a date was set; Delaney would be in Young's office July 28, 1987.

By what was coincidence as far as Delaney knew, ABC's *Nightline* program called about the same time, asking him to participate in a show about the FDA's slowness in acting on AIDS drugs. When *Nightline* learned Delaney would be in Washington to meet Young July 28, the broadcast was set for the night before. And Young was to be on it.

To prep himself, Delaney talked at length by phone to Mansell and Heseltine. Mansell was understandably enraged. He had already gone out on a limb for AIDS. M. D. Anderson was a cancer hospital; Mansell had been treating AIDS patients as medical director of its Institute for Immunological Disorders. Under his leadership, the institute had become independent the previous year, though its doctors remained on the Anderson Hospital staff. It was now the only hospital in the country devoted exclusively to AIDS treatment. Desperate men, basket cases, arrived from all over Texas. Could a few have slipped into the study who were sicker than they were supposed to be? Of course. But willful bias? Mansell was horrified by the charge. Now there was talk that his institute would be closed down by the for-profit corporation that funded and owned it.[27]

Heseltine, who had secure support from USC Medical School administrators, was relatively calm—but no less firm about the results of his study. "Any way you want to look at it," he told Delaney, "there is a drug effect. People on ribavirin who are very sick are likely to get more disease, but only 50 percent of what people of comparable health will get who are on placebo." The drug was dead in the scientific community not because of the trial results but because of FDA manipulation, he insisted. "Cooper and her colleagues testified before the Dingell Committee that we intentionally placed patients who were sicker in the placebo group in order to make the drug look better," he told Delaney. "If she had said that anyplace else, I would have sued that woman's ass for the rest of her life. This was just an outrageous statement."[28]

Now, the FDA was sending an investigator to USC. Heseltine welcomed the chance to clear his name.

From what Heseltine and Mansell said, Delaney figured he had been right about something else, too. The FDA must have deliberately misstated the results of the ARC study. It was still publicizing partial figures from the previous fall that showed more deaths in the ribavirin group, even though final results were now in showing that deaths among the groups were even, and that fewer people on ribavirin had progressed to AIDS.

On the night of July 27, 1987, Delaney met Frank Young in the makeup room at the ABC studio in Washington. Delaney grinned at the sight of Young in his white uniform again, but tried to make the grin seem friendly. Was dress white an effort to project purity or integrity?

As for himself, Delaney had put on a gray suit, blue shirt, and conservative striped tie, and looked ready for a Bank of America training session. He saw Young eye him up and down, and decided Young had been accustomed to gay AIDS activists who dressed in defiantly unconventional clothing, as Larry Kramer did. If Young was expecting another Larry Kramer, he was wrong.

After a few pleasantries, Delaney went right to the point. "I want to talk about the whole issue," he said. "Not just ribavirin, but access to experimental drugs, and the Treatment IND rules and why I think they're failing."

"I think the system's working very, very well," Young said. "You know, the deaths in that last study were greater on the ribavirin side than on the placebo side."

At that, Delaney blew up. "Frank, if you throw that figure out, I am going to call you a goddamned liar in front of twenty million people," he asserted. Delaney was surprised by his own words, but plunged on. "I have the death rate from that study," he said. "Maybe you don't have it yet. But it was equivalent, the people who got the drug and the placebo. You're using old data from a safety-monitoring report early in the study."

Young seemed to freeze.

Delaney softened. "I'll lay off the whole ribavirin argument to-night if you do," he offered. "This isn't the time or place anyway. If we get into that kind of detail, people won't understand it and it will obscure the policy issues."

"Okay," Young said. "As long as you don't pitch the drug, I won't mention it either."

"I'm not here to pitch the drug. I'm here to talk about bigger is-sues."

"Fine."

The program opened with a background report bluntly asserting that "several experimental drugs that prolong life" were caught up in the government's "red tape." And it showed a video of men buying ribavirin at the Regis Farmacia in Tijuana. It said the only FDA-approved drug, AZT, was enormously expensive and owned exclusively by giant Burroughs Wellcome. And it said the govern-ment's testing of experimental drugs was way behind; funds that the National Institutes of Health had authorized for clinical trials were lying around unspent, while promising drugs weren't tested.

The rest of the half hour was turned over to Young and Delaney.

Young began with a stout defense of his agency, saying it was acting on proposed AIDS drugs within 180 days, faster than the FDA had ever acted on anything. "Research may be going slowly," he said. "But there's nothing in the FDA pipeline we're not acting on. We don't do research ourselves."

Delaney agreed that the problem was the entire system of drug testing, of which the FDA was only a part. But he also cited reports from drug companies that "the FDA tied us up. . . . Time and again they point to the FDA as slowing down their progress."

After a commercial break, Delaney and Young were joined by Frank Lilly, chairman of the Department of Genetics of the Albert Einstein College of Medicine, who had just been appointed by President Reagan to his Commission on AIDS. Lilly spoke cautiously, but sided with Delaney. "There is a great problem at NIH" getting drug tests organized, he said. "It's *very* slow."

"We need much more commitment in a lot of areas," Lilly said. "We need—" and he paused long in thought.

"We need a sense of urgency is what we need," Delaney broke in. "And that is what we have not seen from the government up to this point."

That provoked a strong response from Young in defense of the FDA. "Our highest priority, stated in print, is our war on AIDS," he said.

"I beg to differ," Delaney shot back. "If we look at the results, there are a dozen or more drugs that have sat around untested year after year. No one is in charge. No one is leading this effort."

"It takes a while to determine where the leads are," Young said. "Going too rapidly early will lead to tragedies." And he cited suramin—"where a lot of people took a drug that was harmful. We don't want people going off half-cocked and getting hurt," he said.

Delaney decided that getting into specifics on individual drugs would only confuse the audience. "It's the same rhetoric," he said.

Offered a last word, Young pledged, "We will leave no resource unspent to dedicate our lives to bringing drugs forward as rapidly as humanly possible."

"I don't know if it's a guarantee," Delaney said. "But we'll do our darnedest to hold him to that commitment."

As always, there was more to say, but leaving ABC, Delaney felt satisfied he had acquitted himself all right. Young had obviously been to classes in public presentation, and had learned how to reply to a question he didn't want to answer with a speech he had come prepared to give. But Delaney had been to the same classes. On the whole, he felt much more comfortable than he had on *Donahue*.

Suddenly, as he walked toward his hotel, a four-door Honda Accord pulled to the curb and a man motioned for him. Is somebody trying to pick me up? Delaney thought. Then he realized—it was Young.

"Need a lift back to where you're staying?" the commissioner asked. Delaney laughed and climbed in. He'd need his sleep. They were meeting next morning at eight-thirty. Young thanked him for a good, professional discussion on the air, and said he was grateful for Delaney's support on the Treatment IND proposal.

"But you're not living up to it," Delaney said.

"There are differences within the agency over that," Young said as they pulled up to the hotel. "I'll see you in the morning."

When he arrived at the FDA the next morning, Delaney expected to be escorted to Young's office. Instead he was led to a large conference room with a table shaped like a rectangular doughnut, around which were people—lots of them. Young greeted him at the door in his customary whites.

"This is Dr. James Bilstad, my deputy director for biologics research and review . . . Dr. Ellen Cooper, medical reviewer for AIDS drugs . . ." It was the whole FDA high command—the director for drugs, the director for biologics, executive assistants, policy analysts, even the AIDS program director from the National Institutes of Health, the government research laboratories.

Delaney was shaking hand after hand. Then Young was guiding him to a seat next to Young's at the head of the table.

Delaney sat down slowly. My God, he thought. He was in the belly of the beast.

THIRTY-SEVEN

*O*bviously there were going to be major differences. Best to start out nonconfrontationally, Delaney thought. With personal experience.

"One misconception I might be able to clear up," he began, "is your feeling that ICN has been pushing ribavirin as a treatment for AIDS. Much of what the FDA has interpreted as promotional efforts by ICN was in fact initiated by us. It was the government, the Centers for Disease Control, that reported the drug worked on HIV in the test tube. The patients, who had nothing else, tried it and thought it helped them. I have never seen one piece of company literature promoting ribavirin for HIV. In all the dozens of public forums Project Inform has put on, which would be an audience tailor made for ICN, they have never done anything to promote it."

"This fellow Panic has always struck me as a very aggressive promoter," Young said.

"I don't mean to justify all of Panic's behavior," Delaney said. "But ICN has been caught in a squeeze between the pressure from us and other community groups demanding action on the drug and the pressure from you to hold back until you finish your review. We haven't been manipulated. We want the drug."

Delaney told them of talking to Panic and others at ICN, who had emphasized that they didn't know if the drug worked on AIDS. "They were nervous about putting even five million dollars into clinical studies," he said. He looked around the room at his audience. "These don't sound to me like the words of a con man. They said they were reluctant to bet the company's future on this."

The heads nodded, though the only spoken comments were polite and noncommittal. Young looked impressed. But Delaney saw nothing but disbelief in the face of Ellen Cooper, who from all he'd heard was the chief medical decision maker on AIDS drugs. A slender former pediatrician in her late thirties, Cooper's conservative feminine grooming distinguished her from the mix of professorial tweed and white sailor suits favored by her colleagues.

"I don't think you're giving us enough credit," she said finally. "I, for one, was very disappointed we weren't able to approve ribavirin. But it was a matter of the data before us."

"But you continue to quote outmoded data, at least in public," Delaney said. "You testified to Congress about the imbalance of deaths in the ARC study based on early numbers from last December. The final numbers show no imbalance in deaths."

"That's a perfect example," she replied. "You seem to have those numbers, and I don't know how you get them, but they still haven't been submitted to us. ICN never submitted what we asked for. They still haven't."

Delaney found it hard to believe, but Cooper seemed genuinely surprised that he had data and she didn't.

"You seem to want a no-holds-barred deregulation of pharmaceuticals just because there's nothing else available," she went on. "We can't allow that. It's our job to make sure these drugs meet legal standards of safety and efficacy."

"The patient community isn't asking for that at all," Delaney said. "We're not saying there shouldn't be studies, or that there shouldn't be some standard of efficacy. But it needs to be a floating standard, depending on the threat of the disease. The standard of proof for a new headache pill should be different from standards for a fatal disease where there are no effective remedies. You ought to be able to put a drug on the market on conditional approval, to be reevaluated in a year, or only in certain circumstances. You have to start thinking about what might be good for the patient."

And he started recounting the study results again, combining them with some community data and reports he had assembled from private physicians. To his surprise, the doctors seemed genuinely interested, and probed him for details. The doctor from NIH said ICN was cooperating in developing a new protocol, testing ribavirin at higher dosages. Delaney noted that Project Inform had long suggested ribavirin might be more effective in dosages greater than the ones used in the studies.

Then Cooper, too, surprised him by agreeing there might be different interpretations of the ribavirin data. She said she was eager to see how a new panel of statisticians ICN was consulting would assess the results. Delaney said he hoped they would resolve the dispute about the T-cell counts of patients going into the study.

"T-cells are a highly unstable and imprecise measure," Cooper declared, taking Delaney by surprise.

"If that's true," Delaney replied, "then it seems especially unfair for the FDA to attribute the results of the ribavirin study to the T-cells going in, rather than to the effect of the drug. Especially since lives hang in the balance."

Cooper froze.

"That's what I mean about different treatment," Delaney said. "You're asking for all kinds of data, and autopsies, on the people who died in the ribavirin study. But you didn't need them in the AZT trial. The causes of patient deaths in the AZT trial were never verified before you approved AZT. Which is okay. You worry too much about deaths from drugs' being released too early. Nobody ever bothers counting the deaths from drugs that are released too *late*."

He noted that the drug TTPA, which dissolves blood clots, prevented a lot of heart-attack deaths overseas, and at hospitals where it was being tested in the U.S. But emergency crews in the U.S. were banned from using it. "*Why?*" he asked.

"Safety," he was told. Early on the drug had caused fatal brain hemorrhaging in some patients. Everyone agreed that the brain hemorrhaging had been eliminated by lowering the dosage, and Young said the FDA was working on a new review.

"But people a dying of heart attacks every day who could be saved by this drug," Delaney said.

"But you can't say those deaths are our fault."

"To the contrary," Delaney said. "Once you have the suspicion that a drug is going to be helpful then it *is* your fault."

"There's a history of drugs that have been mistakenly approved," Young offered. "We're under real pressure. If we release a drug too early, congressmen like Dingell and Weiss will make our lives miserable."

"Then, doggone it," Delaney said "maybe it's my job to start making Congress responsive when drugs are released too late."

Delaney noticed that no matter how heated the discussions got, Young was unperturbed, even beaming. He seemed pleased that a dialogue with the outside was underway. Delaney remembered what Young had said in the car the night before: "There are differences within the agency." Were Young and his staff divided over how fast drugs should be approved? Young was a political appointee in an antiregulatory administration. The staff was the permanent bureaucracy. Maybe Delaney was giving Young a chance to bring these issues before the staff.

After almost an hour, when the meeting was scheduled to end, Young announced he had to leave for another meeting, but wanted the discussion to continue. He pulled out a speaker box, placed it on the table in front of his chair, and said he would follow the discussion on his car telephone. Then he shook Delaney's hand and left.

Delaney hadn't experienced such a thing before, but the others seemed accustomed to holding discussions with a squawk box in front of the boss's chair.

Delaney brought the topic back to AZT and the licensing advantage it had enjoyed over other drugs. "When there were major side effects in the first AZT studies, you overlooked it. When the blinding of the first AZT study broke down prematurely, you overlooked *that*."

"That was an accident."

"But it still happened," Delaney said. Patients had figured out from blood-work results who was getting drug and who was getting placebo, and the placebo group rebelled. But the study had been accepted by the FDA anyway.

Delaney questioned whether there should even be placebo groups. "It seems damned immoral to give placebos to people with a fatal disease when there's a promising new drug available," Delaney said.

"It may be a promising new drug," Cooper replied, "but it may also be a *dangerous* new drug, or an *ineffective* new drug, and if we don't have a placebo control group, we're never going to know what it is. I know there were problems with the AZT study. But the outcome was so strong it outweighed them."

"If that data had come from ICN instead of Burroughs Wellcome it would have been torn apart," Delaney said.

"Having the National Cancer Institute involved in developing a drug certainly eases its path," Cooper acknowledged. "There are advantages to being well connected in Washington. And to not trying to carry on an adversarial relationship with us. Burroughs Wellcome used people we had worked with before. And the strength of their data just outweighed the other concerns."

The tension was broken by an announcement over the squawk box from Young that he was about to pass CIA headquarters in Langley, Virginia, where radio signals were blocked, and so he would have to go off the air for ten minutes.

When he came back on, Young vowed he would look for ways to help inexperienced companies steer their applications through the FDA approval process more quickly. He pronounced his enthusiasm for the new channel of communication Delaney was providing on issues that disturbed the patient community.

Delaney pledged he would cooperate in keeping the channel open.

The meeting, scheduled for one hour, lasted more than three. It broke up at 11:45 A.M. Delaney left sensing a breakthrough. For the first time, he thought, at least some FDA brass understood that the community's side in the argument was also reasonable.

As soon as he was home, he banged out a letter to Young to summarize on paper what had happened. Among other things, he urged the FDA to resolve the ribavirin controversy publicly, to take the public suspicion off the researchers. He specifically asked that the FDA urge CBS to correct its statement that the drug was harmful. "Lives may well be lost because of what CBS said that day," he wrote.

But as weeks passed there was no FDA response on ribavirin.

Meanwhile, Delaney got a call from a Swedish health worker named Jean Orlef-Morfeldt, who was coming to town and wanted to meet him. Over lunch at the Grand Hyatt on Union Square, Orlef-Morfeldt introduced Delaney to a scientist from a team about to undertake a vast study of isoprinosine and AIDS, with sites in several European countries. Having heard that Donald Abrams had studied isoprinosine, they had been eager to meet with him. They had just come back from Abrams's office. And they were amazed.

Why, they asked Delaney, were Abrams and the FDA so hostile to this drug? All the data they had seen indicated the need for a long-term clinical trial. But the American authorities thought their small, short study was enough to discount the drug. Delaney tried to explain the politics of the situation to them, but wasn't sure he succeeded, considering he really couldn't understand it himself. Like ribavirin, isoprinosine was just made by the wrong manufacturer.

Well, said the visitors, they were going to spend two years testing a thousand people anyway. European countries had a different method of drug testing. After a small test for safety, similar to what the FDA called phase one, the Europeans distributed the drug through hundreds of doctors and awaited their reports. There was less control than in an American test. It was more likely some doctor would mix something up, but the Europeans believed that the larger numbers would overwhelm any errors. Heart and cancer drugs had been tested on tens of thousands of patients, across international borders. That's why many valid drugs came to market sooner in Europe, they said.

Delaney wished them well.

THIRTY-EIGHT

The previous October, 1986, the nursing service Jim Corti worked for had been replaced as contractor of nursing services at Hollywood Community Hospital. He was asked by the hospital to stay on, but chose to take a job he was offered at Midway Hospital, which was opening a special AIDS unit. After all he had been through, it only made sense to concentrate on AIDS patients.

He continued to answer patients' questions. Yes, AZT might be a miracle drug; it was also highly toxic. Some patients said their doctors told them AZT wasn't obtainable. Others were taken off AZT because they couldn't withstand the toxicity. If they asked about alternatives, Corti said to query their doctors about ribavirin and isoprinosine. If they asked further, Corti told them what he knew.

About three weeks after starting the job, he received a warning from the head nurse that several doctors had complained. They didn't want Corti talking about ribavirin or other "unproven" drugs.

He continued to answer questions, being careful to talk factually, expressing as little opinion as possible. Two weeks later, he was confronted by a staff doctor, who told him to "stop talking to patients about modalities other than those practiced in mainstream medicine."

"I don't go running from room to room spreading news about ribavirin," Corti said. "If they ask me, I have to be honest with them."

"Not to my patients, you don't," the doctor said, and walked away.

Three days later, the chief nurse called Corti in again.

"Look, this is how it is," he was told. "You can resign and walk away clean. If you don't, then I'll fire you."

"What are you going to fire me for?"

"For advocating unproven therapies. Advocating that patients use ribavirin."

Corti thought about it a few minutes, and decided he couldn't keep the job and still be effective. He resigned and signed on with a firm that supplied home nurses.

John Upchurch continued to enjoy relatively good health for almost two years after his near death from PCP and simultaneous diagnosis of Kaposi's sarcoma. He had lived more than a year beyond normal life expectancy for an AIDS patient in such a state. He had been taking ribavirin and isoprinosine since leaving the hospital after his recovery, though he knew he was past the stage where they were believed most effective.

Then, in March 1987, he was attacked by bacterial infections. Tests revealed that cancerous lesions were spreading rapidly in his brain. On March 22, he began lapsing into senselessness. Then his thoughts would clear, and he would cry, "Oh, my God, what's happening to me?" He entered St. Vincent's Hospital.

When lucid, he complained of pain. Once, March 26, he asked Corti, at his bedside, "Jimmy, you know how much I love you?"

"John, I think I do," Corti answered.

"No, you don't," Upchurch said. He was crying. He fell asleep. He never said anything again. Over the next two days he would thrash about crying, or sometimes squeeze Corti's hand. Kaposi's lesions began showing up all over his body. When touched he would flinch with pain. He was now where Larry Wardzala had been in 1984.

Upchurch's mother, wrenched and crying, turned to Corti. "How long does he have to go through this?"

"Not very long," Corti said.

As is common with such patients, Upchurch was on a slow morphine intravenous drip in hopes of easing his pain. Corti talked with the medical attendants. The order for morphine was steadily increased.

There was a memorial service. Friends read a eulogy Corti wrote. There were roses, thousands of daffodils, hors d'oeuvres and champagne. At the end, everyone held hands and sang "Auld Lang Syne."

Corti receded from the world after that. He thought about dropping out of the AIDS world. With all the bad publicity, there was less demand for ribavirin. He thought about painting and bicycling, supported by routine nursing work and Upchurch's life-insurance money. He laid plans to go to France for the Tour de France bicycle race in July.

In June, he got some calls from former ribavirin buyers who were interested in a new drug—dextran sulfate. Dextran had been written up in medical journals. In test tubes, it interfered with the virus's ability to attach itself to healthy cells. Word had spread among patients. Some were already buying dextran sulfate from a Santa Monica man named Bob Ring, who insisted on a minimum order of one year's supply, which cost $1,200.

"Sounds like a lot of money up front," Corti told callers. "Try demanding three months' supply. Or just get together with three other buyers and divide a year's supply among yourselves." But he declined their entreaties to get involved.

Just his advice elicited a call from Ring, June 23, 1987, defending his insistence on minimum bulk orders. Ring said he was having the drug made at a small chemical company. But a bodily-absorption problem required a special coating on the drug, and the process was expensive, Ring said. But the drug worked. He implored Corti to stop sowing discord among his customers.

Rather than argue, Corti cut the conversation short and refused to get involved.

He spent six weeks in France. He followed the twenty-four-day bicycle race from start to finish. When he returned home in August, he felt refreshed and ready to grapple again with trouble.

Not much had changed. A good friend was on his deathbed with AIDS. Another friend, Michael Scolaro—despite continuing attacks from AmFAR and the medical establishment for using aggressive therapies—had been appointed director of AIDS research at a major institute associated with St. Vincent's Medical Center.

And Corti's answering machine was overflowing with inquiries about dextran sulfate.

The drug's purveyor, "Bob Ring," had been unmasked. His real name was Rob Springer, and he was claiming amazing results from the drug. Former ribavirin clients were effusive on the phone to Corti, claiming their T-4 counts had rocketed up after they took dextran, and that their skins had cleared of infections. Internal opportunistic infections reportedly diminished also. Springer was telling people that dextran, while not a cure, was the most effective drug yet, including AZT.

But Springer was still requiring large bulk orders—more than many patients could afford. By October, Corti decided to join the fray. He phoned Springer, who, it came out, was about to phone him.

"Goddamn it," Corti began, "people are calling and complaining that they have to buy a whole year's worth."

"And people are calling me because of your badmouthing," Springer said. "I have to sell those large lots to keep the ball in the air. I have to coat fifty kilos at a time. That's about fifty thousand dollars' worth of dextran. Aren't people satisfied with the results?"

"I admit most people are satisfied," Corti said.

"Then can you stop objecting to people about what I'm doing? I've got AIDS myself. Full-blown AIDS. This is my only means of earning a living."

Corti was sympathetic. But there were people who needed treatment and couldn't afford it. He called Delaney. It had been a while, and they had some catching up to do.

"What should we do with this dextran sulfate stuff?" Corti asked.

"I'm hearing a bit about it," Delaney said. "I just don't know."

They had each read articles in prominent journals. The drug had been used safely in Japan for twenty years as a blood thinner for heart and stroke patients. But a recent article in *Lancet* by a Japanese doctor named Ueno said dextran stopped HIV from killing T-cells in the test tube. Ueno's results had been duplicated at the National Cancer Institute in Maryland. Another article, in *Science* magazine, said the drug kept T-cells from clumping, so they couldn't be killed in quantity. Dextran also seemed to work synergistically with AZT, so theoretically a patient taking both could get the same result with a less toxic dose of AZT.

"So how do we get it?" Corti asked.

"An outfit called Ueno Fine Chemicals holds the patent here," Delaney said. "Maybe the same guy who wrote the article. They've applied to the FDA to do a clinical trial next year. Meantime, of course, none of it's getting out."

"This guy Springer seems to have a lock on it down here," Corti said. "He must be bringing it in from somewhere. He sells it out of his apartment in Santa Monica."

"I'm interested," Delaney said.

"Let's not just wait for something to happen."

"Start digging."

As it turned out, someone else had already started digging. Corti got a call from Gil Felts, a West Texan who had bought ribavirin from him. When Felts wanted dextran, Corti had put him onto Springer. Now Felts was flying to Los Angeles for monitoring by Michael Scolaro. He wanted to meet for lunch.

The French Quarter was an open-air restaurant—about fifty tables spread along the sidewalk on Santa Monica Boulevard in West Hollywood. As they sat down, Felts pulled a foil package from his coat.

"This is dextran sulfate," he said.

Corti realized immediately that it was not the same formulation of dextran sulfate Rob Springer was selling.

"So you went to Japan, huh?" Corti asked.

"Yup." Felts spoke in a West Texas drawl. "I can get all I want."

"How long have you been taking this stuff?"

"A few weeks. It started to work almost immediately. Jim, this drug has made me feel better than I have felt in a hell of a long time. I don't know if it's a cure or not, but I sure as hell feel like I can get my day's work done."

"Any—"

"Side effects? Some loose stools. But not bad. I never felt better."

"Sounds great. How much does it cost."

"Seventy-five cents a pill. You take six a day."

Corti's mind started turning the figures: $4.50 a day, times 30 times days times 12 months—"That's even more expensive than Springer's."

"It's in easier-to-take form. And we know it's exactly the same drug Ueno was using in his tests."

"Made by Kowa Pharmaceuticals."

"Yup, Kowa. The same drug. Ueno wants to try to change it where he'd sell it under his own name, but this is the drug they've used in the tests. This is the one that works."

Corti was suspicious about the price. He tried to get Felts to be more specific about his source, so Corti could check it out. But Felts wouldn't say where he got it. He just wanted Corti's network to help him sell his dextran sulfate.

Corti had been to Japan while in the Navy in the 1960s, and had lived part of 1973 in a temple in Kyoto. There was a guy—Harry Kelleher—who had settled in Tokyo and whom he occasionally heard from. Corti called Kelleher. He had copied down the writing from the package Felts had. Could Kelleher scout Tokyo pharmacies for the drug Kowa MDS-300, and call Corti back with prices?

The call came the next day.

"You said your guy wants seventy-five cents a pill?" Kelleher said. "It's only thirty cents."

"Is it difficult to get?"

"It's over-the-counter."

Corti thanked him profusely—and immediately called Delaney.

"It seems rather inexpensive, and it's readily available in the same form Ueno was talking about in his article. I think we ought to move on it."

"Fine," Delaney said. "Do you need any money?"

"I can fund this one myself. It's just an airplane ride, and I know Tokyo."

"I just wish there was more science available. Something that would prove this drug up or down before we commit. But I suppose there isn't."

T H I R T Y - N I N E

On November 12, 1987, Corti took off for Tokyo with $5,000 cash raised from ten desirous buyers, and a change of clothes.

The tourist-assistance booth at the Tokyo bus station hooked him up with a $60-a-night hotel in the business district. The smell of food and flowers pervaded the streets. He flipped open a tourist book a neighbor had given him, and read that "for the gay tourist there is always the East Gate of Shinjuku, with its more than 200 gay bars crammed into a six- to eight-block area." Corti headed straight for it.

Walking the streets, he met an American, who recommended a bar. At the bar, he asked for a hotel recommendation, and was told about the Inabaso Ryokan, a two-story, $30-a-night traditional inn. There were lots of English speakers, and guests slept Japanese-style, on tatamis.

The next morning he checked into the Inabaso, and began looking for pharmacies. The first he tried had never heard of dextran sulfate. The next two knew what it was, but only had about a hundred pills. The pharmacists spoke minimal English, and Corti minimal Japanese, and he was having trouble conveying his desire to buy large lots.

Finally, he found a couple of pharmacies that had large quantities. But for reasons he could not understand, they refused to sell to him.

He tried to contact his friend Kelleher, but now that they were in the same city, Corti couldn't find him. That night he called Scolaro in Los Angeles.

"Michael, I'm in Tokyo. I'm having a terrible time trying to get hold of some dextran. Gil Felts would not give me the name of his pharmacy before I left. Is there any way you can get it out of him?"

"Guess who's right here right now."

"Shit."

The next voice was Felts's. But he still wouldn't yield the name of his contact. He wanted to keep it proprietary.

"Put Scolaro back on," Corti barked. "Michael, this dickhead won't tell me the name of the pharmacy."

"Just a minute," Scolaro replied.

There was a pause of several minutes. Then Scolaro returned, saying, "Jim, Gil wants to talk to you now."

Felts then picked up the phone. "Okay. It's the Mori Pharmacy next to the Fuji Bank near Shinbashi Station." Corti never asked what Scolaro had said, but Felts didn't sound happy.

The next morning Corti put on a plain shirt and tie, and went to the pharmacy. Mori-san and his wife, the owners, proved perfectly hospitable. There were lots of introductions and gestures. Mori-san, in a dark suit and tie, was obviously the business end of the pharmacy and his wife the medical end. They listened carefully, but wouldn't commit to a deal.

"How did you learn about us?" Mori-san wanted to know.

"A person named Gil Felts," Corti replied.

"Who is Mr. Felts?"

"A man from Texas who was here a few weeks ago."

The Moris went off and conferred. Then they returned.

"Ah, yes, we remember Mr. Felts. How much would you like to buy?"

The price was in yen, but came out to thirty-two cents a pill. Corti ordered fifteen thousand pills.

"Very good. We can have them for you tomorrow," Mori-san said. Then he began describing the trip he and his wife had taken the previous summer to Disneyland.

The next evening, Corti had his pills and was on a flight back to the U.S. Thanks to the international date line, he arrived in Los Angeles the morning of the same day he had left.

Within hours, the pills were in the hands of his clients.

Their initial reports were positive. Corti knew some kind of biological activity was going on, if only from the diarrhea they reported. But they also asserted they felt much better.

On December 7, Corti returned to Japan and over four days bought $6,000 worth of pills. He went again over Christmas and bought $10,000 worth. He financed the shipments out of his own pocket, and from buyers. Word about what he was doing spread quickly through the gay community. Through Corti, patients could buy five hundred pills at a time, much less than Springer's minimum order, and at half Springer's price.

Strangers were jamming his phone line again. "I'm a lawyer in San Francisco and a friend of—" Could he get dextran sulfate?

"If you send me down a check," Corti would reply.

He was adding enough to the price of each pill to cover the cost of the trips—about $1,000 per trip—but felt foolish for not tacking any on to cover his other living expenses, particularly his phone bills. As volume went up, he began to cover that, and lower the overall price at the same time. His accounting stayed sloppy. Some people never paid. Some checks bounced. He began asking for cash or certified checks up front, though he didn't always get them.

It didn't matter. The work took his mind off John Upchurch.

The first few trips, he brought the pills through customs in a suitcase without declaring them. But when he mentioned that arrangement to Delaney, the danger became apparent.

"If they decide to look through your bags, they could seize the lot —wipe out a whole shipment," Delaney said.

"You're right. You know what we could do? We could mail it."

Starting with the next trip, Corti began dividing the purchases into individual orders and mailing them from Japan. It cost about $30 a package, but the security was worth it. If one or two packages were waylaid, the rest would get through.

But the need for better security on the U.S. end created a mushrooming operation that in other hands might have threatened security on the Japanese end. Corti chose Room 3 at the Inabaso, on the second floor at the end of the hall. Floor space was measured by the number of tatami mats needed to cover it; his was a five-and-a-half-tatami room with a three-tatami dressing room adjoining. It had large cabinets, perfect for storing the dextran—which was known in Japan as MDS-300. From 15,000 tablets the first trip, he came to ship more than 300,000 tablets in a single visit.

The twenty-two-room inn took in tourists of all nationalities, but was traditional Japanese throughout. Everyone slept on tatami. Doors had real rice-paper fusuma in wooden frames, sliding on wooden tracks. Bathtubs were traditionally square, thirty inches on a side and three feet deep; you washed outside the tub, and soaked only after you were clean.

In such a setting, there was no hiding the fact that Corti was engaged in something other than tourism. Each trip, he would go to a stationery store and buy wrapping papers in every shade of brown, white and gray. He would assemble different kinds of string, twine, and small rope, different kinds of tape and marking pens.

He rose early, before the trash collectors came, and sorted through trash bins, picking out small boxes of different sizes to put the dextran in. He practiced writing in various handwritings. He wanted no one at any American post office or customs station to suppose that all the packages were sent by the same person.

Only Corti's habitual kindness to workaday people, his genuine interest in whomever he met, enabled him to develop such a remarkable operation at the Inabaso without anyone's remarking on it—and blowing his cover. The owner, the manager, and the other guests—the tourists—gave him funny looks when he would enter with bags full of drugs and mailing paraphernalia. But he passed it off cheerfully. He mastered local greetings and courtesies in the Japanese language. No one at the hotel asked him for an explanation, and he gave none. Japanese tradition was not to pry.

Taxis would pull up, the trunk lid would pop open, and Corti would come into the Inabaso carrying two giant-size blue plastic-lined shopping bags filled with the stuff of his trade. The loads got so heavy that he invested in a steel dolly; the manager stored it for him in the basement of the inn when Corti was back in the U.S.

Finally, after many trips, Hakata-san, the young manager, addressed him cautiously: "Corti-san, this time you have a lot of MDS."

Yes, Corti thought, this trip his room was filled so high with dextran boxes that there was hardly room for him to sleep. He decided he couldn't stand the unspoken curiosity anymore. "Hakata," he said, "we've been friends a long time now. Do you know what I'm doing here with all this MDS?"

"No. Do you send it to the U.S.A.?"

"Yes. Do you know what it's for?"

"No, I don't know."

Corti pulled out a clipping from a major Japanese newspaper, *Mainichi Shinbun,* describing the use of dextran sulfate by western-ers to treat AIDS.

Hakata read the article and looked up. "This is a very good cause. Corti-san, you don't look like you have AIDS."

"No, Hakata-san, I don't have AIDS. It's for people I know who are sick."

"Oh, Corti-san. I'm very happy for you."

By early 1988, Corti had to spend several days at the hotel on each trip to process and package the many orders. For customs purposes, each package was labeled dishes, ceramics, slippers, wooden Japa-nese puzzles, or some such item. Hakata was helping him take pack-ages with the hand truck to the small post office three blocks away.

After the second or third time he arrived at the post office with a hundred packages on a dolly cart, a postal official asked him about the unusual shipments.

"I work for a tourist agency," Corti said. "These are gifts the tour-ists are sending home."

Everything was sent registered mail. The official suggested that instead of filling out the paperwork at the post office Corti could take blank forms back to the hotel and do it there. From then on, he came in with the paperwork neatly matched to the packages.

"Oh, Corti-san," the workers would greet him when he came in. The freight bills ran as high as $1,600 a day—a lot of money for a local post office.

The loads increased. The word spread. If he mailed from Tokyo on a Thursday or Friday, the packages would usually be in Los Angeles or San Francisco by the following Tuesday or Wednesday. Some-times packages were a week or two late, but they always came drag-ging in. Some clients wanted dummy recipients to front for them on the U.S. end in order to deflect attention. Corti arranged to send many parcels for such clients to the sister of his recently deceased patient and friend Steven Ingram; she was happy to cooperate.

Among the people showing up at Corti's door to drop off money for dextran deals, two looked familiar. Suddenly he recognized them as the man he had known as Chuck and Chuck's lover, whom Thomas Jefferson had urged him to see more than two years ago. They had been within hours of carrying out a joint suicide pact, the lover sick and Chuck infected. But they had agreed to begin taking ribavirin and isoprinosine, and to see Michael Scolaro. Corti had bumped into them once in Scolaro's office about a year after that.

Now they were at his doorstep, looking fit and reporting good health, both working. They had heard of a new drug that might continue to forestall AIDS, and wanted to try it. Corti put them on his Tokyo mailing list.

FORTY

The first changes Martin Delaney noticed after his *Nightline* appearance in June 1987, were subtle. He was writing a training course in the sale of new payroll services for executives of the First Hawaiian Bank. The bank had expressed delight with programs in negotiating and sales tactics that Delaney had presented for three years running. He was dealing directly with the president of the bank, Walter Dodds. The new training course was to begin in September 1987.

But after the *Nightline* show, Dodds stopped returning his calls. Underlings Delaney spoke to told him, "Oh, yes, we saw you on TV. Everybody saw you. It's being talked about around the bank." Then he was told his project was being postponed. He couldn't get through to Dodds or other contacts.

Just before the *Nightline* appearance, he had been to Hawaii to discuss the job with Dodds and other bank officials. He had quietly mentioned to a vice-president who had been very supportive of his work that the *Honolulu Star-Bulletin* wanted to interview him when he was there, about AIDS issues. The vice-president had told him in no uncertain terms to avoid the interview. "The bank is very conservative about these matters," he was told. And Delaney complied.

Now, suddenly, no senior official of the bank would come on the phone with him. He felt personally affronted, since almost all the executives at the bank had been in his classrooms, and many he considered his friends. Many had told him he was the best training consultant they had ever worked with.

The job never proceeded, and he was never paid for it. Nor was he reimbursed money he had already shelled out to a subcontractor for some materials. Gays he knew in Hawaii told him the bank had a reputation for not hiring any openly gay people.[29] (See note for the bank's response.)

But it wasn't just the bank in Hawaii. Clients stopped calling altogether. He got no more requests from Bank of America, which had been a steady client for years. When he called his contacts at Bank of America, he got friendly conversations, but no work offers.

Until *Nightline*, Delaney was accustomed to annual six-figure billings from his consulting business, which yielded him an executive salary. He had been headed for his biggest year ever in 1987. Then it was as if the work had never been promised. Only a project long underway for Varian Associates continued.

No one had commented over his appearances on local news shows, or on *Donahue*, which aired in the daytime. But after *Nightline* had identified him as a homosexual dealing with AIDS, he had become a pariah in the business world that had provided his living.

Though it hardly compensated for the income shock, he found AIDS work more than enough to occupy him, and more rewarding than the seminars.

Not long after Delaney returned from his meetings with Commissioner Young and other bigwigs at the FDA, someone at ICN suggested that Delaney call Dennis Roth, a Washington, D.C., securities dealer. Roth had pushed ICN stock because of his enthusiasm for ribavirin. As it happened, Delaney had gotten to know Roth back in 1986, when Roth called him after coming across Project Inform newsletters about ribavirin.

Getting back in touch, Delaney learned from Roth that there had been a break in the ribavirin affair. ICN had assembled documentation supporting its claims. Not only that, the documents were said to prove the FDA had willfully deceived the public.

Delaney found Roth furious at the FDA. Roth was convinced ribavirin had been sabotaged by the government. "It goes way beyond AIDS," Roth fumed. "If they allow ICN to put a broad-spectrum antiviral on the market, every big pharmaceutical company in the country will lose sales of cold remedies and a whole slew of other drugs."

Delaney instinctively doubted the existence of a vast drug-industry conspiracy. But something was very wrong.

Delaney's sources at ICN confirmed that a lengthy brief had been compiled. But they said they couldn't send him a copy. ICN was keeping quiet, under orders from its new Wall Street law firm.[30] The lawyers warned that further controversy could interfere with getting the drug licensed, and with a lawsuit ICN had filed against some New York stockbrokers who had allegedly manipulated ICN's stock price.

So Delaney went back to Roth. Roth hadn't been able to lay his hands on the documentation assembled by ICN's law firm, either. But he had learned one secret ICN hadn't disclosed to Delaney. Backed by the FDA, the Justice Department had convened a grand jury to investigate ICN and its chairman Milan Panic on criminal charges of selling ribavirin for use against AIDS without FDA approval!

With that, Delaney thought he had heard everything.

Then the package of documents came in the mail. It bore no return address, but as soon as Delaney saw what it was, he assumed someone inside ICN just hadn't been able to keep the secret any longer.

A twenty-eight-page presentation, prepared by the Wall Street lawyers, was attached to a two-and-a-half-inch pile of supporting documents. Delaney sat down and slowly began to go through it. There was a bibliography of 583 positive articles about ribavirin from scientific journals; some he had read, some he hadn't.

Then came a document he definitely hadn't seen—a 1986 report from the FDA on "New Chemical Entity Approvals," for 1985. "FDA approved 30 chemical entities in 1985," it said, "including three the agency considers to represent important therapeutic gains, 15 representing a modest therapeutic advance, and 12 with little or no therapeutic advantage over existing agents." In the top list—"Important Therapeutic Gain"—along with only two other drugs, was "ribavirin," an "anti-infective."

Then he found copies of letters, as recent as April 1987, from the U.S. Army, seeking FDA approval to use ribavirin in injection form against "epidemic, viral, hemorrhagic fevers" and Lassa fever. These were major health problems in the Persian Gulf, East Asia, Africa, the Caribbean, and other places the Army might be visiting. The letters noted the Army was already using ribavirin against these diseases in aerosol form. A letter from Lieutenant General Quinn H. Becker, the Army Surgeon General, spoke of double-blind placebo-controlled clinical trials underway in China. "It is anticipated that these trials will further prove the effectiveness of Ribavirin," he wrote, adding his anticipation that the Army's "open collaboration will continue into the future."

Turning the pages, Delaney saw familiar scientific articles about the effectiveness of ribavirin in the babies' lung disease, and in the test tube against HIV. There were impressive curricula vitae of the researchers in the HIV tests—the researchers the FDA had publicly accused of possible cheating.

Then came the first two documents that sent a rush of excitement through Delaney. They were previously undisclosed letters from medical professors who had served on the four-person "data, safety and monitoring board" recruited by the FDA to oversee the ribavirin study, just as similar boards oversaw other FDA-approved studies.

One letter, dated February 5, 1987, from Professor Earl E. Shelp, Ph.D., of Baylor University College of Medicine in Houston, was addressed directly to Frank Young. "I write to encourage you to act expeditiously to approve Ribavirin for use by people with HIV infection and LAS," it said. "Clearly the drug is not toxic at a dosage of 800mg. per day. Further, the efficacy of the drug in delaying progression of disease looks quite strong. . . . I encourage the agency to act without further delay."

Another board member, Professor Richard J. Whitley, M.D., of the University of Alabama at Birmingham, had written one letter saying that "both the investigators as well as the sponsors should be congratulated" for the studies, which he called "exciting." Then, apparently having caught wind of the FDA challenges over deaths, Whitley had written again, stressing that his analysis showed "No deaths can be attributed to Ribavirin administration."

Delaney's hands began to tremble as he read. The FDA brass must have had this information long before they torpedoed ribavirin in their congressional testimony and other public appearances in May and June of 1987. They had this information before they publicly labeled the drug ineffective and very possibly dangerous, before they allowed its manufacturer, ICN, to be painted as "charlatans, rogues and knaves." The letters were dated February!

Then Delaney found copies of letters from the Securities and Exchange Commission, dated late December 1986—just before ICN's controversial press conference in January 1987. The letters ordered ICN board chairman Panic to publicly disclose "the current status of the test results of trials of the company's products" before ICN's prospective securities offering could proceed. That is just what Panic had done, and what the FDA called him down for.

Following the SEC letters was a thirty-one-page statement from ICN's resident statistician. With painstaking detail, the company statistician appeared to refute, point by point, the FDA's antagonistic reading of the study data. Even if you excluded the subjects who were sick going into the study, the report said, under the accepted rules of statistics—the Cox statistical model—the superior health of those who took ribavirin could not be explained by chance. It could only be explained by the effectiveness of ribavirin.

Then came four independent statistical analyses, and as he read them Delaney leapt from his chair and began pacing the room.

A three-page assessment from a David Cox of the Department of Mathematics, Imperial College, London, said that while some caution was warranted because the study was relatively small, the FDA was still wrong. To say, as the FDA had, "that the drug clearly does not provide [a therapeutic benefit] would be carrying caution to an almost absurd extreme," Cox wrote. Only the very sickest patients should be dropped from the results, not the great number the FDA wanted dropped. He concluded, "I broadly agree with the [ICN] analysis, which seems extremely thorough and thoughtful."

Joseph L. Fleiss, head of the division of biostatistics at Columbia University's School of Public Health, was even more forceful. He endorsed ICN's analysis as "statistically and scientifically superior" to the FDA's. He said the FDA analysis was "unacceptable and even objectionable." The FDA's decision to leave patients with low T-cell counts out of the study results was, he said, "almost ludicrous" and "possibly disingenuous."

Wilfred J. Dixon, an independent statistician from Los Angeles, wrote a detailed analysis concluding, "There seems to be no evidence that unjustifiable statistical procedures were used" by ICN. He seemed puzzled by the FDA's sudden application of new standards that he said were "too harsh."

And the director of biostatistics at the University of Alabama, Birmingham, also came down heavily on the side of ICN. Its procedures, he said, had adequately discounted the effects of unequal T-cells among the subjects. "I sincerely hope that the FDA will . . . consider an approval for Ribavirin," he concluded.

The experts were unanimous. As Delaney read on, his excitement turned to rage. None of these distinguished assessments had been offered to Congress, the press, or the public. Yet they had all been available. What the FDA had given ribavirin wasn't a hearing. *It was a lynching!* And after banning this valuable drug, the FDA had gone after ICN and the researchers on criminal and ethical charges! These were the people telling AIDS patients what they could or couldn't take to save their lives.

Here, among the documents, were the still unpublicized findings of Bruce Williamson, the investigator the FDA had sent to probe the ethics of the ribavirin study on June 22, 1987, a month *after* the agency smeared the researchers in testimony before Congress and the press and at an international scientific conference. "This was a for-cause inspection," Williamson began, ordered because "certain individuals in the FDA" had "the impression at least that there may have been bias in the study; that patients with lower T-4 counts may have been put on a placebo rather than the study drug, with some intent apparently."

Delaney's temperature rose as he read the determinations of the FDA's own investigator, which the agency hadn't revealed. "I would like to open by saying that I did not find any bias in that regard in the study at all," Williamson declared. "I found the randomization was acceptable. I found no breaking of the code to be able to put patients with any higher or lower counts in any particular study group."

Williamson did say there "may have been a statistical something strange" in the development of AIDS in a few placebo cases. But he said he "would sort of expect" something like that to happen in a study of HIV patients. After reviewing the charts of every patient in the supposedly suspect USC study site, Williamson had found five very low T-cell-count patients: two in the 800-milligram group, two in the 600-milligram group and only one in the placebo group. If anything, the sample had been loaded *against* ribavirin!

Declaring further that there was no unusual clustering of patients with mild disease symptoms either, the FDA investigator proceeded to take his own boss, Frank Young, to task for going public with allegations against ICN without the facts.

Reading further, Delaney discovered that one of the impartial overseers of the study, Professor Shelp of Baylor, had been so upset by the attack on ribavirin that on June 30, 1987, he wrote an impassioned four-page, single-spaced letter to Young's boss, Dr. Robert E. Windom, Assistant Secretary of Health and Human Services in Washington. Shelp had met Windom, formerly of Parkland Hospital in Dallas, back in their native Texas.

Urging the administration to push the FDA to approve ribavirin, Shelp said the drug "conceivably could improve and prolong the lives of hundreds of thousands of people presently infected with HIV but not clinically ill." Saying he was completely satisfied of the drug's safety and impressed with its effectiveness, Shelp declared it was a "great injustice" to continue withholding it from patients.

Delaney stood looking out across the deck at San Francisco Bay, trying to calm himself for the battle ahead. How could this six-pound package of documents not convince any fair-minded person that the FDA had been not merely wrong but morally reprehensibly wrong? And yet none of this information had been made public. To the contrary, the government was pressuring ICN to keep it secret. The company and its chairman faced criminal prosecution and a ban on its drugs. And the hell with the company! People were *dying*!

Delaney went straight to the phone and rang up Dennis Roth, the stockbroker, and started to tell him what he had received.

"I've already got it," Roth said. "It's devastating."

"Peer review is part of the scientific process," Delaney said. "But it doesn't include the commissioner of the FDA running up to the podium and saying you're a crook. There never was any evidence except in Young's mind."

"I know."

"By the way, I noticed one of the statements in the package was from a statistician in England named David Cox. You don't suppose—"

"I don't suppose it, buddy, I found it out," Roth said. "This is *the* Cox—the guy who invented the system."

"The Cox Proportionate Hazard statistical model."

"I'm telling you they went to the guy who invented the system the whole industry relies on to tell what statistics mean. Not only that, this guy Dixon is a major guru, too. And they both endorsed the ribavirin findings. What more do these bastards want?"

"What they *don't* want," Delaney said, "is for a company they consider an enemy to come up with a good AIDS drug."

Roth immediately plunged into a dizzying explanation of how the FDA had distorted the data from the second ribavirin study, on patients who already suffered from the ARC syndrome. Delaney struggled to keep up, as Roth showed that the FDA had counted deaths differently from the way it had counted them in the AZT trial. If you counted deaths the same way, Roth said, "it's the exact opposite of what the FDA said. Patients on ribavirin were only half as likely to die during the study as patients on placebo. For them to present the figures they did—they were just lying."

"Is it possible this stuff didn't get as high as Young and Cooper— that they didn't know?"

"Young maybe. Cooper must have seen it. And if she did, it was her duty to say something to Young."[31] (See note for the comments of Young and Cooper.)

"How are we going to get this out?"

"I'm already writing a draft of a paper," Roth said. "You ought to go over it and fix it up. Project Inform can put this out more effectively than I can."

"I agree. With all the fuss that's already been made about people's motives, this shouldn't come from a stockbroker."

"You'll have a draft on your fax machine by Friday."

"I'm just worried that if they're so determined to block this drug, what we say still won't do any good. But we've got to try."

FORTY-ONE

Days of faxing and phoning between Washington and Sausalito produced a ten-page, single-spaced report with fifteen pages of exhibits. It went out as a memo from Delaney to Congressmen Wyden and Lent, the two who had made the most quotable attacks on ICN the previous spring. Delaney also sent a copy to each other member of the committee.

And he waited for a response.

And waited.

Phone calls brought no congressmen to the phone, and a lack of interest from staff. The hearings were five months old. It was hard to find people on Capitol Hill who even remembered them.[32] (See note for comments of Wyden and Lent.)

"It's not on the agenda anymore," Delaney reported to Roth.

"I know someone whose agenda it goddamned well will be on," Roth replied. "I called the vice-president's office. Bush is supposed to be chairing Reagan's effort to cut government regulation."

"You think we're going to get in to see Bush with this?"

"No, but his chief counsel, Boyden Gray. I assume you're coming to Washington for the big march. I've got an appointment for us with Gray the next day."

On Sunday, October 11, 1987, more than 200,000 people marched through the streets of Washington to protest the government's inaction on AIDS. The next day Delaney and Roth, dressed for business, went through the security check at the Executive Office Building across from the White House.

They entered a big, high-ceilinged, beautifully-paneled office and found themselves shaking hands with Bush's counsel. Gray was a tall, gaunt, and, Delaney thought, Lincolnesque figure. Delaney had been born into a Democratic household and had grown steadily more liberal in his politics as he became exposed to the San Francisco gay scene. He felt a few qualms about offering himself to the most conservative U.S. administration since Coolidge's, to help the Republicans get government off the backs of business. But he was ready to make the most of it. Roth, a trader in biomedical stocks who was furious over the undeserved drubbing he and his clients had just taken on their ICN investments, felt no such reservations.

Gray began by praising the material they had sent him, and explaining that Vice-President Bush had a deep personal interest in the problem. Back in Texas, where Bush went after college to run an oil-drilling business with family money, Bush had a daughter who had contracted leukemia. Bush and his wife heard of experimental drugs that might save their little girl's life, and had tried desperately to gain access to them, Gray said. Despite all the clout of his powerful family, they couldn't. Their daughter died, of a disease that is now curable in most cases. Bush was sympathetic to eliminating impediments to drugs for life-threatening illnesses.

What Bush couldn't understand, Gray said, was why such problems persisted. Frank Young had told them the Treatment IND rule had solved all that.

"The Treatment IND rule is a sham," Delaney said. "And ribavirin is the perfect example." Figuring Gray wouldn't give him much time, he talked quickly, recounting how Treatment IND was originally described and how it developed. He emphasized that the rule affected many drugs and diseases. "It didn't come out the way we hoped. I think it had a lot of trouble from FDA career staffers," he said.

Gray seemed very concerned. "The rule evolved from the vice-president's effort, and I'm his contact with the FDA," Gray said. "This Treatment IND rule was our pride and joy."

"Well, your pride and joy is a lemon," Delaney said. "The system isn't working. You've been sold a bill of goods the same as we have."

"This concerns us very much," Gray said. "We're going to look into it. We've had troubles with the FDA staff in the past, and maybe this isn't so surprising."

Delaney promised to send Gray his file of articles on the problem.

"We will study the matter," Gray said emphatically. "I promise you. And I want you to keep in touch."

Delaney kept his promise, and hoped Gray would do likewise.

Exactly four days later, the FDA produced a hypocritical gesture. Without withdrawing any of its sworn or televised statements about the deadly dangers of ribavirin, or apologizing for them, the agency quietly granted ICN authority to resume clinical trials. After reviewing additional data from the clinical trials reported in January, Young wrote ICN Chairman Panic, "our safety concerns are not of sufficient magnitude to withhold approval of further clinical studies." But he warned Panic not to allow the drug to be used outside the FDA-approved trials. The reason for denying the Treatment IND was gone, but the denial continued.

Delaney continued cranking out newsletters from his laser desktop publishing unit. That October 1987, he published the results of the scaled-down study Joe Brewer had launched of 119 men using ribavirin or a combination of ribavirin and isoprinosine. Remembering their original plans for studies that would meet all the demands of the scientific community, Delaney considered the product a big disappointment. Brewer emphasized its positive results: two-thirds of those in the study asserted subjectively that their rate of deterioration from HIV "slowed, stopped or reversed" while on treatment.

Project Inform's mailing list was now at 35,000, including the counsel to the vice-president. In his writings, Delaney hammered away at the failure of the much-heralded new Treatment IND regulation to provide a single new drug for AIDS patients, despite the fact that ribavirin appeared to have met every criterion announced for the program.

Among his readers was a New York lawyer named Jay Lipner, who had experience with public-interest law in Washington. Lipner had developed AIDS in the spring of 1987. His life limited, he decided to give up his Wall Street practice and devote himself to public-service work. He joined the Lambda Legal Defense Fund, which focused on gay, and particularly AIDS, issues. On hearing his comments about Delaney's work, a mutual friend put them in touch.

Delaney immediately suggested Lipner research the regulations and see if there was any legal basis for the FDA's denials.

Lipner phoned back a few days later. "Have you actually read the Treatment IND regulation?" he asked.

"Well, I thought so," Delaney said.

"When?"

"Back when Young first set it to me for comment."

"That's what I mean. They changed it before they passed it."

Silence.

"You don't believe me." Lipner then talked Delaney through the different published versions of the rule. Young's original proposal had said that experimental drugs could be used to treat life-threatening illnesses unless the evidence indicated that the drug was ineffective or harmful.

"Now look at what's actually in the *Federal Register*," Lipner said. "The way it was adopted, the rule says that Treatment IND should be denied 'if the available scientific evidence, taken as a whole, fails to provide a reasonable basis for concluding that the drug may be effective.' That's proof of efficacy," Lipner went on. "Originally, it was up to the FDA to show why the drug does *not* work. Now, it's up to the company to prove that it *does* work—just like before."

"So Treatment IND is really no change at all," Delaney said.

A slight liberalization, Lipner corrected. A drug could be distributed a little faster after the end of clinical trials, as happened with AZT. But that was it.

"Who made the change?"

"Frank Young must have made it," Lipner said. "Why I don't know. But it hasn't changed the standard of efficacy. It doesn't even say what efficacy is. Efficacy is whatever the commissioner of the FDA says it is."

Delaney felt another blow.

"You know, you didn't use to have to prove efficacy to sell drugs in this country," Lipner went on. The law had required proof of safety and purity. Nothing more. Then, in 1962, there was a scare in Europe over birth defects caused by the drug Thalidomide, which had been sold to women to ease discomfort during pregnancy. Even though Thalidomide was never approved in the U.S., and its problem was not effectiveness but safety, the scare was used to justify sweeping changes in FDA rules. The FDA got a monopoly on how drugs were developed. Long, costly trials to prove effectiveness were mandated. And the number of drugs approved every year dropped to one-third what it had been, Lipner explained.

The result was an oligopoly in the drug business—a tight circle that included the big drug companies, the FDA, and the large academic medical centers that could run the mandated studies. Smaller companies went out of business because they couldn't afford eight or ten years and a quarter of a billion dollars, on average, to test each drug. Ultimately, smaller companies either had to form partnerships with major companies, or sell out to them.

Delaney felt Lipner was giving a long-term context that fit everything Delaney had been seeing for three years. They immediately hit it off. "I just got invited to testify before the President's Commission on AIDS," Delaney told him. "February 20 in New York. You want to come?"

"Sure," Lipner replied.

Meanwhile, the Project Inform newsletter broadcast Lipner's discovery about the Treatment IND language change, under the headline "False Hope: Smoke and Mirrors from the FDA."

A few days later, just before Christmas 1987, Delaney got a call from Tom Jefferson, who had moved back to San Diego that fall and opened a Project Inform–type operation there. Jefferson had recently battled pneumocystis carinii pneumonia—PCP—but seemed to have it under control.

They were chatting about the hotline operation Jefferson had started, when Jefferson exclaimed, "Damn! I've got this rash all over my body. And I've been swelling up all afternoon."

"Tom," Delaney said, "what are you taking for the PCP?"

Jefferson said he had been taking aerosol pentamidine as a preventive, and it had been warding off the disease. But when he moved to San Diego, he had turned for care to the local Veterans Administration hospital because it was free. And the VA hospital wouldn't use a drug that hadn't been approved by the FDA yet.

"So they're giving me this other stuff, Fansidar," Jefferson said.

Delaney blanched. "Drop everything you're doing and get to the hospital," he said, trying to sound grave but not panicky. "Tell them you're having Stevens-Johnson Syndrome. I'm not kidding—you could die from this. It can be treated, but you've got to act right away. The Fansidar doesn't break down in your body for a week, and this allergic reaction will keep going and kill you if you don't treat it immediately."

"Shit!" he said, after Jefferson had promised to head for the hospital and Delaney had slammed the phone down. He explained the situation to Mark Bradley. Intravenous pentamidine was the recognized treatment for PCP. But only recently doctors had discovered that, taken in lower doses as an aerosol, it seemed to prevent recurrences of PCP.

The FDA so far hadn't licensed pentamidine for preventive use. Many doctors, on their own, were converting the liquid form to aerosol and giving it to patients as a preventive. While the FDA deliberated on whether to approve this, some doctors had asked Delaney to help publicize the preventive effects of pentamidine. But at the free government hospital Jefferson was going to, the doctor had administered an alternative drug, Fansidar. Unlike pentamidine, however, Fansidar had a sometimes lethal side effect. Jefferson's doctor either wasn't familiar with it or just didn't see fit to tell Jefferson.

"But you said they can treat it," Bradley said.

"Yeah," Delaney said. "But it takes high-dose prednisone. Steroids. He's already got practically no immune system. The steroids will make him vulnerable to the first infection that comes along. The thing is, pentamidine works better than Fansidar. It's been used by a million people all over the world for forty years. But they wouldn't give it to him because of the goddamned FDA."

On Christmas Day, Jefferson reported from the hospital that he was fine. The syndrome was under control. The big ex-Navy pilot was back in beach-Adonis shape, he bragged.

A few days later, a call came from friends that Jefferson had died of Legionnaire's disease he had probably picked up in the hospital.

"He got it because of the prednisone," Bradley said.

"He got it because they wouldn't give him the drug that would have saved his life," Delaney replied. "Instead they gave him a drug that killed him."

And, he thought, Tom Jefferson was one of the most decent, selfless, capable men he'd ever met.

FORTY-TWO

After what happened to Jefferson, Corti—still busy smuggling dextran sulfate—had to swing into action on pentamidine as well. Patients needed to be able to get the drug even though some doctors wouldn't prescribe it as a preventive because of the FDA ban.

But there was a second issue now, too: price. The manufacturer, Lyphomed, Inc., near Chicago, had charged $20 a vial recently. But when pentamidine's preventive effects were discovered, and the market for the drug mushroomed, the price suddenly leaped to $99. A vial lasted only a few weeks. Patients accused Lyphomed of price gouging, though the company blamed the FDA for refusing to recognize the success of the drug as a preventive, forcing costly new trials.[33] In any event, the FDA's refusal to approve it gave health insurers an excuse not to pay for it. And many patients didn't have medical insurance anyway.

So Corti drove around to various foreign consulates in Los Angeles, and collected phone numbers of pharmacists in countries overseas where pentamidine was sold. He reached some in England who would sell the drug at the equivalent of $35 a vial. Then he found a pharmacist in Frankfurt, Germany, willing to go down to $18 on two-thousand-vial lots. He hopped a plane.

Importing a cheaper form of a licensed drug was a different level of illegality for Corti. It raised different issues from merely bringing in unlicensed drugs. Beyond criminal penalties, he risked a patent-violation suit that might wipe him out. But around the country men like Jefferson were dying for lack of this drug.

On February 20, 1988, Delaney and Lipner waited in the cavernous hearing room in the Metropolitan Life Building in New York for Delaney's turn to testify before the presidential commission. Frank Young and Ellen Cooper were delivering a talk and slide show, arguing that the FDA had been doing a good job, and if it ever hadn't been, Treatment IND had fixed that.

"They are living on another planet," Delaney whispered to Lipner. At perhaps that very moment, Corti was in Frankfurt, picking up a load of pentamidine. Anybody could have seen there was a thirsting underground market for this life-extending drug. But the FDA didn't seem to notice or care.

When the FDA brass had finished assuring the presidential commission that drug marketing in the U.S. was in good hands, Delaney and Lipner were surprised to have Frank Young come up behind them. Young said he knew that Delaney was about to lash into the agency, but bore no hard feelings. He wanted to keep communications open.

Delaney brought up the change in the Treatment IND regulations. Young said he understood their discontent with the change. "But the Pharmaceutical Manufacturers' Association would not live with the original proposal," he said.[34] He asked Delaney to call his office to schedule another meeting on how to improve Treatment IND—and on the back of a business card he scribbled his home telephone number in case Delaney wanted to catch him after hours.

Delaney thanked Young, and said he would be glad to come to Washington again. But when his turn came to speak before the presidential commission, he pulled no punches.

Replying directly to Young's and Cooper's testimony, he said, "They tell you there are no obstacles blocking access to helpful drugs. We have experienced a system in which we are continually denied access to many drugs which have shown promise in early trials.

"They describe a system that is bending over backwards to make drugs available to people in need. We have experienced a system that has denied Treatment IND for drugs with solid Phase I data. We have been denied access to drugs that have passed Phase II placebo-controlled trials to the satisfaction of [government-approved] investigators, drugs that have been proven to the satisfaction of independent world-class experts. We have experienced a system that has delivered a single drug [AZT], which has proven both far more toxic and far less effective than they told us. Yet they continue to spend the vast majority of the federal research dollar developing this drug, while its manufacturer spends nothing and reaps huge profits.

They assure you that a wealth of new Treatment INDs are coming, just around the corner. We have heard that empty promise repeatedly over the past year, but nothing ever comes."

Adopt Treatment IND as it was originally proposed, he told the commission. Or, if efficacy had to be proven, define it. Let it be judged by an independent review board including representatives of the FDA, NIH, private industry, and the AIDS community—not by "one overworked Commissioner of the FDA."

And he called for a national data base on the results of each Treatment IND. Doctors getting the drug would report standardized information, which would then be publicly available.

When he had finished and was leaving the witness chair, two members of the panel approached and asked if they could speak to him in an adjoining room. They questioned him in detail for about two hours. Afterward, one commissioner—Dr. William B. Walsh, founder and president of Project HOPE, a fleet of hospital ships that take medical care to the developing world—stayed behind. Delaney observed to Walsh that the commission had exceeded his expectations, since Admiral James D. Watkins had replaced the original chairman a few months earlier. He suggested that a strong manager like Watkins be placed in charge of the government's whole AIDS effort.

"That's not the way the government works," Walsh said. Then he said that Delaney had been right about the change in the Treatment IND regulation. "I was involved in developing the regulation and evaluating the public comments," he said—and declared that it was the large pharmaceutical manufacturers who got the efficacy rule put back in.

"Why the pharmaceutical houses?" Delaney asked. "Efficacy trials cost them a fortune. You'd think they'd want to relax the regulations as much as we would."

Then Delaney heard Walsh explain that if you're a really big player you don't want the rules relaxed. So long as all those trials are required, only you can play in the club. Treatment IND the way Young originally proposed it would open the door for a lot of smaller companies to get in.[35] (See note for Walsh's contrary account.)

Later, Delaney relayed the conversation to Lipner. "He said the manufacturers forced this on Young," Delaney recalled. "They may dislike the cost of trials, but they dislike the idea of competition even more."

"The FDA could have done whatever it wanted to," Lipner scoffed. The drug companies were just a convenient excuse, he said.

At about the time of the presidential commission testimony, Delaney got a surprising invitation. Donald Abrams, the lead doctor in the AIDS group at San Francisco General Hospital, who had often criticized Delaney in the past, now wanted him to join a committee of lay people that would advise a doctors' consortium Abrams had organized. Delaney agreed, and began traveling periodically to Ward 84 at the hospital to meet with the committee, including Abrams.

In early March 1988, the presidential commission released a report recommending that the federal effort against AIDS mushroom—beginning with $2 billion for treatment programs for intravenous drug users, more subsidy of medical care for AIDS patients, and a doubling of the FDA staff to speed approval of drugs.

The first person quoted in *The New York Times*'s front-page story about the report, in the third paragraph, was Martin Delaney. Delaney's praise for the commission's report was also prominent in *Newsweek*'s coverage. He seemed to have become a leading spokesman for AIDS patients.

But Delaney's liver and neuropathy problems from his hepatitis treatments began acting up again, and at times he was too tired to travel. Jay Lipner went alone to the FDA for the meeting Young had requested over how to improve Treatment IND.

"Young, Cooper, Peck, Bilstad—all the top guys were there," Lipner told Delaney afterward on the phone. "It quickly became confrontational." The FDA officials bragged that the agency had finally given Treatment IND to an experimental AIDS drug—trimetrexate, a new therapy for PCP. Lipner argued that the approval had been only for patients who failed on existing therapies. Other patients wanted it. Besides, the preventive, aerosol pentamidine, still wasn't legally available. When the FDA officials replied with talk about unsatisfactory proof of efficacy, Lipner had snapped back, "So you're just going to let them die, right?" Then Young had suggested that individuals apply to get the drugs under provisions for compassionate use in individual cases, but Cooper and Bilstad had opposed that on the ground there would be too many applications.

"God," Delaney said. "What a mess."

"Cooper was very blunt," Lipner said. "She flat-out stated that if people expect drugs to be released significantly earlier as a result of this regulation, they would be very disappointed. And Young didn't argue with her."

Delaney was just as glad he hadn't gotten into a confrontation with the FDA chiefs himself. He was going to need his FDA contacts.

FORTY-THREE

Corti's trips to import dextran sulfate went smoothly until February 1988. Every ten days to two weeks, he would fly to Tokyo. Before leaving Los Angeles, he would go to the Security Pacific Bank branch at Wilshire and Union, where he would convert the cash and checks people had brought him into American Express traveler's checks, which were worth more than cash in Tokyo. Under the terms of his "value-added checking account," a bank promotion, $10 a month got him unlimited free American Express checks. The bank hadn't figured on a customer like Corti, who was at times converting more than $50,000 a month.

He was impressed by the unusually swift and courteous service the bank provided. Then he learned that the bank gave a bonus each month to employees who sold lots of American Express checks. Whoever waited on Corti usually won.

By this time other dextran buyers had begun arriving in Tokyo, usually after calling Corti to find out where to buy it. One was the lesbian lover of an AIDS-oriented New York City doctor. Though handicapped by deafness, she was in Tokyo buying for the doctor's patients—which impressed Corti no end. She not only took his advice and hung out at the Inabaso, she found other deaf people in Tokyo to pal with, and brought *them* to the Inabaso.

San Francisco patients bought the drug through a lawyer there; after getting Corti's number in Los Angeles, and calling, he began showing up at the Inabaso and buying from Corti's sources. The Inabaso was becoming Dextran Central, Corti thought. When they were in town on the same days, they helped each other wrap packages.

But in February, a package containing five thousand tablets—almost $2,000 worth—was late in arriving at the home of a Chino, California, woman whose brother had died of AIDS, and who had agreed to front for some patients Corti was buying for. Then the FDA wrote her saying it was holding the package. The label listed the contents as a teakettle, the letter said. Instead, the package contained white tablets. Would she please contact the FDA?

Corti immediately called Delaney, who took down the identifying details from the letter the woman had received, and called the FDA officer. Friendly but firm, the officer kept saying, "I have no authority except to follow the regulations as we read them." Delaney asked who in Washington communicated policy to the office. He was given the name of William Schwemmer, the assistant director for regulatory affairs.

He called Schwemmer, identified himself as head of an AIDS organization, and argued that the dextran should be allowed through under liberalized regulations announced two years earlier permitting the importation of a drug for personal use. "I've got a relationship with Frank Young," he explained. "If you need to check my credentials, why don't you call the commissioner and I'll talk to you tomorrow?"

Schwemmer called back the next day saying he had checked with the local office. The problem was mislabeling.

Yes, Delaney said, but people had learned that if the packages were mislabeled they usually got through. If labeled correctly, they would be stopped. Delaney couldn't tell Schwemmer about Corti, whose wholesale smuggling was clearly outside the regulations. Delaney made it sound as if the problem involved only individual patients who were allowed to bring in dextran for their own use.

"You're right," Schwemmer said. Packages labeled "Drugs" were usually held for checking with the FDA, which could take weeks. Customs didn't look at most other packages. "But when they do, if it's not what it says it is, then it gets culled aside. That's what happened with your woman. I'll take care of it."

A week later the package arrived in the woman's mail.

By then, Corti was back in Tokyo. This time, to try to stop the problem, he made sure the packages were at least in part correctly labeled. If the label said "Teakettle," the package contained a teakettle—filled with dextran sulfate tablets. And so on with pots, pans, ceramic dishes, and carved elephants.

But there were more seizures—in Riverside, in Long Beach, in Huntington Beach. Delaney made more calls to Schwemmer, and the packages were released.

Schwemmer insisted he wasn't making any special concessions. "All I'm doing," Schwemmer assured Delaney, "is making sure that all our district offices are following a uniform policy."[36]

Over time, some packages weren't released, but Corti didn't press the cases further, preferring to let sleeping dogs lie. He just factored the cost of lost drugs into the price of his shipments, along with the dollar-yen conversion rate. He also made a practice of bringing ten thousand pills home in his suitcase.

After being bothered enough, Schwemmer suggested that Delaney's friends start following the rules: just identify dextran sulfate on the label instead of saying teakettles, and under Frank Young's ruling about personal use there would be no justification for seizing any parcels. After some cajoling from Delaney, Corti agreed to start labeling the packages accurately. That meant he had to embarrass himself by admitting to all the helpful people at the post office in Tokyo that he hadn't really been sending souvenirs home to tourists all this time. To his relief, they didn't seem to mind.

American authorities weren't so tolerant. When Corti returned home there was a deluge of calls. Almost every package he had sent had been pulled off the customs line and detained. FDA inspectors often took weeks to examine packages, and even then they rejected many.

Schwemmer lamented when Delaney told him the news: "Am I going to have to go out to all these places and show them what to do?"

Not as far as Corti was concerned. The pills were too expensive and too much in demand for such slow procedures. Corti simply resumed mislabeling.

Then a worse problem arose. Suddenly, he couldn't get the drug at all.

Mori, the original supplier, had never been able to handle more than twenty thousand pills in a batch, and so had brought in his wife's brother Arai, who owned a larger pharmacy. But in late March 1988, Arai told Corti that his distributors were refusing to supply the Kowa-brand dextran sulfate in large quantities. Kowa was the brand Dr. Ueno had used in his published studies, and was the preferred brand of Corti's customers. When Corti had tried substituting other brands on a previous trip, the users had complained of much more violent diarrhea.

Corti pleaded.

"Sorry, Corti-san," Arai said. "It won't do any good. It's just not available."

Back at the inn, Corti called Mori and pleaded his case with his original supplier.

"I am very sorry, but I cannot sell you any more," he was told.

"What's going on? We've been doing business for months," Corti said.

"I am very sorry, Corti-san."

The next day Corti made the rounds of pharmacies on the street, buying whatever small lots he could. He tried to stick to the Kowa brand, but picked up some others as well.

Back home, the complaints about diarrhea were immediate—particularly with the alternative brands, but sometimes even with the Kowa brand. Those with the alternative brands felt forced to stop taking the drug.

On his return to Japan, Corti pounded the pavement again, seeking dextran. He was told the distributors would not supply it. At one pharmacy, he lost his temper trying to find out why the curtain had dropped on the dextran supply.

"Get out of my pharmacy," the druggist shouted back at him. "Don't talk to me, get out."

Embarrassed, Corti returned to the pink coin telephone in the lobby of the Inabaso and called Kowa Pharmaceuticals. He reached a Mr. Endo, who said he was in charge of wholesale distribution of drugs to stores. After a polite cat-and-mouse game, Corti asked bluntly, "Why won't you sell us this drug now?"

"Your government has asked that the drug not be sold to Americans," Endo told him. "The American Government told the Japanese Government."

"But who?" Corti demanded, stunned.

"Your FDA."

"Who at the FDA?" Corti tried, again and again.

"Your FDA."

"But I'm in your country. Your laws apply here, not American laws."

"Yes, but you are buying a very large quantity. We know who you are. We were told about you."

Not wanting to lose his temper again, Corti thanked the man.

But the next day, frustrated, he called again, asking the same questions. Who at the FDA told them to cut him off?

"I wish I could help you, but this is what we must do," Endo said. "But, you know, Kowa products are available in other countries besides Japan. If necessary, you may try to obtain it somewhere else."

In desperation, Corti continued to try Tokyo pharmacies. Finally, a druggist told him, "I think I can supply you, but I can't do it from my pharmacy. You need to talk to my father."

The druggist took down the name of the Inabaso. A man appeared there the next day at 3 P.M., the appointed hour. Corti spotted him looking around and made eye contact.

"Are you Dextran Man?" the visitor asked.

Corti smiled. "Yes. Are you from the pharmacy?"

The man motioned him outside to talk. It was snowing.

"I can get you Kowa MDS," the man said right off. "All you want."

"I want a lot."

"How much at a time?"

"A minimum of one hundred thousand tablets."

The man blinked, not expecting so much. "Okay," he said. "But it will be at a premium price."

"How much?"

"Thirty-five cents a pill. And you will need to give gifts to a couple of people."

"Fine," Corti said sarcastically. "How much are the gifts?"

"One hundred fifty thousand yen. About twelve hundred dollars."

"I should receive a discount instead of paying a premium," Corti said. "I'm buying a lot."

"I understand. But you're an American, and it's very difficult for you to buy it here. I have to be very careful when I sell it to you."

"Why is it difficult?" Corti said. "Why do you have to be so careful?"

"I understand there is an agreement between the minister of health in Japan and the American health ministry," the man said. "It cannot be sold to Americans."

"Okay. How soon can you get it?"

"Two days."

"Fine."

"But I need the money first."

"No way!" Corti exploded. "I don't know who you are and I'm not going to give you that kind of money."

The man looked absolutely hurt.

"I'm sorry for insulting you," Corti went on. "It's just not the way I'm accustomed to doing business. I'll give you a twenty-five-percent deposit, and cash for the rest on delivery."

The pickup was arranged in the Roppongi district, next to a Porsche dealership and just down from the Soviet embassy—nowhere near the son's pharmacy. It was another snowy day, unusual for so late in the season, and very cold.

Corti pulled up in a large Mazda taxi, and spotted the man there, seated with a woman in a Datsun delivery truck. Their arms were crossed, and they looked very cold. They were staring at Corti. The man got out and opened the back of the truck.

Corti surveyed the goods. He couldn't count the pills, but was sure there were at least 150,000. Then he counted off the money, in yen, the equivalent of $48,000 for the remainder owed on the pills, plus $1,200 more for the bribes the sellers allegedly had to pay.

The snow was heavy. The man began taking pills out of the van and filling the Mazda taxi—so full that Corti had to sit in the front seat with the driver. When he was finished loading, the man bowed, and shook Corti's hand.

"Thank you," Corti said, bowing back. "We'll need to do it again."

And off he and the driver went for the Inabaso, where packaging materials had been assembled. He carried the pills through the lobby and up the stairs, one box at a time. Hakata-san, the manager, was rolling his eyes.

Corti set to work packaging. He was cold and tired. He had gotten up at four that morning to hear the Lakers game on Armed Forces Radio.

Back in Los Angeles, he immediately called Delaney.

"What the hell is going on!" he snapped. "They're telling me the FDA has ordered the pharmaceutical houses not to sell dextran to Americans."

Two days later, Delaney called back. "It's absolutely not true," he said. "The FDA told me, and I've gone to different sources, not just Schwemmer. They've checked. I believe them."

"You try telling that to the fucking Japanese bureaucrats. If the FDA didn't do it, who did?"

"Nobody in the FDA put the kibosh on this. Get somebody over there to put in writing exactly what he says happened, because I want to push this."

Corti said he'd try. A few days later he was back in Tokyo. Immediately, he tried to repeat the prior deal. But all he got when he went to the pharmacy where the deal had been initiated was a shake of the head. This time there was absolutely no dextran available, regardless of the bribe. He begged for something in writing. He was stonewalled. So it went at every other pharmacy.

By this time, the dextran drought was affecting not only him and his clients but the deaf woman from New York, the lawyer from San Francisco, and groups that had sprung up in Dallas, Fort Lauderdale, Washington, D.C., and other cities around the country. With so many new buyers involved, Corti had actually entertained thoughts of going back to painting. Now there was no dextran for anybody.

He tried Kowa Pharmaceuticals again, and this time was put through to a senior executive named Mr. Ueno—causing some confusion, until he established that this Mr. Ueno was no relation to the Dr. Ueno who had written up dextran sulfate in medical journals. Mr. Ueno volunteered that Dr. Ueno had started his own pharmaceutical house, Ueno Fine Chemicals. Dr. Ueno had agreed to buy all his dextran sulfate from Kowa, repackaging it for sale to the public.

It sounded incestuous. But Corti didn't care what the Japanese did, he just wanted the drug. Mr. Ueno said he couldn't have it. Over and over, Corti pressed for more information about why. The FDA. *Who* at the FDA? No names. Finally Ueno opened a crack.

"The investigator," he said. "The U.S.A. investigator." He would not give names. And he certainly wouldn't put anything in writing.

Nobody was going to put anything in writing, Corti muttered to himself after he hung up. All kinds of mysterious shit was going on here, and if Delaney thought somebody would make a written record of it, he didn't understand the way Tokyo worked.

Furious and discouraged, he headed back to the bar he had found his first evening in Tokyo. Deep into his drink, he was approached by a stranger who persisted in looking at him.

"Are you Dextran Man?" the stranger said.

Corti nodded.

"I know what you want. The Kowa drug can be provided in another country."

"Price?" Corti asked.

"As cheap as you could buy it in Japan." And he gave Corti an address.

There, Corti found a young Japanese exporter who said he dealt in general merchandise—which apparently meant almost anything somebody wanted to buy. Once more Corti heard himself referred to by the comic-book name Dextran Man.

"I can ship it to Hong Kong, Bangkok, or Korea," the young man told him. "You can pick it up there. It's all the same to me, but the best for you is Bangkok because it's the least tax."

"Fine," Corti said. Then he learned that the shipment would take two to three weeks, and that his new friend wanted $1,000 to tide him over, just as a fee. Corti gave him the money. As a gesture, the merchant handed Corti a small amount of the Kowa drug.

In late April, Corti went to Bangkok. The deal was, he paid in greenbacks—$38,000 for 100,000 pills. The trip added $200 to the bargain $700 L.A.-Tokyo air fare he had negotiated. The airlines had responded to fare deregulation during the 1980s by creating a dizzying flurry of deals that were beyond the capacity of most human minds to sort out; Corti had studied United's web of upgrades, downgrades, and off-peaks and learned them.

He was allowed three pieces of luggage, and had calculated exactly what suitcases to bring. His carry-on alone could hold twenty thousand pills. The rest went in the plane's belly with the suitcases. There had been no question but that he had to return to Tokyo to mail the goods. You could not mail packages from a heroin and hash-ish center like Bangkok and expect nine of ten to go through customs unchecked the way packages did from Japan.

He arranged to arrive from Bangkok into Tokyo at about 1 P.M., about an hour before a United plane from the U.S. was due in. He hung around, waiting for the American tourists. When they came, he fell in behind them to go through customs. Asked where he was coming from, he told the Japanese customs man he was arriving from Los Angeles. He and his 100,000 pills were waved straight through.

Would there have been a problem if he hadn't lied? Probably not. But he wasn't taking the chance.

Everything was mailed back from Tokyo safe and sound. Then, coming into Los Angeles with the usual ten thousand pills in his carry-on, he was stopped at customs—the only time that had hap-pened during the dextran runs.

Where had he been?

Like a fool, he later decided, he answered truthfully. "Japan and Thailand."

Schmuck, he told himself. You don't say Thailand.

"What do you do for a living?" the man asked him.

"I'm a writer."

"What do you write about?"

"Bicycle racing. Different sports."

"Could I see a business card?"

Corti gave him a card, which bore only his name and address.

"Who do you write for?"

"*Sports Illustrated.* All of them."

The man wasn't believing a word of it. "I'd like to look in your bag."

And he did, moving aside some dirty socks and underwear, and peering at the rows of boxes of tablets. "What's this?"

Corti looked him in the eye. "It's dextran sulfate. It's medicine for AIDS. I bring it in to help people stay alive."

The inspector was still holding a pair of Corti's undershorts. "AIDS?"

The inspector dropped the shorts, turned to a colleague, and said, "Let this man through." Then, holding his hand away from him, he pivoted and darted into a men's room, apparently to wash. Corti zipped his suitcase, put it back on its cart and rolled it out.

The business with the shorts should have been funny. But Corti was beyond laughing.

FORTY-FOUR

"*T*his is bullshit," Corti screamed at Delaney. "We've been cut off. All I can get out of Kowa is that it's the investigator. The U.S.A. investigator."

"It's got to be Abrams," Delaney said.

"Abrams! How the fuck does Abrams have anything to do with dextran?"

"He's starting a dextran trial at San Francisco General. He's the investigator on the study. Which is ridiculous, because he's been badmouthing dextran for months, saying it doesn't work. But he must have gone over there to Japan. It's the only thing I can figure out. I've been seeing him from time to time at these advisory-committee meetings, and we've got another one coming up. I'm going to press him about it, and go back to the FDA people, too. We've got to find out what's going on."

Bill Schwemmer at the FDA again denied that his office had made any request to the Japanese concerning sales of dextran sulfate, and pledged a new series of inquiries around the agency.

Delaney prepared for a confrontation with Abrams at the next advisory-committee meeting at San Francisco General. What amazed him was that Abrams's reputation around the country was favorable, and growing. Some considered him the most dedicated AIDS researcher in the U.S.

A gay himself, Abrams had grown up in Cleveland and attended Brown University. He had gone to medical school at Stanford, and was attracted by laboratory work against cancer. After graduation, liking northern California, he entered fellowship programs there at the Kaiser Foundation Hospital and then at the University of California/San Francisco, of which San Francisco General Hospital was a part. He was fascinated by the relationship between viruses and cancer, studying under a noted retrovirus researcher, Harold Varmus, who in 1989 would win a Nobel Prize. He moved on to study bone-marrow transplants under another future Nobel Prize winner, Donald Thomas, in Seattle.

Over the radio, in 1981, Abrams heard about an epidemic of a rare form of cancer among gay men. His mind went to work on it. Meanwhile, Dr. Paul Volberding, whom he had gotten to know on one of his fellowships, had taken over as chief oncologist at the U.C./San Francisco hospital complex, and invited Abrams to come with him. There Abrams met Marcus Conant, an older-generation dermatologist, who was among the first to recognize the Kaposi's sarcoma syndrome.

Working with K.S. patients, Abrams was intrigued that they often reported having had swollen lymph glands several years before. He recalled in his early cancer work having met men with swollen glands and night sweats—sure signs of Hodgkin's disease, a form of lymph cancer, he had thought—but who tested negative for Hodgkin's. Then it turned out that patients with a rare form of pneumonia —PCP—had similarly experienced swollen lymph glands several years earlier.

Abrams hadn't known it, but he was piecing together clues of what would become the AIDS epidemic. And when AIDS was discovered, he stayed with it.

But despite Abrams's popularity, and despite his predilection for such playful outfits as pink-striped shirts, blue paisley bow ties, and saddle shoes, Abrams seemed to Delaney to represent everything elitist and wrong about the American medical-research establishment.

When Abrams formed his medical-study consortium on AIDS, some saw it as a sign of his great dedication. Delaney saw it as a power grab that dislodged Abrams's former mentor, Conant. Abrams's consortium gradually replaced the Conant group as the main idea exchange for San Francisco AIDS doctors, though Conant seemed not to mind. Abrams pointed out that the Conant group had been mainly academic, while he, Abrams, was emphasizing the inclusion of doctors from the community.

Abrams said he had established the laymen's advisory committee to the consortium in order to reach out to the community of infected people. But Delaney saw the committee as a paltry bone tossed to patients who were angry over lack of treatment. Patient groups were getting noisier, and being heard. For political reasons Abrams needed to be able to say that he consulted patient representatives. A similar consortium had just formed of AIDS doctors in New York, and it had invited members of the infected communities to join. In contrast, Abrams's advisory community was a separate entity that wouldn't meet with the doctors. Abrams told Delaney he was the only doctor in the consortium who wanted any participation by community members at all.

At meetings, Abrams condemned the unauthorized use of dextran sulfate by patients. If the drug was available on the street, it could contaminate his forthcoming study at the hospital. To Delaney, such complaints were ridiculous. Abrams had already decided that dextran didn't stay in the body long enough to be effective. If Abrams was going to study the drug, Delaney thought, it was for political reasons.[37]

Delaney and another community member accused Abrams in a committee meeting of having blocked the supply of dextran sulfate from Japan. Abrams responded hedgingly, answering questions with questions, then finally denied the allegation.[38] (See this and note 37 for Abrams's account.)

On April 28 and 29, 1988, Delaney was in Washington, invited to testify before Congressman Weiss's subcommittee. He found the mood in Congress improved. Instead of being worried that too many AIDS drugs were being rushed to market, congressmen finally seemed concerned that drug development was not progressing fast enough.

He warned the congressmen not to be taken in by government spokesmen like Frank Young. And he specifically criticized the qualifications of young Ellen Cooper for the job she was doing at the FDA. "I simply cannot believe that she has the depth of experience necessary to pass judgment," he said. "Yet this is the bottleneck through which all AIDS drugs must pass. There is no court of appeal. Dr. Cooper has her way. I don't know of any other situation in the government where there is no accountability."

Again he complained that no one was coordinating an effort to bring new drugs to market in the midst of the crisis. He said the Treatment IND reform had been a sham, and accused the FDA of blocking promising drugs like ribavirin and dextran sulfate.

The next day a top government research scientist, Anthony Fauci, appeared before the committee and made the front page of *The New York Times* with the same charge, that promising drugs were being held up. He called for more funding from Congress. Existing staffs weren't big enough to assign people to shepherd promising drugs through the testing process, he said.

Congresswoman Nancy Pelosi of San Francisco pressed him about dextran sulfate. "Over one thousand people in our community are using it, and I would think that would be a compelling enough reason for you all to study it," she said.

Fauci said protocols to study dextran would be ready in four to six weeks, but that more weeks, or months, would pass before trials were underway. It depended on how quickly the individual study units got the medicine, recruited patients, tested the patients to establish their medical status going into the study, and so forth.

Back in San Francisco after the hearings, Delaney was delighted to find that his friend John James had cornered Abrams for a taped interview for the AIDS newsletter James published. James had obtained what people were saying was a smoking gun.

"As you know, there is a rumor that you were responsible for making it hard for Americans to buy dextran sulfate," James told Abrams. "People assumed you must have called Ueno, and Ueno had a way to get the Japanese companies to stop selling to Americans" to secure exclusive use for Abrams's hospital trial.

Abrams hemmed and hawed evasively. "It's so upsetting to me. . . . How am I so powerful?" Finally, he said, "We're working together, and they realized that the drug was flooding the market. Whatever happened happened, and I don't know how I could have any control over this."

It wasn't quite an admission, but as far as many in the community were concerned, the guilty party had been nailed. Delaney went back to his FDA liaison. "I've checked all around." Schwemmer said, "and nobody in the system [at FDA] has had any contact with the Japanese Government or any of the companies on this issue."

"Will you put that in writing?" Delaney asked.

"Why?"

"I want something to show the Japanese companies so we can start buying this drug again. Something to say the FDA supports the right of Americans to purchase this or any other drug available to Japanese citizens, and that it has in no way asked anyone not to supply this product. There are lives at stake."

Schwemmer sighed.

"And while we're at it," Delaney said, "what about putting a policy in writing once and for all about drug importation? Obviously the guys in the field don't have a clear idea of the policy. That's why I have to keep bothering you every time there's a seizure."

"You're right," Schwemmer said, "maybe it's time. It will have to go to the lawyers."

For weeks, the dialogue dragged on. Delaney and his volunteer lawyers would propose strong wording and the FDA would prune it. Schwemmer acted as a middleman, trying to be agreeable. Corti began waking Delaney with nightly phone calls from Tokyo, cursing and demanding to know where the new statement was. He used the business telephone line, so Delaney had to go stumbling down the hall in the dark at 3 A.M. accumulating minor bruises to get the calls.

Whatever Abrams had said, Kowa was scared to death that none of its other drugs would be approved by the FDA if any dextran got through.

When morning came, Delaney would transfer the pressure Corti was applying to Schwemmer—though he still had to avoid mentioning that a wholesale operation was underway in Tokyo. Schwemmer was folksy and polite. "You've got to be patient with us, we're bureaucrats," he said.

Then he confessed to another problem: "The pharmaceutical manufacturers are having trouble with this," he said. "They're afraid it will create a back channel to get around their pricing structures."

As Delaney had already seen, the companies charged wildly varying prices for the same drug in different countries. They were afraid that legalized importation of drugs bought cheaply abroad would allow entrepreneurs to undercut their higher U.S. prices for the same drugs. Delaney told Schwemmer he would accept wording that banned commercial sale of drugs that got in under the new policy. The drug companies still wouldn't like it, but their only valid complaint would be met.

Finally, June 1, 1988, the letter was ready. Schwemmer, though puzzled by the rush, agreed to fax it that afternoon—on condition that Delaney would keep the new policy secret from the press until the FDA had a chance to announce it on its own.

The letter, addressed to Delaney, said, "The U.S. Food and Drug Administration has not requested any agency of the Government of Japan to restrict sales of dextran sulfate to U.S. citizens traveling to that country. . . . Our view is that U.S. citizens visiting Japan should be allowed to purchase any product legally available in that country to Japanese citizens."

There followed a paragraph warning that the FDA and customs still might search incoming parcels to prevent the commercial distribution of unapproved substances. But it expressly okayed "limited, personal use quantities of dextran sulfate."

Perfect! Delaney knew "personal use" could be interpreted liberally. The FDA wouldn't set a limit, because that might be construed as a dosage recommendation for an unapproved drug.

The fax was relayed to Corti as a prearranged rendezvous at the Hyatt Hotel in Tokyo. Corti decided that the lawyer who was buying dextran with him could most effectively deliver the news to Kowa.

Two days later, the dextran floodgates opened. Japanese distributors drove the price down to twenty-one cents a pill in their competition to get the Americans' business. Two groups from New York

raced to join in, one represented by the deaf lesbian Corti had befriended.

Labels were prepared to accord with the new policy:

> THIS PACKAGE CONTAINS DEXTRAN SULFATE TABLETS FOR PERSONAL
> USE BY THE ADDRESSEE.
> IT IS NOT FOR COMMERCIAL DISTRIBUTION.
> IT IS BEING USED UNDER THE SUPERVISION OF [blank], M.D., TELE-
> PHONE [blank].
> IT DOES NOT POSE A SAFETY RISK.
> THANK YOU FOR ALLOWING THIS TO PASS INTO THE UNITED STATES.

It was the first time since the FDA opened its doors that unapproved drugs could openly be shipped without proof of some individual exception.

On July 23, 1988, Young chose to announce what he'd done—at a
speech before the Second International Lesbian & Gay Health Conference & AIDS Forum in Boston. The hall seated one thousand.
The first three rows were planted with demonstrators from the protest group Act Up, geared for confrontation, wearing costumes with
signs that said, FDA, YOU'RE KILLING ME.

An administration public-relations man started giving Young a
long introduction and was hooted off the stage. Young appeared in
uniform—accompanied, as usual, by Ellen Cooper in tasteful office
clothes and others in uniform. When he was barely into his talk, the
first row of the Act Up contingent got up, approached the stage, and
fell down as if dead. The rest of the group stood up, arms raised,
pointing at their watches.

Young went through his entire speech amidst this display. He
mentioned Delaney and Lipner, but gave no clue that it was they
who had brought about the new policy. Of course, there was no
mention of Jim Corti, who may have contributed most of all to the
new policy, but who had to remain under cover because so many of
his activities were illegal.

A question-and-answer session followed, in which members of the
audience accused Young of being personally responsible for the murder of thousands of people. Segments of the audience interrupted
with chants of "Hey, Hey, FDA, How many people did you kill
today?" Young stood his ground at the podium and answered every
question.

Slowly, the agony and unbridled anger over countless lives lost
was tempered by the knowledge that now, finally, infected persons

might not be stopped from trying to help themselves. Gradually, the crowd reckoned that they might be witnessing a turning point in FDA history. In the end, Young got a standing ovation, even from the Act Up people.

Delaney decided that if it were up to Young things would be much better. He also decided that Young was in many ways a figurehead, who lacked power to make things happen.

The New York Times put Young's announcement on page one the next morning, under the headline "FDA Will Allow AIDS Patients to Import Unapproved Medicines." The same day, the FDA announced in Washington that it was approving human trials of dextran sulfate, a common Japanese drug for twenty years. Delaney was the first person quoted in the *Times* article about the tests, saying they were beginning only because of outside pressure. The tests would be conducted by Dr. Donald Abrams at San Francisco General Hospital, and paid for by Ueno Fine Chemicals of Japan.

F O R T Y - F I V E

As summer turned to fall in 1988, Delaney started getting calls from an aide to George Bush's counsel, Boyden Gray. Time seemed to stand still in Washington—nearly a year had passed since Delaney's meeting in Gray's office. But Gray, as he had promised, was finally leaning on the FDA. With Bush now a presidential candidate, Gray wanted the FDA to reduce the proof of efficacy required before drugs could reach patients with life-threatening illnesses. And he wanted ARC, not just AIDS, defined as a life-threatening illness.

The FDA staff was refusing to budge. It threatened to provoke congressional hearings to persuade the public that Bush wanted to open the gates to quack medicine. After weeks of negotiation, a compromise was reached on October 19, and candidate Bush announced the plan as a triumph of the administration's deregulation policy.

That was an overstatement. Again, the FDA had wriggled out of setting precise standards for judging a drug's efficacy, though it did concede that "the benefits of the drug need to be evaluated in light of the severity of the disease being treated." Many in the gay community condemned the announcement as cheap electioneering.

Delaney was convinced Gray had given the FDA his best shot, and had won a significant though not satisfying victory. And he said so in letters to Gray and some of the skeptics from the gay community. He wrote Jeff Levi at the National Gay and Lesbian Task Force, "As much as I hate to admit it, Bush—not our traditional allies in Congress—is the only one in the last two years who has taken any steps to correct the problem at FDA."

Later, Gray said he had spent more time during the campaign fighting over the FDA regulations than defending Bush in the Iran-Contra controversy. But while Delaney believed Bush and Gray had sincerely tried, he still wondered how much would really change at the FDA.

Eight days after Bush announced the new regulations, the Infectious Diseases Society of America was due for its annual conference, and as luck would have it, the conference that year was at the Bonaventure Hotel in Los Angeles. Delaney was asked to debate patient access to experimental therapy at a plenary session, with more than five thousand leading doctors and medical researchers in attendance. His debate opponent was Dr. Douglas Richman.

Delaney had never met Richman, but knew about him. Now a bigshot in the federal AIDS research bureaucracy (known as the AIDS Clinical Trials Group, funded by the NIH), Richman was known as a traditionalist who opposed relaxing rules to suit the desires of patients. Delaney knew something else about Richman: he had been Tom Jefferson's treating physician at the VA hospital in San Diego when Jefferson was promised a dose of Fansidar. Delaney believed the drug cost Jefferson his life when another drug, though not approved by the FDA, may have protected him.[39] (See note for Richman's contrary account.)

It was far and away the biggest public appearance Delaney had ever made. Recalling his nervousness addressing the Conant group several years earlier, he decided to take a precaution. Before leaving San Francisco, he went to Alan Levin, an iconoclastic local doctor, who had taken an intense interest in AIDS and begun attending Project Inform meetings. Levin gave Delaney a prescription for Inderol, a drug actors use to fight stagefright.

Corti brought several dozen friends to the session for moral support, though he and Delaney took pains to see that there was no heckling or other protest behavior to disrupt the professional tone of the proceedings.

Delaney decided to list, then rebut, the main arguments used by his opponents. He reminded them that the efficacy law had been passed on the false basis of the Thalidomide scare. Thalidomide's problem was safety, not efficacy; no lifesaving potential had been claimed for it. It was a bad analogy.

If an efficacy standard was needed, Delaney said, the current one was unreasonable. "The regulatory mind seems to contend that there are only two options," he told the doctors. "(A) either a drug is fully proven to FDA standards, or (B) there isn't a shred of evidence that it works. Common sense and science alike realize there is often a time during a drug's development when some, but not conclusive, evidence of effectiveness exists," he said. "There are a dozen or more AIDS-related drugs in this stage of development," and he cited Hoffmann-La Roche's ddC and Bristol-Myers's ddI among them. Both drugs were similar to AZT, both were entering second-stage trials, and yet neither was available to patients. Many patients couldn't take AZT; for others, AZT's benefits were wearing off. They needed these new drugs.

"Unknowns will always remain," he said. "The question is, in the final analysis, who should decide which risks are acceptable—the bureaucracy in Washington or the patient whose life is on the line?"

Then, however, Delaney plunged into some new thoughts that had been churning in his mind in recent months. Scientists were concerned that early access to experimental drugs would interfere with clinical studies by reducing the incentive for patients to sign up. There had been considerable argument. Some scientists said free medical care at major institutions would be enough incentive to keep study subjects coming in for trials, even if the drugs were available from doctors. Others disagreed.

Delaney had another idea entirely. From what he had seen, he said, if a disease was fatal, denying patients early access to drugs unless they signed up for a study actually *hindered* scientific experimentation. Letting all patients use these drugs not only wouldn't hurt science, it would *improve* science. Suddenly, his huge audience perked up and began murmuring.

"The real-world AIDS experience," he said, "shows us that the policy of restriction is itself destroying our ability to conduct clinical research. AIDS study centers throughout the nation tell of wide-scale concurrent use of other treatments; frequent cheating, even bribery, to gain entry to studies; mixing of drugs by patients to share and dilute the risk of being on placebo; and rapid dropping out of patients who learn that they are on placebo. . . . Such practices are a direct result of forcing patients to use clinical studies as the only option for treatment. If this trend continues, it will soon be impossible to conduct valid clinical AIDS research in the U.S. Already, serious questions are being raised about the validity of many AIDS trial results."

He pointed to cases of study subjects sharing their dosage with their lovers, unbeknownst to the clinicians. "If patients had other means of obtaining treatment, force-fitting them into clinical studies would be unnecessary," he said. "Volunteers that remained would be more likely to act as pure research subjects, entering studies not solely out of a desperate effort to save their lives."

As he spoke, Delaney felt that wonderful sense of an audience not merely listening but experiencing an awakening. He had hit upon something many of them had thought, but no one had said. He could hear the favorable comments being passed around the room even as he continued talking. When he finished, the applause was enthusiastic—all the more satisfying because he had expected the crowd, like the doctors at the Conant meeting, to oppose him.

For his part, Richman could not have played better into Delaney's hands. He read his prepared remarks, and didn't respond to what Delaney had said. He cited Thalidomide as if Delaney hadn't already addressed it. He cited Laetrile, the old quack cancer cure, as if the doctors didn't know Delaney was talking about drugs that had passed early-stage trials. Richman didn't address the patient-incentive issue Delaney had impressed the audience with. He spoke barely half as long as Delaney had, and received only polite applause.[40] (See note for Richman's account.)

Afterward, it was Delaney whose route off the platform was clogged with doctors waiting to congratulate and question him.

Then, in the back of the room, he spotted a cluster of important government officials: Ellen Cooper, and alongside her Anthony Fauci's deputy Jack Killen, and next to him James Allen, head of the National AIDS Program Office at the Department of Health and Human Services, and some others. The group motioned Delaney over, and they moved to a sitting area away from the main forum. A discussion ensued lasting more than ninety minutes.

Delaney's heart was racing, despite Dr. Levin's stay-calm tablet. Almost everyone was acting as if something important had just occurred. He could scarcely tell who was saying what.

"The way things are going, it's actually damaging the trials."

"It's the exact opposite of what we're trying to accomplish."

Only Cooper held out, taciturn—until Delaney brought up AZT as an example of his point: more patients had signed up for AZT studies after the drug had been licensed than had signed up before.

"That's not fair," she said. "There were no other drugs available, and AZT was very expensive outside the trials."

Delaney just plunged on. "AZT should have been made available after the phase one study," he said. "There was immediate evidence it worked. While the phase two study was going on, limited to three hundred patients, another *five thousand* people died of AIDS."

"We didn't know enough about AZT then," she replied. "You can't pretend they'd all have been saved."

"So what? They'd all have been happy to live another six months," he said. And he was thinking, "Is it up to you to decide, lady?" This was the woman being referred to by some militant gay groups as the "Ice Lady." Now he saw why.

But it was clear to him from the rest of the conversation that Fauci's scientific assistants, and people from the Department of Health and Human Services, were intrigued. He had provoked a new line of thought.

Then he was approached by someone from the prestigious *Journal of Infectious Diseases,* which wanted permission to publish his speech as a paper in the next open issue, which was to be dated March 1989. He agreed immediately.

F O R T Y-S I X

After the FDA's clearance letter was faxed to Tokyo, and dextran sulfate became available again, Jim Corti eased himself out of the business of smuggling it. A network had been established to bring the drug into the U.S. It included a ten-man troupe of Kabuki students from the U.S. whom Corti had met in Tokyo. These were Americans in Japan to study traditional Japanese theater, and they agreed to make monthly buys and ship home parcels. Corti had also made friends with a Taiwanese man, David Chan,[41] whose international-trade business kept him hopping between Asia and southern California; Chan helped coordinate the traffic.

Corti went to France for the month-long bicycle race again. Later in the year, when Japanese suppliers suddenly raised prices, he returned to Tokyo once to help line up new sources, and succeeded in holding the price to nineteen cents a pill.

But dextran was no longer a growing business. Although thousands of patients were using it enthusiastically, the "urge-to-purge" side effect, as the diarrhea came to be called, seemed to increase the longer the drug was taken. Normally, Japanese heart patients took the drug briefly, or in small doses. With Americans now taking higher doses for nearly a year, many were forced to discontinue it because of the diarrhea. Then, Donald Abrams (for the second time) and another FDA-approved researcher at Johns Hopkins reported that dextran sulfate wasn't effective. Much as Abrams had said earlier, the Johns Hopkins researcher reported that dextran didn't stay in the body. Patients who still trusted the government were directed away from the drug.

Delaney thought the Johns Hopkins study in particular was a lot of hokum, based on a faulty method of measuring blood absorption.[42] If the study was right, the Japanese had been using a bogus heart drug for twenty years. Several doctors—including Al Levin, Michael Scolaro, and even Abrams himself—reported rises in T-cell counts for many patients on dextran sulfate, suggesting it might be active. But given the severe diarrhea problems, and with other drugs coming along, Delaney turned his attention elsewhere.

The most talked-about new drugs were ddC (full name: dideoxycytidine), owned by Hoffmann-La Roche, and ddI (full name: dideoxyinosine), owned by Bristol-Myers. Both were antivirals, from a class of chemicals called nucleoside analogs. Ribavirin and AZT were both nucleoside analogs. There were hopes that ddC and ddI would be more potent than either ribavirin or AZT, and less toxic than AZT (though preliminary reports raised the fear of side effects with both new drugs).

Ironically, ddI had been developed in part by ICN, the makers of ribavirin. But ICN had envisioned ddI as an antibiotic. When it didn't work as such, ICN gave up on it without the costly process of securing a patent. So it wound up at a government laboratory. Then along came AIDS. Government scientist Sam Broder at NIH began looking at nucleoside analogs with a fresh eye. Ribavirin still belonged to ICN. But ddI was now on the government's own shelf, as was AZT. So they became the drugs of choice. When AZT seemed to work, and was handed over to Burroughs Wellcome, the government scientists went next to ddI.

After preliminary lab studies showed that ddI had promise against AIDS, the government took sealed bids from drug companies for exclusive development rights under the Orphan Drug Law. ICN put in a bid. But the government chose a big company, Bristol-Myers, to develop and market the drug.

Now, both ddC and ddI were being tested by their respective manufacturers. Neither was commercially available to patients—or were they?

Enter Paul Sergios, who had bought dextran sulfate through Corti. Sergios had moved to Florida, but occasionally called to stay in touch. When he had learned Corti was going to France for the bicycle race in the summer of 1988, he had written, asking Corti to pick up a bovine-thymus drug he was interested in, available from a pharmaceutical company in Milan.

Sergios had been a graphic artist for a corporate public-relations department in Los Angeles. But now he wrote the letter as Dr. Paul Ellis, director of immunology, on the letterhead of "South Florida University." He signed other documents as Dr. Spyros Andropolous of the "Athens Institute of Immunology." Sergios had always struck Corti as wild.[43] But since the thymus promotes T-4 cell growth, the drug idea didn't seem illogical. And since Milan wasn't far off Corti's route, he agreed to investigate.

But the pharmaceutical company wouldn't sell Corti the drug, even for the distinguished director of immunology, Dr. Ellis, without confirming the order on the phone with Dr. Ellis's university. And "South Florida U." wasn't listed in a standard reference guide. To make matters worse, on his way out of the drug company empty-handed, Corti saw two men in the parking lot removing the luggage from his rented Audi 90, having pried open the trunk with a crowbar.

No small physical specimen, Corti dived at them, sending the crowbar flying. He slugged one and kicked the other. But then the first man pulled a gun, even as a crowd began to gather, and the thieves jumped into their own car and drove off with all his clothes. Clutching his camera and shaving kit—all he had retrieved —Corti set about to get himself organized, forgetting about the thymus drug for now.

Months passed, until December 1988, when to Corti's surprise Delaney suggested he give Sergios a call. Sergios—alias Dr. Ellis, alias Dr. Andropolous—didn't fit the typical profile of Delaney's Rolodex entries. But Delaney had been excited by initial reports about ddI, and now word had reached San Francisco that Sergios had his hands on some. Both Delaney and Corti had been besieged by would-be buyers of ddI, and had thought none was available. Corti took on the assignment of squeezing Sergios for his source.

No problem. Sergios gave Corti the name of Dave Wilson, address River Road, Jacksonville, Florida. Several calls put Corti on the phone with Wilson, who said he was in real estate, had come down with ARC, and had begun buying ddI for his own use. He would not tell Corti where he got it. But he sold it for $35 a gram. At a recommended dosage of 750 milligrams a day, the price of a chance for improved health with ddI came to about $800 a month—more than most people could afford.

Buying from Wilson would not only be expensive. As with pentamidine, it would involve Corti in a possible patent violation. Bristol-Myers owned rights to ddI, even though the U.S. taxpayer had paid for its development, and no one else was supposed to sell it.

Corti went back to his potential buyers. "I can get ddI," he told them, "but at quite a price. I'm not going to just send that kind of money to someone I've never met. If a bunch of you will go in on the ticket, I'll go to Jacksonville."

Within a day, eight people had ponied up $7,000 for the trip and, they hoped, the first shipment of ddI. Corti flew into Jacksonville, rented a car, and followed directions to River Road. One look at the neighborhood told him that if Wilson was in real estate, he wasn't just an agent at the local Coldwell Banker. The address led to a Spanish-style stucco manse with a tree-speckled lawn that backed onto the St. Johns River.

"This guy's made a bundle," Corti said to himself.

Then he saw the inside. The opulence reminded him of a scene from the television show *Miami Vice*—hardwood floors trimmed with marble, leather furnishings, and walls painted in muted pastels. With scant introduction, Wilson led him to an upstairs office. He opened a large cabinet, removed a container with several kilos of ddI and began measuring about 200 grams on a sophisticated balance-beam scale.

Corti couldn't help laughing. "Here we are in Florida with a beam scale measuring out a white powder . . ." And Wilson started laughing, too. Corti paid him $7,000 in $100 bills.

It was night. Wilson offered him the spare bedroom, but Corti said he had friends in Tampa he hadn't seen in years, and would be staying with them.

"How'd you get to know Sergios?" Corti asked him.

"Who?"

"Paul, the guy who set me up with you."

"You mean Dr. Ellis?"

Corti laughed. "I don't think his real name's Dr. Ellis."

Wilson laughed. "That's okay. My real name isn't Dave Wilson, either. I'm Dean Shaw."

Corti wondered whether perhaps he should make up another name for himself while they were at it, but decided not to. Instead, he turned to the ddI. "Where is this stuff coming from?" he asked. "Not Bristol-Myers, I assume."

"I can't tell you that," Shaw said.

Corti visited his friends in Tampa, and flew on home.

The initial glowing reports he got from users weren't surprising. It seemed that almost any drug that people started led to comments about how much better they felt. The placebo effect was real. Of course, if a drug could improve the limited time these men had been given to live by their doctors, why not use it? Word spread. Demand was heavy. Corti made several more trips to Jacksonville, then decided to have people deal directly with Shaw by mail.

But $800 a month per person bothered Corti. ddI was becoming known as a "gay, white, rich boy's medicine." Most HIV sufferers couldn't afford to get near it. As weeks passed, the price dropped to $26 a gram. But with people buying ten grams at a time, Corti wanted evidence his clients weren't being ripped off.

"I want to know who you're buying it from and what the price is," he told Shaw on his next visit.

"You know, I'm buying it for myself, too," Shaw said.

"I understand."

Shaw told Corti the source was Raylo Chemical, a company in Edmonton, Alberta, Canada. It turned out that Bristol-Myers's exclusive rights to market the drug in the U.S. covered only human beings. Raylo was authorized to sell it for use on farm animals.

"I told them I have a poultry farm down here," Shaw said. "We are using large quantities of ddI to fend off a chicken virus."

Corti smiled.

"If I can really buy a large quantity, I can get the price down to fourteen or fifteen dollars a gram," Shaw went on. "But I can't always get that."

Back home, Corti called Raylo. From what the sales department said, Corti decided Shaw was telling the truth about prices. The price could drop as low as $6 a gram, but only on huge increments, enough to supply a Frank Perdue–sized chicken farm. But when Corti inquired about buying smaller amounts from the company, he encountered a flurry of suspicious questions—what did Corti want to use it for, and so on. Corti wasn't prepared to answer.

But it was clear other people had tried to buy ddI from Raylo, and the company knew very well why. If Raylo got caught violating Bristol-Myers's monopoly on human-use rights, Raylo might get sued and lose its lucrative business selling ddI for chickens and other critters. On the other hand, Bristol-Myers, in order to secure its monopoly on human-use sales, had to promise the government that it wouldn't make any—until after years of testing and tens of thousands of deaths from AIDS.

Unable to buy from Raylo or Bristol-Myers, Corti hit on another idea—manufacturing ddI himself. Early on in the dextran sulfate episode, when there had been such trouble obtaining dextran in Japan, a friend in the chemical industry in Orange County had suggested trying to make dextran. But because of dextran's peculiar acid-alkaline problems, making it proved trickier than they at first imagined, and they gave up.

Maybe ddI would be easier.

A patient in Boulder, Colorado, who bought from Corti, worked in a chemistry laboratory and said he'd give it a try. At first, the project seemed promising. A related compound, ddA—dideoxyadenosine—was available generically and could be converted into ddI. But the Colorado man tried a batch and reported that the conversion process was prohibitively expensive—$490 to create a mere 100 milligrams.

Corti talked it over with Delaney. The people using ddI reported an increase in T-cells, energy, and weight, a decrease in fevers and night sweats, and a return to normal activity—just what AIDS patients want. But side effects hadn't been checked out. And unless you were selected to participate in the relatively small government-sponsored tests, the drug was extraordinarily expensive.

Meanwhile, Delaney was moving into position to really affect the way the government handled these drugs. He and Corti decided their strategy for 1989 would be to go after the government to force Bristol-Myers to expand its trials and make sure patients could get the drug legally and affordably.

FORTY-SEVEN

Delaney's speech before the Infectious Diseases Society of America attracted the medical community's attention like a five-alarm fire. Speaking invitations poured in from the University of Pittsburgh, Columbia University, and other schools.

A call came from Dr. Robin Weiss of the Institute of Medicine, part of the National Academy of Sciences in Washington. The institute was creating a Roundtable on the Development of Drugs and Vaccines for AIDS, to try to coordinate government and private research, and sponsor scientific conferences. Would Delaney join? Other members were to be Young, government lab chiefs Fauci and Gallo, some university researchers, and some pharmaceutical-industry executives. Delaney jumped at the chance.

Then Fauci's office called, seeking a reprint of the Infectious Diseases society speech. Fauci was both coordinator of the AIDS program at NIH and director of the National Institute of Allergy and Infectious Diseases, one of the National Institutes of Health. Delaney said he'd be delighted to make a photocopy for Fauci.

Not long afterward, the same secretary called and said Fauci was coming to San Francisco to receive an award in January 1989, and would like to spend the rest of the day meeting Delaney and anyone else Delaney thought Fauci ought to meet. Would Delaney like to be his guide for the day? Of course!

Then Fauci himself called.

"I got a copy of your speech," said one of the most powerful scientists in government. "I was really struck by your point about improving the quality of clinical trials by taking the pressure off the patients. That really explains so much of why the studies these days are of such questionable validity—the cheating to get in, people not reporting taking the other drugs they're taking. People are in studies out of a desperate effort to save their lives, not to participate in studies."

Delaney smiled. He felt empowered, knowing he was no longer a voice in the dark.

His home life, however, kept his feet on the ground. Mark Bradley had moved out, then back in, then out again, after some bad scenes. Bradley was a well man, but with a deadly sickness perched on his shoulder, and forced to take personality-bending steroids because of a misguided medical experiment years earlier with suramin; he wondered each day whether that day he would come down with something fatal.

Feeling useless and cooped up in the apartment in Sausalito, his acting career derailed, and with an old history of drug abuse, he sometimes went out and drank heavily. One night he came home in a rage and began ripping Delaney's shirt from around him, screaming, "I'm going to die."

"You drunk!" Delaney cried, throwing him off.

And Bradley was drunk. They exchanged fierce shoves. Bradley tore Delaney's shirt fully away, and headed toward the car again. Delaney wrestled him down on the stairs and pinned him there.

"You're not going anywhere like that," he said.

"You don't understand what it's like," Bradley screamed. "Nobody does."

The stress got to Delaney at one of the community advisory board meetings Abrams had organized. Dr. Merle Sande, head of the Department of Medicine for the hospital and Volberding's and Abrams's boss, was sitting in on the meeting. Ribavirin came up, and Sande casually opined that during the study more people had died on riba-virin than on the placebo.

Delaney had heard this lie once too often. "Are you saying you've done a formal analysis of this data and people did worse on the drug than on the placebo?" His tone was not friendly.

"No, well, I didn't do a formal analysis," Sande said, a bit surprised at the assault. "It's just a general observation here in the hospital."

Delaney blew up. "When you people are questioning our data, you always demand precise statistical analyses. Now you're willing to put this drug down in loose, observational terms." He was nearly screaming. "Have you compared all the sites? I have seen those data analyzed, all the sites, and you're just wrong!"

Everybody including Delaney was startled by the outburst.

When time came for Fauci's day in San Francisco, however, he was ready. Here, at last, was a top-dog establishment scientist who seemed to have an open mind. And Delaney thought he had the perfect issue to achieve Fauci's conversion. The FDA had recently refused to license a drug called ganciclovir, made by Syntex Corpo-ration of Palo Alto. Ganciclovir, while toxic, effectively treated a viral disease known as CMV, which tended to find AIDS patients, blind them with retinitis, and often kill them. Thousands of patients had received ganciclovir under individually granted compassionate-use exclusions, though now that program was threatened by the license refusal.

Meanwhile, another drug against the same disease, foscarnet, a Swedish product, was just entering initial trials and was years away from even an application for FDA licensing. It wasn't yet eligible for compassionate-use distribution. While its efficacy was less certain than ganciclovir's, it had the advantage that a patient could take it simultaneously with AZT; since ganciclovir and AZT both sup-pressed bone marrow in patients, lowering the white blood cell count, they weren't supposed to be taken together.

Delaney had arranged for Fauci to meet three desperately ill AIDS patients who were going blind from CMV retinitis. Driving in from the airport, Delaney casually brought up the licensing denial. Fauci said ganciclovir had seemed like a good drug, and that the AZT problem could be solved by lowering the dose of AZT. That way, the drugs could be taken together. Fauci volunteered that he thought the 1,200-milligram dosage of AZT recommended by the manufacturer, Burroughs Wellcome, and approved by the FDA, was far higher than it needed to be anyway.

Delaney jumped. "That's exactly what *we've* been saying!" he exclaimed. "Several community doctors here saw half their patients dropping off AZT because of the toxicity. So they started giving half doses. And they found that not only at six hundred milligrams, but even with only three-hundred- or four-hundred-milligram doses, they get the same improvements in the blood results and the patients can keep taking the drug."

"We've got a study right now where we're only going to give people three-hundred-milligram doses," Fauci said.

It turned out that Delaney and Fauci shared the suspicion that one reason AZT seemed so toxic was a dosage error. High dosages were a legacy of the government's longtime emphasis on cancer research. Cancer-chemotherapy agents were designed to kill cancer cells; it was assumed that the optimum dose was the maximum that would still let healthy cells survive. So during trials dosage was increased unit by unit until the patient could no longer tolerate the drug being tested. Then the dosage was reduced one unit—one step back from the precipice—and that was deemed the optimum dose.

But the same formula was not necessarily right for a chemical that changed the way the AIDS virus replicated. Agents like AZT (or ribavirin, or ddI) might do their optimum work at doses well below the maximum tolerable. Fauci seemed to share this belief.

"So knowing this," Delaney asked, "how can we keep telling people to take twelve hundred milligrams of this stuff?"

"I can't go out there as head of one institute and say that's what you should do without having a study behind me," Fauci said.

"But in the meantime, you're going to overdose the country on AZT. And the drug is going to look a lot more toxic than it is."

"We have to have the data first," Fauci said.

Delaney told him that a local doctor, Al Levin, was compiling data on his own that had already persuaded him to prescribe only the lower dose.

First stop was a television taping at KPIX-TV. Delaney had provided the interviewer with questions and probable answers—with the proviso that Fauci's schedule at the station would be kept secret to avoid demonstrators. If Act Up protesters found out where Fauci was, they would show up and ruin the experience Delaney had planned—especially at the next stop, the San Francisco Hilton. In a room there, Delaney had already ensconced three sick AIDS patients. Delaney wanted Fauci to be confronted not with the politics but with the humanity of the disease.

Terry Sutton, still in his early thirties, was tall, but gaunt, with dark hollows under his eyes. He had, literally, been pulled from his deathbed, at his own insistence, to meet Fauci. His clothes looked as if they had come from his floor, which they probably had.

"Here I am in the last months of my life," he pleaded. "And I'm trying to save my eyesight. I do not understand how a bureaucrat could sit there in Washington and say what is best for me. They offered me ganciclovir under compassionate use, but I have made up my mind that I don't want it, because I want to continue using AZT. The way you've got it now, I have to take ganciclovir to save my sight, but to do that I have to give up AZT, which I need to save my life. I think it's criminal. I want foscarnet. And I am going to go on fighting to get it no matter what it takes. I know this is going to be the last fight of my life, but that's what I want it to be. Bureaucrats are interfering in my choice."

Delaney could tell by the look on Fauci's face that he was moved. No human being could have remained aloof, he thought. Sutton was angry, as he had a right to be.

Norm Watkins, the next patient, was in pretty much the same shape physically. He walked on crutches. But Watkins was by nature less contentious, more understanding. And he had made a different choice. He wanted the ganciclovir and the AZT, too. "I am willing to trade my bone marrow for my eyesight," he explained to Fauci. But fear of breaking the rules kept doctors from prescribing both.

Delaney wanted Fauci to hear from patients themselves that dual stupidity of not licensing ganciclovir or foscarnet. Foscarnet was being held up by the usual testing roadblocks. The ganciclovir proceedings, Fauci was told, had reached beyond these roadblocks. Thousands of patients had used ganciclovir under special compassionate-use exemptions, and the reports from doctors were unanimous that it worked.

But Ellen Cooper at the FDA, backed by a panel of FDA-appointed physicians who hadn't worked with ganciclovir, was demanding controlled studies before the FDA licensed the drug. Placebo control would mean that a hundred or more patients would be deprived of the drug and willfully condemned to blindness and an earlier death in order to prove that the drug deserved licensing. This was nothing short of unethical, in human if not medical terms, Fauci was told.

When they were done, Delaney summed up with a little talk of his own, trying to provide a transition from the purely emotional to the politically practical.

"I'm moved by what all of you have said," Fauci told them, groping for how to reply. Everyone in the room could see that he was moved. "I really want to help," he added.

Delaney, who prided himself on his professional ability to size up other people's intentions, felt he had gained a real ally. He knew that a lot of other bureaucrats, from either Washington or Wall Street, would be squirming in the seat where Fauci sat, counting the minutes till they were out of the pressure cooker. Fauci had asked to be there. Delaney decided to tell him how to help.

"Do you support the FDA's decision to refuse to license ganciclovir?" Delaney asked bluntly.

There was a pause. "No. It was absolutely wrong," Fauci said.

"Would you say that before a congressional committee?"

There was a longer pause.

"Yes, I would."

"I'll arrange it and let you know the dates."

As they filed out, Delaney extracted another promise: that Fauci would talk to Frank Young to encourage compassionate-use exceptions for foscarnet.

Later, talking about Fauci to his friend John James, the newsletter publisher, Delaney said, "He changed sides for good today. This is a change that will beat Ellen Cooper."

Fauci's award ceremony that evening was crashed by demonstrators. He met with them afterward. When Delaney apologized for what they'd done, Fauci brushed it off. Everything Delaney saw and heard impressed him with Fauci's compassion.

Fauci even called later saying he had intervened to get foscarnet for Terry Sutton. But Sutton refused the personal exception, and demanded access for all patients who wanted it. A few weeks later, Fauci called again saying he thought he had a deal that would please Sutton. Sutton, unfortunately, had died in the interim—leaving behind an angry letter blaming his death on the FDA policy that made him give up AZT.

And once again, Delaney had overestimated Congress. The day after the meeting with Fauci, he had gone to Jay Lipner's friend on Congressman Weiss's subcommittee. He offered some real fireworks if they would hold a hearing on ganciclovir. He promised that Weiss could show, through the testimony of patients and a top government scientist, what happens when the FDA unreasonably withholds a drug.

Lipner's friend, Patsy Fleming, responded stonily, it seemed to him. The congressman was too busy with other issues. There would be no time for more hearings like last year's. No, Delaney could *not* speak to the congressman himself.[44]

He called Lipner. "I thought I sensed a turn-around last year," he said. "That they were going to start pushing for us."

"They're delighted to look like they're supporting us as long as it doesn't go against their other constituencies," Lipner said. "But they're not going to turn around and push the FDA to license drugs faster. Ganciclovir is precisely what they don't want to hear about."

Delaney then went to Nancy Pelosi, the San Francisco congresswoman. She was more sympathetic, but told Delaney she had no relevant subcommittee. If not Weiss or Dingell, she said, the only other congressman who might be able to tell the ganciclovir story publicly was Henry Waxman of Los Angeles, who headed the subcommittee on health.

Waxman's office said, yes, the congressman might hold some hearings over the summer. Maybe then . . . But it was still January.

F O R T Y - E I G H T

The first meeting of the Institute of Medicine Roundtable was in February 1989, in a large formal conference room at the main building of the National Academy of Sciences on Constitution Avenue in Washington. The prestigious cast of characters Delaney had expected was there, except for one. Ellen Cooper apparently hadn't been invited.

Delaney recalled being told a few days earlier that Cooper had been brought to tears by Act Up demonstrators at a speech she had given in New York. The issue had been ganciclovir. The demonstrators had interrupted her with chants of "Murderer, murderer . . ." That was unfair. But maybe it would make Cooper begin to better appreciate the human effect of her decisions.

The meeting began with a round robin in which each member was asked to say briefly what problems the roundtable should address. The first few statements weren't memorable. People were politely testing the water. At his turn, Delaney made his usual points as briefly and politely as he knew how. Then came Fauci's turn.

"I've been going through a change of thinking on this," Fauci said. "I am now convinced that drugs can be distributed early to patients who might benefit from them without interfering with clinical trials. We've got to come up with a mechanism to do it."

Delaney froze. It was one thing for Fauci to stroke Delaney on the phone and say he liked something Delaney had said. It was another thing for Fauci to repeat the sentiments in front of high-level officials to whom he was accountable for every word. Was this a major turning point?

Delaney didn't have to wait long to find out. Frank Young's turn came, and the FDA boss jumped immediately onto the bandwagon.

"I very much agree with that," Young said. "The time is right to provide some more-compassionate system. I can't say how strongly I agree with what Dr. Fauci has said."

When everyone at the table had spoken, no one had disagreed. It truly seemed a landmark.

The talks continued all day, and victories kept falling into Delaney's lap, as if the issues had never been contested. The chief business on the day's agenda was to pick a topic for the group's first scientific conference. A consensus quickly formed around one of Delaney's pet causes—the issue known to scientists as "surrogate markers."

So far, the FDA had placed no value on the ability of an AIDS drug to improve physical well-being. In order to get an AIDS drug licensed, the manufacturer had to demonstrate that the drug improved human survival. This added years and millions of dollars to the testing process. It also often condemned a large placebo group to prove a point by dying without treatment.

Delaney had argued for years that improved T-cell counts or a reduction in symptoms was proof enough of a drug's efficacy. On that basis, isoprinosine, let alone ribavirin, would have been licensed. Companies would have been encouraged to test other drugs that could meet this standard, and some might have been licensed. But Ellen Cooper, with Frank Young behind her, had insisted that only death—and its opposite, longevity—should be the standard by which an AIDS drug was judged.

Suddenly, in Cooper's absence—after years of unsuccessful debate—a consensus formed. A conference would be held to consider a substitute for the longevity standard—a "surrogate marker," such as T-cell counts or the frequency of infection. If the conference was successful, the new alternative indicator might determine very quickly if a drug worked. Delaney's only dissatisfaction was that the conference couldn't be scheduled until the following September, hardly the kind of crisis pace he wanted. But for now it was amazing enough just to see government move in the right direction.

The day was split by a buffet lunch, and Delaney found himself eating and conversing pleasantly with Frank Young. The war isn't over, Delaney thought. But it's now clear we're going to win it.

Eager to pick up on the momentum, Delaney approached NIH and FDA officials between sessions, and arranged to meet a few weeks later to discuss the ganciclovir problem. Lipner would come, and bring two New York doctors he knew who had extensive success treating CMV retinitis with ganciclovir.

By the appointed day, however, bureaucratic gridlock had set in again. Two separate meetings were required because Fauci's staff from NIH and the FDA staff would not meet with each other. They all worked for the same department—Health and Human Services— of the same government. But they reported to rival bosses, and the command chains didn't mix. That alone spoke volumes to Delaney about the federal government's AIDS effort. Fauci's deputy, Jack Killen, recognizing the snarl, at least agreed to provide his meeting rooms for both meetings as a logistical help.

With Fauci's staff present first, the New York doctors presented the case for licensing ganciclovir. To every doctor who had used it, they said, the matter was quite simple. Before this drug, all patients with CMV retinitis went blind; with this drug, they didn't. There were thousands of cases. What more did the government want? If the FDA forced a placebo-controlled study, thousands of people would be condemned to unnecessary blindness.

But it quickly became clear that the argument wasn't with NIH. Fauci and his staffers were already convinced. The problem, Killen explained, was that the manufacturer, Syntex, had been so confident ganciclovir would be approved that it hadn't bothered assembling all the data it could have. No one expected that the FDA advisory committee would reject the data from compassionate-use experience on the ground that it hadn't been gathered with scientific controls. Killen said the researchers were putting additional data together.

"Your argument isn't with us, it's with FDA," Killen said. "We'll supply all the data they ask for, but we can't tell them what to do."

"Well," said Delaney, "the Ice Lady is on her way over here now."

Killen and his staff moved out discreetly before Cooper and several aides arrived. The presentation with the doctors began all over again. But they had barely begun to talk about needless blindings, and the ethics of giving a placebo to patients instead of a valid drug, when Cooper cut them short.

"You're right," she said.

That shut everyone up for a minute.

"We have to fix this," she said. But then, instead of taking the blame on herself, she blamed the advisory committee—outside doctors the FDA routinely asked to assess a company's application for a drug license. The committee on ganciclovir had recommended against licensing until formal clinical trials were held.

Bullshit, Delaney thought. Cooper wasn't bound to accept the committee's advice.

"You can overrule it," he said. "It's in your authority to stand up and say, 'Thank you very much, advisory committee, but we think this is the right thing to do.' What's the advisory committee anyway? You fly in fourteen people who don't know about the drug firsthand, and in one day they review studies and render a decision. Most of that panel didn't even work in AIDS."

"The idea is to bring in people with independent opinions."

"Independent of the people who did the research," Delaney said. "Ganciclovir is an unusual case. Thousands of independent doctors have experience with it because of the compassionate-use program. They're still independent."

"But the committee we had wouldn't approve it. What do you want me to do?" Cooper said.

"Fix it!" Lipner shouted.

"Why don't you recall the advisory committee and set a process in motion to fix it?" Delaney asked calmly.

"I think we can do that," she replied. "But I can't recall them unless I show them something new. First, we'll have to collect more data."

"Why more data?" Delaney asked incredulously. "Just introduce them to some of these doctors who have tried it."

"They've seen that."

"You mean you want to go back to the committee and say that something new has happened, so there's an excuse to reconsider it? Look, Ellen, everybody understands that a mistake was made here. Just admit it."

"I can't just slap the advisory committee in the face. I have to give them new data to make them feel comfortable. I can get it."

Delaney sighed. "Well, it so happens we just met with Jack Killen, who was speaking for Tony Fauci. They're going over the data that Syntex didn't bother to submit the first time, pasting together information from the first fifty patients or so, just trying to figure out how much you'd need."

"I'm thinking in exactly those terms," she said. "If the company had just given us a hundred patients with before and after photos I could have persuaded the advisory committee."

Why, Delaney thought, was she trying to persuade a committee that can only make unenforceable recommendations? Because the FDA didn't have the courage to make decisions. She knew more about this drug than the whole advisory committee put together. That's what she did for a living. But if she went ahead and approved a drug over the objections of an advisory committee, if anything went wrong, Congressmen Weiss and Dingell would be all over it. The advisory committee had to be there to take the blame for a mishap.

"Look," Delaney said. "The NIH guys are already working on it. All you've got to do is get together with them."

"Well, why didn't the NIH people tell me?"

Jesus, Delaney thought. She's looking for NIH help and she doesn't know how to get it. They're in the next goddamned room! Meanwhile, although the FDA wouldn't license Syntex to sell the drug because of a silly dispute over procedure, public pressure would force Syntex to keep *giving* the drug away as a gesture of compassion. And that would demonstrate to other drug companies how much money they would lose if they ever agreed to show a little compassion to sick people.

But Delaney didn't phrase it quite that way to Cooper. There was nothing to be gained by breaking off their working relationship. As he spoke, Delaney studied this woman who held such power over life and death, who had the power to save people's eyesight. And he thought, "None are so blind . . ." [45]

FORTY-NINE

*A*t about the same time, Corti found himself on an airplane to Jacksonville, displeased. He was about to buy $50,000 of ddI from Dean Shaw at $26 a gram when he knew the manufacturer sold it for $14 a gram—$6 in bulk. But the manufacturer wouldn't sell it to Corti. Not only was Shaw raising the price, he had also become irritatingly unreliable about delivery times, and about how much ddI he could obtain. There was obviously a problem with the factory in Canada, and Corti wasn't being told what it was.

Shaw had instructed Corti not to come straight to the house, but to call Shaw's wife from the airport first. She stalled him off.

"You'll have to wait for a couple hours," she said.

Corti wanted to know what was wrong. He drove to the house. Nobody answered the door, though Shaw's four-door Cadillac was in the driveway. Corti found a diner. After lunch and a few more calls, Shaw's wife finally picked up, and told him the bad news: the feds had seized the new shipment at the Federal Express terminal in Memphis. There would be no delivery today.

Shit.

Corti had never liked this arrangement. Given his choice, he would have picked the ddI up in Edmonton and *driven* it across the border. Federal Expressing a drug for agricultural purposes to a riverfront home in the posh section of Jacksonville was bound to alert an inspector with an IQ higher than the room temperature.

He flew home empty-handed, hoping the Shaws would eventually be able to talk the goods through customs. But when he talked to Shaw later, he learned the shipment had been returned to the factory.

Supplies of ddI remained a problem. On the other hand, Corti had come across an ingenious way to help patients without health insurance pay for costly AZT. Now that some aggressive local doctors had found that AZT was equally effective—and less toxic—at less than half the recommended 1,200-milligram-a-day dose, there was a potential pool of leftover AZT.

In other cities, Corti heard of a marketplace in which insured patients got reimbursed for 1,200-milligram doses, but gave half their pills (or sold them at a reduced rate) for use by uninsured patients. That way, double the number of patients could afford 600-milligram doses, which seemed to provide optimum benefit. Corti developed just such a marketplace. Technically, it might have been insurance fraud, but it wasn't being done for profit; lives were at stake.[46]

Corti continued to work part time as a nurse, through a local registry. That, the AZT exchange, plus ddI and continued demand by many patients for dextran sulfate, kept him busy in early 1989.

One day he was having his hair cut in his favorite West Hollywood salon, its other clients a mix of men, aspiring young actresses, and little old ladies. The owner, Dan Evans, was trying to talk Corti into a fashionably short "clone cut," while Corti protested that at his age he wanted to hold on to as much hair as could be kept tidy. As he cut, Evans mentioned a Dr. Kline, a dermatologist from Beverly Hills, who had been in the shop talking about a new drug for AIDS. With one shot, or at most a series of shots, this mystery drug would possibly wipe out the disease.

"Fine," Corti said. "Tell Dr. Kline I'll take a box of it." Rumors about miracle cures were a hazard of his line of work. He heard them everywhere.

"I'm serious," Evans said. "The drug is owned by a Swiss company, Sandoz. It's being developed in San Francisco right now."

"If you hear any more about it, holler and I'll look at it."

Three days later, Scott Eidsen, a friend of Evans's, dropped by Corti's studio for his customary supply of dextran. "You know that drug Dan told you about? It's for real," he said.

At that, Corti got a phone number from Evans, and began calling Dr. Kline, leaving messages. The calls weren't returned. He also called Delaney. Yes, Delaney, too, had heard something was afoot, but he didn't know what it was and had never heard of Dr. Kline.

As days passed, Corti continued to encounter rumors about a new drug . . . a shot or series of shots . . .

Then Delaney called. There was definitive news. The drug was called Compound Q. It came from China. And Delaney had heard that the first person in the underground to draw a bead on some was —Paul Sergios, this time operating as Dr. Robert Elias, who supposedly had a son dying of AIDS.

Well, blessings sometimes came in funny packages. Corti called Sergios.

"Dr. Elias? I hear you have the Chinese drug."

Sergios was stopped cold. "Chinese drug? I don't know what you're talking about. What Chinese drug?"

Corti had expected Sergios would be protective. "The only one that counts," he said.

There was another pause. "How's the weather out there?" Sergios said.

"With a little help the weather could be a lot healthier."

"All right. What do you want to know about it?"

"I want to know if you have any."

"Not yet. But I will. I have some hot leads. Jim, on this one I can't tell you what I'm doing. If I'm successful, I'll share it with you."

"What's the time frame and what's the money?"

"The next few weeks. I don't know the money. And that's all I'm going to tell you."

Corti and Delaney continued to chase rumors without success. Then, suddenly, it was in the newspapers. Dr. Paul Volberding, head of the AIDS unit at San Francisco General Hospital, and an assistant, Dr. Michael McGrath, said they were working in the lab with a drug more promising than any yet seen. It might even be a "cure"—and this was the first time Corti or Delaney could remember seeing the "C" word in print from an establishment physician talking about a particular AIDS drug. Compound Q, the doctors said, could seek out and kill infected cells while leaving healthy cells alone.

The article went on to say that the University of California (of which San Francisco General was a part) and Genelabs, a company in nearby Redwood City that was financed by Sandoz, had jointly patented a version of the drug called GLQ-223.

The next day, April 14, 1989, Delaney got more of the story. Abrams brought Volberding and McGrath in to talk about Q at a meeting of the community advisory board Delaney had been appointed to. The purpose, it seemed to Delaney, was to cut short any attempts by the AIDS community to obtain or use the drug. The doctors kept emphasizing the potential dangers of any version of the drug that came from China, as opposed to the tightly controlled supplies they were using from Genelabs. Chinese products often contained pyrogens—chemicals that produce high fevers—Volberding said. Q from China might have other impurities, not even imagined.

Don't play with yourself, you'll go blind, Delaney thought.

But between admonitions to stay away, he also got some information. The first item he caught, which made his blood boil, was that San Francisco General had been sitting on this drug a long time. Genelabs and the university had gotten their patent approved in January, a year and a half after applying. Delaney wondered if the wait for the patent had delayed announcement of the drug.

McGrath and Volberding said the announcement had been withheld until completion of toxicology studies on mice, which had been done throughout 1988—seeing what dose provoked negative reactions, how deeply the drug penetrated the body over how much time, and how long the drug stayed in the system and at what levels.

Based on these tests, McGrath said, the FDA just a few days before had approved the drug for testing on some human beings. The other event triggering disclosure of the drug at this time was publication of McGrath's article on Q in the new issue of the *Proceedings of the National Academy of Sciences, USA.*

Delays aside, the drug looked exciting. Other drugs, like AZT, slowed down the infection of new cells. Compound Q worked like a laser-guided bomb, selectively finding and killing infected cells, leaving others alone. To test it, McGrath and a scientist at Genelabs had developed a new process. Usually, drugs were tested on what were called "cell lines"—generations of cells reproduced in a laboratory, which didn't necessarily mimic what would be produced in a body. In fact, a consortium of companies had just lost about $200 million testing a drug, Soluble CD4, which turned out to work on the mutated HIV virus in the test tube, but not on the actual virus in real people.

Compound Q was tested instead in whole human blood, so the results would be more reliable. Because whole blood varied from person to person, more tests were necessary. But there had been plenty of time for that while the patent pended and the animal studies were done. In the end, Q seemed to suppress the virus better than AZT, ddI, or ddC.

McGrath told how he had developed Compound Q. He had been intrigued by the way T-cells, after being infected with HIV, died quickly, virus and all. So how did HIV persist in the body to infect new cells? It turned out the virus also infected another kind of cell, macrophages—which help remove bacteria and other harmful matter from the blood. And unlike infected T-cells, infected macrophage cells lived more than a year, allowing the virus to replicate.

McGrath decided to look for a toxin that would kill macrophages. He figured if he could kill them all, while AZT temporarily blocked replication of any stray viruses left in living T-cells, bone marrow would eventually produce replacement macrophages in a virus-free body. The result *might* be a cure. A research chemist from Hong Kong, who stopped by the hospital AIDS unit to talk about something else, heard of his interest and said he could provide a macrophage toxin. He sent two. One worked—trichosanthin, a protein distilled from the root of a cucumberlike plant in China.

Finding "trichosanthin" too much to write all day long, McGrath had given it the name "Q," short for cucumber. The drug had been used in China for more than twenty years to induce abortions and treat certain cancers of the womb; it worked because the cells that form a placenta, both normal and tumorous, are similar to macrophages. Testing and tinkering showed that a dosage and length of exposure could be achieved in the test tube that would kill the HIV-infected macrophage cells without killing the healthy ones.

Delaney listened, fascinated. Then McGrath said he had obtained trichosanthin in late 1986, and had discovered its hopeful qualities soon afterward. Two years had passed. Delaney and two other men who had been asked to join the committee to represent the gay community exchanged glances. In those two years, thousands of people had died.

Volberding said the phase one test would begin in a month or two, and take another six to nine months to complete—single injections to a series of individuals at escalating dosages. At that, Delaney and his two gay colleagues spoke out. Why had it taken so long to get to this point? Why was phase one going to take so long? Why was it aiming to do so little?

Volberding talked about potential toxicity. But, hell, every drug had potential toxicity. The other two gays began to explode. The meeting turned rancorous.

Delaney thought quietly. He and Corti were going to have to take this ball on their own. He would need allies. Something about the way McGrath had talked, his eager-beaver sincerity, appealed to Delaney. In the hall after the meeting, he approached McGrath and struck up a friendly conversation.

McGrath seemed annoyed at the delays, too, and complained that the FDA had kept asking for more animal studies after he thought enough studies had been done. At one point, he even said the FDA had been "unreasonable"—not a sentiment Delaney usually heard expressed by someone from the research establishment.[47]

"Well, it was sure interesting," Delaney said as they headed out. "I'd like to learn more. Could I call you sometime?"

FIFTY

Corti and Delaney hungered in vain for a sample of the new drug.

Then, at the end of the first week of April, Sergios called Corti. A box of Q had arrived in Florida March 25, from a woman surgeon in Shanghai whom Sergios (posing as Dr. Robert Elias) had somehow contacted.

Corti's heart leapt. Now they could have the drug analyzed, find out what it was, make sure it contained nothing obviously dangerous —then, if the signals were all green, try it on somebody.

But Sergios hadn't been thinking along those cautious lines. He told Corti he had quickly injected some newly arrived Q into the buttocks of an AIDS patient he knew named John Fisher.

Corti rolled his eyes and held his breath.

And, Sergios said excitedly, Fisher's T-cells had shot up. The results were absolutely stellar—from one ampule!

Where was it produced? Sergios wouldn't say. And he said he couldn't supply Corti with any.

Corti racked his brain. He longed to get on an airplane, but he didn't know where to go. He called his friend David Chan, the trader who shuttled between California and Asia, who had helped with dextran sulfate. Chan hadn't heard of trichosanthin, but would be on the lookout. Corti called his friend in Colorado who had converted ddA into ddI; he had read the papers, too, but had no idea how to get the new drug. Delaney was also coming up dry.

Corti called Sergios again. Sergios said his Shanghai source could deliver only small quantities. The source had to be kept secret. But John Fisher was still doing great after one dose.

"You know, I practically got myself killed trying to get you that thymus drug in Milan last summer," Corti reminded him. "The least you can do is give me a crack at the Q."

"No."

"What does it say on the label of the box?"

"It says 'Trichosanthin.' The rest is Chinese; I can't read it."

"Then mail me a copy. I can get it translated."

"No."

"Why?"

Sergios wouldn't discuss it.

For two days Corti called Sergios with new ploys, but couldn't get him to budge. Finally, Corti called Delaney.

"Whatever you got to do, Marty, do it," he pleaded. "But get me the goddamned label and I'll get the goods."

Two days later, Sergios faxed Delaney a copy of the label and Delaney overnighted it to Corti.

"What did you do, blackmail him?" Corti asked.

"I didn't blackmail him. I listened to him. I congratulated him on what he had accomplished. I told him I knew he had the best of intentions, but he just didn't have the apparatus to make it happen on a large scale. I told him lives were at stake. I told him he could be a hero, that the community needed him to do this."

"I swear I told him the same thing," Corti said.

"You got to know how, I guess. By the way, the label isn't all I got out of him."

"I suppose now you're going to tell me he sent you some Q."

"Only enough to have analyzed for purity," Delaney said. "I promised him I wouldn't use it for anything else."

Corti tried to conceal his awe. "Where are you going to have it tested?" he asked.

"Well, this is kind of a strange pact, too," Delaney said. "Remember, I told you I've tried to establish a friendly relationship with Mike McGrath?"

"Jesus Christ," Corti sputtered. "You're going to go to Volberding's people with the stuff? Doesn't that risk blowing our operation before we even get started?"

"Take it easy. I'm not telling McGrath where I got it. And Volberding won't know a thing. He doesn't know I'm talking to McGrath. McGrath's a good guy. He told me Volberding low-balled us on the length of the phase one study. Instead of six to nine months, which is already obscenely long, it looks more like a year and a half."

"Then why doesn't he do something?"

"He's doing what he can. I don't think McGrath's any happier about it than we are. Sooner or later, we're going to need to know if the stuff coming from China is exactly the same stuff Genelabs is making. The only way is to compare them, and only McGrath can do that. I told him people on the street are getting this stuff, and he can either help us make sure it's pure, or refuse and take a chance on people poisoning themselves with an unknown substance. He agreed. He's taking a risk himself. I'm sure the secret's safe."

"Congratulations," Corti said.

"Probably the toughest part," Delaney said, "was getting Sergios to agree not to use it again until we get a report back that it's pure. He said Fisher seems to be doing well. But there's tremendous pain around the injection area. And the nurse he got to give the first dose won't do it anymore. I get the idea there are problems administering this drug. I think he'd like you to help him the next time around."

"I guess you've pulled off another miracle,"Corti said.

"Sergios pulled off the miracle. I just got him calmed down."

But now, Corti thought, after they hung up, you need me to pull off a bigger miracle.

Corti studied the Chinese label he had just received and called Chan, who was back in Orange County. Chan drove straight to Corti's studio. He was quickly able not only to translate the box cover, but to decode the factory information, with the skill of a veteran China trader. He then got on Corti's phone and called a physician friend in Shanghai. He was speaking Chinese.

After what seemed an eternity, Chan hung up. "Now, we just wait it out," he told Corti.

That same April 1989, the Gay and Lesbian Health Conference held a major AIDS meeting at San Francisco's Cathedral Hill Hotel. Delaney ran into Jack Killen, Fauci's aide, in a hallway after the first morning meeting.

"You free for lunch?" Killen asked. "Wait here."

He came back five minutes later with Dan Hoth and two other top underbosses to Fauci at NIH. They all headed to a Mexican restaurant across the street.

Fauci had called for a new system to make experimental drugs available to desperately ill people, Killen reminded them as soon as the chips and salsa were on the table. He was ready to follow through. What did Delaney propose?

Delaney talked slowly, determining how radical a plan he could get away with. "What I think the community wants," he said, "is that nobody goes to his grave without a chance to try something that could help. Let me propose something new. Call it 'Expanded Access,' or 'Extension of Compassionate Use,' or whatever. But let people who have run out of options be given access to the next-best-proven therapies. Don't open the door to everything. You need some evidence it's effective. The FDA just won't say how much is 'some,' and that's why Treatment IND hasn't worked. But there's always a queue coming up for each disease, and critical thinking can tell the difference."

"But then it all just comes down again to who's going to make that decision," Hoth said.

For years Delaney had been arguing that the patient and his chosen doctor should make it. But the system wasn't going to let go of control all at once. It would still insist on some policing. Who would make for the friendliest cops?

"The researchers rather than the licensers," he said at last. "We have to start thinking of this as something outside the normal sequence of licensing a drug."

He looked around the table and sensed general agreement.

"You know," Hoth said, "for years, I've administered Category C drugs for cancer. Drugs partially proven, not fully licensed, but made available to patients when nothing else is helping."

"Then you're already doing what I'm talking about," Delaney said.

"The FDA still has to approve it," Hoth went on. "But if the recommendation is coming from the researchers rather than from a drug company, it will be much easier to sell."

Hoth told Delaney to write up a proposal for a program separate from the drug-licensing procedure. Delaney agreed. All the while, he said nothing to these men about Compound Q.

FIFTY-ONE

On April 19, 1989, McGrath called Delaney, excited.

"Wow, that shit you gave me is really good," he said. "It's ninety-nine percent pure trichosanthin. That's at least as good as anything Genelabs has made. No hemolytic activity. No clumping. No endotoxins. Where did you get this stuff?"

That was a secret, Delaney said. But human tests would proceed in Florida.

McGrath pondered what to do. He had been studying possible effects of the drug, positive and negative, in his laboratory for more than two years. He had helped lay the groundwork for a human trial. He had been arguing with his boss, Volberding, for months now. Everything was dragging on too damned long. If Delaney's guys were going to give this stuff to people anyway, maybe he could learn from them. He also felt an ethical obligation to help them avoid mistakes. Among HIV patients, anybody would try anything. He sure didn't want someone dropping dead from this drug if he could prevent it. What would Volberding say? Volberding wouldn't know.

"Make sure you question the subjects about dementia," McGrath began. Delaney sat up, opened a file on his computer, and began typing. "Decreased ability for purposeful movement," McGrath went on. "Muscle pain—they're going to have that. All these phenomena may occur in the second twelve-hour period after taking the drug. So far, all the problems encountered in the animal studies have been transient. But you don't know with people. And seizures . . ."

McGrath instructed Delaney to make sure a neurological examination was done on each patient, looking for a change in reflexes or sense of touch, and told him what blood tests to take. They discussed dosage. The Florida dose had been 60 micrograms per kilogram of body weight. McGrath predicted the effective dose would be about a third of that. The hospital's planned trial would start at a dose of 2 micrograms per kilo and go up to 100. He even told Delaney how to test future samples of Q for likely contaminants.

"This is potentially a very dangerous situation," he stressed. "You could go down to Chinatown and get the root, and distill it, and if you inject that it will kill you. There's an impurity in there called lectin that causes the blood cells to clump. If they clump in the lung, that's called a pulmonary embolism. If they clump in the brain, that's a stroke."

"I know," Delaney said.

"Well, I just want to make damned sure these buyers don't get hold of impure formulations and start shooting up."

Delaney took it all down. When they were done, he immediately called Corti, who called Sergios. The stuff was okay to use, but a lot of precautions had to be taken. Sure, Sergios said. But the nurse who had injected the first dose into John Fisher had developed cold feet about more injections. Would Corti help?

"Two things," Corti said. "I want to talk to Fisher myself first. And I want you to have a doctor fully briefed about what's happening and ready to step in if anything goes wrong."

Sergios agreed, and supplied Fisher's phone number.

To Corti's surprise, Fisher was almost as buoyant about the results as Sergios was. He said he had felt very sore after the shot, and was sick for about a week, like a bad flu. But since then he felt as good as he had ever felt. The AIDS symptoms, even the chronic weakness, had vanished. And his T-cells were way up.

Corti called Delaney, then boarded a plane. Sergios had rented three rooms in the Sunshine Glades Howard Johnson's in North Miami. The motel was right across the freeway from a large hospital. A Dr. Robert Mayer was on call for emergencies. With Sergios's help, Corti set up the rooms with needles, sterile water, and a crash cart of emergency equipment. Then Sergios brought in three patients and two local nurses who treated AIDS patients who wanted to watch.

With a copy of Delaney's detailed notes from his conversation with McGrath, Corti injected the three volunteers in the buttocks muscle with reduced dosages, and waited through the night, regularly noting their vital signs and observing McGrath's checklist.

The next day at noon, Dr. Mayer showed up as promised. Corti was surprised and worried to see a seventy-six-year-old retired pediatrician, looking frightfully gaunt and a bit strange from a hair transplant. But Mayer projected a bouncy attitude of fitness, and made rounds. He and Corti both wrote assessments: the men seemed fine. One was starting to get a fever, but that was no surprise. All three suffered excruciating pain at the injection site; Compound Q killed muscle cells at the site, so that was no surprise either. They were medicated.

By prior arrangement, Dean Shaw stopped by the motel with some ddI. Corti paid him $26,000 for 100 grams, and on April 23 flew back to Los Angeles with it. The three Compound Q patients were forty-eight hours past their injections and seemed to be doing fine. Dr. Mayer had agreed to be responsible for their care.

Meanwhile, Delaney had received an unnerving call from Larry Kramer, the AIDS political organizer in New York. Kramer had heard that Volberding—Volberding!—had been giving Compound Q underground to patients in San Francisco and had been getting great results. Kramer wanted to start a press campaign to try to steamroll the FDA into releasing Q. Delaney had a terrifying vision of backlash —an FDA crackdown on the underground experiments he and Corti were embarking on—or maybe an FDA call to China to stop further sales of the drug. Using all his psychological wiles, he persuaded Kramer that he, not Volberding, was beginning to work with Q, and that it had to be kept secret. If Q turned out to be of value, he promised to bring Kramer in on it. Then he called a mutual friend and implored him to cool Kramer off.

Then *Business Week* quoted an Oakland man who had distributed Corti's dextran sulfate and other health products, saying he was about to import and distribute Compound Q. Delaney called him and extracted a promise not to call any more attention to Q.

McGrath called. It looked like years before Volberding's tests would get Q in patients' hands. New questions had just come in from the FDA, which still hadn't formally approved the initial test. Data to answer those questions could cause more months of delay.

"You know some important people at the FDA," McGrath said. "Do you have any contacts you could go to to try to cut through this?"

Delaney called Ellen Cooper. Besides requesting the new data, he was curious to know if the rumors about underground tests had reached her. He chatted in a friendly way about other things, then mentioned that he'd heard there might be a delay in the human trials of Compound Q. He said how disappointed the community would be if Q was held up, and asked if he could do anything to help.

"It's in the company's hands," she said. There wouldn't be endless requests for more data. The new information the FDA wanted could easily be supplied in time for the trial to get formal approval at an FDA decision meeting April 26—just a few days off.

Delaney told McGrath, who said he'd talk to his contacts at Genelabs. He also said a university lawyer had advised him not to appear to encourage any unauthorized tests. But the lawyer had agreed that McGrath had an ethical duty to steer Delaney away from avoidable dangers if he and his friends insisted on going ahead. For one thing, he said, they should keep documentation careful enough to be submitted to authorities later.

Delaney responded with news from Miami. There were aches and pains all around. But blood work was essentially normal, and everyone felt improved energy. McGrath said all this accorded with his expectations, and recommended two new blood tests.[48]

Then Delaney got a surprise call from AmFAR, the very establishment AIDS organization that for years had turned down every grant request he made. Suddenly an AmFAR official was eager to talk. Gushing friendship, he said he had heard Delaney was involved in underground tests of Compound Q, and wanted to observe. If AmFAR participated, the caller said, it would greatly enhance the credibility of whatever results were obtained.

Fuck you! Delaney said he'd think about it.

A few minutes later, he heard from Corti, in Los Angeles, . . . The same AmFAR officer had just called Corti.

"He said he just talked to you and understood that I was going to China to bring back Compound Q," Corti said.

They laughed, both knowing Delaney had said no such thing. But AmFAR's sudden passion could only mean that expectations were high about Compound Q in establishment circles.

The next day McGrath called, and said a respected New York researcher had just called him with a rumor that McGrath had been giving the drug out underground. McGrath sounded worried. Delaney told him Larry Kramer was identifying the underground source as Volberding. McGrath got a laugh, and seemed to be at ease again.

Meanwhile, someone sent Delaney a copy of the *New York Native,* a radical gay newspaper in New York that had been alleging almost weekly that HIV was not the real cause of AIDS, and that AZT was part of a plot to poison and annihilate gay men. The paper didn't know about the Q importation, but had discovered Delaney's work and run a front-page article under the headline "Is Martin Delaney Dangerous to Your Health?" The article's answer, more or less, had been "yes."

Then Corti called again. David Chan had finally scored. There had been a lot of calls to China. Chan's friends could guarantee a meeting at the factory where Q was made. Then it would be up to Corti to negotiate a purchase. All Chan wanted to know was how quickly Corti could get a visa.

It was done in a day at the Chinese consulate on Fourth Street in Los Angeles. Corti dipped into the dextran and ddI funds in his desk. He visited a local artist who had been buying large quantities of ddI, and talked him into a big loan. He went to Security Pacific and bought traveler's checks, just under the $10,000 limit that would trigger a report to the government.

Corti and Delaney felt the thrill of expectation that night, just as with the early ribavirin and isoprinosine runs. But the spell was broken when separate calls woke both men at 2 A.M., California time. It was April 26. Sergios was reporting a medical crisis in Florida.

One patient Corti had injected had been admitted to the hospital with severe, uncontrolled vomiting, drenching sweats, and shakes. He was not responding to treatment. Delaney cursed himself for not getting McGrath's home phone number. He promised Sergios to call McGrath as soon as he was in his office to find out if this was an expected reaction and whether an antidote existed. Sergios sounded hysterical.

Another call came in at 6:30 A.M. The patient was still in terrible shape. Should Sergios tell the hospital about Compound Q? Right now, the hospital was working on the theory that the patient had a severe gastrointestinal problem of unknown origin. Who was liable for what if they disclosed the experiment? And what if they didn't tell, and the patient died?

If he tells the hospital about the drug, Delaney thought, the hospital will have to report it. In a few hours the FDA is going to rule on whether San Francisco General can get on with the formal test of Q. This could not only delay the test, it could bring the wrath of the FDA down on poor Dr. Mayer—not to mention Corti. Delaney thought of the careers smashed over ribavirin.

"Can the sick guy talk?" he asked.

"Sure."

"What does *he* say?"

"He says he doesn't think this has anything to do with Compound Q. He thinks it's food poisoning. His lover brought him some chicken salad a couple days ago and he wasn't hungry, and then last night he was feeling much better and got hungry and ate it."

Old chicken salad would do it, Delaney thought. But what if it was the drug? He was positive this kind of stomach reaction wasn't in any of the literature on trichosanthin. If they told the hospital about the Compound Q, what was it going to do with that knowledge anyway? Nothing, but maybe panic. The doctors at some hospital in North Miami were no more able than Delaney to seek the right advice, probably less. He told Sergios to hold off for a few hours till he could consult the expert.

He called Corti. They immediately agreed Corti would postpone his trip. Corti reminded Delaney that trichosanthin root powder was sold in Los Angeles as an herb tea. If a cover story was needed, Corti could fly to Florida with a vial of the powder and they could say the patient had taken some. That would tell the doctors to look for an antidote to trichosanthin poisoning without blowing the secret experiment.

"Not bad," Delaney said. "Trouble is, if he doesn't pull out, his parents will explode. They know what's going on. Let's hold off just a while longer."

Delaney called a friend who was close to a Chinese doctor, and asked him to get the doctor's advice. As they were talking, Sergios broke in with news that the patient was responding to anticonvulsive drugs.

At nine, Delaney called McGrath, sounding quite routine. After some chat, he brought up the patient's physical response as if it were a past event. McGrath said there was nothing in the literature or in his own animal studies that would connect such a reaction with trichosanthin. He said steroids were often taken concomitantly with trichosanthin in China. That might help. But there really wouldn't have been enough Q left in the patient's system after several days to provoke a strong antibody response.

"It really sounds like food poisoning to me," McGrath concluded.

The friend called back with word from the Chinese doctor: nothing like this was ever connected to trichosanthin, but they might try steroids.

Delaney passed the word to Sergios, who declared that if the patient hadn't recovered by 7:30 P.M., he was going to bare his soul about the experiment. The patient was arguing against it, insisting that he had food poisoning and didn't want to risk disrupting the flow of Compound Q. But Delaney couldn't disagree with Sergios at all. Soon they would have to come clean. They couldn't risk the patient's life.

Delaney began to have qualms about the whole procedure. Maybe people like Volberding had a reason for going slow. Maybe the drug shouldn't be given to very sick people—one patient in Florida had advanced Kaposi's sarcoma. Patients like that would be the most susceptible to side effects. One the other hand, they also presented the strongest case for getting the drug: they had nothing to lose.

Delaney fretted. On top of everything else, he had to conduct a community meeting that night. He phoned Corti. They agreed that, whatever happened, Delaney would take the public heat. Corti's name would be kept out of it so he would be free to continue to travel and procure drugs. They traded hollow reassurances and hung up. Delaney went back to fretting.

Then came the call from Florida. The hospital had found a positive salmonella culture. The patient was right. This had nothing to do with Q. All it proved was not to eat unrefrigerated two-day-old chicken salad.

That night, Delaney faced the usual packed church, and gave what he hoped was his usual upbeat performance, despite being unable to say a word about what was really on his mind.

The next morning Corti packed $19,000 in $100 bills and traveler's checks in a carry-on. He tossed his American Express Gold Card at the United counter and got a ticket. Calling to say goodbye to Delaney, he got a last warning about reports of student unrest and demonstrations in someplace called Tiananmen Square.

Then he and Chan boarded a plane to Hong Kong.

FIFTY-TWO

*I*n Hong Kong, Corti and Chan tried to book a flight to China. Cathay Pacific, Dragon Air, and CAAC were full up for the next three days. Chan began a long dialogue with several ticket agents in Chinese.

After what seemed like forever, he reported, "We can buy tickets on CAAC and try to go standby."

"Let's do it."

The distribution boarding passes and tickets reminded Corti of pictures he had seen of futures trading on the Commodities Exchange. People were waving bits of cardboard and screaming. That it was all in Chinese made it seem even more pandemonic to Corti. Suddenly Chan raced forward through the mob, screaming for Corti to follow. Clutching his black garment bag and the carry-on that held the cash, he jumped aboard the Airbus right behind Chan.

It was a rough flight. They broke through a low ceiling into the gray Shanghai day and made a teeth-rattling landing.

Chan obviously knew his way around. They converted a small amount of money at the airport and took a taxi to the Shanghai Hilton. Hiltons weren't Corti's style, but Chan admonished him to stay in a big hotel as a way of avoiding trouble.

The Hilton was nearly full, and they had to take an executive suite on a high floor. Chan immediately got on the phone and contacted his doctor friend, who came right to the hotel with his brother. Then they all went to a nearby restaurant for dinner. Corti, a connoisseur of Oriental food, had been looking forward to meals as a happy by-product of the trip.

He was told the Gang of Four had met regularly at this restaurant, though after the meal had been served he couldn't understand why. It wasn't the cuisine or the decor, he decided. He ate uncomplainingly and listened to people talk in Chinese.

When the discussion was over, Chan's doctor friend spoke English to him. Chan had faxed him the label, and the rest had been easy. The next day they would drive to the factory, a good distance outside Shanghai.

Back at the Hilton, Corti called Delaney and told him to be sure to thank Paul Sergios, or whatever he was calling himself that day.

The next morning, Chan, Corti, the doctor, his brother, and the driver piled into a red Fiat taxi and took off in the rain. Everyone was smoking heavily but Corti and Chan, and the taxi wasn't large. The rain meant the windows were closed. They drove more than sixty miles on two-lane roads so full of potholes that it often seemed more like a dirt road than a paved one. They passed farms, and factories that looked at least fifty years old. Corti saw no visible signs of revolutionary, or counterrevolutionary, fervor—just ancient trucks and people by the roadside fishing in streams with tripod poles and nets, much as their ancestors had.

They crossed a glisteningly polluted river right by a chemical factory that was openly pumping a brown-yellow liquid into the river water. And then Corti discovered this was the factory they were looking for. The taxi pulled between two concrete buildings of several stories each, just left of the main road. At least the rain had let up.

Two men came out to greet the car. They spoke primarily with the doctor, who seemed to have arranged everything as promised. He introduced them to Corti and Chan as the plant manager and the quality-control manager. Corti nodded to each of them, and listened to more Chinese conversation. Eventually they were led up a wooden stairway to a dingy conference room and seated around a long table covered with a dirty, tea-stained gray-green oil cloth, joined by another man, the Communist Party clerk.

Chan spoke a slightly different dialect than the others. But he understood everything, and began filling Corti in on what was happening. This was not the normal means of procuring medicines in China, and everyone wanted Corti to know that. Normally, one would buy from a government institute, not straight from the source.

Corti was not impressed with the scientific trappings of the place. The Community Party representative wore a uniform whose top and bottom were mismatched, and tennis shoes. The quality-control manager was dressed in a baseball warm-up jacket and slacks. Corti found himself talking mostly to him, with Chan interpreting.

"Why are you here?" he was asked—a surprisingly elementary question.

"You know why I'm here. I want to buy trichosanthin."

"It will probably be impossible to buy trichosanthin" was the reply. "We have very little of it, and the demand is high." The cancer and abortion uses are explained. "It is not possible," he was told again.

Everyone was being very polite and smiling. What was he here for if it was not possible? They took him into another room and showed him a stack of letters from all over the world, of people wanting to get the drug for cancer. A few letters seemed to connect it with AIDS. But Corti was also shown shipping records. As Chan perused them, he noted that all the customers were in China, except for a Chinese hospital in Singapore that once got a hundred ampules.

That, they seemed to be saying, is why they couldn't sell any to Corti. On the other hand, no one had ever come to the plant to plead for it before, they said. Then they all went back to the conference room, and Corti decided to make his pitch.

"It *has* to be available," he said, with Chan and the doctor both interpreting. "If this drug works for what we think it will work for, you will be saving the lives of tens of thousands of people."

A full hour passed, with Corti repeating over and over how important the drug was, and the Chinese repeating over and over the barriers to supplying it—but not closing the door on him. They showed him a little jar of crystals, about two inches high, and said it took several truckloads of root to make the one jar of crystals. But from that jar could come ten thousands ampules of trichosanthin.

Corti told them he needed a minimum of one thousand ampules. He told them it would be a pivotal adjunct to Western medicine, saving the lives of many people struck by a terrible epidemic. He was being emotional, and the doctor seemed to be supplying a forceful translation. In his mind, Corti kept thinking back to the newspaper article, where no less an authority than Paul Volberding had used the words "possible cure." He could not go back empty-handed.

Corti pounded the table, saying—though very slowly, so the translator could handle it—that if Chinese and American researchers were right, this could be the cure the world has been seeking.

Finally, the quality-control man hit what seemed to be a definitive statement. "It will be very difficult," he said, repeating it slowly, with emphasis. From that Corti deduced that the sale was no longer impossible, and would, in fact, occur; from this point, they were dickering over price. It was time to shift gears, out of missionary, into trader. The quality-control man suggested they all go to lunch.

Corti was led down the street to what seemed to be the main restaurant in the area, a state-run enterprise. Corti had looked forward to real countryside cooking after the disappointing experience in Shanghai. But things didn't pick up.

Once again, they were all sitting over a stained oilcloth. Now waiters were bringing out plates. Some food was recognizable as fish and chicken, but there were parts of animals he wasn't used to seeing— duck feet littering a broth, viscera amidst vegetables, mounds of tiny shrimp to be eaten shell and all.

"What is this?" he asked about one plate.

"Part of the fish," he was told. He didn't ask which part. He was reminded of the dining scene in *Indiana Jones and the Temple of Doom*. "Horrible" was the word that kept coming to mind, but he was determined to be polite, even as an unsightly pile of fish heads, bones, and other indigestible matter accumulated on the oilcloth, tossed there directly off plates or spat out of people's mouths. Corti thought of the yellow-brown river water. Bottled water was poured into their glasses. He hoped it was also used to make the tea.

Well, at least there was no chicken salad.

The conversation was about movies—Western movies that the Chinese had heard of but could not see. One of the men seemed to make a point of bringing up porno films that he had seen once on a VCR. Everyone laughed. Suddenly Corti got the idea that he was now learning some of the bribes that would be required to accomplish his mission.

After lunch, everyone stood and smiled as if the meeting were over. The doctor explained that the factory people would get back in touch with Corti at the hotel. The Fiat taxi collected the group it had brought from Shanghai, and returned there. Corti and Chan waited in the hotel. And waited.

In early evening, the doctor dropped by the hotel and said the factory people had called. They would come to the hotel the next afternoon and bring the goods with them. There had as yet been no talk of price, beyond some VCRs and porno movies.

The next morning, Corti went shopping in Shanghai. He returned to the hotel in the afternoon empty-handed, having found nothing that interested him.

Then the same three men from the factory showed up, along with a woman, who was dressed a notch better and was identified as the plant manager. The other plant manager, it turned out, had been her assistant.

Corti had arranged for the hotel to provide tea, and it turned out to be a fancy service with pastries. The four factory people had clearly never seen anything quite so opulent as this perfectly normal thirty-eighth-floor hotel suite. They went straight for the window and pressed their noses against the glass, gawking; apparently they had never been so high off the ground before. They peered into the open closet door, eying the clothes and camera.

Corti, a little nervous that the scientists he was counting on seemed to be bumpkins in so many ways, asked the doctor if everything was all right. The doctor assured him that they were all very impressed.

A tall, handsome young Chinese man in a hotel busboy uniform filled their teacups. The woman from the factory said they had not brought any trichosanthin; Corti would have to return and make arrangements at the plant. He was asked to repeat for her much of what he had told the others the day before. It was again explained to him that he normally should have bought drugs through the appropriate institute in Shanghai, not by going to the factory. And all they could provide him with was one hundred ampules.

"Impossible," he said. "I must have a thousand."

They went round and round. The busboy poured more tea, and surprised Corti by offering him cream and sugar in perfect English. Finally, the woman manager said that in addition to the hundred ampules, they could also give him tiny crystals that would enable him to make two thousand more ampules by following some secret mixing instructions.

The discussion broke up into smaller groups. Corti found himself in a corner with the quality-control manager and Chan. He realized this was no accident. The quality-control manager had been assigned to give him the price. The hundred ampules would be $5,000, and the raw crystals another $2,000. And, of course, the gifts as described at lunch yesterday.

He was clear about what he was in China for—to find out if Q was really the magic bullet. To hell with the cost, which seemed non-negotiable anyway.

"Okay," he said. But the quality-control manager kept talking.

"One more thing," Chan translated. "It must be in hard currency. They intend to buy refrigerators with it."

It had become perfectly obvious to Corti that the whole price was a bribe. These people weren't authorized to sell anything. What wasn't clear was just what an ampule was really worth. But the cash was handed over.

Someone suggested dinner. On the way out, the busboy gave Corti a knowing smile. "Nine o'clock," Corti said softly.

Soon he found himself back in the same terrible restaurant a few blocks away where the Gang of Four had allegedly met. He spent the meal being grilled on rock-'n'-roll.

Back at the hotel, at exactly nine, the handsome busboy knocked on the door, holding a water pitcher. He had what Corti had come to think of as a strange face with a familiar look. Corti invited him in and asked how he had come to speak such good English. The busboy said he had learned in school, and through family and friends. Corti pulled out a bottle of Campari he traveled with, and offered the young man a drink. He accepted, and stayed the night.

The next morning, getting dressed for the trip to the factory, Corti tuned in CNN on the hotel television, and was amused to see Frank Young in his white uniform speaking to a group of physicians in Washington about cancer drugs. It truly was a small world.

At the factory, the manager gave him the one hundred ampules and the vial of crystals, and explained how the medicine was administered. Each ampule contained a milliliter of fluid holding 1.2 milligrams, or 1,200 micrograms, of the compound. Measure it 15 or 16 micrograms per kilogram of body weight of the patient, she advised. That was half the usual cancer dose. She also gave him printed matter instructing on the use of the steroid Decadron for allergic reactions that sometimes occurred. Corti knew of the drug from his nursing work, and her description of it as an antidote made perfect sense to him, which increased his confidence in the whole procedure. And there were also the "secret instructions" on how to mix the crystals to make more medicine.

Chan had already arranged through the Chinese consulate in Los Angeles to have a television set and VCR delivered to the Shanghai doctor who had served as their interpreter and guide. Corti promised to make similar arrangements for the factory people. They gave him a tour of the factory, apologizing that there was no cucumber root from the field to show him; they were between deliveries. They showed him the laboratories where the root was distilled, and where they also made royal jelly, a popular skin balm. They gave him some samples.

The woman remarked that they expected him back, and that she hoped there would be future sales based on this sample of the product.

Then the factory people got on their bicycles and Corti, Chan, and the doctor got in the taxi, and they drove to another restaurant. Chan explained that the factory people had proposed the same restaurant as the day before, but that he had said Corti might prefer a little variety.

But the table was still covered with dirty oilcloth. There were green vegetables, a big catfish, more small shrimp and chicken pieces, and then the *pièce de résistance*, a huge pot of soup with a dead turtle floating in it, minus its head.

Corti, who had a animal-rights streak, winced. They motioned for him to proceed with the meat, which was inside the turtle.

"I never murdered a turtle before," he said. Chan translated, and everyone laughed.

"You're supposed to pry the shell off the back of the turtle with your hands," Chan told him.

He would have preferred not to, but he did. Under the shell was a garden of stringy flesh. Everyone's chopsticks were raised, but they motioned for Corti to take the first bite. He did—finding the taste funny but not disagreeable. Before he could swallow, chopsticks were flying into the turtle from around the table, and it was quickly scooped hollow.

Back at the hotel, he called Delaney, waking him up in the middle of the night again, and told him the ampules were in hand. Then Corti unpacked the jars of royal jelly from their boxes, gave the jars out to the hotel staff, and repacked the Compound Q into the royal jelly boxes.

He and Chan found a Northwest flight directly to Tokyo. It was several days before the departure date they had forecast when they entered China, causing unwanted suspicion at the airport. Army officers asked to examine their bags. Corti had declared no money coming in, and was carrying more than $10,000 out. Most important, he was determined none of the Q would be seized.

Chan deftly handed hundred-dollar bills to a couple of security and military officers. As Corti filled out his customs form, he could see officers searching the bags of each passenger ahead of him. Just then, Chan came by with an officer in tow, who walked them through passport control and customs without being searched. The officer took them straight to the door of the 747.

They arrived in Tokyo just before a United flight from the U.S. As Corti had done when he carried dextran sulfate from Bangkok, they mixed with the United passengers to go through customs, knowing that passengers on flights from the U.S. were less likely to be searched.

Once in Tokyo, Corti plunged into his dextran sulfate mailing routine. He and Chan mailed half the Q home in multiple parcels labeled teapots and bowls. They bought small sterile bottles from a pharmacy to hold half the powder. The rest of the ampules and powder went into their carry-on bags, and they headed home the next day.

As soon as they reached Los Angeles, Corti overnighted the powder he was carrying, along with a copy of the secret instructions, to Delaney, who rushed it to a chemist in Berkeley, who was waiting for it. The chemist began to try to manufacture injectable trichosanthin.

FIFTY-THREE

Delaney was already feverishly busy planning the national treatment conference that Project Inform was sponsoring the last week of June 1989, built around his campaign for a Treatment Awareness Week. AmFAR surprised him by supplying a small grant; whether its interest in Q caused this sudden largess didn't matter to him. Fauci, the government's top clinical research administrator, agreed to make the keynote speech. The conference should have occupied Delaney full time.

But with the news that Compound Q was coming from China, work on the conference was passed to Project Inform's growing office staff, paid and volunteer. Q offered the chance Delaney had long wanted to demonstrate that he could speed the FDA system by doing a community study of a drug that was about to be distributed. Ed Winger of Immuno Diagnostics Laboratory, a major medical laboratory in San Leandro, near San Francisco, agreed to donate lab work on condition his role would remain secret; Winger did a lot of work for the Volberding group, and didn't want to lose it.

Delaney also needed doctors. And he knew just where he was

going to get them. The morning after Corti had called to confirm the purchase—before the Compound Q was even in the country—he called Alan Levin. Levin was the doctor who had attended Project Inform community meetings, who had prescribed the medicine Delaney took for nervousness before his big speech at the infectious diseases conference, and whom Delaney increasingly liked and trusted.

Levin had been a decorated Marine Corps combat surgeon in Vietnam, then spent a decade doing laboratory research and publishing papers before opening his own office to see patients. He relished controversy. He had testified for veterans who claimed they had been injured by Agent Orange, and joined other medical causes with political overtones. He boasted of having been labeled a quack by respected journals because of such work. He believed American medicine .was suffering under the domination of large corporations and institutions. He loved to talk about the inroads that big military contractors had made in the medical industry.

Levin had shared Delaney's opinion that AZT was so toxic because the recommended dosage was excessive. He had helped prove it by giving lower doses to his patients and achieving equal results. The FDA had eventually adopted the same policy. When a Johns Hopkins researcher had reported that dextran sulfate wasn't absorbed by the body, Levin had tried a different measurement, which showed that dextran was absorbed. He shared Delaney's outrage at the continued use of placebos in AIDS drug trials. He had publicly called Paul Volberding a "Nazi" for refusing to permit subjects in a major AZT study to take preventive treatment against PCP.

But it wasn't just Levin's politics and brassiness that attracted Delaney. Levin and a small clinic group he headed occupied an impressive suite in a downtown San Francisco skyscraper known for its abundance of medical offices. There was even a mini-hospital unit in the building where patients who needed to could spend the night. That would be important in the Q trials.

Moreover, one of Levin's group was Dr. Lawrence Waites, a gay man, who was known to identify closely with AIDS patients. They would trust him. A still more critical factor was Levin's wife, Vera Byers. Not only was she a doctor whose name was also on the clinic roster, but she was director of new product development in clinical immunology at XOMA Corporation, an up-and-coming high-tech pharmaceutical house in Berkeley. XOMA was testing an anticancer drug she had developed. Through her research work, she was associated with the University of Nottingham in England, a major cancer-drug-testing center. She not only knew the big-league research ropes, but her specialty was a class of drugs called ribosome inhibitory proteins. Trichosanthin was a ribosome inhibitory protein.

The combination of her research experience, Levin's politics, and the fully equipped medical facility they could provide would be hard to match. And they had the guts to take the risk. Delaney had mentioned the Q developments to them in social conversation over the past month. Their interest had been immediate. Now, when he told Levin the drug was on its way, and that he wanted to talk about running a trial out of Levin's office, Levin told him to come in that evening. Waites was there, too.

"This drug's going to be brought into the country one way or another," Delaney said. "But it's not like ribavirin or dextran sulfate. This is a chemotherapeutic cancer drug, and people are going to try to inject themselves with it in their kitchens. We need safety and dosage information fast, and we're not going to get it from the government or from Volberding. Can you run a treatment program now that will produce useful study data?"

Levin agreed that the San Francisco General study would be too late to guide community use. He had read McGrath's paper; the drug was similar to those his wife worked on. In fact, he said, she had told him people at XOMA wanted to look at Compound Q. They could not stand by and let the community experiment with no information on this.

"Let's go ahead and do it," he concluded.

Waites was more cautionary. "Let's not decide anything the first day," he said. "We need to do animal studies. We don't even know how to administer it. According to Marty, San Francisco General plans to do it intravenously, and in Florida they've been injecting it in the muscle."

"This is not so big a deal," Levin told him. "If we need animal studies, Vera's connections can get them done."

"Let's think more," Waites said. "This will get a lot of scrutiny. Somebody could die during this."

Levin got up from his chair. "More people are dying right now because nobody's doing the studies."

"The FDA could shut the clinic down," Waites replied.

Delaney decided to break in. "I can't promise anything, but I think I can get McGrath to share what he knows if it's all done in strict confidence."

"That would certainly help," Waites replied.

Levin, too, wanted to talk to McGrath.

When they met again the next day, it was in the evening so Vera Byers could join them. It was clear to Delaney the doctors had been talking about it all day.

A good data base, perhaps unique, was already in place. Levin's office kept computerized records of more than one thousand AIDS patients. Time wouldn't be lost gathering start-up medical histories. There might be drug available for perhaps sixty patients; the doctors would begin culling for good candidates immediately from the hundreds who were clamoring for the drug.

Delaney pointed out that additional sites would have to be used. The FDA liked multiple sites, and there was going to be pressure across the country for access to the drug. He had met some doctors from New York who would probably be reliable, and want in.

Levin, Waites, and Byers leapt to oppose him almost simultaneously. "We've got plenty of patients right here. . . . We can do the whole thing ourselves. . . . We can control it this way. . . . If you go to the other centers it will get more difficult. . . ."

"Probably so," Delaney said. "But there will be tremendous jealousy over this on the East Coast. And we wouldn't even *have* the drug if it weren't for the guy in Florida. I've got to supply him some. Look, this clinic is where the protocol will be written, where the most patients will be treated, and where the data will be assembled. But you can't have it all."

What he was also thinking, but didn't say, was that opponents would jump on Levin's idiosyncratic past to try to discredit the study. Involving other cities would help deflect that.

Heads nodded. Everyone reluctantly seemed to accept the need for other sites.

Byers said she would call Nottingham the next day and see what help her colleagues there could be. But she would have to stay on the periphery; her contributions to this study must be kept clearly distinct from her work for XOMA.

"Don't worry," Delaney said. "We've got a bigger concern than that. Mike McGrath says he'll meet with us and tell what he knows. He could lose his job if it gets out."

There were nervous smiles around the room.

Levin said he and Waites would develop a protocol. Byers noted it would be just like protocols she had already developed for a similar drug. She could supply the forms; all they would have to do was change the specifics as appropriate. Since case-report forms were up to one hundred pages long, that was a big timesaver.

They would need legal protection. It would be critical to have ironclad consent forms from the patients. If anything went wrong, there could be a lot of heat. Delaney said he was sure that Curtis Ponzi, a local attorney who had helped devise language for the new FDA import policy, would volunteer. Ponzi was eager to do more, and would help make sure Delaney and the doctors were protected.

The meeting went so smoothly everyone seemed to lose sight of the fact that they were conspiring to test the limits of the law. No one ever suggested not proceeding—until another doctor on Levin's staff, who had joined the meeting but had sat quietly in the background, let out a whistle. "You boys sound like you're going to war," he said. "I admire what you're doing, but I need that medical license. You better count me out." And he left the room.

Delaney felt a moment of concern. That was one thing *he* didn't have to worry about. Everyone else, however, had committed himself to a profession that required eight years of schooling; in a flash, a committee could take away their ability to practice. Of course, in a way, Delaney had already lost the equivalent of his professional license because of this work; less than two years ago, he was earning a doctor-like income, consulting for banks that now wouldn't hire him. But would Levin, Waites, and Byers risk so much?

They didn't flinch. The meeting continued as if nothing had happened. Byers was obviously fascinated with the science. Levin was eager to show the medical authorities they were out of step with the needs of patients. And Waites, like every gay man in San Francisco, felt a personal stake in finding a cure.

Moreover, they all shared Delaney's concern that trichosanthin posed a potential danger, as well as a potential salvation, to thousands of people. Intense community interest in the drug would quickly lead to wide-scale use regardless of FDA approval. For many, the bloom was already off the rose of AZT, and little else on the horizon promised such hope. A community study was needed. It was the culmination of everything Delaney had given up his career for. It was a return to the original mission of Project Inform.

FIFTY-FOUR

Delaney shared his assessment by phone with Corti in Los Angeles. He was relieved to hear that Corti agreed completely. They couldn't just distribute this drug to all eager buyers as they had other drugs.

There would have to be medically supervised guerrilla trials. And San Francisco would be the focal point. Corti said he had been squabbling with Michael Scolaro over bills charged to AIDS patients,[49] and he didn't know any doctors in Los Angeles he respected and trusted as much as the San Francisco group.

For a second site, the sympathetic doctors they had met from New York probably offered the best environment. Corti would certainly administer the drug to a few desperate patients in Los Angeles, and try to line up some doctors there to monitor them.

Then there was Sergios. They had to deal with him. They would tell him he could run a study site, but a small one, and with careful supervision to make sure he adhered to the protocol Levin and Waites were designing. He would ship his blood work to the lab in San Francisco. He agreed.

Delaney marveled at the way so many strong-willed people with disparate personalities were forming a quick consensus around Compound Q. The work seemed to be defying Murphy's Law. So far.

Ponzi, the lawyer, came to the next meeting at Levin's office, and suggested the patient consents all be videotaped. Every risk would be spelled out for the patients on camera, and they would present their relevant medical histories and accept the risks on camera. It sounded like good advice.

A lab at Stanford had offered to do the animal studies for a cut-rate $1,000. But it was decided to ship the drug by overnight express to Nottingham, where the studies would be done free, and inside of a week, as a favor to Byers. In the tests, the drug was bonded to a radioactive substance so it could be traced, and then was injected into a series of mice. The mice were killed sequentially, over time, and tissue samples were analyzed to see how far the drug had penetrated in the body, how long it took to get there, and how long it stayed.

Precise answers were necessary, because everyone by now agreed the drug would best be administered intravenously. In Florida, the drug had been injected into a muscle; that kept the drug in the body longer, but caused excruciating pain at the injection site because trichosanthin kills muscle tissue.

McGrath arrived, and said he had already done extensive animal testing. The effective life of the drug in human beings after intravenous injection would be seven hours, based on standard extrapolations from the animal studies. Since optimum effect occurred if the drug was in contact with the infected cells for only three hours, there was plenty of margin for error.

Levin questioned whether it was worth waiting for more studies. "Just get it and put it in people," he suggested.

Waites argued again that they couldn't do a protocol until they had animal tests. "This is a Chinese drug, and the other came from Genelabs. They could be two different drugs," he argued.

The consensus was to wait for the new animal studies.

Meanwhile, in Los Angeles, on Sunday, May 7, 1989, Corti offered an injection of Compound Q to Scott Berry, the founder of an AIDS political-action organization called Being Alive. Berry, who had become a friend, had grown gravely sick. His nervous system had been ravaged. He was in pain and could barely walk. He had just announced his intention to commit suicide that week.

Reluctantly, he consented to Corti's plea to give life one more chance, with Q. They consulted Berry's doctor, who did a battery of blood tests so that if a miracle cure occurred there would be numbers to prove it. He was injected in the cottage where he lived on his parents' estate in Bel Air. Before giving him the Q, Corti dosed him with prednisone, a steroid, as both the Chinese and the San Francisco doctors had suggested, to counteract known side effects of trichosanthin.

Corti hated to cause his friend intense pain. But so little was yet known about intravenous administration that Corti felt safer injecting the drug in the muscle of Berry's behind. For the next three nights, Corti slept on the floor by Berry's bed, waiting for problems. Q was strong medicine. Maybe it would kill a man this sick. But if Berry was determined to die anyway, better his death accomplish something. And Berry had agreed.

Daily, Corti drew blood and took it to the doctor's office nearby. Nothing much changed. There was no miracle cure of a dying man. On May 10, Corti went home. Berry was still surrounded by friends. It wasn't long before the call came. Berry had died as he had planned.

FIFTY-FIVE

*T*he results of the animal studies arrived from Nottingham. The doctors were astounded to see how important their decision to wait for the studies had been. When Byers handed the data to McGrath that night, he couldn't believe it, either. The trichosanthin from China had been pure, all right, just as McGrath had learned at Genelabs. But Nottingham found that Q flushed very fast through the kidneys. It stayed in the body in effective quantities only about forty-five minutes to an hour—perhaps less—not seven hours.

"You better go back to your lab and check again," Byers told McGrath. "This stuff is going to have to be infused a lot more slowly than you had planned if it's going to do any good."

McGrath still stared at the results with amazement.

"I'll go back and repeat the studies," he said. "But we're already set with our protocol. We can't change it now, or the FDA will hold us up forever."

Levin and Waites also had trouble accepting the disparity of results between the two labs. "If Nottingham's right," Waites said, "the San Francisco General test will be worthless as to whether the drug works. It won't be in the body long enough to work."

Byers said she trusted Nottingham. "Besides, what if we have two different drugs here?" she said. "We have to go with the test on the drug that we have."

She won the argument. McGrath looked dejected. He had hoped his San Francisco General study would show efficacy. But the main purpose of the study was to test for toxicity. It had to proceed as planned with quick intravenous injections of the entire dose, called a bolus injection. If Nottingham was right, though, the drug would flush out of the patients before it killed the infected cells.

In contrast, the drug Corti had brought from China would be tested in the Levin clinic with a slow, drip-drip-drip intravenous infusion, so the drug stayed in the body the requisite three hours.

With the fundamental questions decided, Levin and Waites were left to draw up the papers. Delaney called the New York contacts he had selected, Tom Hannon and Barbara Starrett.

More than a year earlier, Hannon, an AIDS patient, had helped create Community Research Initiative, a group of interested AIDS doctors and patients in New York. Delaney and Corti had encountered it repeatedly since then. Starrett was among its leading doctors. Delaney knew some of her patients, and her lesbian lover, a deaf woman, had befriended Jim Corti in Tokyo, where they had both shopped for dextran sulfate.

Community Research Initiative was already studying AL-721, an egg product some people said worked against viruses. Though Delaney was suspicious of AL-721 (it never panned out), he admired the group's method, and its ability to attract mainstream support.

Mathilde Krim, a former Sloan-Kettering researcher who had become chairman of AmFAR, supplied AmFAR money to Community Research.

The New York group already had a rough idea of what was going on with Compound Q. Right after arriving in Los Angeles with it, Corti had shipped an ampule to New York as a last shot-in-the-dark for a friend of Jay Lipner's who was near death. Now Starrett and Hannon welcomed the chance to join a national study of Q.

On May 9, 1989, Delaney faxed them a letter outlining the protocol Levin and Waites were writing. They wanted "a body of documented, scientifically valid experience of the safety and efficacy of trichosanthin in HIV infected people in 90 days or less." If the drug really destroyed chronically infected cells, as McGrath's lab experiments had found, or otherwise made patients better, Delaney intended "to use that data to politically force a major change in the planned development cycle for the drug."

Without disclosing that McGrath was a spy in the system, he said he had learned that Genelabs and Sandoz were developing plans for a large multicenter phase two trial, which could be started on short notice. "If our data warrants it (and our political strength is sufficient), we will seek to have that study begin with certain patient profiles without waiting for the completion of Dr. Volberding's phase one study," he wrote. And he would seek immediate compassionate use of Compound Q.

The Project Inform study plan was for patients, taken in groups of three, to receive a dose of Q each week for three weeks. The first patients would get about half the usual Chinese dose, as Corti had been counseled in Shanghai. If all went well, later patients would get the full dose. Both doses were well within the range to be tried at San Francisco General. At least the first three patients at each center would receive the drug in a hospital-like setting, and be monitored for the first forty-eight hours. If sufficient safety was demonstrated, later patients could be sent home after getting the drug. Patients would get prednisone before and after the Compound Q, and would undergo extensive blood analysis.

The supply of drug was limited. Selecting participants would be tough. Compassion couldn't override judgment. Because they wanted to see the results of Q on its own, without other drugs, Levin and Waites were inclined to exclude AZT users from the study. Certainly they didn't want to encourage anyone to drop AZT, so the best subjects were probably those who had declined AZT, exhausted its potential, or couldn't tolerate taking it.

To protect the doctors from retribution by the FDA, it was essential that the Q be handed out by a layman—in New York, Hannon. The FDA regulated the traffic of drugs, but usually wouldn't interfere with the right of physicians to treat or monitor patients as they chose. So patients would bring the drug to the doctor's office, and must be prepared to refuse to say who gave it to them.

"The community is already hysterical about Q," Delaney warned. The entire front page of a recent issue of New York's *Village Voice* was covered with a giant letter "Q"; the accompanying article speculated that the drug might cure AIDS. "This research should be conducted as discreetly as is humanly possible," his letter to the New York researchers continued. "Each new person who learns of what's going on adds to each other person's burdens: demands to talk, to explain, to admit their friends, lovers, etc. We need stern faces and single-mindedness about this project." Even if the drug seemed to work, he said, they would have to resist the temptation to try to rub the FDA's nose in their success.

"All participating physicians (and patients) will be asked to refrain from discussions with the press, and to forswear any premature or preliminary release of data," he wrote. "Such data, especially if it is positive, would only fuel hysterical efforts at self-administration, which in this instance could even prove fatal."

They would inevitably be criticized for what they were doing, he warned. They were taking risks. "We can minimize those for the patient, but must accept a few ourselves. If we succeed, our critics will quickly forget their charges."

Within a few days, Hannon called him, disconsolate. Delaney's proposal had been fine with him and Starrett, he said. But the decision on whether to participate had driven a wedge through Community Research Initiative. Some doctors in the group had gone off the deep end in their opposition to government AIDS policy. They accepted the *New York Native*'s argument that HIV didn't cause AIDS, that drugs like AZT were poisons aimed at killing off gays, and that Delaney was, in the *Native*'s words, "bad for your health."

Now these doctors rejected participation in the study of a drug that killed HIV, which to them was a false enemy. The egg product they were studying, AL-721, hadn't come from the medical establishment; Compound Q had, and worse yet, it was backed by Delaney. Community Research Initiative wouldn't help, Hannon said.

But he and Starrett wanted to proceed on their own with help from allies within Community Research, if that was all right. Starrett's sister and medical partner, Sherree Starrett, a triple-board-certified physician, would help. And the Judson Church, just a few blocks from the Starretts' office in the Washington Square area of New York, had offered its basement as a hospital setting. Two skilled nurses from the gay community had volunteered to help.

That was fine with Delaney, and Corti, too. The other doctors seemed so eccentric they might add to the problem already posed by Levin.

F I F T Y-S I X

On May 11, 1989, Corti injected Fred Wietersen, the current chairman of the organization Berry had started, Being Alive. Wietersen, who owned a successful computer-software company, had been a big supporter of Corti's work, morally and financially. He had yet to exhibit AIDS symptoms. But he had long tested positive, and his T-cell count had dwindled to 150. He was a bull's-eye for germs.

Because of his overtly healthy condition, injecting him was a different step from injecting the deathly ill Berry. It was a new test of both the safety and efficacy of Compound Q. But even knowing that, Wietersen wanted it. After notifying his doctor, he drove from work to Corti's studio, and got the injection on the sofa. Again, it caused great pain at the injection site, but Corti didn't yet have enough information to feel comfortable rushing this drug into the system by infusing it intravenously. Because the drug came in through the muscle, it would enter the bloodstream slowly and not be flushed out at once by the kidneys. Other than the pain, there were no obvious ill effects.

Two days later, a friend and former lover of Corti's, Byron Craig, flew in from Dallas for an injection. He got it in Corti's studio, alongside Scott Eidsen, the friend from the hair salon who had first persuaded Corti to go searching for Q; now Eidsen wanted to try it. Again doctors were notified and blood work was done, prednisone was administered before the Q, and everything seemed to go smoothly.

Two days later came the first sign of trouble—from Craig, who was by far the sickest of the three patients. He complained he was confused, and soon afterward began talking nonsensically. Corti hadn't read anything about mental disorientation in the literature on trichosanthin. But after consulting with Levin and Waites, Corti gave Craig a dose of the steroid Decadron, as the Chinese had recommended. Within hours, Craig was back to normal. After several days, the situation seemed calm enough that Corti decided he could leave town to pick up a load of ddI from Dean Shaw in Florida.

Blood work on Wietersen, Craig, and Eidsen showed no dramatic changes. A week from the day Wietersen had received his first injection, he got another. By this time, Corti had received the dosage news from San Francisco, and infused Wietersen slowly, painlessly, intravenously. He also did something he never did again: he administered a dose to himself. His regular HIV test had come back inconclusive, the first time it hadn't been negative. His T-cell count was down—not below the range to be expected in uninfected persons, but down from what it had been. He was frightened. And he decided that if Wietersen was to try the drug, then he should try it himself.

Word of the Q activity inevitably reached the press, especially the gay press. By now, reporters knew that when a new drug showed promise against AIDS Martin Delaney would be among the first to know how to find it. They began calling him, and he found it getting harder to take his own advice about secrecy. Yet he and Corti had agreed that he would face this heat; Corti's name would stay hidden as long as they could keep it hidden.

"Yes, I've heard that rumor, too," he said over and over when asked whether Q was getting into the country for some kind of underground medical test. "It would be inappropriate to speculate." To one particularly insistent reporter from a local gay newspaper, he said, "If something were going on, I couldn't talk about it. The first thing the FDA would do would be to issue an import alert and try to close it down. If the drug turns out to be really valuable, then the ability to import it should be preserved. Please. Lay off." The reporter got the message and complied.

Meanwhile, Levin and Waites wrestled with what they complained was their most difficult ethical decision: who would get the drug. Practically every patient wanted it. Levin and Waites felt a little like the MacArthur Foundation board selecting recipients for its "genius" grants—except that in this case the wrong choice might do considerable harm. If they gave it to a relatively healthy patient, the drug might kill him. On the other hand, if they chose their sickest patients, they increased the chance one or more would die from disease while the study was underway. That would limit the data they got, and threaten the secrecy of the operation.

They decided to start with patients at the end of their rope—who had already failed on AZT or had never taken it and were near death. Nobody thought Compound Q would miraculously save these patients, but if something went wrong, the cost would be least. The first round would be mainly a test of the drug's safety.

That decided, they still needed patients who were ambulatory enough to make it to the office in downtown San Francisco for three weeks. They picked three, all eager to participate. One was Norm Watkins, a patient Delaney had chosen for Tony Fauci to meet when Fauci had come to town a few months earlier. Watkins now suffered not only from CMV retinitis, but from mycobacterium avium intracellulare, or MAI, which was often the final, fatal opportunistic infection for AIDS patients.

"It'll be great if it helps me," he told Delaney after he heard the news. "But I'm not counting on it. If people learn something, then I'll feel like I've been a help."

Second was Ron Fisher. Like Watkins, he wasn't expected to live more than a few months. Kaposi's sarcoma had already reached his lungs. The third patient, Tandy Belew, was slightly healthier, but suffered from bad thyroid problems and AIDS dementia. Excitement built. The infusion date was set for May 24, 1989. Nurses, the hospital unit in the building where Levin had his clinic—everything was booked and ready.

But, as Delaney had predicted, the more people who knew, the greater the likelihood of exposure. Every patient had a lover, or former lover, or best friend, or parent, who knew somebody. . . .

Hank Plant of the local CBS affiliate, KPIX, had been covering the AIDS story for years, often reporting on Delaney. He had been asking Delaney about Q since April. Suddenly, somehow, he knew—there was a treatment experiment underway, and Delaney had something to do with it.

"We know about the story and we can go with it on tonight's news," he said on the phone. "It would be better with your participation."

Knowing the storm such a story would set off, Delaney offered him a deal. "Hold off. If the doctors are willing to, and the patients are willing to, maybe you can film some of it, on the condition you promise to withhold it until the test is over."

Plant accepted the terms. So did Levin and Waites. The patients were a little more reluctant, but accepted, on condition they weren't compelled to give interviews if they felt uncomfortable. Delaney called Plant back and made the deal. "No airing of the piece until Project Inform decides the dust has settled."

"Or until somebody else goes with it," Plant added.

Plant's presence opened another door. A New York television producer, Allessia DePaulo, had been after Delaney to help with the *AIDS Quarterly* show that Peter Jennings hosted on PBS. DePaulo was coming to San Francisco to film, and also had a pretty good idea something was happening with Q. Hoping to get permission to capture it, she had already pledged that she was working only on a documentary, and that nothing she taped would be released until the Jennings show in the fall. By then, Project Inform ought to have results ready, and would probably *want* publicity. If the CBS TV crew was going to be there anyway, Delaney figured, why not also PBS, which would be most likely to present the trial with the serious tone Delaney wanted? Reluctantly he called DePaulo. The number of TV crews rose to two.

Actually, three. There was also Curtis Ponzi's operation to make a video record for legal purposes. Ponzi's elaborate consents were videotaped, one each night, in the days before the 24th. Ponzi composed a script of potential risks from the drug to be read on camera. Delaney took one look at it and exclaimed, "That would scare the hell out of anyone!"

Each patient brought a personal witness who knew him well, who affirmed on camera that the patient was sane enough to understand and accept all the risks. The videotape concluded with each patient telling potential survivors that if anything happened, no one else was to be held responsible. Byers, and a University of California lawyer McGrath consulted, both said it was the most sophisticated consent they had seen in years of observing such tests.

When 5 P.M., May 24, came, the scene in Levin's office was more chaotic than anyone wanted. Patients from the Levin clinic's normal practice, some with AIDS and others with more mundane ailments, were still in the office waiting room when the TV cameras arrived. Plant and DePaulo both wanted to capture the first infusion on tape, in case Q really proved to be the magic bullet that would wipe out AIDS. Some patients were alarmed, and demanded to know what was going on. Watkins and Fisher arrived on crutches, Belew under his own power, but each with a retinue of friends and an air of excitement.

Each TV crew was given a patient interview, but wanted more. Belew's veins were in bad shape, and the doctors had trouble getting his IV set up right. After a while, Delaney decided the TV crews had taped enough, and he managed to get them out on good terms. Everything was hours behind schedule. But by the time the infusions were over, and the patients and their support groups had gone down the elevator to the hospital area, the atmosphere had grown partylike. Friends had brought in popcorn, VCRs, and tapes.

The patients were surprised to feel nothing unusual. "Was there anything in those vials?" they kept asking. Around midnight, Levin —who had gone home for a nap after the infusions were underway— came in, and Waites left. When morning came, and all seemed normal, the patients, too, were sent home, leaving blood behind for analysis. White blood counts were up—a sign the body was reacting to something—but nothing else had changed.

A day later they came in for examination. Some reported aches and pains, but nothing more. As they left, Delaney remarked to Levin, "This is more intensive monitoring than Mark ever got at San Francisco General during the suramin trial."

FIFTY-SEVEN

*T*he chemist who had been working with the powder Corti had brought back from China phoned. It had failed to produce any drug. The instructions called for mixing the powder with barely measurable amounts of sterile water in laboratory mixing machines that rocked gently to and fro for days. The chemist insisted he had followed instructions to the letter. But the powder would not dissolve. Nothing could be done with it.

The bad news sank in. If the study was to proceed as planned, they would need more drug. The limit on the number of patients had always been the availability of trichosanthin. Unless a problem arose with one of the patients already treated, another group of three patients was to join the San Francisco study in two weeks. New York had set a target date of June 7 for initial infusions.

Delaney called Los Angeles. "Jim," he said, "the powder didn't work. You're going to have to go back to China."

Corti was instantly in touch with Chan's friend in Shanghai, and within a few hours another trip was arranged. He stopped at the bank, and at an "adult book store," where he picked up *Debbie Does Dallas* and a handful of other video titles, and packed his bags.

China was very different at the end of May 1989 than it had been on his prior trip. Hundreds of thousands of students and workers filled streets and squares in pro-democracy demonstrations. The National People's Congress was meeting to resolve a power struggle between leaders who wanted to liberalize the system and those who wanted to crack down violently on the demonstrators. American television networks were sending their prize anchors into China to cover the prospective revolution.

Into this maelstrom flew a single-minded procurer of a drug distilled from cucumber roots. He found that despite the tumult—or perhaps because of it—the purchase was much easier the second time around. Maybe, faced with the unknown, the people at the factory were readier to cash in. He wound up buying 150 ampules for several thousand dollars less than he had paid for 100 ampules on the first trip. And this time the sellers brought the goods to the hotel. He and Chan flew out at the very moment troops were preparing to roll toward Tiananmen Square to finish the rebellion.

"We've got enough to finish the trials at all four sites," he told Delaney proudly. "And more in the future, if the whole fucking country doesn't blow up."

Delaney had some good news of his own. After the first week, all three patients reported feeling better. Watkins had gained back five pounds. Very unusual.

Corti checked on his own patients and found, for the first time, minor improvement. In the second two-week period since starting Q, Fred Wietersen's T-cell count had increased from 150 to 210. Byron Craig's had risen from 90 to 130, and Scott Eidsen's from 150 to 170. The increases weren't enormous, but just the lack of deterioration was impressive. And there were no discernible ill effects from the drug.

Starrett's New York test got off to a good start, too. As in San Francisco, opening night had turned into a party. The patients' friends came to the church. Food was ordered, videotapes were brought (though not *Debbie Does Dallas*), and no ill effects were seen.

But in San Francisco, on the third day after his second infusion, patient Tandy Belew reported slipping back into AIDS dementia. He had been clear-headed for weeks. Was it a natural occurrence? Or, coupled with the confusion of Corti's patient Byron Craig, did it mean that Q had some kind of neurotoxicity? McGrath had mentioned checking for disorientation and neurological damage. Scans and other tests on Belew indicated recurring standard AIDS dementia, which might be unrelated to the drug; his blood markers continued to improve.

The critical blood marker for McGrath had been not T-cells but

P-24 antigen—the core protein of HIV. The more antigen, the more the virus had spread. Since Q was supposed to kill infected macrophages, the first response should be a reduced level of virus and therefore reduced antigen.

Belew's antigen count had been high for months. Entering the study, it was an astronomical 1,100-plus, despite treatment with AZT. Four days after his first infusion, it fell to about 900. By day seven, it was down to 170. After the second infusion, it hit 100. As happy as that should have made him, though, the dementia discouraged him. He turned morose—even stopped shaving. Relating his earlier dementia to a thyroid problem, Waites gave him a thyroid drug and the dementia began to clear. After some hesitation, he got his third infusion, four days late.

The other patients' blood markers improved, too. Watkins's P-24 count fell from 120 to 60. All three patients started with minuscule T-cell counts—under 20. No one expected them to bounce back much, and they didn't.

Also, during his second week, Watkins came down with an ear infection that began to spread. Drug related? Who knew? But Fisher truly improved. Friends and doctors alike noticed. His skin color brightened, and he walked erect, without crutches. There was a lightening around his Kaposi's lesions.

It was decision time for the next group. The trouble with very sick patients was that when something happened you didn't know whether to blame the trichosanthin or the disease. Moreover, if hospitalization was required, it could blow the cover of the experiment, and outside doctors would leap to blame the medication for whatever problem had developed.

They decided to begin treatment on three patients who were a bit less sick going into the study than the first group had been. These would be patients without any active infection. On the other hand, because of possible side effects in the first group, it was decided to try the lower dose again rather than increase it as planned. If dosage was increased in the future, the increase would be only half as much as the protocol originally called for.

On the evening of the infusion of the second group, Delaney met the three candidates in the waiting room. They had already given their videotaped consents, certifying that their condition was stable and they had no active infection.

Delaney launched into his standard reminder that Project Inform was the courier between them and the drug suppliers. The doctors could not be involved in supplying the drug. He asked the patients to follow him out of the office, into the hallway, where he would hand them the drug ampules, which they would then give to the doctors.

Two of the men followed him. The third seemed to have trouble getting out of his chair. He had been introduced as Robert Parr, a native Britisher. Delaney had never met Parr before, but as he walked out to the hall, Delaney thought he looked ghastly, worse than Watkins or Fisher had. He was putting on a good front, dressed in a business suit. But half a minute after they were out of the office, Parr said he needed to sit down. He looked pale, drawn, emaciated. Delaney asked point-blank if he was well enough to proceed.

Yes, Parr said. His problem was a rectal cyst, which made it uncomfortable for him to stand.[50]

That sounded logical. And it was up to the doctors to sort out the patients. Delaney let it pass.

He was preoccupied with Treatment Awareness Week, which, owing to an unfortunate accident of scheduling, was about to gather thousands of people in San Francisco under his hospitality. He even skipped the annual International AIDS Conference, which was held in Montreal in early June 1989, to work on his own affair. But he got an interesting report from Montreal from Barbara Starrett.

Flushed with a feeling of community spirit from the initial New York Q infusions, Starrett took a calculated risk when she ran into Ellen Cooper and an FDA aide at a reception. As they chatted, Starrett set out a supposedly hypothetical situation almost identical to what Delaney had actually organized. And she specifically made Compound Q the drug being tested in her supposed hypothetical example. What would the FDA do?

It wouldn't interfere with any doctor involved in something like that, she said Cooper had told her. The FDA didn't condone the importation and distribution of unauthorized drugs, but a doctor's right to treat his patients in his office was sacred. Based on what she said, Delaney called an FDA official he had grown comfortable talking to. He gave the same hypothetical example Starrett had.

The official, sensing what must be happening, proposed a deal. Send the scientifically relevant details of the study and the results. "Nobody's going to swoop down on you. The agency interferes with the commercial sale of drugs. That's not what's happening here."

Delaney agreed to Federal Express a copy of the protocol to the FDA official at home.

FIFTY-EIGHT

The man on the other end of Corti's phone said his name was Jules Parne. He had just received an ampule of Compound Q by mail from Paul Sergios in Florida, and he needed somebody to inject it.

Sergios wasn't supposed to be shipping his Q around to people who weren't under medical supervision. But, given what they knew, they weren't surprised.

Corti at first refused to infuse Parne. It was a potentially dangerous drug and a doctor should be in charge, he said. Parne pleaded he was dying, and this was his only chance to be saved. Sergios and some friends of Parne from around the country called to plead his case as well. Corti finally gave in. So Parne, very sick, came to Corti's studio, where an IV rig had already been set up. Corti infused him.

Three days later a local friend of Parne's called. Parne had just been rushed to the hospital in a coma. They were afraid he would die. The friend sounded angry at Corti.

"Who's his doctor?" Corti demanded.

He was dismayed to learn that Parne was being cared for by an outspoken opponent of experimental treatments.

"Tell them to give him Decadron, intravenous, about ten milligrams," Corti said.

The caller seemed to ignore him. "What kind of drug is this trichosanthin?" he persisted. "Are you a doctor?"

"Listen to me. He's had one steroid already. Prednisone. He needs a steroid called Decadron, IV. Are you taking this down?" When Corti felt he was finally getting through to the caller, he also supplied the number of the Levin office in San Francisco.

Then he called Wietersen and explained what had happened. If Parne died . . .

Wietersen drove to Corti's studio in his company's truck. Together, they loaded all the Q, the dextran sulfate, the ddI, the intravenous rig, and every other medically related object they could find into the truck and took it to Wietersen's house. If the cops came, the studio would be clean of evidence.

Corti kept checking Parne's condition by phone. The steroids had been administered. Parne was out of the coma. A few days later, he walked out of the hospital. When Corti talked to him, he claimed to be much improved.[51] Corti moved his material back from Wietersen's. But he had already decided it was time to hook up with some physicians. He needed doctors to develop a Los Angeles site for the Q study anyway.

Because of his dispute with Scolaro, he wound up talking to doctors Donald Long and Paul Rothman, who also had large AIDS practices. Rothman was part of the Pacific Oaks medical group headed by Joel Weisman, the West Coast head of AmFAR, who had been much more of an obstacle than an aid to Corti's work so far. But Rothman seemed different. He had supervised patients using dextran sulfate and other drugs obtained from Corti. He seemed well motivated and trustworthy.

Rothman and Long agreed to help. Then Corti and the doctors selected fifteen patients who met the Project Inform criteria—sick, but with no active infections. With money from a few wealthy donors who were infected, they rented a ten-room wing on the ground floor of the Beverly Garland Hotel in Studio City. The rooms were converted into battlefield hospital rooms. And the hotel was near the real hospitals where Rothman and Long practiced, just in case. The hotel wing, isolated from the lobby, offered a secure cover for the operation. Volunteer nurses shuttled in equipment Corti had rented. Volunteer lookouts guarded the hallways.

The videotaped consents from the patients were handled just as they had been in San Francisco. But because of the San Francisco experience, the Los Angeles group changed the protocol a bit. First, they decided there was no more need to take patients three at a time for safety's sake; all fifteen subjects would be infused the same day. Second, because there had been neurological scares, Rothman and Long agreed with Levin and Waites that they would narrow the list to patients most of whom had recently had negative brain scans. Because the brain scan cost about $1,000, a few patients were let in without it, but only when the doctors were satisfied they showed no evidence of dementia or other neurological problems.

On Tuesday, June 20, 1989, the fifteen patients were infused. Rothman was nervous because of his prestigious partners. He stayed away during the actual infusion; Long was there throughout. The patients offered the usual flulike symptoms with low-grade fevers for a few days, but nothing more. Everything seemed to be going well.

F I F T Y - N I N E

As the increasing number of insiders inevitably talked in their excitement about the new compound, more reporters caught wind of the trials. One was Gina Kolata, a former reporter for *Science* magazine who had burst onto the staff of *The New York Times* in 1987 with an unusual stream of front-page exclusives on science, often AIDS.

Like Fauci and many others who were working on AIDS, Delaney had reservations about Kolata's expertise. He felt that at times she wasn't skeptical enough of sources who were trying to promote a story. Twice the previous winter he had felt compelled to write to her because she had reported in the *Times* that he supported positions that in fact he didn't support.

Now, saying she was coming to town on another story, she asked for a meeting. Over breakfast, she told Delaney she had heard about the Q trials from a contact in New York. She tried to persuade him to give her an exclusive on the story. He then tried to persuade her that secrecy was important if the trials were to proceed. In the end, he made the same deal with her he had with CBS and PBS.[52] He would cooperate in giving her information, but she wouldn't run a story until the trial was over.

Next to arrive was Robert Bazell, NBC's national medical correspondent. Bazell came from New York just after Kolata. Delaney found him the most aggressive reporter of all.

"You know, Marty, I could just do a story on this any time I want," Bazell said. "If I can find out about it, it's not much of a secret anymore, is it?"

"Well, until you have some footage you can't do much with it," Delaney responded. "You can bring a crew out here and we'll let you film something. But the release is up to us, not up to you."

"But if the story breaks by other means, then of course I can run with it," Bazell said.

Delaney accepted that as he had with the local CBS reporter before. But nobody had clearly stated just what constituted "breaking" under this agreement.

DePaulo, from PBS, still taped occasional meetings in the doctors' office. Bazell was allowed to tape a patient-selection meeting in Los Angeles, with Corti present. Randy Shilts of *The San Francisco*

Chronicle was also let in on the story; but Shilts, who had written the best-selling 1987 book *And the Band Played On,* chronicling the start of the AIDS epidemic, had long been a confidant of Delaney's, and Delaney trusted him.

Meanwhile, ironically, Delaney and his whole staff were trying to get all the press attention they could for the Treatment Awareness Week conference at the end of June 1989. The theme was optimism —you can treat AIDS and prolong healthy life after HIV infection. The idea was to make people think of HIV infection as a chronic, progressive, but manageable illness, not as a certain short-term death sentence. A commercial was prepared, built around a montage of images of Rock Hudson, Robert Mapplethorpe, and other creative people who had died of AIDS. It ended by asking how much better off the world would be if those men had known enough to be treated in time.

Recently, most of the mainstream gay activist groups that had formerly opposed Delaney on AIDS testing had changed positions. Now almost everyone encouraged high-risk people to get tested. All this buttressed the message of Treatment Awareness Week.

And yet in the very moment of promoting this spirit of openness, Delaney was struggling to keep the lid on a development of consuming excitement. He found himself living two lives, hard-pressed to keep straight who could be told what.

In the hectic days around the start of the conference, Delaney heard disquieting snippets of news about Robert Parr, the sickly-looking patient he had been suspicious of on first meeting. In the rush of events, he didn't even remember who—Levin, Waites—told him what. But Friday, June 16, 1989, three days before the conference was to start, Parr had gone into a coma. Parr had been given his first infusion of Q that Wednesday. The next day, Parr had felt well enough to go home as the others did. But he had returned to the office in the afternoon, complaining of a fever and not feeling well. Many of those who had been infused with Q had suffered low-grade fevers afterward. Parr seemed dehydrated, so was given an intravenous solution to remedy that. Then there seemed to be no reason he shouldn't go home.[53]

Later that night, Waites called Parr's place and got the neighbor who was staying with him. The patient was okay, though still feeling ill. The next morning, Friday, the neighbor called to say that Parr was asleep and unresponsive to shaking.

Waites had the neighbor order an ambulance, and Levin met Parr at the emergency room of Mount Zion Hospital. Levin ordered

Decadron. Not only had the Chinese recommended it and Corti saved a patient with it, but Levin's wife, Vera Byers, had used it successfully in her work with another ribosome inhibitory protein, ricin-A. Twice, patients had gone into a coma after taking ricin-A, and the steroid Decadron had brought them out. Levin told the doctors at the hospital that Parr had been treated with an experimental drug.

For three days, as Delaney welcomed conference arrivers, Parr lay in a coma. But as the conference began on Monday, June 19, Vera Byers passed word to Delaney that Parr was awake and sitting up. After another day, as Parr continued to improve, the hospital moved him out of the intensive care unit.

Delaney resolved to let the doctors handle it. The conference was preoccupying him. He had led off the week with a speech covering five years of AIDS drug history, including smuggling, and got a standing ovation. Mike McGrath gave a major presentation about Compound Q. Abrams, Volberding, and Al Levin were all on the program. But the high point was the appearance Friday, June 23, 1989, of Tony Fauci, the government's top clinical AIDS researcher.

Before Fauci went on, Delaney met with him alone. They exchanged wry observations that ganciclovir had finally been approved under the Treatment IND process; Ellen Cooper had persuaded her committee of outside advisers to go along. Then Delaney revealed to Fauci the whole Compound Q experiment in considerable detail—and waited for a reaction. Fauci seemed neither surprised nor offended, but, rather, intensely curious about what results they were getting. Relieved, Delaney explained that there had been no quick cure for the dying, but there had been significant improvements in blood markers and no unmanageable toxicity—so far; it was way too early to tell. Then they headed for the platform.

And Fauci came through again. He declared that the medical community needed a whole new methodology—a "parallel track" of treatment studies—that would run alongside traditional FDA-sponsored research studies. The new track would allow greatly expanded access to drugs that had passed phase one safety studies and were "possibly effective." It would be open not just to people with AIDS, but also to HIV-infected people who weren't yet ill.

The speech got major national publicity. Reporters from Gina Kolata in *The New York Times* to Randy Shilts in *The San Francisco Chronicle* said it marked a major shift in government policy.

Of course, Fauci said, he couldn't order such open access. It would have to be approved by the FDA, by the researchers, and by the company that owned the drug. But he said he had already begun talking to Bristol-Myers about opening up the forthcoming tests of ddI to such a second, parallel track.

Fauci had earlier come under criticism from AIDS activists for the slowness with which drug trials were proceeding. A year earlier, he had been booed at a speech in San Francisco. Now he had many of the same people applauding him enthusiastically. He praised activist groups for exerting "constructive pressures" on the government. "I ask you to keep it up," he said.

Later, Levin, at his turn at the podium, called Fauci "a hero," and there was more applause.

Delaney couldn't have been happier as he headed to Washington that weekend for another Institute of Medicine Roundtable meeting. "It's going to happen," Delaney told Lipner, who was also attending. "The Fauci alliance was critical. I could never have pulled that off. Not me, not Act Up. It was Fauci getting behind it."

Just before the meeting, Monday, June 26, Delaney thanked Fauci again. Fauci brought up the Compound Q trial. "Marty, you acted like you thought I was going to be upset with what you told me," he said. "What you've done is going to set off a debate about speeding up clinical trials in a way that nothing else you or I could ever have done would have allowed. This is concrete. This is a debate the public desperately needs."

The group planned the fall conference on surrogate markers, and the day sped past.

On their way back to the Holiday Inn, Georgetown, in the late afternoon, Lipner remarked that on a couple of occasions Fauci had seemed to make biting remarks about Frank Young, who had sat there and taken it.

At the hotel, there was a message for Delaney to call Carol, his administrative assistant at Project Inform. It was marked "urgent." He took off his shoes—the soles of his feet still burned when he wore shoes, from the hepatitis treatment nine years before. He loosened his tie. And he called Carol.

SIXTY

"**T**hank God I've got you," she said. "This place has been going crazy. Apparently somebody died. The media is descending from everywhere. There's a guy named Bob Bazell with *NBC News* who says he's going on the air tonight with a major piece saying somebody died in your trial, and he's demanding you talk to him. So is everybody else. Plant called, Shilts called—"

Oh, shit.

"You want all this? *The Washington Post.* Some guy named Vic Zonana from the *L.A. Times. AIDS Quarterly.* Gina Kolata—"

"Hold them off till I find out what happened," Delaney said. He called Levin.

"Parr died," Levin said. "I've been with the media all day long. People are banging on the doors and trying to get in with cameras. It's a real circus."

"What happened?"

"He aspirated. He was doing fine. I saw him Friday night around five-thirty; he was sitting up eating dinner. He said, 'I'm feeling good.' Then sometime later he aspirated—vomited in his sleep and it went right into his lungs, before dawn Saturday apparently. And nobody noticed. They found him blue."

Oh, shit.

"It's the goddamned hospital staff," Levin said. "He should have been in intensive care. Waites and I yelled and screamed at them. But under their damned rules he wasn't sick enough, and they moved him to a medical unit, and now this happens. The thing is, even after all that, they got him out of it. Larry says the resident called him Saturday morning—Larry was on call for me—and said they had him breathing on a tube and his lungs were clearing. But by the time Larry got to the hospital, the staff had pulled the tube out. They say on the request of a brother."

"Oh, shit."

Lipner was tugging at him. "Gina Kolata's on the other phone. She's somehow found us, and she's screaming at me."

"Why is she screaming?"

"She says she thought she had this exclusively. Now the networks are going to beat her. She keeps asking how could we do this to her."[54] (See notes 52 and 54 for Kolata's account.)

"Jesus. Tell her I'll just have to call her back," he said to Lipner, then returned to the first phone.

"We all knew a few people would probably die before this was over," Levin was saying. "We talked about it the first night. But this wasn't even the drug. After ten days, the drug was out of his body. It wasn't the coma, he had recovered from that. This was the goddamned hospital staff."

"I've got to talk to the press," Delaney said. "I'll try to hold them off. I'm flying back first thing in the morning."

"Let's meet here and go over everything we know. There's no reason we shouldn't continue with this protocol. People die every day in tests."

"The patients all know about this, I assume."

"Of course. We've told all the patients and the other test centers. There's no reason not to continue. Not one person wants to pull out."

Delaney's next call was to Bazell, who was in San Francisco. "What does this message mean about a major piece tonight?" Delaney asked. "We had an agreement."

Bazell said he had been on vacation, but got a call from a doctor with admitting privileges at Mount Zion Hospital, who reported that a patient had died after experimenting with Q.

"It's being widely discussed among the doctors," Bazell said. "Hey, if all these doctors are carrying on about it, it's no longer a private story. I'm going to run with it."

"Well, that's damned convenient," Delaney snapped. "The day you get back from vacation, you put the show on the air. You're using this excuse about the patient's death to change the agreement. I don't think it changes anything. People die all the time in these studies. You guys just never hear of it."

"Everybody knows somebody died in a secret underground study," Bazell said. "It's news."

"You don't know how many people died in the suramin study," Delaney replied. "Or the initial AZT study. You guys have been manipulated the whole five years of the AIDS crisis. Parr was one of a hundred and fifty people who died of AIDS Saturday. Parr died trying to save his life. The others, nobody even tried. And the most important thing is that Q didn't kill the guy. He died because he aspirated and nobody pulled him out of it."

It was no use.

Delaney tried the same reasoning with Plant (the CBS man), and the others, arguing on the phone for an hour. They weren't to be dissuaded.

Then Levin called. "They want me to debate Volberding on the *Today* show tomorrow morning," he said. "From what I hear, Volberding went off like Mount Vesuvius when he found out about this. Running around the office steaming, that anybody who's connected with this is going to be fired."

"Look, Al," Delaney said, "we need to go slow till we've figured out where we're at. We've had an agreement all along that I will handle the media. Let me deal with Volberding and the *Today* show."

Reluctantly, Levin agreed. Delaney called the program, and the booker agreed to the substitution. "It's your call," she said. Delaney said he'd be at the studio in Washington in the morning.

As soon as either Delaney or Lipner set down a phone, it would ring again.

"Let's get out of here before you have a heart attack," Lipner said. "I'm starved."

Delaney knew Lipner was on AZT and needed to eat. He called the office and told them to tape the *NBC Nightly News*. Then he and Lipner went out into the Washington heat and found an Italian restaurant.

When Delaney got back to his room, among the messages was one from Carol, his executive assistant.

"It was the lead item they used to headline the Brokaw show," she told him. "Death in Secret Underground AIDS Study."

"Stop answering calls," Delaney said. "Call the clinic and tell *them* to stop answering calls. Just say we're going to have a press conference Wednesday, and we'll give out everything we know then. And that's all."

To be ready for the television appearance next morning, he decided to make one more call—to the Associated Press office in San Francisco, where he had befriended a reporter. When he needed to know in advance what the papers were going to say the next morning, he could call her.

She gave him a rundown, and it wasn't pretty. "Don't worry," she assured him. "You'll still have friends. A lot of people don't read. Or watch television."

Delaney tried to keep the *Today* show segment as low-key as possible. He denied Bazell's opening assertion that Project Inform was skipping the phase one, safety, part of the study. Bazell made it sound reckless.

"We aren't skipping those tests, we're performing them ourselves," Delaney told Jane Pauley, the host. He explained one more time why FDA phase one tests were taking too long in the face of widespread street demand for the drug.

Volberding then came on, accusing Delaney of encouraging desperate people to take a drug that hadn't been tested for safety, and of causing "the disasters that seem to be happening by assuming that we know the dose of this drug." He accused Delaney of prolonging the testing time for Compound Q, not shortening it. He said he feared the FDA would now delay the official study because of "reports of these severe and sometimes fatal side effects of this unauthorized use of the compound." Prospective test subjects would be scared off, too, he said.

"That's fiction—" Delaney began, but was told they were out of time.[55]

SIXTY-ONE

*L*ater that morning reporters were waiting for him at the San Francisco airport. Like paparazzi chasing a movie star, he thought. He told them to wait for the press conference, and raced for Levin's office, where the Project Inform Q trial group was gathered.

"You can't look at a newspaper or turn on the radio without being told we're all under investigation by the FDA," Delaney said. "Has the FDA called here yet?"

"They're about the only people who haven't," Levin said.

"My office hasn't heard from them either," Delaney said. "From the way the press is playing this, you'd think bubonic plague had broken out. At least the papers are saying they don't know for sure whether Q caused his death. The networks aren't being so kind."

Byers said she had seen Parr in the hospital a few days ago and he was sitting up and eating and seemed fine. Levin said Parr had mostly recovered from the coma, but not fully. The swallowing mechanism may still have been impaired. He should have been kept under closer observation.

Waites went over the details of the fatal Saturday, from memory and from notes he had taken from the hospital chart. "I got called at home by the resident about eight A.M. She said, 'Mr. Parr's blood pressure's low. He's responsive only to painful stimuli.' The chart shows there had been a temperature spike at two-thirty A.M. Coarse rales noted on the chest exam."

"So he had fluid in his lungs even then," Levin said. "And nobody did anything."

"The next note is untimed," Waites continued matter-of-factly. "Labored breathing, fast and shallow, patient comatose. Chest X-ray shows right upper lobe infiltrate consistent with aspiration. It also says patient is a no-code." He looked at Delaney. "That means the patient wanted no extraordinary measures to restart his heart if it stopped. He was still breathing on his own," Waites went on. "But they put a tube down his throat to allow more air, and so he could be more easily suctioned and cleared of secretion. They were using fluids to support his blood pressure. I said I was coming in. I got there about ten-forty."

He looked up from his notes. "I rush into the hospital and arrive just as they are putting sheets up over his head. The chart showed the three brothers were at the bedside, one with power of attorney, at ten-twenty, A.M., and asked that the tube be withdrawn. The next thing it shows is ten-thirty A.M., pronounced patient dead."

"You keep saying 'tube,'" Delaney said. "Was he on an artificial breathing machine?"

"No," Waites said adamantly. "He was not on a machine. He was breathing on his own, but he needed an open airway to his lungs so he could breathe more easily. You use these tubes if the airway is swollen, or if there's a lot of fluid. Without it, he ceased to breathe within a few minutes."

"Shouldn't they have waited until you came in?"

"You're goddamned right they should have," Levin barked.

"Absolutely," Waites said, still matter-of-factly. "It's the resident's job to check with the attending physician. That's true of every hospital. At the time, it didn't really hit me. I had a brief conversation with the one brother. He said, 'Well, he died.' He looked very unemotional about it. I said, 'Yes, I'm terribly sorry. If there's anything I can do, let me know.' I got his permission to do an autopsy. Then he said, 'Thank you for taking care of him.' It was a very brief encounter, all done while the nurse was wrapping Parr in a sheet."

Waites got up and walked to the window. "It only kind of hit me later when I was down in medical records going over Parr's chart," he said. "Parr could have lived except for the circumstances. The family came to the hospital, and when they arrived and saw the tube, they said, 'This is not what he wanted, extraordinary lifesaving measures. Pull the tube.' I saw him the day before, and he was smiling and he was doing pretty well. I think he certainly would like to have recovered from this incident, and I have every reason to believe he *would* have recovered. It's not the usual way things are done. Usually the family consults with the physician. But just a resident! A resident is always supposed to consult with the attending physician, which in this case was me."

"Did you ask her about it?"

"Her story to me was that the brother was very insistent that the tube be pulled. We had an argument over it. I told her this was inappropriate for her to make this decision without my being there at the hospital, no matter what the family had said. She was apologetic, but she thought she was doing what the brother with power of attorney wanted done at the time. She was a third-year resident."

"I really think we ought to press criminal charges against the guy," Levin said.

"Was Parr in a coma?" Delaney asked.

"A coma would be totally unresponsive," Waites explained. "This patient, if you pinched him, he would moan. The resident said that. It could be called a light coma. The recovery rate from that is variable. The usual recovery from aspiration is pretty good, given medical intervention."[56] (See note for the sometimes contrary accounts of the brother, the resident, the hospital, and others.)

"I mean it," Levin said. "This is a criminal matter. I think we ought to go after him."

At that point Curtis Ponzi, the lawyer, spoke up. "The brother, having the power of attorney, had a right to decide about the lifesaving techniques that could be used. We can't second-guess the motives of the family."

"But they didn't even wait till Larry got to the hospital," Levin argued. "It shouldn't have been done."

"It would be a terrible legal mess to be pointing fingers of guilt at any particular person during this time," Ponzi said. "You guys could be sued for treating him without an FDA-approved protocol, too."

"I don't care. This wasn't right," Levin said.

Delaney watched the argument get fairly heated.

"Al," Waites said, "the publicity would just be too bad for the whole future development of this drug."

"Larry's right," Delaney said. "Our interest is in the drug. We ought to try to just take a low profile at this stage."

"It's a stand-off," Ponzi concluded. "If they ever threaten to sue, I'll just remind the brother of the circumstances of Parr's death, and I think they'll drop it."

"What did the autopsy show?" Delaney asked.

"The hospital won't do autopsies on AIDS patients," Levin said, outraged. "They say there's too much risk to the pathologist."

"So much for science," Delaney observed.

"Well, science has learned some things," Levin said. "These neurological problems have only occurred in people with very low T-cells. Under thirty. Some under ten. Let's say from now on, no more patients with counts under a hundred. Or with any history of brain lesions or AIDS-related dementia. That would eliminate all known toxicity episodes, and we could try raising the dose as we planned."

Everyone agreed that seemed a prudent step.

After the meeting, Delaney called Corti in Los Angeles to relate what had happened. Corti noted that *The Los Angeles Times* had been relatively kind in its treatment that morning, largely because Paul Rothman had stood up like a soldier. "We would have liked to have done this study formally, and with the approval of the FDA," Rothman told the reporter. "But one person dies from AIDS every thirty minutes. We felt that as long as we proceeded on a rigorous scientific basis, we would be on very strong ground." He said that based on his observation of the fifteen patients in Los Angeles, Q "appears to be the most effective AIDS medication available on the horizon."[57]

The *Times* also quoted other scientists who condemned the trial, particularly James Kahn, the Volberding aide who was running the Q trial at San Francisco General Hospital. Kahn charged that the Project Inform study "lacks proper checks and balances . . . to protect the rights of experimental subjects."

Local television coverage had been more strictly negative, Corti said. The second round of infusions, scheduled for that day, was given at Wietersen's posh five-story house. Corti made every effort at security, not even telling the patients Wietersen's address but having them driven there. Somehow, television news teams found them, though, and more negative publicity followed. Commentators were asking on the air what business a nurse had running an experiment with a drug that might already have killed one patient.

SIXTY-TWO

"You'd think I was the fucking President of the United States," Delaney said when he saw about a hundred reporters and a battery of forty microphones set up for him at the press conference. With him at the table were Robert Pitman and Bob Barnett, the two patients who had been infused with Robert Parr, and some representatives from the People With AIDS Coalition, which wanted to show support for the trials.

Barnett and Pitman had been saying that Parr had confessed to them the night of the treatment that he was actually far sicker than he had let on. Pitman had already issued a press statement saying, "I believe what killed him [Parr] was desperation. . . . I believe that desperation caused him to withhold information about the full extent of his condition for fear that he would be excluded from treatment."

Delaney began the press conference by saying why he had tried to keep the trials quiet. "Look at you! This is why! You've turned this into a circus. This is a private medical affair between these patients and their doctors. Many of them are near death."

Newspaper stories had quoted doctors saying Delaney was doing the trials as a publicity stunt, and suggesting that he wanted to run for public office. "We didn't want this to become public," he said. "When all this is over I'm going to crawl back into the hermit hole I came from and stay there forever."

He also made clear that he and his colleagues saw no reason to stop. "We'll finish what we started," he said. "What we did was ethical, legal, and necessary. You keep asking for our response to an FDA investigation. We welcome an investigation. Everything we do is out front."

And he told them how different that was from the studies the FDA supervised, the supposedly "legitimate" studies. At least five people had died directly from taking suramin in a trial that Volberding ran. The AIDS deaths of some other subjects were probably speeded by the suramin. But that didn't make headlines or lead any network news shows. It was never announced to the public at all. A couple of dozen subjects had died in the AZT trial. How many of those were drug-related and how many disease-related? "You don't know. The sicker the group you work with, the more inevitable will be the case that someone dies," he said.

People certainly died from the disease if they did *not* take Q. There was no approved cure. Even Volberding agreed that Compound Q was promising. Patients didn't have time to wait for a study at the pace Volberding was conducting one.

Moreover, Parr's death appeared not to have been caused by Compound Q anyway, at least directly.

The reason the AIDS patients were at the table with him, he said, was that they knew very well what routinely happened on FDA-approved drug trials, and were glad to finally get it out into the open. It was the FDA-approved trials that were secret. He asked for a show of hands to see how many reporters on this story knew about the suramin study at San Francisco General. Only one hand went up. "How many of you have ever covered a clinical trial before?" Again, hardly anyone.

"The people who run those trials will not discuss anything with

the media," he said. "You people have no idea what goes on inside
those studies. We are accused of running a secret study, and this was
the most public study in the history of medicine. All we were trying
to do was come remotely close to the privacy allowed in every other
study."

And he wanted them to understand that it wasn't just the press that
was kept in the dark during FDA studies. Patients weren't told what
was happening to other patients in the study until much later. "Patients in the suramin study weren't given a chance to back out because other patients were dying," he said. "We immediately let
everyone in our study know what happened to Parr, and every single
person, like the two patients sitting here with me, chose to continue,
because they believe in what we're doing. You're all being given
copies of the protocol, and of activity sheets showing all the monitoring and testing being done. This is not sloppy science, and it's not
sloppy medicine."

Delaney emphasized that Project Inform wasn't recommending
that people take Compound Q; rather it was publicly recommending
that patients in the community *not* take Q until the data was collected and analyzed. And he said that he had been besieged by offers
of free legal help, including from a former chief counsel for the FDA.

The press conference started at eleven and lasted an hour in formal
session. Delaney spent the rest of the day giving private interviews.

Literally thousands of calls poured into Project Inform that week,
most of them fully supportive. "Don't let them shut you down," callers said again and again. But in public about the only favorable editorial comment came from an unusual alliance of parts of the gay
press and the editorial page of *The Wall Street Journal*, which had
long been campaigning for alternatives to the FDA system of testing
and approving drugs. Most of the mainstream press left the impression that the Q experimenters were dangerous fugitives from FDA
justice.

Oblivious, the doctors at Levin's clinic proceeded with the next
nine test subjects. On July 6, Levin issued his planned amendments
to the protocol, excluding the sickest patients. He recommended pre-
cautionary brain scans to weed out patients susceptible to neurological toxicity. And he forwarded a copy to the doctors conducting the
study at San Francisco General,[58] among others, so that prospective
study subjects elsewhere could be protected by what his group had
learned.

Weeks passed, and nobody heard from the FDA. Around mid-July,
agents from the San Francisco office paid separate visits to Delaney,

the doctors, and some patients. But the agents said they were merely "fact-finding." In relaxed interviews of from thirty to ninety minutes, the agents asked not much more information than was available in the protocol. Mainly, the interviewers verified that the drug wasn't sold for profit and that the patients brought it to the doctors, who did not stock their own supply.

In Los Angeles, the test seemed to be proceeding without mishap. In New York, too, the treatment trials at the Judson Church continued in a partylike atmosphere.

The only worsening problem appeared to be money. Ed Winger, who had donated the services of his lab to the study, complained that the work had far exceeded what he had imagined. Unbilled services were over $30,000 and climbing. Finally, Delaney worked out a system whereby Winger would get some money from contributions to Project Inform—still a steep discount from normal prices—to defray part of his cost of doing business.

But even at cut rates, Winger was billing tens of thousands of dollars. Project Inform took in tax-exempt donations, but the Q test was severely pressing its resources. And Corti had borrowed to finance his China buys. The money was supposed to be paid back.

Then a friend of Delaney's told him to expect a call from a man identified as Steve in Los Angeles, whose real name Delaney would never know, but who could provide at least $10,000. That sounded nice. But when the call came, there was a string attached.

Steve wanted to get into the study. He said his lover was the hairdresser of a well-known entertainer who would contribute $10,000 if, in return, Steve could get treated with Q.

"No," said Delaney, bitting his lip as he spoke, "you cannot buy your way into the study. We aren't taking more people right now."

"What about later?" Steve said. "This person, she wants to make a donation to you, and I may want to use Q later."

She. Delaney's mind began to churn out of natural curiosity. He had read that Elizabeth Taylor was upset over the AIDS problem and helping gay male friends. Could it be?

"Your getting into it later is not a question of money," he said. "If we continue the program, we'll judge who gets the drug on the basis of need and medical profile. We'd have to talk to your doctor, or have you visit one of ours."

At the same time, he was thinking, Don't put this guy off entirely. It's ten thousand dollars. "If your entertainer friend wants to contribute," he added, "it would be greatly appreciated."

"I think she will," he said. "But another thing. She doesn't want it known that she's donating. She's worried about liability if anything goes wrong. It will have to be in cash."

Holy smokes.

He called the mutual friend who had put them together.

"I'm really uncomfortable with someone thinking he can buy his way in," Delaney said. "And now he says cash and secrecy. We're an officially tax-exempt organization."

"Marty, it's ten thousand dollars," the friend said. "Take it."

"I don't want my hands to ever touch this. We don't need any problems with the tax exemption. It has to go to Corti. He said costs have been huge, and he needs reimbursement."

"This guy doesn't know who Corti is, or that the drug is coming in through Los Angeles. Nobody does. Let's protect Corti. Look, here's what we'll do. . . ."

Delaney called Steve back and set out the plan. He was to bring the $10,000 to the airport and meet a courier who would match a description to be supplied. He could watch the courier board the plane for San Francisco. The deal was struck. Corti found someone he trusted to carry the money, who was flying north. A brown lunch bag arrived in San Francisco containing exactly $10,000 in $20, $50, and $100 bills. Now the money had to get back to L.A.

Days passed. Nobody seemed to be going to Los Angeles, and Corti was too busy to come up. Finally, Jean O'Leary, a prominent lesbian working as executive director of the National Gay Rights Advocates, agreed to carry the money back down to Corti on a busia guy ness trip. Meanwhile, Corti reported hearing that Joan Rivers, the comedian, had a hairdresser who was sick and looking for Q. As far as Corti was concerned, the case of the mysterious entertainer was solved. The infusions complete, satisfied that the patients were in the hands of doctors, he headed to Europe to watch the Tour de France again.

Levin and Waites continued to donate not only the statistical work and their medical services, but to pay the nurses and even buy dinners for everyone at the infusion sessions. How different, Delaney thought, from FDA-approved studies, in which doctors were often paid top dollar with drug company or taxpayer money.[59] Delaney figured the contributions of the Levin office were worth $150,000. Project Inform picked up the cost of overnight stays in the hospital unit and a specialist to handle difficult needle insertions.

As expected, the Florida study site was what Waites called "the wild card." The protocol was not followed precisely. Infusions would vary from patient to patient, sometimes every three days, sometimes every seven, sometimes less often. Some shots continued to be given into the muscle instead of the bloodstream, also violating the protocol. Forms weren't filled out right. At one point, Waites got Mayer, Sergios's unlikely doctor, on the phone and harangued him. "We're getting laboratory bills for thousands of dollars and you're not following the routine," Waites told Mayer. "And you've never raised a dime to help pay the cost of the trial."

Mayer said he couldn't understand what the problem was, but would try to follow the protocol more closely in the future.

"You'll have to, or we're going to stop supplying everything for your study."

Mayer assured him, and by and large the activities in Florida did become much more regular.[60]

Meanwhile, other money finally began rolling in, thanks largely to all the negative publicity about the Q trials. Through the summer, Project Inform supporters mailed in more than $100,000 in small donations.

SIXTY-THREE

July 20, 1989, Representative Henry Waxman finally held his AIDS-related hearings. By this time, the ganciclovir controversy Delaney brought to him had been settled, and Waxman decided to focus instead on Fauci's "parallel-track" plan. Delaney, in Washington to testify, accepted an invitation from Frank Young to visit his FDA office the evening before. It was the first time they had met without the usual FDA team along; Young had suggested a 7:30 P.M. appointment so they would be alone.

Delaney had long puzzled over Young's constantly being surrounded by staff. At first, Delaney had thought Young liked the protection. Then, a few months earlier, Delaney had been passing time in conversation with Ellen Cooper before a large meeting. Not seeming to make a big issue of it, she mentioned that she and other staffers really didn't respect Young much. They stayed close in order to mind him. "If we left him alone with people, he'd give away the whole shop," she said, only half jokingly.[61] (See note for Cooper's comment.)

Apparently the FDA staff thought Young, a Reagan political appointee, was out to strip them of their regulatory power. That was ironic. If someone was to break the log jam, it seemed more likely to be Fauci, a career government scientist, than Young.

As Delaney walked into the commissioner's office at the FDA the evening of July 19, he felt a further irony. According to the press, Delaney was the FDA's Public Enemy Number One, under heavy investigation for holding lethal and illegal drug trials. In fact, a San Francisco FDA agent had scheduled a "fact-finding" interview with Delaney for the next day, July 20, and had to postpone it a week because of Delaney's Washington trip. What would the agent have thought had he known Delaney was up in Frank Young's office for a private policy consultation?

Young immediately said they couldn't talk about the Q problem, but added, "My only hope is that the patients were treated compassionately."

That struck Delaney as exactly what Young should have said—the sentiment of a doctor toward a patient, not a scientist toward a test subject or a cop toward a suspect.

"We've got some great new decisions coming along under Treatment IND," Young said. "You'll be pleased when you see what we're going to do."

Delaney felt himself being lobbied. He said, politely and low key, that he thought Fauci's parallel-track plan was needed anyway.

"I fear parallel track will just add more bureaucracy, and slow us down getting new drugs out," Young said.

And take power away from your agency, Delaney thought.

When it became clear they weren't going to agree on parallel track, Young steered the conversation to religion—something he knew had been a major part of both their lives. He knew Delaney had been in a seminary, and they talked about it and about Young's own dedication to fundamentalist Christianity. Young proudly told him that the Christian community Young lived in had just taken a group of black women with AIDS into their homes.

"You know," Young told him, "Jesus said, 'What you do to the least of these you do to me.' But"—and he paused—"it's always been difficult for me to understand homosexuality. How men could be that way with each other. But I think you're a fine person, and that shouldn't stand between us." Then the conversation returned to religion.

It was good to be reminded of the human side of your adversary, Delaney thought. He also wondered what all the reporters who were targeting him—not to mention other AIDS activists—would say if they knew about this conversation.

The next morning, at the congressional hearing, Fauci and Sam Broder of the National Cancer Institute, the government's highest-ranking research scientists, seemed restrained in their support of Fauci's parallel-track idea. With them, doing most of the talking, was their boss, James O. Mason, assistant secretary for health in the Department of Health and Human Services. Young was alongside them.

Mason endorsed Fauci's idea, but then talked mostly about the problems that had to be resolved before instituting it: who would be eligible for the drugs, who would pay for them, who would monitor them, who would be legally liable. Mason wanted advisory committees appointed, and outside consultants hired.

Delaney, up next, decided to urge speed. It had already taken too long to get to this point, he said. The basic ideas behind parallel track had been proposed by AIDS activists in testimony to the Presidential AIDS Commission years before.

"We have a crisis facing people with AIDS right now," he said, "in particular that some twenty to thirty thousand people have outlived the usefulness of AZT, and there are thousands of others for whom it was never useful in the first place. These people are, this month, this year, being thrust back into the 1986 reality of AIDS, in which there were no known therapies. And unless we move rapidly on this parallel track, thousands of those people are going to die needlessly. This isn't simply a philosophical discussion. We've heard here today essentially vague generalities about this process. What's going to count in the end is what's delivered."

Treatment IND hadn't worked, he said. Drugs like ddI, ddC, fluconazole (an agent that cures fungal infections that attack many AIDS patients), foscarnet (the CMV retinitis drug) and others "have earned the right to be in the physician's arsenal against AIDS. The fact that they are not already so, the fact that we're having to create a new parallel track or something, is testimony to the FDA's inability or unwillingness to permit early access. There is a large gap between what the commissioner says as the head of the agency, his personal commitments, and what, in fact, the career staffers in the agency have been willing to deliver."

Patient representatives should be included on whatever decision-making bodies were set up to direct parallel track, he said. And the individual patients whose lives were at risk should be able to choose among the available therapies.

"How would you propose that FDA handle the issues of safety?" Congressman Waxman asked.

"Well," Delaney replied, "I think clearly that parallel track does come with a little bit of increased risk. But it has to be balanced against the terrible risk that patients are being asked to take now by not being treated."

Then Waxman expressed concern about drug companies, which "would become nervous about data because they are giving their product to doctors and patients that they don't know and can't oversee."

Delaney saw a representative of the Pharmaceutical Manufacturers Association waiting to testify next. The big drug companies always paid lip service to getting drugs out fast, but then drew up long lists of obstacles to any plan that was proposed.

"I have a feeling," he said, "that drug companies sometimes are anxious to get a drug [approved] while having given it to the smallest number of people possible in order to get it licensed. Before they really find out what happens in large-scale use. That's their problem, not ours. We need that information. And frankly I think this track would get that information much more quickly."

As he predicted, the drug company representative leapt to defend the status quo. "Our society has adopted a system in which studies are done in a reasonable and stepwise fashion, and in which risk is minimized to the extent possible," the witness said. He argued that the existing compassionate-use provision took care of any other patient needs.

Anybody operating under the delusion that the big drug companies are fighting to get out from under the regulatory system ought to hear this, Delaney thought as he listened.

Delaney went back to San Francisco unsure what, if anything, Congress would do. The subject of Compound Q had never come up.

SIXTY-FOUR

According to Levin and Waites, the Miami trial site, for all its early problems, was now forwarding data and blood serum reliably enough so that it could probably be used in the study. The real snag turned out to be Los Angeles. The data had stopped arriving. Winger's laboratory reported receiving no blood samples. All anybody could get from Los Angeles were delays and evasions. Corti, who hadn't expected trouble, was in France.

Delaney decided the problem would have to wait until Corti's return. Once again, he found himself balancing between secret work in the underground drug network and public advocacy of new policies. Jack Killen, Fauci's aide, invited him to start attending the quarterly meetings of the AIDS Clinical Trials Group in Washington, and he did.

Lipner came to visit from New York, mostly as a vacation. But as he was preparing to leave, he jokingly asked, "What's my next assignment?"

Delaney thought over what Young had told him, and what he had heard at the Clinical Trials Group meeting. Bristol-Myers had just completed a very positive phase one study of ddI, and was feverishly planning a phase two study. Corti's underground source for ddI in Florida, via Canada, had become unreliable. If there was ever a candidate for parallel track, or Treatment IND, or whatever you wanted to call it, ddI was it. The FDA in its current mood could probably be swung behind the idea if the company could be enticed, embarrassed, or cajoled into supporting it.

"Your next assignment, should you choose to accept it," Delaney told Lipner, "is to call a meeting of community doctors in New York and somehow get them organized to become part of the ddI process." Lipner knew exactly what he meant, and considered it a brilliant idea. They needed to be able to make Bristol-Myers an offer it couldn't refuse. Act Up had been pressuring the company, but didn't talk Bristol-Myers's language. Lipner started calling doctors as soon as he was back in New York.

Two days later, July 28, 1989, *The Wall Street Journal* published a long front-page account of the Q affair by its highly regarded veteran West Coast medical reporter Marilyn Chase. Because of their reputation for thoroughness and accuracy, *Journal* page-one feature articles have unusually great impact. They are as close to being the last historical word as newspaper articles generally come. Delaney was stunned as he read, especially because the *Journal* editorial page had been supporting the cause he was championing.

The *Journal* news account was not entirely unflattering; the headline read, "Activist Risk-Takers May Gain Legitimacy in the War on AIDS." Midway down the front-page column the story said the Compound Q experimenters were "helping push forward a revolution in American drug development" by forcing a new look at "the issues of the speed of testing and access to drugs." In some ways the article was kind to Delaney, calling him "the architect of the unsanctioned Compound Q study" and recalling his Jesuit and conservative past.

But the more Delaney and Levin read it, the angrier they got. By errors of commission and omission, the story perpetuated the image of them as reckless and dangerous amateurs, who at best might scare responsible professionals elsewhere into working faster.

For one thing, the whole top half of the front-page column was devoted to the death of Robert Parr, which Delaney and Levin saw as minor in its relevance to Compound Q. Worse by far, the facts were wrong. The dramatic introduction of the story had Parr leaving the clinic from his infusion one day, going into a coma the next, and dying the next; the misleading implication was that Q was likely responsible. In fact, more than a week had passed, during which Parr had mostly recovered. The drug had entirely left his body in the first six hours and the lingering reaction to it had long reversed itself.

While the story posed the issue of whether Q killed Parr as an open question, the story then uncritically quoted a series of people from the medical establishment talking as if it were a foregone conclusion that Parr had died from the drug dose. Volberding and his aide Kahn were given their shots to say what a menace Delaney posed, and there was an especially acid remark by Ellen Cooper that "The maximum dose in [FDA] safety studies usually stops well short of death." Even Fauci was quoted calling the project "a mistake," while noting Delaney's good intentions.

The story made it sound as if the only science behind the protocol came from Waites, who was identified as a "pediatrician" (which he had been until the AIDS crisis years earlier had converted him to an AIDS specialist), and Levin, who was identified simply as "an academic with a history of selling unproven biologics among other drugs for AIDS." Levin especially resented the implication that he was profiteering, considering the countless hours and out-of-pocket expenses he was contributing to this project, for which he charged the patients nothing.

To some extent, Delaney's group was the victim of its own need to keep secret the role of such well-qualified research physicians as McGrath and Byers. Still, some things weren't secret—like the University of Nottingham animal studies that had proved the FDA-backed studies inaccurate. Without a hint of the care that had gone into the Q trial, the *Journal* story was misleading and unfair.

Like the television stories, the *Journal* story inaccurately stated that Delaney, Waites, and Levin had skipped safety tests and gone to the full therapeutic Chinese dose. In fact, after long delays for safety tests, Parr and the others had been given the lower of the two planned doses, which was less than half the usual Chinese dose. It was also a small fraction of doses the FDA had authorized for the study of San Francisco General, though the *Journal* story didn't mention that.

And when Delaney read himself referred to as "one of the most radical of the rebels," he rolled his eyes. In New York, gay doctors had refused to work with him because they said he had sold out to the establishment. Did the reporters who wrote these stories know that some patients were trying to import and distribute this drug for unsupervised injection, and that hundreds or thousands of patients might take it without a clue to toxicity if a study wasn't done fast? Stopping such radical and dangerous injections had been a primary objective of Delaney's.

In the end, the whole thrust of the story rested on one anecdote, which seemed compelling because it was told falsely in the lead. Put in that extra week of Parr's life when he mostly recovered, and what did you have to justify all the negative quotes? Nothing.[62] (See note for the *Journal*'s response.)

All test sites except Florida had completed the protocol, and there had been no other such incidents. Waites had discovered that Parr had suffered a head injury in a gay bashing the year before. If only they could check Parr's brain for preexisting lesions—but the hospital wouldn't do an autopsy.

On August 8, 1989, a letter arrived from Carl Peck, director of Drug Evaluation and Research at the FDA. Peck was Ellen Cooper's boss. Delaney, who had just got back the night before from giving a speech in Alaska, read the letter with mixed confusion and relief.

On the one hand, it said matter-of-factly that Project Inform had conducted an unauthorized clinical trial of trichosanthin—presumably a crime. The letter didn't deal with the legal protection that Delaney had provided to the investigators: that the doctors had only treated patients, as they were authorized to do, and that they had responded to Project Inform's requests for data on the patients, with the patients' consent. All that was legal. Of course, it was only a legal fiction, splitting hairs, but that's the way the law was written.

But having offhandedly said that Project Inform had violated the law against unapproved clinical trials, the letter from Peck ordered no sanctions. It didn't order anything, even a cease-and-desist. Peck merely *invited* Delaney and the participating doctors to meet with him to discuss the drug, and *recommended* against initiating any *new* use of trichosanthin before the meeting—which Delaney took to mean that patients already on the drug could continue with it.

Since Delaney had intended to go to the FDA with the results as soon as they were ready anyway, and since the San Francisco and New York sites under his control didn't plan to treat new patients until then, he had no problem with Peck's two requests. But Peck's language bothered him. Peck even said they might be using an impure drug—as if Peck hadn't talked at all to the FDA "fact finders" who had been given copies of the purity reports from both Genelabs and Nottingham.

Delaney tried to call Peck and wound up talking to James Bilstad, director of the Office of Drug Evaluation, whom Delaney had also met at the FDA earlier. Hadn't Peck talked to his investigators? Bilstad said he believed Peck's letter might be unrelated to the investigation—strange, Delaney thought. But they readily agreed to delay their meeting until September, when the data would be ready. And Bilstad agreed that Genelabs would be invited, too. By this time, Delaney was already talking regularly with Genelab's director of clinical research, Roger Williams, who had been very friendly. Williams was eager to learn anything the Project Inform study found out.

In light of all this, Delaney found it hard to reconcile Peck's letter with the coverage it was getting in the papers—which made it sound as if the Project Inform group had been ordered to cease and desist from its Q activities. He phoned his friend at the Associated Press to complain, and was surprised and pleased when she arranged for a toned-down story to go out on the wire, more accurately reflecting the situation.

So maybe everything was okay. The system was successfully being dragged kicking and screaming to reasonableness. If Genelabs was invited to the meeting at the FDA, then the purpose of the meeting was clearly to advance science, not to press charges.

On August 14, 1989, just as Delaney was beginning to feel self-satisfied, McGrath called in a fit. The bastards at San Francisco General, ignoring Levin's written warnings, had given Compound Q to a subject named Charles Weaver who had a T-cell count of 23, far below the limit of 100 that Levin had recommended. They had not performed a brain scan before administering the drug, as both Levin and Rothman had recommended, on the ground that there was no proof, by their definition, that a brain scan would help predict the likelihood of side effects. And the dose they had given was 36 micrograms per kilogram of body weight—more than twice the dose Project Inform had administered, which everybody from Ellen Cooper on down had told the networks and *The Wall Street Journal* was unsafe!

Charles Weaver was in a coma.

Delaney's mind reeled. In *The Wall Street Journal*, these same doctors who gave the fragile Weaver 36 micrograms per kilogram had said Delaney and Levin were risking killing much stronger people by giving them 16 micrograms per kilogram.

"But that's not all," McGrath said.

Delaney braced himself.

"They won't give him Decadron. They say that's not on the protocol and giving him Decadron will interfere with the study."

"But he could *die* without Decadron!" Delaney screamed.

"They won't give it to him. It's a steroid, and they don't want to give immuno-suppressants to an AIDS patient."

"Every problem case we've had, including Robert Parr, pulled out with Decadron," Delaney said. "They're killing this guy for the sake of proving some scientific point, whatever it is."

Delaney was packing to go to Washington the next day to testify before a standing FDA advisory committee that had been assigned to make recommendations on parallel track. He paused to whip out a very blunt press release on Weaver. "Had our findings on this type of side effect been recognized and examined by researchers at SFGH, we feel this incident might have been avoided," it concluded.

Before calling even the first reporter, he called Levin and Waites. After some initial outrage, they decided not to make a show, but to try to save the patient by quietly negotiating with San Francisco General. "Hold off. Go to your meeting in Washington. We'll call these guys and get this straightened out."

SIXTY-FIVE

Delaney arrived at the advisory committee meeting in Washington to find that Act Up had bused at least a hundred demonstrators down from New York. Delaney and others gave talks, and by the end of the day there seemed to be a consensus that the parallel-track concept made sense, and a regulation ought to be drawn up. Delaney urged that the program be run by a mixed committee of researchers, regulators, patients, and the public.

Before a vote was taken, there were comments from the public, mostly the Act Up demonstrators. Larry Kramer arranged to be last in line, to close the meeting. There was some tension, since Kramer had in the past referred to Tony Fauci, who was present, as a Nazi. Now, Kramer skulked dramatically to the microphone, and looked around, while everyone waited uncomfortably.

"You think I'm going to be rude," he observed. "I am. I'm going to be fucking rude." And he began to lecture the committee members that if they didn't vote to support parallel track, they would be responsible for the deaths of many innocent people. Then he turned to his former nemesis and proclaimed in a loud voice, "Dr. Fauci, you're our hero!"

Smiling now, the committee voted to recommend the parallel-track idea to the FDA, and to have James Allen, head of the National AIDS Program Office, nominate a committee like the one Delaney had been proposing to run it.

Back in California, Corti had arrived home from Europe to find his carefully organized Los Angeles study site in shambles. With a few phone calls, he satisfied himself that the study had been tanked by Paul Rothman's medical partners. Rothman denied it was anything so blunt, but there was no doubt in Corti's mind after talking to him that the study had been quietly subverted. The publicity Rothman attracted by publicly defending the study after Robert Parr died had proven too much. Rothman conceded his partners had been concerned about that.

Corti figured that if Q had proven to be the real home-run drug everyone had hoped, Rothman might have ridden out the storm. But with subtle results, and uncertainty about whether the drug worked, it was a different story. The controversial newspaper and television accounts were too much to bear for an office that did its own share of FDA-approved research. But nobody wanted to admit that, and so nobody had notified Project Inform so that replacement doctors might be found.

The study was simply cut loose. Contemporaneous records required for peer review were never filled out. Instead of sending the blood samples to Ed Winger's lab in San Leandro, near San Francisco, Rothman had begun having the samples analyzed in Pacific Oaks's own lab. While the lab was good enough for the patients' safety, its data would not be fairly comparable to the data from Winger's lab, where the patients' original blood values had been established. Even the best labs did things differently, and it was a well-established scientific principle that the lab that performed the baseline studies—what shape a patient was in starting out—had to do the subsequent test studies as well. Without that, no matter how good the labs were, for scientific purposes you had apples and oranges. When Corti asked him about it, Rothman made a remark about cutting out Winger's lab to save money. But at the time Winger's lab had been working free.

Corti told Rothman that his failure to ship the blood to the common laboratory and submit reports in timely fashion would render the Los Angeles results invalid. Waites had already told Rothman pretty much the same thing. And Rothman had replied that Corti and his friends at Project Inform were just disappointed because the Los Angeles trial hadn't produced positive results to match those in the other centers.

Corti pointed out that Rothman had already told the *L. A. Times* that based on his observation of the fifteen patients Q seemed to be the most effective medication yet for this disease. That was premature, Rothman said, and out of context.

Wasn't it true, Corti demanded, that his partners, including Joel Weisman of AmFAR, had reined him in?

"That's definitely true," Rothman conceded. "They questioned the legality of what we were doing. They were very concerned that since we did so much FDA-sanctioned research that for me to be a spokesman for an underground trial could jeopardize that."[63]

"Shit," said Corti, mostly to himself.

"That's just great," said Delaney sarcastically when Corti told him the news. But they still had 19 subjects in San Francisco, 17 in New York, and 15 in Florida. That was only 51 instead of the 60 originally planned. But it was still a study. Waites, Levin, and Byers promised to have numbers and graphs ready in early September.

What especially galled Delaney was the way establishment doctors continued to treat him as a pariah, while *they* were the ones not giving the lifesaving drug Decadron to Charles Weaver, the patient on the official Compound Q trial run by the University of California at San Francisco General Hospital. And Weaver continued in a state variously described as comatose or semi-comatose.

Waites said Weaver's lover had come to the Levin office begging Levin and Waites to take over the case. The lover said that a neurologist at the hospital, Dr. Robert Messing, had recommended using Decadron, but Dr. James Kahn, the Volberding associate in charge of the study, was refusing. According to Waites, the lover said Weaver's doctors had told him they wanted to follow the natural course of Compound Q and see what would happen. Levin had shrieked that this, in the face of a known cure, sounded like Nazi experimentation.

Waites called Messing and Kahn, separately, and got slightly different stories, but no satisfaction. Messing pointed out in Kahn's defense that many doctors, not just Kahn, were reluctant to give immune-suppressing steroids to an AIDS patient already suffering from a suppressed immune system. But Messing confirmed that he had recommended Decadron on the patient's chart, based on what he had heard of Levin's results, and he was holding to that against Kahn's decision otherwise.[64] (See note for accounts of Kahn and others.)

Levin and Waites huddled over what to do. They concluded they could not seize control of the case despite the lover's request. Levin argued decisively that Decadron had to be administered early if it was to bring the patient out of a coma without brain damage. After so many days, he said, it was unlikely Weaver would ever fully recover his faculties no matter what they did. It was important they not give the San Francisco General group the opportunity to blame them for the outcome.

August 24, 1989, ten days after Delaney had written his press release that was never released, he faxed Paul Beninger, a medical officer he had met at the FDA. Saying he was writing "on an urgent matter which calls for your immediate attention," Delaney recounted in detail the Weaver situation and the refusal to administer Decadron.[65]

Delaney paused as he wrote and thought back to what *they* had said to *him*. According to *The Wall Street Journal*, in a front-page story, "Dr. Paul Volberding, AIDS chief at San Francisco General Hospital, condemned the action [Delaney's Q tests] as a disservice to patients. 'Bad medicine,' said his colleague Jim Kahn, who is running the official Compound Q study at the hospital." Then the *Journal* had quoted a New York AIDS specialist saying, "It's dangerous. They're experimenting on human beings." Delaney muttered a curse. *Who the hell do they think they are to say that about me and then let this happen to Charlie Weaver?*

The next day, he called Jeff Lifson, chief scientist at Genelabs, to talk about Q data.

"You must have really put the heat on the FDA over this Weaver case," Lifson said. "Beninger called here. Said, 'What the hell is going on?' " Lifson said that after the FDA prodding he had called the trials group at San Francisco General. Whether or not it was Delaney's doing, within hours they had started Weaver on Decadron.[66]

But, as Levin had predicted, Weaver recovered only partially. He became able to make eye contact and move his limbs. But he never regained full use of his mind. He was moved to a hospice.[67]

Not long after the Weaver episode, at the end of August, Delaney got a call from a lawyer at the Department of Health and Human Services. AIDS director Jim Allen was inviting him to join the parallel-track advisory committee.

Meanwhile, another official of the agency that was supposedly investigating him asked him to speak at the FDA's every-other-month conferences on health fraud. Delaney agreed, hoping to discourage the desperation treatments some people were pushing, such as coffee enemas, urine injections, and typhoid vaccine. He tried to define the line between legitimate unorthodoxy, with a scientific basis, and fraud.

S I X T Y-S I X

AIDS drug trials were never going to be either speedy or humane unless efficacy could be measured by some other yardstick than the death rate of patients. Other measures were available. Every AIDS patient in America wanted his T-cell count to increase and his P-24 antigen count to diminish. But even if you had a drug that could accomplish both, you couldn't get to first base with the FDA under the current rules.

As people like Ellen Cooper argued, nobody had proven that if a patient cut his P-24s and increased his T-cells he wouldn't die of AIDS anyway. On the other hand, death always came in direct proportion to the fall of T-cells. A lot of patients longed for the chance to try a drug that increased them, if only the rules could be changed so that researchers might bring forth drugs that would work on these markers.

The government's Institute of Medicine Roundtable had scheduled intensive hours of scientific presentations and panels at the National Academy of Sciences building in Washington September 11 and 12, 1989, to see if a switch to surrogate markers could be justified. Eighteen people had been nominated to the roundtable, which was assigned to recommend a solution after the conference. Looking back at it, Delaney's inclusion seemed nothing short of miraculous considering he had first been exposed to the drug approval problem in a dusty Tijuana *farmacia* less than five years earlier. The other seventeen members were Young, Fauci, and Gallo; a top scientist each from Walter Reed Army Medical Center, the Veterans Administration, and the National Cancer Institute; senior medical professors or department chairmen from five leading medical schools; senior executives from four big drug companies; and, inescapably, two lawyers.

But it was a nineteenth person, not even formally on the round table but on a couple of pivotal panels, who seemed to play the biggest part. She was Ellen Cooper. For a day and a half, the speeches had been fairly predictable, including Delaney's. After the panels, the roundtable members closeted themselves for a discussion—except that the nineteenth member sat in. Because an FDA scientist seemed useful, no one objected.

Delaney had learned to predict how things were going to go with Cooper by her tone of voice the first time she spoke at any meeting. She seemed to come equipped with two voices: one deep and masculine, which presaged a posture of guarding the temple of science from the barbarians, and the other warm and feminine, which signaled a mood of conciliation. The day a few months earlier when she had backtracked on ganciclovir in front of the doctors Delaney had brought to Washington, she had spoken in her feminine voice. Today she came out sounding to Delaney like the troll under the bridge.

"We have scientists arguing for it, and scientists arguing against it," she said—which was fairly to be expected, since the panels had been set up to articulate the controversy. "Therefore, as regulators, we cannot say this is the right thing to do. Our hands are tied if there isn't scientific consensus, and I don't see scientific consensus here."

Statisticians from the AZT and other studies had been assigned to reexamine all data to see what would have happened had the blood markers been used in those studies instead of longevity. They had just testified that they hadn't completed this arduous chore. They could not yet affirm scientifically that an improvement in T-cells correlated to living longer.

"That data isn't in. We can't act till we get it," Cooper concluded.

As the afternoon dragged on, she seemed to have no real support on the rest of the panel, but also no passionately outspoken opponent —except one. Delaney felt the urge to argue, but in this crowd he knew he didn't have the stature to win. The man who came forward was Tony Fauci. Fauci was determined to move ahead with surrogate markers.

Any clinical doctor will tell you, Fauci finally burst out, that the decline of T-cells is the hallmark of the disease. "Not only is it the hallmark, the CD-4 cells [T-cells] are the primary organ of dysfunction. They are the organ that is being damaged by the disease."

It was clear to Delaney that Fauci was really angry at Cooper's obstinacy. Fauci sat at the end of a long table; Cooper and Delaney were across from each other at its midpoint. The other end of the table seemed dead as the tension built between Fauci and Cooper. It struck Delaney that Fauci must feel chagrined to be paired as equals with her in the first place. Cooper was a mid-level FDA staff person with a few years' experience. Fauci was one of the world's most-renowned immunologists, the head of a great institute. Delaney could read the frustration in his reddening face. He began talking faster.

Delaney decided that Ellen Cooper must look at Tony Fauci the same way she looked at the drug companies: animals ready to bolt the pen if she didn't guard the gate.

At one point after Cooper had gone so far as to argue that no one had proved increased T-cells were a good thing, Fauci replied in a fury, "You can define AIDS as declining T-cells. One does not have to stretch one's imagination too far to figure out that if a drug stabilizes or increases the CD-4 cell count it very likely will help the patient."

Young sat at the table, strangely silent. He seemed to be deferring to Cooper. She was saying things that would play very well to the appropriate congressional oversight committees. No drug company was going to slip any shortcut science onto the drugstore shelves during her watch.

The lines seemed drawn. Once Delaney tried a low-key interjection, about his difficulty in understanding why people were hung up over absolute certainty, when most patients would be thankful for a chance just to roll the dice.

But it did no good. The FDA was the elephant at the table, and Cooper seemed to be running the FDA.[68] (See note for Cooper's contrary account, and Fauci's confirming account.)

After the meeting, the Institute of Medicine staff wrote a report essentially saying there was no consensus. It consisted mainly of academic observations. At one point it even conceded that researchers were confident that reduction of P-24 levels was a sign the virus was being fought. But it said the researchers were "unable to explain why this reduction occurs." So, pending an explanation, it just called for more clinical studies to "clarify the value of these and other potential surrogate markers."

You couldn't argue with the facts. You could just argue that if you were dying of a virus you didn't care exactly how or why a drug stopped the virus. You just wanted it stopped.

From what he could sense of the meeting—and his profession *was* reading people's attitudes at meetings—Delaney suspected that the drug-company executives and other scientists there would have voted with Fauci on a secret ballot if it had come to that. But science was governed by consensus, not democracy. Why had the scientists and drug companies not gone to bat for Fauci? Why had he been out there swinging alone? Delaney wondered how many of the salaries of the people sitting at the table could be affected by the determinations of the FDA.

He was glad to be flying back to San Francisco. Levin, Waites, and Byers had put the finishing touches on the Q study. The press and public were invited for an unveiling of the results Tuesday evening, September 19.

The Q summer of 1989 had begun with the publicity over Parr's death, spoiling what should have been the most glorious public event of Delaney's life, the first Treatment Awareness Week. Now, he hoped, it would conclude with the glory of announcing a successful community-based drug study.

Q hadn't proven to be the miracle cure everyone had hoped for. It held promise of slowing the disease. But the main thing Project Inform had proven was that it could do in a few months what the government took years to do: give desperate patients a clear idea of how safe a new drug was likely to be and a working idea of its possible effectiveness.

But he had barely unpacked his bags when Lipner called with an air of foreboding. Gina Kolata was working on a story for *The New York Times* about somebody's having just died from the Compound Q trial.

"*What?*"

Delaney couldn't imagine what this was about. He did not relish calling Kolata; she had misunderstood their arrangement about the Compound Q story back in June, and had exploded in anger on the phone over losing what she thought was to be an exclusive. But Delaney had to call her now.

"How convenient!" she answered. "I was just going to call *you*." And she told him the story.

The dead man's name was Scott Sheaffer, and he had been infused with Q by Dr. Barbara Starrett, Kolata said. He had flipped out mentally and begun deteriorating physically. Twice he had gone to the hospital. Both times Starrett, in order to protect the secrecy of the study, had withheld from the hospital the fact that he had taken Compound Q. The second time he had died.

"That would be a violation of our protocol," Delaney said. "I'd be stunned if she did that." He cautioned Kolata that deaths commonly occur in clinical trials involving terminally ill people, and said he would call Starrett to find out what had happened.

It was the next day, Saturday, before he could get hold of her.

"I just found out Sheaffer died," she explained. "It wasn't because of Q. It was more than six weeks later, August 25. He had had three bouts of PCP going back eighteen months before he ever took the Q. Plus neuropathy and other infections. Scott wasn't even my patient. He was a volunteer at the Community Research office. He heard the doctors talking about the Q study and begged me to give him some. He wouldn't take AZT, because he believed this *New York Native* business that it was poison. But Q came from cucumbers, and cucumbers are natural, so he'd take that."

"Jesus."

"Yeah. So, anyway, he had the neurological reaction you've described with other patients, except not as bad. He certainly wasn't in a coma. But he needed IV hydration, and his roommate had been fighting with him and couldn't take care of him, so I put him in a hospital. He came out of it over the same weekend—in on a Friday, discharged Sunday. I have him on videotape the next Tuesday night, just fine, telling the other patients his story and asking for more Q."

"Did he get it?"

"Of course not. He said he wanted to get it the next week then. Obviously I wouldn't. But the point is we went through this procedure with every patient on videotape. We tell them, 'We want you to know that this is what happened with Scott, do you want to be infused again?' "

"What about this business that you wouldn't tell the hospital he had taken the drug?"

"That's nonsense. I told people if they had to go to the hospital, to say they were on an experimental drug, but not to say what it was, to call me. I told the doctors at the hospital it was an experimental drug. They didn't ask which one. I told them what to do. And I called Al Levin and he was going to call them. Sheaffer walked out Sunday fine. I told all this to Kolata. I don't understand it. I'm going to have to call her again."

"What happened when he died?"

"I didn't even know it until afterward. I wasn't his doctor. I called the doctor, and he said Sheaffer had gone in the hospital with neuropathy, but seemed to be okay, then died. They're not even sure why. But everyone's satisfied it wasn't Compound Q."

"Well, Gina Kolata isn't. You better call her back. And find Sheaffer's doctor and get him to talk to her. Somebody's got to educate that woman."

Delaney talked to Starrett again on Sunday and got a sanguine report. Kolata had said the story really wasn't about Starrett, but about community trials in general. Sheaffer's doctor, Jeffrey Wallach, had also talked to her, and assured her there was no reason to think Sheaffer's death was related to Q.

Delaney went back to preparing for Tuesday night's big public meeting to announce the trial results.

SIXTY-SEVEN

*E*very Tuesday the *Times* devotes its third of four sections to science, calling the section "Science Times." The lead story on the front page of this week's section was Kolata's. The headline said, "Critics Fault Secret Effort to Test AIDS Drug. Third death may undermine attempts to shortcut time-consuming Federal rules."

The story began ominously, "A New York man participating in an unorthodox private study of an AIDS drug has died." In the next breath, it linked the death to the testing procedures. Without saying anything good about the Project Inform study, Kolata reported it was being "sharply criticized by many advocates for people with AIDS, ethicists . . . and leading academic AIDS researchers."

The article continued, spreading misinformation as it went. "Unlike federally approved studies," it said, the Q study hadn't established procedures to protect "desperate patients . . . from being harmed by the research. The study did not start with a very low dose of the drug to look carefully for evidence of dangerous side effects. In addition, because of the secrecy of the study, the doctor who administered the experimental drug to Mr. Sheaffer did not tell either of two hospitals where he was admitted that he had taken the drug, leading doctors to provide what may have been inappropriate treatment.

"The doctors working on the study may even have violated their own ground rules by admitting Mr. Sheaffer to the study before he had first tried and failed other conventional treatments."

Finally, after this lengthy indictment, which pretty well staked out the *Times*'s determination of what happened, Levin was allowed into the story to dispute the charges. Sheaffer, he said, "knew exactly what he was doing," and "there is no evidence whatsoever that compound Q caused his death." Then there was a typically brash Levin statement that undercut his credibility more than anything else. He accused the FDA-backed university physicians of being "more interested in aggrandizing themselves than in stopping AIDS," and said that because of this Project Inform was keeping these doctors "out of the loop." It looked as if Levin were confirming the charge that Starrett's secrecy had endangered her patient.

What should have been printed was the opposite—that from the beginning Project Inform had invited onto its design team the FDA-backed university researcher who developed Compound Q as an AIDS drug in the first place. Of course, McGrath's role had to be kept secret to protect him. Still, the readers were misled.

Turning to the inside pages where the story was continued, Delaney confronted two pictures. One was of him, and it was labeled "George Annas, professor of health law, Boston University School of Medicine, questions private trials." The other, which had the name Martin Delaney under it, depicted a scraggly, bushy-bearded man who looked like a turn-of-the-century Russian revolutionary, or maybe one of the Smith Brothers—at any rate, 180 degrees from the perpetually cherubic-looking Delaney. How much worse could this get?

A lot.

After the quotes from Levin came the usual piling on of doctors and "ethicists" attacking the study—and, strangely, Delaney thought, even some people from the AIDS community, like Act Up member Mark Harrington, whom Delaney hadn't expected to come down against him so strongly.

And there was Dr. Bernard Bihari being asked by Kolata whether Compound Q had caused Sheaffer's death. "We have to assume it may have," Bihari proclaimed. Bihari was the same doctor the Dingell subcommittee in Congress had relied on to "assume" under oath that ICN had raised the Mexican price of ribavirin as a plot to gouge American patients illegally. Bihari might be wrong, but his assumptions could be devastating. Recently Delaney had learned that Bihari's assumption about ICN had ignited a grand-jury investigation of the company that was still in progress. Michael Scolaro, Nikki Gramatikos, and ICN executives were being dragged in to testify. Why, Delaney thought, did the national press and government investigators always seem to nail their targets with the same small cast of accusers?

Then Delaney saw something he knew would hurt Starrett terribly. After Sheaffer was hospitalized with his neurological reaction, the *Times* said, "Dr. Starrett said she did not tell the hospital doctors that the man had received Compound Q because 'it would not have made a difference in his treatment' and because she feared 'it would blow everything up and I would not be able to complete the study.' "

Now Starrett herself seemed to be confessing to covering up the Q test and, in the *Times*'s words, "leading doctors to provide what may have been inappropriate treatment." Starrett was being made to look like someone whose determination to finish her study was riding roughshod over the interests of her patients. How incredibly unfair! If ever a doctor was giving selflessly of herself out of an almost bleeding-heart concern for her patients, it was Starrett. She wasn't getting a dime for this; it was costing her. Levin, maybe, you could say had a political agenda, although he, too, was making great personal sacrifice for the patients. But for purity of motive Starrett was on line with Mother Teresa.

Starrett told Delaney she had informed the hospital that Sheaffer had taken an experimental drug, and what to do about it; she just hadn't named the drug, and the hospital staff hadn't asked. She said she had explained this to Kolata, too. If Kolata knew that, it was downright dishonest not to say so, or at least print Starrett's side of the story. Moreover, whatever medical steps had been taken had been the right ones, because Sheaffer recovered and went home in two days. And he was on videotape attesting to his recovery and seeking more Q two days later, though Kolata didn't choose to report that and, Starrett said, refused to look at the videotape.

As for the second hospitalization, Dr. Wallach told Delaney that he hadn't mentioned the Compound Q experiment to the hospital only because Sheaffer ordered him not to. Sheaffer, who still volunteered at the community research group, was afraid that, if people found out he was in the experiment, he would be besieged with requests for access to Q. Wallach wasn't protecting anything but his patient. Neither he nor Sheaffer thought Q had anything to do with the hospitalization. Sheaffer went in for his neuropathy, which he had had before he took Q. Q had never been linked to neuropathy. Wallach said he had told Kolata this, but none of it was in the story.

What Kolata wrote was: "Dr. Starrett said she did not tell the doctors at Cabrini [the second hospital] of the Compound Q treatment either." Thus Kolata blamed Starrett by name for not telling the hospital about the Q treatment, without mentioning that by Starrett's and other available accounts Starrett wasn't aware Sheaffer was even *in* the hospital. He wasn't her patient. She learned of the hospitalization only after he died. How dishonest!

But there seemed to be a lot of dishonest things about Kolata's story. She knew that the two other patients who died after participating in the Q study died from causes unrelated to Q. Ron Fisher had died because his lungs filled up with Kaposi's sarcoma and he couldn't breathe, not because he had taken compound Q a month earlier. And she knew there was a lot of evidence that Robert Parr's death wasn't caused by the drug, either. Why lead a story with three deaths when none of them likely related to the drug? Comparable FDA-approved trials had higher death rates—which she didn't bother to mention—and they didn't make big news.

Then, he read, "Mr. Delaney said he was 'stunned' Dr. Starrett did not inform the hospitals that Mr. Sheaffer had taken compound Q." Delaney hadn't told Kolata that Starrett didn't inform the hospitals. He told her he didn't know a thing about it. He just said he would have been stunned if it had been true—and it *wasn't* true, or at best it was a deceptive half-truth.

She reported that "Two earlier deaths of test subjects provoked a federal inquiry, which is still underway." What inquiry? The FDA hadn't rebuked Delaney. Everybody from the commissioner on down had invited him to meeting after meeting to seek his advice and support on drug issues.

The last judgment on Compound Q in Kolata's story, no surprise to Delaney, was given to James Kahn, the distinguished government-approved scientist at the University of California in San Francisco. Of course, Kolata didn't mention that Kahn's patient, Charles Weaver, had spent ten days in a coma or near-coma for lack of Decadron until Delaney pressured the FDA to intervene (although Kahn maintained that he prescribed Decadron as soon as he was advised to do so).

Delaney was still glaring at the article when Starrett called.

"The story is just incredibly misleading and unfair," she said. "This man wasn't even my patient. He didn't die of Q at all. This accuses me of keeping the drug secret from the hospital, and that isn't true. It even quotes you as saying—"

"I know, Barbara. We've got to prepare a written point-by-point answer, and get it off today—as much as I hate to, with the Q meeting starting in a few hours. But she can't be allowed to get away with this."

"Martin, this is *The New York Times*. This could destroy my career. It makes me look like I care nothing about my patients. I've done everything with the patients in mind, you know that."

"Of course, I know that. Barbara, has anybody from the government, or medical society, or any regulatory board said anything to you about this?"

"Not one word."[69]

"What I have trouble understanding," Delaney said, "is why people like Mark Harrington came out against us." Kolata quoted Harrington saying Sheaffer "was healthy and stable" before he took Compound Q, after which, Harrington said, "his decline was so rapid. It was like nothing I have ever heard of in AIDS."

"For Christ's sake," Delaney told Starrett, "Harrington knows lots of people who died much quicker than Sheaffer."

"Of course, he does. I just talked to him, and he's very upset. He says he never met Sheaffer in his life and that Kolata knew that, that he was commenting from some description from the roommate."

"He never *met* Sheaffer? How can the *Times* quote him describing how rapidly Sheaffer deteriorated?"[70]

"There are other things people deny," Starrett said. "I've talked to Joe Sonnabend. According to Kolata, he's the doctor that first brought the mysterious death of Mr. Sheaffer to light. That's not true. Joe was told about the death the day it happened. He says she blew something he said all out of proportion to make it sound like there was a cover-up. He says he knows there was no cover-up and he never complained about one. And he says he knows Q didn't cause Sheaffer's death.[71] Then there's Sheaffer's doctor, Jeffrey Wallach. He says he told Kolata over and over the Q wasn't responsible for Sheaffer's death, but she wouldn't print that."[72] (See notes 70, 71, 72 for the accounts of Harrington, Sonnabend, and Wallach respectively.)

"You know, it's interesting how she does this," Delaney said. "She says Sheaffer's death 'has led to an outcry among some prominent members of the community of advocates.' And then whom does she quote to justify saying there's an outcry? She quotes Bihari, that's who. And Harrington, who disowns it. This is just her, basically, saying these things."

Delaney pounded out a two-page, single-spaced letter to the *Times*. Starrett wrote her own letter asking corrections, as did Wallach and some others. The paper printed none of it.[73] (See note for Kolata's account.)

SIXTY-EIGHT

The September 19, 1989, community meeting of Project Inform was moved from its usual setting at the community church to a hall in the Mission district, to hold the five hundred people who turned out, including doctors and the press corps. With the sting of the *Times* article that morning still in him, Delaney refused to allow TV cameras in, though TV crews were outside doing interviews on the street. "You'd turn this into a circus if I let you inside," Delaney told them. "This is a potentially dangerous drug."

Corti, Delaney, Waites, Levin, and Byers all spoke. Delaney introduced Corti as the AIDS folk hero of San Francisco. The crowd cheered. When Levin was introduced, the crowd rose and cheered again. Delaney could see tears in Levin's eyes as he delivered the test results.

It was heartening that this audience understood what the project had accomplished, as so many people outside didn't. This audience knew that regardless of Q's curative limitations, having come this far so fast was a major achievement. The conclusions spilled out over two and a half hours, including questions from the audience.

The speakers detailed their findings, emphasizing that the sickest patients, and any patient with evidence of infection of the brain or nervous system, shouldn't take the drug. Others should also approach it with caution. Efficacy was less certain, but there was reason for hope and further study. Because of the dosage variations in Florida, only the 19 San Francisco and 17 New York patients could be used to judge efficacy.

Of 18 patients with positive P-24 antigen counts going into the study (P-24 antigens don't show up in patients until the virus is well spread in the body), 12 showed a desired drop in the counts, averaging 50 percent. All 6 patients with very high P-24 values experienced declines averaging 67 percent. Levin said he considered these results particularly significant because they occurred in patients in whom AZT was failing to control levels of P-24 antigen.

T-cell counts also rose—by 12 percent among all San Francisco patients and 42 percent among all New York patients. The effect of the drug peaked several weeks past the last dose, after which the improvements started to reverse themselves.

Levin reminded the audience that the results came from only three doses. AZT achieved its superior numbers after prolonged use. Whether Compound Q would provide continued improvement after prolonged dosing awaited more tests.

Q also correlated with improvements in other blood markers, such as the ratio of T-4 cells to T-8 cells, which some doctors considered more important than the overall T-cell count. T-4/T-8 ratios rose 16 percent in San Francisco and 43 percent in New York. And the fact that Compound Q, unlike other drugs being tried, actually killed infected cells provided a new tool for further laboratory research.

On the other hand, Delaney said, the unexpected complexity of Q meant that more testing would be necessary than he had originally hoped. Unlike its reaction to such drugs as AZT or ribavirin, the human body formed an antibody to Q, which might neutralize some of Q's toxicity, or its effect. The antibody could bring new symptoms. At any rate, dosage was tricky and still unresolved. The jump to a late-stage trial couldn't be made yet.

Finally, the medical team declared that it was writing up the study formally for submission to a scientific journal.

Afterward, McGrath told Delaney that, despite what Kahn was saying, the University of California team had learned a lot from the Project Inform study, particularly about side effects and how to treat them.

"You have behaved extraordinarily responsibly," he assured Delaney. "Project Inform is really keeping a lot of people from taking impure formulations of this drug. Because you're doing that, a lot of lives are not going to be lost."

Mark Roh, the FDA official, called Delaney the next day to compliment him on his presentation. It was the right balance, Roh said, between the promising news people wanted to hear and a warning that the study didn't prove Q worked.

Waites reminded Delaney of the time-consuming animal tests that Waites and Vera Byers had insisted be repeated before they administered any trichosanthin. The team at San Francisco General thought it had already done enough tests, and had settled on a fast infusion, which wouldn't have let the drug in the body long enough to work. After Project Inform's tests showed a slow infusion was necessary, the university team had adopted that process also.

"If we had gone ahead without that test," Waites said, "Q would be a dead drug now."[74]

The usual critics' choir was muted, but present. Gina Kolata in *The New York Times* gave the data straight, though she also rehashed the

three deaths, and spent several paragraphs quoting a medical professor who said AZT test results had been stronger, without noting that
AZT patients were healthier to begin with, and that AZT results were
based on long-term dosage whereas Compound Q subjects got only
three doses.

But worse, in the *San Francisco Examiner* and *Los Angeles Times*
Mathilde Krim of AmFAR was quoted casting doubt on the accuracy
of the Compound Q data—this after AmFAR had practically begged
to get in on the study. Delaney had finally allowed the organization
to send two observers, but as soon as Parr's death was made a national scandal on network television, the two observers had fled like
frightened rabbits, pretending they had never been involved. And it
was Krim's AmFAR colleague, Joel Weisman, who had pressured his
partner, Paul Rothman, into effectively scuttling the Los Angeles
quadrant of the study by halting his cooperation with the San Francisco protocol.

Delaney wrote Krim an outraged letter, denouncing her unsub-
stantiated attack on his integrity. She did not reply.[75]

For Delaney, however, the real test of the team's Q work was to
come October 6, 1989, at FDA headquarters in Rockville, Maryland.
The day before, he met with Nancy Buc, a former FDA general counsel, now a Washington lawyer, who had volunteered to defend him
if he needed it. Buc heard everything, read the protocol and consents, and said she was convinced Delaney's team had done no
wrong—and that the FDA would not want to prosecute them and
face losing in court. That let Delaney sleep a little better.

The next day, Drs. Mayer and Starrett showed up for the FDA
session, along with Delaney, Waites, a legal associate of Ponzi's, and
Roger Williams, director of medical affairs at Genelabs. Sandoz,
Genelabs's partner and patron, also sent three representatives. More
important than anything they said was the unspoken signal that Sandoz had decided to try to make Project Inform an ally, not a compet-
itor, in getting this drug tested.

Delaney aimed to duplicate the presentation made in San Francisco as much as possible. But it seemed wise to substitute the
gentle, soft-spoken Larry Waites for the shoot-from-the-hip Al Levin,
at least before this crowd.

And it was a crowd—nearly fifty people. Delaney had expected
perhaps a dozen people from the FDA, and was stunned to find
several dozen. Teams came from the antiviral division, the statistical
division, the pharmacology division, the general counsel's office, and

the office of regulatory affairs. Cooper, Bilstad, and Peck were all there, though not Young. When the meeting opened, the first decision made was to find a bigger room to accommodate everyone.

After the procession had straggled down the hall to larger quarters, Peck began in a professional and unemotional tone, assuring the visitors that the meeting was not to be seen as a punitive hearing. Nobody was on trial. The agency was interested in what they had done, why, and what results they had achieved. "My goal is to bring this event into compliance so the questions will end," Peck said. Then he introduced the important decision makers in the room and invited Delaney to present his case for Compound Q.

The FDA people had all been given the chance to study in advance the protocol and printed results. Delaney had even forwarded samples of the drug Corti had brought from China. How should he begin now? He thought back to what Frank Young had said: "I only hope, Martin, that the patients were treated compassionately."

Delaney told them that providing the best, safest care for the patients had been the objective from the beginning. He told them where the drug had come from, and emphasized that because it wasn't the Genelabs drug they had taken exceptional care to test it, both at Genelabs and at the University of Nottingham. The reports on purity and quality had been unanimous.

He asked what results the FDA got from the samples he had sent. He saw only blank looks. He wondered whether the FDA even had the capacity to test a highly purified single-chain protein like Q. He decided just to bring on Waites, who presented the study data.

"The question now," Delaney said when Waites had finished, "is where to go from here. What is the right dose? What is the best way to administer it? We want to do another round of testing—a test with ten or twelve small arms, maybe just eight or ten people in each, with a broad range of dosing and length of time of infusion. And we want the patients to have a chance, if they want, to continue treatment after the test is over. Call it compassionate use, or make it part of the Genelabs–San Francisco General Hospital study, or whatever you want, but the FDA should lend its auspices to the patients' continuing on the drug."

There was a pause as he concluded. Then Delaney's worst fear materialized. Peck turned directly to Ellen Cooper.

"Ellen," he said, "what do you think? Do we know enough about the drug to go ahead?"

They held their breaths. Cooper looked slowly up from her notes.

Exactly what she said went straight past Delaney. All he heard was the voice—the soft, woman's voice. They had won.

"Yeah, I think we can do that," she was saying when he tuned in. Then she turned to the Genelabs and Sandoz executives who were seated behind her. "I think these people should be able to work out something like that, and we'll certainly go along with it."

You could almost hear the collective sigh as tension eased all over the room.

Peck made it official. Project Inform and the companies should jointly design a protocol and submit it, he said.

Afterward, in the hall, Williams, the medical director at Genelabs, seemed amazed. "You guys work some kind of special magic with the FDA," he told Delaney. "They never been so cooperative with us one on one. You should come to all our meetings with them."

David Winter, the executive vice-president who headed the Sandoz delegation, was also very congratulatory. "I've been following you guys for years," he said. "Everything you've done till now was just setting the stage. This was the first real act. This is a real step forward in the history of drug development with the FDA."

For all the congratulations, though, there was a big unspoken issue. Might as well raise it now, Delaney thought.

"This is all going to cost money," he said.

"Yes, let's talk," Winter said, and handed Delaney a business card.

After everyone parted company and headed to various offices, restrooms, and exits, Delaney was approached by an official from the FDA pharmacology department, whom he had been briefly introduced to.

"I've been watching your work for the past four years," said the man, whose name Delaney had forgotten. "The new era really began today. This was the real turning point."

It was almost the same thing Winter, the Sandoz executive, had just said. Obviously, this was not the FDA's normal way of dealing with the pharmaceutical industry. For Project Inform it was bending over backward. But why? This is what the FDA should always do, Delaney thought—act in collaboration with the industry, to try to get drugs out, while still making sure that the public was warned of deceptive claims or safety risks involved in taking a particular medication.

Back in San Francisco, Delaney began frequent talks with both Sandoz and Genelabs. Nobody said so, but he began to get the idea he was competing with Genelabs for Sandoz's money, and that the competition was close. He had his staff put in for a million dollars from the European drug giant. Maybe if they shot high enough, they would actually get 50 or 75 thousand.

Meanwhile, word came that Charles Weaver, the patient who had been deprived of Decadron for ten days while on an FDA-approved study, had died, as Al Levin had predicted he would, without ever regaining normal brain function. Delaney observed that no national newspaper ran a front-page story accusing the University of California of killing test subjects—now or during the suramin trial. The *Today* show didn't call. Alone, he could not help but compare the propriety and ethics of the University of California researchers with those of Project Inform's band of renegades.

SIXTY-NINE

On October 10, 1989, Delaney arrived at Harvard University, where he had been invited to appear on a panel with Ellen Cooper, Fauci's assistant Dan Hoth, and Jerry Groopman, a Harvard AIDS researcher. The subject was the value of community-based research.

Groopman had been a vocal opponent of the Q study, quoted on network news. He portrayed the Project Inform team as unauthorized blunderers, giving drugs to patients with no rules and hurting them in the process. Groopman and his group at Harvard had locked horns with Levin before on Agent Orange and other issues. Groopman's associates had sold their expert testimony to companies trying to fend off lawsuits brought by injured people who had hired Levin as their own expert.[76]

Several hundred people crowded into an auditorium at Harvard for the presentation. Cooper talked in general terms about trial designs, and Hoth did a little breast beating about all the good drugs that had come out of the government labs. The newest boast was that aerosol pentamidine had finally been approved under Treatment IND—too late for Tom Jefferson, Delaney thought.

When his turn came, Delaney argued that community-based studies can produce results closer to reality than pristine academic studies. The community understood the way patients were going to weigh risks and rewards better than any professor did, and could test experimental drugs as they were used in real life. Without naming Groopman, who was next to him, he said he felt frustrated that his team was being unfairly attacked by traditional researchers who hadn't bothered to look at the careful safeguards Project Inform had used.

Groopman—tall, thin, balding, fiftyish—rose, red-faced. "I came here prepared to deliver an address," he said. "But I can't go forward without responding to what Mr. Delaney has said." With that, he tore into community research in general, and Project Inform in particular, without qualification. "This isn't science, this is secret underground studies," he said. "The whole study was done in secret until it was exposed by the press. It had no oversight."

After three or four minutes of this, he announced, "I can't go on," folded his papers, and left the podium. Titters and murmurs swept the audience of medical-school faculty and students. Cooper and Hoth glanced nervously at each other.

Delaney had anger to propel him. He got up and said, "I don't have to take this in silence. This wasn't secret. There has never been a study done more in public than this. The press was recording it on videotape from day one. We just wanted the study done before it was publicized. Lawyers said our informed consent was the most sophisticated they had ever seen.

"In fact, it's the typical university study that really operates in the underground. Do any of you here know how many people died in the suramin study at San Francisco General Hospital?" Delaney didn't say so, but Mark Bradley had remarked the other day that as far as he could tell he was the only subject left alive.

"Did Gina Kolata do a front-page story in *The New York Times* about deaths in the suramin study? Were there any front-page stories about how many people died in the AZT study? This is the first time the press was let in to see a study. Three people died, all apparently for reasons unrelated to the drug. In the suramin study, sixteen people died at one site. In the AZT study in twenty-four weeks there were twenty-five deaths. Now people are acting like this is the first death that's ever happened in a research study. And the researchers who have had a press blackout on every study have the gall to get up and lead the attack on us. The least they could have done was have the professional courtesy to shut up."

As he talked, Groopman returned to the table. When Delaney had finished, Groopman rose to deliver another round. "This is just outrageous," he fumed. "Our studies are completely open to the public."

That statement cocked more eyebrows than Delaney's. Someone in the audience went to a microphone set up in the aisle for questions, and interrupted. He began rattling off the particulars of some study Harvard Medical School had done that Delaney had never heard of, and complaining that people had tried to get this or that information and couldn't. Groopman began sputtering and finally sat down.

For the rest of the hour, as Groopman sat mostly silent, Cooper, Hoth, and Delaney resumed the kind of polite discussion of pros and cons everyone had expected. Now that Cooper appeared to be on board the Q study, no one was interested in offending anyone.

Afterward, the panel was led upstairs for a planned dinner with a tableful of faculty dignitaries. Delaney was seated next to Groopman. Thanks to Groopman's embarrassing rejoinder from the audience, Delaney was feeling almost sorry for him by this time, and certainly preferred to mend the dispute rather than maintain it.

"I wish we had had the chance to talk this out before going in front of the group," he began. "I really didn't have any ill feelings for you. You just didn't have a lot of the facts about our study before you spoke."

"Oh!" Groopman shot back. "We're going to get lectures from you on how to do research. Thank you very much."

It was uncomfortable, even ugly. Delaney spent the rest of the dinner talking to others.

SEVENTY

Back in July, when Jay Lipner had been in San Francisco on vacation, Delaney had suggested that Lipner organize some New York doctors to try to open a community arm of Bristol-Myers's ddI studies. If it worked, it could be the first big test of what Delaney had been dreaming of for four years—what Fauci had dubbed the "parallel track."

Lipner had received a quick positive response from a dozen local doctors with big AIDS practices. Then he had attended an official meeting in Washington in late August, called to determine who would be eligible for the ddI trials. Bristol-Myers representatives and all the relevant government officials were on hand. Quietly, during breaks, Lipner broached to them the idea of a community-study arm. And they agreed to meet in New York with Lipner's doctors.

Lipner's progress was so good, that with Delaney's travel schedule and work with Compound Q, they decided Lipner would handle it on his own. The meeting was in Lipner's law office. Cooper showed up. Fauci sent an assistant. Bristol-Myers sent a team. Lipner brought ten community doctors.

The Bristol-Myers group, mostly scientists, reaffirmed that their chief executive had committed the company to make the drug available. They knew Young and Fauci were publicly committed to establishing a parallel track. But it quickly became clear that what Bristol-Myers had in mind was making ddI available only to people who couldn't tolerate AZT and so had nowhere else to turn.

That was when Lipner's doctors went to work. They pointed out that there were far more patients who had taken AZT and for whom the effects of AZT had worn off than there were patients who couldn't tolerate AZT in the first place. Besides that, Bristol-Myers was setting the standard of intolerance for AZT too high. As long as AZT was the lone drug available, only people with dangerously high anemia were going to forgo using it; but there were plenty of people with milder but still significant anemia for whom ddI was a better choice than AZT, and they should have the chance to switch.

As Lipner explained it to Delaney later, he was glad the senior business people from Bristol-Myers hadn't attended. Company doctors, listening to the community doctors, had agreed to give away much more ddI than the business people had originally envisioned. Prior unsuccessful use of AZT was still a requirement, but the standard for proving a patient's lack of success on AZT was greatly liberalized. The floodgates had been opened for a true parallel-track-like experience, even though the official parallel-track committee hadn't decided on the rules of the program yet. ddI would be available in October 1989.

In mid-November, Delaney was on one of his regular phone talks with Sam Broder, head of the National Cancer Institute. Delaney had been encountering Broder at conferences for months. In April 1989, when Broder visited San Francisco for a medical conference, Delaney had invited him to meet with some patients in a rented hotel room, much as Fauci had a few months earlier. Like Fauci, Broder had become an ally, frustrated at the FDA's sluggishness. Today he seemed particularly worried.

"If we don't get another drug or two out this year, I think we've got a terrible problem," Broder told Delaney.

"ddI or ddC?" Delaney asked.

"Well, both of them."

"Do you think we know enough to put them out?"

"We know they're both active against the virus," Broder said. "They both reduce the level of virus in patients, and they both increase CD-4 counts, and we know their side effects. How much more than that do we need to know?"

"Well, you know FDA is going to want a lot more than that," Delaney said.

"That's the problem," Broder replied. Some researchers were complaining that AIDS patients weren't enrolling in the formal ddI studies. They were signing up instead for Lipner's early-access program with private physicians. By and large, the researchers complaining about the diversion had opposed parallel track from the beginning. But if what they were saying was true, a disaster was approaching. Clinical studies had to proceed, and the parallel-track idea had been sold on the notion that patients wouldn't be siphoned away from the studies. That had been Delaney's brainstorm. Delaney better have been right.

Delaney started calling doctors to see what was happening. What he learned was that administrative snafus and last-second changes in the protocol had slowed the schedules at Bristol-Myers and some of the trial sites. The FDA-approved clinical trials had been weeks late getting started. As a result, the expanded-access program for private doctors opened before the clinical trials did.

A major guarantee that parallel-track supporters had offered to opponents of parallel track was that the clinical trials would open first. Only patients who didn't fit into the clinical trials would get early access to the drugs from their physicians. Therefore, the trials would be sure to fill up. Furthermore, they no longer would use placebos—a death sentence for half the subjects—which had scared people off. Instead, they would match new drugs like ddI against the standard treatment, AZT, as a control group.

The problem now was that the ddI trials were stalled. So patients were naturally going to the only available source—their private doctors. Doctors told Delaney that they had called Bristol-Myers's 800 phone number and San Francisco General Hospital before starting patients on ddI. Clerks at San Francisco General said they couldn't process new test subjects for a while. Bristol-Myers was telling them the Bay Area studies had no openings. So doctors and patients were starting off on their own with the drug.

Delaney wrote Broder November 20, 1989, with some suggestions. They had a marketing problem with the trials, but it was no reason to backtrack an inch on the expanded access. The patients were ready. The trial sites needed to think about the patients' needs, and coordinate their marketing message better. And the results obtained by private doctors ought to be collected and tabulated as part of the study. There was no good reason to begrudge private doctors who wanted to start their patients on a promising AIDS therapy.

The next day the disaster Delaney and Broder both feared struck —once again through the pen of Gina Kolata. The headline across the front page of *The New York Times* read, "Innovative AIDS Drug Plan May Be Undermining Testing." According to Kolata, the new parallel-track plan was essentially a failure before it really began. "In the first test of the new system, almost 20 times as many people have flocked to free distributions of the new drug ddI than have signed up for the clinical trial, leaving researchers in despair over whether they will ever be able to complete the formal study."

Delaney groaned as he read it. Only 75 patients had volunteered for the clinical trials, which required 1,900; but 1,300 patients had applied for the drug privately, she wrote. It sounded awful. Couldn't she at least have called some of the people he had called, and balanced the story? If the trial sites were turning people away—some hadn't even opened yet—of course more people weren't enrolled! And she blamed Fauci, who she said had agreed to the program "after numerous discussions with advocates for people with AIDS."

Who were the researchers she said were "grim"? Delaney looked for likely suspects—and found them. The doctor who was quoted most in support for Kolata's thesis was Douglas Richman of the University of California at San Diego, who was quoted in five different parts of the story, saying things like "As it is designed, parallel track will not work. What was actually put in place is an invitation to disaster. It will prevent us from finding drugs that will help people."

Richman was the doctor who had debated Delaney a year earlier at the Society for Infectious Diseases meeting, when Delaney had suggested the parallel-track idea. Richman had publicly opposed the whole notion from its inception. And he had been Thomas Jefferson's doctor at the time of Jefferson's death, something that Delaney, rightly or wrongly, still resented.

The next most-quoted source of support for Kolata was Dr. Jerome Groopman of Harvard—the man who had, just six weeks earlier, exploded into a vituperative, *ad hominem* attack against Delaney and the whole Compound Q project, disrupting a scholarly debate and dinner; Groopman, like Richman, was a committed opponent before the ddI trials had even begun.[77]

And the last quote in the story, nailing down the thesis, was from Don Abrams. Kolata buttressed her one-sided analysis by quoting expressions of concern that, in a neutral context, might not have backed her up—including a statement from Broder. After opening the story with ten full paragraphs arguing that researchers were generally alarmed that parallel track was causing a shortage of research subjects, Kolata quoted Fauci and Dan Hoth saying it was way too early to draw conclusions. Fauci said he was optimistic about the ddI clinical trials, and noted that the expanded access had begun before the FDA-approved studies began, so this was not really a test of his parallel-track plan anyway. Readers who persisted into the bowels of the story could also get a quote from a Bristol-Myers spokesman saying the company was pleased with the clinical-trial enrollment so far. But for any reader who wasn't studying diligently, it was too little, too late.

What Delaney saw happening was that some establishment researchers who had a big career stake in the existing system and opposed change were ready to take advantage of the administrative problems in the trials' start-up to try to stop parallel track before it started. Gina Kolata had become an eager and powerful shill.

The proof would come eventually, as the trial did or didn't fill up. Meantime, Delaney fired off an angry letter to Richman, accusing him of attacking parallel track without knowing what it was; the rules, which took great pains to protect clinical trials, were just being finished. The private doctors taking part in the expanded-access program shouldn't be held responsible for delays in starting the ddI trials.

The reply from Richman was a pleasant surprise. Instead of continuing the duel, Richman accused the *Times* of having distorted his views. "I must say that I was annoyed and frustrated by your letter for the simple reason that you are arguing with a position I did not take," Richman wrote. He said Kolata had used his words "for her own purposes." He also enclosed a copy of relevant parts of a letter he was sending to Fauci, along similar lines.

"I suspect that Gina Kolata has not always accurately reported what you thought you told her," he wrote Fauci. "Although I believe it is important for investigators to try to educate the public and to honestly express their beliefs," he wrote, "I am now clearly aware that Ms. Kolata is not the medium through which to do this."

Fuel enough! Delaney wrote a long, impassioned letter to Max Frankel, executive editor of the *Times*, complaining about the story and Kolata's work in general, and enclosing the partial copy of Richman's letter to Fauci. But in the anger of the moment, his negotiating facility deserted him and he didn't write the kind of precise, factual analysis he could have, or that the *Times* might have been more impressed by. The *Times* didn't print his letter or reply to it.

SEVENTY-ONE

*E*ver since the FDA meeting in October, which tacitly approved the first Compound Q study by authorizing a sequel to it, Levin and Waites had been administering Q from China to all patients they thought might benefit from it without risking a neurological reaction. Corti was still importing it from the factory near Shanghai, mostly using his friend Chan, the import-export dealer, as a courier.

Despite what an average network watcher or newspaper reader might expect, demand for Q had skyrocketed after the publicity over Robert Parr's death. Patients, at least, saw through the alarmist posturing of the "experts." If people were sick with AIDS, they wanted their best shot at treatment, even if it didn't carry a guarantee of effectiveness.

Buyers' clubs also existed in Dallas and San Francisco, and their orders helped finance Corti's purchasing. The original South Florida Q team had dispersed; Sergios had lost his excitement over the drug, and Dr. Mayer was opening a clinic in the Caribbean to pursue his interest in ozone and other unconventional treatments. But a replacement Q program had started in Fort Lauderdale, run by Lenny Kaplan, head of a group called Fight For Life, and his wife, a registered nurse. Corti flew to Florida frequently to help them get started, giving treatments in a local gay-oriented resort motel, the Caribbean. And in Los Angeles, Corti was administering the drug to scores of patients, either in his studio or in a suitable place convenient to them.

The New York scene was disturbing, though. Starrett and the nurses she had worked with had been frightened off by Gina Kolata. No one was willing to administer Q for fear of losing his medical or nursing license—although no action was ever taken against the people who had been named in *The New York Times* stories.

So Corti flew to New York periodically himself to administer the drug. Some doctors agreed to follow the patients if someone else, namely Corti, would do the infusions. So, added to the normal expense of taking an imported drug, patients had to organize and pay

Corti's air fare. One patient invited him to a posh house in Rye to administer the drug, though after two doses a local nurse agreed to step in and do it. Some patients—including two who were prominent in the fashion industry, whose names Corti agreed never to reveal— preferred to fly to Los Angeles for treatment.

Calls seeking his help getting treatment came from around the country. Corti was amazed more people weren't willing to administer it. Patients hadn't been frightened off by the publicity, but doctors and nurses had been.

From everything he heard, as long as the toxicity standards established by Levin and Waites were followed—no T-cell counts under 100, no history of neurological problems—there were no adverse reactions.[78] Some people evaded the standards, however.

Late in the fall of 1989, a patient in Atlanta died after getting the drug secondhand from another patient using the Dallas buyers' club. A doctor had been following the patient, who turned out to have had substandard numbers. The doctor agreed not to make a public case over the death.

Corti himself succumbed to the persistent pleas of a Los Angeles man to give him the drug even though Corti suspected the man was too sick. His doctor knew he had a T-cell count of only 50, but the patient lied to Corti. Three days after his infusion, the patient was in the hospital with a 106-degree fever and was comatose. He died soon afterward. Corti and the doctors involved resolved to screen patients carefully before going forward again.

Then Corti got a desperate call of another sort, from a San Francisco AIDS patient, who was stuck in Hong Kong with the biggest Q load ever. The patient had cleverly managed to crack the Chinese Government's official drug-dispensing institute, which had agreed to sell him large quantities of Compound Q through standard channels, without his having to go to the factory.

But the man had become a victim of his own success: when he went to China to pick up the drug, some bureaucrats at the institute discovered he was infected with HIV and detained him. After some harrowing days, he talked the Chinese into letting him leave with the three thousand ampuls of Q he had bought. But now he was stuck in Hong Kong; he didn't know whether the Chinese had tipped off U.S. Customs, and he was afraid he and the drug would be seized if he tried to enter the U.S. Could Corti help?

Corti was ambivalent. This guy had been out to make a big profit catering to desperate patients. Corti recognized his name from a previous profit-making deal. Normally, Corti tried to thwart profiteers, not cooperate with them. But at stake were three thousand ampules of needed Q.

Corti said he would fly to Hong Kong and guide the shipment back, but at a price: one-half the shipment, or fifteen hundred ampules, plus air fare. The man agreed. Corti met him in Hong Kong and did his usual diversion to Tokyo with multiple mailings. The goods got through.

More important, though, was the message it gave Corti: the Chinese Government had realized that Q could become a source of foreign exchange. It would make the drug available relatively easily, so long as HIV-positive people didn't enter the People's Republic to get it. The number of distributors, including nonprofit groups, would inevitably expand. Corti decided he could ease himself out of Q-importation work.

Meanwhile, Delaney, Waites, and Roger Williams of Genelabs agreed on some basics for the new study Levin and Waites would run with the Genelabs drug. Some problems remained. Delaney, Waites, and Levin were holding out for fewer treatments than Genelabs proposed; the Project Inform group had concluded that after two initial treatments the discomfort of more weekly doses outweighed the extra benefit for a while. A month or so after the first two weekly doses, the drug should be resumed, about monthly.

There was also some disagreement with Genelabs over which and how many different blood markers would be used to chart efficacy, and which lab was best suited to do the blood work. Different labs measured P-24 in different ways. But a protocol was agreed upon in fairly record time.

Then something seemed to go wrong. Genelabs dragged its feet submitting the protocol. Delaney pestered Williams about why. Finally Williams told him: James Kahn of the University of California San Francisco General Hospital AIDS team had called. Kahn declared that if Genelabs proceeded on the study with Project Inform, Kahn's hospital team would halt its continuing FDA-approved study of Compound Q. Could Genelabs afford to sacrifice its university medical team in order to work with community researchers?[79]

Then pressure had begun to snowball from other sources in the AIDS Clinical Trials Group, unidentified to Delaney, though he could imagine who they were. Project Inform and particularly Al Levin weren't to be dealt with. Lots of patients allegedly died in their studies. If Genelabs associated itself with these people, its reputation in legitimate medical circles was destroyed.

"That sounds like a fine, professional way to work together to end an epidemic," Delaney told Williams. "This is blackmail. Rumors. Nobody with a shred of data or knowledge could say that."

But doctors were saying it.

"I now believe the medical community exceeds even the patrons of a typical hair salon in malicious gossip," Delaney told Williams. "Well, we absolutely will not roll up our tents and crawl away without the biggest, noisiest fight you've ever seen." Three years earlier, Project Inform had made ICN roll back its price increase for ribavirin, and the organization was a lot stronger now.

Delaney liked and trusted Williams. Williams was getting instructions from his company, not caving in because of personal cowardice. But Delaney had to make the company see that caving in to pressure from the research establishment would not just be wrong, it would cost Genelabs money.

Finally, on December 1, 1989, whether because of Williams or for some other reason, Genelabs decided to bite the bullet and submit the protocol.

Then the problem became the FDA. Delaney felt sure Peck and his FDA associates were getting similar pressure from the same researchers. He knew many researchers were, as they said, dedicated to upholding medical standards, and Delaney had no doubt that people like Ellen Cooper felt that impulse strongly. But the system was also, as Al Levin said, a river of grant money that community doctors threatened to dam.[80] Where did the professional impulse stop and the profit impulse start? It wasn't always easy to tell, but against Delaney they were working together.

A few days after getting the Project Inform–Genelabs protocol, Ellen Cooper announced one immediate change, without necessarily approving the rest of it: the proposed number of patients would be reduced from 100 to 10. And the dose was to be held at a puny 16 micrograms per kilogram of body weight, even though Kahn was giving much higher doses at San Francisco General. Studying their own results, and the hospital's, Levin, Waites, and Delaney pegged the optimum dose at probably around 24 to 36 micrograms per kilogram. The San Francisco General study planned doses of 100 micrograms. For Project Inform to study 10 patients at a suboptimum dose was getting nowhere.

Meanwhile, the FDA continued to sit on plans for using the Genelabs drug to treat patients treated in the original study, even though Levin had submitted all the requested data on the patients weeks before. Genelabs was ready to supply the drug as soon as the FDA okayed it.

Then someone from Act Up showed Delaney a letter Peck had sent. Act Up had written him, questioning delays in the new Q study. Replying, Peck blamed the delays on Delaney and Genelabs.

On December 7, Delaney fired off an angry three-page letter to Peck. He flat-out rejected Cooper's reduction of the study to ten patients. The FDA had every bit of information it asked for about the original Q trial. Why hadn't the FDA approved continuation of those patients—and made clear that doctors everywhere would not be under a cloud for administering the Chinese drug?

As for the whisper campaign to pressure Genelabs into removing Levin, he told Peck, "Over our dead bodies! I don't know what the agency's opinion is of him, or where it gets the right to question his participation. In the last three years, he has been prophetically right on key issues of AIDS treatment: on early intervention with AZT, on the need to drastically lower the dose of AZT, on aerosolized pentamidine dosage and application, and most recently on the correct treatment of trichosanthin-induced CNS [central nervous system] dysfunction. In every instance, his knowledge was years ahead of the official pronouncements of the medical establishment and the FDA. He achieved this not by intuition but by extensive data collection, far exceeding that of any other clinic in the country—a key point in our decision to work with him and Dr. Waites. That his success and outspokenness has embarrassed the academic research centers is their problem, not his. . . . We urge the agency not to pick a fight over him or the involvement of his clinic in this program."

The FDA yielded, and Cooper soon agreed to a protocol to treat seventy to eighty patients at varying doses.[81] Half were to be at Levin's office. Some would be at a medical group Larry Waites had selected in Los Angeles. The rest would be in New York, where Barbara Starrett—who hadn't given a dose of Q since Gina Kolata's article was published—was persuaded she could emerge from hiding and begin treating patients under the full auspices of the Food and Drug Administration.

And Sandoz, the giant drug company, gave Project Inform $250,000 to conduct the study. Don Abrams's protests were reported in the newspapers, but they didn't stop the grant or the study. Delaney had come a long way from the Regis Farmacia. The quarter-million dollars was almost beyond his dreams.

While the Q episode was unfolding, the FDA, whose work often seemed paralyzed by dread of scandal, was hit by scandal anyway. Three drug reviewers pleaded guilty to accepting bribes from companies that manufactured generic drugs. Frank Young, the evangelistic Christian physician who had become Delaney's strange sometimes-ally, sometimes-antagonist at the agency, resigned as top boss. He had nothing to do with the bribe taking, but was expected to run an agency where such things didn't happen. He landed a job as deputy assistant secretary for something-or-other in the Department of Health and Human Services.

SEVENTY-TWO

*A*n immediate effect of Project Inform's new relationship with Genelabs and Sandoz was an invitation for Delaney and Waites to attend the every-other-month meeting of Compound Q researchers. Levin was invited, too, though he had little patience for such things and didn't attend. When Roger Williams of Genelabs called to tell Delaney the time and place of his first meeting, Delaney asked how the doctors from San Francisco General Hospital would react to his presence.

"It's up to us, not up to them," Williams said. Right now, he said, the University of California group resented sharing academic credit with Waites and Levin. But the problem would be solved.

Still, Delaney noticed that when the meeting started at 5 P.M., Kahn, who headed the study at San Francisco General, wasn't there.

The Project Inform team had more information than the other researchers by this point, and McGrath deferred to them. Some clinicians from other research sites were cool at first, but ultimately listened to what Delaney and Waites had to say. Williams, who chaired the meeting, broke into the reports of other researchers several times to point out that the Project Inform team had already announced the same findings.

At around 7 P.M., Kahn arrived, in time to give the last presentation. He chose to convey his distress that people in the community looked at trichosanthin as a treatment instead of as an experimental agent. It shouldn't be used as if it were a treatment, he said.

Preaching, Delaney thought. Still, when the meeting was over, Kahn talked civilly to Delaney and Waites. Delaney could sense that Williams was working hard to broker a marriage between the warring camps. It was in his company's interest, and society's.

Over Christmas 1989, Corti took time off from setting up Q-infusion clinics around the country to visit a friend in Paris who was sick with AIDS. Through the friend, he met the project coordinator for the largest French national private AIDS organization, who urged Corti and Delaney to meet with AIDS researchers and support organizations there.

So Corti returned to France in February 1990, with not just Delaney, but also Waites and Corti's friend Fred Wietersen. Among the first stops was the office of Luc Montagnier of Paris's famed Pasteur Institute. Montagnier was best known for his long dispute with Robert Gallo of the U.S. National Cancer Institute over which of them deserved credit for discovering HIV. Both had announced the discovery in 1984 after considerable exchange of information and biological specimens between their labs. Because of the striking similarity in virus samples, beyond even what one would expect in molecular structure of the same virus, Montagnier charged that Gallo had willfully or inadvertently claimed credit for "discovering" a virus that the Pasteur Institute had already discovered and sent to the U.S. for further study. Gallo insisted his virus came from the blood of an American AIDS patient. Hefty royalties from the HIV antibody test were at stake, but the pride of the two scientists was even bigger cause for a fight.

What most interested Delaney and Corti, however, wasn't who discovered the virus, but who discovered how to cure people who were infected by it. And Montagnier's lab was considered the most prestigious AIDS research center in Europe. They spent hours with Montagnier, discussing his new, still-unpublished theory that a small form of bacteria called mycoplasma was a hidden co-factor that made HIV so destructive; lack of mycoplasma, he implied, was why some people carried the virus without symptoms for so long. If he was right, it opened a new door for researching a cure.

Delaney and Corti were struck that Montagnier seemed a less significant figure in his own lab than his reputation had led them to believe. His office was not as posh as some other researchers' offices, and he seemed occupied more by administration than science. Another official of the lab privately scoffed to the Americans about the mycoplasma theory. But at least Delaney and Corti now had direct contacts among France's leading AIDS researchers.

Other meetings followed. There was lunch with half a dozen prominent AIDS doctors in Paris, and then meetings with officials at the French equivalent of the American FDA. The French were way behind the U.S. in community organizing, and they knew it. The doctors kept probing for ways to rouse the high-risk population in France to get tested and seek early treatment. They wanted to know how local doctors could organize to keep data on speculative drugs.

But there was also petty backbiting against Montagnier. He was an administrator, not a scientist. Why was he getting all the credit? He was spending precious research money on lawyers to fight with Gallo. To Delaney and Corti, this was sadly reminiscent of scenes of the FDA and NIH glowering across the table at each other. Why couldn't everybody, in whatever country, just focus on curing this disease?

That night, Delaney lectured on the success of community organization in the U.S. By now he was lecturing regularly to large community groups throughout the U.S. His first lecture overseas packed five hundred people into a lecture hall, while others who couldn't get in watched on a simultaneous television transmission.

While in Paris, Corti also made the rounds of pharmacies, picking up five thousand tablets of a drug called Roxithromycin, at $2 a tablet, on request from the Dallas buyers' club. Some recently published research suggested that the antibiotic, not available in the U.S., might work against toxoplasmosis, an opportunistic infection common in AIDS. Corti was skeptical, but it was a fairly benign pill and might as well be tried.

Back home, all the official ddI trials had finally opened. Kolata was wrong. Patient recruitment was meeting its goals.

The real problem turned out to be not a drain-off of trial subjects, but something else: far more patients had signed up for the expanded-access arm than the company had originally anticipated—eventually over twenty thousand. The parallel-track rules, though drafted, hadn't been adopted yet, and under existing FDA rules Bristol-Myers couldn't charge for the pills. The company had to give the drug away as a compassionate gesture. That was costing $50,000 to $75,000 a day, and tying up about fifty Bristol-Myers employees, much more expense than the company intended before Jay Lipner and others talked Bristol-Myers's doctors into expanding the program. Furthermore, the money was buying the company nothing but good will; there were as yet no clear FDA rules to allow the results of the expanded-access arm to be used in getting the drug approved.

The worst part, Delaney felt, was that every big drug company in the country was watching. The lesson seemed to be that any gesture of charity by a drug company would only create the demand for so much more charity as to be intolerable. Free drugs for all was no way to encourage expanded access.

Delaney had sensed such a possibility back when the protocol for the second Q study was being negotiated. He and Genelabs had intentionally avoided any suggestion that Genelabs might donate the drug to all legitimate comers. This was acceptable in the case of Q because Corti and others were still bringing Q in from China. It seemed stupid to Delaney that FDA rules denied patients the chance to take Q under safe medical conditions, and drove them instead to take it at home. But if that's how the FDA "protected" patients, at least Q was available. With ddI, and doubtless other drugs still to come, there was no alternative source for the popular market.

There had to be a way out. At meetings to draw up the parallel-track rules, it was at first suggested to let the drug companies recoup out-of-pocket costs during expanded access. They could wait for profits until the drug was approved.

But as reasonable as this idea sounded, the drug companies would have none of it. The cost of making a prescription drug was as carefully guarded as any secret in the industry. Much or most of what consumers paid for drugs was reckoned to be the cost of years of research and testing, not only for that drug, but for all the other drugs the company had worked on unsuccessfully. The companies feared that if anybody found out how cheap it was just to make pills, men and women across America might rise up against druggists. Counterfeiting and smuggling might proliferate. Drug companies would rather forgo some income than 'fess up to their costs.

Privately, several company representatives warned Delaney that what they were really thinking of doing was ducking the problem by shifting drug development overseas. They faced a no-win situation at home. Under expanded access, they could lose their shirts. On the other hand, if the government gave up on expanded access, the companies would be picketed and boycotted by Act Up, and come off in the press as ruthless skinflints.

And as if things weren't bad enough, Gina Kolata showed up again. This time Delaney had only himself to blame. Foolishly, *he* had called *her*.

It started with a routine committee meeting he had attended of the Aids Clinical Trials Group in Washington. News was announced that six people in the ddI trials had died of a newly discovered side effect of ddI, pancreatitis. Everyone agreed the deaths were solely attributable to the drug. One of the pancreatitis deaths had come from the official trials group, and five from the expanded-access group (which had ten times as many patients).

It struck Delaney as a perfect example of what he had been trying to tell reporters about the unexpected Compound Q reaction. Any strong experimental drug can produce added illness or death. That's why they had trials. The Compound Q reaction, if properly treated, didn't lead to death the way the ddI reaction did, but such things happened.

He called Kolata at the *Times* and tried to educate her. He said he had just sat through a committee meeting at which it was disclosed that six people had died from side effects of ddI. Nobody had gotten excited. It was normal for some people to die in such studies.

He realized almost immediately that he had made a mistake. She seemed electrified by the news of the six deaths. She had a scoop. She fished for more details. Jesus, thought Delaney, how could I have been so stupid? He tried to deflect her questions.

She just got her answers elsewhere. When the story came out on the front page nearly a week later, March 12, 1990, the pancreatitis toxicity problem had been relegated to the back seat. What replaced it in the lead was this news: of the first 700 patients in the hospital trials, two had died. Of the first 8,000 in the expanded-access program, 290 had died. That was more than ten times the rate of the hospital trials.

Dr. Groopman's colleague at Harvard Dr. Thomas C. Chalmers was immediately quoted calling it "A disgrace, an absolute disgrace. I think it's a painful way to learn the lesson, but maybe it's the only way they'll learn that, to my mind, they did the wrong thing."

There was "enormous demand" for ddI by AIDS patients, Kolata said. "But," she reported, "critics have said the expanded access program represents a dismantling of the FDA, makes it extraordinarily difficult to recruit patients for clinical trials and places patients at great risk of being harmed by experimental drugs. With the new data on death rates, these critics say their worst fears are being borne out, even . . . " And that's where the front-page portion of the article stopped. It contained eight paragraphs, and not a word running contrary to Kolata's thesis. Tucked away around the local news on page B-8 the sentence continued, "though the causes of the deaths are not known."

They sure as hell aren't, Delaney thought. The death rate was probably due to AIDS. The expanded-access patients by definition were much sicker than the hospital-study patients were. The hospital-study patients were accepted only if they seemed candidates to survive the two-year study. Their counterparts in expanded access were required to have already failed on AZT, indicating that many in the expanded-access group were in a much more advanced state of disease before ever going onto ddI. Many had organ degeneration. In the hospital study, only one of three sections was for people who could not take AZT, and most of those were probably patients who had negative reactions to AZT, not patients whose disease had progressed beyond where AZT was effective. Mere participation in the expanded-access program indicated desperation.

For thorough readers, Kolata eventually gave Bristol-Myers a chance to explain. In the expanded-access program, a company spokesman said, "we're dealing with a very, very sick population." The company said that except for the five deaths from pancreatitis, all the expanded-access deaths were attributed to AIDS and its complications. Those readers who waded deeply enough into the story learned from Fauci that not enough data was available to give any meaning to the death numbers Kolata reported—the individual deaths would have to be profiled first.

Then Kolata quoted at length a research doctor at Cornell who complained that side effects from ddI had been greater than expected. He accused Bristol-Myers of not informing doctors soon enough about bad reactions.

Delaney almost gave up. Not only was Compound Q killing people. Now ddI was killing people as well. Didn't anybody realize that AIDS was killing a lot more people than these drugs were?

It was scant consolation, but *The Village Voice* ran a devastatingly critical piece about this newest AIDS story of Kolata's, pausing to fault her other stories as well. Fauci, Richman, and others were quoted saying she had distorted their remarks, or ignored evidence contrary to the thesis she was expounding. Two people said she even came to them with prepared quotes that "I need somebody to say," and one said she tried to pressure him to say her words "if you want your name in the *Times*." The *Voice* also quoted unnamed sources at the *Times* saying that editors understood the problem and were reining her in, but if so, it was hard to tell from reading the paper.[82]

SEVENTY-THREE

More bad news followed. Between formal sessions at a Washington meeting, Ellen Cooper dropped hints to Delaney and others that initial reports were arriving from the statisticians assigned to look at surrogate blood markers. And they weren't saying what people like Delaney expected them to say. The results were far from complete, but Cooper seemed to be preparing everyone for a negative finding. Delaney arranged to have lunch with her, to pry further.

The statistical work had been transferred away from a firm in North

Carolina to statisticians at Harvard University—whose foot-dragging medical center Delaney was beginning to equate with the University of California's. In addition to the Harvard group's personal attacks on him, Delaney believed the group had prematurely condemned some possibly useful drugs to the scrap heap. Corti was already scouting places overseas to buy the drugs.

Now the FDA's statistical contract had been switched to Harvard —on the ground it could handle more work faster. But the switch gave the conservatives at Harvard a say in the outcome of tests that were conducted elsewhere.

Delaney thirsted to see the statisticians' numbers without Cooper's spin on them. But he would have to wait. Cooper assured him nothing would happen until the data was in, and that could take months.

Later, back in San Francisco, Delaney learned that the FDA's new antiviral advisory committee had met, and voted resoundingly against using surrogate markers, at least for now. The most experienced AIDS doctor on the committee, and thus one of the strongest voices, was Don Abrams.

The ddI trials were underway. If CD-4 cells—commonly referred to as T-cells, of which CD-4s were a particularly important kind— were adopted as an acceptable marker, ddI could be licensed fairly quickly. If not, two or three years would pass before Bristol-Myers would be able to demonstrate a survival difference. The same was true of ddC at Hoffmann-La Roche.

In the bigger picture, a finding against surrogate markers thwarted the development, let alone approval, of all sorts of drugs. Many were made by small biotech firms that couldn't afford the lengthier, costlier trials required if death was the end point.

Delaney called Sam Broder again. Broder was probably the single person most responsible for taking drugs like ddI and ddC off the shelf and applying them to AIDS. Now he had been appointed head of the whole National Cancer Institute. He was Gallo's boss and Fauci's bureaucratic equal. Would Broder continue to be an ally in the coming war over surrogate markers?

Delaney didn't have to wait long for an answer. He told Broder about the new surrogate marker problem.

"I'm very aware, and very discouraged," Broder said. "I don't know what we're going to do. It's not good for people to be put in a situation where they're begging for their lives from a central government authority. If we don't have another drug out here real soon, we're going to be in deep trouble. You know what's happening with AZT. Huge numbers of people have already been on it too long. And probably the best thing is to use these drugs together. I don't know if ddI or ddC is better than AZT, but I'll bet used together they're better than any one of them."

And using them together would mean lower doses and probably less toxicity, Delaney noted—happily surprised at the candor he was getting from a government official.

"What is the matter with them that they can't see the link between CD-4 and this disease?" Broder went on. "It's staring them in the face. You don't have to be a rocket scientist to know that stopping the decline in CD-4 is what you want from a drug. The FDA doesn't seem to get it. This same kind of conservatism almost killed AZT. When the advisory committee looked at AZT, there was this tendency to immediately accept the negatives about the drug, but not to accept the incontrovertible truth about the positive. We were this close to killing AZT off because it was too toxic. Where would we be if that were the case? They just don't understand what it's like working with a life-threatening disease."

Broder said he had fought the same fight a decade earlier with cancer. He had shown the FDA new drugs that could shrink tumors. But the FDA had demanded long-term studies to prove that shrinking tumors made people live longer. Was there a cancer patient who didn't want to shrink his tumor? So the studies went on, and the longer they went on, the greater the chance that unforeseen variables would produce a negative outcome. There were suicides, happenstance infections, all sorts of routine deaths that would be counted as a negative result of the study.

Broder seemed glad for a chance to vent his anger. Delaney felt confident he had identified an ally. He even sensed in Broder's tone of voice a little bit of the cowboy spirit of Al Levin—a man willing to take risks, and passionate about getting answers.

They continued to talk regularly. Later, Delaney heard that Broder had actually shouted at Cooper at one meeting, where she continued to question how much it helped an AIDS patient to increase his CD-4 count.

SEVENTY-FOUR

A lot of patients coming to Corti for Compound Q were under the care of Joel Weisman, Paul Rothman, or one of their colleagues at Pacific Oaks medical group. As far as Corti was concerned, Rothman and his senior partner Joel Weisman were responsible for torpedoing the Los Angeles arm of Project Inform's Q study. After that, Corti was reluctant to treat Pacific Oaks's patients on the ground that he wouldn't administer Q without a cooperative doctor on hand in case something went wrong, and a patient needed hospitalization.

But the patients kept coming. And suddenly, early in 1990, they were saying that Weisman had caved in. The patients had pleaded with Weisman to allow them to take Q. These patients mostly were no longer benefiting from AZT. They said Q, with its risks, was what they wanted. And their desperate pleas had been enough to turn Weisman around. He had pledged to continue monitoring the patients and to care for them in an emergency.

To Corti, it was all too good to be true. He called Weisman.

"It's a long time since we've spoken," Corti began.

"Too long," Weisman said.

That seemed to confirm that the door was open.

"There's a lot of patients from Pacific Oaks who have come to me and want Compound Q," Corti said. "And I'm reluctant to do it without knowing how you guys will react if a worst case should appear."

"Worst case meaning—"

"It could mean all the way to death."

Weisman responded with questions about the circumstances of the infusion. Corti explained he administered Q only with remedies at hand for any likely emergency, and listed some of the drugs on his crash cart. He was trained to use them. Furthermore, he only gave infusions close to a hospital. His studio was six blocks from St. Vincent's.

"It sounds fine to me," Weisman said, adding that he hoped it achieved some benefit for the patients.

Corti sighed. The Q infusions could continue.

While they did, another potential curative was being heralded by the gay press in the spring of 1990—a new form of interferon. Interferon was a natural protein produced by the body to shore up the human immune system in time of infection. For years, doctors had been studying it as a possible anticancer agent. It had been approved for use in Kaposi's sarcoma. Suddenly, word was out that small oral doses of a kind of interferon known as alpha interferon worked against AIDS. The *New York Native* ran story after story about a Kenyan doctor who claimed to have given oral alpha interferon to 101 AIDS patients; all supposedly became healthy again, and 10 supposedly began testing negative for the virus.

The mainstream press treated these accounts skeptically, but many

AIDS patients wanted to try the drug anyway. Reading what he could, and telephoning around, Corti came across a familiar name as one of those hoping to get the drug to distribute it—Lenny Kaplan, a Florida man who had started a Compound Q clinic with Corti's help. Corti visited Kaplan, who offered him some of the drug in liquid form and showed him how it was being used.

More important, Kaplan directed him to the source—Joseph Cummins, a veterinarian in Amarillo, Texas, who had developed oral alpha interferon for use in cattle. Cummins told Corti that his small, easy-to-administer oral doses of the drug had worked wonders on various cattle maladies.

Figuring to capitalize on his discovery, Cummins began licensing arrangements with companies that produced interferon for cancer experiments, to make the form of the drug that seemed to work in cattle. Then, by coincidence, someone who worked with Cummins contracted AIDS from a tainted blood transfusion. Terrified and having tried everything else with no success, the associate began taking oral alpha interferon. He went a year with no infections. He gave some to other people he knew with AIDS, and they claimed to do well.

Cummins said he had arranged with doctors from Texas Tech University to start a long-term test of oral alpha interferon in AIDS patients, which was still going on. Eager for faster results, however, he contacted some Kenyans who had bought the drug from him for cattle. Since Kenya faced an AIDS epidemic of frightening proportions, Cummins suggested human trials there. A doctor was found and Cummins flew to Kenya with the powder. After two months' of testing, the doctor told a medical gathering in Tokyo in February 1990 of his alleged spectacular success. That started the rash of news reports.

So Corti and Delaney flew to Amarillo and discussed dosing and side effects with Cummins. They all agreed that Corti and Delaney would organize a study to see if the sensational Kenyan results could be replicated.

Again, they needed a supervising doctor. After his unsatisfying experience with Scolaro and Rothman, Corti found another Los Angeles doctor with a large AIDS practice, Robert Jenkins. Jenkins had approached Corti at a medical meeting to talk about Compound Q, and they had struck up a quick friendship. When Corti called, Jenkins agreed to administer and monitor oral alpha interferon in L.A. Delaney and the Levin office found some eager volunteers in San Francisco.

Rothman called. His boss, Weisman, having dropped active opposition to the cause, Rothman was starting a new community-based medical-research organization in Los Angeles. It would be called "The Search Alliance," and he invited Corti and Delaney to join the board. Well, Corti figured, this was serendipity. He decided to trust Rothman again. And so oral alpha interferon became The Search Alliance's first project. Corti's friend Jenkins agreed to join the group.

In April 1990, less than two months after reports of the drug had surfaced, Corti and Jenkins had organized a study of two months, just like the one in Kenya. Since interferon had been given for other purposes in far larger doses, toxicity didn't seem a problem. A hundred volunteers were chosen and their start-up blood levels taken.

The study subjects were far from the only patients taking the drug; they were just the only ones being monitored in an organized fashion for some kind of scientific assessment of how it worked. The buyers' clubs that had sprung up in Florida, Dallas, and San Francisco to distribute dextran sulfate, Q, and other drugs were selling oral alpha interferon. A New York group was putting interferon on communion wafers and distributing them.

Blood work on the Search Alliance patients was studied every two weeks. After a month, Corti, Delaney, and the doctors they worked with were satisfied that nothing remotely like the dramatic response claimed in Kenya was occurring. No one was improving, and some patients were even deteriorating. Mark Bradley and several infected friends had begun taking the drug, and saw their T-cells decline. They dropped it pronto. Jenkins and Waites had to tell patients who suffered such declines to discontinue the drug.

A statistician was hired to analyze the data, and The Search Alliance released its findings in June; the results made *The Los Angeles Times*. Unfortunately, the results were that the Kenyan miracle hadn't happened.

Some people wanted to continue taking the drug despite the findings. Sadly, many black patients wanted it, based on a confusion of desire and pride, because the original results had been reported by an African. Some counterculture groups and radio stations continued to tout the drug. After all he had been through, Corti felt he had no right to stand in the way of an informed patient's judgment, and he continued to give the drug to those in Los Angeles who wanted it, along with a warning that it did no discernible good and might bring a drop in T-cells. At least, Corti felt, judgments could now be made on the basis of facts if the patients wanted to face them.

Other "cures" were being offered for sale with far less scientific basis. A Los Angeles radiologist was arrested for selling a potion called Viroxin, made in his kitchen. Some patients died. The radiologist defended himself with the claim he was doing the same thing Project Inform had done with Compound Q, and he asked Delaney and Corti to testify for him. Satisfied the potion lacked any scientific basis, they refused. The defense didn't fool the FDA, either.

When an Encino, California, doctor was featured on television news programs claiming a breakthrough, Delaney and Corti went to his office. The doctor claimed to have a device that measured frequencies supposedly emitted by different diseases, for which the doctor claimed to have cures. To test him, Corti brought two vials of blood, one from a dying man, the other from an uninfected one. The doctor described them exactly backward, ascribing numerous ailments to the healthy person and giving the dying man a clean bill of health. Corti and Delaney paid him an admonishing goodbye, and later informed the FDA.

Several crates in the Project Inform office were filling with hundreds of such phony cures.

But Delaney and Corti were careful to keep open minds. Some of the first and most effective drugs they had latched on to, ribavirin and isoprinosine, continued to be labeled quackery by the establishment. Where there was a reasonable basis in science, new treatments deserved a look even if they seemed longshots.

One such substance was N-acetylcysteine, an amino acid sold in Europe as an over-the-counter tonic. A husband-and-wife chemist team at Stanford had come across the odd fact that people with HIV tended to have low levels of a blood chemical called glutathione; N-acetylcysteine inspires the production of glutathione. What did that mean? No one knew. It might mean that glutathione was a natural enemy of HIV, and that ingesting N-acetylcysteine would block the spread of the virus. Or it might be just a coincidence.

A liquid form of the substance was licensed in the U.S. as an antidote for an overdose of Tylenol. But it was expensive and noxious to use. Corti went to Italy, where it was cheaper in the form of an Alka-Seltzer-like tablet, and brought back quantities of one brand of the substance. Later, he learned it was available as a bulk chemical in Japan for much less money still, and he had Chan bring back forty kilos; a chemist Corti knew in Boulder, Colorado, agreed to produce tablets from the chemical, and soon Corti had two thousand bottles of pills. They were sold quickly.

Then a San Francisco firm started marketing the pills at about the same price, and Corti quit. Besides, by then lots of people were taking it. While it wasn't a miracle cure, Stanford scientists found it had direct antiviral activity, and it seemed to work positively on blood markers. Fauci got interested, and soon official tests were underway at Stanford, with financial help from Project Inform.

SEVENTY-FIVE

*T*he International Conference on AIDS, held every June since 1986, was scheduled for San Francisco in 1990. Delaney had long since become part of the city's AIDS establishment. He had been invited by the mayor's office onto a task force of some twenty people to try to unite the city on the issue, and to construct a plan for coping with AIDS in the future.

The task force included the local archbishop, the president of Levi Straus & Company, and Paul Volberding, among others. In anticipation of the international conference, the group appealed publicly in the spring of 1990 for early testing for high-risk groups and early, government-paid drug intervention for those who tested positive. As much as anything, the group tried to build bridges, not only between the medical establishment and community organizers like Delaney, but also between the Roman Catholic Church and the gay community, which in many cities, like New York, were practically at war with each other.

The host institution for the conference was to be the University of California. Volberding was conference chairman, and Don Abrams was appointed to head the committee reviewing papers on social and public policies. Abrams was to select a dozen people to work with him. Delaney hardly expected to be one of them after Abrams's many derisive public comments about him and his consistent opposition to everything Delaney fought for. But there it was, a letter from Abrams, inviting him to join the review committee.

Sure, Delaney thought. You want to use my name to make your committee look like it's balanced, so you can say you consulted everybody about what to publish. And he didn't reply.

But then Abrams called, and repeated that he really wanted Delaney to help evaluate the papers.

"I've got to ask if this is sincere," Delaney said. "You're dumping all over me in the press, and now it's kiss and make up and let's do the conference together."

"Oh, gee," Abrams replied. "You know, the press is always trying to play us off against each other. This conference this year is San Francisco's collective responsibility. Whatever we think of each other, you're part of San Francisco's AIDS environment."

So Delaney joined the committee. Maybe it was a peace offering.

Then someone in the New York group called to say he had just attended a speech by Robert Gallo, the renowned government scientist who was mired in controversy over his claim to have discovered, or co-discovered, HIV. After the speech, Gallo had been challenged by someone in the audience over the lack of progress on AIDS drugs. In his leap to defend his laboratory at NIH, Gallo mentioned that a new drug against Kaposi's sarcoma was in the works. Did Delaney know what Gallo might be talking about?

No, but he would find out. Kaposi's sarcoma was one of the main killer diseases of the AIDS syndrome. Cure it, and you extend a lot of lives.

Delaney didn't know Gallo well enough to call him, but wrote a letter instead. Delaney had developed a knack for how long or short, detailed or simple, harsh or conciliatory to make a letter to get the desired rise out of the recipient. If this drug cures Kaposi's, Delaney wrote Gallo, it should enable him to put all the nonsense about the virus discovery behind him.

The dispute was being fueled mainly by the continued pursuit of a newspaper reporter, John Crewdson of *The Chicago Tribune*. After the original claims of Montagnier, the Frenchman, had mostly been forgotten, Crewdson had reignited the furor with a fifty-thousand-word article, the size of a book, building a case that Gallo had committed scientific fraud. The Department of Health and Human Services had been compelled to announce a new investigation. Crewdson moved to the *Tribune*'s Washington bureau, continuing to dog his prey in new articles, none of which resolved the issue.

Delaney wrote Gallo that unlike Crewdson, people with AIDS didn't care who discovered what in 1984. They wanted a cure in 1990. If Gallo would develop this drug fast, he would be remembered for that, not some petty argument.

Delaney sent the letter Federal Express on a Thursday in early June, before the international conference. Delaney's phone rang at 8 A.M. California time, on Sunday, three days later.

"Hello, Martin? This is Bob Gallo. Look, I checked you out. I talked to Sam Broder, I talked to Tony Fauci, I talked to my publisher. They say I can trust you, and I'm going to lay it on the line with you. Why don't you come to Washington? I'll tell you everything. Not only that, I'll *show* you everything."

Wasn't Gallo going to be in San Francisco for the big AIDS conference as scheduled?

No, he had a sudden speaking engagement in the U.S.S.R.

Well, then, Delaney was coming to Washington for another Institute of Medicine Roundtable meeting June 28. He could see Gallo afterward.

The date was sealed.

Delaney then did the same thing Gallo had done—he called Fauci and Broder. "Can I trust him?" he asked.

They laughed. Gallo, they assured him, was nothing like the moral bankrupt whom Crewdson was describing in the newspapers.

First came the big conference. Delaney's longtime detractors at the university had not only put him on the committee, they had scheduled him to deliver a plenary speech on community research. Delaney presented his paper before five thousand people, including the world's scientific elite, at San Francisco's Mosconi Hall.

Community-based research was proceeding too slowly, he said, because the establishment research community was loath to accept what community doctors could do. In fact, he said, community doctors sometimes had research advantages over their university counterparts.

The Levin-Waites clinic, because it was treating its own patients, compared the medical histories of Compound Q subjects going back a year before the trial began; normally, histories started at the beginning of the trial. In the case of Q, the longer history provided a much more graphic picture of the effectiveness of the drug than even a placebo comparison could have. The relatively small improvement in T-cells after the trial began looked much more significant when set against the background of a year of steady T-cell decline. Delaney was careful to say he wasn't making final conclusions about the drug, only about the value of using community doctors to study drugs.

He also talked about the problems of waiting for traditional publication in peer-review journals before releasing the results of trials. The report of the Project Inform team on the original Compound Q experiment was still in line for its eventual publication in a future issue of the *Journal of AIDS*.[83] But better data already was rolling in from the new study built as a continuation of the earlier one.

On the panel to review what Delaney said was Arnold Relman, editor of *The New England Journal of Medicine*. Running perhaps the nation's most esteemed and orthodox medical journal, Relman guarded the gate of establishment research procedure against barbarians like Delaney. Given the floor, Relman immediately denounced Delaney, as he had before in the press—this time for putting out incomplete data. "You have no right putting out data until it's been reviewed by a peer review process and published in a scientific journal," Relman said.

The two then exchanged verbal blows of rising intensity.

"Who appointed you to be the guardian of what can and can't be said publicly on scientific matters?" Delaney said.

"This is the scientific tradition of peer review and objectivity," Relman said.

"How can you talk about objectivity when eighty-nine percent of your revenues come from advertisements from drug companies?" There were laughter and applause for Delaney.

If data was to be believed, Relman said, it should be submitted to a scientific journal like his.

"I'd be happy to give you the data if you could give me some assurance you're going to publish it," Delaney retorted. "If I give the data to you, I tie up my article for a year while nothing else happens." That line also went over well with the audience, which included a lot of research physicians who resented the time-consuming traditions of scientific publication; under the accepted rules, a journal like Relman's could sit on a paper indefinitely, and the paper could not be submitted anywhere else in the meantime.

"We will only agree to review your data, and nothing more," Relman said.

"Well, that's my point," Delaney replied.

When the moderator—the medical chief of San Francisco General Hospital—ended the session, Delaney and Relman moved on to a press conference, where the cameras were waiting. Tempers flared again. Relman called Delaney irresponsible. Delaney complained it was offensive to him to be called irresponsible on national television by the head of *The New England Journal of Medicine*. All he was doing was what hundreds of others were doing at the conference when they presented papers with preliminary data. The only difference was that he was a layman. The exchange made ABC's *World News Tonight* and the *CBS Evening News*.

Relman later issued a statement saying that the figure 89 percent for the amount of revenue accounted for by drug-company advertising was wrong. Delaney replied that he had read the figure in an article, and that Relman hadn't offered a correct percentage. For all anybody knew, it was even higher.

Among the many establishment researchers who approached Delaney with congratulations after the press conference was Jim Kahn,
the doctor who had been running the clinical trials of Compound Q
at San Francisco General Hospital. Their previous words had not
been cordial, especially after the delay in using Decadron on Charles
Weaver and Weaver's death. But now Kahn greeted Delaney warmly
and congratulated him. Kahn said Delaney's work had inspired him
and his team to move ahead faster. Delaney thanked him and tried to
be gracious.

Nice compliments. But Delaney still worried that all this concern
with his methodology meant that Q itself was being mistakenly
shunted aside as a failure. The drug was suffering from excessive
expectations. Press speculation—fueled by Volberding's early comments as well as by the gay community—had been that Q would rid
the body of HIV. Instead, the Project Inform study had indicated that
Q was just one piece of the puzzle.

The data showed lower P-24 antigen levels, higher T-cells, and
other improved markers. Patients said they felt a lot better. The data,
however, was just averages, the kind of thing the FDA liked. Looking
over the individual cases, Delaney sensed the drug had a strong
positive effect on some patients—maybe a third—and little if any
effect on others.

He was heartened later to hear Sam Broder say much the same
thing. "The effects of these drugs are subtle, not dramatic," Broder
told him. "Unless you study them in a precise way, you may not see
a statistically significant benefit." But Broder said he thought there
were many good drugs around.

This disease was unusual in the different ways it affected different
people. Delaney reasoned that drugs for the disease had to be looked
at as having potentially different effects on patients, too. As usual, Al
Levin had made a telling point during one of his recent emotional
tirades against the entire medical establishment: with all the research going on, no one seemed to be studying how the genetic
makeup of individual patients might be affecting the way HIV
worked in each body. Yet that might be the key to defeating the
disease.

Shortly after the conference in San Francisco, Arnold Relman announced his retirement as head of *The New England Journal of Medicine*. Fauci phoned Delaney that very day.

"Chalk one up for you, Marty," Fauci joked. "You got him to re-
tire."

SEVENTY-SIX

*F*or Delaney, the most important part of the International AIDS Conference was hearing about the raft of new drugs being prepared for testing in the laboratories of big pharmaceutical companies.

A new generation of the family of drugs called reverse transcriptase inhibitors was in the works. These drugs challenged the process by which HIV alters and then takes over new cells. The first generation had included ribavirin, suramin, and AZT. Now there were new drugs of this type, the most promising of which, tibo derivative and BIRG-587, were being developed in Europe, where fewer bureaucratic hurdles had to be cleared.

There was also a new breed of drugs called protease inhibitors. They disrupted HIV's enzyme production after it had taken over a cell, confounding the virus's ability to move out to another cell. Delaney discussed the new drugs with Corti, who was already aware of them and scouting for samples. Delaney flew east.

By the time the Institute of Medicine meeting let out in Washington, and Delaney could reach Gallo's lab in one of the maze of buildings on the vast NIH campus in Bethesda, Maryland, it was nearly 5 P.M. The famous scientist's office, on the top floor, was wallpapered in plaques, certificates, and testimonials from all corners of the globe. A large table groaned under the weight of medals he had won, displayed in their cases. The place was a defensive fortress. Why? Delaney needed no reaffirmation of Gallo's accomplishments. Even Gallo's enemies didn't deny them. What Delaney wanted was the skinny on the new Kaposi's sarcoma drug that Gallo had alluded to.

But before Delaney could ask about K.S., Gallo handed him a pile of documents so heavy it might break a toe if he dropped it. Delaney saw at once that they were documents rebutting the charges of the newspaper reporter John Crewdson. Crewdson, it seemed, had sent his accusations and supporting documents to hundreds of scientists. So Gallo had responded in kind by handing out his defense.

Delaney had already done some preliminary reading. There were unusual genetic similarities between the viruses discovered in the U.S. and France. Based largely on that, Crewdson had assembled a strong circumstantial case that Gallo's original HIV might have come from France. Many scientists had come to suspect that at some point, perhaps much later, Gallo had realized, without admitting it, that a trace of serum containing the French virus had contaminated his own serum, leading to his "discovery." But nobody was sure.

On the other hand, it was widely acknowledged that Gallo had reproduced the virus in mass quantities so it could be used in laboratory experiments, something the French hadn't done. Without that achievement, merely isolating the virus wouldn't have been worth much. And Gallo's heralded cancer work, which put him in charge of his lab to begin with, was likewise unquestioned.

In the past, when people were talking about the Gallo controversy, Delaney would say, "If you've got to investigate your most successful general, you ought to wait till after the war's over to do it. I want him in the laboratory working on a cure for this disease."

Now, sitting across Gallo's desk, listening to the scientist's defenses against the journalist's charges, Delaney said, "You know, this is not what people with AIDS want you to be doing. Can't you just put this guy aside and get on with your work?"

"No, I can't," Gallo said. "Sam Broder wants me to ignore it, too. But my integrity's been challenged. I have to defend my honor. Sam would defend himself, too, if it were happening to him."

Gallo allowed that a speaking invitation in the U.S.S.R. wasn't the only reason he had skipped the International AIDS Conference in San Francisco. At least in part, he had avoided the meeting because "every time I'm in public, forty reporters start asking me about the Crewdson stuff." Gallo constantly referred to "the Crewdson stuff," and how much damage it was doing, not only to his work but to the work of others in the field.

"Everything the scientists here do is followed by a Freedom-of-Information Act request [from Crewdson]," Gallo said. "Every travel voucher. The only way to disprove these allegations is to go back and rerun the experiments. We've had to redo every experiment from the mid-1980s. You tell me how this is helping AIDS research."

Gallo's lab had more than twenty-five isolates of the HIV virus on its own when he was accused of expropriating the Montagnier virus. Why did he need to steal anything?[84]

Then he swung around in his chair. "Hey, the afternoon's over," he exclaimed. "If you don't have any plans tonight, why don't you come to dinner with my wife and me."

"Thank you, I'd like that," Delaney said. He had complained in the past about having to stare at four hotel-room walls at night on trips to Washington.

"I need a swim first," Gallo said. "There's a pool at the house. It's five minutes away. Why don't you come on over? I'll lend you an extra swim suit. It's relaxing."

And so Delaney found himself in the passenger seat of Gallo's several-year-old Nissan Maxima. Once again, Gallo was on the defensive, rebutting charges without even seeming to notice he was doing it. "This is the fanciest car I've ever owned," he said. "My wife has a Chrysler." Crewdson had called into question the royalties Gallo got from the HIV antibody test that emerged from experiments on the virus. Who was entitled to the money was a big part of the dispute with the French.

Delaney had to agree that Gallo didn't look like a man getting rich off stolen property. The house was a pleasant suburban two-level ranch house, not out-of-line for a man of Gallo's stature. It was furnished like the house of an academic, loaded with books and journals and pictures of trips Gallo had taken. Delaney, lured by now into playing detective, was scrutinizing a wall of pictures, including Gallo and Montagnier together, in happier days.

But Gallo really wanted the swim, and verbally nudged Delaney toward the pool. They plunged into the water, under great arching trees. It was as relaxing as Gallo had promised. More than that, it finally seemed to take Gallo's mind off Crewdson and send it back to AIDS science.

And suddenly Gallo was quizzing his guest. Did Delaney think a second virus might be involved in inducing Kaposi's sarcoma and lymphoma in AIDS patients? Was Delaney satisfied with the existing explanations for the epidemiology of AIDS—the way it was spread and how far it had reached in the population? And what kind of results could really be expected from Compound Q? How did it work?

They soaked more than two hours, talking nonstop. Delaney was drinking orange juice. Gallo was drinking vodka. The time flew past, Delaney mesmerized. Gallo was one of the few scientists he could recall who really didn't seem to have formed an opinion about a subject before he saw the data on it. Gallo thirsted for facts, about Compound Q and everything else. Then Delaney thought: here he was, an activist from San Francisco, sitting in the pool discussing basic science with the most quoted scientist in the world—who seemed genuinely to want to know what Delaney had to say.

They were talking about the action of lymphocytes, and suddenly Delaney asked if it wasn't "crazy—you, Gallo, asking me about lymphocytes."

"No," Gallo responded. "I understand you have no scientific training. But people have come to respect your opinions about these things."

They discussed the way the virus destroys T-cells. Again, Delaney was struck by Gallo's unusually open mind. Gallo was interested in the possibility that what most people accepted as orthodoxy might not be true—about how the immune system was destroyed, how drugs worked, everything.

Then Gallo said, "I want you to know everything, including my personal life." And out of nowhere he disclosed that he had carried on a lengthy affair with an acclaimed scientist who once worked in his lab. And he named her. "Sooner or later you're going to hear that not only did we have an affair but I fathered a child with her. It's not something I'm very proud of, but I won't deny it. What an awful thing that was to do to my wife! My wife, who was my childhood sweetheart."

"She knows?" Delaney said lamely.

"She knows about it, but we don't talk about it," Gallo said.

"Well, I don't think it reflects on your scientific integrity," Delaney said, recovering. "In fact, I don't think it's any of anybody's business. I can't imagine someone using it against you in the virus dispute."

"*Spy* magazine has already thrown it in my face," Gallo said. "I want you to understand what did and didn't happen with the French. There are things I did that I'm not proud of. But they're not the things I'm accused of."

As he told the story now, he had always intended to credit Montagnier's lab along with his own for having isolated HIV. But in authorizing the initial research papers for submission to journals, Gallo had begun with papers about his own work. Thoughtlessly, he had bypassed the French contribution, planning to honor it in future papers —never realizing, he said, the impact the first papers would have in the press.

Then, while Gallo was traveling in Europe, news stories erupted over the initial papers. He was summoned home for a press conference to be given by his boss, the Secretary of Health and Human Services. "Around the press conference, the pace of activity was furious," Gallo said. He shared the stage, but failed, he said, to dilute the tone of American gloating by properly crediting the French. He regretted that. But he hadn't done anything dishonest. And, given the many isolates he had, it never occurred to anybody that he would be accused of stealing the virus.

"I understand what you're going through," Delaney said. "Even if you had taken the French virus, you still grew it in culture and made the blood test possible. You saved tens of thousands of lives. Congratulations!"

"But I couldn't go through life with that accusation hanging over me," Gallo said.

Was Gallo's denial believable? As far as Delaney was concerned, it could be sorted out later. Somehow, this scientist had to be steered back to AIDS, and the new K.S. drug they still hadn't talked about.

Gallo's wife came back to the house and begged off dinner. So Gallo and Delaney, on their own, left the pool, dressed, and headed off for an Italian restaurant, The Pines of Rome, in Bethesda. The maitre d' and waiters all knew Gallo as he came in.

At the first opportunity, Delaney brought up the new K.S. drug, and got Gallo talking. Gallo's lab at the National Cancer Institute had been working on Kaposi's sarcoma more than anything else for several years. It was the chief cancer associated with AIDS. The idea was to isolate the factors that made the lesions grow.

Whenever a scientist thought he had located an explanation for a tumor's growth, standard practice was to search for a compound to counteract it. Gallo's lab sent letters to companies around the world, seeking compounds with certain characteristics, not explaining precisely what the projected use of the compound was. Thousands of compounds were sifted.

And one emerged, Gallo went on. Its working name was SP-PG, and its discoverer was Daiichi Pharmaceuticals of Japan. As is customary in the drug development business, Daiichi replied to Gallo's request with a sample, while retaining all rights to the drug if Gallo found a use for it. Most drug companies were glad to have a scientist like Gallo tinkering around with their compounds; who knew what he might find?

With the first small sample, Gallo found that the compound seemed to halt the Kaposi's growth factor. SP-PG actually shrank Kaposi's lesions in mice. Gallo tried to get more drug. But Daiichi was cautious. The company knew it had a potentially forceful anti-cancer agent in SP-PG, though it was thinking more in terms of breast cancer than Kaposi's. SP-PG, however, had proven hard to cultivate. Only tiny amounts could be produced. Until some other way could be found to grow, or synthesize, the drug, any application that was discovered would be merely academic. And the company may have feared Gallo would synthesize the effective agent in SP-PG, and leapfrog its patent.

Daiichi kept promising to send Gallo more drug, but didn't. Every time a shipment was due, a letter would arrive instead, offering some excuse for delay.

It was especially frustrating for Gallo, he said, because someone he had met through business, and whose advice he often sought, had an exceptionally close friend who had recently been diagnosed with K.S., and was dying from it. Not understanding FDA regulations, the sometime adviser wanted Gallo to try the drug on his close friend. Before the FDA said a drug was ready for human testing, no scientist could legally or ethically do it. But the situation was frustrating, and made Gallo all the more eager to proceed with further lab work that might justify human testing of SP-PG. Right now he had a measly 200 milligrams of the drug—the equivalent of one AZT tablet.

Gallo wanted to know how to allay Daiichi's fears, and pry loose more of the drug. Delaney said he had run training sessions on negotiating with Japanese. His partner, Jim Corti, had lived for a while in Japan, and penetrated the pharmaceutical industry there to get dextran sulfate. Maybe Delaney could help.

Gallo said a team from Japan was coming to his lab to discuss the drug July 26, 1990—just a few weeks off. If the Japanese would sign a standard international cooperative research and development agreement, their investment would be protected and they might accept Gallo's help, which could speed the synthesis of the drug. Would Delaney care to sit in and offer his suggestions? This was more business negotiation than science.

It was the chance Delaney was looking for. He accepted the invitation, and went straight to work.[85]

SEVENTY-SEVEN

A little more than a week later, Delaney wrote Gallo what he called "a brief tutorial on Japanese business relations." Delaney singled out elements of the Japanese style that were working against Gallo and might explain the way Daiichi had been treating him:

There was the traditional Japanese assumption that foreigners were being as cagey and tight-lipped as the Japanese themselves were in business.

There was the Japanese style of group decision making, which discouraged individuals from taking action on their own. This often left foreign counterparts to be strung along, frustrated, while a group back in Tokyo plodded toward consensus.

There was Japan's decision to make pharmaceuticals a target industry world-wide, following the success of the Japanese in electronics and automobiles.

There was Japan's lack of sympathy about AIDS, which was considered a disease born of and borne by Western decadence.

And there was the traditional belief of many Japanese in their own racial superiority.

On Gallo's side, Delaney said, was the extreme concern of Japanese with public honor (something, though he didn't say it, that Gallo could surely relate to). Although Japanese could be ruthlessly mercenary in private dealings, a threat to their public honor could produce different results. "The trick," Delaney wrote, "is to find ways to put them in the public spotlight without offending them enough that they withdraw altogether."

Soon afterward, he was in Washington for an AIDS Clinical Trials Group conference, and Gallo invited him to attend a meeting of the lab staff. The weekly meetings of the seventy-member staff were renowned in research circles; Gallo grilled his scientists relentlessly on their projects, a kind of instantaneous peer review that they seemed to value.

Afterward, Delaney and Gallo talked, and Gallo, for once at least, seemed free of the Crewdson obsession. His mind was on a new problem. The Japanese delegation had said there were certain matters it wanted to discuss only with Dr. Shuji Nakimura, a Japanese citizen on Gallo's staff who had spent a lot of time on the Daiichi drug. During the meeting with Gallo and staff, the Daiichi executives wanted to be able to huddle with Dr. Nakimura behind closed doors. Some of Gallo's other staff were insulted by this demand.

Delaney said he could understand why the other scientists were insulted. "It's inherently racist," he said. "They must realize that you work as a team. Besides, it's contrary to American law. You should probably reject it. But not prior to the meeting. They might use it as an excuse to cancel again."

Gallo also let Delaney know the identity of his sometime adviser whose close friend was dying of K.S. He was Robert Gray, a prominent Washington public-relations man and now chairman of Hill & Knowlton, one of the world's largest public-relations companies. Gray had broken into the big time as President Eisenhower's appointments secretary, and more recently had assisted William Casey in running Ronald Reagan's 1980 presidential campaign.

Gray had headed his own Washington public-relations firm called Gray & Company, which handled international business, including with Japan; the firm was said to have links with the CIA, sometimes supplying cover for agents. Eventually, Hill & Knowlton bought it out.[86] Delaney called Gray, who, with his high-level experience and government connections, seemed ideally placed to make the necessary subtle challenge to Japanese honor.

It had been a busy summer for Gray. Two senior employees were stricken with AIDS, and his very close friend was dying. On top of that, he represented Middle Eastern interests that were on the brink of crisis. Saudi Arabia was an old client, Turkey a current one, and he was about to represent Kuwait. All three countries bordered on Iraq, which had been demanding that Kuwait curtail its oil exports to levels set by treaty, and stop taking oil from a field that overlapped the two countries' border. In July 1990, Kuwait and Saudi Arabia were trying in vain to get the Bush administration to drop its neutrality and side with Kuwait. That way, they hoped Iraq's ruler, Saddam Hussein, would be warned against using the army he was assembling near Kuwait.

In the midst of the Persian Gulf tension, Gray agreed to take part in a formal dinner for the Japanese the evening of July 26, after the big meeting that day; Gallo and Delaney would attend.

Came the big day, and Gallo scheduled Delaney to arrive at his office shortly after the meeting with the Japanese began. Delaney waited in the foyer while a secretary signaled Gallo he was there. A while later, Gallo emerged, looking concerned.

"How's it going?" Delaney asked.

"I don't know. They're being inscrutable." Gallo instructed Delaney to wait.

After fifteen minutes or so, everyone started to file out of the office. Gallo introduced Delaney to the group as "someone who works with our institute, and helps us with regulatory problems. He's someone you should get to know."

The Japanese each bowed and gave Delaney a business card. For all they know from that introduction, he thought, I'm commissioner of the FDA.

Then Gallo got him in a corner. "They've agreed to send more of the compound," he said. "They've taken a copy of the cooperative research and development agreement, and they're talking like they're going to sign it."

Then he said, "They want to go into the office alone with Nakimura now."

In fact, Delaney could see the Japanese-American separation physically taking place. Should he oppose it?

He decided the Nakimura issue probably wasn't worth fighting over at this stage. But he told Gallo what he would have told a paying client: "If he works for you, and you're his boss, you have a right to ask him to submit a report on this private meeting."

Gallo said he'd do that.[87] Then, as the Japanese disappeared behind the door of Gallo's office, Gallo added that they had rejected his offer of help with the technical problems in producing the drug.

"They say it's their duty to solve these problems themselves."

"Do they have a secure patent on this?" Delaney asked. "Maybe they're stalling until they get one."

"I think they have one," Gallo said. "But nobody ever looked."

After ten or fifteen minutes, the group emerged from the office. It was an awkward moment. The Americans wanted to ask Nakimura what had happened, but couldn't because the Japanese were still hanging around. Finally, Nakimura had to leave for another meeting, and only after he was gone did the Japanese excuse themselves until the dinner that evening.

After a trip to Gallo's house to change neckties, Gallo and Delaney headed for the dinner at the Jockey Club. On the drive over, Gallo suggested that Delaney try to develop a personal relationship with Yasukai Osada, the general manager of Daiichi's research laboratories and the senior man in the Japanese delegation.

As they entered the club and greetings were exchanged, Delaney could see that Gray already knew Osada and the people with him. At the suggestion of Gallo and Gray, Delaney sat on Osada's right, a symbolic position suggesting that Delaney was the person Osada should most be talking to. Delaney explained that he ran a group called Project Inform, which helped people with AIDS.

After repeated toasts to eternal friendships, and some getting-to-know-you chat, talk turned to regulatory approvals. Gallo mentioned that one of his worst regulatory experiences was with the HIV test he had developed using antibodies from the newly isolated virus a few years back, and that Japan had been greatly affected by the delays in approval. The test had been designed for use not just to screen patients but to screen the blood supply. Gallo had argued that the experimental version of the test should be used immediately to screen blood even while it was still being considered for licensing; even if the test turned out to be imperfect, he had contended, it was better than letting the blood supply go unchecked. But he had been turned down.

Japan got blood supplies for hemophiliacs from the United States. In the three months his test had been held up after he wanted to start using it, Gallo said, the HIV infection rate of hemophiliacs in Japan rose from zero to 13 percent. Delaney saw the Japanese faces freeze in horror, as they realized that in that single three-month period was created the principal incidence of AIDS in Japan. Gallo didn't mention the FDA by name. But had the test been used when he wanted it to be, Japan might have been spared much of its AIDS infection.

Once past that jolt, the dinner settled down. A coy dance was unwinding. Despite their assurances earlier in the day, the Japanese were now asserting that they didn't want to begin human testing of their SP-PG drug until they removed some impurities they had thus far been unable to remove. Gallo was angling for the drug—now. He could deal with the impurities, he said. The sides went back and forth, politely. Everyone observed that even after Gallo completed further animal testing, the FDA would have to go through a lot of slow formalities before human testing could begin. Suddenly, as they were getting into dessert, Gray, who had been polite and hardly heard from to that moment, burst out emotionally.

"I just don't understand it," he said. "If this stuff, even in its currently impure form, cures K.S. in the animals, and appears to have no toxic effects, I just can't understand why we can't start testing it in human beings now." He went on to talk about all the Japan bashing that was going on in the United States, and told the Daiichi group that this drug offered the Japanese a chance to overcome that. He appealed to the Japanese sense of international understanding.

Gallo and Delaney listened admiringly, knowing that at that moment Gray's friend was near death from Kaposi's sarcoma. The Japanese just kept saying, "I understand." Delaney sensed they were shaken and uncomfortable at the sudden emotional appeal.

When Gray was finished, Gallo deftly turned the tone of the conversation more businesslike without losing Gray's momentum. "Yeah, we don't see any toxicity with this," he said. "I just don't see why we don't go ahead with testing this now. Just because there's an impurity in it doesn't mean it's a harmful impurity."

The Japanese still seemed nervous and pressured. Delaney took a stab at bringing them around. "I agree with Bob [Gallo]," he said. "Patients for whom this is a life-threatening condition would be more than glad to take their chances with the impurities to hope to get the same results as in the mice."

Then one of the Japanese made what he thought was a pertinent joke. "Well, we don't want to have another Compound Q situation on our hands," he said with a chuckle.

Delaney's smile vanished. "What do you mean by that?" he asked.

"Well, you know, if you go too early, you have all these toxicities. There will be problems."

"Wait a minute," Delaney said, trying to stay diplomatic. "I'm the guy who set up that study. In the first place, the toxicity was manageable. And in the second place, this is a risk the patients are willing to take. The faster you get started, the faster you are going to be able to solve these problems."

The smiles were gone now all around. Gallo, Gray, and Delaney were squaring off against the Japanese and an American consultant they had brought along, a former pharmaceutical-company executive. "Even if we agreed," the consultant said, "the FDA would never allow us to go ahead as rapidly as you want with human testing. I would have to advise against doing that."

"I think that's good advice in general," Delaney replied, "but I think the FDA is willing to be more flexible when it comes to AIDS. In all politeness, I think I have more experience than you in dealing with the FDA on AIDS drugs, and the rules are different."

All this debate had burst out across the table. Suddenly, Delaney heard a voice to his left in the quiet, personal tone, reminiscent of the beginning of the dinner. It was Osada, the senior Daiichi official, speaking so the group couldn't hear him. "Martin," he was saying, "we should talk about this further."

"I would love to," Delaney replied, in the same tone.

"If you come to Japan, you should come to Daiichi."

"I've never been to Japan. I would love to come."

"Then you should take this as my invitation."

The conversation turned polite. The Japanese repeated their assurances that a new shipment of the drug for lab tests would arrive soon. Delaney wasn't quite sure what had just happened. But he decided that if he was going to Japan he was bringing Jim Corti, who knew Japan and its customs inside out.

The next morning, Delaney asked Gallo about the trip. Gallo thought it might break the log jam. If Gallo wanted him to go to Japan, Delaney asked, could Gray pay for it? Gallo said Gray had already offered to.

Weeks passed. The drug didn't arrive. Gallo couldn't continue the studies. Perhaps more important, the cooperative research agreement wasn't returned; in Washington, the Daiichi team had promised that its lawyers would promptly send the agreement back signed. Gallo wrote to Daiichi. His letters weren't answered. Gallo told Delaney he was mystified and angry.

Broder, head of the whole cancer institute, said he was disgusted. "They're incompetent maybe," he told Delaney.

Gray's friend died of Kaposi's sarcoma. So did a lot of other people. Delaney would have to go to Japan.

SEVENTY-EIGHT

Corti was still a bicycle-racing freak, and his trips to France for the Tour de France race every July were part of his life. They were also about the only breaks he allowed himself from his stressful eighty-hour, seven-day weeks—the only times he wasn't wakened at 6 A.M. by calls from the East Coast, and didn't have to stay up until past midnight to call Europe.

After the 1990 race, he stopped in Paris to see his friend there with AIDS. Accompanying his friend to the hospital for a checkup, Corti fell into conversation with a doctor, who mentioned that scientists at the Merrieux Institute, a research center, thought they had struck gold.

If the Merrieux scientists were right, an already-available antibiotic known as clarithromycin could stop MAI, mycobacterium avium intracellulare, a main killer of AIDS patients along with Kaposi's sarcoma and PCP. MAI was a tuberculosis-like organism that attacked people with depressed immune systems, leading to fevers, lethargy, and gradual wasting. Because the infection blocked the absorption of nutrients, patients literally starved to death. In autopsies performed on AIDS victims, nearly all showed MAI. There was no recognized effective treatment.

Clarithromycin had been developed by Abbott Laboratories outside Chicago. But, like ribavirin and many other American drugs, under the crazy licensing rules clarithromycin was for sale in Europe and nowhere close to licensing in the U.S. Abbott had directed the drug at the European market in large part because the testing process was so much faster there. While clarithromycin seemed to be an exceptionally powerful and broad-spectrum antibiotic, it wasn't expected to perform miracles other drugs couldn't perform. Stopping MAI would be a miracle.

So Corti talked to the doctors at Merrieux. They had given ten MAI patients clarithromycin, and ten the standard treatment for MAI—a regimen of four drugs that most physicians agreed was basically ineffective. All the patients started out very sick. The patients on clarithromycin all got much better. After a few weeks, the groups switched treatments. The patients who went off the clarithromycin suffered reversals. The other group was relieved of symptoms.

If this was true, there was only one question for Corti: Where to buy this drug? In France, it was still undergoing testing. It wasn't licensed for sale.

Back home, Corti logged his computer onto a medical data base and found more than one hundred articles on clarithromycin. He started reading. The drug was legally available in Italy and Ireland to treat bacterial infections. No unusual side effects were associated with it. He talked to the doctors and Delaney. Everyone agreed that clarithromycin had to be tried.

But Delaney was also hot on another drug. Not long after the meeting with the Japanese over the Daiichi drug SP-PG, Gallo and Sam Broder had begun talking excitedly about a discovery Broder had made. Looking methodically for substances with a molecular structure close to that of SP-PG, Broder found an almost identical structure in a drug called pentosan polysulfate. And unlike SP-PG, which was impossible to come by, factories overseas would turn out pentosan polysulfate as fast as you'd pay them to. It was used as a blood thinner in the treatment of heart ailments and phlebitis, among other things, in various countries, though not the U.S.

Because low toxicity was already established, Broder planned to import some pentosan quickly and start human tests as soon as the FDA would let him, to see if it worked the same as SP-PG had worked in mice. Of course, Broder couldn't give an experimental drug like pentosan to Delaney. But knowledge was power. If Corti was going to Europe for clarithromycin, he could also get pentosan polysulfate, and maybe the patients wouldn't have to wait for Broder.

Corti began calling around. Lenny Kaplan, the Florida man whom Corti had set up to administer Compound Q, knew a doctor in Munich. The doctor, Selmon Lichtenstein, had a large AIDS practice and had come to Kaplan to find oral alpha interferon when that was a hot item. They had kept in touch by phone. Corti should call him.

Lichtenstein told Corti he would be glad to run down clarithromycin and pentosan, and that Corti should come ahead to Germany. Pentosan was cheap, available over the counter without even a prescription. Clarithromycin, though, was expensive—$4.20 a pill in Italy.

Corti tried some pharmacies in Ireland, getting their numbers from an Irish telephone directory at a library. The price was marginally lower than in Italy, but quantities were limited.

So Corti started collecting money for a trip to Germany. Delaney and Dr. Robert Jenkins agreed to put up $2,500 each. So did Paul Rothman—which, as far as Corti was concerned, absolved Rothman of any remaining guilt he retained from the Compound Q trial. Corti himself coughed up a like amount, giving them $10,000, enough to buy more than 2,000 tablets.

Corti flew into Frankfurt, rented a car, and drove to meet Lichtenstein in Munich. They hit it off immediately. Lichtenstein turned out to speak perfect English and be well versed in most of the AIDS drugs Corti had dealt in. He had been administering Compound Q in his office. It turned out pentosan was close in formulation not just to SP-PG—which Lichtenstein hadn't heard of—but also to dextran sulfate, which both men had worked with.

"So we were really on the right track with dextran," Corti observed.

Lichtenstein called his regular pharmacist, who turned out to be on vacation. A few more calls located a substitute pharmacist, who quickly delivered ten cases of pentosan for about $1,200. The clarithromycin was harder to find, but the druggist finally said she had located a supply in Lugano. Corti said he'd drive there the next day and buy it. But a bridge was out near Innsbruck, and traffic was backed up. When he told the druggist, she said she'd pick it up by train, and transact some other business in Italy at the same time.

That gave Corti a chance to stay in Munich a few days and develop a friendship with Lichtenstein. These were the heady days when barriers between East and West Germany were falling, and two evenings in a row Lichtenstein and his stunning blond girlfriend took Corti out for dinner and a share of the excitement. Days, Lichtenstein introduced Corti to a group of AIDS patients, all of whom looked forward to hearing how Corti fared with the two new drugs.

By the time Corti was back in California, Delaney had obtained a copy of Broder's protocol for the NIH study of pentosan. In fact, two of the eight patients Broder accepted for the test were referred to him by Delaney—San Francisco men who went to Washington in hopes of being cured of Kaposi's sarcoma. As soon as word arrived that Broder had given a potentially effective intravenous dosage without encountering obvious toxicity, Corti turned his supply of the drug over to Jenkins, Rothman, and Waites for duplication of the procedure on the West Coast.

They immediately sensed biological activity. All three doctors reported yellow halos appearing around the blood-purple Kaposi's lesions, like a scab forming around a sore. Broder called from Washington with exactly the same story.

"We're seeing activity," he told Delaney excitedly.

And then the doctors noticed a slightly perceptible lightening of the lesions themselves. What they were seeking was a result known as anti-angiogenesis—a halt in fresh blood supply to the tumor. Tumors couldn't grow without a blood supply. That's why Daiichi had intended SP-PG for other kinds of tumors—breast and lung. If pentosan worked, who could tell how widespread the uses of the drug would be?

There was an air of exhilaration. Maybe it didn't matter if the Daiichi drug wasn't arriving. Pentosan might be its twin.

Meanwhile, Jenkins gave clarithromycin to one test patient with MAI. Although MAI patients didn't have cancerous lesions like Kaposi's patients, they generally felt much sicker than the Kaposi's patients did. Until Kaposi's attacked the internal organs, it resulted in little more than disfigurement. MAI sapped the body throughout.

The Merrieux dosage of clarithromycin was high, six to eight pills a day, about three times the usual dose to cure bacterial infections. Everyone waited to see what would happen. Before the week was out, Jenkins's patient was claiming almost complete relief. The fevers and sweats stopped, appetite was restored and energy returned.

There were no blood markers to reflect the mostly subjective symptoms of MAI. The organism's presence in the body was detectable mainly in bone-marrow samples, which were too hard to get to check regularly as one would a blood sample. But something positive was happening.

Jenkins began clarithromycin on a few other patients. Rothman, who had been awaiting word on Jenkins's first test patient, then started half a dozen patients of his own. The results were as quick and as striking.

The patients proclaimed clarithromycin a stunning success. Word swept the patient community, and demand soared. At forty or fifty pills per patient per week, the original batch of two thousand pills was dwindling. Nobody knew how long a patient should stay on the pill at this dose, but the Merrieux experience suggested patients shouldn't withdraw from it soon. Corti would have to go back for more.

Inventory wasn't the only problem. Because clarithromycin wasn't approved by the FDA, insurance companies wouldn't reimburse patients who took it. At $200 a week, the drug would be unfairly limited to the wealthy. Corti had to try to bring down the price.

He called Selmon Lichtenstein in Munich. Lichtenstein's regular pharmacist was back from vacation. For an order of 5,000 pills, the price was negotiated down to about $3 a pill. When Corti reached Munich, he learned the pills were cheaper because they were coming from Abbott's Irish operation. He determined to try to make his own deal with Abbott. Even at $3 a pill, the treatment was too costly.

S E V E N T Y - N I N E

*I*f it hadn't been for the continued death and suffering they saw around them, Corti and Delaney would have had considerable cause to gloat as summer ended in 1990. It wasn't just the new drugs they had brought to suffering patients or their new influence on national decision making. Events were vindicating even the work they had done in those first early days in 1984.

In the summer of 1990, the study of ribavirin that had been so thoroughly trashed by the FDA and Congress in 1987 was published in a respected, peer-reviewed scientific journal, the *Journal of AIDS*. The "summary" section at the beginning of the article disposed of all the charges that Frank Young and Congressman John Dingell had made, and the network anchormen had reported, about differences in the various test groups. When all entry discrepancies were accounted for, the numbers were still clear: If you had HIV, you were significantly less likely to advance to AIDS in a given period of time if you took ribavirin than if you didn't. In other words, if you legalized ribavirin, more people would live healthier longer.

That was just what the statisticians, ethicists, and others had said back in the summer of 1987. But for political reasons the drug had been politically sunk in the United States. In the summer of 1990, the government of Ireland licensed ribavirin for use by HIV-infected patients. The director of the Irish National Drugs Advisory Board acknowledged that the test results were "preliminary," not phase three, but said that the results were "as promising as you can hope for" and that patients "cannot afford to wait five years."

Then there was isoprinosine, which was squelched in the United States before it could even get as far as ribavirin got. Years earlier,

Scandinavian AIDS workers had told Delaney that their researchers were going off to conduct a massive study of isoprinosine. In June 1990, the results were published in *The New England Journal of Medicine*.

A dozen doctors with long Scandinavian names had studied 866 patients with HIV who had not yet developed AIDS. Half got isoprinosine and half a placebo. Seventeen of 437 patients on placebo developed full-blown AIDS in six months. Only two of the isoprinosine patients did. And this was without the isoprinosine-ribavirin combination that Delaney had thought would be most effective. Said the article approved by *The New England Journal of Medicine*, "We conclude that treatment with inosine pranobex [isoprinosine] delays progression to AIDS in patients with HIV infection."

Delaney immediately compared the Scandinavian study to the AZT trial that the FDA had interrupted midway in 1987 in order to rush AZT to market. That trial had found that infected, asymptomatic people were two and a half times more likely to advance to AIDS if they took a placebo than if they took AZT. Isoprinosine's figures were stronger. If you could produce the same or better result using this utterly benign drug, why would anyone use AZT instead? Of course, in combination, with a lower dose of AZT to reduce the toxicity, the results might be better still.

At the International Conference on AIDS a week after the *The New England Journal of Medicine* article came out, some of the Scandinavian researchers presented a follow-up. After another six months, thirty-seven more subjects had progressed to AIDS. Seventy-three percent were from the placebo group, and only 27 percent were from the group that had taken isoprinosine.

Even in these circumstances, which Delaney and Corti considered suboptimal, one thing was clear: the drug worked.

But you had to live in some other country to take it. In the United States, the news of isoprinosine's healing power came three years too late. For largely political reasons, ribavirin and isoprinosine had been destroyed as treatments.[88]

But Delaney resolved it would not happen again. Two other drugs were knocking at the gates of licensure: ddI and ddC. For a while, after AZT came out, he seemed to notice a reduction in the number of funerals he attended. Now AZT had lost its punch for those who began taking it when it was approved. People were dying again.

Yet, Delaney sensed, both ddI and ddC were drifting dangerously. Bristol-Myers was stuck in a vise with ddI. On one side, the parallel-track idea had forced the company into a $50,000-a-day giveaway program with the drug. On the other, the FDA's refusal to accept surrogate markers meant that the ddI studies in progress had to carry on two more years until superior survival rates could be proven to statistical significance. Only then could the drug be sold, by which time Bristol-Myers would have suffered a financial disaster from the giveaways. The FDA itself was leaderless. President Bush still hadn't appointed anyone to fill the vacancy created when Frank Young resigned in the wake of the generic drugs scandal the year before.

The rest of the industry saw what was happening—especially Hoffmann-La Roche, which was under pressure from various AIDS groups to make ddC available the same way ddI was. Hoffmann-La Roche had tried to offer a parallel-track public-relations gesture with ddC, but offered it under such restrictive conditions that only a few hundred patients in the country qualified for it. The result was bad press, and denunciation by marching activists. Hoffmann-La Roche was trying to hold off the hordes by promising to seek licensure for ddC before the end of the year. But unless something gave at the FDA, it wouldn't be approved.

The parallel-track idea just wasn't working under these conditions. Delaney had not started out as a big fan of drug companies. But he understood enough about business to see that unless they had some kind of profit incentive, the fight against AIDS was going nowhere. The answer was clear. It was no longer just expanded access to drugs prior to licensing.

August 16, 1990, Delaney sat down and wrote the letter of his life, addressed to Ellen Cooper and her assistant Paul Beninger.

> Privately within the industry [he wrote], they are saying that the expanded access program has slowed the development of ddI and diverted resources from the development of other promising BM [Bristol-Myers] drugs. If Bristol-Myers concludes that it has lost ground because of taking innovative stands in AIDS, all of the industry will feel the blow. But not nearly as much as the AIDS community over the long haul. Of course we want access to ddI and ddC any way we can get it. But if our pursuit is blind and narrowly focused, these may be the last drugs we get the chance to wrangle over for a long time.
>
> The answer has to be regulatory innovation which focuses on early licensure, not just getting drugs to people by convoluted expanded access mechanisms. The fundamental problem with both the ddC and ddI development cycles is that both drugs are being

asked to clear the wrong hurdle. Effectively, that hurdle is proof of equivalence or superiority to AZT, or supplementary value. The proper hurdle should instead be reasonable proof of some degree of efficacy, however limited, against HIV.

With a revised hurdle, I believe the case can be made that both ddI and ddC have already cleared it. Both drugs have demonstrated some degree of efficacy against the primary infection, as measured by reduced viral activity and stabilized or improved immune functioning, as well as other minor laboratory and clinical markers. AZT at best only meets this same hurdle. Yes, there are side effects of both drugs, but they have already been very well characterized. They are, we believe, better understood now than AZT's side effects were at its licensure.

Delaney cited Broder and four other prominent scientists saying that combinations of drugs produced the best results. But patients couldn't try combinations, because AZT now stood alone on the shelf.

Proof of extended survival was no longer a suitable requirement, he wrote. "We will contest it on ethical as well as scientific grounds. We'd rather not make the FDA the battleground for such a fight, but we will if necessary." He pointed out that Broder, head of the National Cancer Institute, and Fauci, head of the National Institute for Allergy and Infectious Diseases, supported him on this, as did yet another presidential commission that had recently gotten around to issuing a report.

The tens of thousands of patients who could no longer benefit from AZT "must be given the unquestioned right to access the next best drugs in the system rather than sit idly by watching the rest of their immune system collapse," Delaney wrote. "This is not simply a narrow group easily characterized by a certain CD-4 level or symptom set. It is in fact just about everyone who has been on AZT for a year or longer.

The solution, then, to industry's problems, the aggravated frustration of patients and FDA's own dilemmas—the moral imperative calls for licensure—now—of both ddI and ddC on the basis of current data. The only precedent such a move will set is how to approve drugs in a national emergency.

Like any negotiated solution, everyone would be given the opportunity to save face. These wouldn't be ordinary approvals. They could include serious post-marketing surveillance requirements with goals and timetables.

In other words, the licensing could be conditioned on the continuation of studies. If the data turned sour, the license could be withdrawn.

The ultimate test of what is best under what circumstances will be worked out either in the post-marketing studies or in the marketplace itself. Each physician and patient will have to undertake some degree of experimentation to determine what seems best for the individual. Until physicians and patients have the opportunity to select their treatment in this way, optimal therapy simply won't be attained by most patients.

In summary: We must seek near simultaneous approval of ddC and ddI, this year. This will be supported by people at the highest levels in the federal research institutes. Industry, of course, will go along.

To the extent that any of this may be characterized as a battle, much of it will have to be fought on your battleground. It may already be time for you to begin conversations with both Hoffmann-La Roche and Bristol-Myers. The only unpredictable variables I see are your own response and the details. Let's get to work!

And he signed it as executive director of Project Inform, and faxed and mailed copies not only to Cooper and Beninger but to the drug companies, leaders in the AIDS movement, and every member of the AIDS Clinical Trials Group executive committee—more than a hundred copies as his fax machine worked nonstop.

Across the nation, phone lines buzzed. The letter catalyzed an eruption of pent-up feelings. From protest groups like Act Up, to scientists meeting in the hallways between laboratories at the National Institutes of Health, the letter burst into conversations, not so much as a new idea but as a signal that it was okay to express an idea that had already quietly flowered in almost every mind in the field.

Broder called. "There's no question that both these drugs are going to be approved, sooner or later," he said. "Why not sooner?"

"If it's going to happen," Delaney said, "why not *now?* Why go on with this charade?"

Broder was on board.

Even some of the conservative researchers Delaney had expected might fight him called up to agree. Thomas Merigan, head of Stanford University's AIDS research unit and senior executive of the AIDS Clinical Trials Group, phoned to say, "I think you've made some important points here. I think we ought to do it."

Contacts at Bristol-Myers and Hoffmann-La Roche called, too. The companies couldn't speak publicly on this, as much as it was in their interest to. They couldn't let it appear that profit considerations were interfering with scientific decisions. But they had received the signal that the goal line was in sight—that the data from the early studies and the expanded-access programs was worth assembling, that the midnight oil was worth burning.

Allies in the gay AIDS movement talked of joining forces for a political push to get the two drugs licensed by the end of the year. Chapters of the groups began to circulate the letter.

Cooper called up angry. "You're trying to pressure me," she said. "This is turning into a political thing."

"The science is there," Delaney said.

"Everybody in the world has seen this letter already," she protested. "That's not pressuring me?"

"I'm doing my job, Ellen. You know what that is."

"Look, if this is what everybody wants to do, let's just get clear about it," she said. "Are you trying to force a purely political approval of the drugs?"

"No," he replied. "I'm talking about researchers who have worked with the drugs. They're convinced of the benefits."

"We need data," she said. "Don't pressure us based on opinion only."

Typical, safe line. He couldn't imagine there was any data she didn't have, but he promised to send more.

Inevitably, Gina Kolata at *The New York Times* got hold of the letter, and wrote about it at length.

Advocates for people with AIDS are urging the Food and Drug Administration to license two new drugs before clinical trials of their effectiveness are completed, and some leading researchers are expressing interest in their proposal [her story began]. The proposal, designed by Martin Delaney of Project Inform, a San Francisco advocacy group, and avidly supported by the AIDS Coalition to Unleash Power, or Act Up, would be the most radical departure yet from the FDA's traditionally cautious approach to testing drugs thoroughly before they are licensed for widespread use.

Delaney scanned to see whom Kolata chose to quote. How she treated the story could affect the success of the proposal. The first scientist she cited was Thomas Merigan of Stanford, who had called Delaney with support as soon as he received the letter. Said the *Times*, "Dr. Merigan, who has been discussing the proposal with other researchers and with advocates for people with AIDS, said the proposal is 'a thoughtful and provocative document that has to be taken seriously even though it's a departure from the norm.' "

The first few quotes in the article were cautiously supportive. An FDA spokesman said, "We'll consider it, but beyond that we can't comment." The obligatory attack against the idea came twelve paragraphs deep into the article, and the opponent she used was a vice-president of some unheard-of pharmaceutical firm in San Rafael, California.

At that point, Delaney knew that the conclusion of his letter had been correct. Scientifically and politically, the world was now on his side. The only unknown variable was the FDA's reaction.

The pressure was closing in on Ellen Cooper.

EIGHTY

By mid-September, 1990, the doctors Corti had given the pentosan polysulfate to were beginning to admit to each other that their early hopes weren't being fulfilled. The patients' Kaposi's sarcoma lesions didn't continue to lighten. Dosage was increased, but that only produced side effects, some of them serious, including a plunge in blood platelets. Broder would continue following his protocol for two more months in Maryland, but the doctors in California stopped administering the drug.

That meant that efforts to get SP-PG from Daiichi were once again critical. Robert Gray, the public-relations mogul, told Gallo he would make a contribution to Project Inform to pay for Delaney and Corti to go to Japan. Delaney got on the phone to Daiichi to set a date.

But while pentosan polysulfate failed, the amazing recovery of MAI patients on clarithromycin continued. Somehow, Corti had to bring down the price. He called Abbott Laboratories in Ireland, and struck up a friendly conversation with the marketing manager, Francis Lynch, who seemed sympathetic to Corti's mission. Lynch told him that the same firm that sold to Corti in Milan, Pharmatalia, supplied clarithromycin to Ireland as well, but much more cheaply than it sold the same pills in Italy. Lynch said the price in Ireland was equivalent to only $2.60 a pill, nearly 40 percent off the Italian price. Working for Abbott, Lynch couldn't supply the pills directly to Corti.

Well, could he recommend any pharmacists who stocked it?

Yes, there was Maurice O'Connell, who owned the Teren Ure

pharmacy in Dublin. Lynch offered to talk to O'Connell, after which Corti could arrange to meet him. In no time, Corti was on a plane to Dublin with more money. He and O'Connell arranged for regular shipments via Federal Express.

As calls for clarithromycin increased from around the country, so they also did for ddC. Hoffmann-La Roche obviously wasn't going to enter into a meaningful expanded-access program for ddC because of the cost. People wanted the drug. Initial fears about high toxicity, provoked by problems in Hoffmann-La Roche's phase one tests, had eased since it was discovered that dosage could be cut way back. ddC was many times stronger by weight than ddI or AZT, and so only a little need be used. That also meant the drug ought to be much cheaper than ddI or AZT.

Another thing distinguished ddC from the other drugs: it was a common, easy-to-obtain chemical. Although Hoffmann-La Roche had a patent on its use against AIDS, reference books listed at least fifteen firms that manufactured it for laboratory research. Already someone had figured out how to produce it as tablets; a Dallas group was advertising them at $150 for a month's supply at the new, lower dosage. Not only was that ridiculously overpriced, since the chemical was cheap, but callers said the Dallas group wasn't keeping up with demand. Hundreds of patients were back-ordered.

Corti chatted up the head of the Dallas group, who disclosed the tablets were coming from a gay man in San Francisco, Ken X (name withheld because of obvious illegal activity), who ran a health-food distributorship. Corti called him. Ken X had the ddC tablets made by friends who worked at a small pharmaceutical lab. The friends made the tablets whenever they had spare time. In a good month, Ken X was funneling several hundred bottles to Dallas, each containing about a two-month supply.

By now, Corti had already polled the demand and found that buyers' clubs in New York, Dallas, Fort Lauderdale, and Washington, D.C., were ready to buy more than two thousand bottles immediately.

"Let's do something that counts," Corti told Ken X. "You're established in this. I'm not trying to take your business away from you. But this needs to be out there in quantities. Do you have the facilities for doing that?"

Ken X said his friends were turning out all they could.

"Then I've got to find a lab that can do more."

Besides the quantity problem, Corti was bothered that nobody was analyzing the San Francisco product for weight or impurities. Nucleocide analogs like ddC were sometimes contaminated with plutonium or beryllium. And with the dosage now tiny, weight precision was important. Corti took some tablets to an independent lab and had them analyzed; everything was in order, but that didn't mean it always would be.

Corti remembered years back when a flash-in-the-pan product called DNCB had seemed promising. His friend Bob Alexander, who ran a chemical-supply company, had introduced him to a customer who owned a small pharmaceutical laboratory near Los Angeles. The lab owner, Sherman X (name withheld because of obvious illegal activity), was neither gay nor infected with HIV. But he had thought nothing of producing an unlicensed drug for a good cause and a small profit. The DNCB hadn't worked, but the same guy might be willing to produce ddC.

He was.

He studied the drug and declared that ddC would be easy to bulk up into easy-to-take form by mixing it with a standard filler, which was no doubt what Ken X's friends were doing in San Francisco. Sherman X recommended producing it in capsules rather than tablets. The cost would be a bit more, but the drug would stay potent longer; exposure to air could weaken ddC. Sherman X said he could turn the drug out cheaply in his off hours in batches of two thousand bottles.

It was all arranged. But when he was back home, Corti began to worry. Manufacturing a drug in violation of a drug company's exclusive patent might offend the government more than mere smuggling did. Hoffmann-La Roche might apply pressure. He had a few long, soul-searching talks with Delaney.

He decided to invite some large buyers' clubs to collaborate, sharing the cost and responsibility. But the clubs in New York and San Francisco turned him down.

"They won't do it," he explained. "Either their board of directors won't go along with it, or the guys that run the clubs are afraid."

"Puts you out in the cold if anything happens," Delaney said.

"Making the capsules seems easy enough. What worries me is if something goes wrong. I'm a rookie at this. I don't want to hurt anyone or hurt what we're doing."

"Look," Delaney said, "get the best advice you can on how to test the stuff, and go ahead. This is going to be a temporary thing, but somebody's got to provide an alternative to AZT. I know and you know it shouldn't be us, but who else is there?"

"I guess I'm in," Corti replied. "You know, this is the most illegal thing I've done yet. If the feds come after me, my position's going to be that I'll make it for a certain period of time, but the minute Hoffmann-La Roche gets a license to sell it, I'll stop cold. I don't want to be accused of going after their business."

"Sounds reasonable," Delaney said. "Just keep the price as low as you can so no one could complain you're profiteering."

The scheme almost capsized at the start because of the Wisconsin chemical company Corti ordered the ddC from. He found the drug in the company's catalog, and felt comfortable with the marketing man he talked to. But then the man called back saying the finance department had screamed. The order was too big for laboratory research. Most people bought 100 milligrams. Corti was buying hundreds of grams. The company was going to notify the Drug Enforcement Agency. Corti urged the man to calm down the finance department, and said he'd just cancel the order.

The next company he talked to also must have sensed Corti's illegal intent. Instead of threatening to turn him in, however, it just demanded payment in cash. There was something scary about the tone of the transaction, and Corti backed off. He called Ken X, who agreed to supply 200 grams he had obtained from a local manufacturer until Corti could locate a source for big quantities.

As Sherman X went to work, Corti had the drug analyzed three times—once as a raw material, once as it was mixed, and once after it was in capsules.

He printed labels on a dot-matrix printer, identifying the drug as ddC and warning that it should be kept cool and dry. He photocopied the labels in sheets to be cut out and glued on the bottles. Before a bottle was shipped, he had sample capsules checked again at the labs.

The lab tests were an added expense, but even so, the capsules could be sold for under $35 a bottle, about one-fifth the price for a monthly dose that the Dallas group had charged.

With Sherman X now cranking out thousands of bottles of ddC, Corti and Delaney boarded the flight to Tokyo for the Daiichi meetings. They arrived October 3, 1990, giving them a day to rest. For October 5, Delaney and Osada, the research chief, had mapped out a day of meetings, a tour of the Daiichi facilities and a ceremonial dinner.

Daiichi had just moved into new quarters, and was eager to show them off. But when the group sat down to talk, Osada said he wasn't in charge of the dealings with the U.S. anymore; SP-PG had moved from the research division to the medical-development department.

He introduced Delaney and Corti to the deputy general manager of the development department, a young assistant, and a senior scientist. Also joining the meeting was a young woman who was introduced as the person responsible for continuing research on the drug.

The first big issue was exactly who Delaney and Corti were, and why they were there; the Japanese had a hard time understanding. No, they didn't work for or represent the government. But no, they weren't trying to secure a share of the patent for themselves, either. They were representing the interests of patients. The patient community was paying their expenses.

They weren't sure the Daiichi team believed them, but everyone pressed on to a long discussion of FDA regulations and how Daiichi would get its drug approved. Delaney sensed right away that Daiichi had been coached by an American consultant who had lived with the FDA system before AIDS, and didn't know it was rapidly changing. The Daiichi team believed drugs always took at least five, and more likely ten, years to clear, and that the cost would always exceed $200 million. They were frightened that getting sidetracked with Kaposi's sarcoma might delay SP-PG in the really lucrative solid-tumor market.

Delaney decided to sell AIDS as an opportunity for them to get SP-PG approved faster for all applications. The company, he said, ought to use the fast track that was developing for AIDS drugs in order to get SP-PG approved early. Working with the National Cancer Institute was the fastest way to get approval. Once SP-PG was in American drugstores, numerous hurdles would be eliminated if tests later showed it also worked against breast cancer and other tumors.

He could see he had sparked their interest and curiosity. But the first thing they wanted to know was whether he was looking for a consulting fee from them. What did he really want? Was he from Act Up, a group they had apparently been warned to steer clear of?

"All I want—all—" he said, "is your most sincere commitment to the development of this drug for K.S."

He saw them flinch at the word "commitment."

He stressed he wanted openness and honesty from them. If they were straightforward, he would try to use his influence to help the drug in the U.S. If they weren't he would leave.

They adopted a tone of surprise. Did he think matters had been unclear till now?

Delaney avoided the temptation to roll his eyes. The pace of development, he said, had been much slower at every point than the Americans had been led to expect. The Americans were confounded that the cooperative research-and-development agreement hadn't been returned as agreed. And where was the drug Daiichi had promised? Just as Delaney and Corti were leaving for Japan, Daiichi had announced it was sending another 200 milligrams to Gallo—a paltry amount that still hadn't arrived.

The Japanese seemed to think drug companies were always in a contentious relationship with the U.S. Government. Delaney stressed over and over that cooperation in AIDS research could lead to a similar spirit when it came to cancer in general.

The woman in charge of researching the drug said there were still serious problems producing it, including the persistence of at least two impurities. She showed pictures of the drug—microscope blowups revealing the impurities. She estimated it would take two or three years' more work to get ready for human testing. And it would be particularly difficult to get FDA permission for such tests, she said, because right now Daiichi thought SP-PG ought to be given concomitantly with steroids, and their consultants had told them that drugs taken concomitantly with other drugs were always a problem.

Somehow, somebody had given this company a faulty primer on how the American pharmaceutical industry worked, Delaney was now convinced. And the company had swallowed it whole.

Forget the private advice you've been getting, he told them. Talk directly to NCI, the National Cancer Institute, and the FDA. Anything else was a waste of time. The steroid issue could be finessed. Just eliminate it from the initial protocol and add it as an amendment after the protocol was approved. He had been through that with Compound Q. And Gallo had already told them to forget the impurities for now. They might turn out to be no problem at all. Drugs that came out of U.S. Government labs with a seal of approval had a big boost with the FDA. AZT was a perfect example of that.

Gradually, the Japanese seemed to be believing him. They acknowledged that some of the advice they had been getting was contradictory. But on one issue they held firm: they would not accept Gallo's help in growing the drug. They believed they were more advanced than the Americans were in their ability to do this.

Delaney reminded them that early in the meeting Osada had explained the delays by saying Daiichi lacked experience in fermentation work. NCI would have that experience, he told them.

The Japanese acknowledged there were problems, but wouldn't budge. They didn't want to discuss it further.

Were the problems purely technical, or were they financial, Delaney wanted to know. There were ways of raising money.

No money was needed, he was told.

The group moved from a conference room to Osada's office. The development men left and came back later, as the discussions continued. Osada went off to do some work.

Then Osada came back and took the conversation on a new tack that surprised Delaney. They had heard Gallo was going to be fired for stealing the HIV virus. Was it true? They had also heard that a Gallo assistant named Salahuddin had been banished from NCI in a scandal, and had been a key factor in the work on SP-PG. And they had heard that Nakimura, the Japanese on Gallo's staff, was going to leave, too. Wasn't NCI thus being crippled in its ability to do anything with SP-PG anyway?

So maybe *that* was the problem.

Gallo had fired a technician, a non-Ph.D., named Zaki Salahuddin a few months back. Fortunately, Delaney had spent enough time shooting the breeze with Gallo to have heard the story. Salahuddin and his wife had been operating a company on the side; without disclosing his interest in it, he had contracted with it to do work for the government lab. Gallo had liked Salahuddin and his work, and on inspection didn't think any extraordinary fees had been paid to Salahuddin's company, or that the taxpayers had been robbed. But he felt betrayed by Salahuddin. Rules had been violated, and Gallo had to fire the man. Salahuddin pleaded guilty to two federal felonies and was sentenced to repay $12,000 and perform 1,750 hours of community service. But it was ludicrous to think that Salahuddin's loss seriously impaired the research capabilities of the National Cancer Institute.

The more they talked, and Delaney tried to allay Osada's fears, the more Delaney suspected that Salahuddin himself or someone close to him had approached Daiichi. Salahuddin now worked at a lab in California, Osada said. Osada acknowledged that a source in America was urging Daiichi to finish the SP-PG research in collaboration with Salahuddin's new lab, instead of with the NCI. They had even heard that Nakimura was going to work with the California lab.

So! Gallo had gained unsuspected and unwanted competition in getting hold of this drug. Worst of all, Daiichi, not knowing which lab to work with and confused by the stories it was hearing, had decided to just wait and see, further delaying the development of SP-PG.

Once again, Delaney told Osada that Daiichi ought to deal directly with the government scientists. But Osada kept pressing him on Salahuddin—half a dozen times—creating all sorts of suspicions in Delaney's mind. He finally stressed that because of Salahuddin's financial transgression, dealing with him instead of NCI could derail the drug.

Without stating a final decision, Osada changed the subject to Gallo. Given the Salahuddin problem, the last thing Delaney needed that day was just what had happened—publication of another story in the American press that Gallo was going to be investigated yet again over the Crewdson charges. And Delaney was left to learn about it from Osada, who added gratuitously that all these newspaper articles aroused further caution about a joint research agreement.

Thanks a lot, Crewdson, Delaney thought.

He said the government probably had no choice but to formally investigate each new allegation, but that there was no reason to think Gallo was on shakier ground now than before. Sensing that it might help, Delaney from that point began referring to Broder as well as Gallo as the scientists Daiichi ought to work with.

Eventually, the air began to lighten. Osada seemed finished with heavy questions. Corti—who had agreed to let Delaney negotiate the issues—felt able to join in. Delaney, tired of the tension, felt rescued when Corti's easy social banter took over. At the ceremonial dinner that night, they presented Osada with a gift, a sculpture made by a German artist from pieces of the Berlin Wall, which Osada seemed to appreciate. Corti held forth with stories of Japanese experiences that seemed to flatter and entertain the Daiichi team. Dinner concluded with profuse thank-yous on all sides. The Daiichi team claimed to have been much enlightened.

Back home, Delaney learned the 200 milligrams of SP-PG had arrived at Gallo's lab, as promised. Gallo would at least be able to repeat the mouse experiments, a requisite to publishing the data. And Delaney set about writing a long, detailed report for Gallo and Broder of everything he had seen and heard, stressing that they might have an unsuspected Salahuddin problem, that the Japanese were worried about the size of the market for a K.S. drug, and that Crewdson also posed an obstacle.

He advised Gallo and Broder to write Daiichi linking themselves to Delaney's visit. This would help reinforce Delaney's message that Daiichi could get its cancer drug approved faster if it worked *with* the government agencies on AIDS instead of scheming against them. It would also help with the Salahuddin and Crewdson problems.

Delaney asked to see the letters before they went out. "It is important to be careful how anything I've said here gets back to them," he said. "Their whole approach to business relations is loaded with nuance and subtlety. This guarantees that their relations will often be confused and full of misinterpretation. Once your letter has been received and acknowledged at their end, I will send a further letter urging an increase in the quantity of the drug immediately. I will also remind them of the need to meet with yourselves and the FDA as soon as possible to discuss the minimum requirements for filing the IND [application for a license to test a new drug on human subjects]. They clearly have this confused. I hope this has been useful."[89]

EIGHTY-ONE

*F*ive thousand new clarithromycin pills arrived at Corti's studio by Federal Express from the pharmacy in Ireland. Corti now had a team of assistants to sort, deliver, and mail the pills and collect checks. After two months, twenty doctors in the Los Angeles area alone were encouraging the drug's use. Clearly it worked. But everyone was reminded of its limitations when the first patient to have licked MAI with the drug died two months later—of Kaposi's sarcoma.

At the University of Miami Medical Center, Dr. Margaret Fischl completed a study using low doses of ddC and AZT in combination. Surrogate-marker results were much better than with AZT or ddC alone, and in a year only a handful of patients had progressed to AIDS. Back in the mid-1980s, such an experiment would have meant nothing until a year had passed and some medical journal published a peer-reviewed article about it. Now the ink wasn't dry on Fischl's preliminary lab data before phone lines carried the news around the country. Patient told patient, friend told friend, doctor told doctor. More orders poured in to Corti in Los Angeles, and Sherman X got instructions to crank up production of their bootleg ddC.

Corti had also been drawn to another underground drug. For several years, a researcher named Candice Pert had been aggressively promoting a drug called peptide T, which supposedly blocked receptor sites on T-cells so the virus couldn't enter. Other researchers disputed Pert's claims. Corti watched Michael Scolaro try it on seven patients, who got precious little benefit, and they gave up on the drug. Bristol-Myers had made a deal with Pert to develop peptide T, but the company, too, dropped it when it didn't seem to do much. Small amounts of peptide T continued to circulate in the underground thanks to a believer in Colorado, who imported it from a company in Denmark. But Corti stayed away.

Then, in October 1990, a patient Corti knew in Los Angeles began suffering from AIDS dementia. Fading in and out of coherence, as a last shot he entered a small study of nasally administered peptide T being done at the University of Southern California. After two days on the drug, Corti saw—actually, *heard*—a big change. The patient's sentences started making sense again. The dementia ended.

Through that patient, Corti learned of other success stories in the trial—but each case involved a patient who had suffered neurological symptoms, mainly dementia. Perhaps Pert hadn't correctly understood her own drug, which wouldn't be the first time that had happened in science. Maybe for some reason it worked only on the virus's activity in cells of the nervous system.

Other people heard of the development, too, and started calling Corti for a supply. The Colorado man wasn't importing it anymore. Corti called a local manufacturer. But, just as he had experienced with ddC, the company smelled what he was up to, and said it could only sell the drug for an approved scientific study. It turned him down.

From the Colorado man, Corti got the name of the Danish supplier, a firm called Carlbiotech. Over the phone to Copenhagen he struck up a relationship with the general manager and negotiated a price. Then he hopped another plane. At Carlbiotech, he met the man he'd talked to, who fully understood and approved what Corti was doing. Corti turned over $10,000 and picked up about fifteen grams of peptide T, enough to begin treating sixty patients. Coming home, he stopped in Munich to see Selmon Lichtenstein again.

The peptide T came as a powder. Once back in California, Corti took it to a friend's pharmacy in West Hollywood. Under a protective hood, using mask and gloves, the friend mixed the drug with a sterile saline solution to make a liquid and put it into vials. Patients then withdrew the liquid into a syringe and gave it to themselves just below the skin, not directly into a vein; some used it as a nasal spray. It continued to relieve the dementia and some other neurological effects of AIDS, while having no apparent effect on the loss of T-cells. The official tests at USC plodded on.

Meanwhile, Delaney's staff had collected the endorsement of hundreds of AIDS-concerned organizations around the country on a petition to have the FDA review ddI and ddC immediately. President Bush finally appointed a new FDA commissioner, David Kessler, who was both an M.D. and a lawyer; Kessler had spoken in general terms in favor of easing the way for drugs to get to market. Delaney wanted to confront him with an opportunity immediately.

He prepared a fact sheet that was widely handed out, noting that ddI and ddC weren't new drugs, but had extensive testing histories —consistently *successful* testing histories, if you recognized the validity of T-cell counts, P-24 antigen counts, and other surrogate markers. In a large phase one trial of ddI, 88 percent of AIDS and ARC patients were alive twenty-one months after starting ddI, compared with 50 percent of a similar group treated with AZT in a previous test and 25 percent of a similar group untreated.

If only the facts were all that mattered! But that was never the case.

Thanks to the persistence of Paul Boneberg—who had first enlisted Delaney in the politics of AIDS five years earlier—San Francisco Congresswoman Barbara Boxer agreed to deliver a signal to the FDA that the consumer-protection bloc in Congress wouldn't attack with hearings if ddI and ddC were approved on available data. Boxer's consumer-protection credentials were bulletproof after years of gathering them, and she got thirty-five colleagues to sign a green-light letter to the regulators.

The support statements were to be presented, and a big publicity effort made, the week of November 12. The key players would all be in Washington for the quarterly AIDS Clinical Trials Group meeting. On November 2, Delaney wrote Cooper and Beninger again, letting them know what was going to happen.

He credited them with wanting to get the drugs licensed, too, but wrote, "I am not yet confident that a clearly defined standard has been established against which the data will be analyzed. Contrary to what you may think, I for one am not pushing for a solely political approval decision. Yet we keep coming back to this point year after year." The companies didn't even know whether to apply for licenses, because they didn't know what standard would be used to judge the application. Rejections cost time and money.

The law called for "substantial evidence" of efficacy. But what did that mean? "There are no scientific absolutes operating here," he wrote. "It is a political decision, made many years ago, which the agency has since interpreted as best it could. The extent to which that interpretation reflects the intent of Congress is uncertain. The challenge before us all is to define or redefine the standard in a way which is neither scientifically irrational nor politically insensitive. I don't believe we have to choose blindly between these poles."

He proposed a formal conference to discuss "just what is or should be meant by 'substantial evidence.' " Participants would include Cooper, Beninger, Fauci, Broder, top researchers working with ddC and ddI, new FDA Commissioner David Kessler, the head of the latest Presidential AIDS Commission, someone from the Institute of Medicine, and some patient representatives. He noted that Kessler had called for greater outside consultation in the licensing process. This was a chance to make that happen.

Cooper called him soon after she got the letter.

"We could probably go along with that," she said of a conference. "But the proper forum legally is the FDA antiviral advisory committee."

Bureaucracy rides again, Delaney thought. All the FDA really had to do was tell the companies it would accept data on surrogate markers. The companies would then submit the data and the drugs would be approved. Delaney had just proposed a conference to give the FDA justification for doing that. But then the FDA would be left with its antiviral advisory committee still on record recommending against surrogate markers. Cooper was saying the only way forward was to go back and have the advisory committee change its advice. That way, if the FDA was criticized, it could point a finger at the committee.

"Fine," Delaney said. "Let's call the committee. All I'm trying to say is, rather than have just the FDA be forced up against the wall here, why don't we call together a national group of experts to look at these markers, specifically for ddI and ddC?" He suggested a lunch to discuss it during the coming AIDS Clinical Trials Group meeting in Washington.

They found a table in the atrium at the center of the hotel lobby.

"The only way to approve drugs this quickly would be on the basis of surrogate markers, the CD-4 tests," Cooper said.

"Well, maybe it's time we did that," Delaney replied.

"The advisory committee was against it."

"I thought we were here to talk about how to turn the advisory committee around," he said. Sometimes he felt all the letters and phone conversations from himself and others vanished down a well. He reminded her that the top researchers, Broder and Fauci, had swung around behind the surrogate markers. As she replied, he heard her downshift into her low-pitched voice.

"I think Fauci and Broder are convinced that CD-4 is a surrogate marker no matter what the data is," she said. "Fauci and Broder are going to shove CD-4s down everybody's throats no matter what."

Then she dropped her bombshell. The long-awaited report was coming in from the Harvard statisticians about how the AZT study would have turned out if surrogate markers rather than survival had been the yardstick. The report wasn't complete, but what was done so far wouldn't help the case for ddI and ddC. The statisticians were concluding that CD-4 wasn't a good marker, Cooper said. And the drug companies hadn't designed the new ddI and ddC studies well, she added. "I'm beginning to think that the studies won't prove efficacy unless they demonstrate that the drugs work better than AZT."

Delaney froze. "But you said all along they didn't have to be superior to AZT, just the equivalent."

"We don't really know the efficacy of AZT yet," Cooper said. "We're comparing one unknown to another." After six months of the AZT trials, she explained, the patients on placebo were allowed to go on the drug. From that point, there was no control group.

What difference does it make? Delaney thought. AZT's already licensed. It works. There have been multiple studies. And you, lady, approved the design of all the Bristol-Myers studies before they began. Why are you questioning them now? He wanted to throw his hands up. He was in regular touch with researchers and regulatory-relations officials at Bristol-Myers. They were agonizing over how their ddI data was going to be judged. The woman who would decide was still musing over it as if it were some interesting metaphysical puzzle.

Delaney ached to know what the statisticians at Harvard had really concluded, without Cooper's spin. The dogma of statistics was beginning to remind him of the dogma of Roman Catholicism. That's why he had dropped out of the seminary.

As they talked, she reverted to the idea that you couldn't use CD-4 cell counts unless you proved that they exactly predicted the survival outcome of a study. If those were the rules, not only were ddI and ddC shackled, but a lot of other drugs on the shelf would never even be tested. None of the interesting drugs developed by independent scientists, none of the small companies that had spun off from university research labs, could ever attract the investment needed for the kind of study she now demanded. She seemed to be sending everybody back to square one.

Was this really doomsday for AIDS drugs? Or could it just be the rhetoric of her long-standing caution, which would, in the end, yield to reality?

"Look," she said, "I want to get these drugs out if I can find a way."

"The way you can do it is by bringing everybody into the process, as we discussed. Bring in the researchers. Share the decision. Get yourself off the hot seat."

But the FDA would be reluctant to share power. All Delaney could do was keep the pressure high, and enlist prestigious research scientists at the trials group meeting to the cause.[90]

EIGHTY-TWO

The clarithromycin that was developed in Chicago, manufactured in Milan because it wasn't legal in the U.S., then shipped to Ireland, where it was sold at radically lower prices than in Italy, was then sent by Federal Express through its headquarters in Memphis to Los Angeles for dissemination to patients all over the U.S., including back in Chicago.

To pay for this bizarre trade, Corti sent his Dublin pharmacist, Maurice O'Connell, cashier's checks in the tens of thousands of dollars, drawn on Corti's local Security Pacific Bank branch. The money was coming in from individual patients and buyers' clubs in various cities, augmented by contributions Corti secured from a few wealthy gay businessmen who wanted impoverished patients to be able to get the drug.

In early November 1990, the second shipment of five thousand pills didn't arrive. Under Corti's instructions, O'Connell phoned him with the Federal Express shipping details each time O'Connell sent an order. The November shipment had been sent in one parcel to seven names, all at one Los Angeles address, belonging to a friend of Corti's.

The seven names were a fig leaf of homage to the FDA's rule about only importing for personal use. Because the maximum dose at the Merrieux Institute trial was eight pills a day, Corti figured 720 pills could be called a 90-day supply for one person, and thus a 5,000-pill order could be called a personal supply for seven people. In reality, each order was brought by the recipient to Corti's studio, where it was sold to many more people in smaller lots.

The first time this ruse had worked. The second time it didn't.

Corti called Federal Express, which said the FDA had seized the parcel in Memphis. Corti called the FDA in Memphis, and was told the shipment didn't meet the terms of the import policy. Shipments had to be broken down into individual cartons for each of the seven people named, and sent to seven different addresses. Corti said that would cost about five times as much money. The man said he had to follow the rules.

Well, what of the pills now being held in Memphis? The FDA man there said the package couldn't be released without approval from his boss in Nashville. Corti called the boss in Nashville, who told him to call Marvin Blumberg in Washington. Blumberg was a functionary in the FDA's consumer-protection bureaucracy. Corti knew his consumers were more interested in being protected by clarithromycin than by Marvin Blumberg. But at 3:30 P.M. Washington time Corti called Blumberg. A secretary answered. Blumberg, she said, worked an early day, and had just left. Corti could reach him the next morning at 7.

That night, Corti stayed up till 4 A.M., California time, and called. There, bright and early, was Blumberg, as promised. But Blumberg still refused to release the clarithromycin. He said he would have to discuss the matter with Memphis.

Corti resorted to an old list of phone numbers from Tijuana smuggling days, and found a woman in Pete Wilson's office. Wilson was on his way out as senator from California. He had just been elected *governor* of California. The woman told him to fax her the information and said she'd see what she could do.

A half hour after sending the fax, Corti called Blumberg again. Nothing doing. He kept calling. He had Delaney call Blumberg's boss.

Finally, Blumberg offered a deal. If in the future Corti would meet the conditions of the import policy, Blumberg would counsel the local office to release the clarithromycin this time. Corti agreed to make Federal Express the beneficiary of Blumberg's diligence, and from now on the clarithromycin would be individually packaged and addressed to seven locations. The consumers who were being protected would be charged extra for it.

By then, shipments had risen to ten thousand pills every two weeks. Corti and his volunteer helpers were dealing with hundreds of people in his studio and by mail. Of course, many couldn't pay.

Typical was a patient named Carl Willis, who heard about Corti from a friend and called to buy clarithromycin. He was desperate— near death from MAI. Corti, following routine, insisted on knowing his doctor. But Willis was a patient at 5P21, the Los Angeles County

Hospital AIDS unit, which Corti knew meant he had no insurance and would be treated mainly by a physician's assistant, or P.A.

"Have the P.A. call me," Corti instructed.

But Willis called back later saying the hospital staff were all too busy for that.

Corti agreed to sell Willis eighty-four tablets, a two-week supply at the minimum Merrieux dosage of six a day. Once Willis was past the MAI, Corti told him, he might be able to cut the dosage in half, but probably would have to keep taking three clarithromycin a day as long as he had a depleted immune system. And to keep the FDA at bay, Willis would have to bulk-order future supplies; Corti couldn't sell it retail.

Several weeks later, Willis called back to say the drug wasn't working. Corti observed that the supply would have run out, since Willis had bought only two weeks' worth. Willis said he had decided he couldn't afford six pills a day, and that he had decided to stretch the supply out and only take three a day. Corti told him to have the physician's assistant call, or Corti would have nothing more to do with him. And he hung up in a fury at the way the system treated these people.

Later that day, a P.A. from the hospital called. "We've had patients talk about clarithromycin, but we don't know much about it," he said. "Very few people who come here can afford to take it." Corti told him of the experience at Merrieux and among the Los Angeles doctors who were administering clarithromycin. And the physician's assistant said he would discuss it with Willis.

The next day Corti got a phone call and visit from Willis, who was clutching $240 in $1 and $5 bills for his eighty-four pills. He said he had collected it from relatives.

"Are you going to take this stuff like your P.A. says?" Corti asked him. Willis promised to follow the dosage.

Corti crossed his fingers and gave Willis the pills, throwing in a few dozen extra out of spur-of-the-moment compassion.

Willis called back within days reporting he felt well again.

Corti decided to see if he could save some money by having O'Connell in Dublin double up patients' names, two to a box, so each box could contain 1,440 pills. If he was aware, Blumberg at the FDA didn't object. But the agency did require the prescribing doctors' names to be on the packages. By December 1990, several dozen doctors were recommending the drug. Corti was supplying O'Connell with names of doctors in Los Angeles, New York, Atlanta, Miami, Dallas, San Francisco, San Diego, and Portland, Oregon, to put on the packages. Some were AIDS Clinical Trials Group physicians; they were working on trials of other drugs for the FDA, while quietly prescribing for their own patients a drug the FDA wouldn't recognize.

Corti and Delaney tried to get Abbott Labs to run U.S. trials on clarithromycin as an MAI treatment and preventive. But Abbott proved difficult to deal with. An executive in charge of the drug became impossible to reach, was reported on long-term vacation, and then was removed from his job in a scandal over criminal allegations in his personal life. His successor also proved hard to reach.[91]

In early December, Corti got a call from a nurse at Children's Hospital in Los Angeles. Children with AIDS were sometimes a sore point with gays who had the disease. The kids were often paraded in public as "the innocent victims"—as if infected gays were "guilty." But now the doctors at Children's Hospital had heard about the success of clarithromycin, and were sending out this sub-rosa feeler to see if the parents of young MAI patients could buy pills through Corti. He said to feel free to give his name and number to any such parents. Dozens came to buy pills.

One family, the Montalvos from San Bernardino, brought their eleven-year-old son Ricky. Ricky was a hemophiliac with AIDS, suffering from MAI. The family was poor, but brought money. As he frequently did, Corti said he was throwing in a few extra pills, but actually gave the family double what they paid for. He had by this time lined up several wealthy gay businessmen who were infected with HIV, who were throwing in thousands of dollars to subsidize clarithromycin for the less fortunate.

The irony was that the standard treatment for MAI, a mixture of four pills and an intravenous infusion that everyone agreed didn't halt the disease, cost more than $150 a day. Yet it was routinely given out at hospitals and paid for by insurance companies because the drugs in it were all approved by the FDA for other diseases. Clarithromycin, which clearly *did* halt MAI, cost a pittance by comparison. But health-insurance companies wouldn't pay for it because the FDA didn't recognize it. So a lot of patients couldn't afford to take it.

Clarithromycin cleared up Ricky Montalvo's MAI so well that the family wanted to make sure he stayed on the maintenance dose while he went to Washington to take part in a special program at NIH. Corti found himself remailing a newly arrived shipment of pills to Ricky at his room at NIH, where the doctors either approved or ignored Ricky's taking them. So, Corti thought as he mailed the package, it takes an underground smuggler in Los Angeles to get an American-created miracle drug to the ivory tower of medicine, which officially refuses to recognize it. And it has to be routed through Milan, Dublin, and Memphis.

EIGHTY-THREE

Delaney had a long-scheduled speaking and organizing trip to Australia in late November 1990, followed by a return to Washington in early December for more AIDS drugs committee meetings. Once again, the heavy travel started to catch up with him. He was continually weakened by lack of liver function, continually sore from neuropathy in his feet—all the result of the hepatitis drug test a decade earlier. He kept wishing in his heart of hearts just to go home and go to bed, to sleep for days.

December 3, before catching his now habitual red-eye overnight flight from San Francisco to Washington, he faxed another letter to Cooper and Beninger. This time, he formally called for a meeting of the antiviral advisory committee as Cooper had suggested, "to collectively explore how the existing data can be used" to get ddI and ddC approved. "This should include intensive discussion of the role of surrogate markers," he said.

Anticipating the statistical results Cooper had warned of, Delaney said that "any effort to evaluate these drugs" only by comparing them to the original AZT study "would be scientifically, ethically, and morally flawed. Discussion should also be made of the impact the presence or absence of these drugs will have in the national fight against AIDS."

A decent discussion would require a two-day meeting, he said. And he repeated his list of proposed speakers—Fauci, Broder, the head of the Presidential AIDS Commission, and so forth—this time adding community doctors like Waites, Conant, and Robert Jenkins, whose patients took ddI.

This was not, Delaney was sure, what Ellen Cooper wanted to read. The sheer weight of the names of the respected scientists who a few years ago would have been on her side, but who now were storming the gates with Delaney, must have been intimidating.

The next day, in Washington, they chatted outside the meeting room during a coffee break about the problems of busy schedules. As the group filed back in to listen to more talk, she turned to Delaney and said, "Sometimes I wonder whether it's worth all this."

Within a week, Cooper called to say Delaney would get the antiviral committee meeting he wanted. She sounded grudging. "This is
turning into a political process," she told him.

The committee would meet the first week of February to discuss
surrogate markers. Delaney wanted to know why it couldn't be
sooner. People's schedules, she said. The staff was assembling the
list of witnesses, and would be in touch. He quickly reached Merigan, Fischl, Fauci, and others to let them know what was coming.

Meanwhile, hundreds of letters a day were pouring into the FDA,
asking for whatever it took to get ddI and ddC licensed. Some were
copies of a sample letter printed in the Project Inform newsletter,
then signed and mailed. Some came in to Project Inform's own office,
which forwarded boxloads to the FDA.

Cooper was making her own preparations. She put her thoughts
about the situation on paper and sent them in the form of a letter to
Bristol-Myers and Hoffmann-La Roche. Just as in the lunch with
Delaney in November, she made no final pronouncements, but
seemed to embrace all the old ideas everyone else was giving up.
Page after page, she mused over all the problems that ddI and ddC
would have if the companies tried to get them approved with existing
data.

Delaney learned about the letter in a phone call from a steaming
Sam Broder. Broder wouldn't say where he got it, but obviously the
companies were circulating it. Faced with a broadside that seemed
to say there was no way the FDA would approve their drugs, they
were seeking allies.

"She just cut off every possible direction," Broder said. "It's like
we're back to square one."

Delaney tried to talk Broder into sending him a copy of the letter.
He wouldn't. But he read parts of it aloud on the phone. "I don't
know how we'll ever get this stuff done now," Broder said. "What
does she think she's doing?"

Delaney finally got a source at Bristol-Myers to read the entire
letter to him over the phone, but no one would send him a copy.[92]

On another trip to Washington, Delaney had dinner with Fauci.
"Who is she to tell us what is and isn't a fact?" Fauci said. "Why is
hers the voice of science, and ours not? She's talking beyond her real
station. She's a mid-level FDA staffer who's thirty-nine years old.
She doesn't have the credentials or history Broder or I or the others
have."

Jay Lipner told Delaney he had spoken on the phone to Fauci,
and Fauci had referred to Cooper as "that girl."

If the scientists were angry, the companies were devastated. It looked like doom for their drugs.

Delaney was dealing in devastation of all sorts. One of the patients who got an early dose of pentosan polysulfate, in hopes that it would cure his Kaposi's sarcoma, was a good friend. He had been euphoric when the drug seemed to work, and despairing when it failed. With his lungs filling with K.S. lesions, and with no other recourse, he went on chemotherapy to keep from choking to death. The chemotherapy pummeled his white blood count, leaving him open to a sinus infection, which promptly set in. It was an infection most people would shrug off quickly, but which could kill in this case.

Delaney knew Schering-Plough, the drug company, was testing a drug to bring back the white blood count in such emergencies. Without identifying himself, he called Schering-Plough for the drug for his friend under a compassionate-use exception. The official he was given to talk to refused his request; the official said Schering-Plough had agreed with Act Up that it would make the drug available for people on ganciclovir, but not in other cases. Obviously, this was an attempt to protect the company from a costly Bristol-Myers giveaway-type situation.

Delaney screamed that anyone whose life could be saved by the drug ought to be able to get it. "If you made a deal, it's a bad deal," he said.

In frustration, he identified himself, and threatened to bring in the press if Schering-Plough wouldn't release the drug.

He was told he would have to talk with someone higher in the company, and to wait. Finally, someone higher called him.

"I know who you are," he was told. "We'll make an exception in your case."

Delaney said he'd accept that for now, but wanted to develop a plan for any patient with this problem.

Larry Waites, the patient's doctor, and Schering-Plough dutifully completed the forms necessary to get the compassionate-use exemption from the FDA. Then Waites called, and said the FDA first wanted an independent review board to certify that the case merited a compassionate-use exemption, a process that could take weeks.

"This is insane," Delaney said. "This is emergency treatment, not a clinical study. Review boards don't control treatment."

Delaney went to the review board that Project Inform had affiliated with for the extended Compound Q studies. The board had a meeting coming up, and agreed to discuss the matter. Meanwhile, Delaney's friend, who had been hanging by a thread, died.

It was the third death of a close friend in the weeks before Christmas 1990. Delaney called the review board and told them they could drop the case. Grief-stricken over the loss of this latest friend, Tim Lowe, Delaney wrote angrily to the review board and FDA complaining of "such a stupid bureaucratic step."[93]

Someone else had suffered a loss in the past year. Donald Abrams's lover had died. He had attended the funerals of some physician friends, as well. Whether that was responsible for what happened, or whether it was other factors, is something Delaney was never sure of. But as Delaney's ddI-ddC initiative approached its crisis, Abrams came in from the cold.

For months, Delaney had felt Abrams warming toward him in their occasional phone calls or encounters at organization meetings. In a published scientific article about alternative therapies earlier in the year, Abrams had treated Delaney's work impartially and respectfully. He didn't exactly say that Project Inform had helped people by bringing unapproved drugs into the country, but he pictured a Delaney filling a logical vacuum left by the failure of science, and praised Delaney's research in an acknowledgment.

But now Abrams stunned Delaney. He did more than just endorse Delaney's plan to get ddI and ddC quickly on the market. Under Abrams's leadership, the study group he had formed of more than a hundred doctors, the Community Consortium, prepared a separate "Citizen Petition" to FDA Commissioner Kessler. Abrams was the first of eleven board members, all physicians, to sign it.

It opened by asking Kessler "to exercise his authority under [existing laws] to expedite the evaluation and decision on marketing approval" of ddI and ddC, adding, "We believe that it is both imperative and possible for the FDA to reach a decision on approval of New Drug Applications (NDA) for these drugs by 1 March 1991."

The arguments that followed—covering seven single-spaced pages, followed by several pages of scientific references—were arguments Delaney had been making for months: the loss of effectiveness of AZT, the advantages of using drugs in combination, the unacceptable cost to Bristol-Myers of the expanded-access program, and so on. But now all these arguments bore Donald Abrams's signature.

And at the end of the petition, Abrams called for approval criteria to include surrogate markers—not just T-cell counts but "improvement in the quality of life (e.g., improved functioning, weight gain, and decreased incidence of opportunistic infections)."

If Delaney could have put those words in Abrams's mouth in years past, he figured, he could have won a lot of battles. On the other hand, if Abrams hadn't stood so rigidly in the defense of conservatism for so long, maybe his words wouldn't have had the impact they did now. Abrams had been appointed one of the eleven members of the FDA advisory board that would make the decision. His endorsement of surrogate markers was important enough to merit coverage in *The New York Times.* The story was accompanied by a picture of Delaney—correctly identified this time.

On December 17, 1990, Project Inform sponsored a coordinated round of press conferences in New York, San Francisco, Los Angeles, Philadelphia, Baltimore, Washington, Miami, and Dallas, each co-sponsored with a local AIDS support group to increase local coverage. They got a lot of publicity.

The pressure was snowballing.

On December 19, late at the end of another long workday, Ellen Cooper quietly typed a brief message on her computer screen, and directed it at the electronic mailbox of her boss, Carl Peck. She was, it said, requesting to be transferred to another job. Then she added, "I guess I'm just burned out." And she went home to her husband and four children.

The next day, Delaney got a call from Don Abrams.

"Did you hear our friend Ellen resigned?" he said.

"No." In fact, it was a shock to Delaney.

"And what's worse," Abrams said, "is that everybody claims you and I did it."

Delaney was speechless a moment. "You know, I can understand why she's mad at me," he said. "But I can't understand why she'd resign."

He called the FDA and got confirmation from secretaries, but couldn't reach Cooper. He had always relished tilting lances with the FDA and its outmoded philosophies. But in his eyes it had never been Ellen Cooper herself at fault. Suddenly, it was personal, and he felt bad. He had taken lunch and dinner with her, called her at home on weekends. There was never any question of her motivation or integrity. She wasn't doing it for money. Recently, at least, she sure couldn't have been doing it for popularity. She worked hard for the taxpayers in defense of rules she deeply believed in. And they were rules that at some time, in some place, were important. She was just blind to an emergency. Corti and others liked to call her "the ice lady." But it wasn't compassion she lacked. It was common sense. She was just wrong.

Delaney called Carl Peck, expressing concern. Peck assured him he shouldn't take the blame. "Maybe we were wrong at the agency," Peck said. "We were wrong to urge her to keep working on this. The pressure was enormous."

Peck couldn't spell it out, but Delaney understood. Cooper was about to be forced either to go against her principles and approve drugs that didn't meet her standards, or face a lynch mob that by this time might even have included Peck himself. She refused to do either.

Delaney urged Peck not to let her departure delay still further the advisory committee meeting she had set for February. Peck said he had decided he would personally take over her responsibilities, and that he saw no reason anything need be delayed.

A few days later Delaney finally got through to Cooper herself.

"It wasn't your fault," she said. "It was everything."

The *Times* gave her resignation a three-column headline and picture. The reporter was Gina Kolata, and—Delaney smiled to himself as he read it—of course she got the story wrong. It began, "In a move that is widely viewed as boding ill for the approval of new AIDS drugs . . ."

And which scientist did Kolata find who said that Cooper's departure would impede the approval of AIDS drugs? Jerome Groopman of Harvard, Delaney's old nemesis. Kolata quoted no one to the contrary. Obviously, she was 180 degrees off point.

It was sad to see a good person take a fall, Delaney thought. But the departure of Ellen Cooper opened the door to a possible golden era for the development and marketing of drugs for AIDS and other life-threatening illnesses.

E I G H T Y-F O U R

*O*n February 13, 1991, the FDA's antiviral advisory committee, with a half-dozen or so voting members and about as many "consultants" appointed for this session, filed into a meeting room at the Holiday Inn Crown Plaza in Rockville, Maryland. They took seats around a U-shaped table. Milling about before them was an audience of more than a hundred drug-company executives, reporters, AIDS patients, and other interested parties.

Because it was nearby, the Holiday Inn Crown Plaza was a common site for FDA meetings. It was a place many who gathered there had grown to hate because of its association with boring speeches and nights far from home. But this was, quite possibly, the most important meeting on AIDS drugs yet held there.

Bristol-Myers alone had sent a dozen people, from secretaries taking transcriptions on up through senior vice-presidents.

Carl Peck opened the meeting by praising the contribution of Ellen Cooper in the fight against AIDS, and pointing her out in the audience for applause. So, Delaney thought, she cared enough to come even though it wasn't her job anymore. By contrast, he hadn't seen Frank Young attend an AIDS meeting since Young exited the FDA a year earlier.

After a speech emphasizing the gravity of the decision before the committee, Peck started calling witnesses—the Harvard group of statisticians who had analyzed the data on surrogate markers that was collected but never tabulated during the 1985–87 AZT tests. This was the report Cooper had been hinting about for a year: to what extent did AZT's effect on surrogate markers predict the survival of patients?

Anastasios "Butch" Tsiatis spoke for the Harvard group, and he proceeded exactly as Delaney had anticipated: in an emotionless, academic, monotonic polysyllabism familiar only to the practitioners of his narrow craft. Nobody but statisticians would understand it. The letter "p" popped up frequently as part of an equation. And the word "probability."

Delaney had caught onto this game during the months he spent in 1987 analyzing how the ribavirin data had been misconstrued even by scientists. Statisticians invited themselves to be misunderstood. Through practice, however, Delaney had learned that if you stayed awake and hyperscrutinized, you still wouldn't exactly understand a statistician, but you could sometimes get his drift, which put you way ahead of the rest of the room.

Tsiatis was saying that his group had tabulated and studied the CD-4 cell counts and other blood markers of patients during the original AZT study. Even though the cell counts couldn't be used in the study, the researchers had taken the data down on the possibility it might mean something.

Long minutes into the presentation, Delaney thought he heard Tsiatis, though never changing his tone, say something to the effect that patients whose T-cells stabilized had lived longer than others. If so, that would directly contradict what Cooper had been saying. A few minutes later, Delaney thought he heard something to the effect that people whose T-cells had gone up more had lived longer than people whose T-cells had gone up less.

Delaney looked around the room and saw people, even the panel members, staring blankly or looking at their watches or in a few cases nodding off. Seated next to him, though, was Broder's top deputy, Bob Yarchoan, who was there to testify for Broder and the Cancer Institute. They exchanged glances. Yarchoan had caught the same thing Delaney had caught. Did anyone else?

So far, it sounded like good news. But now Tsiatis was talking about a problem. People understood the word "problem," and perked up. There was a problem. But what was it? Well, as far as Delaney could make out, the benefits people got from AZT, at least in that trial, sometimes exceeded the benefits that their CD-4 levels would have led a scientist to predict. CD-4 counts alone were not a complete predictor of the longevity and other benefits of the drug. Did this make the counts invalid as an indicator? Tsiatis didn't seem to be saying that.

"That isn't the question anyway," Yarchoan said into Delaney's ear. "The question is whether CD-4 levels correlated with something meaningful, not whether they accurately predicted everything."

People were looking at each other, not understanding. Tsiatis had said the word "problem" and then talked a long time. It must be a big problem. Then, with nothing that sounded like a conclusion, he suddenly stopped talking.

The committee members began to question him, but so inarticulately that Delaney could tell they were confused. Most of the questions concerned the "problem" about the AZT performance deviating from the CD-4 counts. And Tsiatis's answers were just as opaque as his presentation had been. Eventually the panel seemed to just give up.

Yarchoan turned to Delaney. "I think a lot of people didn't get it," he said.

"I think you're right."

"I think," Yarchoan said, imitating the statistician, "that the number of people who accept CD-4 as a legitimate marker is directly proportional to the number of times you hear the data presented."

Delaney laughed. "It has to be repeated," he said. "Why can't these guys ever single out what's important and what's not?"

"It's sure a mass of data," Yarchoan replied.

And during the ensuing break, they went over what each of them thought he had heard Tsiatis say. Toward the end, Tsiatis joined them. When Delaney said bluntly that he didn't think people had understood, Tsiatis looked puzzled.

A little later, Yarchoan presented the work he had been assembling with Broder ever since today's committee meeting had been scheduled two months ago. The Cancer Institute had gone back to the records of every patient treated with antiviral drugs in its own studies since 1985. It was a lot of work, but it produced a startling conclusion: as long as CD-4 counts were kept above 50, he said, patients survived. Only one patient had died with a CD-4 count above 50, and that count was just slightly above 50. No patient on AZT with a CD-4 count of over 50 had ever developed lymphoma.

In contrast with the statisticians' report, there was no doubting what Yarchoan was saying. You could tell when death would come based on the number of CD-4 cells a patient had. How could anyone deny it was a valid marker?

Something else struck Delaney: whatever the outcome of this meeting, the process had already changed substantially. Never before would the results of a study such as Yarchoan had just described have been able to affect a policy decision so quickly. It was just like the AZT-ddC-combination study Fischl had just finished at the University of Miami, which was already affecting clinical practices nationwide.

In years past, both studies would have had to sit up to a year on Arnold Relman's desk at *The New England Journal of Medicine*, or on some other scholar's desk, while teams of scientific "peers" nit-picked them. Only after the interminable process required for formal "publication" by an accredited journal would anyone pay attention to facts that might save lives.

It wasn't that peer review was a bad idea; in the long run, it was needed, and if there were flaws in Yarchoan's and Fischl's data, they would still eventually be found by that process. But in a crisis, you also needed to consider the best information available at the moment. Until now, the system had refused to accommodate that. Things were changing.

After lunch, two witnesses were left before the floor would be opened for public comments. There was another statistician, from the University of California, who had done a study. And there was Delaney. Peck asked Delaney to go first.

Delaney had come prepared with a beautiful speech. But he decided to leave much of it aside. The key witness here was Tsiatis of Harvard, and hardly anybody had understood a word he had said. So, after a brief opening, Delaney began a translation.

"Unless I heard him wrong," Delaney said, "Mr. Tsiatis, the Harvard statistician, sat right here this morning and said that people treated with AZT whose CD-4 counts rose lived longer than those who didn't, and those whose counts rose higher lived longer than those whose counts didn't rise so high. He also said that those whose counts stabilized lived longer than those whose counts continued to fall. And finally, he said that those whose counts fell slowly lived longer than those whose counts fell quickly. That's what the statistician from Harvard said. How can anyone any longer reject CD-4 as a valid marker for drug approval?"

As he spoke, he could see looks of bewilderment on the faces of the committee members. Did Tsiatis really say what Delaney was saying? Feeling he had them hooked, he plunged further. He also explained Tsiatis's other point that seemed to hang them up: Yes, some patients on AZT improved even more than their CD-4 levels alone would have predicted. But that didn't invalidate CD-4 levels as a predictor of longevity. In fact, he noted, that is exactly what Dr. Yarchoan of NCI had just said CD-4 was: a valid predictor. Tsiatis had pointed out a reason to continue considering many factors, not a reason to reject CD-4.

With that now clearly on the table, Delaney moved fast to make the point he had intended in his prepared text: A refusal by the committee to accept surrogate markers could "mean the downfall of the regulatory system as we know it for AIDS." It was a rash statement. But, he explained, they all knew what was really behind this meeting. "The FDA is being asked, perhaps even forced, to license ddI and ddC on the basis of loose historical controls—phase one data and a hodgepodge of uncontrolled surrogate-marker data. I assure you, this is not what we activists desire. It's just the only option the system has offered us.

"Had FDA instead exercised leadership and validated the markers, effective, controlled studies of both these drugs could have been completed swiftly, and strong controlled data would now be available measuring their activity as well as their performance relative to AZT. These drugs might be on the market today and the subject of effective post-marketing surveillance.

"Let's pretend that we had decided in 1986 to accept surrogate markers. Now, look back at every drug and every study we've had since then and ask yourself these questions: Is there any drug we would have approved inappropriately based on the markers? Or is there any drug we would have rejected inappropriately? Would we have made any mistakes? If the answer to that is no—as we believe it is—then we have wasted six years.

"I argue that acceptance of the marker today does not constitute the collapse of the regulatory system, as some seem to fear. On the contrary, the use of such markers in controlled studies is the only way to *save* the system. The bedrock of drug regulation, as laid down by the Congress, is not the use of survival endpoints, but the use of well-controlled data. The realities of AIDS are such that you will lose the option of developing well-controlled data on survival. In the coming years, there will simply be no way to force patients to be good little research subjects for years on end, sticking to a fixed protocol while a steady stream of newer and more promising compounds comes under the light of clinical study. Grand designs for master protocols and years-long combination drug studies are a fiction which will never be realized in this epidemic or any other epidemic of life-threatening disease.

"Patients, physicians, and researchers already have rejected placebo-based studies with survival endpoints. As more and more drugs come along, fewer and fewer patients will accept long-term commitments to single-drug therapies. The pressures seen to license ddI and ddC will become standard procedure, with the agency again and again asked to approve drugs in the absence of controlled data. There is no other future possible if you remain fixed on survival endpoints.

"In the coming months, you will either be forced to abandon controlled data, as is the case today, or abandon the use of survival endpoints. The choice is yours, but it seems clear that the regulatory system as we know it cannot long survive in the absence of controlled data. Taking this step—acknowledging the validity of CD-4 as a marker in HIV—is not only inevitable, it is essential for the public health system of this country."

The audience applauded enthusiastically. But as Delaney suspected, the committee focused on his translation of Tsiatis. Fred Valentine, an immunologist from New York, led the questioning, looking troubled. "I thought you said—" he began, and then repeated what Delaney had said about Tsiatis's conclusions from the AZT study: that patients with higher CD-4 counts had lived longer.

"I'm not sure I heard him say that," Valentine said.

"Butch Tsiatis is sitting right there," Delaney replied, pointing. "Ask him."

Tsiatis went to the microphone. Valentine requestioned Delaney on each point, then turned to the statistician.

"Yes, I did say that," Tsiatis said. "I thought you heard it." Then Tsiatis proceeded to elaborate, and within seconds had lost everyone again in statistical language. Valentine cut him off, and methodically reviewed each of Delaney's summary points: the higher the CD-4 improvement, the greater the longevity; the slower the fall in CD-4, the greater the longevity. Each time, Tsiatis responded that this was exactly what he had said, and tried to expand on it, with Valentine fighting to keep the main points precise.

The committee members were throwing looks of revelation at each other. Delaney sat down again, feeling triumph.[94] Then he noticed that someone new had joined the audience—David Kessler, the new FDA commissioner. It was the first time Delaney had seen him.

For months now, Delaney had held off asking for a meeting with Kessler. He had taken Peck's advice, which made sense, that Kessler's first months were already too full of lengthy intrusions from congressmen, pharmaceutical executives, and other people, leaving not enough time for the homework Kessler needed to do to decide the crises at hand wisely. Delaney had exchanged letters with Kessler, but nothing more. Now they would meet.

The final statistician was an anticlimax. A known skeptic of markers, he opposed adopting them. But a statistician as well, he mumbled a lot and left people confused about what he meant. He was dismissed with a quick thank-you-very-much.

Then came public comments, which were limited to two minutes each. Most of what was said was predictable and mercifully short. Someone from the *New York Native* got up to argue that all these medicines were poison and that HIV didn't cause AIDS anyway. Then something made Delaney sit up. Some guy from New York he had never seen before was making a militant statement, and said, "You know, we're duplicating ddC, and we'll do it for all these other drugs if you don't approve them."

Now Delaney knew what he had to talk to David Kessler about. Inevitably, Kessler had become aware that someone was illegally making and selling Hoffmann-La Roche's drug ddC. Not only had it just been mentioned from the floor, but at the last two FDA antifraud conferences Delaney had attended, the illegal ddC manufacture had been brought up in front of FDA officials, and artfully dodged.

Corti was more and more afraid of going to jail. He talked about a possible arrest frequently in conversation. Reporters were onto him. CNN, *The Wall Street Journal,* the big California dailies had all called, asking questions. The rumor seemed to be that he was making ddC at home in his kitchen sink. Mostly, he shrugged off the reporters and suggested they call Delaney.

And while Corti acted on high principle, the work of some buyers' clubs was open to legitimate question. One advertised oral alpha interferon as a cure-all, despite studies showing the drug was ineffective. Another had turned itself into a low-grade Walgreen's, publishing unverifiable claims and urging people to buy all sorts of drugs at quoted prices. Recently, for example, it had touted an animal dewormer as a surefire T-cell booster.

Some clubs were increasing the ddC price significantly above Corti's wholesale rate, raising the specter of big profits.

As the meeting moved into a break before the committee's actual deliberations, Kessler approached Delaney and apologized for missing the first part of his presentation. Peck had urged him to hear it, he said.

After a few pleasantries, Delaney brought up the comment made from the audience about counterfeiting ddC. "I assume you're aware of it," he said. "Our position is that we'll be happy to make sure it stops, but not until the real drug gets approved. There are other issues about the buyers' clubs we need to talk about, though."

Kessler seemed pleased that Delaney had brought it up. He was receiving reports of abuses by the clubs, he said, and was under increasing pressure to address the issue. He told Delaney to call his office the following Monday for an appointment. Kessler said he was worried about claims of selective prosecution. Delaney knew exactly what he meant. If the FDA waived its rules for one group, that might allow real criminals to escape sanction. Selective prosecution was a valid legal defense: the FDA couldn't prosecute someone for violating a law that wasn't generally enforced.

To Delaney, the talk was a positive sign. Kessler had signaled that he didn't want to close down Corti's operation or the buyers' clubs if they could just find a rationale that didn't cause problems elsewhere.

Delaney promised to call. After that, Kessler exited the meeting with Peck, leaving Beninger to be chairman when the critical vote was taken. At that point, Delaney was convinced that victory was assured, or Kessler and Peck wouldn't have left.

On his way back to his chair, he saw Ellen Cooper and approached her. She had said nothing at the meeting. Now she seemed cold.

"You have to be careful with this, or you could do yourself more harm than good," she told him.

"What do you mean?" he said.

She just gave him a look, and turned and walked away as the meeting resumed.

Polled for comments, some committee members expressed doubts about using P-24 antigens as a marker, because not all patients had the antigens. But there was scarcely any discussion at all. Beninger went down the line asking the committee members if they believed CD-4 cells were a valid marker by which to evaluate AIDS drugs. Each one answered, "Yes." It was unanimous.

The end was almost anticlimactic. Some reporters gathered around Delaney. "It looks like you won this one," a reporter said.

"This is the signal the companies needed to start getting ddI and ddC approved," he told them.

But suddenly, or maybe not so suddenly, he felt very tired . . . exhausted . . . he wanted a taxi and to get on the plane back home.

EIGHTY-FIVE

*T*he week after the surrogate-markers committee meeting, Delaney was on the phone, as promised, with the new FDA commissioner, David Kessler. Kessler had engineered a conference call including his general counsel, Joseph Lovett, and regulatory-affairs director, Gary Dykstra; Delaney had his own lawyer, Curtis Ponzi, participating on his side. Kessler himself bowed out after a few minutes.

Delaney and Ponzi urged the need to distinguish what the buyers' clubs were doing from the kind of fraud the FDA was in business to stop. The buyers' clubs weren't commercial operations. They could be regulated from within the community they were serving. Delaney talked gingerly about the ddC manufacture, never acknowledging that he knew who was responsible. The underground wasn't trying to violate any patent or sabotage commercial prices, he said. But until Hoffmann-La Roche was ready to sell it, the drug had to be made available through other means. It was saving lives.

"On that issue, we'll fight with everything we've got," Delaney said.

So far, Delaney and Ponzi had done substantially all the talking. But the conversation was headed for a turning point. What Delaney and Ponzi had been saying, the FDA already knew. The question was how the FDA planned to respond. Did the FDA understand the difference between Corti's guerrilla action to save lives and drug fraud? In short, how safe was Jim Corti from jail?

"Yes," said Lovett, the general counsel, "we understand the difference. We'll tell Dr. Kessler how you feel." And he quickly directed the conversation to the buyers' clubs. The signal to Delaney was that the FDA would continue to turn a blind eye to the ddC distribution, but that the agency felt it had to do something about the buyers' club violations.

Delaney agreed that some clubs were run according to the whims of individual founders, who might have been courageous in starting the clubs but were not always wise in running them. Delaney could campaign for the clubs to make themselves responsible to a board of directors or scientific advisory board. And Project Inform could exert pressure on the worst offenders.

"We have a lot of influence, both through what we write and through personal relations," he said. He didn't say it, but there was also the matter that the clubs needed Jim Corti's drugs.

Delaney offered to go after groups to install formal procedures and become more accountable. That seemed to satisfy the FDA people for the moment. The conversation left Delaney feeling they had time to straighten out the worst offenses, and that if they did, the FDA was not going to go looking for trouble. He talked to Corti, who immediately began jawboning the problem groups.

By 1991, Corti's work had expanded. A growing support staff of volunteers and minimally paid assistants now helped Corti import and distribute clarithromycin and other drugs, and spread the word about what they could do and how to use them. Among his favorite collaborators was an HIV patient named Mike Slattery, who had started devouring the medical journals and other literature about the disease that jammed Corti's mailbox. They talked at length about potential treatments, including the Daiichi drug SP-PG that Corti and Delaney had gone to Japan to pursue. Slattery had been under the care of doctors at Los Angeles County/University of Southern California Medical Center.

One day, Slattery came back from USC with news: there, working at the medical center, was Zaki Salahuddin, the lab technician whom Robert Gallo had fired for patronizing his family-owned firm with business from Gallo's government laboratory. Corti had told Slattery about Salahuddin's contributions to SP-PG research, and the strange interest that Daiichi officials had in him.

Now Slattery said that Salahuddin and another researcher at the Los Angeles County/University of Southern California Medical Center—like Salahuddin a member of the Sikh religion—had formed a private research lab housed on the grounds of nearby Huntington Memorial Hospital.

What was going on? Corti immediately went to see Salahuddin.

Salahuddin complained that he had been wronged and victimized by Gallo. He said that even though he had contracted with a company he quietly owned, he felt that wasn't out of line—it was "the way business is done." He said he had been made a scapegoat. He blamed the whole episode on miscommunications. He contended that he had been a significant member of Gallo's team. He also complained about Corti's friend Delaney, who he said was now working for Gallo. Delaney, he said, was calling up USC on Gallo's behalf and urging the university to get rid of Salahuddin.

Corti listened to all this, not believing or disbelieving. Maybe, he thought, Delaney had grown too close to Gallo. What mattered was what Salahuddin was up to that might help HIV patients.

Salahuddin said he thought Daiichi could develop SP-PG with Salahuddin and his friend at USC, not Gallo. He said Shuji Nakimura, the Japanese researcher on Gallo's staff whom the Daiichi executives had insisted on talking to alone, was coming to work with the California group.

Salahuddin explained for Corti why pentosan polysulfate, the apparent cousin of the Daiichi drug, hadn't worked, and why Daiichi's SP-PG would. He said Daiichi was parceling out the drug so frugally not because it was being obstreperous, but simply because it didn't have much. Culturing the SP-PG was so difficult, and so slow, that 100 milligrams—a fifth of an aspirin tablet's worth—was a major batch. Until someone showed Daiichi how to produce the drug faster, there would be no usable quantity. Salahuddin said he wanted to devise that process for Daiichi.[95] (See note for Salahuddin's contrary account.)

Corti decided that under the circumstances there was no more he could do, but passed the information on to Delaney—who denied having called USC about Salahuddin.

Corti continued to distribute and administer the Compound Q that his friend David Chan supplied from China.

Meanwhile, Vera Byers was tabulating and writing up the results that the Levin-Waites group was getting from the new test of Q in San Francisco. Under the protocol, a patient's blood results while taking the drug were compared with his results the year before he started treatment; that way, each patient acted as his own control, and no one was forced to take a placebo. There seemed no doubt that most patients did better on Q than they had before. About 60 percent stabilized or increased their T-cell counts.

EIGHTY-SIX

*P*eptide T was still relieving AIDS dementia cases. A presentation at the International Aids Conference in Florence in June 1991 testified to it. But suddenly a supply problem developed. Corti had called Carlbiotech in Copenhagen to arrange a third pickup of peptide T. Because of the drug's high price—about $10,500 for enough to treat just sixty cases—Corti wanted to bring it in personally rather than trust it to Federal Express. But Henrik Krogen, Carlbiotech's vice-president for sales and marketing, suddenly said no.

Corti had dealt amiably with Krogen in arranging the first two pickups. But now Krogen said he had signed a new deal with the United States Government to supply peptide T for official drug trials. He said the FDA had insisted that as a peptide T supplier for U.S. trials, he could not sell it for export to private Americans.

Corti knew from experience with dextran sulfate that Krogen might be wrong about what the FDA wanted. Krogen might have mistaken the jealous words of an American research physician for government policy. But rather than spend months haggling with the FDA again, Corti settled on a simpler solution: he would buy the peptide T using the address of his friend in Paris. Krogen said that would satisfy Carlbiotech, so long as Corti could display an airline ticket from Copenhagen to Paris and prove he had a Paris address. Corti was glad for the excuse to stop and see his friend and enjoy a few French meals.

But another problem ensued: transporting the drug into and out of France subjected it to the French value-added tax, increasing the cost by 22 percent over the already high price. Corti solved that problem with the help of Derek Hodel, who had bought drugs through Corti and was now running a buyers' club in New York.

Hodel had told Corti about a nonprofit foundation in London that could buy drugs on the continent without paying the value-added tax. The foundation could then pass along the drugs to other nonprofit organizations like Hodel's and Corti's without paying a further tax. Hodel had used the foundation to buy clarithromycin, but Corti could just as well use it to buy peptide T. So Corti went back to Krogen at Carlbiotech, and Krogen agreed to sell the peptide T to the foundation in London. Corti picked it up there and carried it back to the U.S. in his carry-on. Through the foundation, he even negotiated a quantity deal with Carlbiotech that dropped the price a bit, and a decline in the price of the Danish krone helped neutralize his added transportation costs.

After that, Corti also began using the London foundation to bring in clarithromycin at lower prices. So, too, with other drugs. He had read about an antibiotic called azithromycin. Like clarithromycin, azithromycin was purported to be an advanced offshoot of the common American antibiotic erithromycin. Pfizer held rights to the drug in the U.S., though it wasn't licensed yet by the FDA. Azithromycin was believed to work on MAI, as clarithromycin did, but also to tackle two common AIDS infections that clarithromycin didn't touch —toxoplasmosis, a disease of the central nervous system, and cryptosporidium, an acute diarrhea.

Corti called Selmon Lichtenstein, the Munich doctor who had lined him up with clarithromycin and pentosan polysulfate. Yes, Lichtenstein said, azithromycin could be obtained from a source in Yugoslavia. He gave Corti a phone number. Corti made a deal on the phone, rounded up money from the usual sources and flew into Zagreb.

As China had been in 1989, Yugoslavia was beset by overriding political problems when Corti arrived in 1991. He was met at the airport by a man who came prepared to exchange 1,500 pills for $7,500 cash—$5 a pill. Corti made the transaction and returned to Frankfurt on the same plane.

Dr. Robert Jenkins, part of The Search Alliance, tried the drug on patients in Los Angeles. In MAI cases, azithromycin produced the same effect as clarithromycin had—though, since it cost more than twice as much as clarithromycin, there seemed to be no advantage to using it. Against the two other diseases, the drug didn't seem to do much. Corti tried calling the Yugoslavs back to see if he could finagle a break in price, but never was able to reach anyone at the phone number again. So much for azithromycin.

ddC was rolling off the tables of a secret pharmaceutical lab in Southern California by the thousands of bottles in violation of the rights of Hoffmann-La Roche. Suddenly, however, Sherman X, Corti's lab friend, developed cold feet. Making the drug was too dangerous, he abruptly decided. He wasn't going to manufacture ddC anymore.

Had someone from the government contacted him? Corti could only wonder. But he had to find another source. The drug worked. Alone or in combination with other drugs, ddC delayed the onset of AIDS. Dr. Margaret Fischl's studies at the University of Miami had shown particular benefit from a combination of AZT and ddC in low doses, and many patients were using it that way. Corti was supplying buyers' clubs all over the country. Thousands of patients were already relying on him, and the demand was growing each day.

While ddC continued to undergo official trials, doctors nationwide were referring patients to buyers' clubs in various cities, some of which got the drug from Corti. That was much easier than trying to get the drug from Hoffmann-La Roche under the company's narrowly restricted "expanded-access" program. The program required doctors to fill out complicated paperwork proving that each patient had failed on AZT and ddI. It was easier just to give out a buyers' club phone number, which is exactly what hundreds of doctors did.

Because ddC worked less well as a lone drug, and was most useful in combination, Hoffmann-La Roche was slower compiling data for its FDA application than Bristol-Myers was with ddI. Licensing could take a while. If Corti didn't find someone to replace Sherman X to manufacture ddC, the patients would be cut off.

By now, Corti had grown to trust and depend on Dr. Selmon Lichtenstein in Munich. And sure enough, Lichtenstein was able to suggest an alternative supplier of ddC.

The supplier was in Czechoslovakia. Once more, Corti flew to Eastern Europe. He was concerned, however, that shipping the drug from a suspect East European country would be more than customs or the FDA could accept—especially in such quantities. ddC was a prophylactic drug, of potential benefit to every HIV-infected person. So requested quantities would far exceed the volume of, say, clarithromycin, which treated a particular illness.

But the Czech pharmaceutical concern had an answer. Officials said they could easily ship the medicine to a destination in northern Mexico, where Corti's agents could pick it up for transport back to the U.S. overland in smaller loads.

Right back where we started, Corti thought.

And the Czech factory was prepared to crank up capacity, turning out thousands of bottles—more than a million tablets—a month. Immediately, the pills started flowing again. Bulk boxes of fifty thousand pills each were brought across the border into the U.S. by a patient's grandparents in their Winnebago, hidden amidst laundry and fishing tackle. Then the shipments were bottled in Corti's studio for distribution around the country. And the wholesale price stayed low, under $30 a month for each patient, even with travel and shipping costs from Czechoslovakia through Mexico included.

Also by the spring of 1991, Corti was supplying between twenty-five and fifty thousand clarithromycin tablets a month. The drug was leading him for the first time to heterosexual clients in large numbers. Treatments for the early stages of HIV infection tended still to attract predominantly gay men, because they were the ones who had themselves checked for the virus early. But when infected heterosexuals and children came down with MAI, the diagnosis led them to Corti and clarithromycin.

His mail contained letters like this from grateful parents:

Dear Jim,
Traci is doing well on clarithromycin, no need for other MAC medications. A new lease on life, she just celebrated her 27th birthday. Thank you! God bless you.

The drug gave him sudden respectability in polite scientific circles. In the spring of 1991, he was invited to speak about the underground traffic before the FDA's AIDS Research Advisory Committee in Bethesda, Maryland. When he got there, he discovered that of nine doctors from around the country on the committee, at least two had referred patients to Corti for illegal clarithromycin.

And as he told them about the success of clarithromycin, and the need to license it, he thought: This whole adventure has come so far that while the FDA still won't approve my drugs, the doctors it appoints to its advisory committees are my customers. He stopped in his prepared talk and said, "Here I am trying to convince you of the value of this compound, and two of you listening to this have already come to me to buy it for your patients."

They offered no sign of reaction.

Then a patient returning from Mexico with an antifungal drug that was available there reported a new phenomenon: clarithromycin was on sale in Mexican pharmacies, for about $2 a pill, under the trade name Klaracid. There had been no announcement from Abbott, the manufacturer; the drug just appeared on shelves one day. Mexican availability of clarithromycin would certainly simplify Corti's life, because many patients or their relatives could pick up their own drug, as they had with ribavirin and isoprinosine in the old days. And the price was about the same, shipping costs considered.

But could Corti be sure of the quality? One mistake in supplying an offshore drug could kill somebody. Corti tried again to get through to George Anelian, an Abbott Laboratories executive in charge of clarithromycin. Anelian had proven elusive in months past. But this time Corti made it through the marketing people and secretaries to

Anelian, who confirmed that Klaracid was the same clarithromycin Corti had been buying in Europe, with the same quality guarantees.

Corti wondered to himself whether Abbott, having learned of clarithromycin's success with MAI, had knowingly gone into Mexico to short-circuit the FDA testing system and tap the American AIDS market immediately. Few Mexicans could afford the drug.

Anelian said that Abbott would soon test the drug for American licensing, both as a treatment for MAI and as a prophylaxis against recurrence for those who had recovered from it. As Corti dictated, Anelian took the names of some doctors who regularly prescribed Corti's clarithromycin to their patients and followed the patients' progress. These community reports could be a big help to Abbott. And Corti asked Anelian to discuss the prospective tests with Delaney.

Then Corti called an old friend whom he hadn't seen in several years—Robert Castro of the Regis Farmacia in Tijuana.

"Hello, Jim!" Castro exclaimed. And they chatted awhile before Corti announced he wanted to come to Tijuana to discuss a deal.

"What's the deal?"

"You got a drug down there called Klaracid, real name clarithromycin?"

"Yeah, I got about ten bottles of it."

"Well," Corti said, "I want a thousand bottles."

"A thousand? You know the price of this stuff?"

"Yeah, I know."

Castro laughed. "I guess we've come the whole circle," he said.

"You mean the whole enchilada. Yeah, I guess we have."

"But have we done any good?" Castro asked.

"I hope so," Corti said.

Castro called back saying he could supply lots of up to ten thousand pills, to be paid for in advance. Corti came calling with a $17,000 certified check for his first purchase. Eventually, Castro knocked the price down to $1.65 a tablet in bulk—about the same as the Dublin price, considering shipping costs.

Then, in a research magazine, he read that a new drug was about to go into preliminary testing on human subjects at the University of California at San Diego. It was one of the more powerful, second-generation reverse transcriptase inhibitors that had been discussed at the International AIDS Conference at San Francisco.

Knowing how many years the university trial could take, Corti had one of his chemists create a sample of the drug based on a diagram of its chemical structure as printed in the magazine. Then he had the sample independently analyzed. It turned out that the research drug had a nitrate loop at the bottom that was missing from the drug Corti's chemist had produced. They weren't sure it was the same drug.

There had to be another way. Corti needed a sample of the actual compound, to achieve precise duplication. He phoned around until he found an AIDS patient who had been signed up for the university test. Would the patient agree to sneak out one dose of the drug instead of taking it? That way he might allow replication of the drug and, if it worked, speed it to help tens of thousands of patients.

The patient agreed. Corti was on his way again.[96]

E I G H T Y-S E V E N

*T*he FDA advisory committee's approval of T-cells as surrogate markers for AIDS had signaled Bristol-Myers that it could apply for a license for ddI now, two years before the phase two longevity tests would be finished and analyzed. Proving that the drug had a positive effect on patients' T-cell counts seemed a cinch, using data that was already in hand.

Bristol-Myers pledged to have an application before the FDA within thirty days. The FDA pledged to act on it with unprecedented speed. Trusting to nothing, Delaney kept in almost daily touch with both organizations. And he was glad he did.

A source on the Bristol-Myers development team told him that officials of the company were still wary of their own good fortune, and planned to file a limited application—perhaps just for use on children and patients who were failing on AZT, the two groups covered by the expanded-access program.

In the long run, Delaney knew, once a drug was licensed for one use, doctors could prescribe it as they chose. No one was going to investigate the lengths to which physicians went to learn if a patient was really unable to take AZT, or whether the patient was simultaneously taking AZT with the ddI. Once it was in the drugstores, it was fair game.

Nevertheless, it was important to test the FDA's new limits. The drug company ought to take a stand that its own drug worked, and not impose limits the FDA hadn't requested.

In that spirit, with the help of Bristol-Myers's public-relations staff, Delaney arranged a meeting in the company's New York headquarters with the executives in charge. He prepared a written analysis of why they should go for the broadest license they could—at least as broad as AZT's. They were, after all, related drugs.

Bristol-Myers turned around. On April 2, barely missing the thirty-day goal, the company applied for the broad license. The FDA promised to respond within thirty days. But when the scope of the data overwhelmed the agency's best intentions, it asked for a little more time. Eventually the critical advisory-committee meeting was scheduled for the third week in July 1991.

FDA Commissioner Kessler, meanwhile, was speaking out for a new system for the early approval of such drugs. He called it "conditional approval." Essentially, it was what Delaney had proposed to Ellen Cooper and Paul Beninger the previous August.

In outline, a company would be allowed to sell, for profit, a drug that had shown itself safe and had shown significant activity against a disease. But the license would be "conditional"—granted only if the drug company agreed to complete the requisite long-term studies by a specified date, after which the FDA would again review the drug. The company could then be granted an unconditional license, or told to withdraw the drug from the marketplace. Patients needed for long-term studies would still be shepherded into those studies.

Besides the obvious advantage of speeding the drugs to market more effectively than either Treatment IND or parallel track had been able to do, Delaney saw two other advantages to the conditional-approval idea. Smaller companies would be better able to compete with the majors; they could finance at least part of their drug trials with income from sale of the drugs. And second, if Kessler could talk the insurance industry into paying as it would for other approved drugs, more people could afford treatment.

As with the previous expanded-access programs, no congressional action was necessary. It was merely a matter of Kessler proposing the new procedure and nobody mounting a successful attack on it in the challenge period. Delaney wanted to help Kessler with the plan, and help was needed on two fronts where he had influence.

Some congressmen from the consumer-protection bloc were quick to try to kill the idea before it even got off the ground. Weiss called it a Republican plot to deregulate the industry. An aide to Waxman also attacked the idea publicly, trying to avert any FDA move in advance with threats of congressional reprisal. Delaney began lobbying the consumer-protection group to back off.

On the other extreme, some gay groups, suspicious of Kessler, were trying to get Congress to legislate conditional drug approval. A Republican congressman from California, Tom Campbell, submitted a bill to force the new system through. In Delaney's judgment, debate over this bill would just give the consumer protectionists a platform. The best way to get conditional approval was to keep Congress out of it. He began lobbying the gay groups who supported the bill, and the congressional Democrats who faced conflicting advice over how best to help their afflicted constituents.

Persuading Daiichi Pharmaceuticals to sign the Cooperative Research and Development Agreement and supply more SP-PG, if there was more, was another matter. For a while, Delaney had seemed to be getting nowhere. A letter in February from his contact Osada, in Tokyo, had sung the same old tune of amiable delay. Gallo was repeating studies he had already performed, as required for a scientific article he wanted to publish. Delaney was getting phone calls from others in the AIDS network who were aware of the negotiations with the Japanese and demanded to know their progress.

Then, in the spring, surprising scientific advancements were announced in Switzerland, at a world conference on anti-angiogenesis —the process of stopping the blood supply to tumors. Anti-angiogenesis was precisely the method by which the Daiichi drug worked. If someone else found another way to block angiogenesis, Daiichi might lose its projected bonanza.

The other entrant in the race was Judah Folkman, a Harvard researcher and friend of Gallo's, who had come up with a drug called fumagellan. Early on, fumagellan appeared to work much like SP-PG on many tumors. Folkman had brought a Japanese chemical company in to help him grow it. So far, this hadn't produced the expected speedy synthesizing, and fumagellan was still scarce. But Delaney saw the announcement as a shot across Daiichi's bow.

On top of that, Farmatalia, the company from which Corti had obtained his original quantities of clarithromycin, revealed that it, too, was working on an anti-angiogenesis drug—a supposedly detoxified version of suramin, the drug that had proved so deadly to research subjects at San Francisco General Hospital in 1985.

Delaney decided it was time to strike. After clearing the idea with Gallo, he wrote to Osada at Daiichi on April 8, 1991. He hurled a blatant, double-pronged threat. First, he noted the challenge of competitive drugs, and mentioned the rival Japanese firm working with Folkman. Come to the dance with us now, or we find a new partner, he said, in effect. And second, Delaney baldly threatened mass demonstrations by gays and their supporters against Daiichi, to take place at the Japanese consulates in New York and Washington, and, possibly, at Ortho, the American drug company Daiichi was working with on a promising antibiotic.

"I have successfully asked the more militant groups to trust Daiichi's sincerity and competence," he wrote, "but many groups have now grown impatient with me, as well as with Daiichi, and I do not fault them. They have set a deadline of approximately one month. Please, the best solution is a prompt response before any actions are taken."

He didn't refer to Gallo by name, but did say, "The potential for SP-PG is very great, and there is no faster way to develop it than through collaboration with the National Cancer Institute."

"I hope you do not find this letter disturbing," he concluded. "It is intended to alert you to these problems in advance, in a spirit of friendship as we felt in Tokyo. Please let me know of your plans and response, and I will attempt to communicate them to other interested groups in the United States."

Within two weeks, Osada and the Daiichi team came around, docile as puppy dogs. In May 1991, they were in Washington, signing the Cooperative Research and Development Agreement, and hinting that the synthesis problems had been overcome. Gallo credited Delaney with this achievement—"Delaney solved the Salahuddin problem," he said.

But just as quickly, Gallo was sidetracked by another attack from Crewdson. An outside researcher was accused of misusing a prospective vaccine made from a chemical obtained from Gallo's lab, injecting it in some people, including himself, without adequate study. There was no reason to believe Gallo had authorized this premature human experimentation, and the substance had been marked "for lab use only." Such substances were routinely exchanged among scientists, just as Gallo had obtained the drug SP-PG from Daiichi, and no doubt they were sometimes misused.

But because it was Gallo, and Crewdson was watching, this case was suddenly all over the papers. Congressman Dingell pounced on it. In response, a bureaucrat in a recently created NIH branch called the Office of Protection from Research Risk had demanded stringent new accounting procedures for routine lab samples, discombobulating labs all over Bethesda. Gallo became so preoccupied with the inquiries that Daiichi's phone calls were going unreturned.

In May 1991, the Justice Department dropped its long-standing criminal investigation into ICN's alleged illegal distribution of ribavirin. No charges were filed. ICN entered into a civil settlement, neither admitting nor denying violations of FDA regulations, but agreeing to pay $600,000 in costs. Case closed, except for the people who had died who might still be alive if they had taken ribavirin.

Peter Heseltine, the ribavirin researcher whose ethics Ellen Cooper had questioned in congressional hearings, was promoted to full professor and made associate chairman of the medical department at the University of Southern California. In the summer of 1991, he was running an FDA-approved study of peptide T. His former colleague Peter Mansell, who had been verbally booted off the platform by FDA Commissioner Frank Young at an international AIDS conference, and publicly humiliated on the network news, had a rougher time. He lost his job in Houston and for a while was without work. But the Health Protection Branch of the Canadian government hired him as chief outside consultant on drugs; he was also hired as a consultant to the AIDS Clinical Trials Group in Canada.

Karl Johnson, ICN's chief doctor at the time of the supposedly rigged ribavirin trials, had an ironic new job—running the AIDS Clinical Trials Group Operations Office, which supervises drug study protocols, including most AIDS drug studies. Technically, he was employed by a private concern that contracted with the trials group to run the office, but Johnson worked at NIH headquarters with the agency's senior officials. And he continued to tell anyone who asked that ribavirin was a great product, which would effectively delay the onset of AIDS in people with HIV, if they could get it.[97]

While Kessler promoted FDA liberalization through conditional approval of drugs, his bureaucracy was often mired in its old ways. In late May 1991, the FDA put a hold on tests at Stanford University of a promising T-cell booster known as PEG-IL, because of stroke-like reactions in four of the hundreds of patients who had been given the drug. Delaney reached out to Broder, Fauci, Gallo, Dr. Thomas Merrigan at Stanford, and Kessler, urging them to get the trials resumed.

All the patients in the study had T-cell counts under 200 and declining. Delaney had seen the preliminary data, which showed the immune cell counts rising uniformly and substantially for the sickest patients. It wasn't conclusive. But, he wrote, it was "remarkable in light of the lukewarm effects of virtually all other treatments in this class of patient. Where there is an important decision about risk vs. potential benefit, we strongly feel that decision must be made by the patient, not the bureaucracy."

Three weeks after Delaney went to Kessler and the others, the FDA reversed its position and the trials of PEG-IL continued.

There was a lot of evidence Kessler was really trying. The week before the critical advisory-committee meeting on ddI in mid-July, 1991, Delaney was among several dozen people invited to a conference in Annapolis, Maryland, sponsored by a nonprofit health-and-environment group called the Keystone Center. Keystone was run mostly by conservative mega-corporations, with a few representatives on its board from academia and organized labor.

Barely after pinning on his standard-issue plastic name tag, Delaney began to sense that this conference was differentiated from the many others he had attended on drug access by the conspicuous presence of insurance executives. He began to suspect the unseen hand of Kessler, who must have realized that health insurers were vital to the conditional-approval plan. If the insurers wouldn't cover the drugs, the plan would lose a lot of its meaning.

So insurance moguls had been sprinkled in among the usual attendees—Abrams, some FDA staffers, and some drug-company executives, academics, and congressional aides. And soon into the opening-night reception, Delaney felt himself being pulled aside by John L. Cova, director of Medical Technology Assessment of the Health Insurance Association of America.

As Cova talked, Delaney began to understand how the insurers perceived what was happening. To them, the pharmaceutical industry was trying to shift the cost of drug development to the insurance industry, by asking insurers to pay for drugs still in trial. Nevertheless, the insurers saw advantages to sharing this cost in some cases. If a new drug kept people out of the hospital longer, it would save insurance companies money in the long run.

So the insurance industry was rethinking its policy of not paying for experimental treatments. The industry wanted to encourage the next generation of drugs. But, Cova said, the industry needed to do this of its own accord, without pressure. Good guys, like Cova, were working to bring the industry around. But if the industry was bullied in public, the bad guys would fight back, and maybe defeat the farsighted approach of the good guys.

Here was one more group asking Delaney to hold off the militant activists. But Delaney sized Cova up as sincere. He promised nothing, except to keep a close eye on what happened. He now believed, though, that the insurance industry could be brought into the fold, like the regulators and the drug companies. Common sense was on his side.

The real battle was to be the next week in Washington. What happened to ddI would determine what happened to a potentially endless line of other drugs. The FDA was about to say whether a drug company could legally sell a drug that appeared to work against the main marker of a disease, without waiting for the completion of control-group longevity studies.

EIGHTY-EIGHT

*E*ver since the Seventh International AIDS Conference in Florence, Italy, the month before, Delaney's neuropathy—the terrible pain in his feet from side effects of the hepatitis treatments he had taken at Stanford a decade earlier—was worse than he could ever remember it. He checked in at Stanford again to see if anything could be done. His condition was complicated by remnants of the liver dysfunction that had brought him to the experimental treatments in the first place. At times he felt so fatigued he didn't think he could walk across the room.

The doctors ran their usual tests and told him the condition was unchanged—that is, permanent. Their advice was typically unhelpful—try to avoid heat, stress, and exertion; those things would exacerbate the problems. And rest a lot.

He checked out in time to catch the all-night red-eye flight to the Keystone Center meeting. After that, he traveled to Washington for a political dinner at Bob Gray's house, then returned to San Francisco. He made a quick trip to Houston to talk to doctors setting up a regional drug trial, and to address a large patient group, then returned to San Francisco to attend a memorial service for a friend. The next night, he took the red-eye again to Washington, which was its usual steamy caldron in mid-July. Before the ddI hearing Thursday and Friday were three days of AIDS Clinical Trials Group meetings. He had fought hard to become a voice at those meetings, but had come to dread them.

The Clinical Trials Group supposedly met about drugs, but really, to a large degree, met about money. Every researcher who attended paid his mortgage, and impressed his romantic partner, with money from drug companies or government grants. And what these scientific conferences determined was who would get the money. Each researcher, whether forward-thinking or Neanderthal in his ideology, wanted the money. Each worked for a university or other institution that expected him to bring it home to pay for a staff or laboratory, as well as his own salary.

This week the squabbling was particularly bitter. The proposal most favored was for a vast, multicenter study on the benefits of combination therapies. It was guaranteed to spread the wealth to the maximum number of research centers. Some three thousand patients would be studied. Half would get therapy on one drug, and the other half would be split among two different sets of combinations.

How, Delaney kept asking anyone who would listen, could you possibly go back in time and ask fifteen hundred AIDS patients to stick to a single therapy for two years? Nearly every researcher at the recent international conference in Florence had concluded that a combination therapy offered the most hope. Now, to prove that point, the American doctors intended to ask fifteen hundred people to sacrifice what was left of their health.

The issue dominated discussions in the primary-infection committee of the group. Delaney was among the dozen people on the committee. Most members represented institutions that stood to get some of the $18 million the study would cost. One, and Delaney's most vocal opponent, was Douglas Richman of the University of California at San Diego, an antagonist from way back.

But Richman had loudly advocated combination therapies. Why, Delaney asked in the committee meeting, would Richman want to condemn fifteen hundred people to a single drug if he believed so thoroughly in multidrug combinations?

It was science, Richman said.

It was money, Delaney thought. Project Inform would try everything to shut this study down, he said. He pointed out that the patients were well educated by now. "They're not going to sign up for the study. I'll campaign against it."

"There are a lot of patients who don't read your newsletter," Richman shot back. "There are all sorts of people who can't afford combination therapy. We'll get them in the study."

At that, Delaney exploded. "Yeah, let's experiment on the poor!" And he said probably more than he should have, accusing Richman of talking out of both sides of his mouth.

Margaret Fischl, whose combination AZT-ddC experiment at the University of Miami had already validated the combination-therapy idea, gingerly tried to bridge the gap. They could modify the protocol to protect patients who failed on a single therapy.

Why let them fail at all? Delaney asked. The trial was a waste of badly needed resources. "The AIDS Clinical Trials Group should be using its money to find new therapies, not to fine-tune what's already there," he said.

But as he looked around the room, he could see the vote was ten to one against him. The more moderate members of the committee, like Fischl and Thomas Merrigan, offered further concessions to protect the patients. If any arm of the study began to fail or lag according to a certain preset standard, that arm would be opened up and the patients allowed to switch to a different arm with a therapy combination that was achieving superior results.

In the end, he felt he had achieved as much as he could have, and even congratulated the group on conducting a reasonably fair negotiating process with him after the angry confrontation.[98]

Still his feet got worse and exhaustion began to set in. To save energy, he decided not to switch hotels from the Holiday Inn in downtown Washington, where the ACTG conference was being held, to the one ten miles away in suburban Bethesda where the ddI hearing would occur. He figured that when the ACTG researchers moved out, the downtown hotel would be quiet and he could rest.

He was wrong. Just as the ACTG members were checking out, hordes of born-again teenagers from the Christian Youth Foundation descended on the hotel for their annual meeting. Hundreds of kids who had never been out of their parents' sight or seen anything bigger than Oklahoma City were screaming with delight just to ride the elevators up and down. Their suitcases were everywhere, except in their rooms.

Feet hurting worse than ever, Delaney elbowed through the rowdy lobby and made it to Bethesda Thursday morning. In the hall between the men's room and the meeting room, as people slowly filed by gripping their coffee cups, Delaney found David Kessler. Kessler warned him it would be a roller coaster. "The first day may not look so good," Kessler said. "The problems all go on the table on day one."

Delaney had already discussed the plan with FDA staffers, the ddI researchers and Bristol-Myers officials. What Kessler was saying was in line with what he'd already heard. After the drug-company presentation, featuring some of the researchers, the FDA staff would challenge the data along traditional lines. The company would show T-cells had increased, but the staff would argue that without a control group you couldn't prove the drug caused the improvement. The company would argue that it had created a control group of data from similar patients who had taken placebos in earlier studies of other drugs—"historical controls," they would be called. But the statisticians would denigrate that approach. On day two, however, the drug would be rescued. Other FDA staffers would introduce the notion that there were new methods of analyzing data.

But as Kessler started to explain the new analysis, suddenly Gina Kolata of *The New York Times* was there next to them. Delaney knew his briefing from Kessler was over. Just as suddenly, there was Marilyn Chase of *The Wall Street Journal,* then people from CNN and NBC, and half a dozen other reporters.

All at once Delaney realized what this was about. That Tuesday morning, Chase had broken a big story in the *Journal:* counterfeit ddC was for sale all over the country, provided by an AIDS drug underground. She had even quoted Jim Corti, identifying him as "a major link in ddC's underground distribution chain," though she didn't reveal Corti's real role as the manufacturer. Kessler had declined to be interviewed for the article, and the FDA had issued a vague statement of "concern."

This was the potential hot story that Delaney and Kessler had begun to deal with gingerly, and here was the whole press corps aiming to pin them down on it. Microphones were being shoved in Kessler's face. What was he going to do about this?

"Gee," Kessler said, "I've been so busy looking at ddI all week I haven't read the newspapers. I don't know what you're talking about." And he made some comments about the ddI hearings, excused himself, and darted off. Delaney, relieved, tried to shrug the matter off as a tempest in a teapot. He really wanted to ask Kolata if she was surprised that the ddI trials were fully enlisted and the drug was up for licensing despite her "scoop" in the *Times* that expanded access had torpedoed the research process. But then the hearing started.

The room was much like the one for the surrogate-markers hearing in February. There was a table for the committee—eight voting members and roughly as many kibitzers. Carl Peck again was nonvoting MC. A couple of hundred people were in the audience, and Delaney was not surprised to see that one of them was Ellen Cooper. As best he could figure, NIH, Bristol-Myers, and Hoffmann-La Roche accounted for about a third of the total.

Kessler had been right on target about the content of the day. But he hadn't warned Delaney about the pace. As slide after slide of heavy data was tediously explained, the perspiring audience, mostly in business suits, squirmed on uncomfortable folding chairs. It was close to one hundred degrees outside, and the room was too crowded for the air conditioning to cope with. The television lights were like small furnaces. Delaney remembered his doctors' advice to avoid heat.

Morning finally ran into the lunch break. Delaney had planned to meet the head of the Pediatric AIDS Foundation for lunch, but the foundation head left word she would be late. He waited in the wide hall outside the meeting room, watching everyone else file out. The television crews packed their gear and left. He sat alone on a bench next to a staircase that wound down to the hotel's first-floor lobby, and nursed his feet. He had taken to wearing soft-soled shoes that didn't quite go with a business suit, but felt better. He kept the laces loose.

He stopped wondering where the foundation head was, and began to enjoy the solitude and cooler air. Suddenly his eye caught another lone figure coming up the stairs. It was Ellen Cooper. She sat down on the bench next to him. He was glad to see her in circumstances where they didn't have anything to argue about. They talked about California. She said she was thinking about taking a job in industry there.

Inevitably, though, the conversation drifted toward what they were both at the hotel for, the ddI hearing. Delaney said how pleased he was at the spirit of collaboration that seemed to be growing between the FDA and the drug companies, to try to bring the best drugs to market. It was a new spirit, and everyone felt a little strange, but the FDA staff and Fauci's people had actually worked with Bristol-Myers to try to put together a winning case for ddI. It wasn't that the government doctors particularly wanted to help the drug company; it was that they believed ddI could, at least for a while, maintain the health of HIV-infected people who would otherwise wither and die.

"It's what I was asking for in my letters to you last year," he said. "It's a vision coming true. This is what we wanted all along."

"This is all a mistake," Cooper told him. "What I'm concerned about is the process. The agency has become an advocate for the drug. It's lost its objectivity. That's wrong. The FDA's job is to decide whether the data submitted for a new drug meets the legal standard. It's not a question of whether researchers and doctors out there feel that it works. For a regulatory agency, you have to have data. If the company doesn't show statistically significant efficacy, then the drug just doesn't get licensed. It's simple."

It used to seem simple, Delaney thought. He realized how critical Cooper's resignation had been to the process he was pushing. If she had still been around, none of this would have happened. He thought back to something Fauci had told him about her a few weeks earlier. "She's still in that mode that this is black and white," Fauci had said. "It doesn't matter that there are umpteen thousand people out there who need the drug. It doesn't matter to her that five thousand clinicians working with the drug are convinced it is helping their patients. If the data don't prove statistically significant efficacy—"

Delaney put Fauci's conversation aside. "I understand what you're saying," he told Cooper. "The agency is taking a risk doing things this way. But who takes the risk doing things your way? If in another year and a half the evidence comes in that the drug works, as everyone believes it will, who takes responsibility for all the lives that were lost?"

"Well," she said, "you have expanded access."

He could have reiterated why that wasn't working. But why argue? He had won. The new commissioner agreed with him. They were allies. She had lost. She was there as an outsider.

Delaney and Cooper had been through a lot together. He shared her commitment. He understood, intellectually, her point of view. But for now she was a symbol of what he felt he had beaten—the old FDA.

After a silence, they talked some more about California. Then his lunch date showed up and he left.[99]

The afternoon proceeded as scheduled. Some FDA staff members attacked the data. But as far as Delaney knew, that's what was supposed to happen—a public display that the agency had been diligently skeptical—and it would all be reversed the next morning. He had no inkling of a problem.

EIGHTY-NINE

Delaney ducked out of the hearing a bit early to keep another appointment. He had been invited to the Vice-President's office at the Executive Office Building adjacent to the White House. A call had come to the Project Inform office for a meeting, and this had been the convenient day. The caller had been sketchy about the purpose. Delaney assumed Boyden Gray had something to do with the invitation. Gray had continued as Bush's chief counsel when Bush moved into the presidency. Now Delaney didn't know if he was coming face to face with Dan Quayle, about whom he had enjoyed the same jokes everyone else told, or some lesser authority.

He was greeted by John Cohrssen of the President's Council on Competitiveness, and Angela Antonelli of the Office of Management and Budget in the White House. Someone from the Competitive Enterprise Institute, a business lobbying group, had also been invited to sit in.

The administration team began by praising Kessler, and left no doubt the new commissioner had Bush's full support. But they wanted to know about the Campbell bill, the effort to get Congress to legislate accelerated approval of drugs. What did Delaney think of it?

He was reluctant to say, uncertain whether his listeners would understand the subtlety of the situation. Conceptually, it was a swell bill, he told them. But tactically it was stupid. "The last thing we want is to get Congress into this now."

"Gee, that's what we think, too," he was told. "We were afraid you guys were behind this."

At that, the atmosphere eased. The administration officials wanted suggestions on how to expedite putting the new conditional-approval plan in place.

Delaney thought a minute.

"You know," he said, "the only time the FDA staff gets recognition is when it's punitive—when a bad drug is suspected of getting through. If Kessler succeeds with this, you ought to bring in Kessler and all the top brass, including from NIH, invite them to the White House for lunch, get their picture taken with the President, and give them all certificates of commendation."

As he spoke he saw them grab pens and notepads and start writing.

"These guys are always browbeaten by Congress when a drug causes harm," he said. "But they're never criticized for the lives lost when new drugs move too slowly. The system rewards caution and discourages innovation. The executive branch can't change what Congress does, but it can offer a counterbalance. Make a big noise about what they're doing now. And do it for people all the way down the ladder in the agency who are helping make this ddI approval happen. This would be the first time in the history of the FDA anybody rewarded innovation. And you'll probably enjoy the lunch."

They were smiling as they wrote. And, he thought, you probably like this idea because it won't cost you much money.

"What else?" they were asking.

Money, Delaney thought. Getting the health insurers to pay for experimental treatments.

"Another issue," he said, "is that the whole conditional-approval plan hinges on the patient's ability to get reimbursement. The insurance companies don't want to pay and the government doesn't want to pay. In fact, a lot of activists working in AIDS have opposed Kessler's idea precisely because they think insurance companies will say these are still experimental drugs and reject the claim, and right now, under the expanded-access program, ddI's free. You and I know the drug companies can't keep donating their products, but by the same token you can't just throw this cost back on the people who are sick, a lot of whom can't work."

Thinking as he spoke, Delaney suggested, "Why not have the President call a meeting of the health-insurance industry. Bring in the pharmaceutical companies, the FDA, the NIH along with them. Have the President himself kick it off, saying, 'We have a national emergency here. I want you to solve this problem, which affects all people with life-threatening illnesses. I want you to come to an agreement over who pays for what.' It won't cost the administration anything but leadership."

Unless the answer they come up with is a new government health program, he thought, but he didn't say it. His listeners seemed pleased, and were still scribbling. They asked for more ideas.

He thought of conversations he had just had with Gallo, Fauci, and others during the ACTG meetings. The latest Crewdson-Dingell campaign over the premature human injection of a substance from Gallo's lab was really interfering with research. The Office of Protection from Research Risk had buried the NIH in red tape in order to ensure that no outsider could misuse a substance from a government lab. Fauci was fuming that there were hundreds of substances in his own refrigerator at any given time whose origins or destinations he couldn't tell you. He was already short-staffed, and if every researcher had to account for what happened to everything that came and went the research itself would be significantly impeded.

Gallo was even more upset, because not only was his lab suffering like all the others, but his own alleged lack of accounting was the cause of everybody's new problem. Sam Broder was mad. Every researcher Delaney had talked to about it was grousing.

If the administration wanted to help science, Delaney said, it ought to look into whether this single episode really warranted such a massive disruption of all government research facilities.

The two administration officials said they were unaware of all this, and seemed much impressed. They kept Delaney talking for an hour and a half, and thanked him profusely.

Then he taxied back to the Holiday Inn and fought through hundreds of rambunctious Christian Youth Foundation revelers and their luggage, cluttering the lobby and hallways, to get to his room and get his shoes off.

NINETY

By the early summer of 1991, Jim Corti had found his system of delivering bootleg ddC from Czechoslovakia had grown unwieldy, despite the appreciable fortitude of the grandparents of an AIDS patient, who smuggled the capsules from Mexico into California in their Winnebago.

For one thing, testing the drug was difficult. Samples had to be sent from Czechoslovakia to Los Angeles by regular mail, because Federal Express shipments were more likely to be seized by customs. Corti had the samples checked for purity by a friend who worked in the laboratory of a well-known institution, who could run the complicated high-resolution liquid chromatography test free on the institution's costly equipment. Then he had the samples tested for potency by Truesdail Laboratories in Tustin, California, which gave him letters of certification. The samples came out fine and he sent word back to Czechoslovakia to forward the shipment of capsules to Mexico. But what if a batch didn't come out fine—what would he do to correct a supply problem so far away?

Security was another concern. Reporters, particularly Marilyn Chase of *The Wall Street Journal*, were onto the fact that illegal ddC was flowing in what obviously was an organized underground operation. Publicity might force the FDA to crack down. And how much did the reporters and the FDA really know—enough to trace the operation to him? Enough people at the buyers' clubs knew who he was and what he was doing that the secret would be hard to keep.

Weighing even heavier on his mind, his good friend and supporter Fred Wietersen was incapacitated by an AIDS-induced stroke in early June, and was obviously headed down the inevitable path to death.

At a wine tasting in West Los Angeles, Corti got to talking to some men who owned a laboratory in Orange County. They proclaimed themselves libertarians—people who believe in minimizing (if not eliminating) government involvement in the lives of citizens. As they got further into conversation about Corti's work, the possibility of a deal became obvious.

By the third round of Chardonnay, it was agreed that Corti would come look at their lab to consider its suitability for taking over the manufacture of the ddC capsules. Bringing the production close to home would simplify both quality control and distribution. Since the vast majority of what the capsules contained was easily available inert material, local production made sense all the way around if secrecy could be assured.

The lab checked out—clean, modern, and thoroughly satisfactory. The next step was to find a source of adequate quantities of raw ddC. As Corti had already discovered, manufacturers recognized immediately that anyone ordering more than a tiny amount was probably planning to infringe on Hoffmann-La Roche's exclusive right to market the drug for human use. American companies seemed to want no part of that, even though Hoffmann-La Roche couldn't market it yet for lack of FDA approval.

Corti turned again to Selmon Lichtenstein in Munich, and the pharmacist Lichtenstein had introduced him to who was good at obtaining hard-to-get drugs for AIDS patients. Corti had often remarked that unlike in the U.S., where medical personnel specializing in AIDS often tend to be gay themselves, in Germany there was no such correlation; the pharmacist was married with two children. And he came up with a ddC supplier: Pharma Waldhof, in a northern suburb of Mannheim.

Corti placed an order for 300 grams, $30,000 worth. That would be enough to produce 3,000 bottles containing a two months' supply of 400 ddC capsules each. And he flew to Munich with the cash. The order had to be placed by a pharmacist. But after the order was placed, rather than wait for the shipment, Corti rented an Audi 90 in Munich and drove the 300 kilometers to Pharma Waldhof. To his surprise, the company was part of the mile-square, fenced-off compound of Boehringer, the large German-based international pharmaceutical firm.

In the seven- or eight-story Pharma Waldhof building, he went through receptionist after receptionist, finally locating the official who had his order from the pharmacist in Munich. The official gave Corti documents that would allow him to pick up the drug at a laboratory in another building on the compound.

Corti hopped in his car and suddenly found himself at a security checkpoint. Guards began scrutinizing the pickup documents he had just been given in what seemed to Corti to be worrisome detail. He couldn't understand their objections. Suddenly Corti heard an American voice behind him: "What do you need?" The voice turned out to belong to a former U.S. Army officer, now dressed in a business suit and working for Boehringer security. He looked at the documents and spoke in German to the guards. A German official in a business suit appeared and looked at the papers.

"Where is this going, and who do you represent?" he asked.

"It's going to do AIDS research in Bangkok," Corti said. Ever since dextran days, Corti had been spending more and more time in Thailand, where he had a lover and where he had undertaken the uphill task of counseling the flourishing male-prostitution industry on AIDS safety. "I represent the Anglo-French AIDS Consortium in Bangkok," he said, and gave the address of a private group there that promoted patient care and sexual safety.

The men eyed him, and then gave directions to the lab where he could pick up the drug. He wondered whether they had believed him, or whether they guessed what he was really going to do with the ddC and just didn't care. No matter.

The lab was in a three-story building. Its shiny white tile floor looked clean enough to perform surgery on. The clerk produced the ddC in a sealed, white plastic jar that said "Pharma Waldhof." Corti asked for a copy of the order that said "Boehringer" on it; if there was ever a problem, he wanted to be able to prove the drug had come from a Rock-of-Gibraltar source.

And he drove back toward Munich on the Autobahn. It was a warm afternoon. He couldn't help but notice the bicyclers, all ages of men, with their colorful jerseys and flashing spokes, streaming across the overpasses above him, and disappearing into the forest on either side. What fun it looked! He longed to be with them. Maybe one of them had someone like John Upchurch waiting at the end of the ride to take him home. Corti searched in his mind for a metaphor for the disaster that had diverted him to this mission—for why there would be no John Upchurch waiting for Corti at the end of his ride today.

And as he approached Munich, the metaphor presented itself. The road sign announced a turnoff for Dachau. That's what he was fighting, he decided. Another holocaust.

Back at the pharmacy, he said that if this batch worked out, he would place a new order for a full kilo of ddC, $100,000 worth, in a short time. And he returned to the pension where he was staying. There, he found a fax from a friend in Los Angeles: a copy of Marilyn Chase's story in *The Wall Street Journal* describing the secret ddC network and mentioning Corti, though not recognizing his real role. With $30,000 of ddC in his carry-on bag, Corti felt a chill. What might lie in wait at customs?

He called Delaney.

NINETY-ONE

Delaney got the message when he returned to the Holiday Inn. It said urgent. Despite the hour—it was 2 A.M. in Germany—he returned the call.

"What the hell's going on?" Corti demanded. "Are they going to be meeting me with indictments at the airport when I get back?"

Delaney told him what Kessler had said to reporters that morning. "I don't think you have anything to worry about," Delaney said.

Corti sounded relieved and said he'd go back to sleep.

For Delaney, sleep and relief had become close to the same thing.

Back in Bethesda the next morning for the conclusion of the ddI hearing, Delaney detected a negative buzz before he even got near the hearing room. People in the hallway were saying the advisory-committee members had made extremely negative comments the evening before.

Delaney saw an FDA staff member who he knew supported ddI. "Yesterday was terrible," the staffer said. "It's going down the tubes."

"Looks gloomy," one of the reporters said. "All they could talk about were problems of using a historical control group, and how could you be sure the patients had exactly the same profile."

Delaney thought back to Kessler's warning. "Yesterday was supposed to be about problems, so the agency could demonstrate that it's aware of them all," Delaney told the reporter. "That should turn around today."

"It sure doesn't sound like it."

As the meeting began, Paul Meier, a statistician from Chicago and a voting member of the panel, was holding forth. Delaney knew Meier tended to be conservative and was not a likely ally. But Meier represented the statistical expertise on the panel. And he had found one after another statistical flaw in Bristol-Myers's data, particularly regarding the historical controls. Then others joined in, expressing their concern.

Maybe, Delaney thought, they were just showing off how smart they were, to get on television or in *The New York Times*. But the hearing was so one-sided!

At the first break, he found the Bristol-Myers contingent. They were despondent. He visited the FDA people who had presented the negative case the day before. They were worried they had gone too far. The application was in real trouble.

Delaney decided to go to bat. Instead of returning to his usual seat, he usurped one in front, by the door the committee members used to enter and leave during sessions, to get water or go to the bathroom.

The first one up was Don Abrams. Delaney followed him out.

"How's it going?" he asked, and Abrams gave a very pessimistic view.

"Everybody's beating up on ddI," Abrams said.

"Showing off how much they know about statistics," Delaney agreed.

"I tried to speak up for it last night," Abrams said. "But Kessler cut me off. He wouldn't even let me talk."

Delaney wondered why, and resolved to ask Kessler about it.

"Don," he said, "I can't do much standing out in the hallway. If the committee's causing a problem, you're going to have to get angry. We've got tens of thousands of people for whom AZT isn't doing anything."

"I know," Abrams said. "I know."

"So get angry about it. Speak up."

"Every time I get angry, people tell me I'm too emotional. I don't want to lose what influence I have."

"Don, if there's ever a time in your life to get angry, it's today."

There was no doubt now about Abrams's support. Delaney hoped only that Abrams would throw into this fight the same force he had once used to try to stop such drugs. One really strong speech might shame the committee away from its concern with statistics and "P values," toward the desperation of the patients.

The next committee member Delaney managed to corner was Paul Meier. Meier had always struck him as well intentioned, but a true believer in the religion of statistics.

"It's not just a question of statistical proof," Delaney argued. "There's a profound need for patients to have this drug. You can't oppose this and make it sound like an ethical decision."

"But you already have ddI under expanded access," Meier said.

"Paul, expanded access is just a word. It doesn't do what you think it does. The medically indigent don't get access at all. Physicians literally have to lie their way into expanded access because of the unrealistic rules about having to fail on this drug or that drug before you can take some other drug. Patients are supposed to watch their immune systems collapse before getting help. I don't care what the statistical models show, we need this drug."

Delaney could see a pained look on Meier's face. He was more worried than Delaney had given him credit for.

"I'll do what I can," he said. "Maybe we could have some sort of limited approval for those who can't take AZT."

"Put whatever you want on the label," Delaney said. "But let the physicians decide whom they want to prescribe it for."

"I'll tell you what I'll do. I won't vote against it."

That was as much of a commitment as Delaney could have hoped for from Meier. If the statistical expert abstained—if the statistical expert could accept ddI—who else on the panel could object?[100] (See note for Meier's account.)

Neil Schram, a Los Angeles nephrologist, was the next person at the committee table to go out in the hall. Schram had done some AIDS work, and Delaney knew him.

"Neil, we don't have a lot of people on that committee today. You've got to help us."

"Well, I would. But I see problems with the data."

"If the data was solid and convincing, we wouldn't be doing anything unusual here. The point of all this is that we are doing something unusual. We need this drug."

"Delaney," Schram snapped, "maybe we should go to Congress and ask them to give *you* the authority to license drugs in this country."

"I think I could do a better job than some people," Delaney replied. And as Schram walked off, Delaney cursed the structure that made this handful of "experts" the arbiters of whether people could or couldn't take the medication of their choice for a fatal illness. He took his seat again.

The FDA staff was now presenting its different statistical way of approaching the data, a system known as an "area under the curve" analysis. Call it anything, Delaney thought, it was still statistics. This wouldn't rescue the drug. Who even understood it?

He thought about all he had been through—the seamy streets of Tijuana, the suramin crisis and Bradley's near death, winning the pricing fight with ICN, piloting the drug flights with Winterhalter, the alliance with Corti, the excitement of Corti's uncanny ability to procure each new drug, the disillusionment at discovering how ribavirin and isoprinosine were sabotaged, the vow to fight back, the exhilarating days of the Compound Q trial, the devastating publicity after Robert Parr's death, the eventual vindication, the alliance with the world's leading scientists, expanded access, parallel track, the successful assault on the surrogate-markers barrier—now all to fail because of this one committee?

Delaney went back to the hallway. Suddenly David Kessler followed him, gave him a tug on the arm, and headed for the stairwell. "Someplace private," Kessler ordered.

When they got there, the FDA commissioner opened up, anticipating Delaney's question. "Last night, Abrams started telling the group he felt constrained by not having the 'conditional approval' system available yet," Kessler said. "I stopped him, because I don't want them thinking that's a way out. I want them to deal with this drug on the basis of the data that we have. The minute we use the word 'conditional,' we give the insurance industry an excuse not to pay for the drug. I'm urging you, if you talk to the media on this, don't use the word 'conditional.' "

"I'm with you on that," Delaney said. "But what if we lose? I'm really concerned that some of those committee members are digging in to reject it."

"No, don't worry," Kessler said. "I'm sure we'll approve it one way or another. If we have to, we can always go back to some sort of conditional approval. But I'd rather see the committee make a real decision. We put a great deal of work into this and we believe it's the right thing to do."

Good God, Delaney thought. Is this the FDA commissioner taking responsibility? Is this real life?

"I'm not as confident as you are about the committee," Delaney replied. "What if it has to be a conditional approval?"

"I might have to do it on a conditional basis, without calling it that," Kessler went on. "Make some kind of conditions with the company."

"Would the company go for it?"

"The company will take anything we give them," Kessler said. "I need to know how you'll respond."

"We'll be behind it." Delaney was surprised Kessler had any question about this. "As long as we get the drug out there."

"Don't talk to the media," Kessler instructed. "We have to try to get them to approve it on its merits first. We haven't played our strongest card yet."

"What do you have?"

"An early peek at the trial data." He was talking about the ongoing large-scale trial, which wouldn't end until late 1992. "What the data shows corroborates what we're saying. It shows in the first six months the same pattern of CD-4 response."

"It looks," Delaney beamed, "like we're going to get ddI before this day is out, one way or another."

Kessler eyed him earnestly. "Martin, one way or another, we'll get it approved."

Delaney felt a wave of elation. Success was guaranteed.[101] (See note for Kessler's demur.)

They walked their separate ways back toward the room. Delaney stopped at the door and leaned against the wall panel. At the committee table, someone was droning on about the new statistical system. He looked at the empty chair. If he sat down in it, he would never have the strength to get back up again. His feet hurt.

He was booked on the night flight, but there was also an afternoon flight. He called and made a reservation. Then he went outside to the taxi queue.

He thought of Corti, still on the trail of new compounds around the world, still cranking out illegal ddC. Maybe the days of running from the law were fading. Victory was within sight. Relieved, he sank into the airliner seat and let his tired body give way to quiet sleep.

His car was where he had parked it. As he headed for the Golden Gate Bridge and Sausalito, he picked up the car phone and dialed his friend at the Associated Press. What was the news from the FDA drug meeting? he asked.

She looked. "There's stuff coming on all the wires," she said. "They passed ddI. Lots of talk about a dramatic change in policy. The dawn of a new day. *The New York Times*'s story begins, 'In a decision that sets new standards for drug approval . . .' Here's a quote from Kessler, 'A lot of precedents are being set.' Kessler 'said the process of speeding ddI's journey to the market sets an example for the approval of other drugs for AIDS and other serious or life-threatening diseases, like cancer and Alzheimer's disease.'"

"Is there anything about what happened at the meeting?"

"Yeah. Donald Abrams made what was described as an impassioned speech just before the final vote. He said this wasn't about statisticians' arguments. 'It's that we profoundly need patients' treatment, and I'm getting frustrated waiting,' Abrams said."

"What was the vote?"

"Five for, two against. And Paul Meier, a statistician from Chicago, abstained."

Delaney smiled and thanked his source. He was still weary, but the drain he had felt climbing into the taxi in Washington was gone. Almost instinctively, his hand reached back to the telephone. He needed to connect with those who had taken the long march with him. He called Paul Beninger at the FDA in Rockville to congratulate him. Beninger raved about the job the FDA staff had done in the previous weeks, assembling the new data.

He called Fauci, who had also done herculean work to push through the surrogate markers and ddI.

"How different it is from the old FDA," Fauci said. "You look at all the data and you can't conclusively say you've proven the drug's efficacy yet. The old FDA would have just stopped there. What Kessler did was say, We have all these other facts, and he made a rational decision."

At home there were messages from a dozen reporters, wanting comment. He called some.

There was another call. Mark Bradley had just come back from the doctor with startling news. His T-cell count had risen to 947, about normal. Once it had been under 100. Just two years before, when he had begun Compound Q, it had been under 200. Diligently, over all these years, Bradley had taken combination therapies, the best available. The only time he had ever been hurt was when he trusted his care to the system rather than his own judgment.

But those, too, were the old days. Today, San Francisco General Hospital had been on their side.

Today, HIV infection was not a death sentence, at least not one you measure on a calendar. HIV infection was becoming a manageable, long-term chronic illness. A lot of people died from it. But a lot of people were still alive.

At last, Delaney went to bed.

POSTSCRIPT

On December 17, 1991, Jim Corti took some capsules from the latest batch of ddC to Truesdail Laboratories for testing. The next day, the results came back. The capsules averaged 0.253 milligram of drug each—within a perfectly acceptable hair of the targeted 0.25. Corti told his libertarian associates in Orange County to start releasing the batch to the buyers' clubs that placed orders, and he took off for Thailand.

A month later, Hoffmann-La Roche sent the FDA some samples of ddC capsules it said had recently come from buyers' clubs, and complained that the contents were irregular. On Friday, January 24, 1992, clubs in New York and San Francisco were called by the FDA, which requested samples of the ddC capsules they were selling. Each club agreed to turn over samples.

The following Monday, January 27, the *San Francisco Chronicle* carried the headline "Black-Market AIDS Drug Seized in S.F. for Tests." The story began, "Investigators from the U.S. Food and Drug Administration, acting on warnings about potential safety problems with the black-market AIDS treatment ddC, have seized samples of the drug from underground buyers' clubs in San Francisco and New York."

Delaney never could learn who had leaked the story, but in fact there had been no raids or orders to cease and desist. He and Derek Hodel, head of the New York buyers' club, were in Florida at a conference of buyers clubs the Friday the FDA called. It was decided to halt sales of the drug at the buyers' clubs immediately, and to stop further shipments from Corti's operation. Corti hastened back to the U.S. Both the sellers and the FDA ran new tests.

The FDA reported to Hodel February 7 that the samples taken from Hodel's group ranged from a low of 64.8 percent of the intended 0.25 milligram to a high of 188.3 percent. It said a batch from another site—apparently Florida—didn't show improper variations. But a batch from a third site—apparently San Francisco—ranged from 0 percent to 230 percent of the intended dose, though the average content of the batches from all sites were much closer to the intended 0.25 milligram.

The content fluctuations among the capsules indicated such poor quality control, the FDA said, that "one could not be assured that the product is free of contaminants," though, so far, its tests hadn't found any. "The use of any product produced under unlicensed conditions poses serious potential public health risks as demonstrated by this lack of product consistency," wrote Randolph F. Wykoff, director of the FDA Office of AIDS Coordination, to Hodel. "We request, therefore, that you strongly encourage your customers who wish to take ddC to explore the options for obtaining legally produced ddC through the existing expanded access program or ongoing controlled clinical trials." That was the extent of the FDA's action.

The underground's own tests showed much less variation. New tests run on individual capsules by Corti at Truesdail Laboratories showed a variation of only from 76 percent to 160 percent of the intended dose, with most capsules much closer to the intended 0.25 milligram. In several tests ordered by the underground, no capsules approached either zero or 230 percent. Delaney, in a press release, noted that even the highest dose found by the FDA, an apparent aberration, didn't reach levels associated with serious side effects.

Still, it was an unacceptable performance. The relatively tiny quantities of ddC hadn't been adequately mixed with the filler to assure a uniform product.

Corti noted that in the suspect batch the libertarians' lab had substituted a generic filler for the name brand used previously.

Delaney said there was enough blame to go around. Corti had been away a lot. The laboratory had not warned Corti that the tests he had been ordering were inadequate for his purpose; the tests merely showed the average content of batches of capsules, rather than variations among individual capsules, which would have been revealed only by more exacting tests. Delaney himself had assured everyone that adequate tests were being run without educating himself on exactly what tests were desirable. And the buyers' clubs, which Corti had asked to be partners in the manufacturing process, and help with the testing, had ducked responsibility.

Delaney and others immediately began negotiating with Hoffmann-La Roche to increase the expanded-access program. The company agreed to open the program to all AIDS patients with a T-cell count under 300; it had been requiring a count under 200. Delaney was pushing the company to include everyone with a count of under 500. But he really believed the drug should be open to all, noting,

"Every drug that's worked in sicker patients has worked better in weller patients."

Ironically, the bad ddC batch received less publicity than it otherwise might have because reporters on the FDA beat were preoccupied with an erupting scandal over Dow Corning Corporation's silicone gel breast implants. Delaney was fond of pointing out that, unlike the breast implants, the bootleg ddC hadn't harmed anyone, and unlike Dow Corning, he and the buyers' clubs had supplied the FDA immediately with every scrap of information they had. Dow Corning was accused of withholding damaging information about its product for many years.

By March, when Hoffmann-La Roche was still keeping thousands of desirous ddC consumers off its expanded-access list, Corti resumed the manufacture of imported ddC, using yet another Orange County production center, and running product tests that he was persuaded were up to industry standards. The buyers' clubs were being instructed to do their own quality-control testing as well.

Derek Hodel of the New York club summed up what Delaney and Corti were also saying: "It is everyone's responsibility to quality control this, and we dropped the ball. Food and Drug's response was entirely appropriate and entirely professional. We've all acknowledged that the buyers' clubs are not equipped to have the same kind of quality control as Hoffmann-La Roche. We would be better off if we could get drugs from the drug companies. We have never said the buyers' clubs are how people should get their health care. It's a matter of desperation. This highlights how serious the problem is. I would hope that the powers that be learn from this experience as we have. I would hope that the need to take this risk doesn't come up again."

As this book was being sent to the printer, the FDA said it still hadn't found any evidence of impurities or other safety hazards in the bad batch of ddC, but was still testing.

Meanwhile, on April 21, 1992, an FDA advisory committee voted to recommend licensing ddC. Though the licensing would be only for use in combination with AZT, once the drug arrived in stores doctors could prescribe it as they and their patients thought best. Hoffmann-La Roche, the manufacturer, began talks with the FDA over when the drug would be approved and what the label would say. And while they talked, thousands of bottles of ddC were rolling off the line at Jim Corti's new lab so that patients who depended on the drug could stay supplied—illegally, but with the clear awareness of the FDA.

On April 25 and 26, 1992, at the Four Seasons Hotel in the George-town section of Washington, Project Inform gathered several dozen leading research scientists from around the world for a ground-break-ing off-the-record scientific meeting to try to shift the focus of re-search to a promising new area. Studies were continuing on ways to control HIV. But Delaney had decided that more attention should be paid to fighting the disease from the opposite direction.

A leading French scientist, Jean-Claude Chermann, was trying to restore the immune systems of persons infected with the virus. If T-cells could be replenished as fast as they were killed, maybe peo-ple could live with HIV and not get AIDS.

In 1984, Chermann, working at the Pasteur Institute in Paris, had helped isolate the AIDS virus; it was that virus that Luc Montagnier, the institute's administrator, claimed was then stolen by Robert Gallo at the National Cancer Institute in Maryland. Now, at the University of Luminy near Marseilles, Chermann was working with thymic hu-moral factor, a drug that might pick up the work of the thymic hor-mones that promote T-cell growth. And, Delaney reasoned, there were other scientists with similar ideas.

So, after talking it over with Fauci and Gallo, Delaney convened a conference without the usual formal presentations and press cover-age. He prepared and mailed out several pages of questions that could be batted about informally: what progress was being made and what obstacles were being encountered in the development of vac-cines, gene therapy, bone marrow and thymus transplantation, and so on.

Chermann and some French colleagues flew in. Fauci and Gallo attended. So did Jonas Salk, Tom Merigan, and other researchers from universities and nonprofit institutes, from as far away as Aus-tralia and Italy. Including Gallo and Fauci, thirteen senior scientists showed up from NIH, the Army and the Department of Veterans Affairs. Half a dozen drug company representatives attended—in-cluding Ellen Cooper, who was now working for Syntex, the com-pany whose drug Gancyclovir was at first rejected and then, after Delaney and others yelled, approved by an advisory committee Cooper worked with at the FDA.

The Project Inform conference was praised by participants, in-cluding those from the NIH. But, as usual, Delaney wasn't relying just on talk. Unbeknown to most attendees at the conference, another secret drug trial was going on without the FDA's approval. With Chermann's cooperation, Corti and Delaney had obtained some thymic humoral factor in France and smuggled it into California.

There, some patients they lined up began taking the drug as an arm of the French study.

Before making the drug available, Chermann had insisted on going to California to set up testing standards compatible with those he was administering in France, and Delaney committed himself to supplying research data according to the French protocol. He smiled at the idea that the lab work for the study was being done by workers at a branch of the University of California Medical School, though the research leaders at the school weren't told of it.

As this book goes to the printer, the operation is still a secret. By the time the book is published, Delaney and Corti hope to have some handle on whether, and how well, Chermann's new drug works.

AN AFTERWORD BY
MARTIN DELANEY

*T*hroughout its development, author and subjects alike struggled with the inherent limitations of what could be said in any book of this type. In fairness to the many people whose contributions are not chronicled here, it might be best to think of this book in terms of what it is and what it is not. *Acceptable Risks* is but the story of two of the many people who fought this epidemic. It is not a broad history of the period, of the changes in federal drug regulation, or even of the movement of people with AIDS fighting for their rights.

No story of the fight for change in FDA regulatory policy or AIDS research policy is complete without acknowledgment of the contributions made by a band of pioneers operating under the banner of Act Up. Although Act Up universally provided the muscle of our movement, a small subset of the group also fought at the negotiating tables and in the offices of researchers and government officials. Beginning in 1988 much of the work attributed to myself herein was accompanied by similar activity, sometimes coordinated, sometimes independent, by the Act Up New York Treatment and Data committee, most often spoken for by Jim Eigo, Mark Harrington, David Barr, and Peter Staley. In later years, "T & D" groups evolved in Act Up chapters elsewhere, such as Act Up Golden Gate, Boston, and San Francisco, and made their own contributions. Other books in development will chronicle the details of this important, related work.

Similarly, this book is not the tale of the overall works of my own organization, Project Inform, which on its own became a powerhouse of AIDS education, activism, and research. Carol Adams, too often assumed to be my secretary, is in fact the heart of the group's administration, while its financial growth and integrity have been ably attended to by Bob Elkins. A dozen or so other staffers and literally hundreds of deeply committed volunteers rounded out the team. Without their willingness and ability to run and expand the home office and to serve the needs of nearly 100,000 constituents, I would have been unable to do much of the work described in *Acceptable Risks*.

Finally, both Jim Corti and I must acknowledge the incredible work of so many individual patients and their lovers, friends, and families, and others in our community who are no longer with us. This book only hints at their strength, compassion, and ingenuity. With few exceptions, this community has acted in an amazingly self-less and giving manner, putting community needs ahead of personal ones. No book could adequately tell this tale. I believe history will one day note that the giving and caring by the gay community, and by its straight supporters, during this time of crisis is without precedence.

—Martin Delaney

AN AFTERWORD BY
THE AUTHOR

This book is the story of Jim Corti and Martin Delaney, based on what they told me and what I have learned from other interviews and research. Thus, in some important respects, it is a joint undertaking, and Corti and Delaney between them will share 40 percent of the proceeds. They have reviewed the manuscript, but I am, under our agreement, the final arbiter of its content.

In going back over their stories with other participants, even their occasional enemies, I found their accounts consistently trustworthy except for the kind of occasional detail almost everybody would stumble over, and surprisingly little of that. The gist of what they said was consistently confirmed by a consensus of other observers, with only rare exceptions that are noted in the text and explained in the notes.

Obviously it was impractical or impossible to corroborate everything they said. For some events, they were the only living witnesses. Generally, under the circumstances, I felt I could rely enough on their accounts not to clutter the book with attributions for statements based on the word of two people who are effectively colleagues as well as sources.

For parts of the story I thought might be particularly contentious, however, I have called on my own research. For example, in writing the scene in which Delaney discovers the Dingell Committee's perfidy on ribavirin, I did not rely on Delaney's memory for details but independently obtained the document package he received, interviewed many of the persons whose names were in the documents, and wrote from that. What appears are not allegations by Delaney, but fact that I am satisfied is documented, and which I would report anywhere independent of Delaney. In many cases such as this, I found the story of Delaney and Corti to be an entertaining (I hope) vehicle for reporting what seemed to me to be good news stories.

Readers, I notice from the best-seller lists, seem to favor having dialogue set forth explicitly, even though it was spoken years ago and nothing but the fallible device of human memory was there to record it. In this book, much more than in any previous nonfiction book of mine, I have undertaken to cater to this reader preference for detailed dialogue. To help, I have often used the exact words people spoke to me in interviews in 1990 and 1991 as the best guide to words the same people said when trying to make the same points in other situations in years past. I have tried to reach participants in the recounted conversations and confirm the words spoken. At times I have negotiated consensus versions when memories produced minor differences. I have also made some wording deletions in quoted material—for example, changing "has been in a semicomatose condition" to "has been semicomatose"—but never to change meaning.

For further convenience in telling, I have sometimes taken incidents or conversations that were told me separately concerning the same approximate time and put them into a single scene. While everything portrayed actually happened, it is possible, for example, that incidents portrayed on one smuggling trip in this book actually happened to the same people on two different smuggling trips at about the same time. But since there are neither records nor memories of precise dates, and since there is no effort to mislead and every effort for simplicity of telling, this seemed the best way to handle it.

I have bowed to the request of Martin Delaney's lover that a pseudonym be used to protect his acting career, and he is known here as Mark Bradley. In other places, all noted, I have used pseudonyms to protect people who were engaged in lifesaving work, but who could still be prosecuted for the illegal nature of their activities.

With these stipulations, all persons, dialogue, and events in this book are real; the scenes happened in the sequence described, and reflect what the participants were doing and saying according to the best available evidence. Where I found disputes, I have stated them in the text and notes.

Because of the current state of libel law I have reluctantly decided to omit certain information. I have learned from experience that while accuracy and adherence to professional journalistic standards still affords some protection under the law, for a freelance this protection is not nearly enough. I have faced litigation in a multitude of courts for years over a single matter, which I cannot describe here for fear of provoking still more lawsuits. That numerous judges have dismissed the libel claims and none has challenged the accuracy of my work, has not stemmed the flow of new litigation that has to be defended.

The courts also decided that a previously unpublished historical document, which I obtained through an intermediary from the files of former CIA Director Allen Dulles and quoted from extensively, was subject to copyright protection and that I therefore violated the copyright by quoting from it in a 1984 book. I was ordered to allocate to the document's author 2.6 percent of profits from future sales of the book, but his attempt to enjoin the book was denied. Still, I was unable to circulate the book for years while the case was being decided.

When a journalist or historian, though confident of his facts, is haunted by the specter of litigation and feels compelled to omit a name here and there, to paraphrase when he could quote, or to be general when he could be specific, he risks misleading the reader. Unfortunately, that is a lesser evil than the thought of years of litigation. The public's need for good journalism is ill served when lawyers become a bigger part of the process than editors, and that is now the case. The system ought to be changed.

I owe a special debt to John S. James, author of *AIDS Treatment News*, a bound volume of which was invaluable in keeping straight the names of various drugs and the diseases they are aimed at.

I have already thanked Ellen Sackstein for her help in editing the manuscript. Others who contributed valuable suggestions include Ellen Levine, Fonda Duvanel, Ann Patty, Alice Barstow, Elizabeth McNamara, and a research physician at a major teaching hospital who has asked not to be identified but whose many donated hours were an important help to this book and are greatly appreciated.

An enormous debt is owed to Arthur Eisenberg of the New York Civil Liberties Union and a group of lawyers he has helped assemble whom I have heard refer to themselves as the Kwitny Bar Association. Although their work didn't concern this book, without their help in defending lawsuits relating to other matters I doubt I would have been able to write it. Among them are Hariette Dorsen; Kenneth Norwick of Norwick & Schad; Steven Krane, Peter Falkenstein and James M. Strauss of Proskauer, Rose, Goetz and Mendelsohn; Earl Ward of the New York Civil Liberties Union; Arthur Amron of Debevoise & Plimpton; and last—only because they alone are getting paid in full for their efforts—John Lankenau and Rob Balin of Lankenau, Kovner & Bickford. They get not only my deepest thanks but a certified exemption from every lawyer joke I've ever told.

Judges may not think it's right to thank them for their decisions, since they are presumably following the law and doing no favors. Nevertheless, I feel gratitude toward the following men and herewith express it: U.S. District Judge Richard Owen; Judge John G.

McCarthy of the New York State Supreme Court, Suffolk County; U.S. District Judge Raymond J. Dearie; U.S. Circuit judges Lawrence W. Pierce and J. Daniel Mahoney; U.S. District Judge Charles M. Metzner sitting on the Second Circuit Court of Appeals; and the judge in Kings County Criminal Court who spoke his wisdom so fast I didn't even get his name, but who decided that my utterances, which the other judges ruled weren't libelous, also weren't criminal.

Thanks to Ron Bernstein for putting this deal together.

Thanks to my housekeeper, Kathleen Fish, for making a livable space to write, to my daughters Carolyn and Susanna Kwitny for the meaning they give to life, to Mark Malone for all the mileage I've run on the tennis court, and to Ellen Levine, Tony Scaduto, and Stephanie Trudeau for being such incredibly understanding friends.

And to Marty and Jim for the privilege of getting to know them.

Finally, I would like to answer a central question that there was no convenient place to answer in the telling of the story without imposing thoughts of my own on other people. It is the question Ellen Cooper raises when she suggests that people who support the right of patients and doctors to decide on treatments must therefore oppose the existence of the FDA, or any government effort to regulate drugs. This suggestion presents a dilemma between control and anarchy, a dilemma I have heard expounded by many persons on both sides of the issue. Some want to increase the FDA's power to rid the market of unsafe or unproven treatments; some say the FDA is a bureaucratic intruder and should be disposed of.

These attitudes overlook a distinction that seems to me so obvious that I cannot understand why more people don't see it. It is one thing for people to use the power of their government to make sure they are forewarned about the dangers that may lurk in some other people's plans to make money selling drugs. It is another thing for government to be able to tell us what we can or cannot do with that forewarning if we get sick.

I know of no more perfect example than the Dow Corning silicone breast implants described in the Postscript. Years passed before Dow Corning confessed, and the FDA publicized, the dangers of these implants. Considering what we now know, and considering the many women who had implants in ignorance, one could argue that in certain respects the FDA's powers, and budget, need to be increased. Yet now that the information is available, by what right does the FDA tell women and their doctors that they may not make a fully informed use of this treatment? For many women who might, all things being equal, prefer to have larger breasts, the surgery is now no longer worth the risk. Many women who have already had the surgery are justifiably angry that they weren't aware of the known, or knowable, dangers at the time. But for other women, who may face severe psychological or physical trauma, can anyone but they themselves best weigh the risk and benefit, so long as they can find a qualified physician who agrees and is willing to take responsibility?

Other cases in this book, such as that of ribavirin, are almost as clear. The doctor and patient, after full disclosure of available information, are best placed to decide what drug to use. One can imagine different cases: for example, does a woman have the right to risk her unborn fetus by taking Thalidomide in order to relieve relatively minor symptoms of her pregnancy? Even in that case, however, it is hard to imagine that very many women would want to take the Thalidomide.

The vast majority of cases seem subject to the general distinction I have made here. We need a strong, unbiased agency, empowered to compel disclosure, to probe for and broadcast the best current information on the benefits and dangers of available remedies, and to make sure medical remedies aren't misrepresented. The FDA is the institution in place to fulfill that function. But does that mean we have to tolerate a government agency that tells us what we can and cannot take to save our own lives? I cannot see why one requires the other.

NOTES

1. Eventually, four years later, he died anyway—three and a half years past his life expectancy when he began taking the drug. Of course, there were patients who didn't take ribavirin and who also lived beyond the six months. And there were men like Cahoj's lover, Randy Wendelin, who did take ribavirin and was still alive in the 1990s.

2. Quotes in this section are to everyone's best recollection; I have taken some wording from what Roh said to me in an interview in 1990, which he said also reflected his views at the time of the 1985 meeting. Roh says he can't recall exact words from that far back, but that he may have said exactly what Delaney and Boneberg recall his saying, or at least said words to that effect. A videotape of the meeting was made, but can't be located.

Roh told me that he may actually have been aware of ribavirin and isoprinosine at the time of the 1985 meeting, but publicly denied knowing of them because FDA policy forbade him to discuss them. Roh also said that he has been working quietly within the FDA for years to achieve some of the same policy changes Delaney has fought for publicly, and that this quiet approach has been effective in many areas. For years, while doing this, he said, he has been taunted by "AIDS vigilantes" who wait outside his FDA office and call him "a murderer" when he goes in or out.

Roh said in the 1990 interview that he had felt constrained from expressing his defense before Boneberg's audience—including that other FDA officers, who dealt with AIDS issues, had declined to come to the meeting, leaving Roh, reluctantly, to fill the breach. There is more about Roh later in the story.

3. Volberding told me this "doesn't sound like the kind of conversations I usually have with patients." He said he didn't recall the conversation or whether he had any conversation at all with Bradley before the study. Asked what, specifically, he disagreed with, he said only, "I would never have said ribavirin and isoprinosine were dangerous, toxic drugs," but "that they were probably not very active." In evaluating his response, the reader should consider the FDA audit of the suramin study, and Volberding's published reply to an article about the study, both of which are summarized later in this book.

4. Knight did not return numerous phone calls with detailed messages that these events would be described in this book. Rogalski, however, dug out Upchurch's records and read me his and Knight's entries, which provided a definitive source for this account. In defense of the earlier diagnosis of bronchitis, it is possible that Upchurch, hoping for the best, didn't disclose all his symptoms.

5. As noted, Knight didn't return my repeated phone calls. Weisman, interviewed in November 1990, said Upchurch had survived "one of the worst illnesses I've ever seen." He praised Corti and Delaney, saying, "I think they've done an incredible job of pushing the drug issue. I'm definitely fans of both of theirs."

6. In the *International Journal of Tissue Reaction.*

7. In the journal *Cancer Research.*

8. The young doctor supervising the trial told me in an interview, regarding the events of that day as recounted in the text, "I have absolutely no recollection of any of that. I know he [Bradley] has made those allegations. I don't believe that there's any substantiation for that. The patients on the study were followed quite closely by the physicians in the clinic. I find it unlikely that such a thing occurred. As far as remembering any of that, I can't at all. You're asking me things seven years after the fact."

The staff physician who examined Bradley and gave him hydrocortisone told me in an interview, "It's a lot of detail that I don't completely remember, but I guess the gist of it is correct." When I asked him how the blood results could have sat around for a month, he replied, "I don't have an answer for that. Some of the [blood samples] go to outside labs. The results sometimes come back to the doctors and sometimes don't. Sometimes they get directed to the data managers. I can't say when the results [of Bradley's prior blood test] came back. I don't know." When I said I wanted to eliminate any vagueness, and asked whether Bradley had complained that the delay had been a month, and whether there was a substantial possibility he was right, the doctor replied, "Yes, that's true." He said he had a clear recollection of Bradley's being highly upset.

9. I filed a Freedom of Information Act request with the FDA for any information about the suramin study. I learned that in the spring of 1986, before the results of the study were officially published, the Food and Drug Administration ordered a formal investigation of Dr. Volberding's handling of the study, based on a complaint from an unnamed subject. The FDA's summary of findings from that investigation run five paragraphs. The first four merely detail the methods the FDA followed in the investigation. The fifth paragraph says, in full:

> Several deviations from the protocol for the Suramin study were noted and discussed with Dr. Volberding and staff on 4/17/86. Objectionable conditions noted included the failure to revise the consent form to reflect amended protocol of 8/8/85; failure to determine the [blood] serum levels of the drug as specified by the protocol, change in the drug treatment schedule for patients without documentation or explanation of the change and failure to follow the toxicity grade levels as explained in the protocol. Five patients were administered increased doses of the test article prior to signing the revised consent form.

Beneath the summary is the following finding, in full:

> As a result of the inspectional observations noted during the data audit for the Suramin study, it appears appropriate that a letter issue from the Office of Drugs to the clinical investigator regarding the deviations from the protocol for the study.

In the many detailed pages that follow, this sentence appears:

> Although several deviations were noted as related to the Suramin study, Dr. Volberding's performance as related to clinical studies on investigational drugs appears to be adequate.

The suramin study was written up by Dr. Volberding, his young prodigy, and eight others in the March 23, 1987, issue of *The American Journal of Medicine*. The writeup covered not only the San Francisco General group, but eighteen other men who were given the drug at other hospitals. In standard scientific fashion, the writeup includes a summary, which says in full:

Forty-one homosexual men with the acquired immune deficiency syndrome (AIDS) or AIDS-related complex were treated with 0.5, 1.0, or 1.5 g of suramin weekly for up to six months. In no patient evidence of symptomatic improvement or regression of Kaposi's sarcoma shown. Opportunistic infections developed in 16 patients during therapy. Only six patients (15 percent) became human immunodeficiency virus (HIV) culture-negative during treatment, despite documentation of adequate serum suramin levels. All but one of these six have had disease progression. Decreases in the numbers of total T4 cells with time were observed in both AIDS and AIDS-related complex subgroups. Toxicity was significant and consisted of fatigue, fever and hepatic and renal dysfunction, all of which were observed most frequently with the 1.0 or 1.5 g dosages. Fatal hepatic failure developed in two patients, and adrenal insufficiency was documented in eight patients. Suramin is a toxic agent that shows no virologic, immunologic or clinical benefit in patients with HIV-related disease.

Drs. Volberding and Abrams and a colleague defended the study in a letter published in *San Francisco Magazine* in 1988. They were responding to an article in the magazine that had criticized the study. Their letter said:

In using experimental drugs in a new disease such as AIDS, one of the most important considerations is to observe the patients very carefully for side effects which are either unusual or unusually severe in nature. This was done in the Suramin trial and when it became apparent that the toxicities were unacceptable, the trial was stopped. The Suramin study is an example of how a clinical trial should be conducted. Trials such as this one, which document drug toxicity in a small number of patients, prevent potentially harmful drugs from being distributed to large numbers of patients in the community. Quite in contrast to the impression in the [magazine] article that this trial was flawed in design, we consider it, in fact, to be a model that should be followed as we test other new drugs.

The suramin research group's lengthy reply didn't mention that the FDA had sent the writers a letter rebuking the study for "deviations from the protocol" and " objectionable conditions," following an investigation the FDA had initiated because of a complaint about the study. To the contrary, the doctors told the public, "The Suramin study was one of several clinical trials audited in the course of a routine FDA inspection. It is also a matter of public record that the study easily passed that audit. The implication that the Suramin trial was improperly conducted or poorly managed has no basis in fact."

Volberding's statement to the public appears untrue, based on the FDA audit document, then private, which I have since obtained.

The conversations here between Volberding and Bradley are based on

Bradley's recollection, and Delaney's recollection of what Bradley told him immediately after the conversations. When I interviewed Volberding, he said the conversation with Bradley "doesn't sound like me. None of this sounds at all reminiscent of any conversation I've had." But when I tried to go point by point, beginning with whether Bradley had suffered adrenal failure, Volberding said he didn't want to talk to me anymore and asked that Delaney call him. He added, "That's all, thanks," and hung up. I advised Delaney of this; Delaney tells me he has approached Volberding several times to discuss the issues, but that Volberding never seemed interested.

Certain AIDS-associated infections—CMV retinitis and tuberculosis—can cause adrenal damage. Bradley did not suffer those or any other AIDS-associated infections. It's unknown if any other suramin trial subject who suffered adrenal damage contracted these infections, but it's unlikely they all did.

The young doctor referred to in the text told me, "The original warning of adrenal damage was not a major concern of ours because it had occurred only in some animals, not others, and never in humans. But it was noticed at the end, and the study was brought to a quick halt after that."

The wording of the published findings of the suramin study leaves the door open a crack on the number and cause of deaths. The most straightforward interpretation, it seems to me, is that at least two people died from liver failure brought on by the drug, and that other patients' deaths also may have been caused by, or speeded by, the drug. Delaney and Bradley insist that at least five patients died directly from the suramin, and the 1988 magazine article certainly suggests there were more than two.

The young doctor who supervised the study continues to assert to me that "it is not clear at all that anyone treated with suramin died as a direct result of the drug." He says the two hepatic deaths referred to in the study results involved patients who had liver disease before entering the study. Regarding the apparent untruths in the letter that he, Volberding, and others signed, he says the FDA told him its investigation of the study was routine rather than for-cause, and that "the reprimands were reprimands that occur in the course of clinical trials. The FDA investigators felt that those weren't complaints that warranted any other action than to point out the issues at hand."

10. Five years later, in 1991, the use of steroids in PCP treatment became an official government recommendation.

11. The doctor in question absolutely denies talking about an HTLV-3 license plate, or hearing anyone else do so. Gramatikos, whom I found to be generally reliable, is just as absolute in asserting her detailed memory of the incident. The virus was later renamed HIV.

12. In a telephone interview January 18, 1991, Michael Gottlieb absolutely denied ever comparing Scolaro to a voodoo priest, or making any other such disparaging remark about Scolaro. He did, however, criticize Scolaro for talking to the press about the ribavirin clinical-trial proposal. Gottlieb said ribavirin had always been a low-priority drug, and at the time of Scolaro's intended study "was already looking like an inactive antiviral." He made other disparaging remarks about ribavirin and isoprinosine.

Gottlieb said that he was a member of a large committee that decided on AmFAR grants, and that he had only one vote on the committee, the same as every other member. He said he did not remember Scolaro's specific grant application.

Scolaro, Gramatikos, and Corti each volunteered to me, in independent interviews, the story about the "voodoo priest" remark. They recalled other patients who chose to see both Scolaro and Gottlieb who reported that Gottlieb had strongly criticized Scolaro and said he had no business treating patients for AIDS. Scolaro said he later encountered Mathilde Krim, co-leader with Gottlieb of AmFAR, at a social function. He said she was nice to him and encouraged him to apply to the organization for financial help on a future project.

13. Rigler did not return my telephone messages. His secretary, Joe Medina, told me January 18, 1991, that he remembered Scolaro's proposal's being turned down. "Perhaps Mr. Rigler didn't feel like helping," he said.

Michael Gottlieb told me, "Lloyd occasionally sought my counsel on AIDS issues," but said he couldn't remember the Scolaro proposal.

14. To this day he remains so convinced. Isoprinosine seemed to work because this particular kind of encephalitis was brought on by immune deficiency caused by a prior disease. Even if the results of the study were controversial, it is worth remembering that isoprinosine, in widespread use in many countries, has been shown to have no serious side effects. While the FDA might not be satisfied by Glasky's proof of efficacy, the question remained that if the drug *might* work on a serious disease—just as with AIDS—why not try it?

15. The exact words here are Glasky's to me in a January 1991 interview.

16. In a 1991 interview, Abrams said he couldn't remember exactly what he had said at the meeting Conant arranged, but that he had changed his views considerably in the meantime. "I was young then," he said. "I thought I knew everything. A lot of us have since modified our positions."

Abrams also said that his views at the Conant meeting were influenced by an episode he had not talked about publicly prior to my interview with him. A few months before the Conant meeting, in the fall of 1985, Abrams said, he had been asked by ICN, the manufacturer of ribavirin, to visit the ICN office. He said ICN officials took him there after a speech he gave in Los Angeles. He said they had asked him there to advise them on a protocol for a study of ribavirin, but instead solicited him to buy the drug to sell to his patients. He said he denounced that on the spot as unethical, and ever afterward remained highly suspicious of the company.

When I asked ICN about this, a spokesman replied, "The company told Dr. Abrams that if he had AIDS patients, ICN would give him the drug for free under a compassionate IND [an FDA-approved means of distributing a drug still under testing], in exchange for medical data [on how the patients reacted to the drug]. Dr. Abrams declined. All matters involving Abrams were fully investigated by the Justice Department and the FDA."

In our 1991 interview, Abrams expressed admiration for much of Martin Delaney's work. Abrams will reappear in the story.

17. In an interview on July 17, 1991, most of which Delaney attended, Johnson generally confirmed the accuracy of what Delaney remembered while urging that it be toned down for publication. Asked if he had a problem with the account of the conversation printed here, he replied jokingly, "My lawyers might." Asked if it was factual, he generally confirmed it,

finally adding, "I don't remember saying 'sons of bitches.' " But Delaney remembered it and Johnson didn't deny it.

18. Brokaw's intended involvement appears to have been a false rumor. Delaney could never find out where it started, but made the most of it in negotiations with ICN.

19. To satisfy those who contributed funds, Brewer and an employee, Bill Woods, eventually produced a retrospective study of about 150 patients. But by Brewer's own account, "We weren't finding out anything significant. By the time the study was done, it was old news."

20. Abrams told me in 1991 that he didn't remember the degree of sickness of the patients in the study, but that in general he was in charge of caring for early-stage patients and so he probably chose them for the study.

21. Dr. Young told me in an interview that his son's injury was not a factor in the evaluation of ribavirin.

22. Volberding says the statement about earning part of his living from drug-company grants is correct as it applies to him. Abrams says that unlike many other researchers, he arranges his grants so that none of his own salary is ever paid for by drug companies. "I'm funded by the University of California, San Francisco," he says. But he acknowledges that grants from drug companies and other private support groups go to the university to pay the costs of the studies that have occupied much of his work time. The drug companies pay for the patients' care, lab work, nursing staff, and other costs, allowing the studies to take place.

He explains: "I don't think patients should be paying for research on drugs that have no known efficacy. It's very unusual that a university can pay somebody a hundred percent of their salary, so professors have to be responsible for getting grants. My salary comes 50 percent from NIH [the National Institutes of Health]. My salary comes from a conglomerate of various funds. I personally have never felt comfortable having my salary subsidized by a drug company." But, he says, "some of my colleagues support portions of their salary" by charging off time spent to drug company grants.

23. I found no further reference anywhere to such side effects, or to an ICN cover-up of them. As the reader will see from what follows, there must have been no evidence to support these anonymous allegations, because the committee went after ICN vigorously at every opportunity. The FDA never withdrew its approval for use of aerosol ribavirin in sick babies. The allegation of dangerous side effects appears to have been so wildly untrue as to suggest the source may even have fabricated it to try to torpedo ICN in the press behind a shield of anonymity, when the company wasn't around to defend itself. Like much else in this section, it is a cautionary tale for editors; government sources can lie just as other sources can.

24. Levi said in an interview February 19, 1991, that he preferred not to try to recount the conversation, and doesn't "have a lot of faith in [his] recollection. I'm perfectly willing to let you have just Martin's version of all this. My position has moved since 1987. I'll be honest with you. I do not want to reopen those old wounds," he said.

25. Weiss's aide Patsy Fleming says she doesn't know exactly why the hearings were held, and that the staff member in charge has departed. But she emphasizes that Weiss was always very interested in maintaining FDA standards, and that he has since changed his position regarding the use of

experimental drugs in cases of AIDS and other life-threatening illnesses; he now strongly supports such use, Fleming says.

26. During a telephone interview June 8, 1991, I asked Bihari if he had investigated before testifying. He said he hadn't. When I told him about the price agreement and the peso collapse, he said, "That sounds like a good cover story to me. I don't know anything about that. This is the first time I heard." Dr. Bihari will reemerge later in our story.

When I questioned Dingell's staff, April 8, 1991, I was told by an aide that the person in charge of those hearings, Patrick McLain, was no longer working for the congressman, and that people now on staff didn't remember them. I was advised to call McLain at his private law office. Told about the contradictions to Bihari's testimony, he said, "His testimony was under oath. He can speak for himself." Asked if he would comment about apparently unfair representations of the ribavirin trials presented by other witnesses, he said, "No." Asked why ICN wasn't allowed to defend itself at the hearings, he said, "I do not have a perfect recollection whether we discussed with the company their interest in testifying. It is not routine to have every party that might have some interest in a particular issue testify before the committee." Asked if he wanted to make any other comments, he said, "I am perfectly comfortable in the regularity and the responsibility with which the subcommittee conducted those hearings."

27. Mansell tried in our interviews to belittle the incident. He said the institute was eventually closed because it was losing money, not because of the ribavirin episode. But he also said Anderson hospital transferred him to oncological work and wouldn't allow him to see AIDS patients. He left, and for a long time was out of work. See later in the text for what finally happened.

28. The words are as he spoke them to me in interviews in 1991, and presumably a fair reflection of the similar remarks he made to Delaney on the same topic in 1987. In fairness to Cooper, she didn't accuse Heseltine of actually falsifying the data, she just said he may have falsified it. But from his perspective, considering that it was sworn testimony before Congress with full news coverage, the loss of distinction seems easy to understand.

29. Mr. Dodds didn't return my many phone calls, either—even after I left detailed messages with aides about what Delaney had said. Eventually, I called the bank's public-relations department for a corporate response, and was told, after the question was researched for five days, "It's absolutely not true that Martin Delaney was not hired for reasons due to his homosexuality. He was using the consultative selling approach, and we made a policy change within the bank to go to a more aggressive approach." When I asked, I was told that consultative "is a softer approach to selling, that basically involves getting to know your client." Also, I was told, the bank decided "to go to local trainers for reasons of cost." When I asked if that was why Dodds wouldn't even return Delaney's phone calls, I was told, "I don't know."

30. The firm was Finley, Kumble, Wagner, Heine, Underberg, Manley, Myerson & Casey, which later broke up amidst charges of misconduct. But the firm had many reputable clients, and I found no reason to be suspicious of the work done in the ribavirin case.

31. Dr. Young says the reports of the various statisticians and investigator Williamson were "all reviewed by the FDA." He says decisions about such

matters "are not made by the commissioner," but, in this case, by Dr. Cooper and her direct superior. "The reaction of the agency is public record," he says, though he acknowledges that the "only comments made publicly were at the Dingell hearing." He says it would "not be appropriate" for him to comment further on the matter.

Dr. Cooper says, "My recollection is that the final data on the ARC study was not in" when the Dingell hearing was held in May 1987, just one week before the data was presented publicly at the International Conference on AIDS; but she acknowledges, "I honestly forget when they got the ARC study in." She adds that "all that bringing in of outside consultants didn't come in until after" the Dingell hearing. "We didn't ignore anything that was submitted," she says. "It's just that they did not cause us to change our position. I think the statisticians were just addressing the issue in the LAS [swollen lymph glands] study about more patients having been assigned to the placebo group. We reread them and took them into account. There wasn't enough of a change to change the overall assessment of the drug. It doesn't mean that the statisticians' letters were wrong," she says, but that the fate of the drug was determined by more than "just the statistical questions."

As for the letters and data supportive of ribavirin that were sent to the FDA before the Dingell hearing, she says, "It's very difficult for anyone at the agency to reiterate five years later everything that goes into an overall judgment." She says, "It's very unlikely that any data on ribavirin would have been submitted that I would not have seen," and that Dr. Young "would have been aware of" it, too. Of the testimonial letters from impartial academic medical authorities, she says, "That's not data, that's interpretation. We were aware that the company, and at some point their consultants, the statisticians and others, we were aware that the arguments they were making were different from the ones we were making. Our position didn't change. It's not to say there's never a difference of opinion. If another group of people looked at the same data the agency looked at, they might have [had] a different opinion. That doesn't mean one was right and the other wrong."

In general, Dr. Cooper emphasizes that public statements by her and Dr. Young about the ribavirin studies were hedged. "If the issue is whether the ARC data showed that ribavirin caused death, you couldn't make that conclusion. We certainly didn't come to the conclusion that it caused death," she says. Regarding Dr. Mansell, the Houston researcher, she says, "The FDA to my knowledge never said that Mansell did fool with the assignment [of patients in the study] or bias the results. What we were talking about was, 'What's the likelihood of that [the assignment of patients] happening by chance alone?' And the FDA statistician gave those statistics that it was unlikely. I would certainly agree that there was no evidence that Mansell did anything wrong. What was discussed at the May hearings was, 'What's the likelihood?' "

I asked if there wasn't unfairness in the mere raising of the possibility that ribavirin caused death, and that a medical researcher had committed fraud to promote a phony AIDS treatment, in testimony during public hearings before Congress, without giving the company or the researcher a chance to respond, considering that it led to widely printed and televised news items disparaging the drug and the researcher. She replied, "You know how the news media does. They take a statement that says it may be, and they say it causes something. I think that's just a lack of sophistication about the interpretation of data."

I asked if, in retrospect, Dr. Mansell wasn't owed some statement by the FDA that its investigation had vindicated him. "I would not be opposed to that," she said. "I don't know that a request ever came in that that be done. The agency is generally so busy with things, it's unlikely that would have happened without it's being called to our attention."

She also said that more recent studies had vindicated her conclusion that ribavirin isn't effective. Asked which studies, she cited a Spanish study. Asked for specifics about it, she said, "We didn't see any of the actual results," but that it showed no evidence of efficacy—"at least that's what we've heard." Other scientists, including the head of the FDA office that supervises drug study protocols, have said the opposite; more information about ribavirin's effectiveness will be presented later in this book.

32. Congressman Lent's office says, "He based what he said on information provided for him by the FDA, and he believes he should be able to rely on what it said." Lent's spokesman said that the FDA reasserted its position in a communication to another member of Congress, which Lent was given a copy of, in August 1987; that would be after the FDA had received the full documentation from its own investigator and from ICN's outside consultants. I asked to see a copy of this communication, but Lent's office refused to supply it, giving no reason except that I couldn't force the congressman to turn it over because the Freedom of Information Act doesn't apply to Congress.

Congressman Wyden's office says its failure to respond to Delaney's pleas "is not unusual in the least. We oftentimes don't respond to constituents outside our district," which is in Oregon.

33. Lyphomed said it had to raise the price to recover the cost of trials to prove to the FDA that the drug worked as a preventive. The original cost of licensing the drug as a treatment had been unusually low because pentamidine had started out as an orphan drug—a drug the government developed that worked against a disease so rare that special encouragements were needed to make production profitable for a private company. The staff of Congresswoman Nancy Pelosi investigated the price increase, and came away satisfied that Lyphomed's explanation was correct.

Still, it's worth noting that in the case of pentamidine, as with Burroughs Wellcome's AZT, an unintended effect of the Orphan Drug Act gave a legal bonanza to a drug manufacturer. PCP, like AIDS itself, was a rare disease at the very beginning of the epidemic, and so drugs against it qualified for subsidies. But authorities knew that the disease was spreading exponentially, and that there would soon be a mass market for the drug.

34. While not specifically denying this remark, Young told me in a telephone interview that the decision to weaken his original proposal had been influenced by many sectors, but mostly the congressional committee led by Representative Ted Weiss, the consumer-protection advocate from New York. Young said he had come to Washington "looking for ways to get drugs to the desperately ill more expeditiously. It was a major part of my agenda, and Martin [Delaney] became an interesting ally. Where it really changed

was the Weiss hearing. We were beat around the head and shoulders pretty badly. If I were to point to one thing that swung it, it was the Weiss hearing."

35. These words are from a verbatim account Delaney gave me of the conversation. He said he remembered certain phrases like "only you can play in the club" precisely. Walsh said he remembered talking to Delaney, but not the contents of the conversation. When I read Walsh the quote "That's not the way the government works," he replied, "That sounds like something I would say." And he agreed that his old friend Frank Young sometimes called him for "guidance and advice" on FDA matters, maybe including Treatment IND. But when I read Walsh the rest of the conversation as Delaney recalled it, he stoutly denied blaming the big drug companies. He said he could prove, by correspondence, that the Pharmaceutical Manufacturers Association had supported Treatment IND. But when he found the correspondence, it turned out to be about a different issue more than a year later. He then said he had "no idea" why the regulation had been changed in 1987, but that he thought the manufacturers would have supported Treatment IND.

Hearing that, Delaney adamantly reaffirmed his original account. Because the companies later disparaged a similar plan (parallel track) while paying lip service to the need to spread experimental drugs to patients, I suspect that in private they may well have taken the position on Treatment IND that Delaney describes.

36. In my phone interview with him March 8, 1991, Schwemmer told me, "Martin's a pretty good guy. I would like to be portrayed as a typical Washington bureaucrat, someone who was just trying to do my job. Some people thought I tried to bend the rules. I don't want to be portrayed that way."

37. Delaney and another member of the committee, Terry Beswick, say Abrams repeatedly contended that popular use of the drug would interfere with his study. Abrams told me the study was fully enrolled and so he hadn't been worried about protecting it. But he also volunteered that at least one test subject had increased his dosage with dextran bought on the street, and that this was a problem. He agrees he spoke out frequently for years against the lay use of drugs not approved by the FDA.

In my interview with Abrams in his office March 5, 1991, he said his study had indeed been "caused by political pressure." He gave this account of his involvement with dextran sulfate:

After attending an AIDS conference in Paris in 1987, he had flown to Japan for another meeting, where he was introduced to people from Ueno Fine Chemicals. They told him of their positive results with dextran sulfate in vitro, and said the results had been duplicated by Broder at NIH. Abrams said he would do a phase one trial. The trial was delayed for several reasons, he said—because of a disagreement over whether the dose should be oral or intravenous, because AZT seemed to be a preferred drug, and because Abrams found NIH "not interested" in dextran. When the trial finally took place, Abrams reported that dextran showed little or no effect, which he attributed to the drug's propensity to break down into sugar so quickly that it didn't stay in the body. Just when he was ready to drop it, however, he told me, community support for the drug swelled and NIH responded by urging him to do a phase two trial.

38. When I asked Abrams if he had told the Japanese to stop selling dex-

tran sulfate to Americans who weren't part of his FDA-approved study, he said, "I didn't have to speak to the Japanese. They were very well aware of it. It gets me very discouraged and depressed to see people investing so much time and money in something [dextran sulfate] we really don't know anything about." I repeated the question, suggesting a clear-cut yes or no. He replied, "I don't remember if there's something I've said that could have had such an impact. I'm not sure."

39. Richman says he prescribed the Fansidar at Jefferson's own request, and tried to discourage Jefferson from using it. "This hasn't ever been discussed in public because I was accused of murdering him," Richman says. "He requested it after reading all the literature, and I thought it was a reasonable thing and I approved it. I prescribed many of the things he requested after discussions with him. He was a very knowledgeable, intelligent person, as knowledgeable as anybody. He's the only patient I ever prescribed Fansidar for. I remember he said this is what he wanted, and I remember trying to discourage him."

Delaney says that if Jefferson requested Fansidar, it was only because Richman wouldn't give him aerosol pentamidine. He says Jefferson told him often that pentamidine was the drug he sought, and that he was angry he couldn't get it in San Diego.

When I asked Richman whether Jefferson had requested pentamidine, he replied, "You're asking me for details. My memory is that this [Fansidar] is what he wanted." When I pressed Richman on whether he would have been willing to prescribe pentamidine if Jefferson had asked for it as his first choice, he said, "I can't remember." At some point, he said, the hospital did begin using aerosol pentamidine, but he wasn't sure when. "I don't remember those details," he said.

His memory cleared, though, on another matter. Saying it had been "painful" to hear repeated public statements blaming him for Jefferson's death, he said, "He was killed by his friends as far as I'm concerned. He was taken out of the hospital against medical advice, dragged out by some friends who accused us of murdering him when he was in the early stages of treatment for a treatable disease. The accusation was he was not allowed to die in dignity" in the hospital.

Delaney says he learned after Jefferson died that some friends in San Diego had removed him from the hospital at his own request after he was told he would have to go on artificial life-support systems. Delaney says he was told that Jefferson himself had determined his case was hopeless.

40. Richman says they were each asked to give prepared remarks, and he did. As to any failure to respond to Delaney's points, Richman told me, "He's just a very good debater." When I asked about the specific contents of his remarks as Delaney related them, he sent me a copy of his remarks published in *The Journal of Infectious Diseases*. There isn't any mention of Laetrile or Thalidomide in the published remarks, but Delaney says Richman talked about them in front of the audience.

41. "David Chan" is a pseudonym, for reasons that will become obvious later.

42. Since dextran sulfate was a blood thinner, the Johns Hopkins researcher checked for its presence in the body by measuring bleeding time after one dose against bleeding time before the dose. But Delaney reasoned

the drug took multiple doses to work. Later, Levin ran his own blood tests, vindicating Delaney's theory.

43. I confess he struck me similarly in my phone conversation with him February 15, 1991, as I tried to get his version of the events Corti had described to me. At first, Sergios said he wouldn't talk, because he was working on a book of his own about these events. Then he said he would cooperate with me if I supplied a notarized statement guaranteeing him the right to review the galleys for this book—start to finish—before I could publish it. When I said this would be impossible, he said he trusted Corti but didn't trust Delaney, and wanted to know more about me. He said he was interested only in "historical autobiographies" and wanted to know "how many historical autobiographies" I had written. When I listed my previous publishing history, he said he would consult his attorney about how to proceed, then call me back. He never did.

44. Fleming told me July 12, 1991, that she didn't remember the details of the conversation, but that she would never have told Delaney he couldn't speak to Representative Weiss. "It isn't possible to do a hearing on every issue that comes up," she said, adding, "Approval of ganciclovir should have been made much earlier. It affected many, many people."

Delaney replies that he has tried many times to speak directly to Weiss, and has always been cut off by the staff.

45. Cooper says the gist of the conversation recounted here "is basically accurate," but emphasizes that she wouldn't have said the advisory committee had made a mistake. "Most of these things, it's not right or wrong," she says. "It's a matter of judgment at the time. I'm pretty careful not to say somebody was wrong on a matter of judgment." But, she notes, "we don't have tapes of that conversation. I don't want to get into some kind of battle over whether I did or did not use this word."

46. Eventually, the government itself lowered the recommended dosage to 500 milligrams a day, reducing Burroughs Wellcome's sales income, and also curtailing the ability of uninsured patients to get insurance-subsidized treatment.

47. McGrath, whom I interviewed repeatedly in 1991, agreed he believed this at the time, but says he now has come to believe that at least some FDA procedures were necessary. "This is the first drug I've ever been involved with," he said. "And it was Genelabs's first drug. We thought we were working incredibly hard to get this drug on line as rapidly as possible. I, as a first-time developer, may not think that it's reasonable to ask so many toxicology studies. In retrospect, it was not excessive." McGrath said he is up for a tenure decision in 1992.

48. McGrath, Delaney, and Corti had slightly different recollections of the exact contents of the phone calls in this section, but no more than to me would be consistent with the passage of time. Fortunately, a search of Delaney's computer's memory yielded some precise and detailed notes Delaney was taking in those hectic days, and I have used them as the definitive guide.

49. The disagreement has ended amicably since then.

50. A different account of this story will be given later.

51. After a time, Corti resumed administering Q to Parne off and on for more than another year, but then lost track of him.

52. Kolata says she met with Delaney at his request while she was in San Francisco on another story, and that he volunteered news of the Q trials, and offered her an exclusive if she would sit on it. He vehemently denies this, and reasserts the story in the text.

53. A very different account of this story will be given later.

54. In a telephone interview July 22, 1991, Kolata told me she remembered reaching Lipner. "I said, 'How come this is coming out and you said it wasn't going to come out? How come one of these [networks] is coming out with it? We were told we were all going to be told at the same time. Maybe I did say, 'How could you do this?' " She agreed she may have been angry or upset.

55. This description comes from a videotape of the program.

56. Waites's words here are as he spoke them to me in several conversations in 1991. That, according to the group's recollection, is the best indication of the words he used at the time.

The brother in question, who worked for Robert Parr's real-estate company and now owns it, told me a very different story when I interviewed him March 16, 1991. He also said several things that were flatly denied by all other witnesses I could find. He promised to supply me names of five witnesses, and phone numbers of at least three, who would verify what he said, but he didn't call me back as promised, and after that wouldn't return my numerous phone messages.

The brother said that what Levin and Waites provided "wasn't care. It was gross negligence. Robert was not that sick. He really was not that ill. This Dr. Levin persuaded Robert to quit taking his vitamins and go on this regimen [Compound Q], which he proposed. Robert discussed going on this Compound Q with me, and I was totally against it. He felt there was no point living the way he was living. It was either do or die. He had a completely wrong understanding about how the test was being done. He explained to me that he was going to be in a hospital or clinic environment while the test was being done. [Instead] he was left to sleep in an office corridor. There was no monitoring. There was not someone there at all times [as promised]. Robert told me. He went in early one evening to get this treatment. The treatment was not until eleven o'clock at night. He was left to sleep on a bench the whole night. A friend brought him home."

Everyone connected with the test flatly and angrily denied this description of the procedures. From my own examination of the Levin office, the corridors outside, and the hospital area on another floor, and my talk with an administrative nurse in the hospital unit (which is a separate entity from the Levin office), who remembered the trials clearly, I found the brother's account impossible to believe. I asked to speak to the friend who brought Parr home, and the brother said he would be unable to locate him. I could find no phone listed in the friend's name.

Continuing with his story, the brother said he talked to Robert right after Robert returned from the infusion. "I said, 'Robert, what is going on?' He said, 'I had no idea I was going to be injected with this thing and within a few hours sent home. I was told this drug was dangerous. It would either kill you or cure you.' He told me it was going to be done under strict supervision. It's a known fact from the use in China that one of the side effects is an inflammation of the brain."

Although this side effect did emerge from the Project Inform study, I have found no evidence that it was known from use in China.

"About noon that day he said he was not feeling good," the brother went on. The brother's account of the rest of that day is identical to Waites's account, including Robert Parr's trip to Waites's office, an intravenous feeding for dehydration, and going home to bed while the friend kept watch.

The brother said he got a call from the friend the next morning saying he couldn't wake Robert. The friend called an ambulance, while the brother came over. "Robert was in bed, his eyes rolling around, blood coming out of the sides of his nose. I called Levin. He said I was overreacting, that this is a normal reaction. Levin wanted to send Robert to his HMO. Levin said, 'You're panicking.' But he finally said, 'Bring him to Mount Zion and I'll be waiting for him. But don't tell them what was going on, it was a secret test.'

"The ambulance crew asked if he was taking any drugs," the brother went on. "I said no. They said, 'It looks like he's overdosed. We should pump his stomach out.' At that point, I told them exactly what had gone on. He was admitted. The man who examined him said, 'Why was he given an injection?' There was no evidence he even had AIDS. He had weight, his skin color, everything [was all right]. When we got to the hospital, Dr. Levin was there. They all disappeared for two or three hours. When he came out, Levin said, 'It doesn't look good. Robert's in a coma. If he comes out of it, it will be a miracle.' "

So, the brother said, he called his family in England and the other two brothers flew to San Francisco immediately. "From what Dr. Levin said, it seemed final," he told me. Levin, Waites, and Delaney all insist that was never the prognosis, and they never would have said such a thing.

"The doctor at Mount Zion was not in agreement with anything Levin was doing," the brother said. "It's known Compound Q causes this swelling. There is something they administer with the Q that stops the brain from swelling. If he'd been in here with that he wouldn't have gone into the coma."

I am convinced, after talking with the living parties and looking at written records of the test procedures, that Levin and Waites routinely gave the steroid prednisone before and after administering Compound Q, to combat known side effects as determined by the Chinese and American scientists.

A week later, on Saturday, June 24, the brother said, a nurse called him at 8 A.M. and said Robert had died. The three brothers went to the hospital. "When we got there, he was sitting up in bed. He had a tube in him. And his chest was going in and out from the tube."

Throughout his telling of the story, the brother kept referring to a "nurse." Since the resident on duty was a woman, I asked if perhaps he was referring to the resident physician. He insisted, "It was a nurse. There was no doctor present. She said, 'As soon as I take the tube out, this will stop and he will be dead. Technically, he already died. We put this tube in for your benefit.' She said the only other thing they could do now for him is brain surgery. Robert had specifically said he didn't want that, if we felt it would not do him any good. She said it would not do him any benefit whatsoever, it would just be for the benefit of the doctors and scientists and all these people. She said, 'My advice to you is to let me take this tube out and let him pass on peacefully.' I felt that the way all this had gone down, he should not suffer one more minute. So we discussed it, my brothers, while the nurse was there, and we decided she should take the tube out. As soon as she took the tube out, he stopped [breathing] immediately. There was no response.

"She said nothing about consulting a physician. Considering Robert's condition, he begged me not to let him suffer if there was no chance of him surviving. It was all done within minutes of arrival at the hospital, and to my knowledge without talking to any doctor. She was extremely helpful and she explained things very carefully. She said two or three doctors had seen him and that Dr. Levin had already been in and nothing could be done for him."

Given that Levin had gone to Lake Tahoe after seeing Parr in relatively good shape the night before, I believe Levin's and Waites's assertions that Levin did not see Parr after the aspiration.

The brother also recalled a scene of "panic" at the hospital. "There was vomit all over the place," he said. "On the sheets, the bed, the floor, the walls. Obviously they had a very hard time trying to revive him." Waites says he didn't see any such scene when he arrived. The brother pledged to put me in touch with his two living brothers who were there, and to get me the name of the woman he had talked to at the hospital from the papers he had. He never supplied these.

At first, he said that until I raised it in a question to him, no one had told him that Levin had wanted to bring criminal charges against him. A bit later, he reversed himself and said his lawyer had told him Levin had threatened to do this, but that he didn't believe his lawyer. He said that a wrongful death suit he had wanted to bring against the doctors wasn't filed because his lawyer had "screwed up." Waites told me a deal had been struck under which the lawyer had promised not to bring a wrongful death suit and Levin agreed not to file criminal charges against the brother. The brother said he was unaware of such a deal. Ponzi, Project Inform's lawyer, says there was no formal deal, but he may have linked the two in conversations with both sides, which would explain how Waites got this impression.

Then the brother asserted that a second death had occurred in the Q trial at the same time. "The guy in the next room died the very next day from the same thing. The guy tried to commit suicide he was in such agony. He had had Q." Delaney, Levin, and Waites all deny this vehemently. The brother promised to find the name of the second alleged Q victim, but then didn't return my calls. A second patient, Ron Fisher, did die, from the Kaposi's sarcoma that had infiltrated his lungs extensively before the trial began, and which the Q failed to stop (although it did lower Fisher's P-24 antigen count). The pain and breathing difficulty became so great that Fisher ended his own life by increasing the morphine flow on his intravenous tube. "This death is considered unrelated to trichosanthin," Levin noted for the record.

Said Parr's brother, summing up his feelings, "Robert's life was lost for nothing. All they know is that Q makes the brain swell up and kills them. *You* try and make any sense out of it."

The resident who was on duty when Parr died, now in practicing medicine, told me she had seen Parr the night before, and found him all right. That morning, she said, he was "semi-comatose. He was less responsive, and having trouble breathing." She said he couldn't talk, but that she doesn't remember what his responses were otherwise. She said she notified the attending physician, but doesn't remember what he said.

She agreed it was incorrect procedure not to have talked to Waites or Levin before pulling the tube. "I know my practice is not to do things like that without consulting the attending physician. Now that I am the attending physician [on other cases], I don't expect things like that to be done without consulting me. I know it was an important incident." She insisted she doesn't remember anything she or Waites said to each other that morning, but remembers they talked. "I don't really feel comfortable talking about it any more without talking to the people at the hospital."

I urged her to talk to them, check her records, and get back to me. After that, she didn't return my phone messages.

After several rounds of telephoning, Mount Zion issued the following statement: "We strongly believe proper care procedures were followed, but to answer your questions in detail would require Mount Zion to release confidential medical records and information, and California law prohibits us from doing so." A hospital spokesman wanted it stressed that Mount Zion was independent at the time of Parr's death, but since then has become part of the University of California at San Francisco medical school complex along with San Francisco General Hospital.

57. Rothman says his original statement to the *Times* added the words "to be tested," which the *Times* deleted. I cannot see that the extra words change the meaning of the statement at all, but Rothman says in his opinion they do.

58. I have questioned several of the San Francisco General doctors mentioned here. Only one said he recalled seeing Levin's missive, but none challenged that it might have been sent. I have a photocopy, and tend to believe Levin that he sent it. He was certainly vociferous at the time about the conclusions he reached.

59. A doctor experienced in FDA-approved clinical studies at a prominent medical institution, who kindly agreed to read and comment on the manuscript for this book, noted, "Most studies are run by putting in a lot of personal overtime—without pay!—on the part of the investigator."

60. When I asked him about this, Mayer said, "They [the San Francisco group] paid for it. It was quite expensive. We sure filled out a hell of a lot of forms. There might have been an error or two. You can't always be 100 percent. I remember Levin remarked something about we had left a few things out." As to not following the protocol on dosing, he said, "I remember somebody making remarks about it. I can't remember who it was or what he said. We did our best."

61. Cooper says, "I don't recall ever having said the FDA staff didn't respect Dr. Young. I think Young wasn't afraid of being out front on issues. But like anybody in his position, he can't possibly know the details of every area he's in charge of, and so brings his key officials along with him."

62. Marilyn Chase was a colleague of mine for many years at *The Wall Street Journal,* and I developed much respect for her. I know that the editing process at the *Journal* is probably the most rigorous in daily journalism. I have been mystified for months, as I have been shown each new flaw in the story, as to how this could have happened. It may be a lesson that even the best reporters and institutions can be undone by a tendency to rely on official authority.

When I questioned Marilyn, I told her about the chronology of Parr's last week, and said I thought the evidence I had seen showed she had given too little credit to the care Delaney and his colleagues had put into the study, and too much credence to his critics; I did not reveal the previously secret details, such as the role of Dr. Michael McGrath. I received this reply from her bureau chief at the *Journal*'s San Francisco bureau, Greg Hill:

Marilyn Chase asked me to help her respond to your inquiry about our page one story of July 28, 1989. I have reviewed both the story and related spot coverage of Compound Q. We stand by the coverage as valid, fair and balanced. All of the stories, for instance, give ample space to the views of Martin Delaney and/or Alan Levin. I would offer the following points:

1) If Mr. Parr died 10 days after his last Compound Q treatment, rather than four days, it's curious that neither Mr. Delaney nor Dr. Levin ever suggested the story was in error.

2) The failure of doctors to perform an autopsy makes it impossible to rule out the possibility that Compound Q played a role in Mr. Parr's death.

3) All our coverage of this incident, both the page one story and spot news coverage, included the fact that Mr. Parr awakened from his coma, before he vomited and developed aspiration-pneumonia, leading to his death.

4) Whether the death of Mr. Parr occurred four days after treatment, or a week later, doesn't rule out the role of Compound Q as a contributing factor to Mr. Parr's death. Indeed, major organ damage from drug toxicity could require a period of several days to several weeks before causing death.

5) All sources including supporters of the experiment acknowledged that Compound Q was a potent drug with potentially dangerous toxicity, and that the death of Mr. Parr was possibly drug-related.

6) The factuality, impartiality, and longevity of Marilyn's coverage of the AIDS epidemic speaks for itself.

(In reproducing the letter here, I have corrected a numbering error that I'm sure was inadvertent.)

As to why he filed no written complaint at the time, Delaney responds, "By then we had gotten a sense of the futility of trying to correct things. One, the papers seldom bothered to print our letters, and two, nobody saw it if they did." In addition, he says "Marilyn Chase is someone I respected," and he considers her errors to have been due to a lack of information rather than to the antagonism he saw in some other reporters.

That the *Journal*'s news columns sometimes disagree with the paper's editorial page stance surprises many people besides Delaney. But the staffs and editors are distinct, as are their missions—news versus opinion—and the paper has liked it that way.

63. This quotation consists of words Rothman spoke to me in a telephone interview June 28, 1991. It is as close as Corti remembers to the words Rothman spoke to him in the late summer of 1989. I took from Corti the phrase "rein in," and tossed it at Rothman, which triggered his response.

In another interview four days earlier, Rothman had told me, "At the time of the trials, some serious questions were raised about the propriety of it within my own practice. The practice as a whole wanted some clarifications of the risks involved, and legal issues had to be resolved about a non-FDA group." He repeatedly stressed he "was never directly involved with" the infusions themselves.

In addition to what is reported in the text, Rothman gave me this account in the two interviews: His relationships with Corti and Delaney were and are very good, but were strained for a few months following the Q trial. "When it became evident a month after the trial began that our patients were not getting improvements in either T-cells, P-24s, or clinical findings," he said, "there was an open dispute that developed. There was a rumor started that we had sabotaged the study to make these doctors and Project Inform look bad. I personally have never seen any improvements. A lot of patients feel that they're doing well, but I have not seen any objective improvements in any of them"—including, he said, patients he has seen since the trial who continue to receive Compound Q from Corti. Rothman said half the original fifteen patients have since died of AIDS.

I asked him about the quote in *The Los Angeles Times*, in which he said observation had showed Q to be the most effective medicine he knew of, and he told me that if you added the phrase "to be investigated," it changed the meaning. "That's a far cry from saying it's a beneficial medication. I saw no benefit," he said.

Regarding the paperwork delays, he said, "I had very little control over it. Yes, that was delayed greatly, but I was one of twenty people working on this. The clinical forms were delayed several months. There was certainly no attempt on anyone's part to thwart the study." According to Delaney, it was up to Rothman and Rothman alone to submit the data. Delaney says the results from Los Angeles didn't come in until after the study results were announced to the public September 19, and formally to the FDA October 6.

Rothman agreed that "Initially, I know they wanted the lab work for the entire program to be sent to Immuno Diagnostics [Winger's lab]. But after a while that became impossible, because Immuno Diagnostics said it couldn't provide free lab work after the trial." Asked if he knew that the other sites had all continued to use Immuno Diagnostics during the trial, he replied, "I have no idea."

He said Delaney at first had accused him of botching the administration of the drug. He said that because of advice from a Chinese doctor he knew the Los Angeles infusions were given much more slowly than those elsewhere, lasting as long as six hours. He said Delaney had speculated that maybe the slow dosing accounted for the poorer results, preventing the drug from ever reaching therapeutic levels in the patients' bloodstreams. He acknowledged that was possible, but said Delaney and Waites had approved the slow dosing. Delaney denies he or Waites ever approved such slow dosing, and Corti insists the dosing in Los Angeles was exactly as it was in San Francisco, not more slowly as Rothman says.

64. I interviewed Messing by phone on July 5, 1991, and Kahn on July 8. Kahn came up with a different story than the other principals I could reach. He insisted that as soon as Messing recommended Decadron, he put Weaver on Decadron, but that the drug had no clear effect.

Messing agreed with Waites and Levin that there had been a prolonged disagreement over Decadron, and that Kahn had rejected his advice. But, unlike Levin and Waites, Messing stressed that he thought Kahn had been reasonable although wrong, and he denied having heated arguments about it such as Weaver's lover had described. He denied ever hearing Kahn advocate letting Q take its natural course for experimental reasons. Asked if

Levin hadn't written the hospital advising against giving Compound Q to a patient as sick as Weaver, and providing case histories in which neurological reactions had been reversed with Decadron, Messing replied, "Yes, but that's not literature. Because something worked once, it could be a coincidence. That [Project Inform's] study hadn't been published [then]." Messing said he first saw Weaver about four days into his hospitalization, and that Weaver's lover had been frantic to get him on Decadron, despite the risks.

"My opinion now is that steroids are indicated" for a reaction such as Weaver's, Messing said. "And that's based mostly on Project Inform's experience. Anecdotally, it has an effect. Clinically, it will probably never be tested. The FDA hadn't yet come out [when Weaver became comatose] in favor of listening to studies that were done outside FDA channels. They were talking about it, but it was still pooh-poohed."

Delaney adds further that Decadron is now part of the FDA-approved protocol for continued tests of Compound Q.

Kahn said he didn't recall seeing anything from Levin regarding reactions to trichosanthin, though he would check his records. But he did, in our interview, volunteer serious charges that Levin had abandoned a patient, Robert Parr, for 72 hours after having Parr admitted comatose to Mount Zion hospital. I was able to determine, from many other accounts, that Levin or his partner Waites provided consistent care for Parr, and that Kahn's charges were untrue.

Kahn told me the FDA had required that the first three patients in his study have T-cell counts less than 100, and that while Weaver wasn't one of those, most of his early patients, including Weaver, had such low counts.

Kahn said that when Weaver went into a coma, "Neurologists were called immediately, and we went by the recommendation of all the experts. The experts included pulmonary physicians, cardiologists [and] neurologists. When he [Messing] recommended to us that we should start steroids, we followed it. The same day."

Told that this contradicted others' recollections, Kahn advised me to see the chart. But he said the chart was private, and said he couldn't send it to me, or put me in touch with Weaver's family, who might be able to obtain it. He said he would consult with Messing and others and get back to me. He didn't.

About one point he was adamant: "Our focus has always been on the welfare of the patients and the subjects of our trials. For anybody to suggest that a study is more important is outrageous and a complete lie."

65. In determining what I think really happened in the Weaver case, I relied in large part on these detailed contemporaneous records Delaney and I found as we plumbed old files from the recesses of his computer memory, dated by the computer to show their entry. Delaney himself had forgotten about these documents until we came upon them. Unless there was an elaborate, long-concealed scheme to defraud me on this point, I have to accept the chronology that Delaney's computer provided (including the unsent press release), buttressed by the memories of Delaney, Waites, and Messing, interviewed separately.

66. In both my phone conversations with Lifson, he seemed very nervous and hesitant. At first he said the quote Delaney gave me was too "dramatic," and "fundamentally at odds with how I speak." But he declined to tell me

what actually was said in the conversation "to the extent it did occur" until he had discussed it with other people. I asked how other people could tell him what he told Delaney, and he replied, "There were a number of interactions with Beninger and others and I would need to check my recollections with the facts as they occurred at that time." He continued to resist my specific questions, but at one point said, "It was a dramatic incident. It was dramatic in real life."

Later he told me that from his records calls were made in the sequence Delaney describes, and Decadron was administered to Weaver right after this sequence of calls. But he said, "My understanding is that after a careful consideration of the pros and cons a decision had already been taken to start him on steroids," so it's not "particularly accurate" to say there was a causal relationship. He also pointed out that only the treating physician could make the drug decision, adding, "Certainly I and other people at Genelabs were interested in this patient but not in a position to determine his care."

Beninger didn't return my repeated detailed phone messages.

67. Kahn told me he still doesn't think there is a proven association between Decadron and the improvement Weaver showed, which he said was slight; it might have happened anyway, he said. Messing said, "After the Decadron he became more alert, but he was still cerebrally impaired. There was eye contact and so forth. He did become more responsive [after taking Decadron]; he could move an arm, or blink his eyes."

68. Cooper told me in an interview January 30, 1992, that she attended the meeting because Young asked her to, "because I knew more about these drugs than anybody at the agency." She absolutely denies that she ever insisted on longevity as an endpoint, or opposed any use of CD-4 cells as a marker.

"I was one of the ones who said that CD-4 counts along with some kind of clinical data, lesser clinical parameters like weight loss, likely would make a good case for efficacy," she says. "I never said and would never say that increasing the CD-4 count isn't of benefit. The issue is whether CD-4 counts themselves, whether there is enough data to rely on CD-4 counts alone as the only indicator of efficacy. Opportunistic infections were always considered valid endpoints. That I insisted on survival is absolutely wrong. Martin [Delaney] has said that a number of times. Survival is something you're going to want to look at, but in terms of approval of a drug, CD-4 counts plus some kind of clinical data, if it was convincing, if it showed a difference, would likely be some kind of a basis for approval. I've heard from several sources over the years that Martin would really like to eliminate the FDA. This is one way of trying to make a case to do that."

Delaney, whose sentiments on the subject are abundant in this book, doesn't want to do away with the FDA.

When I asked Fauci how his version of the meeting compared to Delaney's, as expressed in the text, he said, "Martin is remarkably accurate in what he said. I don't see anything I could disagree with." I then asked him what he thought of Delaney in general.

He replied: "Martin Delaney manifests such a keen insight, intelligence, rationality, common sense and sensitivity that I have grown to admire and respect him greatly over the years. He is particularly superb at written analyses of complex problems. After reading some of his responses to misguided activities or policies, I find myself wishing that somehow I could convince him to work with us here at the NIH. However, he has broader areas to cover, and I am afraid that confining him to only one aspect of the problem would restrict his talents and his potential contributions. He is extremely effective at just what he is doing. I've thought about this a lot. It is nearly impossible to quantify his impact. But if you look at the influence that people outside the government who are exerting pressure on the traditional processes have, he is unquestionably at the very top of the heap. He combines an activist's zeal with an extremely rational, well-thought-out analytical approach, which is a fantastic combination. I really enjoy working with him. He is so analytical tearing apart nonsense—he does it as well or better than anybody I know."

Cooper told me she remembered discussions on these topics, and that "I'm sure" the account given here is "a paraphrase of what was said, not verbatim."

69. Which she says remains true in late 1991.

70. I interviewed Harrington July 11, 1991. He told me that he never knowingly laid eyes on Sheaffer, and that Kolata knew he was merely relaying someone else's description when she quoted him as an authority on Sheaffer's deterioration. He repeated the phrases Starrett has him saying in the quotation above. He said he didn't remember saying some of the things Kolata quoted. He said that many people with AIDS decline and die more rapidly than Sheaffer did. And he said that he knows others who died as Sheaffer did who never took Q. He accused Kolata of having misused passages from a written statement he said he gave her stating how he thought community trials should be set up; he said she quoted the statement in a context that seemed to be critical of Delaney, which he said he never intended. He praised Delaney and expressed regret for the way his words were portrayed in the article.

71. I talked to Sonnabend July 10, 1991. He told me someone had asked him to look at some data from the Q test, and that he noticed one patient, identified only by a number, had dropped out after one infusion. "What happened to him?" he said he asked. "Oh, he died," he said he was told. He said he made no further comment because then, and now, he thought the matter "meant nothing." He said he mentioned the death casually to Bihari, who became upset. "I had no idea why he [Sheaffer] died," Sonnabend told me. "I didn't connect the death to Q. He praised the study Delaney organized for its toxicity findings. He said he was very displeased with the way Kolata had used his name in her story.

In addition, Starrett supplied me from her files a signed statement by Sonnabend from the time, dated September 28, 1989, saying, "I have <u>NEVER</u> [his double emphasis] believed that there was a cover up and in fact expressed this opinion to those who said there was."

72. In the story, Kolata quoted Wallach, attributing the death to "cardiorespiratory arrest," which means his heart and breathing stopped. Starrett and others argue that everyone in a sense dies of this, and that the quote made Wallach sound foolish.

I interviewed Wallach July 11, 1991, and he said he agreed. He said, "I spent over an hour with Gina Kolata on the phone shortly after Scott died explaining to her that the death was not attributable to Compound Q at all, and that sudden death in people with AIDS had occurred many, many times before. She used that silly statement about cardiorespiratory arrest. He came in complaining of an inability to walk because of peripheral neuropathy [a condition that predated his taking Compound Q]. Q was at least six weeks prior. I saw him the day before [he died], and he was fine, lucid, talking. It could have been a pulmonary embolism, it could have been anything." Wallach reaffirmed that contrary to the implication of Kolata's story, Starrett was unaware of the illness and death until she got a call from Sheaffer's roommate after Sheaffer had died.

73. I discussed this by phone with Kolata July 22, 1991; I offered to come see her, but she said she wanted to do the interview quickly by phone, as she was busy. She asserted her story was absolutely accurate, but said that after two years she could not remember "details" and eventually hung up on me when I persisted in trying to elicit explanations for various statements she had made. After that, I reinterviewed witnesses whose word directly contradicts hers; they maintained their stories and in one case proved in writing she had told me an untruth about a critical point. In the end, I am satisfied that, by the weight of the evidence, the version presented here is fair. It is a painful portrait of my profession, journalism, and should be seen by the reader not as what the profession usually does, but as what it is sometimes capable of doing and must guard against. It is certainly not typical of *The New York Times*'s methods. The *Times*'s general reputation for professional standards needs no defense here. But Kolata's story about Starrett, even on cursory examination, let alone close scrutiny, seems terribly wrong. It shows the consequences when a powerful newspaper fails to maintain its professional standards.

Though I find many distressing issues raised by the story, the most critical to me is whether Kolata knew four things either before publication without printing them, or after publication without correcting them. One is that Starrett contended she had told St. Clare's Hospital that she had given Sheaffer an experimental drug, regardless of its name, and how to treat the reaction. The second is that Starrett and Wallach (Sheaffer's doctor) say that Starrett (who believed Sheaffer had recovered from the Q reaction) didn't know Sheaffer went into Cabrini Medical Center more than six weeks later to get treatment for a longstanding condition, and consequently couldn't possibly have told Cabrini about the Q dose—the information Kolata accused Starrett of willfully withholding from Cabrini. The third is that Wallach contended Sheaffer's death was almost certainly unrelated to Q. And the fourth is that Sheaffer was on videotape six weeks before his death, after his final Q infusion, having recovered from the reaction and asking for more Q. Each point drives to the heart of the story, and to have omitted any of them—let alone all of them—would seem to me to be a gross and willful misleading of the reader.

On each of these points, and other important points as well, the evidence, including Kolata's defense of her story, persuades me that the version I have presented in the text is fair.

Kolata said, "I completely agree with Martin Delaney that people always die when they're deathly ill and they're taking a drug. But this was kept secret. And there's something funny about that. Starrett didn't want anyone to know that she had given an illegal drug because she could lose her li-

cense. The point of that story was that there is a cost to these secret underground studies. The roommate of this guy Scott was very, very upset about
this. He was very concerned that Starrett's reaction was to try to keep it
quiet."

Kolata said Starrett "called me several times [over the week-end preced-
ing the story] crying hysterically and saying her license could be taken away.
She sounded a little bit crazy. She went on and on and on and she was
hysterical. I do not remember the doctor of Scott Sheaffer calling me, but
maybe he did. Starrett was hard to forget."

Starrett says she cried because Kolata persisted in saying she had withheld
word of the experimental drug from the two hospitals when Starrett kept
telling her otherwise. Starrett says she was worried about losing her license
because of that, not because of the Q involvement. "She was accusing me of
a cover-up," Starrett says, adding that she repeatedly urged Kolata to look at
the videotape of Sheaffer taken after his release from the hospital, and that
Kolata refused. Kolata hung up on me before I could ask her about the
videotape.

When I tried to go over facts in detail, Kolata repeatedly refused, saying
words like these, which I took down at one point: "It's been more than two
years. I am not going to sit here and be cross-examined. I cannot continue
these questions about this article. It's been two years. We received the
letters from Dr. Starrett and Dr. Wallach, and when I went over them and
showed them to my editors, we decided that the article was accurate." When
I asked which editors, she said I was asking "too much about the internal
workings of *The New York Times*."

As to her source for saying that Starrett hadn't told the hospitals, she said,
"I don't know whether Starrett told me or Delaney told me or the roommate
told me that she had not informed the hospitals."

But about one thing she was adamant: "This [my own questioning of her]
is the first time I heard [of] her saying that she told the hospital [about an
unnamed experimental drug and how to treat the reaction]. If she had said
that, I would have put it in the story. She wrote several letters. Her letter
did *not* say that she told them he was taking an experimental drug and how
to treat it [Kolata's emphasis]."

After talking with Kolata, I interviewed Howard Grossman, a physician
then on the staff of St. Clare's who heard of the controversy right after the
article and checked out Sheaffer's chart for the critical period. He says, "In
the chart, it does say that Barbara told the staff at St. Clare's that he [Sheaf-
fer] was on experimental medication." Grossman told me there were several
different notations to that effect, and that Starrett had advised on how to
medicate Sheaffer. Grossman recalls that Sheaffer walked out of the hospital
fine about a day after he came in.

After reading the chart, and Kolata's story, Grossman says he called Kolata.
"I told her I had looked at the chart and that none of the stuff [she had
written] was true. She said that she stood by her story because that is what
Barbara said to her. But the chart says Dr. Starrett said he was on an experimental medication."

Patient charts aren't publicly available, and Grossman says he cannot ethically obtain Sheaffer's chart to show to me. But one critical thing Kolata
told me can be tested against a written record: her statement that Starrett's

protest letters after the article failed to say what Starrett is now telling me. In this, the record shows Kolata told me a bald untruth. Starrett's October 20, 1989, unprinted letter to the editor of *The New York Times* says, "Ms. Kolata states that I did not tell two hospitals about Compound Q. In Scott's patient chart at St. Clare's Hospital there were several entries by doctors mentioning my name and reference made to patient having a drug reaction with an experimental therapy." The *Times* ran no correction. Moreover, it is a fair inference that if Kolata didn't tell the truth about what the letter said, she may also be wrong about what Starrett and Wallach told her. If Starrett wrote such things the day after the article, it's easy to believe she said the same things on the same subject when she talked to Kolata several times at length two or three days before the article.

Kolata hung up before I could ask her how to get in touch with Sheaffer's former roommate, who she several times said was a major source of her story. Others told me the roommate, who they emphasized was not a lover, was in a fight with Sheaffer, apparently over money. Says Wallach, Sheaffer's doctor, "Scott was crying to us many times that his roommate wouldn't help him, threw him out. Gina knew there was a domestic problem. She knew that in advance, and didn't print it."

Starrett and Wallach are adamant that they told Kolata at length, in advance of the article, that Starrett was unaware when Sheaffer was hospitalized at Cabrini, and that this final hospitalization before his death came about because of a preexisting neuropathy, unlikely to have had any connection with Compound Q. As I talked on the phone to Kolata, she told me she had located Wallach's letter to her after the article, and read me a passage saying Starrett was uninvolved in that hospitalization, and that Wallach had withheld news of the Q from Cabrini on his own authority at Sheaffer's insistence. After reading it, she continued to maintain that her accusation against Starrett for having failed to inform Cabrini was accurate and needed no correction.

Kolata raised to me the issue of motivation. "Delaney says I am out to get him because the Q story broke," she said. "I do not carry grudges. I do not decide I am going to call somebody because they are crazy about [favorably inclined toward] me. I don't think that anybody who knows me would say that I would lash out at Martin Delaney because of the Compound Q story. Somebody thinks that I personally set out to write this story to make Martin Delaney and Compound Q look bad. The implication of your questions seems to be that I was avoiding anything that would detract from the story, and that's just not true."

I asked her to justify the statement that Starrett's alleged secrecy about Sheaffer's having taken Compound Q was responsible for "leading doctors to provide what may have been inappropriate treatment." She replied, "They did not know what was wrong. I don't know—I have to see my article again. He was thrashing around incoherent. They were holding him down. [Obviously, she was referring to the first hospitalization, supervised by Starrett, which resulted in a quick recovery, as testified to by other doctors and by Sheaffer's own videotaped statement.] I think the appropriate treatment was to give some sort of steroid."

Steroids, of course, were Levin's therapy. I asked if she knew whether Starrett had put Levin in touch with the hospital. She replied, "I'm sorry, it has been too long since I've written the story." I asked whether, if Levin *had* told the hospital about steroids, it would invalidate her accusation against Starrett. She replied, "I'm sorry, it is too long [afterward] to answer these detailed questions."

When I asked if she knew of any possibly inappropriate treatment that had been given to Sheaffer after his Q reaction, as her story states, she again said she could not remember. At one point, she explained, "I cannot continue with these detailed questions because it has been two years. If you had written six hundred stories, you wouldn't remember either. I think that story was accurate and correct. I think that article was completely accurate and I don't think I unfairly castigated anybody."

I asked her about Delaney's contention that she violently misquoted him by taking his statement—that he would have been stunned if Starrett had done what Kolata alleged—and making it seem that Delaney agreed with the allegation and was stunned by it. She replied, "I asked him and that's what he told me. If he had later told me that he didn't think that was true, I would have put that in."

I wanted to get her reaction to my observation that Delaney could not possibly have corrected a misquotation before he saw it in print, and that after he saw it he wrote a letter denying it. I wanted to ask her about the other people, like Harrington, Sonnabend, Wallach, and Dr. Douglas Richman, who say Kolata misquoted them or distorted their views in the story.

But at this point she cut me off, saying, "I don't have any more time. I quoted him as I heard him at the time. This is not a lawsuit. I just don't like this. I don't have a good enough memory from two years ago. Lots of times things look different when you look back on it. I have too much to do. I'm not going to go through what somebody did or didn't say two years ago. This is it. Goodbye." And the line went dead.

I waited a day, called back, and left a message on her answering machine. Two days later, she called back and warned me she had "detailed, dated notes on all my conversations and you better be very careful what you write." I said I was glad to hear she had such notes, and wanted to go over them with her. She replied, "I don't have time. I can't even tell you how many things I'm working on now. I've already spent a lot of time with you." I immediately raised the issue of the videotape, which Starrett said Kolata refused to look at. Starrett emphasized the videotape both in her letter to the *Times* at the time and in her continuing conversations with me. It seemed to me that for a reporter to have assaulted the professional integrity of Starrett as Kolata did while refusing to look at proffered videotaped proof to the contrary would be a gross deviation from journalistic ethics. Kolata said she was "busy" and "won't go into it." She warned me again to be careful because she has "detailed, dated notes," then once more said "Goodbye" and hung up.

74. McGrath says the Nottingham studies were influential, but that he thinks his team at San Francisco General would soon have reached that conclusion anyway.

75. Krim told me in February 1992, "I was quoted out of context and that made my remarks [appear] more pejorative than they were intended to be." She said she didn't reply to the letter because its tone was "very harsh," but

that she later made up with Delaney. "I think he is an extremely bright guy and a courageous person and has rendered enormous service to the community," she added.

By then, Weisman and Rothman had also become outspoken admirers of Delaney and Corti.

76. I regret that this section was written without input from Groopman. I left numerous detailed messages both on his answering machine and with his assistant, but he never returned my calls. The statements in this paragraph come from Levin and Delaney. The description of the meeting is based mostly on Delaney's account. Cooper and Hoth say it conforms to their recollections, except that they don't recall Groopman's leaving the podium; they say it may have happened, and Delaney says it did.

77. One participant on the panel, Dr. Daniel Hoth of the National Institute for Allergy and Infectious Diseases, told me in an interview, "Jerry made some pretty outrageous statements. He really was coming across as not understanding of the community perspective, not sympathetic."

78. There were some allergic reactions of the type that happen with many drugs, but experienced medical personnel knew how to manage them.

79. In an interview, Kahn at first told me, "I don't remember that being true. I don't remember that conversation with Roger at all." Then he said his statement about closing down the university study was "only if they were going to come in and do my study—if there was going to be an instant that we were going to add an investigator that I didn't know the quality of their work or how the data was going to be cleaned up." Then he said he hadn't singled out Project Inform. "I would have reservations working with anyone if I did not know the quality of their research," he said.

Williams told me in an interview that Kahn had delivered the threat exactly as Delaney recounted it, and as it appears in the text.

80. A research and treating physician from a prominent institution, who kindly read this manuscript to advise me, objects that there is less research money available than Levin seems to think.

81. Cooper says she had merely sought more detailed information before going further. In general, however, she told me she thinks Delaney is guilty of "high-handed arrogance. He's telling the agency what it can do and can't do, and when. I think that's sad, when that happens to a regulatory process."

82. Kolata had cut off all conversation with me before I could question her about this story. I did tell her there were other stories I wanted to question her about.

83. It was published in Vol. 4, No. 12, 1990.

84. According to the case against Gallo, the French lab had found a more virulent strain of HIV, which made it easier to work with than the viruses Gallo had obtained from American patients. Gallo, of course, disputes that, and the sides respond endlessly. The Gallo-Crewdson argument has taken on almost religious overtones. I had hoped to avoid detailing it here, but have had to include some background because of Gallo's importance to this story, and Crewdson's importance to *him*. When I met Delaney, just as he was getting to know Gallo, he was neutral on the dispute. Since then, he has swung around to support Gallo's side; it's worth noting, however, that in supporting Gallo Delaney also furthers the mission that drives his life, help-

ing AIDS patients get well. I don't see it serving the purpose of this book to wade further into the dispute, let alone try to resolve it.

When I called Crewdson for his comments, he denied passing around large piles of documents supporting his cause, which Gallo had said justified his own preoccupation with handing out piles of documents. Crewdson said the sources he had talked to in preparing his articles, about 150 persons, had requested copies of the articles and that was all he had sent out. I asked to see Crewdson's main article on Gallo, which won the George Polk Award for excellence in journalism. The next day, I was startled to find a Federal Express man lumbering up my steps with a parcel bearing Crewdson's return address, containing two thick, carefully assembled and bound volumes of photocopied articles from the *Tribune* and other publications about Gallo and related matters; the photocopies weighed in at five pounds.

I asked Crewdson about Delaney's feelings that whether or not Gallo claimed undue credit in 1984, the persistent pursuit of the scientist, and his need to respond, was slowing down the fight against AIDS. Crewdson responded: "Do I feel responsible if Gallo's research has suffered? No, I don't. Anyone who thinks I am responsible for holding back research is the kind of person who likes to cut off the messenger's head."

85. July 17, 1991, in his office, I asked Gallo about their meeting, as Delaney had described it. And I asked how Gallo happened to bring Delaney into such a delicate matter so quickly.

Gallo said: "He [Delaney] is one of the most impressive persons I've ever met in my life, bar none, in any field. He should have gone into science. I'm not the only one around here who's said we could use him in the labs. I was impressed by his knowledge, his judgment, and his ability to think. If I were infected, I would sure follow what that guy is doing. He's got his mind on the goal of getting rid of the thing.

"He came here one day asking questions, not as my friend. I've never seen a businessman know an area he's supposed to know with this amount of savvy. He knew who everybody was, and understood the arguments. He saw to the core of everything. He had his own arguments, about the blood test, and the infection of children. He bridged science and the gay community better than any other person by far. I remember his talking to me in a personal way about his hepatitis and his Irish and personal background. He can be charming, warm and open, but it's never very many seconds before he's back to the business at hand.

"I saw this guy's personality. We went into the swimming pool for hours. I trusted him. I took a chance. I decided to invite him to the meeting with Daiichi."

Gallo and I went through the other events Delaney had described to me, as they are about to be related. But Gallo said the main thing Delaney had done for him was to make him "far more concerned. In science we want to dot 'i's' and cross 't's.' He makes me think more quickly of what could be done at any point for people who are dying."

86. Gray says if he had any agents under cover, he's not aware of it. He says he does consult the CIA before taking on foreign clients to make sure he isn't working against "the best interests of the United States. They've never told us to take a client, but if they recommended against it, we'd walk

away from it. On that thin reed," he says, "many in the press have written about some interrelationship."

87. Gallo later told me he didn't feel comfortable asking Nakimura for such a report, and didn't.

88. Having questioned them, I accept that Delaney and Corti believe energy is better spent encouraging new therapies than trying to get the government to change its mind about old ones. But I must say that if I learned tomorrow that I had been infected by HIV, based on all that I know from writing this book, I would go to Mexico on the first flight and start a course of ribavirin and isoprinosine in tandem while weighing some of the more advanced but more toxic treatments that have emerged in recent years.

89. In my interview with him, Gallo was unbounded in his praise of Delaney's long report. He said Delaney seemed to have "infiltrated the whole place. If I sent five guys from my team over there, they'd come back with one percent of what he did. They'd see something [in the laboratory], get distracted, and spend six hours before they got back to business. He went over there and allowed me to understand what their problems and fears are. He elbowed into them in a good way. He worked a political strategy very well."

90. Cooper again denies that she opposed the use of surrogate markers altogether, but merely said the markers had to be measured in controlled studies at recognized research centers. "The quality of expanded access data is never very high," she says. "The company asks for information and may or may not get it, and doesn't have any way of assessing its quality." Nor, she says, was she insisting on placebo controls, but believed that a patient might be his own control, with blood markers after he went on the drug compared to markers before he went on the drug. "If it was good quality and showed a measurable response where you could basically make the case that it was due to the drug, that might be adequate," she says. As will be seen later in the text, however, the question became whether she posed such excessive standards as to destroy the practicality of surrogate markers.

She says the remark he quoted from her about Fauci and Broder "certainly is an overstatement of anything I may have said," although she says she can't recall exactly what she did say.

91. The successor also failed to return my telephone calls in the summer of 1991.

92. I have been unable to obtain a copy either. Cooper says she "may have a copy," but that it's up to Bristol-Myers to release it. Bristol-Myers's public-relations staff transferred me from one person to the next in my search for the letter and answers to other questions for this book, and then stopped returning my calls.

Cooper did describe for me her view of the contents of the letter, which I found to be revealing on the issue of why many important people, not just Delaney, constantly think she is saying one thing when she insists to me with impressive sincerity that she is really saying another—not just in this letter, but on the issue of surrogate markers and even about ribavirin.

She says the letter expressed her view that CD-4 counts along with some clinical data can provide an acceptable standard for proving efficacy; that alone would seem to put her in near lockstep with all the people who say they violently disagree with her. But in describing what else she said in the letter, she made it seem as if the other clinical data would be so difficult to attain that I can understand why people interpreted the letter as saying that surrogate markers could never prove efficacy.

The additional data, she said, should involve the frequency of onset of opportunistic infections among persons taking the tested drugs. "The question I raised in that letter," she told me, "was how you interpret O.I. [opportunistic infection] data over a year or two in the context of when patients are taking a lot of prophylactic therapies—in comparison with 1986 when the original AZT study was done. One would anticipate that now, in 1990, there would be fewer O.I.'s because of prophylaxis."

In other words, in the years since the original AZT study, patients had gained access to many of the therapies already described in this book, from aerosol pentamidine to clarithromycin; even though no exact data had been assembled, it stood to reason that these therapies were warding off opportunistic infections and making people healthier. The people trying to get ddI and ddC approved wanted to use the historical AZT data as a control, so as not to force test subjects to take placebos and not to wait many years before getting the drugs approved. Now she was telling them that even if the ddI and ddC patients came out healthier, there was no way to tell whether this was because of the ddI and ddC, or because of all the other therapies people were now taking.

"It's not that we knew for sure how effective those agents were, but the presumption would be that they were delaying the onset of O.I.," she told me. "It was purely a scientific issue that should be considered."

One observation that could be made about this statement is that for purposes of ddI and ddC approval, she was willing to "presume" that the other remedies were effective. Yet those other remedies had been held up for approval or not approved at all because she and other officials at the FDA wouldn't make that "presumption."

As regards the letter under discussion, her statement indicates that she thought she could engage in interesting philosophical discussions in an academic climate, without anyone's noticing that she was the regulator in charge of deciding the matter, in the balance of which hung thousands of lives—and, one must add, millions of dollars.

She made other remarks to me indicating she had come to recognize this. "The way it was received," she told me, "was that the FDA is setting up new hurdles and only going to look at mortality data, and that wasn't what was intended. I guess I can understand in retrospect how people might have looked at it that way, how people might interpret that as another hurdle that the FDA was setting."

This might also help explain how Cooper might, under oath, before Congress and national television, think she was musing about the unusual nature of some ribavirin data, and naïvely not understand that, by her words, the United States Government was hurling a deadly accusation (which turned out to be untrue) against the total work of some career scientists, with sweeping impact on them, their families, the companies whose drugs they tested, and the thousands of people whose health depended on their reliability.

93. These boards, officially known as Institutional Review Boards, are required for federally approved drug studies. One of the points critics had

seized on when Project Inform's original Compound Q trial became public was its failure to have such a board, which the FDA system regards as providing independent protection for patients from possible mistakes by researchers. Delaney had tried to create a review board for the Compound Q trial, but found that the red tape of doing so would have delayed the program by many months. At the first chance, he affiliated with an existing board he thought would be sympathetic. Obviously he was dismayed when in Tim Lowe's case it "protected" a patient by delaying access to the one drug that might have extended his life awhile.

94. My interview with Tsiatis was almost a parody of everything Delaney had prepared me for. After considerable discussion, most of which I had a hard time following, I decided that what he was trying to tell me was this: Everything in the account in the text is correct, but one important thing is missing. Tsiatis also told the committee that the fact that a drug increases CD-4 is not necessarily a sign that the drug is beneficial, because the drug could do other things that would harm the patient, more than compensating for the help it did in increasing his CD-4 count. At least when I read him the above, he said it was "a fair statement."

95. Corti says he was led to believe that Salahuddin and his friend had formed a private laboratory, housed on the grounds of Huntington Memorial Hospital, a short drive from the University of Southern California medical center. Salahuddin denied to me that he was affiliated with a private company, and said he had been hired as a professor by the Department of Medicine at USC, and that the lab was provided by USC and Huntington. In our interview, he recalled telling Corti that he *wanted* to continue working on SP-PG after leaving Gallo's laboratory, but said Gallo had made it impossible for him to do so. He acknowledged that he had continued to talk frequently to officials from Daiichi, but only because "they are my friends." He acknowledged that he had brought in Shuji Nakimura, the Gallo staffer who had met separately with Daiichi officials at their request, as an associate in the USC lab. And he acknowledged pleading guilty to two felonies, though he insisted they weren't crimes of "moral turpitude."

96. The drug, BIRG-587, proved ineffective.

97. He told me in my interview with him July 17, 1991.

98. Richman says, "I think he's distorting things. There are good examples in medical history where the less complicated regimen is safer and just as effective. He acts as if he knows what the answers are going to be to everything, and that's not good medicine."

Merigan says Delaney was very helpful to the committee. "It really helped the committee make a more informed vote, by seeing the problems that the patients would have with the protocol. What happened was we made some changes in the protocol. We made the protocol more patient-friendly."

Merigan, however, challenges Delaney on one point: the financial incentive. Congress had already allocated the money, through NIH, to the AIDS Clinical Trials Group. "All these centers were getting funding whether they voted yes or no," Merigan says. "They don't gain anything whether they vote for it or against it. They are insured the funding until the end of the grant period." If the one protocol had been rejected, he says, "There are innumerable things to be done. There are many other protocols."

Delaney responds that in a large sense the money was allocated, but it still had to be expended to justify new appropriations. "This was such a big and expensive study it took away the opportunity to work on a number of smaller ones. It made their life easier that they had one large study." And by studying new combinations of known drugs, he says, "they were trying to bet on the surest thing. It was bound to show something publishable. And they have big staff overheads winding down from their last large study. Merigan admitted to me once that if the study wasn't approved, he was going to have to be laying off staff."

99. When I went over this conversation with Cooper, she disputed a number of things Delaney remembered her saying, but then restated what seemed to me the same thoughts in different wording. So in several instances, I simply substituted words she spoke to me over the telephone for words Delaney recalled her saying that day.

She also expressed concern over "the suggestion that when I was at the FDA, there was a war between the FDA and the drug companies over AIDS drugs. Nothing could be further from the truth. Touch base with drug companies whose applications were approved. Burroughs Wellcome. They very much welcomed the cooperation."

I asked her whether, if she had still held her former job, she would have thought ddI should have been approved at that time. She replied, "Based on that data—well, I think—I don't know. I would have asked for different data."

100. Meier says he "did not and would not" tell someone how he was going to vote, and that he ended the conversation with Delaney noncommittally. Delaney remembers a promise. Meier says his abstention was "unpredictable" because it depended on procedural circumstance. He says, "I felt strongly that it was improper to vote on approval without first determining what further studies and requirements should condition such approval. Had such a vote been held first, my decision on whether to vote for a conditional approval would have depended on the requirements to be imposed." That seems to me consistent with Delaney's account, because, as the reader will see, Kessler had already ruled out conditional approval at that stage.

Meier says, "I do not have a side. I am trying as best I can, fairly and accurately and within the guidelines of science and common sense, to perform a difficult task. I will continue to do so, and I will continue to 'call them as I see them.' It is my practice to try to keep an open mind so long as deliberations on a matter and mutual consultations are still going forward."

I know of no information—certainly not Delaney's account in the text—that would contradict this statement from Meier. My own opinion is that Delaney's account depicts Meier as a person of the highest integrity, conscientiously doing the painful job of balancing his scientific and human responsibilities in an enormously difficult matter.

101. On first approach, Kessler replied in writing that the three conversations with Delaney recounted in this book took place, but that the second two—at the ddI hearings—weren't as Delaney gave them to me. He said he didn't tell Delaney that he would approve ddI regardless of the advisory committee's recommendation, but otherwise wasn't specific.

I went back to Delaney, who reasserted the conversations as he originally recalled them to me, and said he would talk to Kessler. He called back saying he had met with Kessler about it, and that FDA lawyers were nervous that parts of the conversations might make it appear Kessler had violated Securities and Exchange Commission rules by disclosing information that would affect Bristol-Myers's stock price. But Delaney said he thought some changes, which were agreeable to him, would satisfy the commissioner. The result was the version printed: most significantly, I took the advance description of the ddI session out of Kessler's mouth and put it in general narrative, and I removed the word "guarantee" from Kessler's mouth and let it find its way into Delaney's ear of its own accord.

Kessler again chose to respond in writing, insisting that he didn't brief Delaney about the meeting before it took place, or assure him that ddI would be approved if the committee opposed it. He even denied saying that he wanted the committee to approve ddI on the basis of the existing data, asserting that he had merely said he wanted the committee to "evaluate" ddI on the basis of existing "options."

Finally, after all deadlines for the book had elapsed, Kessler phoned me in a conciliatory tone, not changing his position but saying he didn't want to seem in disagreement with Delaney. He read me, then faxed me, a letter Delaney had written him before I changed the text according to Delaney's suggestions. Delaney, a skilled negotiator, had obviously crafted the letter with an eye toward his need to work well with Kessler in the future.

It concurred that Kessler hadn't said he "guaranteed" approval for ddI if the committee turned it down. But the letter added, "You did, however, express confidence repeatedly that the drug would be approved, one way or the other. . . . You did, by implication and expression of your own confidence, leave me with the assurance I felt I needed." In two interviews with me, one soon after the conversation with Kessler, Delaney had put the specific word "guarantee" in the commissioner's mouth.

Delaney's letter to Kessler agreed that Kessler "did not advise me of the strategic plan" for the meeting in advance. Delaney said others at the FDA had told him beforehand what to expect at the meeting, suggesting that he and Kessler merely discussed the public agenda. To Kessler, these statements constitute Delaney's endorsement of Kessler's objection to the version in the text.

But just two days earlier, Delaney had reasserted to me that the version in the text, in its current form, is correct, and that it does not conflict with the letter he wrote Kessler. He said he thought Kessler was reading more into the text than is there.

Because Delaney's accounts of other conversations were so consistently confirmed, because he was so certain and consistent in recounting these two conversations soon after they happened, and, frankly, because I don't think Delaney would have left that meeting without the guarantee he says he felt he got, I have settled on the text as it is.